Waubonsee Community College

THE BEST PLAYS OF 1934-35

THE BEST PLAYS
OF 1934-35

AND THE
YEAR BOOK OF THE DRAMA
IN AMERICA

EDITED BY

BURNS MANTLE

DODD, MEAD AND COMPANY
NEW YORK -   -   -   1966

INTRODUCTION

THERE are prophets who, being encouraged, will foretell the eventual amalgamation of the living theatre and the mechanical theatre of the screen. The argument runs that the screen drama, having become articulate and bright with color, is more than ever dependent upon the legitimate drama as a supply source of both material and the actors with which to interpret it. This, they conclude, will naturally force the producers of screen drama into the play-buying and play-producing field, which their abundant capital will make it possible for them to dominate.

The prophecy is far-fetched, as such prophecies frequently are found to be in the windy alleys of the theatre, though not as foolish as it may at first sound. There is a compromise around some not too distant corner through the working of which stage and screen will naturally be drawn into a closer relationship than any that has previously existed. They are, by the continued scientific expansion of the one and the established and historic stability of the other, being gradually drawn into a sort of co-operative dependence one upon the other.

As a result these post-depression years in the theatre have become years of experiment. The producers of pictures have either learned, or are learning, that when they rush hysterically into the Broadway market and snap up both actor-talent and author-talent still in a positively green state of development they are not only paying outrageously for the experiment but getting little out of it.

Actors and authors so grabbed have learned, or are learning, that a Hollywood offer, with options, is frequently not only a depressing experience, but one that milks them dry of inspiration in a few months and tosses them back upon the theatre heap with nothing left to sell.

And producers have learned, or are learning, that although by a newly developing law of averages the names and personalities so ruthlessly snatched away from them come creeping back to the theatre in varying stages of artistic decline in from three to five years, it is profitless to wait for them. Better go immediately about the business of developing new talents.

The application of the prophecy to this introduction to "The Best Plays of 1934-35" is found in the fact that in the legitimate theatre this has been a most important experimental season. Motion picture play and talent scouts by the dozen have flocked to the Broadway theatres, and to the summer theatres that followed in the wake of the regular season, searching for playwrights, actors and directors who might be worth a provisional bid.

Motion picture producers financed a half dozen legitimate theatre managers in the production of plays last season, and discovered in several instances that their percentage of profit, counting the comparative insignificance of their investment, gave them a sweet return without lessening the value of their interest in the play they bought for later screen production. This discovery has prompted them to announce a closer and more definite coöperation with Broadway play producers during the season of 1935-36, and given their imitative competitors a plan of action to copy. As a result, there is a prediction current that something like 70 per cent of the capital employed in the production of legitimate plays in the immediate future will be supplied by the larger motion picture interests.

This cannot be accepted as an altogether healthy sign of the times, but the threat it contains is not, in fact, as ominous as at first appears. Motion picture promoters have discovered, or are discovering, the wisdom of raising the standard of their output if they are successfully to compete with the rapidly improving foreign films. This promises a continuation of at least present standards in the theatre. They also now realize, or will shortly realize, that it were better to permit their pearls of great price in the author and actor line sufficient contact with the theatre to guarantee their seasoning, their competence and their audience appeal.

There was, as has come to be expected, the usual divergence of opinion regarding the play of American authorship most entitled to the Pulitzer award as the best of the year. There were five or six candidates that may be catalogued as generally acceptable, and one among them that was voted outstanding. This was Lillian Hellman's "The Children's Hour," dramatically the most powerful of recent contributions to the theatre. "The Children's Hour," however, happens to be based upon a legal action of the last century in the courts of Scotland which was a test of the libel laws in fact but included a free reference to an unnatural sex attraction as a basis of the libel. This reference, though superficial and lacking in offense to any adult mind so far as the play is concerned, did produce a taint of unwholesomeness in discussion that unquestionably had an effect upon a critical estimate of the drama's worth.

The Pulitzer award was given to "The Old Maid," a strongly sentimental drama concerned with the maternal urge which Zoe Akins has extracted with skill from a story of old New York written some years ago by Edith Wharton. In addition to "The Children's Hour," the awarding committee also passed by Maxwell Anderson's "Valley Forge" and Robert Sherwood's "The Petrified Forest."

The Anderson drama has, for those whose family roots are struck deep in American soil, a strong appeal in the beauty and eloquence of its presentation of a human Washington who became, by grace of God rather than the help of the Continental Congress, the father of his country. It is bold drama in the sense of refusing to compromise with a soft patriotism, and also in its employment of a boldly spoken text. And a weakened drama in that it introduces a romantic note that some way does not meld smoothly with the generally accepted character of Washington, despite Rupert Hughes, or the situation as developed in the play.

Mr. Sherwood's "The Petrified Forest" combines the virtues of effective melodrama with an interesting philosophic content uncommon in dramas of so patent a theatrical base. The fact that Leslie Howard intelligently and modestly assumed and expressed the virtues of the somewhat visionary hero was undoubtedly of vast help to the play.

Samson Raphaelson's "Accent on Youth" provided the most appealing romance of a season that was weak in this type of play, retelling the love story of sentimental bachelors and romantic middle-aged professors to the great delight of a playgoing public that is in itself largely middle-aged and reminiscent. There were those who thought that it, too, should have been considered by the awarders of prizes.

"Merrily We Roll Along" is a stunt play in the sense that it was written backward in open defiance of all the traditional laws of dramaturgy extant. Following the career of a fallen hero back from his fall to the inspiration of his nobler ambition as a college graduate is a little like listening to and revisioning the virtues of a dead man at his wake. A none too cheerful experience. But there were many points in the drama's favor, not the least important of them the fine opportunities given its actors and its director. Individual scenes were expertly staged and directed by George Kaufman who wrote the drama with Moss Hart.

Two character comedies of superior quality and appealing to widely different publics were Clifford Odets' "Awake and Sing," a study of Jewish-American home life in the Bronx section of New York, and "The Farmer Takes a Wife," a story of the closing days of the Erie Canal peopled with racy native American "canawlers" of the early fifties.

"Lost Horizons," which may prove a bit confusing in the reading, seeing that many of the scenes are presumed to have been taking place simultaneously, is a drama fascinating in theme and provocative in conclusion. Not since "Outward Bound" dealt objectively with death and the soul's flight has any play created more definite expressions of praise and dispraise among its supporters. This play is an editor's choice. It was not given a general endorsement by theatre supporters.

The single play of alien authorship included in this season's list is John Van Druten's "The Distaff Side," an amiable and interesting discussion of feminine problems as they might credibly have agitated and affected an English middle-class family. It brought Dame Sybil Thorndike to America for the first time in many years and she spent a happy winter in making innumerable good-will conquests as one of England's fine actresses.

This volume brings the Best Play series to seventeen, if we include the volume containing the 1909-1919 record. It is the pious hope of the editor to go back one day to 1900 and come forward to 1909, which will complete the record of the American theatre from 1782 to the present day by bridging the single decade so far uncovered by the theatre's historians.

The usual record of performances given and the casts employed are included in the pages of the year book, for which your approval is again respectfully solicited.

B. M.

Forest Hills, L. I., 1935.

CONTENTS

CONTENTS

THE BEST PLAYS OF 1934-35

THE BEST PLAYS OF 1934-35

THE SEASON IN NEW YORK

FOR purposes of classification this may be spoken of as the record of the second theatrical season following the depression. There is some slight disagreement as to just when the depression ended, if ever, but there is no call to go into that, our interests being theatrical and not political.

The second season out of the depression was less exciting than the first. You who follow these chapters of record will recall that in the Spring of 1933 we watchers of the drama were sitting at the bedside of an ailing theatre a little fearful lest the patient begin picking at the coverlet almost any moment. You may recall, too, that after an anxious summer we enjoyed the pleasant shock of seeing the patient arise and walk and laugh again.

The recovery continued through the Winter. The Fall was filled with hope and renewed activity. But gradually the season took on a settled appearance. There were more performances of distinction than there were plays of distinction. A goodly percentage of our better dramatists either stayed on in Hollywood or, coming home, made but a brief visit and returned. The more successful plays of the year were written for the most part by novices. Which is a promise for the future as well as an achievement for the present.

There is not much to choose between Junes in the theatre. They are all pretty dull. In the old days it was the custom for Florenz Ziegfeld and George White, and occasionally Earl Carroll and John Murray Anderson to organize a vieing contest. One would vie with another for the honor of producing the nakedest and most amusing revue with the hope of establishing it for a Summer run and a Fall tour. Mr. Ziegfeld most frequently was the winner.

The last few years, or since the depression, followed by the talking pictures, the theatre season proper has come to a full stop in May and remained stopped until late August or early September. It was so this year. We closed the record officially on June 15. We could as reasonably have closed it June 4, when

3

Mr. Carroll produced his "Sketch Book" at the Winter Garden. Nothing happened after that. Nothing worth mentioning.

Nor was it any different last Spring. Pauline Frederick, who had been hopping about the West with a fairly labored comedy called "Her Majesty the Widow," tricked herself into the belief that it was good enough entertainment for Broadway and brought it in. Broadway decided it wasn't. James Barton, the dancer, replaced Henry Hull as the second of the Jeeter Lesters in the somewhat amazing "Tobacco Road," already approaching its second year (it is up to 700 performances at this writing and still going) and that gave the lingering reviewers something to write a column about. Barton was reported never to have played a legitimate rôle before this engagement, and the nerve of him, thinking he could replace the actor who had won all the season's medals for the best characterization of years and years, amused the experts. It was later admitted that Barton, as a youthful trouper, had had quite a bit of stock company experience. His Jeeter may have lacked histrionic polish and something of the authority supplied by the experienced Hull, but it was good enough to carry all the essential values of the part and the former burlesque comedian and eccentric dancer was duly acclaimed. Later James Bell succeeded Barton in the part. Being one of our better character actors his success was assured.

It was a good month for theatre restaurants, too. They were a novelty in those days. Two were flourishing. One was the Casino de Paree, with an expensive vaudeville revue on the stage and a variety of dinner and supper menus served on tables where orchestra seats had formerly been fastened to the floor. Billy Rose, who doubles the rôle of Fanny Brice's husband with that of being an active producer of bizarre reviews, having started the Casino successfully, organized another for the former Hammerstein theatre, a huge and handsome playhouse which Arthur Hammerstein had built to the memory of his father, Oscar, and later lost to the mortgagors. This was called "Billy Rose's Music Hall" and was opened with considerable hoop-la. There were to be 100 Singing Waiters and 100 Lonely Hearts, these last to serve as hostesses and dance partners for visiting strangers and adventuring summer bachelors whose wives had gone to the country. The authorities put a stop to the hostess idea and the singing waiters gradually sang themselves out. The Music Hall, past the novelty of its flashy opening, proved an expensive experiment and was closed up. There is, it appears, not support enough for more than one of these costly restaurant theatres, even on gay

Broadway. The Casino de Paree was later closed and a Folies Bergère was opened in what was built as the Earl Carroll Theatre, featuring the French troupe imported for the second year of the Century of Progress in Chicago. This has, by report, done very well.

In late August Walter Huston got back from Central City, where he had played Othello at the summer festival, and the run of "Dodsworth" was resumed with Fay Bainter and the original cast. This served as a sort of semi-official opening of the new season, which came burgeoning in a week later with "Life Begins at 8.40," a better than average Shubert revue featuring Bert Lahr, Ray Bolger, Luella Gear and Frances Williams. The town, being show hungry, took avidly to "Life" and kept it playing for more than two hundred performances, or until March. An attempt to approach if not to match this success with a second revue called "Saluta!" with Milton Berle as the chief comedian failed definitely a few weeks later. A Bronx "Saluta!" in other words.

The second excitement of the season was provided by the arrival of the D'Oyly Carte Opera company from London. Curiously, it was the first engagement this famous organization had played in New York in fifty years and, much to the general surprise, its success was immediate. For the several weeks of its engagement a succession of capacity audiences attended the Gilbert and Sullivan revivals. They began with "The Gondoliers" and continued on through a list of twelve favorites, no one of which seemed to please the delighted audiences more than another. "Patience," "Iolanthe," "Ruddigore," "The Mikado," "H.M.S. Pinafore," "The Pirates of Penzance," even "Trial by Jury" and "Cox and Box," were rapturously approved as new discoveries. It was a happy inaugural for the season.

Frances Starr, married and settled happily in Washington, still hears the call of the theatre occasionally. There was a play called "Lady Jane" ("The Old Folks at Home" it was in London with Marie Tempest) and Miss Starr liked that. She came to New York to play it, the story being that of a mother who had the frankness to declare that "many a marriage has been saved by an unsuccessful infidelity," and then to put her own married daughter in the way of such an experience. It was rather an obvious theatrical arrangement, however, and caused little stir. Lila Lee of the pictures played the daughter. Owen Davis dashed off one of his book dramatizations, this one called "Too Many Boats," but that, too, was much too close to the theatre to have any attractive contact with life. And Laurence Rivers, Inc., tried a hillbilly drama smothered in accents called "Tight Britches," an honest attempt by John Tainter Foote and Hubert Hayes to relate the tragedy of a mountain boy who wanted to be a preacher but had difficulty saving his own soul after a lustful servant girl seduced him. He never got to preach his first sermon, which convinced his loyal aunt that he was foredoomed as a little boy too big for his britches.

A minor September tragedy was the Elmer Rice experience as an independent producer. Mr. Rice, who had had a considerable success as the director of his own plays, "Street Scene," "Counsellor-at-Law," "We, the People," etc., decided, with Mrs. Rice, who is the managerial end of his family, to lease the Belasco Theatre and devote himself to the intelligent drama of protest. He had two plays written and ready for staging. The first, called "Judgment Day," was a vivid dramatization of the trial in Berlin of the young man accused of having burned the Reich. The second, "Between Two Worlds," related the adventure of a youthful communist who, returning disgustedly to Russia after an unhappy experience in capitalist Hollywood, seduces a restless parasite, a capitalist's daughter, on shipboard and thus helps to readjust his own thought and that of the young woman regarding the state of the world and its more individual social conflicts. "Judgment Day" suffered from an excess of passionate hatred of the Hitler inquisition. "Between Two Worlds" proved too casual a statement of fairly uninteresting conclusions to stir emotional response. With the failure of the second play Mr. Rice retired from the theatre forever and aye, remaining completely aloof for several weeks. Then he agreed to assist with the formation of the Theatre Alliance, which is to operate actively and coöperatively on a subscription basis the coming season.

A succession of comedies of admitted virtues but more faults included Charles Divine's "Tourists Accommodated," Ruth Langner's adaptation of "The Bride of Torozko," a study of English undergraduate life, "First Episode," and a more serious adventure by a famed psychiatrist, "A Ship Comes In." These lasted no longer than their producers' capital. Quicker failures were Samuel Shipman and Alan Dinehart's "Alley Cat" and Nat Dorfman's "Errant Lady."

The situation brightened perceptibly the next few weeks. Norma Krasna contributed a taut little melodrama, "Small Miracle," giving graphic cross-sections of city life within the space of an evening spent in the lounge of a theatre while a play was on.

It was repeated on the screen as "Four Hours to Live." The George Kaufman-Moss Hart drama that ran backward, "Merrily We Roll Along," caused considerable discussion and aroused a good deal of interest. Dame Sibyl Thorndike came from London with John Van Druten's placid but pleasant domestic drama, "The Distaff Side," and Max Gordon (in partnership with the Rockefellers), having taken over the smaller of two huge theatres in Rockefeller Center, opened it with a production of "The Great Waltz" that set the town buzzing with aye and nay opinions but finally swung into its stride as the season's No. 1 show piece. What the Hippodrome revues were to this theatrical capital twenty years ago "The Great Waltz" became in 1935, making thousands of tourists and metropolitan suburbanites supremely happy.

About this time Bert Lytell, having found a play by Emmet Lavery having to do with miracles and the faith of the Jesuits, called "The First Legion," determined to produce it, also on faith and a little borrowed capital. It came at a time when theatre competition was fairly keen and was rather neglected by the older and busier reviewers. Gradually, however, the play began to find a public of its own, largely though not predominantly Catholic in make-up. Twice the engagement was extended in New York. Later, on tour, a similar experience was enjoyed in Boston, Philadelphia and Chicago, and a successful Pacific Coast engagement followed. "The First Legion" tells a holding story of three young priests temporarily shaken in their conviction that the cloistered life is the life for them. A seeming miracle that cures a fellow priest is explained away by a man of medicine, but another and simpler miracle, the healing of a crippled child, takes its place to restore the faith of the doubters.

Francine Larrimore, who has not been very fortunate the last few seasons, did what she could for and with a folk play of New York's East Side called "Spring Song," written by Bella and Samuel Spewak. But what she could do was not enough. Owen Davis came again with an honest little character comedy of his own New England, called "Spring Freshet," but New Yorkers would have none of it. An elaborately planned Theatre of Young America, which had been in the throes of organization for many months, finally emerged in Columbia Circle with a fantasy called "The Chinese Nightingale," by Hans Schmeidel and Lasar Galpern, who served as director. Children young enough to appreciate it had nothing but their enthusiasm to offer, and their parents and guardians failed to stand back of them. As a result the Children's theatre is another dream temporarily shunted back into the limbo from which such dreams periodically emerge.

An expansive adventure in showmanship this season was that of Arch Selwyn of the theatre and Harold B. Franklyn of the radio. They joined forces and pooled bookings. Their first attraction was a super-vaudeville billed as "Continental Varieties," which they gave in the Little Theatre after they had redecorated that miniature monument to the career of Winthrop Ames and made of it a gem-like continental music hall. Their first bill was headed by a famed diseuse, Lucienne Boyer, who has been the toast of Paris and beyond for some years, and Vincente Escudero, the Spanish dancer who can stamp you a rhythm with his musical heels or snap you one with his talking castanets more excitingly than any of his competitors. There were others, including a polite little French barman who poured any liquor you might call for from the same pitcher of pure spring water. It was expensive entertainment and classy as anything, but the exclusive public for which it was intended was shortly exhausted.

The Messrs. Selwyn and Franklyn went on with their program, producing a little later an elaborately staged musical entertainment, "Conversation Piece," written by the gifted Noel Coward for the also gifted Yvonne Printemps (a darling of Paris when she was Mme. Sacha Guitry), and shortly after that a second expensively staged music play, "Revenge With Music," written by Howard Dietz and Arthur Schwartz. Never a more promising assortment of authors and performers, and yet with all their promise there was not a hit among them. Shortly after the firm of Selwyn and Franklyn was dissolved by mutual consent.

It was a great season for unexpected disappointments. The Theatre Guild had waited with calm assurance until October before it made a first production. This was James Bridie's "A Sleeping Clergyman," which unhappily developed soporific tendencies a few weeks later. Laurence Schwab, who had a record of successful productions before his announced retirement, came back to the theatre with something called "Dance With Your Gods," a voodoo drama of slightly muddled story, and this failed. "Lost Horizons," with as fascinating a theme as any drama has offered in many seasons, was beautifully staged by Rowland Stebbins, but could do no better than a precarious run of seven weeks.

A quiet little comedy of the Southern mountain country, "Bridal Quilt," written by the actor, Tom Powers; a mystery drama chasing a corpse through a hotel and called "Order,

Please," adapted by Edward Childs Carpenter; a holdup comedy, "Hipper's Holiday," by John Crump—all these were quick failures.

One spot of brightness about this time was the production of "Personal Appearance," a first comedy by Lawrence Riley which Brock Pemberton was fortunate in inducing Gladys George to play. Miss George is a comedienne of the Mae West school whose pert style is most popular just now and she helped to lift Mr. Riley's fairly commonplace play into line with the few definite popular successes of the winter.

Sean O'Casey's "Within the Gates," representing that interesting Irishman's departure from the drama of realism with which his first success was gained and his arrival at the drama of symbols and poetic philosophies which it is his contention will provide the important drama of the future, was received by a divided press and a slightly mystified public. "Within the Gates" is a play of the dream world of a poet's imagining existing within the confines of Hyde Park. Through the gates dance a Dreamer to represent the idealists, a Bishop to recall the confusions of the church, a Young Harlot to plead for the frailer humans. A variety of atheists and agitators, conformists and radicals, all performing before an animated frieze of depressed and unfortunate poor, completed the pictures.

There were demonstrations by those who hailed the drama as the most inspiring of recent contributions to the theatre, paired with the eloquent silences of a mystified majority. When interest slackened in New York "Within the Gates" was sent on tour, but did not get far. The Mayor of Boston banned it as a slap at religion and the more sacred traditions of Massachusetts thought. Its producers concluded a fight would not be worth its cost. Mr. O'Casey returned to London, presumably to work upon another play of similar character.

Eva LeGallienne, who had been touring with her Civic Repertory company, returned to Broadway with a production of "L'Aiglon" which the previously reported Arch Selwyn and Harold Franklyn also helped her stage. It was the most ambitious of the recent LeGallienne ventures, but it served to carry her only a short distance. Reports that she would return shortly to her Civic Repertory home in Fourteenth Street are denied by the re-lease of the theatre she formerly used to the Theatre Union for a continuation of its propagandist laboratory.

There was a noticeable dearth of music plays last season. Expenses of production were too great; salaries, thanks to the competition of radio and Hollywood, were too high and the risks much too heavy to invite capital. A second production in the revue class, following ten weeks after the season opened with "Life Begins at 8.40," was a little something cooked up and assembled by Jack McGowan and Ray Henderson called "Say When." It was cut pretty closely to Broadway's measure, with Harry Richman as a chief attraction and such minor favorites as Bob Hope and Dennie Moore, Cora Witherspoon and Taylor Holmes, Nick Long, Jr. and Charles Collins to provide support.

Tallulah Bankhead, who had been fighting through an illness, found herself recovered in early November and appeared with personal success in a drama called "Dark Victory," written by George Brewer and Bertram Bloch. The play took but light grip of the public's interest, however, and a month or so later Tallulah was ready to take up rehearsals for a proposed revival of "Rain." Her performance of the popular Sadie Thompson brought her added paragraphs of praise, many of them extravagant, but again there was no great interest indicated in the John Colton-Clemence Randolph play. Too many, apparently, had seen all they wanted to see of Sadie during the four years she lived with the late Jeanne Eagels, and the many engagements she has played in stock and on the screen. Miss Bankhead found still a third play for a short spring run, a comedy by Adelaide Heilbrun, flippant as to speech, diaphanous as to story, and pretty empty as to logic. "Something Gay" was its name.

The Abbey Theatre Players came back for two weeks of repertory with their Irish comedies. Their reception was again cordial but their business was nothing to brag about. There was a romantic tragedy centered about the life of the late Emily Dickinson called "Brittle Heaven," intimating that the poetess found inspiration for her love verse in a passion she acquired for the husband of Helen Hunt Jackson, her best friend. Dorothy Gish played the poetess. Josephine Pollitt and Frederick Pohl wrote the play, which lingered briefly.

"The Farmer Takes a Wife," extracted from Walter Edmund's novel, "Rome Haul," had an interesting historical background having to do with the last days of the Erie Canal as a popular waterway. June Walker, Henry Fonda, and Herb Williams, a favorite of old vaudeville days, gave it a racy performance. It did nicely for a month or two, but missed the wider popular success anticipated. Fred Stone had a fling at the drama in a Civil War play written by Sinclair Lewis, novelist, and Lloyd Lewis, a writer of drama reviews for the Chicago *News*. "Jayhawker" it was called. "Ace" Burdette, a likable liar who talked his way into the Senate and tried to fix up a truce between General Grant and General Lee that might have ended the war in 1864, gave Stone a chance to prove that he has a sense of character better than any the average musical comedy comedian can boast. But the play proved weak in that its first scene was its best. Interest dwindled as the story ran toward a theatrical conclusion.

Two outstanding successes of the November list were "The Children's Hour," a tense tragedy by Lillian Hellman, a fairly complete history of which will be found in this volume, and "Anything Goes," a happy musical comedy which Guy Bolton and P. G. Wodehouse started and Howard Lindsay and Russel Crouse finished. Music and lyrics by Cole Porter were selling factors, and a superior cast that included Victor Moore, Ethel Merman and William Gaxton made firm friends with practically all the playgoes of the town.

A farce that had its extravagantly amusing moments but found a consistent pace as entertainment hard to sustain was called "Page Miss Glory." Philip Dunning had a hand in writing it after Joseph Schrank had begun it and Dorothy Hall played the heroine. The Group Theatre, still a bit set-up over its success of the previous season with "Men in White," produced with a generous disregard of expense a drama of the early gold coast of California called "Gold Eagle Guy." There was free praise for the production and for the individual work of the actors engaged, but not as many playgoers as expected were interested in the play. The hero, a ruthless sailorman from off a windjammer, fought his way to the top as the head of a great steamship company in the sixties and seventies and died finally in the earthquake of 1906. He failed to stir that emotional reaction popular play heroes should command, though he was played to the hilt by J. Edward Bromberg, a favorite of the Group Theatre acting company. After an uphill fight for sixty-odd performances the play was withdrawn.

"Post Road," a clever mixture of farce and exciting melodrama, overcame the handicap of a story that had to do with the kidnaping of an infant. Lucille Watson was popularly cast in this comedy, playing the head of a family that unwittingly gave house room to a gang of crooks engaged in the kidnap racket. She was too quick for them, and saved the child. Will Hays, however, even with this happy ending, refused permission for a screening of the story. The Lindbergh case and the Hauptmann trial were still too fresh in the public mind.

The Theatre Union, devoted to the drama of protest in Fourteenth Street, staged an interesting bit of propaganda detailing a mutiny of sailors in the Austrian navy in 1918 near the close of the great war. "Sailors of Cattaro," written by Frederick Wolf and adapted by Michael Blankfort, stirred the radical following of the producers and played through ten weeks.

The Theatre Guild's second try was with Maxwell Anderson's "Valley Forge," which may have been a little too uncompromisingly American for the mixture of races making up New York's playgoing public. Nor was it completely to the liking of the native element, presenting George Washington as a very human hero fighting a Continental Congress that included many cheats and grafters prepared to sell their country to the enemy for a promise of trade gains, as more fully appears in a digest of the play printed in the pages following. It was a noble production and the Guild actors, led by Philip Merivale, did nobly by it. But after the subscription list had been covered there was no popular demand for the play.

As the holidays approached the number of plays produced fell off, as usual. Nor were there any of quality, save the "Romeo and Juliet" which Katharine Cornell brought in the week of the twentieth. Miss Cornell had devoted the previous season to a road tour that extended over something like 75,000 miles of territory, playing "Romeo and Juliet," "Candida" and "The Barretts of Wimpole Street." This was the first time she had permitted New York to see her Juliet and she was a bit anxious as to the outcome. As it turned out her opening night was catalogued as one of the most satisfying events of the recent theatre. Cheers for her gentle Capulet were loud and long and praise for her production and her company was heavy with superlatives. She continued with "Romeo and Juliet" for the ten weeks following, which approaches the record for Juliets.

Good entertainment came with the holidays. S. N. Behrman's philosophical "Rain from Heaven," with Jane Cowl returned to the local stage following a considerable absence, was one of the better plays of the season. Through its assorted characters Mr. Behrman expressed definite conclusions as to many social and political evils afflicting the world, the evil of the Nazi inquisition in particular. The Theatre Guild was the producer, and a tour followed a Broadway engagement of twelve weeks. Samson Raphaelson's "Accent on Youth" delighted a succession of large audiences, once it was settled and had become known as an appealing bachelor's romance. Nicholas Hannen, a comparative

newcomer from England, served the author as a playwright con-
vinced there could be no great love romance in which an old
man and a young woman were the principals involved. How
wrong he was the play, as hereinafter printed, relates. Constance
Cummings played the heroine during the major part of the run.
When Mr. Hannen returned to England he was succeeded by
Kenneth McKenna, and when Miss Cummings departed Claudia
Morgan took her place. The comedy continued successfully into
June, and was a great favorite with the summer stock companies.

The first week of 1935 brought two outstanding successes:
The first, Robert Sherwood's "The Petrified Forest," with Leslie
Howard amiably regathering all that huge public that came to
adore him when he played "Berkeley Square" and "The Animal
Kingdom"; the second, Zoe Akins' "The Old Maid," deftly extracted from an Edith Wharton novel of some years back. The
Sherwood play and the Howard performance were tremendously
popular from the first, but "The Old Maid," lacking critical support, started slowly. Matinees were capacity from the first, the
play making a particularly strong appeal to women. Gradually
those men who were dragged to see it came away grudgingly admitting that they had had a good time. By early spring the
play's success was assured, and when it was given the Pulitzer
award over both "Valley Forge" and "The Petrified Forest," it
enjoyed such a boom in attendance that it easily ran through the
summer. Two superior performances by Judith Anderson and
Helen Menken were important factors in this success.

Eddie Dowling organized a revue called "Thumbs Up" that
was both cleaner and brighter than most of the Broadway output.
It included the missus, Sister Ray Dooley, the surviving member
of that Dooley family which made life a lot brighter for thousands
of playgoers during the early years of the century. Thomas
Mitchell staged and played in an amusing comedy by Dorothy
Bennett and Irving White called "Fly Away Home." A father,
separated from his wife when his children were young, does not
see them until they are grown. Meantime his wife has pursued
her theories as to the liberal and quite unconventional rearing of
the youngsters. The father finds them, to his amazement, much
better equipped to discuss the facts of life with him than he is
with them. Another of J. B. Priestley's trick comedies (you may
recall "Dangerous Corners") was brought from London by a popular English comedian, Edmund Gwenn. "Laburnum Grove"
was the title. The story had to do with an eminently respectable
citizen of an exclusive suburb who, by his own startling confes-

sion, made his money counterfeiting. His family simply could not believe him, which was probably just as well for the family, and kept the play going for two hours.

Noel Coward suffered his second defeat of the year, which was a record for Coward, with the production of his "Point Valaine." The Lunts, Lynn Fontanne and Alfred, were its important personages and each gave a splendid performance. Even they could not save the play, which was a fairly unpleasant recital concerned with the adventures of unattractive humans. The story of a hotel keeper in the West Indies who took her primitive Russian waiter as a lover and denounced him when he dared assert his claims in opposition to those of a younger guest whom she also had favored. The Russian, emotionally crushed, jumped into the sea.

The Theatre Guild took over a contract which the unhappy firm of Selwyn and Franklyn had held with Charles B. Cochran for the importation of Elizabeth Bergner in her London success, "Escape Me Never." Miss Bergner came variously hailed as a flaring genius and an actress whose stage creations placed her in a class with the Bernhardts and the Duses. It was rather a fearful handicap to overcome, and if there was some slight hesitancy on the part of the local reception committee in granting all these virtues it was not slow in admitting the little Austrian to a place among the inspired comediennes of her time. Margaret Kennedy's play was interestingly superficial, Miss Bergner playing a waif who was picked up by one of the eccentric Sangers of "Constant Nymph" fame. They lived together, were finally married, and suffered numerous unhappy experiences, including the death of the young woman's child by a former companion. In the end they were still unhappy. Hugh Sinclair played opposite Miss Bergner and the play's success, through their aid, was consistently sustained. At the end of twelve weeks Miss Bergner decided she would rest, and though there was a clamorous demand for more performances the engagement was closed.

"Three Men on a Horse," a farce that had been bouncing about from one manager's office to another, fell finally into the hands of Alex Yokel who interested the Warners of Hollywood. Produced in late January the farce was an overnight success, and before Spring had settled there were four or five companies playing it between the two coasts. It is a racy affair relating the adventure of a timid greeting card writer who picks winning horses with such unerring success that he is shanghaied by a trio of gamblers and forced into the job of professional dopester. All goes well until they force him to place a bet on his own judgment. That, he explains, breaks the charm. Anyone can pick winners so long as he does not bet.

Pierre Fresnay, who had been the leading man playing opposite Yvonne Printemps in "Conversation Piece," being still in town after that play closed, arranged a production of André Obey's "Noah," an appealing fantasy relating the adventure of the captain of the Ark in much the same fashion that Marc Connelly told the story of the creation in "Green Pastures." M. Fresnay, a graduate of the Comédie Française, gave so fine a performance in the name part that he immediately jumped to the head of practically every play reviewer's list as the best actor of the season. "Noah," however, appealed to a small public only.

The Theatre Guild's fourth production of the season was Bernard Shaw's amusing but discursive "Simpleton of the Unexpected Isles." The Guild arranged a competent and carefully staged production, the cast including Alla Nazimova, Romney Brent, Rex O'Malley and McKay Morris. The reviews were a bit whimsical when they were not regretfully frank in reading the good gray dramatist out of the picture as an aging and garrulous bore. The Guild subscribers were loyal, but the general populace would have none of this older Shaw.

The Group Theatre found a success with which to follow "Gold Eagle Guy" in the first full-length play of its newly discovered member dramatist, Clifford Odets. This was "Awake and Sing," the Jewish-American folk comedy that is included with this year's best plays. It ran successfully into the Summer. "The Bishop Misbehaves," a placid comedy to which Walter Connolly added a measure of charm playing a Church of England Bishop whose fondness for theoretical crime detection involved him in as pretty a plot as any he had ever studied, enjoyed a moderate mid-Winter success. "The Green Pastures" came back for a fifth-year celebration, giving the late Richard B. Harrison a chance to play his 1265th performance as De Lawd before a weakening heart could bear him company no longer. The play, with Mr. Harrison's understudy, Charles Winter Wood, taking up the rôle, continued the anniversary engagement for nine weeks.

Dennis King, having nothing better to occupy him at the moment, produced a farce called "Petticoat Fever" and, though it was a trivial affair, the King performance was engagingly buoyant and at popular prices it ran on for many weeks. When Dennis wearied, Oscar Shaw took up the rôle. The Theatre Union did another strike play, "Black Pit," in Fourteenth Street and sold enough tickets to labor and radical organizations to guarantee a run of eleven weeks. The Group Theatre, having actors on its hands and under contract, decided to produce two other Odets plays, "Waiting for Lefty," which he had written for a benefit performance, and "Till the Day I Die," a dramatization inspired by correspondence from Berlin at the height of the Nazi inquisition. These proved tensely dramatic exhibits and drew a considerable public outside the natural response of liberal organizations.

Katharine Cornell made a third production in April, that of an anti-war play called "Flowers of the Forest," written by John Van Druten. Its reception was unfavorable, though the virtue of the Van Druten protest and the worthiness of the production were admitted. Miss Cornell decided not to force a run and withdrew the play after five weeks. Brock Pemberton, whose "Personal Appearance" had developed into a huge success, also agreed to embrace motion picture capital to the extent of agreeing to stage a melodrama written by Commander Frank Wead, once high in the navy's aviation forces, called "Ceiling Zero," with Warner money. The play, having a second act that is the most thrilling of any recently produced, gathered a good deal of praise, and played through until mid-July.

Grace George, who had been resting and reading plays for what seemed to be ever so long, found a drama she liked in an opus by Edward Chodorov called "Kind Lady." It belongs to the gooseflesh group, relating the thrilling adventure of a kind lady who was tricked into letting a gang of crooks into her home. The crooks thereupon boarded up the house, announced through the press that the lady was traveling abroad and proceeded to wear her down to the point of signing papers that would have put them in possession of her fortune. She contrives to outwit them in the end, which is well. Otherwise audiences probably would have died in the aisles. Miss George heard herself acclaimed one of the fine actresses of this time after she played this beleaguered heroine.

A melodrama that various managers had been threatening to produce for ages, entitled "A Trip to Pressburg" in the original German, finally appeared as a dramatization by Arthur Goodrich ("So This Is London" and "Caponssachi") titled "A Journey by Night." It proved a fairly dull and routine affair and was shortly put back in storage. A group of Moscow Art Players, led by Michael Chekov, nephew of the great Anton, played a repertory of Russian comedies and dramas, but attracted little attention save from their own people. Ernest Truex, always on the lookout for a timid man comedy, found one in "The Hook-up," telling the romance of a Seth Parker of radio who had to agree to marry a member of his troupe in a nationally broadcast radio wedding in order to save an advertising account. As a farce "The Hookup" had its moments, but there were not enough of them.

As a concluding gesture the Theatre Guild decided to produce a revue. This would be its sixth and final play in keeping with its subscription agreement. It took over the structure of a revue called "Parade," planned for the Theatre Union, which was basically radical. The sketches were satirical digs at the New Deal and the ensemble numbers slaps at the extravagance of a capitalistic society. What may be described inelegantly but truthfully as the "bellyache" entertainment has to be exceptionally clever if it is to prove attractive, and "Parade" was far from exceptional. Whatever the subscribers may have thought of it they kept mostly to themselves, but four weeks and "Parade" had passed.

The Players' Club wound up the season, as it so often does, with dignity and with success. With George Cohan's consent and coöperation they revived the pacemaker of all the mystery comedies, Earl Derr Biggers' "Seven Keys to Baldpate" which Mr. Cohan fashioned into a drama in 1913. It was a revival studded with names and pointed up with fine performances. Otis Skinner read the foreword. Audiences were large, the Players' benefited accordingly, and enthusiasm ran high. Dozens of mystery plays have come and gone since "Baldpate" was a season's hit, but of them all it is the most likely to endure. Cohan on this occasion played his own hero for the second time. He was forced into the cast by accident when Wallace Eddinger was hurt in an automobile wreck on the way to the try-out performances in Hartford in 1913. Eddinger afterward took up the rôle for the New York run and a subsequent road tour.

If we must have statistics, and a good many supporters of these volumes feel that we should have, there were 110 dramatic performances during the season and twenty-eight that were musical, including eleven Gilbert and Sullivan revivals.

There were less than the usual number of revivals, being fourteen in all. None of these prospered unusually, except the Cornell "Romeo and Juliet." Twenty-seven of the produced plays were of foreign authorship and importation, eighteen coming from England, three from France, two each from Austria and Spain, one each from Hungary and Germany.

THE SEASON IN CHICAGO

By CHARLES COLLINS

Dramatic Critic of the *Chicago Tribune*

STRIVING to take the cheerful view of Chicago's theatrical annals during the calendar year from June 1, 1934, to June 1, 1935, I will launch myself into the subject with the buoyant declaration: The drama holds its own! This will serve as a reassuring slogan which hews fairly close to the line of truth. Yes, I can testify without sense of perjury that the drama has held its own in this weakened sector—but as if by a finger-nail clutch on the edge of an abyss. There have been times when it seemed to be clawing its way vigorously back to safety; there have been other times when it seemed to grow faint and yield itself up to oblivion.

The statistics of the season are not completely reassuring; they do not fairly indicate the slight advance toward partial recovery which, I believe, has been made. After much struggling with a strangely miscellaneous batch of theatre programs and much perplexity over the classification of the many odd fish in the collection, I have arrived at the figure 41 for the total of theatrical engagements. This seems to be a shrinkage, for the preceding year gave me 43. Border-line cases enter into this business of theatrical score-keeping so often, however, that the slight decrease is of no importance. It probably grew out of my own vagaries over such items as Cornelia Otis Skinner's exploits in costumed elocution and "The Drunkard's" status as a cabaret show.

These 41 Chicago theatrical engagements or bookings, several of which represent repertories with abundant catalogues, may be subdivided as follows: Plays, 28; operettas, 9; revues, 4.

By approaching the subject from what might be called the architectural or real estate point of view, one gets a different and more discouraging story. There were only 8 theatres in part-time use; the year before there were 13. Moreover, one of the playhouses that figured in the 1934-1935 season, to the extent of one booking—the Cort—has already been demolished.

Here is the score by bookings for theatres in occasional use: Grand Opera House, 7; Harris, 6; Erlanger, 5; Selwyn, 3; Blackstone, 4; Cort, 1; Studebaker, 2; Auditorium, 1.

Playhouses which did not answer to the roll-call at all were the Apollo, the Garrick, the Punch and Judy, and the Princess, which have been converted into cinemas; and the Illinois, which stands mute and apparently useless.

Under present conditions there are only four Chicago theatres that may be counted on for a reasonable degree of operation— the Grand Opera House, the Harris and the Selwyn, which are managed by the Shubert firm; and the Erlanger, which is controlled by the survivors or heirs-at-law of the once magnificent Erlanger syndicate. The others get what stray bookings they can snatch out of the air, and these are few indeed. My figure of 1 for the bookings at the Auditorium does not do justice to the activity of that great old opera house, which is coming back into its own as a civic amusement center. Its only contribution to the drama for the year was "A Midsummer Night's Dream" in Max Reinhardt's style, but it sheltered operas, grand and comique, Russian ballets, concerts and recitals of all kinds.

The greatest event of Chicago's stage season was something entirely off the beaten track of professional showmanship. Broadway had nothing to do with it. The Actors' Equity Association, I suspect, got no dues out of its participants. Everyone said, in advance, that it would fail—everyone, that is, except myself, who had a spell of clairvoyance—and it turned out a unique and extraordinary success. I refer to the Old Globe Theatre of the second summer of A Century of Progress.

Shakespeare in abbreviated form for the masses, six and seven performances a day, in a playhouse which reproduced the atmosphere of Queen Elizabeth's era. That was the Old Globe idea, and it worked, to the surprise of the cynics who maintained that World's Fair crowds wanted nothing that rose above the peepshow or county-seat carnival level of intelligence. It was a hit at its start, before an invited audience of shivering intellectuals on a cold spring night, and it continued a roaring success for five consecutive months.

Thomas Wood Stevens, whose career has been spent largely in art and little theatres, gets the credit for the Old Globe achievement. He made the excellent condensations of the texts, and attended to most of the stage direction. For auxiliary, he had B. Iden Payne, now director of the Shakespeare Memorial Theatre at Stratford-on-Avon. But none of it would have been possible without the devoted coöperation of the young and spirited players, who without faltering went through a grind of acting that no other Shakespeareans in history ever tackled. It was a feat that required physical stamina and spiritual exaltation as well as art, but they finished as strong as champions; and when it was all over, of course, they shed tears of regret.

The leading rôles were admirably played by Carl Benton Reid, John A. Willard, Miss Jackson Perkins and Miss Irene Tedrow. The plays given were "The Taming of the Shrew," "All's Well That Ends Well," "A Comedy of Errors," "A Midsummer Night's Dream," "As You Like It," "Julius Cæsar," "Macbeth" and Marlowe's "Doctor Faustus." After the Fair closed, the Old Globe company set up its Elizabethan stage in McVicker's Theatre, in conjunction with cinema bills, and in the Studebaker Theatre. At the latter location they added "King Lear" and "Twelfth Night," in longer versions, to their record. Then they went on a tour of midwestern cities and college communities. They are spending the summer of 1935 at the California-Pacific Exposition in San Diego, where another Tudor playhouse has been built for them.

Another special event of stimulating effect was Max Reinhardt's staging of "A Midsummer Night's Dream" in the Auditorium. New York had no hand in this affair, either; it came from California, where it had been given in Los Angeles, San Francisco and Berkeley as a "festival" production under the sponsorship of a state commission. It was a production of great visual beauty—lyric theatricalism in the grand romantic manner —which sustained Reinhardt's international reputation as a master-mind of stagecraft and organization. The acting was not notable, except in the case of the two juvenile comedians from the motion picture studios who played Puck—Mickey Dooley and Georgie Breakston, urchins of 10 or 12. Nini Theilade's dancing, as a spirit of the enchanted woodland, matched the shimmering loveliness of Shakespeare's lines.

Chicago's playgoers, who are building up a reputation for reluctance about stepping toward box-offices, went for this Reinhardt spectacle in a large way. This successful affair, which came early in the season, marked a turn in the tide. Before "A Midsummer Night's Dream," it seemed as if the city might be denied the pleasures of the legitimate theatre; after it, the plays begin to arrive, in fair number and of improved quality. The advance in quality, rather than quantity, is, in fact, the most encouraging aspect of the season.

At this point a roll-call of titles is in order. After rejection of the casuals, the unclassifiables, the amateurs making a bid for general patronage, and the God-awfuls that had nothing to offer but a pious purpose, my catalogue for Chicago's stage year of 1934-1935 is as follows:

Old Globe Theatre Company (Shakespeare); "Fresh Fields," with Margaret Anglin and Alexandra Carlisle; "The Milky Way"; Gilbert and Sullivan by veterans of the Aborn revivals ("The Mikado," "The Pirates of Penzance," "Pinafore"); "Ziegfeld Follies" (the Billie Burke-Shubert production); "No More Ladies" (only one member of original New York cast); "The Pursuit of Happiness," with Tonio Selwart; "As Thousands Cheer," with Clifton Webb, Dorothy Stone, Helen Broderick and Ethel Waters; "A Midsummer Night's Dream," staged by Max Reinhardt; "Romance," revival with Eugenie Leontovich; "Ah, Wilderness," with George M. Cohan (Theatre Guild Company); "Petticoat Fever," with Dennis King (première here, prior to New York run); "Stevedore"; ("Roberta," with the original company; Earl Carroll's "Vanities"; the Abbey Theatre Company of Dublin in dramatic repertory, two engagements (ten full-length plays, 4 one-act plays); "L'Aiglon," with Eva LeGallienne; "Continental Varieties," mixed bill of music and dancing, with Lucienne Boyer, Escudero, Raphael and Nikita Balieff; "Sixteen," with Shaindel Kalish (Chicago production); "Ode to Liberty," with Ina Claire; the D'Oyly Carte Opera Company of London (Gilbert and Sullivan; 6 full-length operettas, 2 one-act pieces); "The First Legion," with Bert Lytell; "Life Begins at 8.40," with Bert Lahr, Ray Bolger, Luella Gear, Frances Williams (the complete New York company); "Rain from Heaven," with Jane Cowl and John Halliday (Theatre Guild production); "Three Men on a Horse," special company for Chicago run with Jack Sheehan in central rôle; "Mary of Scotland," with Helen Hayes, Ian Keith and Pauline Frederick (Theatre Guild production); "Hollywood Holiday," with Bebe Daniels, Ben Lyon and "Skeets" Gallagher; and "Laburnum Grove," with Edmund Gwenn.

One must admit that this is a good list. One must also admit, however, that for the Second City of the nation and the fourth of the world, it is a decidedly meager representation in a great cultural activity.

An outstanding event was the first engagement of the Abbey Company from Dublin, world-famous interpreters of their racial drama. They thrived here as they did during their visit of two years before, but it became evident, when they submitted several of their new plays, that the vein is running thin. A refreshment of inspiration or a change of policy is needed at the Abbey.

The season reached its highest point of playgoing enthusiasm when the D'Oyly Cartes of London arrived with their admirable presentations of the Gilbert and Sullivan operettas. They were received with a glowing affection which recalled the theatre-going mood of the Victorian and Edwardian era, before the movies and the radio and the night-clubs stripped off most of Thalia's garments and left her the most dejected Muse among the sacred Nine. The last performance of the fortnight ended with that almost extinct manifestation of popular approval, a spontaneous ovation, of a fervor unparalleled in my playgoing experience of thirty years around this town.

Other engagements that brought out the customers in great numbers were those of "Roberta," "As Thousands Cheer," "A Midsummer Night's Dream," "Mary of Scotland" and "Three Men on a Horse." The latter comedy had reached its tenth week when the season crossed the Summer dead-line, but was still running strong. In the second week of June it remained as the only specimen of the "legitimate" left on the Chicago stage. It wins the long run honors of the year, "going away," as the race-track form writers put it.

A striking curiosity of the year is found in the history of the showboat Dixiana, which has been operated in a backwash of the north branch of the Chicago River since August, 1934. This craft is, strangely enough, Chicago's most successful claim to status as a "producing center," to date. It was built by a group of Chicago business men, more or less innocent of "show business"; it is without doubt the biggest and best showboat, in equipment, that can be found upon the waters of the earth; and its revivals of melodramas representing the American folk-theatre of the 1890s and 1900s have aroused much merriment in the town. The performances are not the arty burlesques of the Hoboken and Greenwich Village style of smart-alec humor. The plays are acted with melodramatic sincerity, and the rôle of comic satirist is assigned to the audiences. Community singing of ancient ballads and moss-backed variety turns help to create the atmosphere of whoopee among the customers. A restaurant and bar on the commodious craft also contribute to the picnic mood.

The Dixiana, thus far, has staged the following examples of barbaric and maudlin American taste in drama: "No Mother to Guide Her," "The Convict's Daughter," "The Fatal Wedding," "Human Hearts," "The James Boys in Missouri," "Nellie, the

Beautiful Cloak Model," "Bertha, the Sewing Machine Girl,"
"Forgiven at the Altar," "The Little Outcast," and "While the
City Sleeps."

My notes on Chicago's stage history for the year include a
large group under a caption of "Miscellaneous," which does not
figure in my score-keeping. Here are some of the entries: Summer drama "festival" at Woodstock, Ill., with Orson Welles,
Michael MacLiammoir, Hilton Edwards and Louise Prussing, in
"Trilby,"¹ "Hamlet" and "Tsar Paul"; Offenbach's "La Vie
Parisienne" and "Tales of Hoffman," by the New York Opera
Comique Company (semi-professional) at the Auditorium; two
engagements of the Monte Carlo Ballet Russe at the Auditorium;
a week of Cornelia Otis Skinner's "monodramas"; two elaborate
revues in theatre-restaurant style at the French Casino; five or
six semi-professional productions of drama by the Uptown Players in the Chicago Woman's Club Theatre; and ambitious amateur
affairs by the score.

Box-office business, in general, has been moving slowly uphill.
Chicago's playgoers, however, seem to want miracles or nothing.
Deserving plays that have not been highly publicized have a
hard row to hoe. The city's tradition has always been to import
its amusements, insisting upon the biggest and the best, or at
any rate the most stylish. This course, through the generations,
has brought about an attitude or point of view which may be
characterized as that of the Superior Provincial, deficient in the
sense of discovery and inclined to be snooty and stand-offish
about anything that does not wear a label of approval by the
Olympians elsewhere. But that is another story.

Explicit historia spectaculorum Chicaginiensium 1934-1935.

THE SEASON IN SAN FRANCISCO

By George C. Warren

Drama Editor of *The San Francisco Chronicle*

THE theatre in San Francisco had hard going during the year beginning June 1, 1934, and ending May 31, 1935. At several times during that period no legitimate theatre was open. However the town saw many of this and last season's New York successes, and at the moment of writing has both "Tobacco Road" and "Accent on Youth" running at the Curran and Geary Theatres respectively.

There has been less Coast production than for several years, with Homer Curran and Henry Duffy as the adventurers in the field, sometimes with success; at others at a loss. Since January there have been more companies from New York come across the continent on the report of big business in San Francisco and Los Angeles than has been the case in a number of seasons.

Both Mr. Duffy and Mr. Curran have had difficulty in getting casts for the New York successes, and the haste with which the motion picture producers have turned out pictures from current New York plays has stopped the staging of many of these plays.

The year began with Conrad Nagel and Violet Heming in John Van Druten's "There's Always Juliet," which had fair success, and was followed shortly afterward by Mordaunt Shairp's "The Green Bay Tree," acted by Edward Cooper as the sybarite and Walter Armitage as his protégé. Lucille Ryan, advised by Louis Owen Macloon, was the producer.

Keith Winter's "The Shining Hour," with Jane Cowl, Pat Somerset, Joyce Carey, Leo G. Carroll and Eily Malyon, was staged by Henry Duffy, but met with a chilly reception. The next important production was "Mary of Scotland," done by Homer Curran. Helen Gahagen was the Mary, Violet Kemble-Cooper the Elizabeth, and Ian Keith the Bothwell.

"Men in White," produced by Henry Duffy, had Roger Pryor, Henry Kolker, Betty Lawford and Lorin Raker in the leads. It followed the picture made from the play and so failed to draw.

Max Reinhardt's fantastication of "A Midsummer Night's Dream," presented at the Memorial Opera House, had twelve

24

performances to immense audiences. Walter Connolly was the
Bottom. The play was given for two performances in the Greek
Theatre at Berkeley. The comedy began in Faculty Glen and
then the audiences walked to the Greek Theatre for the final act.

The city had William Thornton and Fritz Leiber, each for two
weeks, in Shakespearean repertoire, and the Ziegfeld "Follies"
with Fannie Brice, Willie and Eugene Howard and the Presser
Sisters as the featured players. Business was very big.

Homer Curran produced Kaufman and Hart's "Merrily We
Roll Along" with Douglass Montgomery in the Kenneth Mc-
Kenna rôle, and such other players as Erin O'Brien-Moore,
Frieda Inescort, Virginia Cherrill and Irene Franklin. Walker
Whiteside came for two weeks in "The Master of Ballantrae" to
rather light business, and the Abbey Players played three weeks
to sell-out houses in their familiar repertoire.

"As Thousands Cheer," with Dorothy Stone, Ethel Waters,
Margaret Irving, Porter Hall and Hal Forde did three and a half
big weeks, and Henry Hull in "Tobacco Road," with Mary
Servoss, and Otto Kruger in "Accent on Youth" bring the year
to its end, so far as the professional stage is concerned. In immediate prospect are Bert Lytell in "The First Legion"; Percy Kil-
bride in "Three Men on a Horse" and "Petticoat Fever" with
Dennis King, Doris Dalton and Leo G. Carroll.

Community, University, Children's and Little theatres were busy
and some produced surprisingly well. The Pacific Little Theatre,
attached to the College of the Pacific at Stockton, offered Euripi-
des' "Medea" in its open air theatre, with DeMarcus Brown directing. The tragedy was done as a melodrama, with Medea
garbed in gay colors almost as a gypsy might dress, with the result of making the classic modern and fast moving.

At Carmel-by-the-Sea a pageant was presented on the grounds
of the Carmel Mission church where Fra Junípero Serra lies
buried. George Marion wrote the pageant and himself acted Fra
Junípero. Frank Sheridan, Helen Ware, Fred Burt and other
professional actors were in the cast. The pageant is called "The
Apostle of California," and celebrates the founding of the line of
missions from San Diego to San Francisco, the work of Serra.

Carmel also saw a production of Martin Flavin's play, "Sunday," that city being the home of the author. Hattie M. Smith,
graduate of the Yale School of the Drama, is giving the art
colony in Carmel the first regular summer season of plays, presented on week ends from June to September, beginning with
Ervine's comedy, "The First Mrs. Fraser." This is the first

summer season planned in the State.

Children's theatres have been busy in San Francisco, where there was a season of 16 Saturday performances, backed by the Board of Education, and well attended. Palo Alto also has a children's theatre headed by Hazel Glaister Robertson, and a short season of Saturday plays for children was given at Mills College, Oakland, and sponsored by the Women's clubs of Oakland, Alameda and Berkeley.

The Ronald Telfer Players gave a season of Shakespeare's plays, well done and capably acted, and including "Much Ado About Nothing," "The Two Gentlemen of Verona," "Love's Labour's Lost" and "Richard II." In the latter Frances Creel, daughter of Blanche Bates, acted the Queen.

Under the direction of Edwin Duerr the Little Theatre of the University of California presented a series of plays, chief among which were Jean Girardoux's "Intermezzo"; Sidney Howard's "Yellow Jack," done on an architectural stage, and "The Doctor for a Dumb Wife," a combination of Molière's "A Doctor in Spite of Himself" and Anatole France's "The Man Who Married a Dumb Wife," Duerr, the director, having done the writing. This group also produced Pirandello's "Henry IV."

A new group, headed by Philip Mathias, who is also its director, taking the name of the Pine Street Players, has its own theatre and produces only original plays. Among them was an experiment along the lines of the ancient Commedia dell'Arte. A theme was given to the actors and they supplied dialogue and action. The piece was called "The Living Lie," and was most interesting.

Baldwin McGaw offered several well-rehearsed plays, among them being Ibsen's "Peer Gynt," and "The Cricket on the Hearth" in a new dramatization by Gilmor Brown, head of the Pasadena Community Playhouse. At Mills College, Oakland, Marian L. Stebbins, a pupil of Yvette Guilbert, presented the old morality play, "Gibour," in which Guilbert had presented Mrs. Stebbins in New York some years ago. This group at Mills also made a production of Chista Winsloe's "Girls in Uniform."

The Community Players of Palo Alto, who have a splendidly equipped theatre, the gift of Mrs. Louis Stern, gave regular performances once a month, offering their plays for three nights. Some of them were Maxwell Anderson's "Both Your Houses"; "Squaring the Circle," a soviet farce, and a Browning evening with "In a Balcony" and "Pippa Passes" as the plays. Ralph Emerson Welles is the professional director of this group.

An outdoor performance in the Woodland Theatre at Kentfield of Josef and Karel Capek's "The World We Live In" was the most important of the productions of the Ross Valley Players, who have Cameron Prud'homme for their director. The Wayfarers continued to stage plays for a week every two months, two originals, "A Preface to Morals" and "Escape," among them. The most important production of the Dramatic Council at Stanford University was "The Doctor's Wife," an original play by Eric Linders in which Dr. Margery Bailey, of the faculty, played the title rôle.

At this university, Stanford, a course in Shakespeare is being given this summer under William Thornton, an alumnus of the University, who for several seasons has been touring the West in Shakespeare's plays. A production of "Othello" by the students at this summer school will be an event of August.

THE SEASON IN SOUTHERN CALIFORNIA

By Philip K. Scheuer

Assistant Drama Editor of the *Los Angeles Times*

UNLIKE most cities, Los Angeles more or less officially launched her 1934-35 season by staging a production not indoors but out. This was Max Reinhardt's conception of William Shakespeare's "A Midsummer Night's Dream," in Hollywood Bowl. Despite the direst predictions of the wiseacres, the whole of this end of the state, it appeared, pack-jammed the 14,000-seat amphitheatre for the eight performances commencing September 17 of 1934. The gross was in the neighborhood of $130,000, a record.

Setting and Shakespeare together combined to evolve a memorable evening. The emphasis, of course, was all on setting, although the essential buffoonery shone through, particularly during what might be described as the "afterpiece," or show within a show. The musicians' shell had been removed, and a torchlight procession came winding over the hills into Prof. Reinhardt's specially prepared wood.

Greatest individual triumph was scored by young Mickey Rooney as the impish Puck. Walter Connolly played Bottom, with Julie Haydon as Titania, Evelyn Venable as Helena, Olivia de Havilland as Hermia, and Sterling Holloway, John Lodge, William Farnum and Frank Reicher in the company. Nini

Theilade was première danseuse.

Reinhardt duly transferred his spectacle to the films, this marking also the beginning of his capitulation to Hollywood. A second Bowl production, "Twelfth Night," was in preparation for the summer of 1935, possibly with Katharine Hepburn.

Long talked-of, the Hollywood Theatre Guild started out ambitiously enough. Twelve dramas were promulgated and subscriptions sold on that basis, but only two materialized. The first was "Kitty Dooley of Times Square," by Raymond Bond, who also acted the lead. The Bliss-Hayden Little Theatre group was behind this one, a harmless, wisecracking comedy above the local average for this sort of thing, but rather "dated" in its theme: the problems of two- and four-a-day vaudevillians.

Expectant subscribers who made their way to the Hollywood Playhouse to witness the second of the series—also independently produced—were surprised to find pickets with banners circling 'round and 'round the lobby. The banners proclaimed that the actors inside were being woefully underpaid ($2 per week was the mean average) and demanded that something be done about it. What made the situation unusual was the fact that one of the two plays on exhibition was Clifford Odets' "Waiting for Lefty," a decidedly anti-capitalistic document from the New Group Theatre.

This dissension in the ranks of presumed comrades was fairly indicative of the unsettled state in which much of the Southern California drama found itself toward the close of the season, although the circumstances were exceptional. Odets' dual bill had already met with opposition at Laguna Beach, where it was tried out; and earlier in the short run at Hollywood, the director had been kidnaped and beaten, allegedly by Nazi sympathizers who objected to a slight to Hitler in "Till the Day I Die," the "curtain raiser." But few denied the advent of a playwright of great promise; and the cast, consisting largely of unfamiliars, received approbation.

Los Angeles continued to be the center of all south-state activities, with no road shows appearing anywhere outside. Stock—the Savoy—flourished briefly, three weeks, in San Diego, with some attendance reported at the "tab" Shakespearean versions in the reconstructed "Globe Theatre" at the California-Pacific International Exposition. A commentary on the disordered and unpredictable condition of "the road" is contained in the facts that "The First Legion," with Bert Lytell, made the jump to Los Angeles direct from Philadelphia, that "Three Men on a Horse" hopped straight from Montreal, and that the Ringling Brothers-Barnum and Bailey Circus left town after five days with $220,000 in receipts—an all-time Coast high.

"Three Men on a Horse," with a second-rate troupe, did well at the Biltmore. The house record for the season was toppled in one week by Billie Burke's "Ziegfeld Follies," with Fannie Brice and the Howard Brothers. "As Thousands Cheer" arrived in April, with Dorothy Stone and Ethel Waters, but the fleeting topical nature of this Moss Hart-Irving Berlin extravaganza militated against its attaining sell-out proportions.

Touring repertory did unusually well, the Abbey Players of Dublin meeting with rather extraordinary favor, in their fortnight at the Biltmore. "The New Gossoon," "Juno and the Paycock," "Playboy of the Western World," "Drama at Inish" and "The Far-Off Hills" were included among the offerings. Two weeks of Fritz Leiber, and the same for William Thornton, were sufficient to bring out most of the bibliophiles who hide away between Shakespeare seasons. Young Thornton, variously made up to represent Hamlet, Lear, Petruchio, Shylock, Richard III and Romeo, and sponsored in toto by "The Shakespeare Guild of America," displayed a quality ingenuous enough—and hence unorthodox enough—to be interesting. Leiber, it may be noted, returned later to go into the cinema.

Cornelia Otis Skinner, alone peopling the boards with the Empress Eugenie, Henry VIII's ladies and the "loves" of Charles II, was extended a polite welcome back by her admirers. Conversely, a whole troupe of Scottish Players failed to elicit half the response at the Philharmonic Auditorium. Peripatetic Walker Whiteside reached into a voluminous old sleeve and pulled out "The Master of Ballantrae," which he staged, all with a faint odor of must, at the Biltmore.

Henry Duffy's El Capitan Theatre, which has operated practically continuously since it opened in 1927, moved into the ill-defined 1934-35 season with "Goodbye Again," presenting Conrad Nagel and Sally Bates, "The Milky Way," with Hugh O'Connell and Jean Dixon, and "Her Master's Voice," with Billie Burke. Norman Krasna's melodrama, "Small Miracle," followed in due course, Joseph Spurin-Calleia (now merely Joseph Calleia) trekking westward for the engagement and staying on for the talkies. More auspicious than any of these was the run of Samson Raphaelson's comedy, "Accent on Youth," with Otto Kruger and Martha Sleeper, which lasted eight weeks. Mark Reed's "Petticoat Fever," starring Dennis King, came after.

Homer Curran relighted the Belasco in September for a Coast production of Maxwell Anderson's "Mary of Scotland," which did fairly during a two-weeks tenure. Helen Gahagan, Ian Keith and Violet Kemble Cooper were the principals. In February the Kaufman-Hart "Merrily We Roll Along" appeared, Douglass Montgomery, Erin O'Brien-Moore and Frieda Inescort portraying the leads. Attendance was so-so. Subsequently Jack Kirkland and Samuel H. Grisman put on Kirkland's "Tobacco Road," Henry Hull, Manhattan's No. 1 Jeeter Lester, resuming the interpretation locally. Theatre-goers, shocked into attendance, sustained it for two months at the Belasco and later at the Hollywood Music Box, whither it traveled via San Francisco.

Sentiment attached to the revival of Somerset Maugham's "The Circle," which was done at the Hollywood Playhouse with Mrs. Leslie Carter. The R. C. Sherriff war play, "Journey's End," took a new lease on life at the same place, with Colin Clive and later John Warburton featured. Lucille Ryman produced the Siftons' "Blood on the Moon," with indifferent results, at the Mayan, which afterward housed two journeyman pieces by Willis Maxwell Goodhue—"Pop Goes the Weasel" and "Chickens Come Home." The virtue of novelty was discernible in "Woman on Trial," by Ayn Rand, a courtroom affair which placed the responsibility of verdict-rendering squarely up to alarmed Playhouse spectators. Barbara Bedford, Mozell Brittone and Morgan Conway headed the cast.

Support of Little Theatres—first-night support particularly—by screen celebrities lent an impetus to these unofficial activities. Pasadena Community Playhouse continued to be a focal point, with such dramas as "The Brothers Karamazov" (the Reginald Pole version of Dostoievsky, with Pole directing and Hans Von Twardowski and Martin Kosleck leading the company), and "Gallows Glorious," by Ronald Gow, an Englishman, among the more ambitious efforts. The latter history, based on that of the John Brown of body fame, included Hobart Bosworth and Rosamond Pinchot in its ensemble.

Maxwell Anderson's "Both Your Houses," Elmer Rice's "Judgment Day," Lynn Riggs' "Roadside" and Dr. Cecil Reynolds' "The Mystery of Broadwalk Asylum," the last a première, also appeared on the Pasadena roster, along with revivals of "Hedda Gabler," "The Virginian," "Anna Christie," "She Stoops to Conquer" and "The Return of Peter Grimm." J. C. and Elliott Nugent projected a comedy of the depression and the NRA, "The World's My Onion," with the elder Nugent and Douglas Wood,

which was more or less favorably described. Of three whilom
dramas by Martin Flavin, two were proffered at Pasadena. These
were "Amaco," a stylized indictment of the machine age, badly
"dated"; and "Achilles Had a Heel," an excursion in expression-
ism reminiscent of the O'Neill of "The Hairy Ape" and "Emperor
Jones." The latter piece, noteworthy if only because it revealed
the eminent Walter Hampden in blackface, developed considerable power in its treatment of two men in a zoo. John Wray was
the other man.

The Bliss-Hayden people sponsored "Sunday" (formerly
"Every Day Is Sunday"), the third Flavin play, which retails the
disintegration of a family.

Among the various groups presenting "firsts"—actual or im-
plied—was the Spotlight Theatre, with "Torquemada," a potent
discussion of Spanish Inquisition evils, by Theodor Dierks; the
Gateway Players, with "Embers of Haworth," still another investigation of the Brontë Sisters, by DeWitt Bodeen; the Beverly
Hills Community Players, with "World Without End," in which
Tiberius Cæsar reappeared on earth, as a modern captain of
finance, by Mears Pitcher and Dickson Morgan; and Lela Rogers'
Hollytown Theatre, with Marie Bercovici's "Strangers All." The
latter was filmed, with May Robson.

The Beverly Hills Little Theatre for Professionals moved into
Hollywood with two of its comedies, offering them to the more
general public at the Vine Street. These were Lea Freeman's "A
Widow in Green" and John Entenza's "A Notorious Lady."

Among the oddities, "The Drunkard" remained preëminent, entering its third bibulous year at the Little Theatre Mart. An ill-
advised attempt to cash in on its popularity was made with "The
Drunkard Repents," at Tony Pastor's. In downtown Los Angeles, the Musart bade vehemently but vainly for extended notice
with "Stevedore" and "Sailors of Cattaro," while the Olvera
Street, in the Mexican quarter, essayed "East Lynne" and Molière's "A Doctor in Spite of Himself." Frederick Hollander's
second revue intime, "All Aboard," was a disappointment and
soon darkened the quaint Tingel-Tangel. At the barn-like Philharmonic, dollar-top operetta did very well indeed with "The
Vagabond King," "The Chocolate Soldier" (with Charles Purcell)
and "Blossom Time."

Although studio-promoted stage shows were already a reality
in Manhattan, progress in this direction was slower on the Coast,
with rumors rife but unsubstantiated. The affiliation of Henry
Duffy, veteran local producer, with one of the larger picture com-

panies, was expected to result beneficially. Studios continued to try out plays with their own "junior" talent in shuttered playhouses, privately, with attendance limited to personnel.

But the question of just what ultimate good might come to the theatre from a closer liaison between the two mediums remained unanswered. The final desideratum, obviously, was for the commercial theatre to do what the screen could not, the experimental theatre to do what the commercial theatre would not. At the other extreme lay the danger that the theatre would become a testing house, a laboratory, for the movies.

Meanwhile attendance figures climbed over those of the previous season, ten playhouses being lighted in the spring of 1935. The fatal Coast habit—that of acquiring a reputable play for production and then stinting on those refinements whose sum total is Theatre—persisted to some extent, and the "service charge" evil (i.e., "free" passes plus a "nominal" box-office fee) had not yet been wiped out. But the signs were unmistakable that a public eager for the good things of the drama would continue to support them as occasion arose.

THE CHILDREN'S HOUR

A Drama in Three Acts

BY LILLIAN HELLMAN

IT was late November before anything resembling a definite dramatic sensation had been scored by any one of the new plays of this particular season. Then Lillian Hellman's "The Children's Hour" struck Broadway like a thunderbolt, in the phrase of Whitney Bolton.

It was a first play, and not too much had been expected of it. It was also a play written upon a subject of such delicacy that reference to it in the theatre usually is confined to the vulgarized comment of burlesque comedians and the writers of tasteless sketches for topical revues. That would be the subject of unnatural affections harbored by persons of the same sex.

In place, however, of providing the major theme of "The Children's Hour" this disturbing subject becomes by nature of the tragedy largely incidental to it. The true theme is the curse of scandalmongering and the whispering campaign, the kind of vicious lying that may easily wreck the lives of innocent persons.

Miss Hellman, building her play upon a story basically similar to, if it were not suggested by, that told by a William Roughhead in his report of a famous case tried in the Glasgow courts of the last century, reveals her subject with such absence of untoward suggestion and attacks it with such honesty that, to this editor, the play is entirely free of offense.

"The Children's Hour" attracted a good deal of attention, was excitingly acclaimed by its reviewers and drew large audiences for a period of months.

The study room of the Wright-Dobie school for girls, housed in a converted farmhouse near the village of Lancet, is large, comfortable and unpretentious. When it is not being used for study purposes it automatically becomes the living room of the school.

This late afternoon in April the class combining sewing and elocution is here assembled. Under what would be the watchful eye of Mrs. Lily Mortar, ex-actress and teacher of elocution, if Mrs. Mortar were not at the moment leaning comfortably back in a large chair with her eyes closed, Peggy Rogers is reading from "The Merchant of Venice" to seven fellow-students.

Peggy has arrived at Portia's quality of mercy that falleth like the gentle rain. At the moment it is falling in tones that are sing-sing and tired. Peggy is bored. So, too, is the sewing class which is not even sewing with any enthusiasm. Evelyn Munn, for instance, is using the time to cut Rosalie Wells' hair, and not making any too successful a job of that.

Mrs. Mortar opens her eyes suddenly and is properly shocked. First at the haircutting and then at the atrocious reading of one of her favorite speeches. Mrs. Mortar can remember when she spoke for Portia with proper feeling:

". . . And earthly power doth then show likest God's when mercy seasons justice. We do pray for mercy, and that same prayer doth teach—"

Mrs. Mortar has skipped three lines, Peggy points out, but Mrs. Mortar, insisting that she never has missed a line in her entire stage career, refuses to credit the statement.

It is during this moment of some excitement that Mary Tilford carefully squeezes herself through the door. "She is an undistinguished-looking girl, except for the sullenly dissatisfied expression on her face," and she is clutching a slightly faded bunch of wild flowers.

Mrs. Mortar abandons Shakespeare for the moment to demand Mary's excuse for coming late to class. Mary explains that she had taken a walk and, seeing the wild flowers, had stopped to pick them for Mrs. Mortar. The whole thing had taken much longer than she had thought.

The class has settled again to some sort of study attitude when Karen Wright comes quietly into the room. "Karen is an attractive woman of twenty-eight, casually pleasant in manner without sacrifice of warmth or dignity. She smiles at the girls, goes to her desk. With her entrance there is an immediate change in the manner of the girls. They are fond of her and they respect her."

Karen is quick to take note of Evelyn's haircutting and Rosalie's distress as to how she is going to look. And quick, too, to note the faded wild flowers which Mary Tilford is putting into a vase. She wonders where Mary found them. Mary found them near Conway's cornfield, she thinks.

"It wasn't necessary to go so far," quietly remarks Karen. "There was a bunch exactly like this in the garbage can this morning."

The suggestion throws Mrs. Mortar into a good deal of temper, which she expends on Mary, accompanied by charges of the girl's other recent lapses. She would have gone on at length, but a bell is heard calling another class. As the girls file out Karen asks Mary Tilford to stay.

"Mary, I've had the feeling—and I don't think I'm wrong—that the girls here were happy; that they liked Miss Dobie and me, that they liked the school. Do you think that's true?"

"Miss Wright, I have to get my Latin book," replies Mary evasively.

KAREN—I thought it was true until you came here a year ago. I don't think you're very happy here, and I'd like to find out why. (*Looks at* MARY, *waits for an answer, gets none, shakes her head.*) Why, for example, do you find it necessary to lie to us so often?

MARY (*without looking up*)—I'm not lying. I went out walking and I saw the flowers and they looked pretty and I didn't know it was so late.

KAREN (*impatiently*)—Stop it, Mary! I'm not interested in hearing that foolish story again. I *know* you got the flowers out of the garbage can. What I do want to know is why you feel you have to lie out of it.

MARY (*beginning to whimper*)—I *did* pick the flowers near Conway's. You never believe me. You believe everybody but me. It's always like that. Everything I say you fuss at me about. Everything I do is wrong.

KAREN—You know that isn't true. (*Goes to* MARY, *puts her arm around her.*) Look, Mary, look at me. Let's try to understand each other. If you feel that you *have* to take a walk, or that you just *can't* come to class, or that you'd like to go into the village by yourself, come and tell me—I'll try and understand. I don't say that I'll always agree that you should do exactly what you want to do, but I've had feelings like that, too—everybody has—and I won't be unreasonable about yours. But this way, this kind of lying you do, makes everything wrong.

MARY (*looking steadily at* KAREN)—I got the flowers near Conway's cornfield.

KAREN (*sighing*)—Well, there doesn't seem to be any other way with you; you'll have to be punished. Take your recreation periods alone for the next two weeks. No horseback-riding and no hockey. Don't leave the school grounds for any reason whatsoever. Is that clear?

MARY (*carefully*)—Saturday, too?

KAREN—Yes.

MARY—But you said I could go to the boat races.

KAREN—I'm sorry, but you can't go.

MARY—I'll tell my grandmother. I'll tell her how everybody treats me here and the way I get punished for every little thing I do. I'll tell her, I'll—

MRS. MORTAR—Why, I'd slap her hands!

KAREN (*ignoring* MRS. MORTAR)—Go upstairs, Mary.

MARY—I don't feel well.

KAREN (*wearily*)—Go upstairs now.

MARY—I've got a pain. I've had it all morning. It hurts right here (*pointing vaguely in the direction of her heart*). Really it does.

KAREN—Ask Miss Dobie to give you some hot water and bicarbonate of soda.

MARY—It's a bad pain. I've never had it before.

KAREN—I don't think it can be very serious.

MARY—My heart! It's my heart! It's stopping or something. I can't breathe. (*She takes a long breath and falls awkwardly to the floor.*)

They send for the doctor and carry Mary to her room. Martha Dobie, Karen's partner in the school, a nervous and high-strung young woman about Karen's age, is as distressed by the problem of Mary Tilford as Karen, but neither can think of anything to do about it. Mary is the spoiled darling of her Grandma Tilford, and Grandma has been very kind to the Wright-Dobie school through its early struggles. Neither of them is eager to speak to Mrs. Tilford about her grandchild, nor at all convinced Mrs. Tilford would believe anything they might report. Martha thinks perhaps they might ask the doctor to do it.

"That would be admitting that we can't do the job ourselves," protests Karen.

"Well, we can't and we might as well admit it," answers Martha. "We've tried everything we can think of. She's had more attention than any other three kids put together. And we still haven't the faintest idea what goes on inside her head."

"She's a strange girl."

"That's putting it mildly."

"It's funny. We always talk about the child as if she were a grown woman."

"It's not so funny. There's something the matter with the kid. That's been true ever since the first day she came. She causes trouble here; she's bad for the other girls. I don't know what it is—it's a feeling I've got that it's wrong somewhere—"

"All right, all right, we'll talk it over with Joe. Now what about our other pet nuisance?"

"My aunt the actress?" laughs Martha. "What's she been up to now?"

"Nothing unusual. Last night at dinner she was telling the girls about the time she lost her trunks in Butte, Montana, and how she gave her best performance of Rosalind during a hurricane. Today in the kitchen you could hear her on what Sir Henry said to her."

"Wait until she does Hedda Gabler standing on a chair. Sir Henry taught her to do it that way. He said it was a test of great acting."

Martha is agreed that Mrs. Mortar should be deftly eased out of the school if it can be done, and Karen thinks it can. Fortunately they are now in a position to scrape together enough money to send Aunt Lily somewhere.

Their talk turns to Dr. Cardin, who is reported on his way over. Karen is expecting to marry Joe Cardin. After the term is over, perhaps, when the school is out of debt and paying for itself.

The thought is not pleasing to Martha. For one thing Karen's marriage will interfere with their vacation together.

"I had been looking forward to some place by the lake—just you and me—the way we used to at college," says Martha.

"Well, now there will be three of us," answers Karen cheerfully. "That'll be fun, too."

MARTHA (*after a pause*)—Why haven't you told me this before?

KAREN—I'm not telling you anything we haven't talked about often.

MARTHA—But you're talking about it as *soon* now.

KAREN—I'm glad to be able to. I've been in love with Joe a long time. (*Continuing with papers.*) It's a big day for the school. Rosalie's finally put an "l" in could.

MARTHA (*in a dull, bitter tone*)—You really *are* going to leave, aren't you?

KAREN—I'm not going to leave and you know it. Why do you say things like that? We agreed a long time ago that my marriage wasn't going to make any difference to the school.

MARTHA—But it will. You know it will. It can't help it.

KAREN—That's nonsense. Joe doesn't want me to give up here.

MARTHA—I don't understand you. It's been so damned hard building this thing up, slaving and going without things to make ends meet—think of having a winter coat without holes in the lining again!—and now when we're getting on our feet, you're all ready to let it go to hell.

KAREN—This is a silly argument, Martha. Let's quit it. You haven't listened to a word I've said. I'm not getting married to-morrow, and when I do, it's not going to interfere with my work here. You're making something out of nothing.

MARTHA—It's going to be hard going on alone afterwards.

KAREN—For God's sake, do you expect me to give up my marriage?

MARTHA—I don't mean that, but it's so—

Dr. Cardin has come through the door. "He is a large, pleasant-looking, carelessly dressed man of about thirty-five." His greetings are cheery and he is not at all surprised to hear that their little Mary has a pain. . . .

Martha is staring out the window when Mrs. Mortar sweeps through the door in a plainly flustered state. She has just been asked to leave the room while Dr. Cardin examines Mary. It seems to Mrs. Mortar that under such circumstances an older person should be present, and it seems to Martha that her Aunt Lily is extremely silly to think so.

The doctor's snub is but another humiliation for Mrs. Mortar. Karen, she reports, has been consistently rude to her, for all she has worked her fingers to the bone for little or nothing.

It is plain to Martha that Aunt Lily is not happy at the school and that she should have a change. If she would like, she can go back to London now and visit her old friends for the first time in twenty years. Now that the school is doing better it probably will be possible for Martha to let Aunt Lily stay on in London after her visit.

"So you want me to leave?" slowly decides Mrs. Mortar.

"That's not the way to put it," corrects Martha. "You've wanted to go ever since I can remember."

MRS. MORTAR—You're trying to get rid of me.

MARTHA—That's it. We don't want you around when we dig up the buried treasure.

MRS. MORTAR—So? You're turning me out? At my age! Nice, grateful girl you are.

MARTHA—Oh, my God, how can anybody deal with you?

You're going where you want to go, and we'll be better off alone. That suits everybody. You complain about the farm, you complain about the school, you complain about Karen, and now you have what you want and you're still looking for something to complain about.

MRS. MORTAR (*with dignity*)—Please do not raise your voice.

MARTHA—You ought to be glad I don't do worse.

MRS. MORTAR—I absolutely refuse to be shipped off three thousand miles away. I'm not going to England. I shall go back to the stage. I'll write to my agents tomorrow, and as soon as they have something good for me—

MARTHA—The truth is I'd like you to leave soon. The three of us can't live together, and it doesn't make any difference whose fault it is.

MRS. MORTAR—You wish me to go tonight?

MARTHA—Don't act, Aunt Lily. Go as soon as you've found a place you like. I'll put the money in the bank for you tomorrow.

MRS. MORTAR—You think I'd take your money? I'd rather scrub floors first.

MARTHA—I imagine you'll change your mind.

MRS. MORTAR—I should have known by this time that the wise thing is to stay out of your way when *he's* in the house.

MARTHA—What are you talking about now?

MRS. MORTAR—Never mind. I should have known better. You always take your spite out on me.

MARTHA (*impatiently*)—Oh, don't let's have any more of this today. I'm tired. I've been working since six o'clock this morning.

MRS. MORTAR—Any day that he's in the house is a bad day.

MARTHA—When *who* is in the house?

MRS. MORTAR—Don't think you're fooling me, young lady. I wasn't born yesterday.

MARTHA—Aunt Lily, the amount of disconnected unpleasantness that goes on in your head could keep a psychologist busy for years. Now go take your nap.

MRS. MORTAR—I know what I know. Every time that man comes into this house, you have a fit. It seems like you just can't stand the idea of them being together. God knows what you'll do when they get married. You're jealous of him, that's what it is.

MARTHA (*her voice is tense*)—I'm very fond of Joe, and you know it.

MRS. MORTAR—You're fonder of Karen, and I know that. And it's unnatural, just as unnatural as it can be. You don't like their

being together. You were always like that even as a child. If you
had a little girl friend, you always got mad when she liked anybody else. Well, you'd better get a beau of your own now—a
woman of your age.

MARTHA—The sooner you get out of here, the better. Your
vulgarities are making me sick and I won't stand for them any
longer. I want you to leave—

There is a noise outside the center doors. Martha breaks off,
"angry and ashamed," crosses to the doors and opens one of them
quickly. Evelyn Munn and Peggy Rogers are standing on the
staircase. It takes Martha a moment to collect herself. Then
she asks the girls what they are doing there. They were, they
explain, going upstairs and then decided to stop and see how
Mary Tilford was. They didn't really mean to listen, but they
couldn't help—

The children are sent to their rooms. The incident has convinced Martha more than ever that Mrs. Mortar is not the best
of influences for the school. "When you're at your best you're not
for tender ears," says Martha.

"So, now it's my fault, is it?" shrills Mrs. Mortar. "Just as I
said, whenever he's in the house you think you can take it out on
me. You've got to have some way to let out steam and—"

Dr. Cardin has come in from Mary's room. Mrs. Mortar
sweeps majestically past him on her way out. She is just keeping
her hand in, Martha explains, in case Sir Henry is watching from
above.

Dr. Cardin has nothing interesting to report about Mary. He
could have managed a better faint himself. He's related to Mary
and her grandmother, but they are a different branch of the
family.

"You can look at Aunt Amelia and tell," he says; "old New
England stock; never married out of Boston; still thinks honor is
honor and dinner's at eight thirty. Yes, ma'am, we're a proud old
breed."

He has no definite idea what may be wrong with Mary. She
has always been difficult and her grandmother's spoiling has not
helped. He has no intention, however, of taking the matter up
with Mrs. Tilford. He is marrying Karen, but he is not writing
Mary into the contract.

"Forget Mary for a minute," pleads Cardin. "You and I have
got something to fight about. Every time anything's said about
marrying—about Karen marrying me—you— (She winces.)

There it is. I'm fond of you. I always thought you liked me. What is it? I know how fond you are of Karen, but our marriage oughtn't to make a great deal of difference—"

Martha has pushed his hands from her shoulders, exclaiming— "God damn you. I wish—" She covers her face with her hands and stands so for a moment. When she takes her hands away she holds them out to Cardin, contritely. "Joe, please, I'm sorry. I'm a fool, a nasty, bitter—"

"Aw, shut up," says Joe, putting an arm around her. She is leaning her head against his shoulder when Karen comes in.

"Your friend's got a nice shoulder to weep on," says Martha.

"He's an admirable man in every way," admits Karen.

Mary, Karen reports, is busy putting her clothes back on. Martha tells her of the incident of the listening children at the door and it is Karen's decision that the girls will have to be moved away from one another. . . .

The news of separation is imparted to the girls. Peggy and Evelyn both protest against the change, and Mary is shrill as she starts to cry. They are always mean to her, according to Mary. She gets blamed for everything, too. She wants to see her grandmother. She wants Cousin Joe's help.

Cardin is entirely unsympathetic. He thinks Mary had better lie on the sofa until she gets through trying to work herself into a fit. "The next time she faints, I'd wait until she got tired lying on the floor," he advises them.

Karen has walked to the door with Dr. Joe. They are barely out of the room when Mary throws a cushion after them, and kicks a leg of the table, toppling over an ornament that falls and breaks, to the dismay of the others. One of Miss Wright's favorite gifts, too!

Mary doesn't care. She'll think of some way of explaining. She'll find some way to go to the boat races, too. If she can't go she won't let them go. She'll think of something.

Peggy and Evelyn tell Mary of their being caught listening at the door. And about the quarrel between Dobie and Mortar. And what Mortar said about their wanting to be rid of her.

Rosalie Wells pops in to advise them they had better be moving their things before Miss Wright comes, but Mary isn't going to be cheated out of hearing what Dobie said to Mortar by any such interference. She sends Rosalie back to do the moving, and when Rosalie refuses to go Mary reminds her that she better had —if she wants to wear Mary's gold locket and buckle to town next time. The mention of the jewelry has a strange effect upon

Rosalie and she goes obediently to do the moving.

Mary has returned to the cross-examining of the eavesdroppers.

"Now, what do you think of that?" ejaculates Evelyn in an excited lisp. "What made her tho agreeable?"

"Oh, a little secret we got," smiles Mary. "Go on, now, what else did they say?"

"Well," exclaims Peggy, feverishly, "Mortar said that Dobie was jealous of them, and that she was like that when she was a little girl, and that she'd better get herself a beau of her own because it was unnatural, and that she never wanted anyone to like Miss Wright, and that was unnatural. Boy! Did Miss Dobie get sore at that!"

"Then we didn't hear any more. Peggy dropped a book."

"What's unnatural?"

"Un for not. Not natural."

"It's funny, because everybody gets married."

"A lot of people don't—they're too ugly," corrects Mary.

Suddenly Peggy remembers a copy of Mademoiselle de Maupin they have in their room. If Rosalie finds that she's sure to blab. But Mary is reassuring. Rosalie won't say a word. And as for the book—she's finished it. Peggy can have it next. And there's *one part in it*—

Mary has decided that she is going home. She's going to tell her grandmother that she isn't staying at school any more.

"I'll tell her I'm not happy," says Mary. "They're scared of Grandma—she helped 'em when they first started, you know—and when she tells 'em something, believe me, they'll sit up and listen. They can't get away with treating me like this, and they don't have to think they can."

Mary doesn't know exactly how she is going to get home, or just exactly what she is going to tell Grandma when she gets there, but she will think of something. She can always do better on the spur of the moment, says Mary. And Peggy and Evelyn have got to help her go. They've got to lend her money.

"I've got to have at least a dollar for the taxi and a dime for the bus," figures Mary.

"And where you going to find it?" wonders Evelyn.

"See?" adds Peggy, hopefully. "Why don't you just wait until your allowance comes Monday, and then you can go any place you want. Maybe by that time—"

MARY—I'm going today. *Now.*

EVELYN—You can't *walk* to Lanthet.

MARY (*goes to* PEGGY)—You've got money. You've got two dollars and twenty-five cents.

PEGGY—I—I—

MARY—Go get it for me.

PEGGY—No! No! I won't get it for you.

EVELYN—You can't have *that* money, Mary—

MARY—Get it for me.

PEGGY (*cringes, her voice is scared*)—I won't. I won't. Mamma doesn't send me much allowance—not half as much as the rest of you get—I saved this so long—you took it from me last time—

EVELYN—Ah, she wantth that bithycle tho bad.

PEGGY—I haven't gone to the movies, I haven't had any candy, I haven't had anything the rest of you get all the time. It took me so long to save that and I—

MARY—Go upstairs and get me the money.

PEGGY (*hysterically, backing away from her*)—I won't. I won't. I won't.

(MARY *makes a sudden move for her, grabs her left arm, and jerks it back hard and expertly.* PEGGY *screams softly.* EVELYN *tries to take* MARY'S *arm away. Without releasing her hold on* PEGGY, MARY *slaps* EVELYN'S *face.* EVELYN *begins to cry.*)

MARY—Just say when you've had enough.

PEGGY (*softly, stiflingly*)—All—all right—I'll get it.

(MARY *smiles, nods her head.*)

THE CURTAIN FALLS

ACT II

Agatha, Mrs. Tilford's sharp-faced, querulous, middle-aged maid, is surprised and not a little suspicious to see Mary Tilford, slightly disheveled, home on Wednesday. Mary has come probably for the Wednesday fudge cake, thinks Agatha, and she has a quite positive idea what she would do about it if she were Mrs. Tilford.

Mrs. Tilford, however, is greatly worried about Mary and anxious to be reassured that she is well. Mary is well enough. She had walked most of the way home, she explains, and she has run away from the school. If her grandmother were to send her back before dinner, as she threatens to do, Mary knows they will just kill her.

Mary is crying hysterically now, and to quiet her Mrs. Tilford has to promise not to send her back immediately.

"I fainted today!" reports Mary, after she has crawled back into her grandmother's lap and is quiet again. "I had a pain in my heart. I couldn't help having a pain in my heart, and when I fainted right in class, they called Cousin Joe and he said I didn't. He said it was maybe only that I ate my breakfast too fast and Miss Wright blamed me for it."

Mary thinks perhaps her heart is a little better now, but she still feels weak. Much too weak to bear going back to school and being punished terribly by that Miss Wright. Can't she stay until the first of the week and help her grandmother celebrate her birthday?

Mrs. Tilford is past celebrating birthdays and she doesn't want Mary to grow up imagining that she is always being mistreated. She is happy to have Mary with her. Happy in the memory of their years together when Mary was a baby. But she knows school is the best place for Mary and back she shall go directly after dinner.

Now Mary is threatening hysteria again, protesting shrilly that her grandmother does not care what becomes of her, whether she is killed or not. Seeing this is a wrong attack, she is humble again and sorry. She is scared, she wails. Scared of the dreadful things they will do to her. Mary knows things, and that's why Miss Dobie and Miss Wright are down on her. Mary knows secret things about them. Things Peggy and Evelyn know, too. Things they had overheard Mrs. Mortar say. That's why the teachers had changed her room; that's why she was being punished.

"Run along, Mary," says Mrs. Tilford, impatiently. "I hope you get more coherent as you get older."

MARY (*starting for the door*)—All right. But there're a lot of things. They have secrets or something, and they're afraid I'll find out and tell you.

MRS. TILFORD—There's not necessarily anything wrong with people having secrets.

MARY (*coming back*)—But they've got funny ones. Peggy and Evelyn heard Mrs. Mortar telling Miss Dobie that she was jealous of Miss Wright marrying Cousin Joe.

MRS. TILFORD—You shouldn't repeat things like that.

MARY—But that's what she said, Grandma. She said it was unnatural for a girl to feel that way.

MRS. TILFORD—What?

MARY—I'm just telling you what she said. She said there was something funny about it, and that Miss Dobie had always been like that, even when she was a little girl, and that it was un-natural—

MRS. TILFORD—Stop using that silly word, Mary.

MARY (*vaguely realizing that she is on the right track, hurries on*)—But that was the word *she* kept using, Grandma, and then they got mad and told Mrs. Mortar she'd have to get out.

MRS. TILFORD—That was probably not the reason at all.

MARY (*nodding vigorously*)—I bet it was, because honestly, Miss Dobie does get cranky and mean everytime Cousin Joe comes, and today I heard her say to him: "God damn you," and then she said she was just a jealous fool and—

MRS. TILFORD—You have picked up some very fine words, haven't you, Mary?

MARY—That's just what she said, Grandma, and one time Miss Dobie was crying in Miss Wright's room, and Miss Wright was trying to stop her, and she said that, all right, maybe she wouldn't get married right away if—

MRS. TILFORD—How do you know all this?

MARY—We couldn't help hearing because they—I mean Miss Dobie—was talking awful loud, and their room is right next to ours.

MRS. TILFORD—Whose room?

MARY—Miss Wright's room, I mean, and you can just ask Peggy and Evelyn whether we didn't hear. Almost always Miss Dobie comes in after we go to bed and stays a long time. I guess that's why they want to get rid of us—of me—because we hear things. That's why they're making us move our room, and they punish me all the time for—

MRS. TILFORD—For eavesdropping, I should think. (*She has said this mechanically. With nothing definite in her mind, she is making an effort to conceal the fact that* MARY'S *description of the life at the school has shocked her.*) Well, now I think we've had enough gossip, don't you? Dinner's almost ready, and I can't eat with a girl who has such a dirty face.

MARY (*softly*)—I've heard other things, too.

MRS. TILFORD (*abstractedly*)—What? What did you say?

MARY—I've heard other things. Plenty of other things, Grandma.

MRS. TILFORD—What things?

MARY—Bad things.

MRS. TILFORD—Well, what were they?

Mary—I can't tell you.

Mrs. Tilford—Mary, you're annoying me very much. If you have anything to say, then say it and stop acting silly.

Mary—I mean I can't say it out loud.

Mrs. Tilford—There couldn't possibly be anything so terrible that you couldn't say it out loud. Now either tell the truth or be still.

Mary—Well, a lot of things I don't understand. But it's awful, and sometimes they fight and then they make up, and Miss Dobie cries and Miss Wright gets mad, and then they make up again, and there are funny noises and we get scared.

Mrs. Tilford—Noises? I suppose you girls have a happy time imagining a murder.

Mary—And we've seen things, too. Funny things. . . . I'd tell you but I got to whisper it.

Mrs. Tilford—Why must you whisper it?

Mary—I don't know. I just got to. (*Climbs on the sofa next to* Mrs. Tilford *and begins whispering.*)

Mrs. Tilford (*trembling*)—Do you know what you're saying? (*Without answering* Mary *goes back to the whispering.*) *Mary! Are you telling me the truth?*

Mary—Honest, honest. You just ask Peggy and Evelyn and— (*After a moment* Mrs. Tilford *gets up and begins to pace about the room.*) They know too. And maybe there're other kids who know, but we've always been frightened and so we didn't ask, and one night I was going to go and find out, but I got scared and we went to bed early so we wouldn't hear, but sometimes I couldn't help it, but we never talked about it much, because we thought they'd find out and— Oh, Grandma, don't make me go back to that awful place.

Mary's final excited plea reaches Mrs. Tilford belatedly. She pauses while she frames a course of action. No, Mary will not have to go back to school. She can go upstairs now and get ready for dinner.

For a moment Mrs. Tilford stares after her grandchild as she disappears. Slowly she puts on her eyeglasses and crosses to the phone book. She dials a number and starts to call Miss Wright. She changes her mind. Dials another number and asks for Dr. Cardin. She would have Joseph come to see her right away. She wishes he could come at once. It isn't about Mary's fainting —yet in one way it's about Mary. But let him come as soon as he can—

She has hung up the receiver and sits for a long moment in a state of indecision. Then she picks up the phone again and dials another number.

"Mrs. Munn, please," she says, when the connection is complete. "This is Mrs. Tilford. . . . Miriam? . . . This is Amelia Tilford. I have something to tell you—something very shocking, I'm afraid—something about the school and Evelyn and Mary—"
The curtain falls.

A few hours later Mary Tilford is lying on the floor in front of the living room couch working on a puzzle. Agatha is bustling up the stairs with an armload of blankets and pillows. Agatha is peevish again. This time because Rosalie Wells has been asked to spend the night with Mary and is quite likely to get the best of the bed quilts dirty. How does Agatha know about Rosalie? Agatha heard Mrs. Tilford telephoning Mrs. Wells, all the way to New York, "three dollars and eighty-five cents, and families starving!"

Rosalie arrives a moment later. Mary's greeting is to hide and make strange sounds of welcome. Rosalie is quite frightened. It might be a werewolf. But Mary, coming into the open, laughs at that idea. No werewolf would pick Rosalie.

It's funny about school, Rosalie thinks. She hopes she isn't being taken home to stay. She doesn't want to stay at home. Peggy and Evelyn and Helen and Lois were also sent home last night, Rosalie reports. Could it be scarlet fever, does Mary think?

Mary knows what it is, but it's a secret. And maybe she told her grandmother that Rosalie told her what it was. Maybe—

Rosalie is of a mind to go right straight and tell Mrs. Tilford that she didn't; that she didn't tell Mary anything. Rosalie doesn't intend to let Mary get her in trouble again. She's going—

"Wait a minute, I'll come with you," slyly smiles Mary.
"What for?"

MARY—I want to tell her about Helen Burton's bracelet
ROSALIE—What about it?
MARY—Just that you stole it.
ROSALIE—Shut up. I didn't do any such thing.
MARY—Yes, you did.
ROSALIE—You made it up. You're always making things up.
MARY—You can't call me a fibber, Rosalie Wells. That's a

kind of a dare and I won't take a dare. I guess I'll go tell Grandma, anyway. Then she can call the police and they'll come for you and you'll spend the rest of your life in one of those solitary prisons and you'll get older and older, and when you're very old and can't see anymore, they'll let you out maybe with a big sign on your back saying you're a thief, and your mother and father will be dead and you won't have any place to go and you'll beg on the streets—

ROSALIE—I didn't steal anything. I borrowed the bracelet and I was going to put it back as soon as I'd worn it to the movies. I never meant to keep it.

MARY—Nobody'll believe that, least of all the police. You're just a common, ordinary thief. Stop that bawling. You'll have the whole house down here in a minute.

ROSALIE—You won't tell? Say you won't tell.

MARY—Am I a fibber?

ROSALIE—No.

MARY—Then say: "I apologize on my hands and knees."

ROSALIE—I apologize on my hands and knees. Let's play with the puzzle.

MARY—Wait a minute. Say: "From now on, I, Rosalie Wells, am the vassal of Mary Tilford and will do and say whatever she tells me under the solemn oath of a knight."

ROSALIE—I won't say that. That's the worst oath there is. (MARY *starts for the door.*) Mary! Please don't—

MARY—Will you swear it?

ROSALIE (*sniffling*)—But then you could tell me to do anything.

MARY—And you'd have to do it. Say it quick or I'll—

ROSALIE (*hurriedly*)—From now on, I, Rosalie Wells, am the vassal of Mary Tilford and will do and say whatever she tells me under the solemn oath of a knight.

MARY—Don't forget that.

Mrs. Tilford has come in. The bell is ringing and she thinks it is probably Dr. Cardin. The children will find some fruit and milk in the library and they are then to go to bed.

It is difficult for Mrs. Tilford to explain to Dr. Cardin why she has sent for him and what she has to tell him. It is not about Mary's fainting. It is much more serious than that. Something that has happened since he last saw Karen. Something that affects them all.

She asks about his plans for marrying Karen, and wonders that it does not strike him as unusual that Karen has suddenly decided to make these plans definite.

"She has not suddenly decided anything," Dr. Cardin answers with some spirit. "The school is pretty well on its feet, and now that Mrs. Mortar is leaving—"

"I've heard about their putting Mrs. Mortar out."

"Putting her out? Well, maybe. But a nice sum for a trip and a promise that a good niece will support you the rest of your life is an enviable way of being put out."

"Don't you find it odd, Joseph, that they want so much to get rid of that silly, harmless woman?"

"I don't know what you're talking about, but it isn't odd at all. Lily Mortar is not a harmless woman, although God knows she's silly enough. She's a nasty, tiresome, spoilt old bitch. If you're forming a Mortar Welfare Society, you're wasting your time. It's not like you to waste your time. Now, what's it that's really on your mind?"

"You must not marry Karen!"

Before Cardin can learn any reason for this startling statement there is a commotion at the door. A moment later Karen Wright, followed by Martha Dobie, has burst into the room. They are equally excited. Angrily Martha faces Mrs. Tilford.

"We've come to find out what you're doing," she says.

"What is it?" demands the mystified Cardin, kissing Karen.

"It's crazy! It's crazy!" almost shouts Karen. "What did she do it for?"

Mrs. Tilford is trying to protest that they should not have come. Dr. Cardin is demanding to know what the mystery is about. No one can coherently answer him until finally Martha says:

"I'll tell you, I'll tell you. You see if you can make any sense out of it. At dinner-time Mrs. Munn's chauffeur said that Evelyn must be sent home right away. At half past seven Mrs. Burton arrived to tell us that she wanted Helen's things packed and that she'd wait outside because she didn't want to enter a place like ours. Five minutes later the Wells's butler came for Rosalie."

"What was it?"

MARTHA—It was madhouse. People rushing in and out, the children being pushed into cars—

KAREN (*quiet now, takes his hand*)—Mrs. Rogers finally told us.

CARDIN—What? What?

KAREN—That—that Martha and I have been—have been lovers. Mrs. Tilford told them.

CARDIN (*for a moment stands staring at her incredulously. Then he walks across the room, stares out the window, and finally turns to* MRS. TILFORD.)—Did you tell them that?

MRS. TILFORD—Yes.

CARDIN—Are you sick?

MRS. TILFORD—You know I'm not sick.

CARDIN (*snapping the words out*)—Then what did you do it for?

MRS. TILFORD (*slowly*)—Because it's true.

KAREN (*incredulously*)—You think it's true, then?

MARTHA—You fool! You damned, vicious—

KAREN—Do you realize what you're saying?

MRS. TILFORD—I realize it very well. And—

MARTHA—You realize nothing, nothing, nothing.

MRS. TILFORD—And that's why I don't think you should have come here. (*Quietly, with a look at* MARTHA.) I shall not call you names, and I will not allow you to call me names. It comes to this: I can't trust myself to talk about it with you now or ever.

KAREN—What's she talking about, Joe? What's she mean? What is she trying to do to us? What is everybody doing to us?

MARTHA (*softly, as though to herself*)—Pushed around. We're being pushed around by crazy people. That's an awful thing. And we're standing here— We're standing here taking it. (*Suddenly with violence.*) Didn't you know we'd come here? Were we supposed to lie down and grin while you kicked us around with these lies?

MRS. TILFORD—This can't do any of us any good, Miss Dobie.

MARTHA (*scornfully imitating her*)—"This can't do any of us any good." Listen, listen! Try to understand this: you're not playing with paper dolls. We're human beings, see? It's our lives you're fooling with. *Our* lives. That's serious business for us. Can you understand that?

MRS. TILFORD (*for the first time she speaks angrily*)—I can understand that, and I understand a lot more. *You've* been playing with a lot of children's lives, and that's why I stopped you. (*More calmly.*) I know how serious this is for you, how serious it is for all of us.

CARDIN (*bitterly*)—I don't think you do know.

MRS. TILFORD—I wanted to avoid this meeting because it can't do any good. You came here to find out if I had made the charge. You've found out. Let's end it there. *I don't want you in this house.* I'm sorry this had to be done to you, Joseph.

CARDIN—I don't like your sympathy.

MRS. TILFORD—Very well. There's nothing I mean to do, nothing I want to do. There's nothing anybody can do.

CARDIN (*carefully*)—You have already done a terrible thing.

MRS. TILFORD—I have done what I had to do. What they are may possibly be their own business. It becomes a great deal more than that when children are involved.

KAREN (*wildly*)—It's not true. Not a word of it is true; can't you understand that?

MRS. TILFORD—There won't be any punishment for either of you. But there mustn't be any punishment for me, either—and that's what this meeting is. This—this thing is your own. Go away with it. I don't understand it and I don't want any part of it.

MARTHA (*slowly*)—So you thought we would go away?

MRS. TILFORD—I think that's best for you.

MARTHA—There must be something we can do to you, and, whatever it is, we'll find it.

MRS. TILFORD—That will be very unwise.

KAREN—You are right to be afraid.

MRS. TILFORD—I am not afraid, Karen.

CARDIN—But you *are* old—and you *are* irresponsible.

MRS. TILFORD (*hurt*)—You know that's not true.

KAREN (*goes to her*)—I don't want to have anything to do with your mess, do you hear me? It makes me feel dirty and sick to be forced to say this, but here it is: there isn't a single word of truth in anything you've said. We're standing here defending ourselves—and against what? Against a lie. A great, awful lie.

MRS. TILFORD—I'm sorry that I can't believe that.

KAREN—Damn you!

CARDIN—But you can believe this: they've worked eight long years to save enough money to buy that farm, to start that school. They did without everything that young people ought to have. You wouldn't know about that. That school meant things to them: self-respect, and bread and butter, and honest work. Do you know what it is to try so hard for anything? Well, now it's gone. What the hell did you do it for?

MRS. TILFORD (*softly*)—It had to be done.

CARDIN—Righteousness is a great thing.

MRS. TILFORD—I know how you must feel.

CARDIN—You don't know anything about how I feel. And you don't know how they feel, either.

MRS. TILFORD—I've loved you as much as I loved my own

boys. I wouldn't have spared them; I couldn't spare you.

CARDIN (*fiercely*)—I believe you.

MARTHA—What is there to do to you? What can we do to you? There must be something—something that makes you feel the way we do tonight. You don't want any part of this, you said. But you'll get a part. More than you bargained for. (*Suddenly.*) Listen: are you willing to stand by everything you've said tonight?

MRS. TILFORD—Yes.

MARTHA—All right. That's fine. But don't get the idea we'll let you whisper this lie: you made it and you'll come out with it. Shriek it to your town of Lancet. We'll *make* you shriek it—and we'll make you do it in a court room. (*Quietly.*) Tomorrow, Mrs. Tilford, you will have a libel suit on your hands.

Mrs. Tilford is of the opinion that such action would be very unwise. It would be wrong for them to try to brazen the thing out, to let their pride bring them so much pain.

Mrs. Tilford has no right to take a child's word for what she alleges to be true, protests Karen. Particularly a child of Mary's character, a strange, bad girl who has always hated them and without reason.

Now Dr. Cardin demands that Mary be sent for. Nor will he be put down by Mrs. Tilford's refusal to subject the child to such a scene. She is taking the responsibility now, Mrs. Tilford insists. She had taken no action until she was convinced that what she had been told was true. Her only thought was to get the children away. There will be no more talk about what has happened or about Miss Wright and Miss Dobie. Now they can get out.

Cardin will not have that. "When two people come here with their lives spread on the table for you to cut to pieces," he says to Mrs. Tilford, "then the only honest thing to do is to give them a chance to come out whole. Are you honest?"

"I've always thought so."

"Then where is Mary?"

Cardin has gone to the library and called Mary. She comes in and "stands nervously near the door, her manner shy and afraid." Cardin has faced her. He tells her quietly that many people lie. In fact everybody lies all the time. Sometimes they have to, sometimes they don't.

"I've lied myself for a lot of different reasons," says Cardin, "but there was never a time when, if I'd been given a second

chance, I wouldn't have taken back the lie and told the truth.
You're lucky if you ever get that chance. I'm telling you this
because I'm about to ask you a question. Before you answer
the question, I want to tell you that if you've l—, if you made
a mistake, you must take this chance and say so. You won't be
punished for it. Do you get all that?"

"Yes, Cousin Joe."

"All right, let's get started. Were you telling your grandmother the truth this afternoon? The exact truth about Miss
Wright and Miss Dobie?"

"Oh, yes."

"All right, Mary, that was your chance; you passed it up.
Now let's find out things."

Mrs. Tilford would again save Mary further questioning, but
Dr. Cardin is determined to have the truth now. He begins to
cross-question the child, though not with great success. Mary
has always liked Miss Wright and Miss Dobie. They just don't
like her. Mary is sure she is always being punished unjustly.
Just because Evelyn and Peggy overheard Mrs. Mortar say what
she did about Miss Wright—

"My aunt is a stupid woman," exclaims Martha. "What she
said was unpleasant. It was said to annoy me. It meant nothing more than that."

Mary rushes on. All the little things she remembers she would
twist into evidence against her teachers. All the girls were talking, she says. All the girls thought it was funny, the sounds they
heard in Miss Wright's room.

"One night there was so much noise I thought somebody was
sick or something and I looked through the keyhole and they
were kissing and saying things and then I got scared because it
was different sort of and I—"

"That child—that child is sick," exclaims Martha, her face
distorted with disgust.

Mary repeats her charge—that she looked through the keyhole
of Miss Wright's room and saw—

"*There's no keyhole on my door!*" interrupts Karen. And
slowly repeats that information for Mrs. Tilford's benefit.

Now Mary thinks it maybe was the keyhole in Miss Dobie's
door. It was there she heard—

But Miss Dobie shares a room with her aunt at the other end
of the house. Let Mrs. Tilford come and see!

Now Mary is flustered again, and threatened with more hysteria. "Everybody is yelling at me," she shouts. "I don't know

what I'm saying with everybody mixing me all up. I did see it!
I did see it!"

Mrs. Tilford takes charge now. Excitedly she must know the
truth—the real truth. Determinedly she pins Mary down to facts.
And then Mary quiets down and explains. It was Rosalie who
saw. It was Rosalie who had told Mary all about it. It was
Rosalie who said she had read about it in a book and knew.

"You ask Rosalie. You just ask Rosalie," shouts Mary. "She'll
tell you. We used to talk about it all the time. That's the
truth, that's the honest truth. She said it was when the door
was open once and she told us all about it. I was just trying to
save Rosalie, and everybody jumps on me."

Disgustedly the others are leaving. Mrs. Tilford calls them
back. She is plainly worried now, and pitifully puzzled. She
goes to the library door and calls Rosalie. The child comes hesitantly to the door. She is plainly frightened as she makes nervous
little bows to everybody. Mrs. Tilford takes her hand and leads
her into the room.

"I'm sorry to keep you up so late, Rosalie. You must be
tired." And then, speaking more rapidly: "Mary says there's
been a lot of talk in the school lately about Miss Wright and
Miss Dobie. Is that true?"

ROSALIE—I—I don't know what you mean.

MRS. TILFORD—That things have been said among you girls.

ROSALIE (wide-eyed, frightened)—What things? I never—I—
I—

KAREN (gently)—Don't be frightened.

MRS. TILFORD—What was the talk about, Rosalie?

ROSALIE (utterly bewildered)—I don't know what she means,
Miss Wright.

KAREN—Rosalie, Mary has told her grandmother that certain
things at the school have been—er—puzzling you girls. You,
particularly.

ROSALIE—History puzzles me. I guess I'm not very good at
history, and Helen helps me sometimes, if that—

KAREN—No, that's not what she meant. She says that you
told her that you saw certain—certain acts between Miss Dobie
and myself. She says that once, when the door was open, you
saw us kissing each other in a way that— (Unable to bear the
child's look, she turns her back.) women don't kiss one another.

ROSALIE—Oh, Miss Wright, I didn't, I didn't, I didn't. I
never said such a thing.

MRS. TILFORD (*grimly*)—That's true, my dear?

ROSALIE—I never saw any such thing. Mary always makes things up about me and everybody else. (*Starts to weep in excitement.*) I never said any such thing ever. Why, I never even could have thought of—

MARY (*staring at her, speaks very slowly*)—Yes, you did, Rosalie. You're just trying to get out of it. I remember just when you said it. I remember it, because it was the day Helen Burton's bracelet was—

ROSALIE (*stands fascinated and fearful, looking at* MARY)—I never did. I—I—you're just—

MARY—It was the day Helen's bracelet was stolen, and nobody knew who did it, and Helen said that if her mother found out, she'd have the thief put in jail.

KAREN (*puzzled by the sudden change in* ROSALIE's *manner*)—There's nothing to cry about. You must help us by telling the truth. Why, what's the matter, Rosalie?

MARY—Grandma, there's something I've got to tell you that—

ROSALIE (*with a shrill cry*)—Yes. Yes. I did see it. I told Mary. What Mary said was right. I said it, I said it— (*Throws herself on the couch weeping hysterically;* MARTHA *stands leaning against the door.* KAREN, CARDIN, *and* MRS. TILFORD *are staring at* ROSALIE; MARY *slowly sits down.*)

THE CURTAIN FALLS

ACT III

It is late November. The living room of the Wright-Dobie school has a changed look. "It is not actually dirty, but it is dull, dark and uncared for." The windows are shut, the curtains tightly drawn.

Karen Wright is sitting in an armchair staring at the walls. Martha Dobie is lying on the couch, her face buried against the pillows. For a moment neither moves. Then Martha turns over to remark, dully, that the room is cold. She wonders what time it is. Karen doesn't know, and doesn't think it matters.

Time matters to Martha. She must know when the hour for her bath arrives. It is the one thing she has to look forward to all day. The one thing she has to do that keeps her in touch with the full life. It would be better for Karen, says Martha, if she were to have some one thing to focus her attention on.

"You wake up in the morning and you say to yourself, the day's not entirely empty, life is rich and full; at five o'clock I'll comb my hair."

They are silent again. The phone rings, and rings again. Neither pays any attention until the persistent ringing forces Karen to walk across the room and lay the receiver off the hook.

It is probably about time to think of dinner. Neither is hungry. Neither has been hungry for days. But Joe is coming. He's late. Martha thinks perhaps she will cook eggs, and fix potatoes with onions, the way Karen used to like them.

"It's a week ago Thursday," muses Karen. "It never seemed real until the last day. It seems real enough now, all right."

"Now and forever after."

KAREN (*suddenly*)—Let's go out.

MARTHA—Where to?

KAREN—We'll take a walk.

MARTHA—Where'll we walk?

KAREN—Why shouldn't we take a walk? We won't see anybody, and suppose we do, what of it? We'll jus—

MARTHA—Come on. We'll go through the park.

KAREN—They might see us. Let's not go. We'll go tomorrow.

MARTHA (*laughing*)—Stop kidding yourself.

KAREN—But Joe says we've got to go out. He says that all the people who don't think it's true will begin to wonder if we keep hiding this way.

MARTHA—If it makes you feel better to think there *are* such people, go ahead.

KAREN—He says we ought to go into town and go shopping and act as though—

MARTHA—Shopping? That's a sound idea. There aren't three stores in Lancet that would sell us anything. Hasn't he heard about the ladies' clubs and their meetings and their circulars and their visits and their—

KAREN (*softly*)—Don't tell him.

MARTHA (*gently*)—I won't.

There are footsteps in the hall and the sound of something being dragged across the floor. It is the grocery boy with his deliveries. He brings the box into the room, staring at them strangely and giggling. He has done this for several days. Karen's nerves are ready to snap under it. Martha finally faces the boy, thrusting her hand in the air:

"I've got eight fingers, see? I'm a freak," she shrills. The
boy is still giggling as he backs out.

MARTHA (*bitterly*)—You still think we should go into town?
KAREN—I don't know. I don't know about anything any
more. (*After a moment.*) Martha, Martha, Martha—
MARTHA (*gently*)—What is it, Karen?
KAREN—What are we going to do? It's all so cold and unreal
and awful. It's like that dark hour of the night when, half
awake, you struggle through the black mess you've been dream-
ing. Then, suddenly, you wake up and you see your own bed
or your own night-gown and you know you're back again in a
solid world. But now it's all the nightmare; there is no solid
world. Oh, Martha, *why* did it happen? *What* happened?
What are we doing here like this?
MARTHA—Waiting.
KAREN—For what?
MARTHA—I don't know.
KAREN—We've got to get out of this place. I can't stand it
any more.
MARTHA—You'll be getting married soon. Everything will be
all right then.
KAREN (*vaguely*)—Yes.
MARTHA—What is it?
KAREN—Nothing.
MARTHA—There mustn't be anything wrong between you and
Joe. Never.
KAREN (*without conviction*)—Nothing's wrong.

Again there are footsteps heard in the hall. They think Joe
has come. It is Mrs. Mortar. She arrives with a small suitcase
in her hand, smiling coyly.
They stare at Mrs. Mortar briefly. Martha welcomes her with
extravagant politeness. Mrs. Mortar is a little puzzled. She is,
she admits, glad to see the old place again. And them. She
would like some tea, and perhaps a little brandy.
Suddenly Martha is off the sofa and is facing her aunt with
fire in her eye and bitterness in her tone.
"Where the hell have you been?" she demands.
"Around, around," smiles Mrs. Mortar. "I had a most interesting time. Things—"

MARTHA—*Why didn't you answer my telegrams?*
MRS. MORTAR—Oh, Martha, there's your temper again.

MARTHA—Answer me and don't bother about my temper.

MRS. MORTAR (*nervously*)—I was moving around a great deal. (*Conversationally.*) You know, I think it will throw a very revealing light on the state of the new theatre when I tell you that the Lyceum in Rochester now has a toilet back-stage.

MARTHA—To hell with the toilet in Rochester. Where were you?

MRS. MORTAR—Moving around, I tell you.

KAREN—What difference does it all make now?

MRS. MORTAR—Karen is quite right. Let bygones be bygones. As I was saying, there's an effete something in the theatre now, and that accounts for—

MARTHA (*to* KAREN)—Isn't she wonderful? (*To* MRS. MORTAR.) Why did you refuse to come back here and testify for us?

MRS. MORTAR—Why, Martha, I didn't refuse to come back at all. That's the wrong way to look at it. I was on a tour; that's a moral obligation, you know. Now don't let's talk about unpleasant things any more. I'll go up and unpack a few things; tomorrow's plenty of time to get my trunk.

KAREN (*laughs*)—Things have changed here, you know.

MARTHA—She doesn't know. She expected to walk right up to a comfortable fire and sit down and she very carefully waited until the whole thing was over. (*To* MRS. MORTAR.) Listen: Karen Wright and Martha Dobie brought a libel suit against a woman called Tilford because her grandchild had accused them of having what the judge called "sinful sexual knowledge of one another." (MRS. MORTAR *holds up her hand in protest.*) Don't like that, do you? Well, a great part of the defense's case was based on remarks made by Lily Mortar, actress in the toilets of Rochester, against her niece, Martha. And a greater part of the defense's case rested on the telling fact that Mrs. Mortar would not appear in court to deny or explain those remarks. Mrs. Mortar had a moral obligation to the theatre. As you probably read in the papers, we lost the case.

MRS. MORTAR—I didn't think of it that way, Martha. It couldn't have done any good for all of us to get mixed up in that unpleasant notoriety— (*Sees* MARTHA's *face. Hastily.*) But now that you've explained it, why, I do see it your way, and I'm sorry I didn't come back. But now that I'm here, I'm going to stand shoulder to shoulder with you. I know what you've gone through, but the body and the heart *do* recover, you know. I'll be working right along with you and we'll—

MARTHA—There's an eight o'clock train. Get on it.

Mrs. Mortar—Martha.

Martha—You've come back to pick the bones dry.   Well, there aren't even bones anymore.   There's nothing here for you.

Mrs. Mortar (*sniffling a little*)—How can you talk to me like that?

Martha—Because I hate you.   I've always hated you.

Mrs. Mortar (*gently*)—God will punish you for that.

Martha—He's been doing all right.

Mrs. Mortar is going to her room.   She will wait there temporarily if Martha should want to apologize.

"I'll call you when it's time for your train," Karen says firmly.

Joe Cardin has arrived.   He is still worried about their staying so closely indoors.   He has taken Karen in his arms.   She has a feeling that imperceptibly he draws away as she would kiss him. Joe would laugh that idea away.

Joe has news.   He has sold his place.   In response to their excited inquiries and protests he further announces that he and Karen are being married this week and the three of them are going far away.   It's all fixed.   They are going to Vienna, and they're going quick.   He is to have his old place back over there and there will be enough for them all to live on, modestly.

Martha thinks she will not go with them, but Joe is determined. After a time, if she wants to leave, that will be all right.   But for the present they will stick together.

"I'll be going back with a pretty girl who belongs to me," cries Joe to Karen, when Martha has gone back to the kitchen.   "I'll show you off all over the place—to Dr. Engelhardt, and the nurse at the desk, and to the fat gal in the cake shop, and to Fischer. (*Laughs.*)   The last time I saw him was at the railroad station. He took me back of the baggage car. (*With an imitation of an accent.*) 'Joseph,' he said, 'you'll be a good doctor; I would trust you to cut up my Minna.   But you're not a great doctor, and you never will be.   Go back where you were born and take care of your sick.   Leave the fancy work to the others.'   I came home."

"You'll be coming home again some day," says Karen.

"No.   Let's not talk about it," protests Cardin.   And again, when she sensitively picks up a note of pessimism in his voice, he says to her, quite seriously:

"Karen, there are a lot of people in this world who've had bad trouble in their lives.   We're three of those people.   We could

sit around the rest of our lives and exist on that trouble, until in
the end we had nothing else and we'd want nothing else. That's
something I'm not coming to and I'm not going to let you come
to."

"I know. I'm sorry."

Now Karen would take a part in the planning. She hopes
they can have a baby right away, as he had always hoped they
would. Yet, vaguely, Karen feels there has been a change in
Joe's feelings about that, too. Suddenly she knows that never
again can they be quite as they were. She feels that they have
both known that for a long time. She knew the day they lost
the case.

"I was watching your face in court," she says to him. "It was
ashamed—and sad at being ashamed. Say it now, Joe. Ask it
now."

"I have nothing to ask. Nothing—" And then he adds,
quickly, "All right. Is it—was it ever—"

KAREN (*puts her hand over his mouth*)—No. Martha and I
have never touched each other. (*Pulls his head down on her
shoulder.*) That's all right, darling. I'm glad you asked. I'm
not mad a bit, really.

CARDIN—I'm sorry, Karen, I'm sorry. I didn't mean to hurt
you, I—

KAREN—I'll say it for you. You wanted to wait until it was all
over, you really never wanted to ask at all. You didn't know for
sure; you thought there might be just a little truth in it all.
(*With great feeling.*) You've been good to me and loyal. You're
a fine man. (*Afraid of tears, she pats him, walks away.*) Now
go and sit down, Joe. I have a lot of things to say. They're all
mixed up and I must get them clear.

CARDIN—Don't let's talk any more. Let's forget and go ahead.

KAREN (*puzzled*)—Go ahead?

CARDIN—Yes, Karen.

KAREN—You believe me, then?

CARDIN—Of course I believe you. I only had to hear you say
it.

KAREN—No, no, no. That isn't the way things work. Maybe
you believe me. I'd never know whether you did or not. You'd
never know whether you did, either. We couldn't do it that way.
Can't you see what would happen? We'd be hounded by it all
our lives. I'd be frightened, always, and in the end my own

fright would make me—would make me hate you. Yes, it would; I know it would. I'd hate you for what I'd thought I'd done to you. And I'd hate myself, too. It would grow and grow until we'd be ruined by it. (*Sees him about to speak.*) Ah, Joe, you've seen all that yourself. You knew it first.

CARDIN (*softly*)—I didn't mean it that way; I don't now.

KAREN (*smiles*)—You're still trying to spare me, still trying to tell yourself that we might be all right again. But we won't be all right. Not ever, ever, ever. I don't know all the reasons why. Look, I'm standing here. I haven't changed. (*Holds out her hands.*) My hands look just the same, my face is the same, even my dress is old. We're in a room we've been in so many times before; you're sitting where you always sit; it's nearly time for dinner. I'm like everybody else. I can have all the things that everybody has. I can have you and a baby, and I can go to market, and we can go to the movies, and people will talk to me and— (*Suddenly notices the pain in his face.*) Oh, I'm sorry. I mustn't talk like that. That couldn't be true any more.

CARDIN—It could be, Karen. We'll make it be like that.

KAREN—No. That's only what we'd like to have had. It's what we can't have now. Go home, darling.

CARDIN (*with force*)—Don't talk like that. No matter what it is, we can't leave each other. I can't leave you—

KAREN—Joe, Joe. Let's do it now and quick; it will be too hard later on.

CARDIN—No, no, no. We love each other. (*His voice breaks.*) I'd give anything not to have asked that question, Karen.

KAREN—It had to be asked sooner or later—and answered. You're a good man—the best I'll ever know—and you've been better to me than— But it's no good now, for either of us; you can see that.

CARDIN—It can be. You say I helped you. Help me now; help me to be strong and good enough to— (*Goes toward her.*) Karen.

KAREN (*drawing back*)—No, Joe! (*As he stops.*) Will you do something for me?

CARDIN—Anything but leave you.

KAREN—Will you—will you go away for two days—a day— and think this all over by yourself—away from me and love and pity? Will you? And then decide.

CARDIN (*after a long pause*)—Yes, if you want, but it won't make any difference. We will—

KAREN—Don't say anything. Please go now. (*For a moment he stands looking at her, then slowly puts on his hat.*) And all my heart goes with you.

Joe is at the door. "I'll be coming back," he calls. For a moment Karen stares after him. "No, you won't. Never, darling," she says quietly, and turns into the room. . . .

Martha is in from the kitchen. There will have to be some food for Mrs. Mortar. "When the hawks descend you've got to feed 'em," she says. And Joe. Where's Joe?

Martha is distressed by what Karen tells her. It must not happen that way. Karen must call Joe back. Or go to him. But Karen can do no more. She wants to go away, too, now. She and Martha. But where can they go? In the big places where they might get jobs, they would be known. In the small places it would be even worse. There's no place they could go, nor ever will be.

"We're bad people. We'll sit. We'll be sitting the rest of our lives wondering what's happened to us," says Martha.

Karen has gone to the fire. The room is suddenly cold again. Martha continues seeking an explanation for what has happened, and what is likely to happen; seeking justification and understanding. Now she goes to Karen and demands that she listen.

"I have loved you the way they said," says Martha, tragically. "You're crazy!"

MARTHA—There's always been something wrong. Always—as long as I can remember. But I never knew it until all this happened.

KAREN (*horrified*)—Stop it!

MARTHA—You're afraid of hearing it; I'm more afraid than you.

KAREN (*her hands over her ears*)—I won't listen to you.

MARTHA—Take your hands down. You've got to know it. I can't keep it any longer. I've got to tell you how guilty I am.

KAREN (*deliberately*)—You are guilty of nothing.

MARTHA—I've been telling myself that since the night we heard the child say it; I've been praying I could convince myself of it. I can't, I can't any longer. It's there. I don't know how, I don't know why. But I did love you. I do love you. I resented your marriage. . . . I never felt that way about anybody but you. I've never loved a man.—I never knew why before.

Maybe it's that.

KAREN (*carefully*)—You are tired and sick.

MARTHA (*as though she were talking to herself*)—It's funny; it's all mixed up. There's something in you, and you don't know it and you don't do anything about it. Suddenly a child gets bored and lies—and there you are, seeing it for the first time. (*Closes her eyes.*) I don't know. It all seems to come back to *me*. In some way I've ruined your life. I've ruined my own. I didn't even *know*. (*Smiles.*) There's a big difference between us now, Karen. You feel sad and clean. I feel sad and dirty. (*Touches* KAREN's *head.*) I can't stay with you any more, darling.

KAREN (*shaken*)—All this isn't true. We'll pretend you never said it; you'll have forgotten it tomorrow.

MARTHA—Tomorrow? That's a funny word. In all those years to come, Karen, we would have had to invent a new language, as children do, without words like tomorrow.

KAREN (*crying*)—Go and lie down, Martha. You'll feel better.

Martha looks slowly about the room. She is very quiet now. At the door she turns, looking again at Karen. Then she goes out. Karen sits quietly alone. There is no sound in the house. A moment later a muffled pistol shot is heard. Again the silence.

Suddenly Karen springs from her chair. Mrs. Mortar appears on the stairway, greatly excited, calling Martha. She has heard a shot. Karen has rushed out of the room. Now she comes back, slowly, her face ashen, her hands waving helplessly. Mrs. Mortar goes into the other room, and is back again, demanding that something should be done. A doctor should be called.

Karen knows that isn't any use. In a little while they will send for someone. Let Mrs. Mortar quit crying. She need not worry. She will be taken care of. "When the hawks descend they must be fed," she repeats.

The doorbell is ringing. Karen doesn't move. Mrs. Mortar goes finally. Mrs. Tilford and the maid, Agatha, are at the door. They follow Mrs. Mortar into the room. Agatha would plead with Karen to see Mrs. Tilford. All day she has been trying to telephone. She's been trying to get Dr. Joe, and can't. She's a sick woman, is Mrs. Tilford. She's old. It's going to kill her—

Finally Karen agrees. Mrs. Tilford comes into the room. "She is a sick woman; an old woman; her face, her walk, her voice have changed. She is feeble."

"I had to come," she says, stretching out her hand, which Karen does not notice. "I know now; I know it wasn't true—" "What?"

MRS. TILFORD (*carefully*)—I know it wasn't true, Karen.

KAREN (*shuddering*)—You know it wasn't true? I don't care what you know. It doesn't matter any more. If that's what you had to say, you've said it. Go away.

MRS. TILFORD (*her hand to her throat*)—I've *got* to tell you.

KAREN—I don't want to hear you.

MRS. TILFORD—Last Tuesday Mrs. Wells found a bracelet in Rosalie's room. The bracelet had been hidden for several months. We found out that Rosalie had taken the bracelet from another girl, and that Mary—that Mary knew that and used it to force Rosalie into saying that she had seen you and Miss Dobie together. I—I've talked to Mary. I've found out. (KAREN *suddenly begins to laugh*). Don't do that, Karen. I have only a little more to say. I've talked to Judge Potter. He will make all the arrangements. There will be a public apology and an explanation. The damage suit will be paid to you in full and—and any more that you will be kind enough to take from me. I—I must see that you won't suffer any more.

KAREN—We're not going to suffer any more. It's all too late. Martha is dead. (MRS. TILFORD *gasps*.) So you've come here to relieve your conscience? Well, I won't be your confessor. It's choking you, is it? (*Violently.*) And you want to stop the choking, don't you? You've done a wrong and you have to right that wrong or you can't rest your head again. You want to be "just" don't you, and you wanted us to help you be just? You've come to the wrong place for help. You want to be a "good" woman again, don't you? (*Bitterly.*) Oh, I know. You told us that night you had to do what you did. Now you "have" to do this. A public apology and money paid, and you can sleep again and eat again. That done and there'll be peace for you. You're old, and the old are callous. Ten, fifteen years left for you. But what of me? It's a whole life for me. A whole God-damned life. (*Suddenly quiet, points to door.*) And what of her?

MRS. TILFORD (*she is crying*)—You are still living.

KAREN—And I don't know why.

Mrs. Tilford would convince Karen that she is not there to relieve her own feelings, but to try anything that promises help for Karen. Let Karen take anything she will that Mrs. Tilford can give her. The future holds nothing for Mrs. Tilford but darkness, however long the years may be. As for Mary, she can't send her away. "Whatever she does, it must be to me and no one else," she says. "She's—she's—"

"Yes. Your very own, to live with the rest of your life," answers Karen, quickly. "They will be years of darkness; you're right. It's over for me now, but it will never end for you. She's harmed us both, but she's harmed you more, I guess. I'm sorry."

MRS. TILFORD (*clings to her*)—Then you'll try for yourself.
KAREN—All right.
MRS. TILFORD—You and Joe.
KAREN—No. We're not together anymore.
MRS. TILFORD—Did I do that, too?
KAREN—I don't think anyone did anything, anymore.
MRS. TILFORD—I'll go to him right away.
KAREN—No, it's better now the way it is.
MRS. TILFORD—But he must know what I know, Karen. You must go back to him.
KAREN—No, not any more.
MRS. TILFORD—You must, you must— Perhaps later, Karen?
KAREN—Perhaps.
MRS. TILFORD (*after a moment*)—Come away from here now, Karen. You can't stay with—
KAREN—When she is buried, then I will go.
MRS. TILFORD—You'll be all right?
KAREN—I'll be all right, I suppose. Good-by, now.
MRS. TILFORD—You'll let me help you? You'll let me try?
KAREN—Yes, if it will make you feel better.
MRS. TILFORD (*timidly*)—And you—you'll take the money?
KAREN (*tired*)—If you want it that way.
MRS. TILFORD (*with feeling*)—Oh, yes, oh, yes, Karen.
KAREN—Is it nice out?
MRS. TILFORD—It's been cold. (KAREN *opens the window.*) It seems a little warmer, now.
KAREN—It feels very good.
MRS. TILFORD—You'll write me sometime?
KAREN—If I ever have anything to say. Good-by, now.
MRS. TILFORD—You will have. I know it. Good-by, my dear.
(KAREN *smiles, shakes her head as* MRS. TILFORD *exits. She does not turn, but a minute later she raises her hand.*)
KAREN—Good-by.

THE CURTAIN FALLS

VALLEY FORGE

A Drama in Three Acts

By Maxwell Anderson

THE New York Theatre Guild began its season in October with an English comedy by James Bridie called "A Sleeping Clergyman." It was a pleasant but not at all an auspicious opening. In December a second play was ready. This a native drama, as native as the history of "Valley Forge," the winter of 1777-78.

Again, while there was definite pleasure in the acceptance of the play, there was lacking that stirring enthusiasm that Guild audiences stage so perfectly when a "Mary of Scotland" or a "Strange Interlude" or a "Mourning Becomes Electra" stirs them to approval.

"Valley Forge," being, in a way, Maxwell Anderson's answer to the critically inspired query as to why he should concern himself so eloquently with the histories of Elizabeth of England and Mary of Scotland and overlook the romantic and heroic figures of his own country's history, was immediately subjected to a devastating comparison. It was not, the subscribers were practically unanimous in agreeing, as good a play nor as moving an entertainment as the Anderson studies of foreign rulers.

They could have as truthfully answered each other, had an interest in fairness to the author inspired them, that neither was the subject of George Washington trying valiantly to hold a ragged army together in the snows of Valley Forge as romantic or colorful or even as glamorous in subject or setting as were the dramas of European courts they were pleased to set against it.

There is, in "Valley Forge," much the same eloquence of speech and force of character drawing that distinguished the more popular Anderson dramas on historical themes. It has its moments, in the estimation of this editor, when in the reading it rises to finer and more thrilling dramatic statements than do the stories of either Elizabeth or Mary. True, that may be traceable to a certain native pride of country that could stir a defense of Washington and the wavering Continentals, even in New York. If so, it is a little to be regretted that a larger percentage of Theatre

Guild subscribers were not also moved by it. The play's run
of seven weeks was much less than it deserved, as drama or production, or as the inspiration of a finely moving performance by
Philip Merivale in the part of George Washington.

It is January, 1778. In a bunkhouse at Valley Forge a section
of the First Virginia regiment is variously disposed. There are
ten or twelve bunks built of saplings against the back wall. Most
of the seats are cut logs. There is a fire in the fireplace, and a
pile of logs beside it. "Three or four of the men still have mess
dishes in their hands, out of which they eat with penknives, or try
to eat, for the food this evening is inedible. . . . The clothes of
the men are dirty, torn, patched, threadbare, and in many cases
almost nonexistent. There are no uniforms. The boots are
worn out—many feet are on the floor. Socks are undreamed of,
a shirt is a rarity. . . . What clothes are still recognizable were
once Colonial homespun, and retain vestiges of the Colonial style.
. . . Long muskets are stacked in the corners, with pendant
powderhorns."

The conversation, rough in the manner of soldiers disgusted
with their billet, leads through the rottenness of the food to the
lack of clothes, and the curse of a Congress that has failed to
provide them. Alcock, a beefy fellow wrapped in a blanket, has
a complaint more personal than the others.

"What this army needs is pants," says Alcock. "If I had a
pair of pants I might stand a chance of getting a pair of boots—
but you can't walk up to a lady's back door without pants on—
not for no purpose whatever. And you can't borrow a pair to
stand sentry duty in!"

Alcock had tried to borrow Teague's leather britches and
Teague, a descendant of the Seminoles, refused the loan. There
are clothes on the way, according to Spad, a red-faced Virginian,
but Alcock, the naked one, knows more about that than Spad.

"There's no clothes coming—you might know that," reports
Alcock, dolefully. "What happened was General Washington
sent a requisition for pants to Congress. And Congress looked at
the officer that brought the requisition and says: 'Pants, my dear
man, is both dear and scarce. We can't send you any pants.
Moreover, the countryside around Philadelphia is full of Quakers
with more pants on than they need. Go out and take the pants
off the Quakers.' Two or three weeks later the officer got back
and reported to General Washington. The air around the General's headquarters turned blue to an altitude of eighty foot and

the Schoolkill River ran backward a distance of some fourteen miles. This went on for quite a spell—and then the General came to enough so's you could distinguish what he was talking about. 'You go back to Congress,' says he, 'and ask 'em if they ever tried to take the pants off a civilian.—Pants,' he continues, 'is one of the inalienable rights of man under the Declaration of Independence and the Ten Commandments. At this moment,' he says, 'I have three thousand soldiers whose pants are wide open from Genesis to Revelations, and while we remain in this defenseless condition there's nothing to stop the British regulars from marching up to York and taking the pants off the Continental Congress, which I rather hope they will do!' I was there when he said it, and, boys, I'd like to be there when he gets his answer back."

The door opens and two women burst in with a flurry of cold. One "is a slatternly workwoman" of middle age and thinly clad; the second "is fairly young and pretty, the widow of a soldier." The young woman goes to a bunk on which Neil Bonniwell, a sick soldier, is lying. She has brought a wisp of straw to put under his blanket and a stone jug of hot broth. The older woman, known as Auntie, has a bundle of what is left to launder for the men.

The women will soon be hearing of the new general orders, thinks Spad. To be sure they will he reads the orders to them from a hand-written scroll pasted on the inside of the doorjamb:

> *"Owing to over-crowded conditions and the scarcity of provender for the troops of the encampment, each company commander is requested to inquire into the status of all camp followers and the like quartered in his vicinity, there appearing to be a remarkable number of women, and especially of pregnant women, established within the lines, and greatly in excess of the allotment for companies under our military articles. Commanders are reminded that six women are allowed to a company, for washing and other necessary duties, but under no circumstances more."*

Auntie will have General Washington know that she is not pregnant, nor has been these twenty years. As for Tavis, the younger girl, that is as may be, but Neil Bonniwell stands ready to marry her, he feverishly cries out. Tavis would quiet him with a drink of broth she stole for him.

"God damn this blasted army!" cries Spad, in sudden disgust.

"This army?" exclaims Alcock, drawing the blanket closer about his bare shanks. "If God was to damn and blast this army every working day for a full year He couldn't do anything to it that hasn't been done. We've got everything from the itch to the purple fever, nothing to eat, nothing to wear, and the coldest son-of-a-bitch of a winter since the lake of Galilee froze over and Jesus walked on the water."

"He could 'a' walked across Chesapeake Bay yesterday and hauled a fourteen-pounder behind Him."

Now Teague, a hunter, from his clothes, has taken up his musket and is prepared to take leave of the company, and take Minto, an oldish, graying fellow, with him. Teague's through with waiting for conditions to get better. They're out of food now, and they've traded about all their cavalry horses for shoats. He aims to get away while he has the strength to walk.

The others would not stop him, nor promise to cover for him if he's caught. They just don't want to know anything about it.

"There was a Hessian Johnny here today with leather boots on—looking for a job as a general—or maybe commander-in-chief," reports Mason Bonniwell. "He stayed long enough to soak in a few fair-sized impressions and then took out for Philadelphia to join up with General Howe."

"They eat over in Philadelphia."

MASON—Sure, the big-hearted patriots of Pennsylvania—we fight for their liberty and they carry their butter and eggs to Philadelphia in a steady stream to feed King George's troops. And you can't stop 'em. Shoot 'em dead and you can't stop 'em.

ALCOCK—King George pays cash and we pay in continentals. Did you ever meet up with a Quaker that didn't prefer a guinea in hand to any amount of liberty in the bush? You can shoot 'em, hang 'em, damn 'em, give 'em the water cure, rip their guts out and fill 'em up with old iron, they go right on selling hogs to the English.

TEAGUE—I'm no Quaker, son, and I'll fill anybody up with old iron that says I'd sell out to General Howe! We're going home, that's all.

ALCOCK—All right, all right. You've read the orders: the new penalty for desertion is seventy-five lashes on the bare back, well laid on—or hanging if there's treason connected with it. Don't get caught, that's all.

TEAGUE—I've never been caught yet.

ALCOCK—How often have you taken French leave?
TEAGUE—Whenever there's nothing to do here I go home.

Lieutenant Cutting, a young officer somewhat better dressed than the others, is followed through the door by a dog. He doesn't know the cur, but it's been following him all the way from the King of Prussia Inn. He has come to warn the men to turn in if they want any sleep. They are to be on parade at five for manual of arms under Baron Steuben. The rest of the day they will spend making cartridges.

A further commotion outside heralds the entrance of Lieutenant-Colonel Lucifer Tench. He has come in search of a squad of men with passable footwear to go on a raiding party to the hay islands below Darby under personal supervision of the Commander-in-chief. It has been reported that General Howe, running short of horse fodder, is to make an attempt to bring in the forage stored the year before in the islands of the Delaware. It is the General's idea to get there ahead of Howe, to cut off his approach and salvage the hay. Tench would take with him a company of outdoor fellows who could do the work, each to draw four days' rations.

Lieutenant Cutting is of the opinion that the order cannot be carried out. Certainly not that night.

"We've drawn the last ration for this regiment, such as it was," says Cutting. "If that dog keeps it on his stomach he'll probably go to meet his maker before morning."

"The supplies for your regiment were sufficient for ten more days."

"On paper, yes. But when they rolled out the last twenty barrels the meat was spoiled. As for the flour, they baked the remains of it this morning."

It occurs to Tench that Cutting is inclined to enjoy the situation. If he has further criticism to register, or would indicate with whom the fault lies, Tench would like to hear it. They are facing each other belligerently when the door opens and an aide appears to announce General Washington's desire that if the matter has been arranged, Col. Tench should rejoin him. Tench goes to explain.

A moment later the door opens to admit "a tall, dark French officer of nineteen or twenty in resplendent uniform." He is followed by General Washington "in shabby boots, a long, much-worn cloak, and an old cocked hat." The men come as smartly to attention as circumstances permit. The fevered Neil rises on one elbow.

General Washington is distressed to hear of the shortage of supplies reported by Colonel Tench. However, a long-expected wagon train has begun to arrive, bringing not only munitions but eighteen long tons of flour and pork as well.

Lieutenant Cutting is ready, then, to begin preparations at once, unless it happens that this be the wagon train that was to have been sent by General Putnam from Fishkill—

"It is," answers General Washington. "Though how you may have learned of that I'm at a loss to conceive."

"I supped this evening with General Conway, who had received a letter from Putnam. And if the information in the letter is correct I very much fear you will be disappointed of your expectations in regard to the salt pork and flour. Putnam was unable to locate mules or wagons to accommodate the food allotment."

There is confirmation of that report in the failure of Colonel Tench to receive the expected bills of lading.

"I should like to hope this report was erroneous," says General Washington, "but some little experience with the commissary department has taught me to credit any amount of ill news from that quarter. It sticks in my crop a little, let me add, that I should receive important intelligence in a manner so singularly circuitous. General Putnam writes, not to me, but to General Conway, and General Conway conveys his intelligence, not to me, but to a junior officer with whom he has supped. Quite by chance I encounter this officer and in the course of conversation these little military details are relayed to me—"

"Sir, I hope I have not offended—"

"Not in the least, sir. I am in your debt for the information, and can only congratulate you and General Conway on the celerity with which you receive dispatches which have not been vouchsafed to the Commander-in-chief."

Washington has turned to go when the young French officer, who has been examining the collar around the dog's neck, stops him to report that the animal belongs to General Howe. An inscription on the collar reads: "Rover, Sir William Howe." Indicating that this rover has roved all the way from Philadelphia.

"I might have known by the fat on his ribs he was no local product," observes the General. "We must see that he is returned." When pen and ink have been brought Washington dictates a letter to Colonel Tench:

"'Sir William Howe, British Headquarters, Philadelphia. Dear Sir: The bearer of this note will return to you a dog of which you appear to be the owner, since he wears your name on his collar. May I say that I was the more astonished to find him at Valley Forge because I believed the desertions to be going the other way. G. Washington.' Choose a reliable man and send him to Philadelphia with a flag. The animal is to be delivered to the General himself with this note and my compliments. (*Indicating* ALCOCK.) This is a man I know. Would the errand amuse you?"

"I'm easy to amuse, General," admits Alcock, "but the fact is I haven't any britches."

"Well, that can hardly be considered a defect of character. Choose a messenger, Lieutenant."

Now Washington would leave, but the soldier Teague, much to the dismay of his mates, indicates a desire to speak to him. Twice he addresses the General before he catches his attention. Then he would ask about the new regulations governing men going home without leave. It is said it means seventy-five lashes if they catch you now.

"The traditional penalty for desertion is shooting at sunrise," replies Washington. "We've been more lenient here."

"But, look, General Washington, it don't make sense. It don't stand to reason—"

When the others would stop him, General Washington requests that Teague be given a chance to say what is on his mind.

It is Teague's idea that it is foolish for him to stay in camp and starve while his woman is starving at home. It would be much better for him to go home during the winter, help to keep his family in food and come back when the fighting is resumed in the spring. He has done it before to everybody's gain. It isn't that he's afraid of a fight. Fighting's ham and eggs to Teague. He and his son are aiming to keep at it until they chase the god-damned red-coats clear out of the Chesapeake Bay and across the Atlantic Ocean, but sitting there starving is something he can't savvy.

"What is your name, sir?" asks Washington, in a friendly tone.

"Teague, sir. Teague's my name."

WASHINGTON—Well, Master Teague, if they catch you they'll give you seventy-five lashes, and that's a good deal to take and live. On the other hand you're quite right from your own angle, and if I were you I'd feel as you do.—But this you should know, sir: if you go home, and we all go home this winter, you won't need to bother about coming back in the spring. There'll be no fighting to come back to.—General Howe will march out of Phila-

delphia and take over these states of ours. If he knew now how
many have deserted, how many are sick, how many unfit for duty
on account of the lack of food and clothes and munitions, he'd
come out in force and wring our necks one by one, and the neck
of our sickly little revolution along with us. So far we've kept
him pinned in Philadelphia by sheer bluster and bluff and show
of arms. We've raided his supplies and cut off his shipping and
captured his food-trains and so bedeviled him generally that he
thinks there's still an army here. But every able-bodied man,
every man that owns a pair of dungarees for his legs and brogans
for his feet, has to look like ten men if this nation's coming
through the winter alive.—What are we in this war for? Are we
tired of it? Do we want to quit?

THE MEN—No, sir. No.

WASHINGTON—I can't blame you if you sound a bit half-
hearted about it.

TEAGUE—I'm not half-hearted about it! Not me! I'm fighting to keep King George out of my backyard! I moved west
three times to get away from his damn tax-collectors, and every
time they caught up to me! I'm sick of tax-collectors, that's why
I'm in it!

WASHINGTON—Then it may be you're here in error, and the
sooner you discover it the better. You'll get death and taxes
under one government as well as another. But I'll tell you why
I'm here, and why I've hoped you were here, and why it's seemed
to me worth while to stick with it while our guns rust out for
lack of powder, and men die around me for lack of food and
medicine and women and children sicken at home for lack of
clothing and the little they need to eat—yes, while we fight one
losing battle after another, and retreat to fight again another
year, and yet another and another, and still lose more than we
win, and yet fight on while our hair grows gray and our homes
break up in our absence, and the best and youngest among us
give their blood to swell spring freshets and leave their bones
and marrow to flesh the hills. This is no lucky war for me. I
thought it was at first. I wanted to astound the world as a military leader, but my head's grayer now and I've had enough of
that. What I fight for now is a dream, a mirage, perhaps, something that's never been on this earth since men first worked it
with their hands, something that's never existed and will never
exist unless we can make it and put it here—the right of free-born
men to govern themselves in their own way.—Now men are
mostly fools, as you're well aware. They'll govern themselves

like fools. There are probably more fools to the square inch in the Continental Congress than in the Continental army, and the percentage runs high in both. But we've set our teeth and trained our guns against the hereditary right of arbitrary kings, and if we win it's curfew for all the kings of the world.—It may take a long time, but one by one, bolster themselves as they will, pour out money as they may for mercenaries, make what victorious wars they can, they'll slip one by one from their thrones and go out with the great wash through this breach we make in their sea walls.—It may not be worth the doing. When you deal with a king you deal with one fool, knave, madman, or whatever he may be. When you deal with a Congress you deal with a conglomerate of fools, knaves, madmen and honest legislators, all pulling different directions and shouting each other down. So far the knaves and fools seem to have it. That's why we're stranded here on this barren side-hill, leaving a bloody trail in the snow and chewing the rotten remains of sow-belly on which some merchant has made his seven profits.—So far our government's as rotten as the sow-belly it sends us. I hope and pray it will get better. But whether it gets better or worse it's your own, by God, and you can do what you please with it—and what I fight for is your right to do what you please with your government and with yourselves without benefit of kings.—It's for you to decide, Master Teague— you, and your son, and the rest of you. This is your fight more than mine. I don't know how long the Congress means to keep me where I am nor how long you mean to stay with me. If you desert they may catch you and they may not, but the chances are they won't, for the sentries are men as you are—hungry, shivering, miserable and inclined to look the other way. Make your own decision. But if we lose you—if you've lost interest in this cause of yours—we've lost our war, lost it completely, and the men we've left lying on our battle-fields died for nothing whatever—for a dream that came too early—and may never come true.

He stands looking a little dreamily at the men, and then at the officers. He has gone now, followed by the others. All save Tench, who has stayed behind to have further word with Cutting.

"I guess the old woman'll get along," says Teague, turning back to the others. "She's brought in her own bear meat before."

It has occurred to Tench that there is something a little strange about General Howe's dog following Lieutenant Cutting. If those be fighting words Tench has every intention of making them good.

Cutting, too, is in fighting mood, but offers explanation first. There had been an exchange of prisoners at General Conway's camp that morning, and it is possible the dog followed the British party into camp. Cutting has no love for the English, nor any desire to see them win. If they should win it will be because Tench, and others like him, insist fanatically upon following a leadership already discredited. He will name no names, but there is open dissatisfaction and Tench knows it as well as he.

"I've served as a brigadier-general under the French colors," says Cutting, "and I'm cast here as a second-lieutenant. There's no place in this army I couldn't fill, and I serve under a captain who sits at table in his stocking feet and got his experience fighting Indians on the Ohio. Why doesn't Benedict Arnold hold a commission? Why is Gates shunted into the northern department? Why are Lee and Conway pensioned off with minor commands—?"

TENCH—I thought we'd come to Conway.

CUTTING—Why, because the army's run for the glory of a little inner clique, of which you happen to be one—

TENCH—And you want it run for a little clique of adventurers that's served in every army in Europe, sworn allegiance to every king and cause in Christendom and turned your coats so often for money that you start undressing every time you see a shilling—

CUTTING—You've served abroad, I believe!

TENCH—I know a man when I see one! Washington's a man —and there isn't one among those you've named that he couldn't eat after dinner, with a little brandy and soda to wash down the taste. You may be a good officer, you may have served with all the duchies and principalities between Turkey and the Swedes, but take care how you align yourself with these foreign swashers who come over to cash in on this revolution—with nothing to recommend them but tarnished epaulets, tarnished reputations and a full set of military mustaches! We've had the clippings and sweepings of every European court dumped on us, mostly younger sons and bastard half-brothers, and leavings that were pitched out when the college of heraldry cleaned house!—I beg your pardon heartily if you're a bastard. I meant nothing personal.

CUTTING—I think you did, though, and I'd take the trouble to quarrel with you if I thought it worth my while. It isn't. You can rate Conway and Lee and Gates as low as you like. They'll hold their commissions long after your Washington's gone back to planting tobacco along the Potomac. He's a beaten man. You heard his speech, and if that wasn't a valedictory I never heard one. He's tired and others are tired of him, and when he goes you'll go with him.

TENCH—Come, come—this is news. When may we expect this happy sequel?

CUTTING—I've said my say.

TENCH—You have indeed—and you've said what I wanted to get out of you—

CUTTING—No doubt you're a tale-bearer, too, to go with the rest of your Colonial virtues.

TENCH—You may be right.

CUTTING—Tell it then. I've said nothing that isn't said from here to Boston, and with added flourishes.

TENCH—Good night, sir. Gentlemen, your pardon for a scene hardly calculated to instill respect and discipline. Good night.

Tench has gone out. Private Spad improvises a leash for the dog. He has visions of a full meal, perhaps of beef and kidney pie, in Philadelphia.

"I hope you over-eat yourself and regurgitate," hopes Alcock.

"Thanks. Always a friend!" answers Spad.

Tavis has turned to comfort the restless Neil in his bunk.

"Lie still, sweet. Lie still and rest," she murmurs.

"This is a poor death to die," mutters Neil.

The curtain falls.

From the ballroom at General Howe's headquarters in Philadelphia strains of Mozart can be heard. The rising curtain reveals three or four "furbelowed and periwigged couples" dancing to the music.

Sir William is among them, his partner a dainty lady in mask and domino. At the end of the room a corner is curtained off for private theatricals later, and there are boxes arranged for spectators. Sir William takes his partner into one of these boxes, where they are screened from the dancers.

Sir William is in a sentimental mood. The beauty of the music, the grace of the minuet, have touched him. He would that his lady had loved a soldier. She had, she says, married one.

"My dear," replies the gallant General, "if I knew his name

I'd be inclined to practice King David's stratagem. Poor man, I'd set him in the forefront of the battle, and then his widow— I'd keep her for myself."

But what of the others? The domino lady would know. What of Mistress Loring? They are but friends, the General swears, and none as fair as she. He has kissed her, impulsively, and she, though surprised, is not angered. She did, in fact, she says, lead him on, but it happens that this once he is not the man. Her love is in another camp, the camp of the rebels in fact, and she would have his leave to go out and see this other man. Now she has removed her mask, and at sight of her beauty he is even more distressed at thought of her on the rebel side.

"Never rebel, dear lady," General Howe cautions. "God sets up kings, and all the prayer books teach us it is irreligious to fight against them."

"Come, be serious," she chides.

"With a woman?"

MARY—Solemn, then, sad—
   doleful. I loved and lost when I was a child.
   I let my love go then, when I might have had him—
   and now it may be too late.

HOWE—See the tears in my eyes—
   you have smitten the rock like Moses.

MARY—When I was a child
   a young man came wooing from Virginia way.
   And we fell in love, but my parents said, No, no—
   this is an Indian fighter; you are rich,
   and may turn out good-looking; let him go,
   and catch yourself a lord. And I let him go
   and caught myself a captain of marines
   or something of that kind. I've never loved him.
   I've wanted what I lost.

HOWE—The Indian fighter.

MARY—Yes.

HOWE—It's someone I know?

MARY—I doubt you've seen him; but you've heard of him;
   he's no less on the rebel side than you on this.

HOWE—Washington?

MARY—I believe
   that was the name.

HOWE—Is this some game you play?

MARY—It would be but a poor game. No, I'm deadly earnest,
I'm not jesting now.
HOWE—What a strange mad thing
is a woman's heart! To remember all this while
and brood on it, and remember. You'd go to him,
and give up all that's civilized to live
on corn bread in log cabins?
MARY—Will it be so long
before we come to terms with the rebels? This
is the last year of their war.
HOWE—A long-headed girl;
you've thought this through.
MARY—Oh, truly.
HOWE—But then I've heard—
the man is married, is he not?
MARY—A widow.
When I refused him he married a widow with land
and a nest of children. Nasty ones, I hope,
with wipey noses.
HOWE—Is there any other kind?
Strange that they're such a pleasure in the getting
and so damp to have about.—Why, no, my dear;
the answer's no. As a gallant to a lady,
here in this ballroom, we may talk, look you,
of anything under heaven; but wars are something
which you have hardly imagined, here in this ballroom.
They're fought with blood and iron. I say, for your sake,
for yours alone, you're not to cross the lines.
MARY—I understand that. If you must refuse, why then,
you must refuse. You have your reasons. Still—
I shall go.
HOWE—Without a pass?
MARY—If necessary.
There comes a time when a woman's desperate
to have her youth. It's come to me, and I'll have it
though all the generals in hell should stand
eyes front and bar my passage. Oh, believe me,
I can make my way.
HOWE—And, being warned, I shall find
a way to prevent it.
      (*The orchestra begins to play Yankee Doodle.*)
Come; the masquerade

is about to begin, and we're to be amused.

MARY—Surely.

Howe pulls back the curtains. The dancing couples drift in, one and two at a time, and face the improvised stage. Major André, an upstanding Britisher, serves as a smiling, satirical master of ceremonies. It is, he says, his sad duty to announce that the program is now to be taken over by General George Washington and his Continental army, "whose services we have acquired for the evening at the expense of three shillings, sixpence, and three twists of local tobacco, very bad."

"In a personal interview which I obtained with General Washington he said in part, 'Yes, sir, by gum, we'll be there, by gum, every man jack of us, by gum!' " mimics André, and the crowd snickers appreciatively.

Now, "amid cheers, jeers and hisses, the curtains are pulled back revealing three ragged soldiers, caricatures of the Continentals, and Washington as impersonated by a British officer on a broomstick hobby-horse, with movable ears. The *Washington* raises his wooden sword.

" 'Stop! Halt! Whoa! Give the password!' " shouts the imitation Washington, with the horse wagging an ear at each command. The first soldier breaks into song. The tune is "Yankee Doodle."

> " 'I am a soldier in a cause,
> I march and fight for freedom;
> I won't obey nobody's laws,
> I never seem to need 'em.

Chorus:

> " 'Yankee Doodle has no shoes,
> Yankee Doodle Dandy;
> For ham and eggs he has no use,
> But he fills up on brandy!
> Clippetty, clippetty, clippetty, clippetty,
> clop, clop, clop, clop, clop; clip!' "

The *Washington* has contributed a clog dance accompaniment. The ladies and their partners are greatly amused. There are several verses, followed by a burlesque drill, with the patriots facing and firing in every direction. One gun kicks its owner over backward and he knocks down the rest of the army. They are sprawling thus when Spad of the Continentals wanders into the room

with General Howe's dog. He stands awkwardly and listens to
the chief actor recite a piece about Washington, ending with—

> " 'I am that Washington on whom you've pondered;
> My head is in the clouds, my feet—in mud.
> My socks are wet, my shirts are never laundered,
> I grind the neighbors' children up for food.' "

"Looky here, mister actor!" interjects Spad, stepping forth
belligerently. The *Washington* goes on—

> " 'In short to put it briefly, men and matrons,
> I'm at the end of what I call my string;
> I'll trade this revolution and its patrons,
> For half a gill of rum—or anything.' "

"You'll have to get up first, then," says Spad, knocking the
actor down.

There is a good deal of consternation at this. General Howe
thinks perhaps it is all part of the show, but Major André wrote
the show and knows it is not. The Washington imitator has
picked himself up from the floor and is squaring off to revenge
himself upon Spad when André and the others rush in and sep-
arate them.

Spad explains his mission and produces the letter from General
Washington. General Howe takes a hand now, thanking Spad
as messenger and asking him kindly to wait and take a message
in return to General Washington. He would also reward Spad,
with money, which the soldier spurns, or with a good dinner if
he will take nothing more.

". . . You have come a long way and I have heard that you
fare but lightly along the Schuylkill," smiles Howe.

"Somebody's been lying like hell, then!" spiritedly answers
Spad. "They told you we were shy of victuals over at Valley
Forge? Listen, last night I threw away more than I ate! I'm
much obliged but I wouldn't be able to accommodate any dinner.
I wouldn't want to take the last few mouthfuls away from a
beleaguered army in straitened circumstances. No, thanks just
the same, I'll go back to my own side, where the cooking's plenti-
ful and excellent."

The soldier and the dog have gone, each in charge of an officer.
André has sent the guests to the refreshment tables in another
room. Mary Philipse still waits on General Howe. Consulting

with André, Howe learns that she is the wife of Major Morris, unhappily a prisoner at the moment. André would vouch for Mary's loyalty with his life.

"She tells some tale of having been affianced to Washington, or having come near it," Howe reports.

"Why, that's no more than truth," André answers. "Her family broke it off. She told you that? But I've heard it often."

Howe repeats Mary's request for a pass through the lines to see her rebel General. It has occurred to him something might be made of that.

He has just heard disquieting news. The French alliance, he has learned from papers taken from a captured packet, is quite likely to become a fact. With French encouragement the rebels could go on for another five years, and Howe is tired of fighting.

"The longer it goes on the more chance they have," the General explains. "At this moment the war is won. Washington's army's a wraith. It lingers on from month to month by miracle. And now, now when I've won my war, the French drop on us and botch the game.—I see one possible hope of making an end of it. If Washington can be reached, and convinced it's useless to go on, the thing is done. He has reason to be discouraged if ever a man had reason. . . . Suppose I sent this lady out of his youth with a message?"

"He'll see her, surely," André agrees. "She might persuade him."

To Mary now Howe admits that he has been thinking she might be of use in making that visit to General Washington. He wants the war to end and tonight he has learned of something that makes it perfect suicide for the colonies to continue. There is to be no French alliance, deceitfully reports the General. The Colonists, he thinks, are as sick of fighting as he is. Washington is a Virginia squire at heart and would much prefer to take his ease and hunt his foxes. Congress is sick of the whole thing. The Boston merchants and Massachusetts officers are plotting to put Gates in Washington's place and sue for peace on any terms.

"They're ruined by the war and losing money every day," says Howe; "no ships, no commerce, markets shot to fatrells, all the fat-backed Puritans screaming over taxes and retching with fear to think how big they signed their names to the Declaration. Washington—he's our man."

"And is he open to reason?" asks André.

"He's a canny gentleman. He knows how bread is buttered,"
answers Howe.

MARY—Then—he will talk with you?
HOWE—Well, that was where I thought you might come in,
    Mistress Morris. You say he loved you once
    and you wish to see him—well, that can be dished up
    into some raggle-taggle gypsy tale,
    all honey and moonlight—
    how you sheer must—must see him; dashed away
    forgetting husbands, wives, proprieties,
    in one sweet sweep of passion—it's no man's brain
    can find the seasoning, but you'll worm your way
    into a friendly meeting—
MARY—I can say this truly,
    with no help of seasoning. And then—?
HOWE—Why then—
    I have no speech prepared—but tell him this
    in your own fashion: The war's gone on too long,
    both sides lose, both are worn down till there's nothing
    left to win should he win. One word from him
    and we all forget and forgive—exchange general pardons,
    live again like men. What beasts we've been,
    we English-speaking brothers, to gash and stab
    and drill each other's brains out all these years
    over one kind of government or another
    when they're all the same! I'm a liberal myself,
    want to see men free, as he does—but, good Lord,
    when has a king balked freedom, when has the lack
    of a king guaranteed it?
MARY—But if I told him this
    I should mean it, Sir William.
HOWE—And I should mean it!
    (*The music begins again.*)
    I mean it from my heart! You think because
    I dance and take it lightly, and play about
    with women, this damned war means nothing to me
    but a colonial interlude, a picnic
    on military lines? I tell you and swear it,
    if I could keep some semblance of victory
    they could have their liberty for all of me!
    Three years is much too much to give a cause
    you never believed in!

MARY—Well—I'll go.
>   (*The dancers are returning.*)
HOWE—And tell him
>   we in this camp know that he's lost, but are loathe
>   to press our advantage home, having held him always
>   as a magnanimous gentleman and a soldier
>   just this side of miracle. You'll say this?
MARY—Yes.
HOWE—And say, too, to give up hope of France.
ANDRÉ—The dancers are returning.
MARY—I'll say all this—
>   but with one difference—that I'll mean it all.
HOWE—Our compact's drawn
>   and a kiss shall seal it. Shall we dance, my lady?
>   (HOWE *and* MARY *take places in the minuet and the scene
>   ends as it began, with several couples dancing to the
>   Mozart music.*)

The parlor of the Colonial house that Washington has taken
for headquarters has been turned into a sort of office. There is
a small desk in it and rather formal chairs are spaced about it.
"A large map hangs on the rear wall, showing Philadelphia, the
Delaware below the city and Valley Forge." There is a conference on now, with General Washington pacing up and down
the room by the window, and with Generals Varnum and Stirling
seated near Lieutenant-Colonel Tench, who is at the desk. Near
the window the Marquis de Lafayette is standing.

Tench is reading the minutes of a previous meeting. Mostly
they have to do with sentences that have been passed on deserters
and other offenders, and their punishments include being "lashed
and cashiered with infamy," or "flogged at a cart's tail for selling provisions to the British." Only one, Samuel Jelliffe, sentenced to be hanged for espionage, is reprieved in consideration
of a bargain he had made with Washington by terms of which
he had turned over documents of inestimable value.

There's an end to business now and "a puke-faced lad" waiting
outside, persistently determined to see Washington, though Tench
has booted him out a dozen times, is brought in by the General's
order. He proves to be the Neil Bonniwell who was ill in his
bunk the time Washington visited the bunkhouse of the First
Virginia.

Neil is there to plead for a chance to serve the cause and the man who is leading it. He knows that he is dying, and he would die fighting.

"There are certain things men have in this world, and I'll never have them," says Neil. "Damn it—let me die for something! I've believed in this war we're fighting—and you, I've believed in you! A man doesn't like to go out forever and not one blow struck for—it sounds like bluster—and that's what it is—but one chance is all I can ever have—that's all I could be remembered for—"

It is Washington's fear that Neil is not fit for service, and it is Tench's idea that the boy is wasting the General's time, but Washington will see what can be done. That is the only promise he can give.

Now Washington would get to the matter for which he has called them together.

WASHINGTON—It's not accident,
    as you may have thought, that you four are here tonight.
    There's a question I ask myself so often now
    I must ask it of someone else. The reports before us
    show us we've neither food nor clothes nor arms
    for the maintenance of an army, nor defense
    if we're attacked. In my last letter to Congress
    I told them we must either starve or dissolve
    unless they sent instant aid. I've written before
    almost as urgently, receiving replies—
    friendly, cajoling, evasive, full of advice,
    mostly unworkable, and a thin stream of goods,
    sufficient, say, for half a regiment,
    and we've foraged for the rest. They're sending tomorrow
    two commissioners to investigate; by the time
    we've satisfied these stool-wits that we're dying
    the men who have gumption left to arise and walk
    will have walked away, and we'll muster nobody here
    but the sick and naked. It's begun already.
    Great bands of marauders shift away from camp
    and range the country like brigands. Some thousand or two
    have put out for home; it's reckoned another thousand
    has crossed the lines to Howe. One-third of our soldiers,
    and those the most able-bodied, have gone—the remainder—
    how they hold out, or why, I don't know.—We can't blame
        them

if they follow their fellows.—Now when our army's gone,
as it seems to be going, Sir William Howe, who's waited
for just this chance, will stroll out in his fat-haunched way
to round us in and we're done for. My question's simply:
Does this end the adventure? Is the revolution over,
or is it worth trying to hold on into spring
when at least there's food to be had?—It will cost lives,
by hundreds, perhaps by thousands.—What it means to me
to say this, I think you know.

He turns to General Varnum as first in rank. Varnum is a
soldier who takes orders. The burden is Washington's, not his,
and he prays that God may help his commander, and that there
may be men to take orders so long as he is there to give them.

General Stirling, too, would stick along with Varnum and knows
there are more than Washington reckons on who will see it
through "until we've eaten the wolves extinct." There'd be enough
food and to spare, blurts Stirling, if all those "moth-eaten drones
who've served abroad and spread their dog-eared commissions in
every company" could be dumped into the river through the ice.

". . . They'd sell you out to Gates, or Lee, or any mother's son
who'd raise their rank by half-a-crown a year—and stain their
good right hands to the bone with ink—not with blood, mind
you—writing their peaching letters to put you out, and Gates in!
What disaffection there is, they've started most of it!"

"Well, we have no evidence of it, and this was not the theme
we met here to discuss," says Washington.

But Stirling *has* evidence. He had been drunk with Conway
and heard him boast of writing Gates. He had saddled a horse
and ridden sixty miles to catch the postman and recover the letter
and has it with him to toss upon the table before them.

Washington takes little note of the letter at the moment. He
will see Conway, and Cutting, too, at Tench's suggestion. But
that will not settle the greater question he has gathered them to
ask. And upon their answer depends, largely, "whether there is
an army—or will be tomorrow, for Gates to covet or me to say
good-by to."

"In a republic treason is not exactly what it seems under a
king," continues Washington. "There are rights of opinion here.
Friend Gates has been winning victories of late, and it may be
he'd be better."

"Now, if you meant that—" protests the fiery Tench.

"I don't, as it happens!" admits Washington. Still, his other question is not answered, and he would have that answer now. Tench rises testily to the challenge.

TENCH—Then I'd see the Congress
    damned in hell, before I'd let them ruin
    our campaign for us! Who is it sits at York
    doling supplies out? A pack of puling grimsirs
    with one testicle among them to keep their wives
    in order and run the state! A school of prissies
    thwarting the war and cadging on the side
    to fur their gowns! This country'd come to you
    with open arms if you said to them once for all:
    I'll take just this and that, and I'll take it now
    when it's needed! One word, one breath from you and you'd blow
    the Congress from here to Maine!
WASHINGTON—A dictator?
TENCH—Why,
    are you so afraid of words? It's that or lose.
WASHINGTON—Has it escaped you, sir, that we fight this war
    against usurpation of power? Should I usurp
    the powers of Congress, which gave me what power I have,
    I'd have nothing left to fight for.
TENCH—I beg your pardon!
    We're in rebellion against the King of England,
    or so I thought.
WASHINGTON—It happens that our Congress
    is the heart of what we fight for, good or bad,
    and I uphold it. Now, keeping that in mind,
    is it possible to go on?
TENCH—No, it is not.
    Last night there was mutiny in the Eighteenth; they objected
    to their food, and little blame to them. The riot
    was quelled only by scouring out the larders
    of neighboring battalions. This will happen again
    and spread. There's no holding men to discipline
    when there's bread in the country, and boots, and bales of clothing
    waiting for shipment, and nothing but plain damned fools,
    sitting in legislature, withholds them! Who gives
    a simple curse for Congress, or theories,

when his guts are rotted out with rotten food
and his toes fall off from freezing?

The men are sick of fighting for "these fastidious wind-bags
that make our laws in session, and draw their pay, and leave us
to die here," shouts Tench.   Tench is a soldier, as Varnum is,
"and a soldier's business is to fight when he has to, run away
when he can, eat if he can get it, drink as much as there is and
stay alive."

". . . I'll fight for the man I believe in,
    but if I'm to fight to make Congress permanent
    they can take their revolution and stick it back
    in the bung it came from!"

It is a plain statement, Washington concedes.   Stirling and
Varnum would reason with the orator.   If his words suggest trea-
son, as they do to Stirling, the whole damned war is treason to
King George, answers Tench.   And if it be a war for liberty, as
Varnum reminds him, then Tench is against them all.   Says he:

"They're all alike, and have one business, governments,
    and it's to plunder.   This new one we've set up
    seems to be less efficient than the old style
    in its methods of plundering folk, but give them time;
    they'll learn to sink their teeth in what you've got
    and take it from you.   To hell with the cause!   I'll fight
    while I'm fed and paid, and I haven't seen much lately
    of either one."

When it comes Lafayette's turn the Marquis is loathe to speak,
yet eager to explain his emotions.   He must, he knows, tell them
things they already know.   That the world they have cut from
the wilderness is a new world; that the air they breathe is a new
and bracing air; that while Europe has thirty kings and a hundred
million slaves, here each man's a king, and each woman bears
herself regally, like a queen.

". . . The air
    of this coast has fired your blood, and while three among you,
    no more than three, hold hard against the old masters,
    the kingdoms lessen and dwindle.   They've felt your breath
    and feared it in the old world.   Lose!   Now the gods

> in heaven hear me, you cannot lose! Bow down
> and humble yourselves if you can! It's not in you to bow
> nor to speak humbly. It's a trick you've never learned
> and cannot learn in this air!—As for these thrones
> that men have bowed to, I've come from them lately, and
>   seen them,
> how they're eaten down with old vices and slimed with worms
> till they crumble into the moats! Lower your muzzles,
> droop your flags! Even so the kingdoms falter
> and go down of themselves!"

It is the name of Washington that is magical in France, Lafayette continues. It is Washington who has fired the determination of a people, led by Beaumarchais and not by Louis, the little, to help the Continentals with men and money and ships, and these will be theirs before the end of spring. He knows, even as they know, that it is too long to wait. Yet if they knew the dreams and faith that rested upon them they "would do this impossible."

The Marquis, rich and spoiled at twenty, has left a young wife whom he loves in France and come to them "because the best life in all this world lives here in what *you* have to do." He knows the silly errors of the Congress, knows of the irritating foreign officers and the privations the men have endured, knows of the lives that have been lost and are to be lost, it may seem for nothing, "for a false dawn, a chimera";

> ". . . Still, soberly,
> in fact—in all soberness—not since Prometheus
> drew the gods' fires in heaven and left them cold
> to bring fire down to men, there's been no action
> better worth risk of stapling to the rocks
> with vultures at your liver, than your defiance
> of Hanoverian kings! There—I've slipped again
> into rhapsody—and again you must forgive me
> since I meant each word."

"You're quite forgiven," mutters Washington.

A little sadly the Commander would know of Tench what's on hand. Enough, thinks Tench, by dint of scratching all together, for three or four days. As for their high purpose, muses Washington, they have that still, despite the dying men about them and the sick men without blankets, or food, or care. He knows

the lines of war they keep, "one middling wind would blow them
with the leaves and heap them in the gullies." And yet—

> ". . . Gentlemen,
> looking back over what you've offered,—each one of you
> has said in his own way—even Lafayette—
> there's no immediate hope.—And since I agree
> that this is true—we should make our preparations
> to break up camp and give over. We should—and yet—
> since it's begun
> and we're in it deep, while we have men and arms
> and a government behind us and a gambler's stake
> in what's to happen, we must still stand here
> and take things as they come."

"This is the man we heard of overseas," says Lafayette.

Yet, if they think he would be a martyr, they will suffer great
disappointment, the General tells them. He'd rather live and
have his fun, with no thought of posing as a St. George and the
dragon. But they have three days and the order's given. They'll
gamble on a change of luck "and face what brand of hell's reserved for madmen."

Lafayette lingers a moment when the rest have gone and there
is a further exchange of confidences and understanding between
them. Washington has been moved by Lafayette's reference to
his wife and hears again of that supreme devotion. There was a
girl in Washington's life, when he was twenty-three, and it might
have been that he could have known such a love. But it came
out otherwise—

Tench has come, still a testy protester, to announce the arrival
of a British major—or one in such a costume, though it's plain
there is a woman inside. She demands to see Washington. She
has a message from Howe.

A moment later Mary Philipse stands in the door in a scarlet
uniform. She stands before him, Mary informs the General, as
one he has long forgotten. She brings a message from General
Howe, his kindest thanks for the return of the dog. There was
a time Washington had sworn never to forget—

Now Lafayette, with some eagerness, would say his farewells
and leave, though Washington, with light embarrassment, would
have him stay as a possible help in an emergency.

Mary is frank in confessing her wish to see Washington again.

Even the enemy costume she wears is a part of her woman's stratagem. "Is a woman never to follow her heart and run after him she loves though she run back twenty years?" she demands. "You read no novels—always the practical man—I can see it. This is love's disguise. It passed me handily in the exchange of prisoners."

"Then you dealt with blind men at either end," smiles Washington. But he is not pleased. War is not a game of blindman's buff with him, nor is he a figure in grand opera to have time for romancing between battles. It's true he remembers the time she meant a heartbreak to him, but "what treasure may lie there lies too deep for dredging."

Mary had expected some such rebuff and has her answer. For twenty years her heart had starved for love. "I'm not light nor given to lightness—nor have I come here lightly," she says, with some spirit. "The one thing worth having in a brief life, I have still to seek. It was mine once, for the taking. It came at your offering and I tossed it away, believing like all young fools it grew on every bush. I'm not young now and I'd risk whatever name the world might give me to have it back again."

"I shall seem ungracious," sighs Washington. "You married Captain Morris, and I am married. We're fixed in our two worlds. The time's run out for pleasantries. It's winter in my bones as well as in the year."

"I'm afraid it is," mutters Mary.

Teague has brought in two bags with which Mary has arrived. Where she shall be put up presents a somewhat awkward problem. The inn is crowded with soldiers. She had tried that. There is no other lodging this side of Philadelphia. Yet, if she is unwelcome, she will find one.

"You can stay here. Hamilton's room is empty," says Washington. "It will cause some conversation. Nothing, I hope, that can't be weathered."

"What a woman's name will bear, a man's should be equal to," answers Mary, and returns smartly to the business in hand.

MARY—Sir, I do bring
    a word from General Howe. He wishes to see you—
    his proposal is general amnesty
    with no surrender on either part—the Congress
    to receive all it's petitioned for, nothing
    reserved, save the king's sovereignty.

WASHINGTON—When you see him
tell him we intend to fight while we can. We've asked
complete independence.

MARY—And still have hopes of it?

WASHINGTON—We still have hopes.

MARY—I can say to you truly
there's no hope for you on the other side. If I
have come unasked, and unwelcome, still it can't be said
I go with the wind. We have news today from Paris
of the French alliance. This is your losing year!
I was willing to lose with you.

WASHINGTON—And your news?
The French will have none of us? Is that your message?

MARY—So the story runs.

WASHINGTON—And so I feared. We must take it
in our stride, if we can. I thank you. No doubt I've been
abrupt beyond all warrant.—Forgive it. I carry
a good many burdens.

MARY—I think no less of you.
I'm sorry for us both.

WASHINGTON—To be quite frank
you lose no lover in me. I'm old and cold
and given over to soldiering. What love
I have is given.

MARY—Sir, would you teach a woman
the art she's skilled in? I read you by your face
and know how deep you've buried what you dreamed
under your soldiering.
A young man has excess of appetite
and eats at every table. When we're older
the body fires less easily. It waits
permission of the mind and memory,
and these come seldom. Young love we've never had
burns underneath and gnaws the upper ground
ready to flame at a breath. For you and me
we must love one another now, or grow old coldly
and make an end to love.

WASHINGTON—It may be so.

MARY—And now, if you'll call the soldier.

WASHINGTON—Yes. (*He goes to the door.*)
Sentry, this lady will occupy Hamilton's room.
(TEAGUE *comes in for the bags.*)

MARY—And good night.
WASHINGTON—Good night.

(MARY *goes out.* TEAGUE, *taking up the bags, gives one speaking look at* WASHINGTON'S *back and departs, shaking his head as*

THE CURTAIN FALLS

ACT II

Early the next morning the men of the First Virginia are beginning to stir themselves in the bunkhouse. There is a dying fire in the fireplace, with as many as can find space stretched or huddled about it. One is busy trying to fill in a chink in the wall. Another is trying to wash his face in a tin of ice water.

Teague is back from guard duty at headquarters with the interesting story of a woman now being housed there. "Howe sent back a bitch in exchange for his dog," he explains characteristically. She may be a lady, but if she is Teague has lost a shilling piece to Alcock.

Now Alcock bustles in happily with the news that he has won the shilling piece. The lady had slept alone. He had put a ladder against her window and peeked. A charming picture—but she slept alone.

"That's your opinion," protests the still doubting Teague.

"Opinion?" snaps Alcock. "Seminole, a man don't live to be as old as I am without being able to tell at a glance whether there's one or two under a log-cabin quilt. More than that, the lady's scarlet breeches were draped over a chair within reach of my hand—but no others to keep company with 'em—and to judge by what little I saw of her she's not the kind an officer and gentleman would get up and leave before time for morning services."

Teague is reluctant to accept his loss on the evidence, but there it is. Nick thinks perhaps he can confirm Alcock's story if he also takes a peek through the window. He is gaily anticipating the adventure as he starts for guard duty.

Spad is back with stories of his trip to Philadelphia. He has seen the enemy and he knows they can be licked. He'd knocked one of them down in his own ballroom. They're a lot of "hermaphroids," declares Spad, scornfully; nothing but musicians.

Spad has also discovered something else. His pockets bulge with ears of corn. The sentries had pushed him off his course and he came out around Mud Island. Enough hay stacked there, says Spad, to "feed through seven lean years and bed down all King Solomon's wives and children." Also about a dozen corn-cribs full of corn and guarded by only three soldiers. One of them's dead now, and two tied up. It is Spad's idea that the boys should go down and take that corn. The English don't even know it's good to eat.

"The current's took all the ice out of the lower end of the island," reports Spad, "and there's three old bumboats frozen in at Print's Landing. We can get 'em out, and we can ferry that corn. I tell you there's nobody watching it!"

Mason, the corporal, thinks he has no right to order a party out, but he'd like to go along. Alcock would like to go, too, but there's that matter of pants.

"You'll freeze off everything you're famous for if you start in that rig," warns Spad.

They are ready now and Teague has his hand on the door latch when Lieutenant Cutting appears. He is surprised at the activity he finds, nor altogether satisfied with Mason's explanation that they were getting ready for roll call. Cutting also notices that Alcock is missing. Let Alcock be found, he barks to Mason, and have the men report for early morning drill.

Mason is not so sure the men will follow him if he issues those orders. They will, answers Cutting, or be answerable to him. There's no two ways to run an army, and he will have absolute obedience or he will put a few of them underground. Let them put down their guns—

In the corner Teague has raised his gun and is aiming it at the center of Cutting's back.

"Don't do anything sudden, Mister Cutting," he calls, "because I'm a nervous man, and liable to spasms in my trigger finger. (CUTTING *turns toward him*.) If you draw that pistol I'll put a slug through your pump, and I never missed yet with this here iron."

They have backed Cutting, spitting threats of revenge at them, back against the wall and tied him there.

"I'll see you all lashed to shreds, you scabby hounds," he shrills.

"You won't see us again, you nor none of you," answers Spad. "We're through with your damn camp and your orders. Catch us if you can!"

The men have recovered their guns and are through the door now. Only the sick Neil and the Lieutenant are left. Cutting

pleads with Neil to untie him. Neil's answer is to get out of his
bunk, take his own gun and follow after the others. . . .

From the near distance Alcock can be heard announcing to the
world in song that he is the son of a unicorn. As he comes
through the door he is busily occupied with trying to bring the
scarlet breeches of Mary Philipse together at the waist. He is
much surprised to find the boys gone and Cutting tied up.

"Well, what do you know about it?" cries Alcock gleefully.
"Somebody left a pair of boots here!"

He has kicked the burlap from his own feet and pulled the
boots from those of Cutting. He puts the boots on and is ready
to go.

"If I follow you for the rest of my life I'll get you for this!"
shrieks Cutting.

"Spew on you!" answers Alcock, turning at the door for a final
Bronx cheer as the curtain falls.

In his headquarters General Washington is sitting alone, writing, or trying to write, with an assortment of goose quills that
irritates him. He is interrupted momentarily by the arrival of
Lafayette, come to report that a proposed meeting with General
Howe at the island is progressing satisfactorily. Howe is approaching by the river, and General Anthony Wayne has blocked
the channel, so there will be plenty of time.

Colonel Tench is in to report the arrival of visitors. "I've
stabled the horses, and have two Congressmen left over," says
Tench. "If you can suggest any disposition for them—"

"We're giving them breakfast here—and you'll stay for it,"
answers Washington; "but I warn you to eat sparingly. Heat the
mess, Rafe, heat it just enough to bring out its qualities."

"Yes, sir."

Congressmen Folsom and Harvie, "fairly young and dressed in
the height of Colonial fashion," are cordially welcomed by the
General, made acquainted with Colonel Tench and invited to a
light collation of army fare. Being starved, the Congressmen are
ready for anything.

WASHINGTON—The order's in
    and we'll be served in a moment. Now, will you mind
    if I make bold meanwhile to open the question,
    and say the last letter which I received from you
    concerning food for the troops, has left me dark
    as to how I'd best proceed? This is how we stand:

The Quartermaster-General was replaced
against my advice, by Congress. Your new man
was most unsatisfactory—gave us, in fact,
almost no coöperation. Food ran low
and I protested, whereon your man resigned
and has not been replaced. It's plain that an army
can't run without a quartermaster, and yet
you've left me so this three months.

FOLSOM—We know it—we know it—
   it's most unfortunate, but there's been some quarrel
   in Congress over appointments. The North and South
   are at odds about the post, each section claiming
   the other's had too much. I've done my best
   to settle the matter.

WASHINGTON—It's not settled yet?

FOLSOM—God, no,
   and I don't know when it will be.

WASHINGTON—The resolution
   passed by Congress, that we live off the country
   until you agree on a quartermaster—if that's
   to be taken seriously, I think you'll find,
   first, there's not that much food without our range,
   and second, if you turn men loose to steal
   and ravage what they need—

HARVIE—Steal? Ravage and steal?

WASHINGTON—What else can you call it? Put in a soldier's
      hands
   the right to take what he wants, and where he will,
   without reprisal, and how long can you hold him
   from rape and wanton plunder? It can't be done.
   Better give up at once than sow the country
   with foot-pads, armed, insolent and bearing pardons
   signed by their officers—

HARVIE—Now, now—

WASHINGTON—You seemed
   reluctant to advise me before breakfast,
   but within three days you'll have a starving mob
   here—one I can't control—one that could eat
   this country clean as locusts. Every moment
   is precious for our plans.

HARVIE—You speak of a mob—
   and truly, it's been rumored here and there
   that discipline is easier to maintain

under the European code of arms
than by our backwoods methods. You've preferred
our native leaders, who fight by hook or crook,
and win or lose by chance. But you might win
more regularly if you could bring yourself
to swallow technical advice. Add to that
that there are methods known for drilling a mob
into an army, and holding it to its task
even under difficulties.

WASHINGTON—The art of war
set down in paradigms, like a Greek declension,
and conned by schoolboys!

HARVIE—Shall we say that Gates was a schoolboy
when he won at Saratoga?

WASHINGTON—Oh, it was Gates
who won at Saratoga? I had supposed
it was the farmers fighting behind trees
American-fashion. The art of war's much simpler
than's set down in the manuals. Get there first
with superior force if possible, and surprise
the enemy if you can. Any fool knows that.
But before you get there with any force at all
you must write a thousand letters to a thousand fools
begging them for the men, the arms, the food,
the chance to get there late!

HARVIE—I beg your pardon!

WASHINGTON—Sir, I beg yours,
but if Congress had wanted me to fail, had set
itself to favor the English, it couldn't have played
its hand more neatly! Will you show me a rule
for holding an army together on air?

Rafe has brought in tins of food and is serving the famished
visitors. One taste is enough for them. Harvie is strangling.
Folsom is wide-eyed with something like horror. Only Tench
makes a show of eating. The beans may be moving, but he is
used to that. Now Folsom has bolted for air and Harvie is curs-
ing Tench for eating and accusing him of intending to poison
them.

General Washington is sorry they have been displeased with
the food, but it is what has been served to several corps of late
for lack of anything better. Later, it may be possible to find
something better for them—after they have settled the matter of

a quartermaster.

Harvie suggests Conway. Washington would resign rather than serve with Conway, for reasons that General Stirling, who has joined the conference, will later make plain.

"Oh, gentlemen, gentlemen, forget that you are Congressmen, forget that I'm an officer!" pleads Washington. "Let's put aside all bickering and rivalries that spring from personal privilege, take our holds together and pull out of this slough! If I've been harsh or defiant or even insulting, I'm desperate, and ready to use the most desperate means to wake you to what's happened, what's happening here! Here is our war come down to a moldy crust— and you in whose hands it lies to help, wrangle over ribbons, men dying meanwhile, our cause dying!"

Conway and Cutting have arrived and are sent for. To Conway General Washington reports how matters stand. He has been mentioned for an appointment. He also has been accused of having indicted a letter to General Gates congratulating that soldier on his success and intimating that it will not be long before he (Gates) will be taking Washington's place.

Conway remembers no such letter. When faced by Stirling he makes light of what he may have said to that officer when in liquor. Neither does he recognize the letter that Washington hands him to identify. Certainly the writing is not his.

The letter, answers Stirling, is a copy of one taken from the saddlebags of Conway's courier and copied. The original had gone on to its destination. Again Conway would deny the charge, but is forced by evidence finally to confess. This he does defiantly, insisting it is not treasonous to hold that one man might be better than another as a leader of an army.

Washington has still further evidence. In an exchange of letters such as reasonably pass from line to line certain notes have contained a cipher—ciphers addressed to Lieutenant Cutting for transmission to General Conway and through him to General Gates. These letters have contained nothing less than "the terms that would be acceptable to General Howe and the English crown if the Continental army were willing to surrender."

"Sir, on my word, I know nothing of this," protests Cutting.

"And I, sir, on my word, say that you do, and am willing to bring it to trial," replies Washington, turning to the commissioners. "You will understand, I think, why I objected to General Conway's promotion."

Folsom and Harvie, a bit flustered, do understand, but as for the trial, they think it would be unwise to risk a scandal.

"For the good of the service, at least, we must keep it quiet," says Harvie.

"For the good of the service and in all common justice, the officers' court must pass on the evidence in hand," answers Washington, firmly.

"But reflect, sir, there are names involved—"

WASHINGTON—Then they'll be damned as black
   as the evidence calls for! What's this sudden concern
   of yours for names! The names of these two here
   mean nothing to me but two who come sucking around
   for favors when they see me, like a couple of squid,
   and squirt their ink at my back!
CONWAY—I give fair warning
   if I'm court-martialed I have three words to speak that'll
      hush it up!
WASHINGTON—Speak them now!
HARVIE—Believe me, sir,
   there's more consequence in what you plan than's plain on
      the surface—
WASHINGTON—What consequence—?
HARVIE—I say no more—
WASHINGTON—Then we proceed—
CONWAY—Will you speak up for me
   or must I speak up for myself?
      (*The Commissioners are silent.*)
   Why, these two knew
   as well as I of the correspondence with Howe,
   and most of the Congress knew it! If I'm a traitor
   they're traitors with me! We were commissioned by Con-
      gress
   to angle for Howe's terms! Well, look at me
   if you like.—Does it surprise you? When a war's lost
   the usual thing's to feel around for bargains
   and that's what's being done!
HARVIE—What he says is true.
   It has not yet been brought to a vote in Congress—
   nor did we wish it published, but this is true.
   There are those among us who know that a war is worth
   what it brings on the exchange, no more. And when
   your stock is going down, it's best to sell
   before it goes to nothing.
STIRLING—What's that? What's that?

HARVIE—Why, I'll say it again. A war, my friend,
   is a tactical expedient to gain
   certain political ends. Those ends being proved
   impossible, the war's without excuse,
   and should be pushed no further than need be
   to gain an advantageous peace.
STIRLING—You say it,
   and I must believe you've said it, but, death of God,
   is this like any other war?
HARVIE—The same,
   or much the same.
WASHINGTON—Sir, I should have supposed
   you'd notify me, before negotiations
   were begun with the enemy.
HARVIE—There was thought of it,
   but you and your army have so much of the hot-head
   in your composition, it was believed unwise
   to open the subject. Besides, there was always doubt
   what reply we'd get from the English, and it seemed best
   not to call off our dogs till we were sure
   we had no need for them.
WASHINGTON—Your dogs, you say!
HARVIE—Nay, that's a figure.
WASHINGTON—Not one I'm inclined to relish!

Negotiations had begun, Harvie admits, after Washington had
lost at Brandywine. When Gates won at Saratoga it strengthened
the opposition. Nor are they moved by Washington's protest
that, with any support at all behind the lines, the Continentals
might have won. A moment later they have admitted that Gates
himself is in their counsels and convinced it were better to give
in while there's still trade on the seas. It is Harvie who states
the case for those who believe "that it's no treason for a government to consider a peace—even in wartime!"

HARVIE—This war began to protect our trade. The merchants
   were being run out of business by subsidies
   to English boats! It cut so deep in Boston
   there was no more profit in smuggling—and all our trade
   was smuggling, anyway! They dumped the tea
   in Boston harbor, and raised a hue and cry
   of "Freedom!" "Down with the tyrant!" Christ, what they

      wanted
    was profits, not freedom. But then the inland boys
    took up the yell, and ran together in mobs,
    and old Sam Adams made speeches, and cock-a-hoop,
    hell-bent, pell-mell—it spread till we couldn't stop,
    spread to Virginia, and a pack of oyster-faced
    backwoodsmen met and signed a declaration,
    and then we were in trouble! Where's our trade now?
    Nobody makes money—not even the money-lenders—
    nobody but the god-damn farmers selling pork
    to the British commissary! It's time to stop it!
    We've got to settle down and live, that's all,
    and why not under King George? If your fire-eaters
    can't make a living in time of peace, why, hell,
    the rest can't make one now!
WASHINGTON—This sentiment
    prevails in Congress?
HARVIE—It does, or it will shortly.
STIRLING—Then fig your Congress!
WASHINGTON—And is this the reason supplies have been with-
      held
    and gone astray—and all our calculations
    upset—to discourage us—and call off your dogs,
    as you put it so tersely?
HARVIE—I should say there's been little stomach
    for expenditures that looked to a longer war
    when peace was in the air.
WASHINGTON—I understand you.
    Nobody cared to win.
HARVIE—What was there to win? We lose more day by day
    than we'll ever gain back!
WASHINGTON—Perhaps we've been unaccustomed
    to thinking in terms of money of some things
    men give their lives for. You may find this difficult
    to comprehend, you who have thought beyond us
    and reckon our lives in dollars.
FOLSOM—But that's not so.
    Harvie forgets himself, and says too much
    and outruns all discretion.
WASHINGTON—I think we know
    how to estimate you both. I shall hope no more
    for any help from you. Make your appointments.

Make any arrangements you like. You need not consult
with me. Make your plans, and be easy.

There will be no court-martial for Conway and Cutting, Washington agrees. ". . . the desire to degrade me and put Gates in
charge, so that he might surrender, was patriotic, and quite in
the fashion."

So far as the ending of the war is concerned, he will attend to
that also, and quickly. Now the Congressmen are visibly perturbed, but Washington has no thought of listening to the protests. All further negotiations with the British he will conduct,
in his own fashion and on his own terms. Sir William will hear
from him, but behind their backs this time.

"I warn you, sir—take no steps without instruction!" pipes up
Harvie. "Your service here is under commission from the Continental Congress— Remember it!"

"You'll take steps without instruction and take them now!"
bristles Washington, grabbing the surprised Harvie by the collar
and the seat of his trousers and turkey-walking him out of the
door. From outside a crash is heard, and then a second crash as
Folsom follows. Washington is dusting his hands as he returns
to the room.

Tench is much pleased with this "good beginning," and Stirling
still fighting mad. They are ready to go forward with the rendezvous at the island, but before they go Stirling must have another fling at governments—

STIRLING—Do you know what I think of governments, by and
    large,
  I mean in general? They're run by pimps
  who get kicked out of hothouses for picking
  the customers' pockets. This one we've got—we made it,
  set it up, picked the best men we could find
  and put them in—and their brains began to rot
  before the year was out. It rots a man's brains
  to be in power, and he turns pimp, and picks pockets;
  the scavengers! At least, when you have a king
  you can chop his head off. I'll be on my way.
  I must be there before sundown.

They have gone now and Washington sits moodily at the table.
From the stairway Mary Philipse appears. She is "cloaked, bon-

neted, and ready for the road," and stands a moment motionless,
looking at Washington. Then she speaks, softly—

MARY—I'm sorry if I disturb you. I'd have gone
   without a word, only I must make my peace
   and ask you to forgive the fool I was,
   for coming here at all.
      (WASHINGTON *does not move.*)
   The camp I came from
   is not like this. I drew my notion of warfare
   from the quadrilling officers that dance
   attendance on Mistress Loring, and the bevy
   of officers' darlings with her. How wrong I was
   I've learned through a night of thinking on my ways
   and yours. You believe in yourself and what you do
   to the verge of martyrdom, and all your men
   have cased themselves in some armor of the spirit
   to have and hold what's their own. I'm out of place here
   with my thwarted love and beribboned misery
   where death walks sentry on your night, too near
   and real for cavalier fancies. I honor you
   and the men you lead, let me say this in saying
   farewell, more than I'd thought possible.
WASHINGTON—Eh, but it seems
   that you were right.
MARY—Not I.
WASHINGTON—I've been a gull.
   They've led me by a ring, like a circus bear
   to fright the children for them. Behind my back
   they make their shabby deals, shilling for shilling,
   men's lives for copper pennies, marked down, sold off
   to die for groats and farthings. The devil drench them,
   these talking swine! We're in their way, we've fought on
   longer than they intended, and they lose money—
   money, by God, hard money! They starve us out
   to make us stop—two or three hundred tons
   of human beeves, pushed out into the dark
   to teach us they lose money, by God, hard money,
   and can't afford it.—This is our bright new day,
   this is our world well lost! The spirit of the eagle
   unconquerable, unconquered! So many crows
   over a stinking sheep in a bogged cow-yard
   would show more nobility!
MARY—But I'm sure you're wrong—

disheartened over some check—
WASHINGTON—You'll return to Howe;
    tell him he can buy our Congress for tuppence
    if he lays out his money shrewdly. Less; let him save
    his cash, and deal out four or five dozen clerkships
    in so many pawnshops, found; they'll jump at that—
    they were born with the souls of under-secretaries,
    and want no more.
MARY—I shall tell him no such thing,
    but that you are brave men, honest, and dangerous.
    Yes, more than he thinks.
WASHINGTON—The revolution's sold out!
    Congress bargains behind my back, asks terms!
    Bargains with Howe!—What's left of the revolution
    you see here, in these windy shacks and starved men
    and the broken boots I wear! What hopes we had
    of the French—you dashed them for me!
MARY—But—are you sorry?
WASHINGTON—No. I shall have my life again, and begin
    to fence my land where I left it. I've been the fool!
    It began to get into my blood, this crusading zeal
    pumped up by the counter-jumpers to fill their tills
    and edge out competition! I've lived hard,
    slept hard, drunk water, made my meals on biscuit,
    for some great end!—They've shown me what that's worth!
    Six feet of earth, if there's that much left undug.
    The corpses crowd in close in this neighborhood—
    some get less than that.
MARY—Then this is the end of the war?
WASHINGTON—This is the end.

Washington will be free again and live again, he promises. But
before the quarrel goes out of his hands he will make his own
bargain with Howe!—Let Mary tell Sir William a meeting waits
only on his pleasure; it is for him to name the place and hour in
fairly neutral territory.

MARY—Sir, I thank you
    for your kindly entertainment at a time
    when you felt less reminiscent than the lady
    who knocked upon your door.—
    Of all men I have known I least like to think
    of you defeated. Defeat seems not for you—
    even in a hopeless quarrel. It's not you that lose,

but the speech-making mongrels over you. Even now
you've a king in yourself, unbeaten, one who has within
what men will follow or a woman serve.

WASHINGTON—Aye, once
I was alive, before so many men
had died around me. The gray years weigh like a mask
and set you hard.

MARY—I know.

WASHINGTON—And this victory
called love, adds well to victory, but defeat's
a dull and lonely thing. I think I've seen you
only as a brightness lost, something I wished for
in a happier year, gone now—might wish for again
if there are years to follow—which I doubt—

MARY—There will be better years—

WASHINGTON—I've given myself
to a footless insurrection, drained out my blood
on a mock heroic altar, made a monk
of what might have been a man. And I'll get for that
what Jack Cade got. Three lines in history,
touching a minor figure in a brief uprising
that died down early in some year of our Lord,
A.D., God quit the beggar. Let us hope
Jack Cade reached out his hand and took what sweets
went by with the years, before they snared him in
and quartered him. Wait for me here. God knows
the years go fast. If I let you leave me now
I'll not see you again.

MARY—And the word to Howe?

WASHINGTON—Why, later
will do as well as now.

MARY—No, I must take it—
or you'll change your mind. But we shall meet again—
If you doubt it—was there ever another meeting
less likely than this we've had?

WASHINGTON—No. Then I'll see you?

MARY—I shall manage.
You must leave these things with the woman.
Let's get the soldiering over, and do it quickly.
After that—trust me.

Tench arrives to announce all in readiness for the ride. It dis-
tresses him a little to think of Mary leaving them broken-hearted,

and he so good at mending broken hearts, but duty calls.

"I betray my cause—but—don't give up yet—hold on while you can—" calls Mary, as they start away.

"Yes? Dear lady, this nation's spending its last heart's blood for a package of liberty," answers Washington. "We opened the package today and it was empty. We ride our last expedition. And so—good-by."

"Good-by!" echoes Mary.

THE CURTAIN FALLS

ACT III

A cold morning light reveals the interior of an abandoned barn on Hay Island. There is a floor covering of hay, ancient and matted, and hay hangs from the rafters. Double doors, one of them hanging from a single hinge, let into the building and a smaller door into the stable.

Alcock, a thigh bandaged, is lying on a truss of hay and Marty, a bandage around his head and over one eye, is playing a jews-harp. Alcock would sing something to the accompaniment of Marty's playing, something about his first love. "Honey o' dark, honey o' rue, where went the kisses I gave to you?" is the refrain. Alcock is still cheerful, despite his wounds. Even about his scarlet pants, which are now ripped and bedraggled.

"This is the kind of war that as soon as you get a pair of britches they shoot 'em out from under you," he sighs.

There is gunfire down the island. Big gunfire, indicating the British are using their heavier field pieces. This is followed by musket fire. A moment later there is the sound of voices outside. Marty and Alcock reach for their guns

The talkers are Tench and Lafayette, looking for a barn that may have been selected for the rendezvous with Howe. As they step into the light, Alcock and Marty lower their guns, and Alcock makes shift to explain their seeming "desertion."

"We found Howe had enough ear corn on this island to make a poultice for the state of Pennsylvania. So we commandeered four old monitors below the hook and ferried over a few loads of it in the night. Then we had a brush with some scouts, and Marty and me got clipped. They laid us in here and went back to their navigating."

Tench and Lafayette have gone to see what the firing signifies when André and a brigadier of Howe's staff arrive. They, too, conclude this must be the barn assigned for the meeting, seeing it is the only one in sight. Alcock and Marty, now joined by Minto, are gentle with the Britishers, suspecting their errand. Minto would have been belligerent, but Alcock soon quiets him.

"These are headquarters birds, you stingaree," Alcock explains, when the Britishers have left; "poll-parrots from headquarters. Their business is talking, not fighting. There's a truce on the island, and they're here to parley-voo. If you weren't a thousand years old and afflicted with all the animal diseases from stringhalt to rinderpest I'd get up and tan your hide off for disregard of an order!"

Now Spad and Oscar have backed in through the stable. They have been trying to head off a squad of British so they can get Neil in the barn. Neil's got a splinter through his chest and is pretty bad. Nick and Teague are next to arrive.

"It seems there's a truce at the moment, and nobody's supposed to shoot anybody," Alcock explains to Teague. "If you see any Hessians they're out of season. There was a couple of English brigadiers here a minute ago. They went back after more."

There is activity down by the river. The men are prepared to defend the barn, and do pick off a few of the enemy who try to creep up. It occurs to Spad, too, that if Tench and Lafayette went down that way somebody better be going along to help them. He takes Nick and they start out. There is a spattering of British bullets against the barn.

Now Andrew has carried Neil in and laid him on a bundle of hay in the corner. Tench, with his musket through a crack, suddenly fires. There may be a truce, as Alcock insists, but the British evidently don't know it. They are learning about it, slowly, however. They have gone back to their boats now and are disappearing.

A moment later General Washington and General Stirling arrive. There is, General Washington admits, something both remarkably strange and remarkably familiar about the place. It seems to him that he recognizes many of the faces. He knows them now, with Alcock's help, as those Virginians he had so feelingly lectured on the evils of desertion. As a result of which advice they had taken the first opportunity to pinion their officer and start out on their own—

"I have no doubt the circumstances might be termed extenuating," admits Washington. "No charges will be brought against you, and you may consider yourselves free of all further obligations to the Continental army. However, your presence is damnably inconvenient. I have appointed to meet here with a British officer for a discussion that will hardly concern you. It would mortify me somewhat to usher him into an apartment overrun by renegade Continentals—"

"Cutting's a renegade, if you ask me," answers Alcock.

It is agreed the men may be moved into the adjoining granary and consider themselves under arrest until they are mustered out. Soon Washington is joined by Lafayette, whom Spad has brought through a line of skirmish fire, which was also against the truce. It seems now that Neil will have to be left in the corner. It would mean his death to move him.

A moment later the British have arrived, André and the brigadier, Sir William Howe and Mary Philipse in an officer's cloak, and two or three officers. It is Mary who makes the introductions.

Washington and Howe are pleased to meet, and pleased to assume a friendship that may not in reality exist. At least their quarrel is not personal. It is also agreed that they shall permit their officers to hear whatever may pass between them.

WASHINGTON—First, let it be understood
  that I bind myself to nothing by this meeting,
  nor have I altered in my loyalty
  to the cause I captain. But you have sent me word
  that if a peace were arrived at now, the king
  would expunge all statutes over which we differed,
  omit taxes of which we complained, and, in simple, grant us
  all objects for which we fought originally,
  except our independence.
HOWE—You may add also
  complete erasure of all charges made
  against you as rebels, so that you're received
  freely and brotherly again among us
  without writ or reprisal.
WASHINGTON—This order would apply
  to all, without exception?
HOWE—Without exception.
  For I'm free to tell you, since it's kept no secret,
  we're sick and sore about this war in England,
  would to God it had never started, and want you back
  on your own terms.
WASHINGTON—Well, frankly, my own terms
  would mean that we never went back at all, for going

would mean we accept the king, but I'm not alone
in these decisions; we have a government,
and plenty in that government are sore
and sick as in your own.   I've lately learned
that some backhanded gesture was made toward you
by members of Congress, and I've come in some pique to say
that if any settlement with the king goes forward
it will first go through my hands.

HOWE—I would I might
speak freely, as you have, but I confess I'm bound
to secrecy in that matter.

WASHINGTON—You may well ask
why I have not gone to Congress, and said to them
what I say to you.   I would answer, I've said my say
to Congress in so many different ways
and wasted so much language, that the thought
of speaking to them gives me gumboils.   I
have come to you directly as a soldier
to warn you there will be no peace, and no peace
can be made effective without me.

HOWE—How well I knew that
you can judge from the fact that I asked you for this meeting,
not content to deal elsewhere, I have my spies out.
There was a time when Congress had control
of your rebellion.   Not now.   The city boys
are weary of it, but all your fighting strength
is ranked with farmers, and while they follow you
and you lead them, there's a war.   We can begin
with that as a basis.   Your word is good with your army
and good with me.

WASHINGTON—Well, there'll be a storm, but if
it's peace the Congress wants, peace it shall have,
only it will be of my making.   It's not too easy
to swallow a king, after your gorge has risen
against him so long—

STIRLING—Now, God forbid this, General,
must we take back King George?

WASHINGTON—God damn you, Stirling!
Do you think it's easy for me?

Before more can be said the boy Neil is heard to raise his voice
in delirium.   He is facing the enemy again, and imagining them
as coming with pikes and arms.   He would call to Tavis that he

is dying. Mary Philipse goes to Neil and holds his hand and hears him say, thinking she is Tavis, that she must let their child be called by his name. She is still comforting the boy as the dark, dark morning gathers him in. Then she covers his face and moves back to the group.

Now there is a further break in the proceedings. Colonel Tench comes uncertainly through the door and goes direct to Washington to report, first the stowing of His Majesty's corn in Clopton's Landing, and second, the lost and wounded in action, among the dead Nick Teague and Lucifer Tench—

"I'm dead enough. My boots are full of blood," he says, when Washington would question the "tasteless joking" of his report.

> ". . . I've had my day
> and it's time for another dog. It's exit, midnight,
> and alas and alack for Lucifer. Sir, I've loved you,
> but if you set your seal to an English compact
> my curse on you.—These dying men have visions
> and that's the gist of mine. Bring on your burlap,
> and the sailor's needle, and sew me in to sleep;
> I'm tired and done."

Washington, with a hurt cry, has followed Tench into the granary. For the time negotiations are halted. General Howe, at Stirling's suggestion, thinks it were better that he and his officers withdraw for the moment from the scenes of private grief.

Mary Philipse stays on. She has a further word for Washington when he reënters. It is the report that the French Alliance has been signed with the colonies. It had been wished to keep the news from him, but it is true. The news fires the imagination of Lafayette—

> "Sir, I beg you, before
> you pledge yourself to Howe, you gather your troops
> and make one final effort—"

WASHINGTON—Gather my troops!
> Have they strength to come together! Gabriel's trumpet
> might rally that vale of bones! Bring me these specters
> with the wind-fed entrails and mouths that open and speak
>   not
> gaping their misery! Summon forth brigades
> and companies from the lazarettes they lie in,

cry, "Lazarus, arise! On to the field!"
This is no mockery. The cerements
are much too tough for miracle. Look about you
at these remnants of dying and deserted men!
What could I offer them to follow me?
What could I say to them? Call them in to me!
Come in! Come in and hear me—you were some of the best,
you skulkers who run the woods! Come in! I've told you
no charge will be brought against you. I'll tell you why
I've come here to surrender. The British staff
waits outside for my word. And the reason I quit
is because I've neither a Congress nor an army.
Congress is through with the war—and the army's through
and running out. Look for them in the woods—
you'll find them there. They root for acorns and pignuts
to fill their bellies—and they had good reason to go
for Congress wanted to quit and sent no food
and men must eat or die. There was a time
when you had shoes and powder for your guns
and fought to rule yourselves. There was hope in the air
and possible victory. If you starved and died
you died for a purpose. That's gone now. If you die
you die for nothing. We've set our feet down now
on a bedrock of despair, and I promise those
who'll follow me further, no chance of victory,
for, by my God, I see none, no glory or gain,
or laurels returning home, but wounds and death—
cold and disease and hunger, winters to come
such as this you have, with our bloody trail in the snow
and no end to it till you shovel each other in
with those at Valley Forge! Close in and take
your place in my ranks if you like it. If you don't,
and none will blame you, go your road as you have
and find yourselves food, and live!

SPAD—You'll take us back?

WASHINGTON—Take you back!

SPAD—I'll go with you!

ALCOCK—Yes, by God!

THE MEN—Come on, you fellows, you heard what he said!
     And so will I!
     We'll go with you!
     Do you mean you'll take us?
     Put me in!

Anywhere you say to go!
That goes for all of us!
ALCOCK—We thought it was over!
We thought it was falling to pieces, but if you meant
what you said about being plowed under, before we stop,
hell, I'm for being plowed under!

The others crowd forward. They are almost gay now, and determined. They tell of the corn they have ferried across the river
—three thousand bushels of it. That's Washington's too, if he'll
take it. Their General looks upon them with a new light in his
eyes—

> "The forge was cold
> that smelted these men into steel—but steel
> they are. I know them now. And now I change
> my answer! Let one ragged thousand of them
> pledge them to this with me, and we'll see it through."

Something like a faint cheer stirs the men. And now Sir William is called again and the conference is brought to an end—

WASHINGTON—Sir William, I have forgotten
what was last said; something of our accepting
kings or princes. It hardly matters now,
for it's better blank. Gentlemen, I am servant
to these men in the rags of homespun. They've heard from
    me
this proposition of the king's, and they
refuse it flatly. This war, to your brief misfortune,
is not mine to end, but theirs. I have my orders
and I'm in your debt for a very fruitless errand
over wild water.
HOWE—Your choice of councilors,
sir, is your own, of course, but may I remind you
that the people of a country are never open
to reason in such matters? They're willing to fight
for the virgin birth, or the freedom of the seas,
or the tomb of Christ, when nobody knows where it is,
or your brotherhood of man—oh, any drivel
that's clean impossible. But tell them once
what a war's really for, perhaps, trade advantage,
or the rights of bankers, and they drop their war like a snake.
This war's for trade advantage.

ALCOCK—Oh, no, it's not!
  It's because we don't like kings, and won't have a king,
    and never will!
WASHINGTON—And there we end.
HOWE—You'll draw out this tragedy further?
WASHINGTON—As far as we must.
HOWE—But you've lost, lost now; your government's opposed,
  your men in draglets—the dregs of what's swept up to eat—
WASHINGTON—We're all too well aware of that.
  And we have lost; we know it; by all the rules of the game
  we're beaten, and should surrender. If this war
  were for trade advantage, it would end tonight.
  It was made over subsidies, or some such matter,
  but it's been taken over. Let the merchants submit
  if that's any good to you, then come out and find
  my hunters and backwoodsmen, and beat us down
  into the land we fight for. When you've done that—
  the king may call us subject. For myself, I'd have died
  within if I'd surrendered. The spirit of earth
  moves over earth like flame and finds fresh home
  when the old's burned out. It stands over this my country
  in this dark year, and stands like a pillar of fire
  to show us an uncouth clan, unread, harsh-spoken,
  but followers of dream, a dream that men
  shall bear no burdens save of their own choosing,
  shall walk upright, masterless, doff a hat to none,
  and choose their gods! It's destined to win, this dream,
  weak though we are. Even if we should fail,
  it's destined to win! If we could hold on till spring
  even now the French would be on our side, and we'd beat you.
  Have you heard that news?
HOWE—I was not aware it had reached you.
  Your work, lady?
MARY—Yes, mine.
HOWE—Why, trust a woman
  and tell the world. Sir, I've been more your friend
  than you know in this matter. This is my last winter
  with the British army here. They'll send someone else
  to fight you, but not me. I'm no Quixote,
  to battle with dreams and windmills. But it's not over,
  make up your minds to that. They'll press you harder
  when I'm gone home.
WASHINGTON—Sir, we engage to stand it.

HOWE—No doubt you will. This spikes our guns for us.
There was a storm promised before we came
and I'd like to beat it back. Come, we must go.
The terms I've offered you will not be offered
by my successor.
WASHINGTON—We should hardly expect it.
HOWE—No,
for I've been too much your friend. Heigh-ho, I'll get
a drubbing when I face England. Good-by!
WASHINGTON—We wish you good morning,
and a fair voyage, Sir William.
    (HOWE *goes out. The officers follow.*)
We owe you thanks too, Madame.
MARY—I hope so.
WASHINGTON—And it will be remembered.
MARY—Why, then, I'm glad.
I know my own destiny, little though I may like it,
and it's not high as yours. There are some men
who lift the age they inhabit—till all men walk
on higher ground in that lifetime. God keep you all
and bring you victory.
    (*She goes out.*)
WASHINGTON—And so we're left
with some years of revolution on our hands.
ALCOCK—Good God,
you shouldn't have put it up to us. I'm standing
in a man's clothes for the first time in a year.
I'd never say die.
STIRLING—We have food for three days.
WASHINGTON—And then
for three more if we can find it—and three more—
if we can find it. And now I think we will!
    (*He goes toward* NEIL.)
Was the brother lost?
STIRLING—Yes, Mason.
WASHINGTON—Mason and Nick and Neil—and Tench. They
    paid
for our three days. You know best who will pay
for days to come. We must bury them here. They died here
and earned their ground.
This liberty will look easy by and by
when nobody dies to get it.
    (*They go toward* NEIL *to take him up.*)

Shall we fire a volley
over our dead?
TEAGUE—No, sir. We'll need our powder,
and dead men don't hear volleys.
WASHINGTON—So be it, then.

THE CURTAIN FALLS

THE PETRIFIED FOREST
A Drama in Two Acts

By Robert Sherwood

- MR. LESLIE HOWARD had gone definitely cinema after his success in Philip Barry's "Animal Kingdom," which followed his previous success in John Balderston's "Berkeley Square." It is impossible at this stage of his career to detach Mr. Howard successfully from any drama in which he appears, on screen or stage. He is one of the fortunate persons of the drama who lend the theatre glamor merely by being a part of it.

For two years he devoted himself to the making of pictures. When he came back to the living theatre it was as the hero of Robert Sherwood's "The Petrified Forest," a melodrama that, for all its superior philosophical content, could easily prove to be something less than satisfying entertainment were it uninterestingly peopled or less than competently played

With Mr. Howard's aid "The Petrified Forest," shown at the Broadhurst Theatre, January 7, after preliminary engagements in Hartford, Conn., and Boston, Mass., sprang immediately into favor as a perfect vehicle for the popular star. When he suffered a minor indisposition there was no thought of attempting the substitution of another actor. The theatre was closed until the star recovered. The engagement continued successfully through the remainder of the season.

At the opening of "The Petrified Forest" it is late afternoon of a Fall day in 1934. The Black Mesa Filling Station and Bar-B-Q lunchroom, one of the lonelier outposts of the eastern Arizona desert, gives its patrons a suggestion of "strenuous if not hearty welcome."

Through double doors at the back of the lunchroom and a large window at the side, a glimpse is caught of red gasoline pumps just the other side of a wide covered porch, and beyond them the sweep of the desert toward distant and purple hills.

There is a lunch counter at the back of the room, and three tables in front of it. The counter is fitted out with the usual coffee urn and cash register. The wall is decorated with familiar whiskey, gas, oil, railroad and beer posters, and a scattering of

NRA, Red Cross and American Legion posters.

At one of the three tables two telegraph linemen are eating hamburger sandwiches and drinking coffee such time as they are not engaged in fairly excited conversation. Across the room from them Gramp Maple, in his late sixties, is sitting by the side of a stove and pretending to read the Denver *Post* while he cocks an eager ear in the direction of the linemen's conversation. Gramp's eyes "are watery and his vision blurred. His skin is like leather that has been dried by a lifetime under the desert sun and worn thin by constant rough usage."

Between Gramp and the linemen is Boze Hertzingler, "a stalwart, bronzed young man who wears dirty white canvas pants and a filthy football jersey on the back of which is a patch with the number 42." He, too, is getting a comfortable load of the linesmen's debate.

This debate appears to be concerned primarily with communism and an approaching revolution. The first lineman is excitedly convinced that both are coming and that both will be welcome, whatever a lot of old fluffs back East may think about it. He is strong for the Russian experiment and all it signifies.

The second lineman, being fatter and more content, indicates an inquiring but not particularly keen interest. Boze, however, would take a hand and put the communistic lineman in his place. Boze has read a lot about that Russian thing in high school and would probably tell what he had read if he were not called away at the moment by Jason Maple, who has just appeared back of the counter and is ready to issue orders like a boss. Jason "is a dull, defeated man of about forty, solemn, bespectacled, paunchy," and wears an American Legion button in his lapel.

Gramp's curiosity stands the strain until he hears the argumentative lineman say something about the Russians' pioneering. He must know more about that.

"I said they're pioneering," repeats the lineman, in answer to a query from Gramp. "They're opening up new territory—and for the benefit of all, not so's a few land grabbers can step in and take the profits after somebody else has done the real work. . . . Those engineers in Russia are building something *new*! (*Turning to his companion.*) That's where they've got it on us. We ain't building—we're repairing. Just like you and me. What do we do—day after day? We climb up poles, and fix the wires, so that some broker in New York can telegraph in a split second to some guy in Los Angeles to tell him he's ruined."

"Well, my friend—when you talk about pioneering—you're talking about something I can tell *you* a few things about," answers Gramp, raising himself with some little effort out of the rocking chair and moving across the room to be nearer the center of discussion.

Jason would stop Gramp. He doesn't approve of any member of the family getting into discussions with guests. But Gramp is not to be stopped. He is there to tell those boys that he came down into the desert from Virginia City fifty-six years ago, and you had to be tough to cross that country in those days. Gramp was a wire-stringer, too. And who was Governor of that territory in those days? General Lew Wallace, that's who. Wallace wrote "Ben Hur" right there in the palace at Santa Fe. Yes, sir. Gramp knew some tough fellows in those days, too. Billy the Kid, for one. Fact, Billy the Kid had once taken a couple of shots at Gramp and missed.

"I'm practically the only man he ever missed," Gramp admits, modestly; "but he was only doing it in fun, so it couldn't hardly count."

"Gabby" Maple has appeared from the kitchen. "She is young and pretty with a certain amount of style about her. Her principal distinguishing feature is an odd look of resentment in her large, dark eyes. She carries a thin book, her forefinger marking the place."

The linemen have finished their hamburgers and are about to go, but Gramp has one more reminiscence he would like to get over. It is about the first message that was ever sent over the wires in the old days.

"General Wallace dictated it, and we sent it all the way through to Washington to President Hayes," reports Gramp. "And do you want to know what it said? It said, 'God save the Republic!' That's what General Wallace told us to say—and he was a great author."

"You better send that same message through again, Pop—because the old Republic's badly in need of assistance," suggests the first lineman, making his way to the counter to pay his check.

Now Jason would take a hand in the discussion. He would like to warn this high-sounding young man that he had better watch out how he talks about the United States of America.

"What do you mean?" the lineman wants to know.

"I mean simply this," Jason is quick to answer. "Belittling our system of government, preaching revolution and destruction,

and red propaganda—well, it isn't a very healthy occupation.
That's all."

GRAMP—I thought you said not to argue with the guests.

JASON—I'm only telling you, brother—for the sake of your own good.

FIRST LINEMAN—So it's unhealthy, eh! How do you think this government was started if it wasn't by revolution?

SECOND LINEMAN—Come on, Nick. We got to get going.

FIRST LINEMAN—Wait till he answers my question.

JASON—The American Revolution was fought to establish law and order. But the object of your dirty red propaganda is to destroy it. . . .

FIRST LINEMAN—And how much law and order have we got? Did you read about that massacre yesterday in Oklahoma City? What kind of law and order is that?

SECOND LINEMAN—Listen, Nick, I got a dame waiting up for me in Gallup and I . . .

JASON—If some of you Bolsheviks would quit preaching disrespect for law, it wouldn't be possible for criminals to . . .

FIRST LINEMAN—Yeah? Do you want to know something? They don't have crime in Russia. And why? Because they've abolished the cause of crime. They've abolished greed! And I'll tell you something else . . .

SECOND LINEMAN—I'm going. (*He starts out.*)

JASON—You got your eats and there's your change. Now kindly get out.

FIRST LINEMAN (*pocketing the change*)—O.K., Mr. Tin-horn Patriot. I only hope I'm around here when it happens. I want to see you when you've joined the mob and started waving the red flag.

Jason is pretty mad. He thinks he should have taken the lineman's name and reported him. Gramp's suggestion that he should mind his own business does not help. Jason hasn't any business worth minding. Certainly not this "miserable little service station on the edge of nowheres." Jason would like to be out getting some place in the world. What chance has he ever had? The war? He joined the army to drive a truck, which was the thing he could do best, and then he was blamed for not coming back with a lot of medals and German scalps hanging to his belt. What Jason wants Gramp to do is to sell the service station—he has already been offered seven thousand dollars for it—and buy

a piece of an auto camp on Redondo Boulevard, near Los Angeles.
"I'd put in a Bar-B-Q service and in a couple of years we'd
have something," declares Jason.

"Los Angeles! My God!" Gramp's reaction is definite. "You
want to go to Los Angeles and Gabby wants to go to Europe.
Ain't they nobody around here that's satisfied to stay put?"

"How about yourself? Were you ever satisfied to stay put,
until you got so damned old you didn't have enough energy to
move?"

"Listen to me, son. In my day, we had places to go—new
places. But, my God—Los Angeles . . ."

Gabby is back from the kitchen to report that the cook's scared.
The Mexicans are saying that the bandit Mantee is headed that
way. It is Jason's opinion Mantee is already over the Mexican
border, and Gramp's idea that the killer is too slick for the Texas
Rangers or anybody else. "He's got Injun blood. He'll fool
'em!" says Gramp.

Jason must go and dress, now. Important Legion meeting.
He thinks perhaps he will report that Bolshevik lineman. Anyway, let Gabby keep an eye on the counter.

"What did that telegraph man say that got Dad in such a
stew?" Gabby asks Gramp.

"I don't know what he said—something about Russia and
pioneering," Gramp explains. "But there's a lot in it, whatever
it was. The trouble with this country is, it's got settled. It's
camped down in the bed of a dried-up river, and whenever anybody says, 'Let's get the hell out of here,' all the rest start to
holler, 'If we move a step the Injuns'll get us.' Well—say—if
we'd been that way in my time, I'd like to know how this country'd ever have got rich enough to be able to support the American Legion."

Two hoots of an auto horn outside have reminded Gramp that
the mail's in, and he has gone to fetch it. Gabby has poured
herself a cup of coffee and resumed reading her book. Boze,
coming in from the gas pumps and seeing Gabby alone, softly
closes the doors and would do a bit of love-making if Gabby were
in an approachable mood. Gabby is moderately curious as to
Boze's reactions, but not at all stirred by his approach. Nor
greatly impressed at his insistence that if she would let him he
could teach her more about love than she'll ever get out of books
of poetry. Even pash poetry.

Boze is considerable boy, and nobody knows it better than
Boze. There's the gold football he wears at the end of his father's

watch chain around his neck. He got that for intercepting a pass and running sixty-eight yards for a touchdown when he was playing for Nevada Tech. If he had been with Princeton, or Minnesota, or any of the big clubs, Boze has an idea he would have made the All-American. He's got press clippings showing the sports writers thought so, too. Boze could have had better jobs than the one he's got if he hadn't been so restless. He's always chasing a rainbow. That's Boze. And he'll catch it yet.

"You'd better look someplace else," Gabby advises him. "There aren't any rainbows around Black Mesa."

"I wouldn't bet on that," says Boze. "You know, Gabby—you're a queer kid. Sometimes you seem too young to know anything. And then—sometimes—you seem like God's grandmother. And reading that pash poetry. That gives me an idea."

"An idea of what?"

"Oh—it's easy to tell when a girl's ready for love."

"How do you tell that, Boze?"

"Well—one pretty sure way is when she starts calling me by my own name for the first time. And another way is how I feel myself. It takes two to make a radio program, you know—the one that's sending, and the one that's receiving. And when I'm with a girl that's cute and appealing, with big, soft eyes—well—I can feel sort of electric waves running all through me—and I can be pretty sure she's doing some broadcasting, whether she knows it or not."

"Have you got a program coming in now?"

"Listen— It's like the hottest torch song that ever was sung. Can't you kind of hear it, honey? (*She looks away from him, but says nothing. He reaches out and takes hold of her hand, entwining his fingers with hers.*) You can call me a sap if you want to, Gabby—but I guess I'm falling in love with you. I'm getting so I want you more than is good for me."

Gabby is still cold to Boze's ardor, even after he has kissed her impulsively and assured her with conviction that she is going to love him a lot. The fact that at that moment the sound of someone approaching from the porch prompts Gabby to warn Boze helps break the spell.

Alan Squier stands in the doorway. He has been in time to realize that he is interrupting an amour, but he considerately looks away and waits. "He is a thin, wan, vague man of about thirty-five. . . . He is shabby and dusty but there is about him a sort of afterglow of elegance. There is something about him—and it is impossible to say just what it is—that brings to mind the ugly word 'condemned.' He carries a heavy walking stick and a ruck-sack is slung over his shoulders. He is diffident in manner, ultra-polite and soft spoken; his accent is that of an Anglicized Ameri-can."

Squier, having taken off his ruck-sack and hat, is prepared to eat what they have to serve. He has been walking and thumbing his way West, he explains in answer to Gabby's queries. His last host had left him ten miles up the road.

"You mean, you were just bumming along?" persists Gabby.

"Call it gypsying," suggests Squier. "I had a vague idea that I'd like to see the Pacific Ocean, and perhaps drown in it. But that depends . . ."

"Where did you come from?"

"Quite a long way, Miss Maple. Is that the name?"

"Yes—that's it. Are you English?"

"No. You might call me an American once removed. . . . But—if you don't mind—"

"The soup'll be right in. The washroom's through there, on your left, if you want it."

"Thank you."

Gabby has gone to the kitchen. Jason has returned resplendent in his Legion uniform of horizon blue, with white Sam Browne belt, rather a startling combination to Alan, passing the legionnaire on his way to freshen up in the washroom.

Now Gramp is back with a new copy of the Denver *Post* and such gossip as Roy Greeley, the mailman, has to relay. They are still saying in the village that the Mantee outfit is headed that way.

"Look! They got the whole story here in *The Post*," exclaims Gramp, holding up the paper. "Oklahoma City Massacre! Six killed—four wounded—two not expected to live. The sheriff's got all his deputies out patroling the roads. They think there's going to be some killing around here."

"Well—if there is—we can't trust that sheriff to do a damn thing. We'll turn out the Legion," threatens Jason.

"You *would?*"

"Certainly! That's what we're there for!"

Jason has thrust his revolver into his Sam Browne belt, taken five dollars from the cash register in case of emergency and left final instructions with Gabby about turning on the neon light when it gets dark.

"It's too bad they didn't wear a uniform like that when they fit the Germans," observes Gramp as Jason, the legionnaire, disappears through the door. "They wouldn't none of 'em have come home."

Squier is back and ready for the food Gabby brings to him. Ready to be entertained by Gramp's amiable gossip while he eats, too, seeing there seems nothing can be done about that.

Gramp is full of the exploits of Duke Mantee and the killings in Oklahoma City. Must be a fine lot of sheriffs, letting themselves get knocked over right in front of the Court House! Gramp knows something about killers. You can always tell them, he says, by the way they hold their chin in. There was Billy the Kid—

Gramp has other reminiscences, too. When Alan confesses to being a writer, it reminds Gramp of old Sam Clemens. Mark Twain, they called him, and he was the biggest liar that ever wrote for the *Enterprise* in Virginia City. Admitted it, too.

"He used to say he did his writing on the principle that his readers wanted everything but the truth, so that's what he give 'em," Gramp chuckles.

When Gramp's supper is ready in the kitchen, Gabby takes over the conversation with Squier. She had heard Gramp say Alan was a writer. That interests her. She met a writer once—Sidney Wenzell of Warner Brothers. Wenzell had stopped at the Bar-B-Q and advised Gabby to come to Hollywood and look him up. Gabby wasn't impressed. Going into the movies had become much too common. The only place Gabby really wants to go is Bourges—(*with a hard g*). She was born in Bourges, but they had brought her to America before she could walk.

"All I know about it," admits Gabby, "is from the picture postcards my mother sends me. They got a cathedral there."

SQUIER—Your mother still lives there?

GABBY—Yes. Dad brought us back here after the war. Mother stuck it out in this desert for a couple of years, and then she packed up and went back to Bourges. We've never seen her since. Some people seem to think it was cruel of her to leave me. But what could she do? She didn't have any money to bring me up. She just couldn't *live* here—and you can't blame her for that. Do you think she was cruel?

SQUIER—Not if you don't, Miss Maple.

GABBY—Well—I *don't*. She's tried lots of times to get me over there to see her—but Dad won't allow it. She got a divorce and married a Frenchman that's got a bookstore. Mother was always a great reader, so I guess it's nice for her. She's got three more kids. Just think of that! I've got a half-brother and half-sisters that can't speak a word of English. I'd sure like to see them.

Squier—Can you speak French?

Gabby—Only what you learn in high school—like *table* for "table." (*She takes a photograph from the book.*) Look—there's my mother's picture. That was just before she married Dad. She had her picture taken smelling a rose.

Squier—She's lovely! And I can see the resemblance.

Gabby—It's hard to imagine her being married to Dad, isn't it? But I guess he looked all right in his American uniform. Mother used to send me a book every year for my birthday, but they were all in French and I couldn't read them. So last year I wrote and asked if she'd mind sending me one in English, and she sent me this one. It's the poems of François Villon. Ever read it?

Squier—Yes.

Gabby—It's wonderful poetry. She wrote in it: "à ma chère petite Gabrielle." That means "To my dear little Gabrielle." She gave me that name. It's about the only French thing I've got.

Squier—Gabrielle. It's a beautiful name.

Gabby—Wouldn't you know it would get changed into "Gabby" by these ignorant bastards around here? I guess you think I use terrible language.

Squier—Oh, no! It—it's picturesque.

Gabby—Well—it suits this kind of country.

Squier—You share your mother's opinion of the desert? (*She nods.*) But you can find solace in the poems of François Villon.

Gabby—Yes. They get the stink of the gasoline and the hamburger out of my system.

As he goes on with his meal Gabby reads a Villon verse to Alan, at his request, and he finds himself staring wonderingly at her as she finishes the refrain:

" 'This is the end for which we twain were met.' "

"You know, that's wonderful stuff," she explains. "But that's the way the French people are: they can understand everything —like life, and love—and death—and they can enjoy it, or laugh at it, depending on how they feel."

"And that's why you want to go to France—for understanding."

"I *will* go there! When Gramp dies, we can sell this place. Dad's going to take his share and move to Los Angeles, so that he can join a really big Legion post and get to be a political power.

But I'm going to spend my part of the money on a trip to
Bourges, where there's something beautiful to look at, and wine,
and dancing in the streets."

"If I were you—I'd stay here, Gabrielle, and avoid disappointment."

Squier, it appears, had lived in France. He was a writer who
spent his time planning to write. A married gigolo who had been
adopted, in a way, by the wife of the man who had published his
first book—"a novel about the bleak, glacier-stripped hills of my
native New England," he explains.

"I was twenty-two when I wrote it, and it was very, very stark.
It sold slightly over six hundred copies. It cost the publisher
quite a lot of money, and it also cost him his wife. You see, she
divorced him and married me. She had faith in me, and she had
the chance to display it, because her husband was very generous
in the financial settlement. I suppose he had faith in me, too.
She saw in me a major artist, profound, but inarticulate. She
believed that all I needed was background, and she gave it to
me—with southern exposure and a fine view of the Mediterranean.
That was considered the thing to do in the period that followed
Scott Fitzgerald. For eight years I reclined there, on the Riviera,
on my background—and I waited for the major artist to step forth
and say something of enduring importance. He preferred to remain inarticulate."

Alan had left his wife after that, at her suggestion (she having
found a Brazilian painter who also needed encouragement), and
had come back to discover America. Thanks to the power of the
thumb he had gotten this far.

"What were you looking for?" Gabby asks.

"Well—that's rather hard to say. I—I suppose I've been looking for something to believe in. I've been hoping to find something that's worth living for—and dying for."

"What have you found?"

"Nothing so interesting as an old man who was missed by
Billy the Kid, and a fair young lady who reads Villon."

Gabby has other accomplishments that might surprise him.
She paints pictures, too. She doesn't show them to many people
for fear of being kidded. When she brings them in she turns
them quickly face down so a cowboy named Herb, who has come
in to buy a bottle of moon, can't see them.

They are both portraits and landscapes, the pictures. At least
there is a portrait of Paula, the Mexican cook. They're queer
pictures and a little puzzling. Squier thinks Gabby is doubtless

"a product of the ultimate French school." . . . "These are somewhat in the Dufy manner—and yet—a lot less conventional. . . . I'm tremendously impressed but also bewildered."

"I'll bet I could improve if I could get to France," says Gabby, with conviction. "You know, they've got some of the finest art schools in the world there. And they've got beautiful things to paint, too—flowers, and castles and rivers. But here in the desert—it's just the same thing over and over again."

There are probably thousands of artists in France who have the same yearning for America, thinks Alan. But Gabby is convinced that with a proper chance she could develop the something in her that is different. Perhaps it is because of her French blood that she understands even better than Alan. No, she does not want to marry a Frenchman. She does not want to marry anybody. She wants always to be free.

Certainly she would take no notice of anyone like Boze. Just because Alan saw Boze kissing her—that meant nothing. Yet, it might mean experience and it is experience, Gabby is convinced, that she needs.

"Do you think I ought to give in?" she asks, frankly.

"Don't ask me, Gabrielle," Squier is quick to answer. "Let your French blood guide you. It's infallible, in matters like that."

GABBY—But you ought to know *something*. You've seen a lot, and you've written a book, and you've been married . . .

SQUIER—I don't know anything. You see—the trouble with me is, I belong to a vanishing race. I'm one of the intellectuals.

GABBY—That means you've got brains. I can see you have.

SQUIER—Yes—brains without purpose. Noise without sound. Shape without substance. Have you ever read "The Hollow Men"? (*She shakes her head.*) Don't. It's discouraging, because it's true. It refers to the intellectuals, who thought they'd conquered Nature. They dammed it up, and used its waters to irrigate the wastelands. They built streamlined monstrosities to penetrate its resistance. They wrapped it up in cellophane and sold it to drug-stores. They were so certain they had it subdued. And now—do you realize what it is that is causing world chaos?

GABBY—No.

SQUIER—Well, I'm probably the only living person who can tell you. . . . It's nature hitting back. Not with the old weapons—floods, plagues, holocausts. We can neutralize them. She's fighting back with strange instruments called neuroses. She's deliberately afflicting mankind with the jitters. Nature is proving that she can't be beaten—not by the likes of us. She's taking the world away from the intellectuals and giving it back to the apes . . . Forgive me, Gabrielle . . . I can't tell you what a luxury it is to have someone to talk to . . . But don't listen to me. I was born in 1901, the year Victoria died. I was just too late for the Great War—and too soon for the Revolution. You're a war baby. You may be an entirely different species, for all I know. You can easily be one of Nature's own children, and therefore able to understand her, and laugh at her—or enjoy her —depending on how you feel. You're the only one who can say whether or not you should yield to the ardors of Number 42 out there. (*He finishes his glass of beer.*) That beer is excellent.

GABBY—It's made in Phoenix. (*She is looking at him intently.*) You know—you talk like a goddam fool.

SQUIER—I know it. (*He is taking out the last of his cigarettes.*)

GABBY—No wonder your wife kicked you out. . . . And no wonder she fell for you in the first place.

Now Gabby has an idea. Alan, by his own confession, has no real plans. Leaving there, he will follow the road and the road leads to the Petrified Forest. That, he thinks, might prove a suitable haven for him.

"Perhaps that's what I'm destined for—to make an interesting fossil for future study," he ventures, musingly. "Homo Semi-Americanus—a specimen of the in-between age."

But Gabby's idea is different. She thinks she would like to go to France with Alan. Nor does the fact that neither of them has enough money discourage her. Someday she will have enough. Someday there will be her share, not only of the lunchroom, but of twenty odd thousand dollars she knows Gramp has put away in the bank in Sante Fe and willed to her. Why shouldn't Alan be a gigolo for her?

"We could go to France, and you'd show me everything, all the cathedrals and the art—and explain everything," enthuses Gabby. "And you wouldn't have to marry me, Alan. We'd just live in sin and have one hell of a time."

It is, Alan admits, a startling proposal, the like of which he never expected to receive. But that isn't all of it. While they are waiting for the inheritance, Gabby sees no reason why she should not have Boze fired and give his job to Alan. Still, Alan is unconvinced, even by Gabby's further argument that, so long as he has nothing else to do, they might as well make a start.

"You couldn't live very long with a man who had nothing else to do but worship you," he protests. "That's a dull kind of love, Gabrielle. It's the kind of love that makes people old too soon. (*He rises.*) But—I thank you for the suggestion. You've opened up a new channel of my imagination which will be pleasant to explore during my lonely wanderings. I'll think of the chimes of Bourges—and you—and sin."

Alan is ready to go now, though still quite indefinite as to where. He has but one request to make of Gabrielle. He would, if she doesn't mind, like to kiss her good-by. Gabrielle doesn't mind, and she quite understands that it will just be a good-by kiss and nothing more.

The kiss is being taken and given when Boze appears suddenly in the doorway. He is all for throwing this fresh guy out, but Gabrielle will not let him lay a finger on Alan. She knows what she is doing.

Alan's bill is thirty cents, which, he agrees, is very reasonable indeed. But, seeing that he hasn't thirty cents, it still presents a problem. The disgust of Boze is again aroused, and this time, whatever the opposition of Gabrielle, Alan is about to be given a bit of a headstart toward his next destination by being forcibly propelled through the door when a car drives up and from the car emerges Mr. and Mrs. Chisholm. "Mr. Chisholm is about forty-five—thin, dry, sharp, persnickety, with pince-nez eyeglasses. Mrs. Chisholm is about ten years younger—rather attractive, rather chic, very world-weary. The Chisholms belong to the topmost layer of society in Dayton, Ohio."

The Chisholms are on their way from Dayton, O., to the Phoenix-Biltmore in Santa Barbara. It occurs to Gabby that they might be willing to give her friend, Mr. Squier, a lift to the coast. Mr. Squier, she explains, is an author and is without a car at the moment.

Mr. Chisholm is not altogether sure, but after he has called his chauffeur, Joseph, and Joseph has made a careful inspection of Alan to make sure he is not armed, he decides to take Alan along.

"I forgot to give you your change," says Gabby, very much pleased with the arrangement as Alan prepares to leave. From the cash register she takes a silver dollar and presses it into his hand. ". . . Perhaps Mr. Chisholm will take you all the way to the coast. When you get there, send me a postcard, with a view of the Pacific Ocean. I like pictures of the sea."

Mrs. Chisholm, returning from the ladies' room, submits, a bit hesitantly, to Alan's joining the party. Alan says his last good-by to Gabrielle with a promise that some day he will find a way to repay the dollar and the Chisholm's Duesenberg disappears up the road.

Now Boze would renew his campaign for the love of Gabrielle. The night is warm, the moon is bright. How about a stroll?

"I'm not so bad, Gabby," protests Boze. "I'm just a big guy with a good heart and plenty of hot blood. And I'm full of love, honey. (*He takes her in his arms.*) And so are you. You don't know it yet—but you are. And when we get out there in the moonlight, you'll be glad I suggested it. Honestly you will, honey sweet. (*He kisses her lips passionately. After a moment, she struggles a little. He relaxes his hold on her. He is confident of progress.*) All right—I'm not holding you against your will. I'm not trying to force you into anything that's wrong."

"I didn't say you were."

"It isn't wrong—except in the minds of old cranks that have forgotten how to love—if they ever knew. My God! It's the most natural thing in the world, for two people, like us, that are young and clean, and . . . Why, it'd be wrong if we *didn't* take the chance when we've got it."

"Do you know what he said?"

"What who said?"

"He said we'd been trying to fight Nature, and we thought we'd licked it, because we've built a lot of dams, and cellophane and things like that. But that's where we're wrong, and that's what's the matter with the world. We've got to admit that Nature can't be beaten." . . . "Oh, well, what the hell! I'll go out with you, Boze."

Boze has kissed Gabby with fervor to stimulate her resolution and they are moving toward the door when suddenly a car is heard outside. A second later a "short, stubby, cherubic gangster" appears in the doorway with a machine gun. He smiles cheerfully as he advises them that so long as they behave themselves no one will get hurt. He is looking for the boss.

This smiling gangster, called Jackie, has been followed by another, "thin, sallow, adenoidal." This would be Ruby. After Ruby comes Duke Mantee, "well built but stoop-shouldered, with a vaguely thoughtful, saturnine face. He is about thirty-five and, if he hadn't elected to take up banditry, might have been a fine left-fielder. There is, about him, one quality of resemblance to Alan Squier: he too is unmistakably condemned. He is hatless and unshaven and wears an ill-fitting suit with a gray prison shirt. Mantee carries no visible arms, but Ruby has another machine gun and a sawed-off shotgun."

"This is Duke Mantee, folks," announces Jackie, pridefully. "He's the world-famous killer and he's hungry."

In a gentle voice and with "effortless ferocity," Duke Mantee takes charge of the situation. He orders a search of the premises and the bringing in of Gramp and Paula, the cook. One table is pulled over nearer the window that Duke may sit back of it with a full command of the room and the door while his back is to the wall.

In the examinations that follow, Paula, the cook, is the only one who shows fear. Paula is desperately eager not to be killed. To avoid that unhappy experience she is quite willing to cook anything and lots of it. Chickens and hamburgers are ordered and Jackie goes to see that Paula gets them.

Gramp is quite thrilled to meet a killer again, though he had known the greatest of them all in his day. He could tell Mantee a few things about killers if Mantee were interested, which he doesn't happen to be.

Nor is there any time. Alan Squier has reappeared suddenly in the doorway, hatless and breathless. The Chisholms had been stopped by bandits about a mile down the road, he reports. The bandits had taken Mr. Chisholm's car—

Duke Mantee has resumed his place at the table by the wall and the others are ranged out fan-like in front of him. Boze is the only restless one. He has a feeling he would like to take a poke at Mantee. Mantee's a gangster and a rat, according to Boze.

"He ain't a gangster," insists Gramp. "He's a real old-time desperado. Gangsters is foreigners. He's an American! And if the sheriffs find out he's here, we'll see some real killing—*won't* we?"

Gabby has turned on the radio and there is a static-accompanied program of sticky music as a result.

"The cops ain't likely to catch up with us—not tonight," says Duke. "So we can all be quiet and peaceable, and have a few beers together, and listen to the music—and not make any wrong moves. Because—I may as well tell you, folks—old Ruby there, with the machine gun—he's pretty nervous and jumpy and he's got the itch between his fingers. So let's everybody stay where they are."

SQUIER—Let there be killing! All evening long, I've had a feeling of Destiny closing in. (*To the* DUKE.) Do you believe in astrology?

DUKE—I couldn't say, pal.

SQUIER—I don't—normally. But just now, as I was walking along that road, I began to feel the enchantment of this desert. I looked up at the sky and the stars seemed to be reproving me, mocking me. They were pointing the way to that gleaming sign, and saying, "There's the end of your tether! You thought you could escape it, and skip off to the Phoenix-Biltmore. But we know better." That's what the stars told me, and perhaps they know that carnage is imminent, and that I'm due to be among the fallen. . . . It's a fascinating thought.

DUKE—Let's skip it. (*He lifts his glass*). Here's happy days.

GRAMP—Yes, *sir*—it sure is pleasant to have a killer around here again.

SQUIER—Yes. It's pleasant to be back again—among the living. (*He raises his glass.*) Hooray! (*He drinks.*)

THE CURTAIN FALLS

ACT II

A half hour later the Mantee boys are finishing the dinner Paula has prepared for them. The others are at the tables where the Duke assigned them seats. Only Gabby is permitted to move about and wait on them.

Gramp has come pretty close to the end of his killer stories. Boze is still courting sudden death by expressing his opinion of this bunch of yellow dogs that has come to the Bar-B-Q. Jackie thinks perhaps it is time something was done about Boze and is standing him against the wall so no one else will be hurt if the sawed-off shotgun scatters when Duke commands everyone to sit tight and listen to the radio. There is a news announcer on the air.

". . . all anxious first off to hear latest bulletins concerning the greatest man-hunt in human history," the announcer reports, briskly. "A monster dragnet has been cast over the entire Southwest from St. Louis to the Pacific Coast. National Guardsmen are coöperating with state police and the famed Texas Rangers as well as countless local posses and Legion posts in a determined effort to apprehend the members of the notorious Mantee gang— to bring to justice this fierce, colorful band of murderers, kidnapers, bank-robbers, perpetrators of the shocking massacre in

Oklahoma City. . . ."

"Take a bow, Duke!" suggests Jackie.

RADIO VOICE—The gang made its escape in two cars, one of which contained Mantee and three other men, the other car containing three men and *one woman*. The Mantee car was seen early this morning at Tularosa and later at Hillsboro in New Mexico. The second car was positively identified at Estelline in the Texas Panhandle when it stopped at the local police station, held it up, and departed with a large supply of guns and ammunition.

JACKIE—Nice going, boys! I don't see how they did it with Doris along to . . .

DUKE—Shut up!

RADIO VOICE—Both cars are undoubtedly headed for the border, but it is considered certain they haven't reached it, due to the number and vigilance of the patrols. War-time conditions prevail on all the roads of Western Texas, New Mexico and Arizona and you know how the officers of the law are in this red-blooded frontier region: they shoot first and ask questions afterward. (JACKIE *indicates his scorn, but the* DUKE *withers him with a look.*) The Governor of Arizona has issued the following statement: "As long as Mantee and his followers are at large a blot of shame will mar the proud scutcheon of these United States. Any citizen who knowingly gives aid or comfort to these public enemies is a traitor to his country and will be answerable before the great bar of public opinion." . . . I'll now give you the scores of the leading football games of the day. Carnegie Tech—13, Miami—7, Washington State—19 . . .

DUKE—Turn it off, sister.

Duke's arrangements for the evening continue. He is determined, whatever his followers may think of his judgment, to stay where he is until the rest of his party catches up with him. The rest of the party includes Duke's lady friend.

Boze, still busting to take the war path, continues to hurl insulting remarks at the Mantee crowd, with occasional slaps at Squier. For one thing, how is Alan going to pay for all the liquor he's drinking? Well, Alan has a dollar. Gabrielle gave him that.

"You were feeling kind of generous tonight, weren't you?" sneers Boze, turning on Gabby, and then back to Squier. "Would you like to know what she was going to give me when those rats showed up? Would you like to know?"

"Well—speaking of rats! Of all the low, slimy, stinking . . ."

"No, Gabby," interposes Alan. "You mustn't blame Boze for anything he says now. He's a man of muscle and he's suffering from the pangs of frustration."

Gabby is not to be mollified. She is good and mad at Boze. Nor does all his pleading for forgiveness move her in the least. There is nothing to hide from Alan, she insists. Boze did start his love-making again after Alan left, and she was on the point of giving in when the gangsters came. She doesn't blame Boze. Neither does Alan. . . .

Gramp's curiosity would trouble him a great deal less if he knew more of Duke's plans. Is Duke going to spend the night there? Duke can't say. Perhaps he will decide to get buried there.

"You'd better come with me, Duke," Alan Squier suggests. "I'm planning to be buried in the Petrified Forest. I've been evolving a theory about that that would interest you. It's a graveyard of the civilization that's been shot from under us. It's a world of outmoded ideas. Platonism—Patriotism—Christianity —Romance—the economics of Adam Smith—they're all so many dead stumps in the desert. That's where I belong—and so do you, Duke. For you're the last great apostle of rugged individualism. Aren't you?"

Boze has returned to his pleas to Gabby. If she knows what it is to be as crazy about anybody as he (Boze) is about her, who is it? Who is she crazy about?

Gabby is not even hesitant in answering. It is Alan. Whatever he is—panhandler, as Boze calls him, or gigolo, by his own confession—Gabby loves Alan and she doesn't think she will ever love anyone else.

"I swear before God, Boze—I wasn't trying to be seductive," Alan protests.

"No—I don't believe you could even try," sneers Boze.

Gabby—After you left, Alan—I felt as if something had been taken out of me—or sort as if I'd come out of a dream. I caught on to myself, and I knew I'm just another desert rat, and I'll never be anything else. I'd better get rid of all the girlish bunk that was in me, like thinking so much about going to France, and Art, and dancing in the streets. And I'd better make the most of what I can find right here—and it happened to be you, Boze. Do you know what I asked him? I asked him to let me go away with him, and live in sin. (*She turns again to* SQUIER.) But you wouldn't have done it, even if we'd had the money—would you, Alan? (SQUIER *is looking straight into her eyes.*) Would you?

SQUIER—No, Gabrielle.

GABBY (*to* BOZE)—You see—he doesn't give a hoot in hell for me. I saw that, plainly enough. And it only made me love him all the more. And that's why I was willing to go out into the moonlight with you, when Duke Mantee came in.

DUKE—I'm sorry, sister. I don't like to interfere with any-body's fun.

BOZE (*with labored insincerity*)—Oh—that's all right. It was probably all for the best.

DUKE—Yes. When I look at you, I guess it was. (*The* DUKE *turns and opens the window at his side about three inches.*)

SQUIER (*still looking at* GABBY)—I'm sorry now that I came back. (BOZE *has darted a look at the* DUKE, *and there is born in his mind an idea: By a sudden, tiger-like leap, he might get possession of the shotgun which is lying on the table.*)

BOZE—I'll take a drink of that stuff. (GABBY *passes him the bottle which has remained on the table.* BOZE *pours himself a stiff one, drinks it—and a moment later pours and consumes an-other. But he is constantly, furiously watching the* DUKE.)

SQUIER (*still looking at* GABRIELLE)—When I went out before —it was the poignant ending to a—an idyllic interlude. But now it's spoiled. I can't go forth quite so gracefully again.

GABBY—You're sorry you heard the real truth?

SQUIER—I told you I'm the type of person to whom the truth is always distasteful.

GABBY—That wife of yours must have been terrible.

SQUIER—Why do you think so?

GABBY—Because she's talked all the heart out of you. I could put it back, Alan.

SQUIER (*with sudden irritability*)—No! Don't delude your-self. If you have love, and don't know what to do with it, why don't you lavish it on Duke Mantee? There's your real mate— another child of Nature.

GABBY—You'd better not drink any more of that rye.

SQUIER—It's not the rye! It's the same disease that's afflicting Boze! Impotence! (*He stands up.*)

Now Alan, with Duke Mantee's permission, has turned to talk with Gramp. Alan would like to know what Gramp intends to do with the Liberty bonds he has in the bank in Sante Fe? Gramp is thinking of leaving them where they are.

"Your granddaughter is stifling and suffocating in this desert, when a few of your thousands would give her the chance to claim her birthright," protests Alan.

"Yes—and maybe give you the chance to steal it," snaps Gramp. "I've heard what you've been saying."

"That's a low way to justify your stinginess. Oh—I know you were a pioneer once. But what are you now? A mean old miser, hanging on to that money as though it meant something. Why in God's name don't you die and do the world some good?"

That's more than Duke can stand. The idea of anybody talking to an old man like that! Duke would do something about that, but at the moment the gunman Ruby pops in to report two men and a woman coming down the road. Probably the owners of the Duesenberg.

"Listen, Duke," urges Squier, after he has set himself right by apologizing to Gramp; "if you had any of Robin Hood in you you'd go to Santa Fe, and rob that bank, and give it to her, before it's too late for her to use it as it should be used . . ."

"She'll get it when she needs it—when she has a family of her own to support—and probably a good-for-nothing unemployed husband. . . ."

As Duke turns to look out the window Boze sees the opportunity he has been waiting for. Making a flying leap for Mantee, he grabs the shotgun and twists it out of the killer's hand. He has Duke covered and backing toward the wall when the Chisholms and Joseph, the chauffeur, come through the door. Seeing the gun, Mrs. Chisholm screams lustily; Boze's attention is distracted and in that split second Duke Mantee whips out a gun and fires. Boze drops the shotgun and grabs his left wrist.

Now Mantee has set the Chisholms down at the center table with Squier, sent Boze to the kitchen with Gabby to have his hand bandaged and announced that any more attempts at interference with his plans will be met with a wholesale slaughter that will take in the party.

The Chisholms are disgusted but helpless. They are hoping to get their car back and their luggage. Duke thinks they probably will recover the car, and he hopes it will not be messed up with bullet holes and blood. Of the luggage he has taken only a small traveling case belonging to Mrs. Chisholm. Duke has a friend who likes rubies, too.

Now Alan, who has recovered his ruck-sack and taken his life

insurance policy from it, has filled the policy in and is prepared
to ask a great favor of Mantee.

"I don't think you'll refuse it," he says to the killer, "because
—you're a man of imagination. You're not afraid to do—rather
outlandish things. . . ."

"What are you getting at?"

SQUIER—This insurance policy—it's my only asset. It's for
five thousand dollars—and it was made out in favor of my wife.
She's a rich woman, and she doesn't need the money—and I know
she doesn't *want* it, from me. I've written on the policy that I
want the money paid to Miss Maple—that young lady in there.
If Mr. and Mrs. Chisholm will witness my signature, I'm sure it
will be all right. My wife would never contest it. She's a good
sort—really she is. Well—what I'm getting at is this, Duke:
after they've signed, I wish—I'd be much obliged if you'd just—
kill me. (*The* DUKE *looks at him levelly.*) It couldn't make any
difference to you, Duke. After all, if they catch you they can
hang you only once—and you know better than anyone else
they already have more than they need against you. And you
can't be bothered by any humane considerations. You'd have a
hard time finding a more suitable candidate for extermination.
I'll be mourned by no one. In fact, my passing will evoke sighs
of relief in certain quarters. You see, Duke—in killing me—
you'd only be executing the sentence of the law—I mean, natural
law—survival of the fittest . . .

GRAMP—My God—he *is* drunk!

DUKE—Sure—and having a fine time showing off.

SQUIER—Of course I'm showing off. I'm trying to outdo Boze
in gallantry. But is there anything unnatural in that? Boze
was ready to sacrifice his life to become an All-American star.
And I'm ready to do likewise. (*He addresses the* CHISHOLMS.)
Can't you see I mean it?

CHISHOLM—I'm afraid I'm not greatly interested in your
whimsicalities.

SQUIER—I don't blame you. But you must remember that
this is a weird country we're in. These Mesas are enchanted—
and you have to be prepared for the improbable. I'm only asking
that you attest to my signature on this . . .

MRS. CHISHOLM—I believe you *do* mean it!

SQUIER—Good for you, Mrs. Chisholm! You're a kindred
spirit! I'll bet that you, too, have been thrilled by "A Tale of
Two Cities."

MRS. CHISHOLM—You're in love with her, aren't you?

SQUIER—Yes—yes, I suppose I am. And not unreasonably. She has heroic stuff in her. She may be one of the immortal women of France—another Joan of Arc, or Georges Sand, or Madame Curie. I want to show her that I believe in her—and how else can I do it? Living, I'm worth nothing to her. Dead— I can buy her the tallest cathedrals, and golden vineyards, and dancing in the streets. One well-directed bullet will accomplish that. And it will gain a measure of reflected glory for him who fired it and him who stopped it. (*He holds up the insurance policy.*) This document will be my ticket to immortality. It will inspire people to say of me: "*There* was an artist, who died before his time!" Will you do it, Duke?

DUKE (*quietly*)—I'll be glad to.

The policy is duly signed and witnessed by the Chisholms. Between Alan and Duke it is agreed that the killing will take place at the Duke's convenience, but preferably, Alan suggests, just before he leaves. Also Alan would like to have Gabby think it was done in cold blood.

Gramp has finished inspecting the policy and is convinced that it is legal. But he is still a little resentful.

"I'd like to tell you just one thing, my friend," says Gramp. "There ain't a woman alive or ever did live that's *worth* five thousand dollars."

"And let me tell *you* one thing—you're a forgetful old fool," replies Alan. "Any woman is worth everything that any man has to give—anguish, ecstasy, faith, jealousy, love, hatred, life or death. Don't you see—that's the excuse for our existence? It's what makes the whole thing possible, and tolerable. When you've reached my age, you'll learn better sense."

Mrs. Chisholm is hoping that Mr. Chisholm heard that, but Mr. Chisholm is not visibly interested.

"That lovely girl—that granddaughter of yours—do you know what she is?" demands Alan, feverishly. "No—you don't. You haven't the remotest idea."

"What is she?" Gramp would know.

"She's the future. She's the renewal of vitality—and courage —and aspiration—all the strength that has gone out of you. Hell—I can't say what she is—but she's essential to me, and the whole damned country, and the whole miserable world."

Not only does Alan believe his own tribute to women, but he feels that Duke Mantee believes it, too. Hasn't Duke refused to make his escape across the border just because he has a rendezvous with a girl?

As to that, the Duke is evasive. He guesses they are all a lot of saps, but he thinks probably Alan is the champion.

With her second drink, and Alan talking that way, the Bar-B-Q has suddenly become quite cozy to Mrs. Chisholm. She even looks forward with enthusiasm to being witness to a murder. At last she is going to see something!

Now Gabby is back. She and Jackie have left Boze tied up in the bathroom. And Gabby is filled with a new idea. The Bar-B-Q is going to get a lot of advertising from this Duke Mantee adventure. Why wouldn't this be a fine time to sell? They'd get more money! Then they could go to Los Angeles, Jason could get another start and probably she could get a job in pictures with the Warner Brothers. It isn't for herself Gabby is asking. She doesn't care what happens to her. But she is anxious to see her father have a chance.

Mrs. Chisholm is quick to lend her support to Gabby, and to Alan, who doesn't want Gabby to give up her life to anything but her own ambition to paint. Mrs. Chisholm knows what it is to have been repressed and starved through a sense of duty to others. She had given up her life, and a chance she once had to play the Nun in "The Miracle," for Max Reinhardt, because of what her family insisted she owed to them. She had gone back to Dayton and the Junior League, the Country Club and the D.A.R.—"and everything else that is foul and obscene."

"Before I knew it I was married to this pillar of the mortgage, loan and trust," she finishes. "And what did *he* do? He took my soul and had it stenciled on a card, and filed. And where have I been ever since? In an art-metal cabinet. That's why I think I have a *little* right to advise you."

SQUIER—You know—it's the damnedest thing about this place. There's something here that stimulates the autobiographical impulse. (*To the* DUKE.) What kind of life have *you* had, Duke?

DUKE—A hell of a life.

MRS. CHISHOLM—I don't believe it.

DUKE—Why not, lady? (JACKIE *returns and sits on a stool at the counter.*)

MRS. CHISHOLM—Because you've had the one supreme satisfaction of knowing that at least you're a real man.

DUKE—Yeh—that's true. But what has it got me? I've spent most of my time since I grew up in jail, and it looks like I'll spend the rest of my life dead. So what good does it do me to be a real man when you don't get much chance to be crawling into the hay with some dame?

MRS. CHISHOLM (*after a slight, thoughtful pause*)—I wonder if we could find any hay around *here?*

CHISHOLM (*past vehemence*)—For the love of God, Edith . . .

JACKIE—*Say!* What's been going on here?

SQUIER—I'm not sure—but I *think* the Duke has had an offer.

MRS. CHISHOLM—He certainly has! And it was made with all sincerity, too.

PYLES—Now, listen, boss—don't you go getting into no hay with her. Because we got to lam it out of here.

DUKE—Thanks very much, lady. When I get settled down in Mexico, maybe I'll send you a postcard, with my address.

SQUIER—Excuse me, Duke—but how's the time getting along?

DUKE—It's just about up, pal.

SQUIER (*turning to* GABBY)—I must talk to you, Gabrielle.

GABBY—You can wait until after they've gone.

SQUIER—I can't wait. I mean—when they go—I go. I have to tell you now that I love you.

GABBY—Now listen, Alan. I got sort of upset by all that blood, and I don't want to . . .

SQUIER—I tell you solemnly that I love you, with all the heart that is left in me.

JACKIE—Are we waiting just to listen to this?

MRS. CHISHOLM—He does love you, my dear. He told us so.

SQUIER—Please, Mrs. Chisholm. I'm capable of saying it. (*He turns to* GABBY.) Even if I'm not capable of making you believe that I . . .

GABBY—Don't make a fool of yourself, Alan. They're all staring at you.

SQUIER—I know they are. But you've got to believe it, and you've got to remember it. Because—you see—it's my only chance of survival. I told you about that major artist, that's been hidden. I'm transferring him to you. You'll find a line in that verse of Villon's that fits that. Something about: "Thus in your field my seed of harvestry will thrive." I've provided barren soil for that seed—but you'll give it fertility and growth and fruition . . .

Gabby has decided now. Perhaps Alan is kind of crazy. Perhaps she is, too. Perhaps that is why she thinks they would be terribly happy together. She had made up her mind—Wherever Alan goes she will go, too.

"I'm not going away, anywhere," Alan tells her, taking her hand in his. "I don't have to go any farther. Because I think I've found the thing I was looking for. I've found it—here, in the Valley of the Shadow."

"What, Alan? What have you found?"

"I can't say what it is, Gabrielle. Because I don't quite know, yet!" He has turned suddenly to face the Duke. "All right, Duke," he says. "We needn't wait any longer!"

From outside come three short, sharp toots of the Duesenberg horn. In a flash the Mantee gang is on the defensive. Duke's orders cut sharply through the room. Then Jason Maple and two other legionnaires come through the front door. One is a peppery little post commander and all three are wearing gaudy sky-blue uniforms. Rudy's back of them with a machine gun and all three have their hands in the air. They are searched and set down on the floor. The Commander of the Post is hoping Mantee has sufficient patriotism not to shoot three veterans of the World War in cold blood, but the Duke's present attitude is in no way reassuring.

The legionnaires were, they admit, pursuing the Mantee gang. The U. S. Cavalry has already caught the others—three men and a blonde. Caught 'em at Buckhorn, N. M., about a hundred miles away.

That news is a poser for Duke. More than that, the country is overrun with posses, Jason reports. One of them is sure to be closing in and he doesn't want the Bar-B-Q shot up. He thinks Duke better get started quick. He has reason to believe the blonde has been talking.

"I'm telling you for your own good, Mantee—they know where you were heading—they've picked your trail—and they'll get you . . ."

The Duke is hesitant, propelled, for once, "into a state of turbulent, agonized indecision." Jackie and Pyles excitedly urge him to come away.

"For Christ's sake, shut up!" yells Duke. "Shut up! Give me time to think!"

SQUIER—No, Duke—don't waste any time thinking. That isn't your game. Don't listen to what they're telling you. You've got to keep going and going and going—

PYLES—Yeah—and go fast.

JACKIE—You've been double-crossed and bitched, and the next thing you'll be layed flat on a marble slab . . .

DUKE—Where'd they take her?

JASON—I don't know. Maybe to Albuquerque.

JACKIE—If we head for there, they'll take *us!*

SQUIER—You want revenge, don't you! You want to go out of your way again to get that blonde who snitched. Don't do it, Duke. Even if she did betray you, don't you commit a worse crime. Don't betray yourself. Go on, run for the border—and take your illusions with you!

JACKIE—He's right, Duke!

DUKE—I told you to shut up! (*He says that to* JACKIE, *but he is looking hard at* SQUIER, *who is talking with passionate earnestness.*)

SQUIER—You know they're going to get you, anyway. You're obsolete, Duke—like me. You've got to die. Then die for freedom. That's worth it. Don't give up your life for anything so cheap and unsatisfactory as revenge.

PYLES—I hear a car coming, boss. We better lam. (*The* DUKE *looks at* SQUIER *curiously, for a moment.*)

DUKE—All right, pal. I'm going. Now listen, folks; we've had a pleasant evening here and I'd hate to spoil it with any killing at the finish. So stay where you are until we're out of sight, because we'll be watching. Better cut that phone wire, Jackie. Pack up the ammunition, Pyles. (PYLES *and* JACKIE *are galvanized into action.*)

SQUIER—Wait a minute! You're not forgetting me?

Before Duke can answer there is another warning toot on the Duesenberg. A car has driven up in the road and a man is getting out. Ruby, outside, has opened fire with his machine gun, much to the distress of Duke. That will only draw fire to the Duesenberg, and he doesn't want that shot up.

Now Duke has deployed his men for the strategy of the getaway. Pyles is behind the counter covering the folks in the room. Jackie has gone to make contact with Ruby outside. The Duke has thrust his machine gun through the window. Everybody not in the fight has been ordered to lie down on the floor. Jackie, returning, turns out the lights. The moonlight illumines the room dimly.

Outside the shooting continues intermittently. One shot shatters a window pane. Jackie is sent back to cover the kitchen. Boze can be heard yelling from the bathroom a demand to be let out.

"It's an inspiring moment, isn't it, Gabrielle?" hoarsely whispers Alan, moving closer to Gabby. "The United States of America versus Duke Mantee!"

Mr. Chisholm, a bit quaveringly, is trying to tell Mrs. Chisholm what to do in case he happens to be killed. The legionnaires are hoping Mantee is not going to let the deputies rush them.

"I feel as if I were sitting on top of a mountain . . . in the middle of Penguin Island. Watching . . . watching the odd little creatures," says Alan. "How do you feel about it, darling?"

"I don't know, Alan. And I don't care," answers Gabby. A moment later she asks: "Alan . . . Alan—when you get to France . . . what do you see first?"

"Customs officers."

"But what's the first real sight you see?"

"The fields and forests of Normandy and then . . ."

"What, Alan?"

"And then Paris."

"Paris! That's the most marvelous place in the world for love —isn't it?"

"All places are marvelous."

"Even here."

"Especially here, my darling!"

Joseph, the chauffeur, has taken to praying loudly. The cries of the tethered Boze and wails from Paula the cook are heard above the din. Jason has begun to worry about the possibility of the gas pumps going up in flames.

"As long as I live I'll be grateful to the Duke," says Alan.

"Alan . . . Alan . . . will you please kiss me," pleads Gabby.

Alan has taken Gabby in his arms. There is a new burst of fire from the Duke's machine gun and with that blast the Duke rallies his men. They are pulling out now. Pyles, sent to call Jackie in, is back to report Jackie dead.

Duke can't understand how Jackie let them get him, but there is no time to go into that. They'll take the Chisholms and the legionnaires and hang them on the runningboard as shields. A second later Duke has herded the hostages toward the door, shouting that so long as they keep their hands up and make plenty of noise none of them will get hurt. Now they are filing through the door, yelling: "Don't shoot— Don't shoot! For God's sake, buddies, don't shoot!"

The Duke follows with his machine gun under his left arm and a revolver in his right hand. He turns at the door to advise those he is leaving.

"You'd better stay where you are for a while. Good night, folks."

"Duke!" Alan has jumped to his feet and is following.

"Alan! Keep down!" cries Gabby.

"Duke!"

"Do you still want it?" asks the Duke, pausing at the door.

"It's no matter whether I want it or not. You've got to . . ."

"O. K., pal," answers Duke, as he fires. "I'll be seeing you soon."

Alan clutches his side and spins around against the counter.

"God Almighty: He meant it!" ejaculates Gramp.

There is a roar of a motor-car disappearing up the road.

A second later the Sheriff and three deputies appear briefly at the door. Finding the gunmen gone they prepare to follow after and shoot the hell out of 'em, taking Jason's car for the chase.

Gabby has helped Alan into a chair by the table. She has sent for Boze, who would know about first aid. But Alan is content. Once he had wanted to live, but he was blinded then, whereas now he can see.

"They were right, Gabrielle," he says. "I mean the stars. I had to come all this way to find a reason. . . . Oh—if people only had guts enough, they'd always find . . . (*He covers his eyes with his hand.*) Death is funny looking when . . . The Duke—understood what it was—I wanted . . . I hope you'll—"

"What, Alan? What did you say? (*She takes hold of his shoulder and frantically shakes him.*) Alan . . . (*He is finally silent. Her lip quivers, but she tightens her face.*) No, don't worry, Alan. I'm not going to be a God-damned cry-baby about it . . . I know you died happy . . . Didn't you, Alan? *Didn't you?*"

Boze and Gramp have come in. Gramp's sure Alan is dead. Mantee couldn't have missed twice.

"Listen, Gabby—here's the funny thing," Gramp goes on. "His life insurance for five thousand berries. He made it out to you, and it looks regular. Said he wanted you to spend it on a trip to France to see your mother. Of course, I don't know if it's collectable, but by God, I'm going to get it to Summerfield in the morning. He was the damnedest feller I ever did see. Couldn't make him out."

Jason has come back to report that Mantee had let the hostages off the runningboard a quarter mile down the road. They are walking back. Alan, he thinks, died a hero's death and should receive an honorable funeral.

"We'll bury him out there in the Petrified Forest," calmly announces Gabby. "That's what he wanted."

She is still standing with her hand on Alan's shoulder as Jason goes back of the counter to phone the sheriff's office. She is repeating softly to herself—

"Thus in your field my seed of harvestry will thrive—
For the fruit is like me that I set—"

Boze (*coming in from the kitchen*)—Boy—it did me good to see that Jackie in a pool of blood. . . .

Gabby (*louder, almost defiantly*)—
"God bids me tend it with good husbandry:
This is the end for which we twain are met."

Jason (*at phone*)—Hello—who's this . . . Oh—hello, Ernie . . .

Boze (*wildly*)—Don't keep *staring* at him . . .

Jason—Jason Maple . . . Say—Mantee was here and escaped south in a yellow Duesenberg, Ohio license plate. Sheriff went after him, but you got to watch Route 71 and send out the alarm to watch Route 60. Yes—we had quite some shooting here . . .

THE CURTAIN HAS FALLEN

THE OLD MAID

A Drama in Five Scenes
Based on an Edith Wharton Novel

By Zoe Akins

THE early voting was against "The Old Maid." The early
voting by New York's professional play reviewers at least. No
more than a third of them were agreed as to its quality or chances
for popularity, the two-thirds majority insisting that it listed far
too sharply toward the obviously sentimental drama and followed
much too closely the older form of emotional drama to satisfy
the alert and boastfully sophisticated playgoers of this day.

The play was brought to New York New Year's week. Because
it was scheduled to open against Leslie Howard and "The Petrified Forest," and because its producer, Harry Moses, had a feeling that Mr. Howard would draw the first-line reviewers away,
even from his two lady stars, Judith Anderson and Helen Menken
(there not being much gallantry among reviewers), there was an
invitation critics' performance given at the Saturday matinee in
Baltimore preceding the Monday opening in New York.

It may well be that seeing the play for the first time under
these unusual conditions affected the judgment of its critics. It
is possible they were fearful of trusting the enthusiasm of those
1,200 Baltimore ladies who crowded the Baltimore theatre that
Saturday. Or felt they must steel themselves against such display
of human weakness and carefully vision the colder, harder attitude of a Broadway first night.

In any event, the verdict, as said, was not too favorable. As
the reviewers had suspected it might be, the New York opening
was reserved and perfunctorily friendly rather than enthusiastic.
But word went forth that "The Old Maid" was unquestionably
a great woman's play and therefore pretty sure to be a strong
matinee attraction.

This proved a truthful prophecy. For months after its struggling start there were no matinee seats to be bought. Women
playgoers from city and suburbs crowded the Empire Theatre,
dragging a small percentage of their menfolk with them. Business steadily builded until late Spring, when, overcoming a divi-

144

sion in the recommendations made by its advisory jury, "The Old Maid" was given the annual award as the best play of American authorship of the season by the Pulitzer prize committee.

Its critics were right in their charge that this drama of maternal yearning and mother love is definitely sentimental, and that it does belong to that school of emotional drama that flourished a generation and more ago. But its enthusiastic supporters are equally right in insisting that it is a human and substantial drama, skillfully and intelligently adapted by Miss Akins from one of Edith Wharton's most characteristic stories of old New York. At the beginning of "The Old Maid," which goes back to 1833, we are in Delia Lovell's room in her parents' country house, "Lovell Place, at Avenue A and Ninety-first Street, overlooking the East River," New York. It is Delia's wedding day. A striking brunette in her early twenties, she is seated before her dressing table while Nora, her maid, much more nervous than she, is arranging orange blossoms in her Brussels veil. The wedding gown is "a high-waisted 'India mull' embroidered with daisies," and there are white satin sandals to match. Delia is perfectly calm, though the orchestra can be heard faintly playing a selection from Gluck, heralding the approach of the ceremony.

Nora's chief concern is the common superstition attending such occasions. Her mistress should be wearing "something borrowed, something blue"—Delia remembers the rest of it: "Something old and something new." If Nora could lend her, say, a garter, that would help—

A knock at the door. Delia's cousin Charlotte has come with a contribution. Something blue, as it happens. A cameo. A present from Clem Spender—

Delia is excited by this. She did not know Clem was even in the country. She thought he was still in Italy.

"He came home today," reports Charlotte. "Just in time for your wedding. He hadn't heard you were going to marry someone else. He thought you must be ill because you'd stopped writing."

The wedding march will be next, warns Charlotte. Delia is emotionally moved. Suddenly she covers her eyes with her hand.

"Oh, Chatty, I'm afraid!" she mutters.

"Of what?"

"Of Clem! Of what he may say or do," answers Delia, excitedly. "There'll be champagne, and if he should take a glass too much— Watch him, Chatty, will you? Be—be kind to him."

"I don't see how anyone could ever be unkind to poor Clem," answers Charlotte, a hard note in her voice. And, as Delia starts to cry she adds, "You won't cry if you keep saying to yourself, over and over: 'I am marrying a Ralston; I'm marrying a Ralston.'"

"Yes, I *am* marrying a Ralston; and I'm glad!" answers Delia, a little defiantly.

Clem Spender, an old sweetheart of Delia's, it appears from what follows, had been in Italy two years. He had gone to study painting. Delia had agreed to wait for Clem, and Clem had promised to come back, if he failed. He had not come. He had not written. Neither had Delia written Clem when she decided to marry James Ralston. She had intended to write, she tried to write—

"I'm fond of Jim," she explains weakly. "It seemed hopeless to wait for Clem. I couldn't bear to be an old maid, Chatty—"

"I shall be an old maid because the man I love doesn't love me," answers Charlotte, coldly. "Not for any other reason. I would have waited for him all my life."

"You think so, but life doesn't stop; one gets lonely; one wants children and a home of one's own."

The first chords of the wedding march reverberate through the house. Nervously Delia adjusts the wedding veil. "Something blue!" she mutters, slipping the cameo into the bosom of her dress and reaching for her bouquet.

"Oh, Chatty—I'm trembling," she adds. Then, recovering her poise, and with her head proudly lifted, she starts for the door as the curtain falls.

SECOND EPISODE

In a room above the stables of her Grandmother's house in Mercer Street Charlotte Lovell has established a day nursery. The room, with a sloping roof, is furnished as a kindergarten with tables of varying heights and chairs of different sizes. A table and student lamp and several comfortable chairs are a concession to adult visitors.

There are several poorly dressed children in the room at the moment. They are amusing themselves teasing Tina, a shy child of five, who stands with her back against the side of the biggest arm chair.

Tina is plainly miserable, but she apparently is accustomed to this treatment. Her lips tremble as the children fiendishly chant that "Tina lives with niggers! Tina lives with niggers!" She is close to tears as one little boy assures her she is sure to turn black herself some day and another shouts that she never even had a poppa or a momma.

The arrival of Charlotte Lovell saves Tina. Charlotte knows at once what is going on and sends the children smartly to their places. Often she has spoken to them about this. Now she may have to speak to their parents.

They are frightened now and quick to deny individually that they had had anything to do with starting the teasing. Not Bennie, or Emma, or Jerry. Nor will Tina tell who it was.

Now the children are being buttoned into their coats and have asked if they may sing a song Bridget has taught them. It is a song of parting, Tina explains, because Miss Charlotte is going to get married and go away for a while. There are several false starts, but the song is finally sung and Charlotte has thanked and dismissed them. All but Tina. Tina stays behind, and Jennie Meade, "a young woman with a pleasant face and shabby clothes," has come to thank Charlotte for what she has done for the children of the poor in the neighborhood. The way Charlotte has taken them when their mothers had to leave them and go to work, and the way she has taught them nice manners and all, is very wonderful to Mrs. Meade. She can't quite understand why a young woman of Charlotte's class could do it, though she has heard it was because Charlotte had made a vow to God that if he cured her of the lung fever she went South to heal she would devote her life to some such work.

Charlotte is inclined to dismiss the subject curtly. She cares for the children because she enjoys the work and them. She plans to go on with the nursery after she is married. There is the problem just now of the time she'll be away on her wedding trip. Perhaps Mrs. Meade would like to come and help Bridget with the children during that time?

Mrs. Meade would love to come, seeing she has no other work just now. And Mrs. Meade will be glad to take special pains with Tina, who needs looking after, as Charlotte explains, to save her from the teasing of the other children.

"Perhaps I ought to explain that she was left with a Negro family when a baby, and still lives with them," says Charlotte.

"The poor little waif! What sort of a mother could she have had?" wonders Mrs. Meade, picking up her own infant, who has been sleeping in a crib. "I wouldn't have done that to you, son— even if you'd had no daddy, and the two of us had had nowhere to go but the river. . . ."

There are callers struggling up the narrow stairway to Charlotte's nursery. They are Dr. Lanskell, a friend and sympathetic aide in Charlotte's work, and Mrs. Mingott, "Joe's Aunt Carrie," who has just arrived from Paris, an amiable though sharp-tongued lady of middle years and definitely individual ideas. It is plain to see that Mrs. Mingott does not altogether approve of Charlotte's good works in the loft of the stable, but she is willing to overlook that. She is quite convinced that Charlotte and her nephew, Joseph, are wise in marrying. Joe is twenty-nine and Charlotte is twenty-seven, though Mrs. Mingott is agreed Charlotte looks six years younger than she did six years ago at her Cousin Delia's wedding. It is a case of now or never for Joe and Charlotte, thinks Aunt Carrie. And how did they ever happen to take a fancy to each other after all these years? Charlotte thinks it must have been because they saw so much of each other after Delia married Joe's brother, James.

When Dr. Lanskell has gone to see how Tina is getting along Mrs. Mingott takes advantage of the moment for a confidential chat with Charlotte. She has wanted to give Charlotte a wedding present, but she has been in doubt as to what Charlotte would prefer.

"My dear girl, I know you've always gone to parties in made-over dresses, and I know there must be things you'd like, but which you've too much pride to ask for," explains the older woman. "There are—aren't there?"

"Of course," answers Charlotte, simply.

"Then tell me, what do you need most?"

Charlotte is slow in replying, stammers a little in trying to, which decides Mrs. Mingott to give her money and let her buy what she wants. It is the very thing that Charlotte had hoped for most. Money—of her own—to do what she most wants to do —that is unbelievably good fortune!

What she wants to do—what she can do with the five hundred dollars Mrs. Mingott proposes to give her—is to keep the nursery going. Not only because she loves it, but because she feels the children need her, too. With that money she will not have to ask her grandmother for help, nor go immediately to her husband. Even if she cannot keep the stable loft she can get a room somewhere, and perhaps hire a woman to help—for a time at least. Charlotte would kiss Mrs. Mingott's hand in gratitude, were she not "tut-tutted" away. . . .

A knock on the door has been followed by the entrance of Delia Ralston, followed by her husband, James, and his brother

Joseph. James and Joseph, both tall and good-looking, are also distinguished by the same mannerisms.

The visit is a surprise. Charlotte, with a trace of resentment, has long wondered why Delia and James have never been sufficiently interested to visit her nursery. She is glad of any excuse that has brought them now. But if they have come to see the children they are too late. The children are all gone—all save one, who has her supper there every day, being more delicate than the others.

That word "delicate" is ominous to James. If the child is not in good health he hopes Delia, at least, will stay away from her. After all, there has been an epidemic of diphtheria, and they cannot be too careful for the sake of their own small daughter. James has been easily upset by the thought of contact with communicable diseases ever since a neighbor's child had contracted smallpox at a circus. Joseph, too, has worried about Charlotte's being so close to these children when she herself is not any too strong. But Delia is not worried. . . .

Charlotte has led the child Tina into the room and proudly presented her to the family. Tina averts her eyes when they stare at her, curtsies shyly for Mrs. Mingott and announces a little fearfully that her name is Clementina. When they ask her what her other name is she is bewildered. She doesn't know any other name. Which occasions a bit of eyebrow-lifting on the part of Mrs. Mingott. There is even more general surprise when Tina doesn't know where she lives, either. They never talk to her about such things, Charlotte explains, protecting the child from her inquisitors.

Now the truth as to Tina's origin has dawned upon Mrs. Mingott. This is the hundred-dollar baby. Isn't she?

"I mean the baby who, according to gossip, was left several years ago on the threshold of one of those disgraceful shanties out on Broadway near Nineteenth Street, with a hundred-dollar bill pinned to its bib," adds Mrs. Mingott, turning to Dr. Lanskell for confirmation. "You remember all the talk it caused. Everyone wrote me—"

"Chatty!" calls Delia, rather breathlessly, speculation in her eyes.

"Yes?"

DELIA—Is this the hundred-dollar baby, Chatty?
CHARLOTTE (*to* DR. LANSKELL, *casually*)—Is she?
DR. LANSKELL (*as if recalling an unimportant fact*)—Yes, yes,

of course. I'd almost forgotten how Jessamine and Cyrus came by the child. (*Smiling.*)   At least, I'd forgotten that sensational hundred dollar bill.

DELIA (*almost accusingly, to* CHARLOTTE)—Didn't you know that, Chatty, really?

CHARLOTTE (*simply*)—I knew only that she was a foundling whom a Negro family had taken in.

DELIA—And you didn't know that she was *the* hundred-dollar baby?

CHARLOTTE—I'd never thought of it.

JOSEPH—Naturally she never thought of it.   I'd rather we changed the subject.

MRS. MINGOTT (*tartly*)—The subject would never have been mentioned if Chatty herself hadn't given us to understand the child was illegitimate.

JOSEPH—She did nothing of the sort.   She never used such a word in her life.   All she said was that the child didn't know who her parents were—

MRS. MINGOTT—She said "a foundling"—

JOSEPH—She thought—

CHARLOTTE (*quietly*)—I knew what the word meant, Joe.

JOSEPH (*giving in a little, but still indignant*)—But that's not the same thing as going back and delving into a scandal that would disgust—that *has* disgusted her.   I'd rather we didn't say any more about it.

MRS. MINGOTT—I'm sorry, my dear boy, that I offended you by a little plain speaking in Charlotte's presence.   But, after all, her work must have taught her some of the unpleasant facts of life.   *I* never knew when I was a girl that people who weren't married *could* have babies.

There is a new interest in Tina now.   Mrs. Mingott would try again to induce the child to talk.   Tina continues to shy away from Mrs. Mingott, but it is evident to that lady that the child has blood.   She can tell by the shape of her feet.

It is not until Delia speaks to her that Tina shows any interest in these callers.   For a second she stares at Delia, then smiles and runs to her.   Now she is in Delia's lap and they are fast becoming friends, much to the discomfiture of James Ralston, who can't forget that the child did cough, however free from symptoms Dr. Lanskell may insist she is.

Delia and Tina are still having a grand visit when James decides it is time to go.   When Delia would put Tina down the

child throws her arms impulsively about her neck and clings to
her. Delia would let Tina keep the cameo she is wearing, but
Charlotte, whose manner has grown suddenly stern, takes it from
around the child's neck and hands it back to its owner.

Delia is excited by Tina's preference for her. She will come
again, she promises, and let Tina wear her chain again. She has
already promised Bridget that she will see that all the children
get new toys. . . .

The others have gone. Joseph and Charlotte are alone. She is
in his arms now and has given him her lips with passionate ardor.
Joseph, too, loses himself momentarily in the enthusiasm of the
embrace, and then reverts quickly to his normal, self-conscious
state. Charlotte realizes that she has embarrassed her fiancé.
Nice girls save such kisses for their husbands. But she thinks
perhaps, as Joe says, that she feels things more deeply than others,
and is quick to show what she feels.

They are in a confessing mood. Joseph admits he has moments
of being jealous of Charlotte's waifs. They take something of
her away from him. And Charlotte confesses that she is still
wondering why he is marrying her at all. There are so many
other girls, younger and prettier—neither her grandmother nor
Delia can understand, either. Yet it is wonderful to feel that it
doesn't matter any more what anyone thinks.

"They've all stopped patronizing me now—now that I'm not
going to be a poor relation all my life—an old maid—to fetch and
carry for everyone," says Charlotte.

She tells Joseph of Aunt Carrie Mingott's present, and what she
plans to do with it. To keep the nursery and continue with her
work. She is hopeful that he, too, will help with the nursery and
come to know the children and their needs as she has.

Joseph has no such idea, neither for himself nor for Charlotte.
After she is married there will be enough to do in her own home
to keep her busy, and, in time, children of her own to care for.
He would be willing for her to give money to the nursery, and to
turn it over to some worthy woman whom he would pay. But
Charlotte must give up the idea that she will be coming here
every day to continue the nursery as she has been doing.

"Because I'm making a good marriage I'm supposed to get rid
of these poor darlings as though they were dolls I'd finished playing with," declares Charlotte, with some feeling. "Oh, no! I
can't! I won't!"

Joseph is a bit startled at the thought of Charlotte's refusal to
give up her work. Even though, as she insists, the children need

her, he, too, needs her. And there is the question of danger to her health that both Jim and Delia pointed out.

"It shows that I'm not unreasonable in thinking of your health," protests Joseph.

"It shows you're a Ralston, Joe," answers Charlotte, desperately. "And afraid of anything that everybody else doesn't do. And afraid of the slightest risk to your own comfort and safety!"

Suddenly they are conscious that they are quarreling and equally unhappy about it. Neither wants to quarrel, but neither will give way.

"I am right; and you are wrong," snaps Joseph. "But we'd better not talk about it any more until we're both more collected."

"It's not fair for you to ask me to give up these children!"

"Very well; it's not fair. But I ask it just the same."

"Then—"

"After all, they're only a dozen or so strange waifs—"

"No. Let's not talk any more. Not now—"

"I won't. I'm going."

"Good-by." Charlotte has repeated the word dully.

"*Don't* say that—yet," pleads Joseph. "After all, what I'm asking isn't much. You'll—you'll see that. . . . I'll be waiting for you to send for me—when you do see it."

The door closes after him. From the other room Bridget appears with Tina, dressed for the street. Charlotte has gathered the child in her arms for a good-by kiss. There is to be no nursery tomorrow, Bridget reminds her. Tomorrow is Saturday and Charlotte is to "jump the broomstick" on Tuesday.

Charlotte is on her knees with Tina in her arms. A servant has come to announce that the dressmakers are waiting for her. They've brought the wedding dress for the last fitting.

"Shall I say you are coming soon, miss?" the servant asks.

"I suppose so," Charlotte answers, her voice flat.

Tina has wandered to a music-box on the table and set it going. Now she is dancing child-like to the tinkling tune.

"Come, Tina; kiss me good-night again, child—"

Charlotte has gathered the little girl into her arms, as the curtain falls.

THIRD EPISODE

It is several hours later. The lamps and candles are lighted in the James Ralstons' Gramercy Park drawing room, and a fire burns in the fireplace. Dinner is over. Delia Ralston and Mrs.

Mingott are waiting the coming of the men from the dining room. Delia is busy under one lamp with her embroidery. Mrs. Mingott is idly turning the pages of a photograph album and studying the portraits through a pearl-handled magnifying glass. The photographs include one of the first Ralstons to arrive in America—"a stubborn, middle-class Englishman who came to the colonies with every intention of living for a bank account instead of dying for a creed," according to Mrs. Mingott. "All our old families were not founded by gentlemen. A great many people came to this country to get on, and for no other reason. And they *have* got on. That's why you married a Ralston, and why my mother married one. And that's why they and their kind have imposed their own rigid ideas on society wherever they've settled and prospered."

Delia has managed to get her way with her own particular Ralston, even to having dinner at six o'clock in place of at noon. She wouldn't let James kiss her for two days—until he agreed to the change in hours—that is how she managed that particular problem.

The talk turns to Clem Spender. Aunt Carrie knew all about that affair. She had watched it from afar, and she is just as well pleased that Delia did not marry Clem, although she is willing to admit that had she been in Delia's place she probably would have succumbed to the Spender charm.

"He's never been back since my marriage," reports Delia, fingering the cameo she wears around her neck. "He brought me this. It's sweet, isn't it? He knew I liked cameos. It's Psyche and Eros."

"Very pretty," admits Mrs. Mingott without enthusiasm.

Clem, it appears, has married a rich cousin and lives in Rome. He has never done much with his painting. The spark's gone, Mrs. Mingott reports.

"Poor Clem . . . Poor dear boy!" mutters Delia, staring at her cameo.

Dr. Lanskell is first to come from the dining room. He is a trifle exhilarated and wants music. If Mrs. Mingott can still sing he would like to hear her. They have gone to the music room to try again an old song.

A moment later Charlotte, wearing an ermine tippet over her cloak, comes through the door. Finding no one she goes to the door of the music room and signals to Delia. When Delia comes she suggests that the door to the music room be closed that they may talk freely.

Charlotte is troubled. It is possible she may not marry Joe.
Even at this late hour she may decide that it is better to change
her mind than to do something she thinks is wrong. She wants
Delia's help. She wants Delia to convince Joe that he is wrong
in insisting that she shall give up her nursery. She cannot give
it up. There really is no danger of disease. There is no danger
of anything—except the everlasting Ralston cautiousness.

"You must try to be sensible, Chatty," insists Delia. "Whether
you agree with the Ralston ideas or not, you must realize that
you'll never have another chance like this. . . . After all, one's
own babies have first claim."

"That's just it," answers Charlotte, firmly. "How can I give
up *my own baby?*"

"Yours—yours?" Delia is frightened, but tries to find refuge
in a pleasantry. "Which of the waifs do you call *your own baby,*
my dear?"

"I call my own baby *my own baby!*" answers Charlotte,
dramatically clutching Delia's wrist.

Slowly, painfully, the story is told. The mysterious trip
South; the help that Dr. Lanskell gave; the love of a man; the
child who is living with Negroes; Charlotte loves Joe now; she
isn't marrying him just to have money for her child; she loves
him and would have loved his children. But she cannot give up
her own child!

"No, no; of course not," Delia agrees, stroking her cousin's
head. "Of course not; we must think of some way—"

CHARLOTTE (*through her sobs*)—If you could talk to Jim . . .
You can make Jim do what you like—and if he could talk to
Joe—and persuade him that no harm can come of my going on
with my nursery—

DELIA—Don't cry like that. I'll do my best to help you, one
way or another.

CHARLOTTE—Oh, Delia, if only you can!

DELIA (*after an instant, but not very hopefully*)—If you
could tell Joe—

CHARLOTTE (*lifting her head, sitting up very straight*)—I
couldn't. He'd never forgive me. He must never know.

DELIA—No; you are right. You couldn't tell Joe. But—
(*Recovering her poise but hesitating to remind* CHARLOTTE *of
memories which must be painful.*) We're talking as if—as if—
you didn't have to—to consider the—the person who—who took
advantage of you. After all, he's your child's father.

CHARLOTTE (*drily*)—No one took advantage of me. I was lonely and unhappy. He was lonely and unhappy. . . . Besides, he never thought of marrying me. . . . People don't all have your luck. . . . But, even if he had wanted to marry me, mamma would never have consented. And so—one day before he went away—

DELIA (*as she stops suddenly*)—He went away?

CHARLOTTE—Yes.

DELIA—*Knowing?*

CHARLOTTE—What was going to happen? No. I didn't know myself then.

DELIA—But afterwards?

CHARLOTTE—No, never. He never knew. He never came back.

DELIA—But shouldn't he have known? After all—

CHARLOTTE (*impatiently, as* DELIA *pauses*)—Why? He couldn't have helped me. He was in no position to marry anyone. Besides, he didn't love me. He loved someone else.

DELIA (*abruptly*)—Where did he go?

CHARLOTTE (*evasively*)—Oh, what does it matter? You wouldn't understand—

DELIA—You won't tell me who it was?

CHARLOTTE—Why should I? I've never told anybody.

DELIA—How can I help you if you don't trust me?

CHARLOTTE (*after an instant, stubbornly*)—Haven't I told you all you need to know?

DELIA (*her voice hard with suspicion*)—Where did he go—out of the country? To—to Italy?

CHARLOTTE—Oh!

DELIA—Then it *was* to Italy . . . It was Clem Spender!

All compassion has gone from Delia's face. Her voice is hard. She does not want to hear the story the sobbing Charlotte would tell her. But hear it she must, on Charlotte's insistence. The story of Charlotte's love for Clem; of his interest only in Delia; of the time Delia, at her wedding, had asked that Charlotte should look out for Clem; of Clem's later coming to her for sympathy; of her great pity for him—

Charlotte has never been sorry; not really sorry; Clem had gone away not knowing of the child; there is nothing left of anything that Charlotte ever felt for him except her baby. She cannot marry Joe if it means giving up her child.

"If you can't persuade Joe that I should be permitted to go to my nursery every day, so I can see my own baby and watch over her, you can at least help me to get out of this marriage as decently as possible without hurting him."

Charlotte is willing to marry Joe without his knowing. She will make everything up to him in other ways and she will take the risk of his ever finding out. She loves Joe—differently—as Delia must love Jim differently—

Delia cannot make a hurried decision. She must have time. She will not let Charlotte go out again. Charlotte must go to Delia's room and stay there until Delia can think of something to do.

"Whatever happens, that child shan't stay with those Negroes," promises Delia, decisively. "I do promise you *that!*"

"You promise that?" echoes Charlotte, a new light coming into her face. "You do promise—to save her?"

"Yes; but I must manage it in my own way. Will you wait? Or shall I send for a coach to take you home now, and see you tomorrow?"

"I'll wait."

Delia has been pacing the floor, "agitated by her memories, her jealousy and the need for action in behalf of Charlotte." James and Joseph let themselves in from the music room and close the door after them. Mrs. Mingott and Dr. Lanskell are still working with their duet.

The young men are eager to talk with Delia alone. Joseph, as James reports, has a problem to settle and wants Delia's advice. Delia admits she knows the problem, having already talked with Charlotte, but is not sure of her advice. Charlotte, Delia reports, is determined to go on with her nursery work, she is not one to care greatly what people will say, and she is not likely to change her mind whatever anyone says to her.

Joseph cannot understand how Charlotte can be more attached to her paupers than she is to the man she is going to marry. He is willing to give her whatever she needs but that, as Delia explains, is not enough. It is her personal care that Charlotte insists she shall give the children. Joseph would even be willing to stretch a point and let her spend some time at the nursery every day, were it not for her health. The Ralstons have all been apprehensive as to Charlotte's health. Her trip to the South, for one thing, and the fact that her father died young, gave them cause to be apprehensive. Can Joseph reasonably permit Chatty to go on taking unnecessary risks? And yet, Joseph has about made up his mind to let Charlotte have her way.

Let her care for her paupers if she wants to. Nothing is important enough to come between them now.

Now it is Delia who is apprehensive. This decision cannot be.
Joseph cannot marry Charlotte, however forgiving he may be.
Charlotte is not well, even as he suspects. She has been cough-
ing blood again. Charlotte cannot marry anyone—

"But—why—why wasn't I told at once?" demands Joe, his
face paling, his voice unsteady.

"Because such—such things aren't easy to tell," answers Delia.

"Delia's right, you know," speaks up James. "If poor Chatty's
ill again marriage isn't to be thought of. Better face the music
now than later. Better get it over with—"

"But I—I can't give her up. I can't—" Tears have filled
Joe's eyes. "I must see her. Where is she?"

"You must let me see her first," cautions Delia. "I must tell
her I've told you. This is hard for her, too, you know, and you
must be tactful and wait until she sends for you."

The concert is over. Aunt Carrie has gone to her room. Dr.
Lanskell is in to say his good nights. It is Joseph's chance to
question the doctor. He would have confirmation of Chatty's
condition. It is true, isn't it, that if Chatty were not cured of
her lung fever when she went South, and if she were coughing
blood again, her condition would be serious, wouldn't it?

It would be a very bad sign, Dr. Lanskell admits, though he
has thought Chatty was perfectly well.

That is enough for Joseph. He starts for the door. He wants
to be by himself, he says, but James follows him out.

Now it is Delia who confesses. She knows what Dr. Lanskell
knows of Charlotte's trip South. Because of that she (Delia) has
decided that Charlotte should not marry.

"You've taken a great deal on yourself, Delia Lovell," warns
Dr. Lanskell.

"You think I've done wrong?"

"I think it's a sacrilegious thing to lay so much as a finger on
another person's destiny," answers the Doctor.

It is Delia's defense that Charlotte had begged for her help;
that she could not let her deceive Joe by marrying him; that she
would make it up to Chatty by taking her child—Chatty's and
Clem Spender's child—and caring for it herself.

Dr. Lanskell will agree to this only on condition that Delia
shall not take Chatty's child from her. Chatty had left Tina
with Jessamine, who had been her own nurse and whom she knew
she could trust.

"No doubt you mean well, my dear, but each of us has the right to love and suffer, to lie or to tell the truth, after his own fashion. And now that Charlotte has put herself at your mercy in telling you her secret—be generous to her. Don't make her your enemy through a mistaken sense of duty. Above all, don't try to take from her the one thing which is really her own. . . . I won't wait for Jim. . . . Good night."

Dr. Lanskell has gone and James has come in with a decanter of brandy and three small glasses. He had left Joe all broken up. He thought perhaps Delia would be needing a drop of brandy, too. James is very proud of Delia tonight and she is not averse to his being nice to her. She is in his arms wondering what he would have done if she had had to tell him about herself what she had told Joe about Chatty. James can't think what he would have done. He does think, however, that it is a good thing for Chatty now that she has her children.

"I suppose a woman must have children to love," supposes James; "somebody else's if not her own."

"Yes, I see no other happiness for her," craftily admits Delia, leaning against his shoulder. "You know, darling—you and I should see that she keeps her babies."

"But suppose she is sent away—to the South again?"

"She may not get worse immediately. And if she isn't, may I tell her that you and I will see that she has money for her nursery, so she won't have to beg of grandmamma? I could give it to her out of my pin-money?"

"Not from your pin-money! Never! But as much as you want from me for Chatty and her paupers."

"Dearest!" Delia has settled farther into James' eager arms, and responds to his kiss. "We might even manage to let her take that little girl—the one she's grown so fond of, to live with her in a place of her own; couldn't we manage that?"

"I don't see why not, if Chatty would like it," agrees James, expansively.

"Oh, she would! I know she would!" answers Delia.

James has gone and is to send Charlotte down. When she comes, eagerly, anxiously, Delia tells her of the plans made for her. She could not have married Joe and had Tina with her, therefore Delia has broken off the engagement. She had told Joe that Charlotte had been coughing blood again, and that had frightened him away.

"He's dreadfully unhappy, of course, but he accepts your decision—" reports Delia.

"My decision!" Charlotte repeats, ironically.
"Well, *mine* then."

CHARLOTTE—But if *I* don't accept your decision—? If I tell him the truth?

DELIA—I thought you couldn't bear to have him know the truth.

CHARLOTTE—But if I should tell him, and he should say he'd forgive me—!

DELIA—If there'd been any hope of that, would you have come to me?

CHARLOTTE—No; but you drive me to think of such follies—

DELIA—Give up follies, Charlotte; and try to realize what it's going to mean to you to make a home for your child. That's what you wanted most, isn't it? To have her with you, and take care of her yourself?

CHARLOTTE (*desperately*)—Yes—but—

DELIA (*impatiently; in a tone of finality*)—Well, I've done what I could. I've made Jim promise to give you a little house of your own and arrange for Tina to live with you. I can't do more; and if you're not satisfied, I must wash my hands of both of you. Unless you're sensible now, *I can do nothing for you or your child.* Remember that.

CHARLOTTE (*goes to the window and stands, considering a long moment. Then she turns back, and speaks at last, brokenly*)— You said—together always—Tina and I . . . ?

DELIA—Yes. I said you should have Tina with you always.

CHARLOTTE—Just ourselves?

DELIA—Just yourselves.

CHARLOTTE—In a little house of our own?

DELIA—Yes.

CHARLOTTE—You're sure, Delia?

DELIA—Quite sure, dearest. Jim has promised because he thinks you're ill and we don't want you to be lonely.

"Then, as Delia waits, Charlotte, crying softly, catches up one of the skeins of bright silk which lie with Delia's embroidery on the table, and drawing Joe's ring from her finger, slips the threads through it; for an instant she stands, still hesitating, letting the ring swing from her hand. Then suddenly she tosses it upon the table, and without looking at Delia, turns to gather up her cloak and bonnet as the curtain falls."

FOURTH EPISODE

A winter evening in 1853, fourteen years later, finds Charlotte and Dr. Lanskell sitting before the fire in the Delia Ralston drawing room. It is the same room, but its appearance is changed. "The movables are now of the Victorian instead of the late Empire style."

Charlotte, "looking much more than fourteen years older, has passed into a different generation; wearing a severely plain dress she sits near the fire knitting. Her hair, now gray, is drawn tightly back from her colorless face in which even her once fine eyes and bright lips have grown indistinct; and she is the typical old maid in appearance as well as manner; harsh and inclined to be tyrannical."

The years appear to have touched Dr. Lanskell but lightly. His step is a little slower, and he nods occasionally before the fire. In the music room there is again the sound of singing. This time it is a quartet of voices, and they are accompanied by a piano in place of a spinet.

Presently a young woman comes from the music room to bring Cousin Chatty her scarf. She is "Dee" Halsey, Delia's married daughter, an unspoiled, self-possessed and mature young woman. Dee knows that it was Tina who was supposed to bring the scarf, but she knew, too, that Tina would forget. She has gone back to the singing now.

"When you consider how pleasant life is in this house, for young Tina particularly, you must feel a deep satisfaction in having managed to give her such a home," ventures Dr. Lanskell.

"If Tina's life has been pleasant in this house, it's Delia who's made it so; not I," answers Charlotte, drily.

"We won't talk of your own sacrifices for the child, Chatty; but Delia's done her best, too."

"Her best to spoil her," snaps Charlotte, in a passion of resentment; "from the day she brought us here to live, after Jim's death twelve years ago! And now that Delia's own girl is married, there's nothing—nothing at all—that Tina doesn't have, or can't have, by asking for it."

Whoever is playing the piano breaks off abruptly. The young people and Delia come into the drawing room, Delia with Dee on one side of her and Tina on the other. She has an arm around each. They are followed by John Halsey, Dee's husband, and Lanning Halsey, his cousin, tall, good-looking young men.

The young people are going to a ball and are, according to

Charlotte, much too slow about starting. They have no right to keep the horses standing so long on a cold night. It is Lanning and Tina who are always the late ones.

There is some discussion about Tina's failure to put in an appearance at the evening's end, too. Twice Dee and John have waited for her when she could not be found and they are not going to do it again.

Tina can see no harm if she prefers to stay and come home with some of the neighbors. She is also getting tired of being continually found fault with by Cousin Charlotte.

"You think mamma spoils me, but she doesn't!" says Tina, angrily, turning on Charlotte. "It's just that *she* understands me—while you don't. Mamma knows what it is to be young and have everyone fond of her—while you—"

"I must see that what's left of that Madeira doesn't find its way to the kitchen."

"I don't want you ever to speak to Cousin Chatty like that again," warns Delia, deeply agitated.

Tina is not impressed. Sulking prettily, she settles herself on the arm of Delia's chair and continues a report of nice things she has recently heard:

"Mr. Sillerton Jackson told Lanning you were lucky to have such a child—now that Dee's married, and you'd be left all alone with just Cousin Chatty in the house, if it weren't for me," says Tina.

"Of course I'm lucky. I know that . . . Cousin Chatty and I are both lucky to have you."

"And even if I'm not your very own, like Dee, I feel as if I were. And I can never thank you enough for taking me in and treating me as if I were."

"Cousin Chatty wouldn't have come to live with me after Dee's father died, unless I'd have you too."

"That's well enough to say, but would you have wanted her without me? Tell the truth, mamma!"

"I wanted you both. Now run and put on your cloak—"

"I'm going—"

They get away finally, with many good nights said and others left for Cousin Chatty. Tina has her key and she hopes Cousin Chatty will not make another excuse to wait up for her. . . .

Delia has stood in the hall, waving a final good-by to Tina. Now she comes idly back into the room and finds her embroidery. Soon Charlotte has come to take her seat at the other side of the table, resuming her knitting. The silence is heavy between them. . . .

Charlotte is the first to speak. She would have Delia know that she noticed her scolding Tina for being disrespectful. But Delia need not mind. Charlotte knows that Tina thinks of her as an old maid: "A ridiculous, narrow-minded old maid." There is reason for that. Charlotte always rehearses whatever she is going to say to Tina so she will remember to sound like an old maid cousin talking, and not like a mother.

Charlotte has a feeling that Tina has changed recently. It is more noticeable since Lanning Halsey has been coming around so often. Charlotte has no objections to Lanning, save that there is talk of his going to Paris to study architecture and has no money. Certainly not enough to marry on. When she thinks that every mother has warned her son that Tina has neither a fortune nor a name it makes her doubly anxious. She is determined that Tina shall have her chance. But what if Tina, at twenty, should decide not to wait—

"Charlotte! Do you know what you are insinuating?" demands the shocked Delia.

"Yes, I know."

"But it's outrageous. No girl who is decent—"

"Even nice girls are not always what you call decent," calmly insists Charlotte.

"I can't imagine what is to be gained by saying such things—even by thinking them. Surely you trust your own child," protests Delia.

"My mother trusted me. . . ."

Charlotte has decided to wait up for Tina. It may be foolish, and she knows that when she was Tina's age and living with Grandmother Lovell she would have resented anyone waiting up for her. Still she thinks she will wait.

Delia has gone upstairs. Charlotte has resumed her knitting before the fire. Now, thinking out loud, she is practicing what she is going to say to Tina if she is late. It is as she imagines an old-maid relative would speak—

"What, Tina? You *walked* home with Lanning? You imprudent child—in this wet snow! And without your boots, too. You shouldn't do these things. . . . You were always a delicate child. . . . Do you know how late it is? I sat up because I couldn't for the life of me remember if you'd taken your latch-key. But don't tell your mamma, or she'll scold me for growing forgetful, and sitting here in the cold. But I've really been very

comfortable—in fact I was beginning to be afraid I'd slept instead of dozed on the sofa—and missed hearing you come in—"

The curtain has fallen slowly to indicate a lapse of several
hours. As it rises a moment later Charlotte is still sitting before
the fire. Her candle has burned low and the fire is no more than
a glow. She is dozing lightly. The sound of the closing of the
outside door awakens her. Hastily she gathers her things together and steps through the door off the drawing room, a second
before Tina and Lanning come in from the hall.
Lanning has followed Tina into the room and closed the door
softly behind him. Now he comes forward nervously and takes
Tina in his arms, obviously to her pleased embarrassment. It is
quite wicked of them to act so, she thinks. Particularly as Lanning is going away—and she wishes he weren't.
Lanning wishes, too, that he were not going, but he isn't worth
his salt in any regular business. If he were, things might be
different with them. He has followed Tina to the fireplace and
she is at some pains to keep him from taking her again in his
arms.

LANNING—Goose! Don't be angry with me. You know I
can't marry anyone, yet. . . . You're shivering. I shouldn't
have made you wait until the carriages were all gone. Sit down.
Let me see if your feet are wet. (*She sits, as he commands.
He drops on his knees, crying out, contritely.*) Heavens, Tina!
You shouldn't have walked in these things. Why didn't you
tell me?
TINA (*in a very little voice*)—I loved it—the snow—and the
moonlight—and the icy trees in the Square—and being with you
—at last—all alone. What are you doing?
LANNING—Taking off your wet slippers and stockings. I loved
it, too; but I should have taken better care of you, just the same.
TINA (*trying to draw away her foot*)—Don't—!
LANNING (*gayly, tenderly*)—Be still, little foot! Why are you
running away when I'm trying to make you all warm again?
TINA—Silly!
LANNING (*setting her bare foot on his knee*)—Now for the
other little foot; both little feet have to be warm—or little Tina—
(*He strips the other foot of its stocking, holds it in his hand, and
looks up at her with sudden alarm.*) Oh, Tina—what if you
should die! You won't, will you—while I'm away? Promise
not to.

TINA (*leaning forward and catching his face in her hands; simply*)—I shall want to. Because you've gone.

LANNING—Dearest—! (*He lifts his face; she bends hers; they kiss. Then she draws back, and his head falls on her knees.*)

TINA (*gravely*)—That's the first time; and I shall never kiss anyone but you—ever—

LANNING—I've no right, but—

Lanning has lifted his face and Tina has bent again to his lips. Suddenly the hall door opens and Delia, candle in hand, stands in the door in her dressing-gown. She speaks sharply to Tina, in a nervous, embarrassed tone, trying not to look at them, and shortly dismisses Lanning. The good nights are strained and awkward. Lanning would thank Delia for not scolding him—

Now Charlotte has heard and come from the other room. She is trembling with anger. It is not Lanning who should be scolded, but Tina. Any boy would act the same with the same encouragement. But it is not to happen again and Delia should see that Lanning does not come again.

Tina would protest such an order; begs Delia not to listen. Lanning also has something to say. Whether he is forbidden the door or not does not matter greatly. He is sailing shortly.

"I'm sorry I've made Miss Chatty so angry with you," says Lanning to Tina. And then, turning to Delia: "It didn't seem a crime to *me*, for Tina to stay on after John and Delia left without her. . . . It didn't even seem a crime to come in with her, and see that she took off her wet shoes. I warmed her feet with my hands—and *that* didn't seem a crime, either; but I apologize, if you think it was a liberty. As I said before, it wasn't her fault, and I hope she'll not be made to suffer for it. Also, as I said before, it can't happen again. Good night. . . . And good-by, Tina."

Tina is sobbingly protesting that Cousin Chatty has driven Lanning away, and Charlotte is answering that no one could have driven Lanning away if he had really cared. Delia is inclined to agree with this statement, but Tina will not have it so. She could have made Lanning care if Charlotte had not driven him away. Charlotte had no business to meddle—

"I'm going, mamma," sobs Tina, as Delia sharply sends her to her room; "but before I do, she's got to know that I'm sick of her fault-finding and her spying and her meddling! *You* can say what you please to me, because you understand me, and I love you; but she's only a sour old maid who hates me because I'm young—and attractive—and alive; while she's old and hideous and dried up—and has never known anything about love! I won't have her interfering with my life, I tell you! I won't have it!"

Delia has dropped into a chair and covered her face with her hands. Charlotte stands by "as rigid as a statue." Tina, starting upstairs, turns at the door to beg her mother to come to her later.

This, announces Charlotte firmly, when Tina has gone, is the end. She can see the mistake she has made and will proceed to remedy it. She and Tina will leave. She will find a place where they can live plainly among plain people, where they will be unknown and their story unknown. Delia has done all that she could. Charlotte is grateful, but—

"Oh, don't let's speak of gratitude!" protests Delia. "What does it matter whether you're grateful or not? It's Tina I'm thinking of—"

"Of course it's Tina you're thinking of," snaps Charlotte; "Tina and Clem Spender!"

And when Delia protests that she has not thought of Clem Spender in years, Charlotte continues, dramatically:

"You've thought of him, whether you knew it or not. A woman never stops thinking of the man she loves. She thinks of him years afterwards in all sorts of unconscious ways, in thinking of all sorts of things—a sunset, an old song, a cameo on a chain—! (*Then she breaks off with a short laugh, and her voice drops to a whisper as she continues:*) *I* know. I've thought of him too. Only tonight it wasn't Tina and Lanning Halsey here— it wasn't those two I saw from the window—sauntering through the icy weather—like lovers in a midsummer glade, not feeling the wind and the cold at all. I saw *us*—long ago—walking home to a darkened house—on just such a night . . . when I didn't know whether there was snow beneath my feet—or daisies. . . . (*Then harshly.*) I suppose you found them in each other's arms. I was afraid to come in—afraid I'd see us!"

Again Delia would protest, would prevent Charlotte's saying such things, until she is stung to a defense by Charlotte's insisting that she and Tina were taken in by Delia only because Delia wanted to give Clem Spender's child a home.

"And suppose that's all true!" answers Delia, at a white heat. "Supposing I couldn't leave Clem Spender's child to the mercy of chance? She's yours, too. And to take her away now—from the life you made such a sacrifice to give her—would be too cruel. Too cruel—to her! Even more cruel to her than to me."

The argument appeals to Charlotte, though she continues to fight against it. She can see no happiness for Tina with Delia, however much is done for her. Delia's answer to this is that while she has not done all she could for Tina, she proposes to do so now. She will adopt Tina legally. She had thought of doing so from the day Tina had begun calling her "mamma" because Dee did.

"Now I realize that if Tina is to be happy, her position must be made unassailable, both financially and socially, and this is the only way I know of doing it," says Delia.

"It isn't clear to me that your adopting Tina would help so much," answers Charlotte, still hostile.

DELIA—You mean you don't see what a difference it will make if I give her my name—the Ralston name, and my money—the money my mother left me? My own child has all she'll ever need from her father—

CHARLOTTE (*cutting her short*)—No, no! I refuse.

DELIA—You refuse? You dare to sacrifice Tina's happiness to your pride?

CHARLOTTE (*bitterly*)—My *pride!* (*Then brokenly.*) *My* pride. . . . What pride have I, except in my child? And that I'll never sacrifice. No, no—it's gone on long enough—this—this mistake! I'm going to take her away.

DELIA (*desperately*)—You are going to sacrifice her, then? Sacrifice her to your desire for mastery! When she might have everything she wants, and you say you want for her—even Lanning Halsey for a husband; a home of her own. (CHARLOTTE *bends her head suddenly, and covers her face with her hands.* DELIA *is quick with her advantage; continuing:*) It's as she said; he will love her if she wants him to. She can make him love her, if there's no reason why he shouldn't. And if she has money of her own, and my name, the Halseys won't find her such a bad match for their son after all. . . . Give her this chance! What mother wouldn't? And if Lanning takes her away from us both, in time, it won't be like really giving her up. Couldn't we just go on loving her together? (*She has dropped down upon the sofa, beside* CHARLOTTE, *and put her arm about her shoulder. Suddenly* CHARLOTTE'S *rigid attitude relaxes, and she reaches for* DELIA'S *hand and lifts it to her cheek. During the instant of silence between them which follows, the door at the back is opened by* TINA, *who stands on the threshold in a dressing-gown. She speaks uncertainly.*)

TINA—Mamma, aren't you coming up? I've been waiting for you.

CHARLOTTE (*in a flat voice, motioning* DELIA *away*)—Go on up with her. . . . I'll come presently. . . . Good night. (*Without a word* DELIA *rises, and takes her candle from the table; then she joins* TINA *in the doorway and the two disappear up the stairs;* CHARLOTTE *watches them without moving as the curtain falls.*)

FIFTH EPISODE

The Ralston drawing room has been prepared for a wedding. There is a lace-trimmed, flower-decked altar in front of the fireplace; there are lilies and dwarf orange trees on each side of the doorway at the back. Most of the furniture has been taken out, and there are groups of small gilt chairs later to be set in place. Every gas jet has been lighted, giving the room an unusual brightness. It is an evening in June, 1854.

Lanning and John and Dee Halsey are there. Aunt Carrie Mingott is commenting upon the scene from her position on the sofa beside Dr. Lanskell. Tina, excited as a bride should be, is everywhere. Just now she is recalling the order of the march to the altar, and stopping to kiss her darling but tired mother. Tina, thinks Mrs. Mingott, is almost too happy. It makes her fearful for the child.

Now Charlotte has come for a final survey of the situation. "She is a grim figure in the pleasant scene, in her dark dress and black apron; when she speaks abruptly, it is with a kind of dull, impersonal satisfaction and to no one in particular."

Everything has been done that can be done tonight, decides Charlotte. There will be more to do in the morning; more doilies to see about; more ice cream, seeing all the Philadelphia connections are coming. . . .

Mrs. Mingott has retired; John and Dee have slipped out into the garden for a walk in the moonlight and to remember their own wedding; Tina is back from saying good night to Lanning. . . . Tina is ready now to go to her room, if Delia will promise to come up later and say good night to her—

"Because tonight . . . it's as Aunt Carrie said," admits Tina. "I *am* much too happy, mamma. And I'm just a little afraid, though I pretended I wasn't. Lanning says we've all been straws whirling about on a sunlit torrent, ever since mamma adopted me, Dr. Lanskell, and his parents decided he might get married, whether he had a profession or not. . . . They've been sweet to me, but if mamma hadn't cared enough for me to give me her name and the money, they'd not have wanted him to care either."

"Nonsense, darling."

"Oh, I *know*, mamma. . . . I know what I owe you. I owe you everything."

Charlotte, from the stairs, attracted by Tina's happy voice, pauses to listen.

"Everything," continues Tina. "Even Lanning; and I'm glad. I used to wonder who I really was; but I don't care now." She has turned to Dr. Lanskell, who is getting ready to leave. "I'd rather have *her* for my mamma than anyone in the world."

Charlotte comes on down the stairs and turns abruptly toward the back of the house. She can still hear Tina going on happily, about her love for Delia and Delia's love for her; of the greater interest Delia had taken in Tina's wedding than she took in Dee's.

"Your Cousin Chatty has been just as much interested as I've been," protests Delia; "and just as generous to you."

"Yes; what do you think, Dr. Lanskell," agrees Tina. "Cousin Chatty gave me all her grandmother's jewels. . . . And my wedding veil. She wanted me to wear the wedding dress that she was going to wear once, too, and didn't; but I told her I wanted to wear mamma's—the one Dee wore last June. It's India mull, and I knew mamma wanted me to, though she wouldn't say so. It seems odd to think that anyone ever wanted to marry Cousin Chatty."

Charlotte has gone. Delia tries to get Tina to go to bed but she still has much to talk about to Dr. Lanskell. There's the beautiful cameo her mother has given her; the very first thing she remembers as a child; a beautiful lady had held her on her lap, and kissed her and put the cameo around her neck—

Tina has gone upstairs now, and Dr. Lanskell is leaving. There is a moment for reminiscence. The Doctor suspects that Chatty takes Tina's happiness as a direct result of Delia's generosity, and Delia admits that she has sensed Charlotte's gratitude ever since she had decided to adopt Tina.

If it had been a mistake for Delia to interfere with Charlotte's marrying Joe Ralston she has paid for the mistake, Dr. Lanskell agrees.

"Chatty's been jealous from that moment in her nursery when the child went to you, instinctively, as to a mother. And no jealous woman was ever easy to live with."

Delia is seeing Dr. Lanskell out when Charlotte comes ,nto the
room again. She stands for a moment before the altar and then,
hearing Delia starting up stairs, calls sharply to her. Delia admits she is on her way to Tina's room; she thinks a word should
be said to the child the night before her marriage on her new
duties and responsibilities; there will be no time tomorrow—

"I understand; but please understand me, too, if I ask you
not to," interrupts Charlotte, harshly.

DELIA (*with an effort at patience*)—I confess I don't understand you, Charlotte. You surely feel that on the night before
her wedding a girl ought to have her mother's counsel.

CHARLOTTE—Naturally. That's why *I* must be the one to talk
to Tina tonight. Just tonight *I* am her mother!

DELIA—Charlotte! *You're* not going to tell her that! Not
now!

CHARLOTTE (*with a short laugh*)—Do you hate me for it as
much as all that?

DELIA—*Hate* you? What a word to use between us!

CHARLOTTE (*somberly*)—It's the word that's been between us
since the beginning. You've hated me from the moment you
knew I was the mother of Clem Spender's child. And there's
been hate between us ever since. Because his child is mine instead of yours!

DELIA (*wearily*)—Yes. I realize now that you believe I've
hated you because you have hated me. Hated me in spite of
everything I've tried to do for you.

CHARLOTTE—Nothing was for me—it was all for Clement
Spender and his child!

DELIA—You said that once before. Well, suppose it was!
Our lives are spent now; and so is Clement Spender's. But Tina's
is ahead of her; and it seems to me that if you loved her as I
love her you couldn't stand here, before her bridal altar, and talk
of hatred. Not here, not in this room, where the very air is
full of her happiness tonight! It's wicked of you, Charlotte!
Wicked!

CHARLOTTE—No, that's not true! I'm not wicked. I wouldn't
have done to you what you've done to me. From the beginning
you've deliberately divided me from my daughter! Do you suppose it's been easy all these years to hear her call you *mother?*
Oh, I know it was agreed between us that she must never guess!
But you needn't have perpetually come between us! If you

hadn't, she'd have had no one to turn to but me. She'd have had to love *me!* But for all your patience and generosity, you've ended by robbing me of my child. That's why I can talk of hatred here before this altar tonight! And that's why—before she's his tomorrow: tonight, just tonight, she belongs to me! That's why I won't let her call anyone else *mother* tonight!

DELIA—Very well; I won't go up to her; it's your right, not mine. And if you want her to know the truth about her birth, it's your right to tell her that, too. As you say—I have intervened in your life—and it's natural you should hate me for it. And that I should be sorry. I've played my part, done my utmost—but I realize now that all my efforts to insure the girl's happiness have ended in failure— (*She breaks off, unable to say more, and sits down weakly, covering her face with her hands, to hide sudden tears.*)

CHARLOTTE (*after watching her an instant with brooding eyes*) —I suppose you imagine it will be a tragedy for Tina—to learn that she's my daughter. Well—we shall see.

Dee has come from the garden. She brings a small bouquet which she had planned to take to Tina. She remembers the night before her own wedding a year ago; how her mother had come to her and everything she had said was lovely, and how it helped—

"I went to sleep certain that whatever might happen to any girl, love and marriage should be a part of it," explains Dee. "Then, just as I was almost asleep, Tina knocked and came in, and gave me a bouquet—like this—that she'd just gathered for me. And she looked at me so oddly, and said, '*You'll* always be happy, Dee,' in such a way that I knew she was afraid *she* might never be. . . . That's why I was glad you adopted her, mamma— although she's a flighty little thing in many ways. She was thinking of Lanning then. And it would have been unfair to have taken her in and then not have stood by her, the way you have— to the end; so she could be happy, too."

Delia has taken the bouquet and promised to give it to Tina. There are tears in her eyes and a happy secret in her heart, for Dee has also told her that John is already making plans for his son's wedding and that one day she will be a grandmother.

Now Charlotte has come again. "There is something quite different in Charlotte's face; she looks at peace." She has come to say that she could not, after all, tell Tina.

"If she's never really belonged to me, perhaps it's because her father never really belonged to me, either," admits Charlotte. "Both were yours. He loved you; so she loved you, too. So I—I decided to say nothing."

Charlotte had stood outside Tina's room and tried to think of something she could say to her without Tina's guessing. There was nothing. Delia is the mother Tina wants.

"After all, she was mine when she was little," Charlotte remembers.

"Come with me, Charlotte—we'll go together—" Delia is holding out her hand. Charlotte does not take it. She has caught a glimpse of Tina in the doorway. She turns quickly and leaves the room.

Tina has come to see what is keeping her mother. She has been waiting. Delia explains that she has been talking to Dee, and that Dee had brought the bouquet. Tina is happy that Dee did not forget.

"Do you want to do something that will make me very happy?" Delia asks, impulsively.

"Anything—you darling!" answers Tina.

DELIA (*discouraging with her tone and a gesture* TINA's *impulse to kiss her*)—Then find your Cousin Charlotte. She's just gone into the garden. And when you've found her, remember this: she didn't marry a man who loved her very much, and who would have given her everything she wanted—because she wouldn't give you up. That's why she's an old maid.

TINA—Oh—! (*With just a hint of reproach in the question.*) Why didn't anyone ever tell me that before?

DELIA—Sometimes people don't think; sometimes they are selfish. But remember—and try to make her glad of her choice tonight. Without telling her that I asked you to.

TINA (*in a low miserable voice*)—And I've always been so horrid. . . . (*She starts toward the window, and stops, as* DELIA *puts out her hand.*)

DELIA—There's one thing more—

TINA (*turning*)—Yes?

DELIA—When you go away tomorrow—at the very last moment, you understand—after you've said good-by to me, and to everybody else—just as Lanning helps you into the carriage . . .

TINA—Yes?

DELIA—Lean down and give your last kiss to Cousin Charlotte.

Don't forget—the very last.

TINA—I won't forget. . . . There she is now, at the end of the walk. (*Then calling from the window.*) Cousin Charlotte—Cousin Charlotte—

She disappears as

THE CURTAIN FALLS

ACCENT ON YOUTH
A Comedy in Three Acts

By Samson Raphaelson

THERE had not been many samples of that popular form of polite theatre entertainment known as high comedy offered during the Fall of 1934. In September Dame Sybil Thorndike had brought over from London John Van Druten's "The Distaff Side" and had done well with it. But for the most part the successful plays were rugged when they were not rough.

Holiday time, however, brought two of the higher comedy type that depend both on wit and worthiness of dialogue as well as the inventiveness of the playwright and the skill in characterization employed by the players. One was S. N. Behrman's "Rain from Heaven." The other Samson Raphaelson's "Accent on Youth."

Raphaelson, previously known for his racial comedy, "The Jazz Singer," and two honorable attempts in comedy writing, "Young Love," which Dorothy Gish, James Rennie and Tom Douglas had played in 1928, and "The Wooden Slipper," in which Dorothy Hall and Ross Alexander were cast last season, found himself in competition with an extensive list of Christmas week authors. As a result his "Accent on Youth," brought in Christmas night, was rather neglected. For several weeks thereafter, too, the comedy attracted no more than casual attention. When it did begin to build an interest the results were highly gratifying. The run was continued well into the spring.

This is a play stemming from the familiar professor's love story and bachelor's romance type of plot. Intelligently treated, it is a formula almost as sure as that involving the lowly but triumphant Cinderella.

Steven Gaye, the playwright hero of "Accent on Youth," has his study in a penthouse apartment in New York. It is a pleasant room, "has many books, comfortable chairs and everywhere the feel of a civilized, highly individual personality."

On the particular October afternoon that the play opens there are three persons in the Gaye study. One is Frank Galloway, "a rather elegant actor of about fifty-five"; another a Miss

Darling, "an actress of about fifty," and a third, Dickie Reynolds, "an athletic, smartly dressed actor of about twenty-six."

All three are reading play scripts. The clicking of a typewriter in an adjoining room is presently interrupted and Linda Brown comes into the study. The readers pay little attention to her. Miss Brown "is twenty-six, dressed quietly, looks like a secretary, is a secretary." She goes smartly to a library table, arranges a sheaf of letters and envelopes she has brought in with her, takes a checkbook from the drawer and prepares to write checks to go with the letters. When the telephone rings she answers it with business-like promptness, telling a Mr. Grindel that Mr. Gaye is out of town, and a Mr. Benham that Mr. Gaye is taking his afternoon nap.

Miss Darling is the first of the three readers to finish her script. She did not have to read the third act because she isn't in that. She likes her part, she tells young Mr. Reynolds. Not only is it Steven Gaye at his best, but it permits her to play herself—just a decent, old-fashioned woman.

Reynolds is also pleased with his part—a smart young athlete. However, Reynolds would like to be sure that he gets the girl in the end. He hasn't read that far. Miss Brown should know.

Miss Brown does know. Yes, the young athlete gets the girl. Genevieve Lang will probably play that part. But, to Miss Darling's dismay, the husband in the play does not return to his decent, old-fashioned wife.

"But he must," protests Miss Darling. "We've been married thirty years—he's left me for a young girl—the young girl goes off with a young man—he's *got* to come back to me—it's not a comedy if he *doesn't*."

That, explains Miss Brown, is just the point. It is not a comedy. This "Old Love" is a tragedy.

Both players find it difficult to credit such a statement. Steven Gaye has never written anything but comedies. And certainly any story in which the boy gets the girl, and an old man runs off with a young girl must be comedy. If it isn't it must be dirty, according to Miss Darling.

DICKIE—It's not dirty if you marry her. If an old man falls in love with a young girl and marries her legally, there's no law against that.

MISS DARLING—Try and tell that to a theatre audience.—And besides, *this* man doesn't marry the girl—he deserts his devoted wife and *runs off* with the girl—everybody will sympathize with *me.* (*Turns to* LINDA.) Don't you think so, Miss—uh—

DICKIE (*volunteers*)—Brown.

MISS DARLING—Miss Brown?

LINDA—I hope not. If they do, the play will be ruined.

MISS DARLING—What!

LINDA (*almost maliciously*)—The audience should hate the wife, love the husband, laugh at the boy—

DICKIE—Laugh at me?

MISS DARLING—Hate me!

DICKIE—Have you ever seen me on the stage?

MISS DARLING—What kind of audiences do you think we're going to have—degenerates? To hate a good wife!

LINDA (*eloquently*)—*Anybody* can leave a bad wife. That's easy. *Anybody* can write a play about it. Everybody does. But it takes a *man* to leave a *good* wife. And it takes a man to write about it.

GALLOWAY (*slamming manuscript on the desk*)—Young lady, will you be good enough to tell Mr. Gaye that I have read his play from cover to cover—and I have never been so grossly insulted in my life. (*He starts for his hat, gloves and umbrella.*) Good afternoon!

LINDA (*going after him*)—Oh, Mr. Galloway—please—you mustn't go! Mr. Gaye will be in any moment. (*With sublime confidence.*) After he has talked to you about it, you'll get down on your knees and thank him (*Takes his hat and puts it back on table.*) for the greatest rôle in your career! (*This doesn't thrill* GALLOWAY.) Please, Mr. Galloway.

GALLOWAY—I couldn't trust myself to stay. (*Turns to others.*) If I played this thing, my career would be over. I've played butlers, tramps, murderers, and fools—but never a lecherous old man!

LINDA (*genuinely astounded*)—Lecherous! How can you say that! (*With exaltation.*) He's a glorious, courageous man standing just this side of sixty, rebelling at convention, surging under the last rhythmic leap of youth in his blood.

GALLOWAY—Young woman, there never was such a man.

LINDA—Yes, there was—and is.

GALLOWAY—Where?

LINDA—Everywhere. The world is full of him. You're one! And if you don't play this part, Mr Galloway—

The door of Steven Gaye's bedroom has opened and Mr. Gaye appears. "Gaye might be anywhere from forty-five to sixty. He has all the ease of a man of the world and all the susceptibilities of an artist. He wears a business suit. He has a pipe in his hand. He is in a very quiet, grave mood."

Miss Linda has returned quickly to her clerical duties. In reply to his queries she reports the work done. He turns then to the actors and is well pleased with their enthusiasm for the play. Both Miss Darling and Mr. Reynolds are ever so pleased with their parts and quite excited about the "different" treatment Gaye has given them. Their echo of Miss Linda's opinion is obvious.

"You know I've been through the throes of nineteen productions," declares the pleased playwright. "I've worked with more actors than I can remember—but never in all my life have I met three actors as brilliant as you. I want to thank you for a new experience, no matter what happens to the play."

Even the elderly Galloway is satisfied with his part. Satisfied but puzzled. That does not surprise Gaye. He admits that he is puzzled, too. There is, for instance, that love scene in the first act. It is beautifully written—

"I think it's the best thing I've ever done," admits Gaye.

"I'm not criticizing the writing," repeats Galloway, reaching for an explanation of his reaction. "I just wonder if I—you know, after all I am sixty—in fact I'm a little over sixty—and me making ardent love to a young girl in beautiful language and frankly admitting that my wife has never done an unjust thing—"

"I agree with you, Galloway."

"On the other hand there's a poetic something in the play—and if a man can catch it with a high heart, with a grandeur of soul—"

"That's what I thought when I wrote it. I'm fifty-one myself; I can smell sixty. And when you're sixty, you're an old man. Personally, it doesn't terrify me. I've had a great time, married, divorced, had sweethearts—no children, but nineteen plays—not a bad substitute. . . . If *I* behaved like that fellow, I'd consider myself an idiot.—You see, I tried to catch the poetry of a man facing old age. I tried the impossible. Poetry is young or it's no good. I visualized a man with guts enough to be unafraid of seeming ridiculous—surging under the last rhythmic leap of youth in his blood. . . . But I'm getting my doubts. You see— it all depends on the actor who plays the part. If he can catch the imagination of the audience—"

"I've played Shakespeare, you know."

"And very well, too."

"Gaye—I think I'd like to try it. I'm beginning to get what

you're after."

The playwright is still in a state of doubt. He has talked Benham, the shrewdest producer on Broadway, into producing "Old Love," his actor friends are agreed it is a good play, and yet he still has his doubts. He asks each of the actors to take a script home and let some members of their families read it. See what red-blooded young America thinks of it—and then they will have another talk.

Gaye is still wondering about the play after the actors have left. He paces the room for a moment. Then he takes Linda away from her work that she may read him that first-act love scene again. He is holding a second script as Linda begins—

" 'I'm old enough to be your father—almost old enough to be your grandfather.' "

GAYE (*interrupting*)—I'll read it. You read the girl's part. (*Reads.*) "I'm old enough to be your father—almost old enough to be your grandfather. I'm sixty. In five years do you know what I'll be? Sixty-five.—When I was young don't you think I wanted you? You just didn't happen to be around, that's all. You came thirty years late. . . . Do you think I'm going to let time cheat me? You came late—but not too late. I want the five best years of your life; but I'll give you my five best years for them. And when it's over, it will be easy for you—because I'll be too old to suffer . . . and you'll be thirty."

LINDA (*reads*)—"I'll—I'll be a queen."

GAYE (*reads*)—"Think of all I've saved up for you—the accumulation of the years—all the trails I've traveled so I can show you the scenery—the wines I've bottled so that you can taste them now—the bitternesses I suffered so I could distill a sweetness fine enough for you. You'll be giving me your youth —but I'll be giving you my life." . . . Can you imagine Galloway saying that?

LINDA—Yes, I can.

GAYE—So can I, as a matter of fact. But when you actually *see* him—or any other old man—

LINDA—It would make me never want to look at a young man again.

GAYE—No, Linda—no. Imagine Galloway alone in a room with Genevieve Lang. Imagine five hundred people peeking through the transom while he talks to her like that.

LINDA—I couldn't. They'd tip-toe away, ashamed of themselves for eavesdropping.

GAYE (*takes glasses off and holds them*)—Not when they've
paid a three-dollar scale for their tickets, they wouldn't. They'd
leer, they'd sneer; they'd think—"the old boob, why doesn't he
settle down in a rocking chair with his silver-haired wife and
dangle his grandchildren on his knee"—and then they'd yawn,
between dirty laughs.

LINDA—I hate audiences.

GAYE (*putting glasses into case and in pocket*)—You mustn't
hate audiences, Linda. Hate human beings if you want to, but
not audiences. People are drab, they're petty, they spend their
days serving each other and loathing each other. But in the
evening—(*He rises and walks toward* LINDA, *then circles the
chair, to end at desk*)—after they have dined, when they get into
street cars, subways and taxis and come together in the theatre,
when the lights go out and the footlights go on—in other words
when they become an audience—they cease being human; they
become divine. I am a playwright—life is nothing to me. It
belongs to the workman, to the poets, to the politicians. I worship at one shrine, the theatre. I must be true to one God—my
audience. . . . What are you writing?

LINDA—What you just said. You might use it in a play.

The Gaye butler, Flogdell, "a person of distinguished bearing
in his late fifties," announces the arrival in the hall below of Miss
Genevieve Lang. It is her first visit to this apartment. "The
last time we saw her was when we were living at the St. Regis,"
Flogdell informs his master. "That was four years ago, sir."

"Do you think we'll like her for the part?" Gaye would know.

"I think she is eminently suitable, sir. She has unction, technique, she'll fill the balcony—"

"In that case, shall we show her up?"

"Very well, sir."

Linda has taken her work back into the other room when Genevieve Lang arrives. Genevieve is "a very attractive woman, very
smartly dressed. Her face is neither too sweet nor too hard."
She refuses to let Gaye bestir himself in greeting her. She wants
a moment in which to take in the room before she concentrates
on the "second nicest man I ever knew."

"Who's the first nicest?" demands Gaye.

"I knew him four years ago—his name was Steven Gaye,"
answers Genevieve, taking off her hat.

Genevieve is interested in knowing how Steven happened to
think of her for the part of his heroine. He is frank in confessing

that the idea was his manager's. Still, he was enthusiastic about the suggestion. He thinks Genevieve is a hell of an actress. Genevieve thinks the part is a hell of a part. But—

A memory of their last meeting creeps in to interrupt the discussion of the play. She can remember having been insane over him. He can remember having been absolutely mad about her. They both recall that they were all set to go to Paris, tickets bought, staterooms engaged, meeting planned for midnight on the boat. Then—

Steven, finishing his packing, got the most hilarious idea for a play he had ever had. He simply had to write it, and write it at that very moment or he would lose it. He cut off his telephone and went to work.

"But there was nothing to keep *you* from answering my radiogram," Steven protests. "I'd have come on the next boat. . . . What happened when you got my message?"

"I jumped into the ocean and I never was seen again," answers Genevieve.

A moment later she has added, dreamily, that he really was a very attractive man—four years ago. Four years do make a difference. Fifty-three, after all, "isn't quite the age to make a girl's heart go pitty-pat."

"Speaking impersonally—as an elderly man of the world to a young woman of the world—at what age would you say a man ceased being—well—just where would you draw the pitty-pat line?"

"Roughly—at forty-nine."

"So that's what you don't like about my play?"

"Your play can't help it—it's that kind of play . . . 'Old Love.' "

"And I can't help it—I'm that kind of man—old man."

Genevieve would change this suggestion of creeping depression. Audiences will probably like "Old Love," even though she doesn't.

The subject has changed to one of immediate plans. What is Genevieve going to do? Wait for another play? Genevieve doesn't know. She might suddenly decide on a trip. She often does, being mildly insane. Gaye thinks of Finland. Has she ever been to Finland? They say Finland is a marvelous place. Why shouldn't they try Finland?

"What about your play?" she asks.

"I hate the goddam play," explodes Gaye.

Genevieve has leaned over and given him a long kiss. She smiles as she raises her head. Her explanation is simple.

"I wanted to see what it would be like," she admits.

"How was it?"

"Not bad. . . . Do you really mean that about Finland?"

"Passionately."

"Do you expect me to believe that I, or any other woman, could make you hate your play?"

"Of course not. I knew the play was all wrong before you came."

Genevieve happens to know that the "Ile de France" is sailing at ten o'clock. Steven would call Linda and have Genevieve make the reservations, but Genevieve doesn't believe in trusting so completely in secretaries. She has her passport and she thinks she can be ready by ten.

A moment later Gaye has taken her in his arms and kissed her. This time there certainly is a pitty-pat reaction. Inopportunely Linda appears with Mr. Gaye's five-o'clock pills. Mr. Gaye promptly tosses the pills, box and all, into the waste basket. Genevieve is troubled. Steven may have only been experimenting. Steven is troubled, too. He is afraid Genevieve has only been acting. But again they are agreed that Finland should be tried. Genevieve will rush back to her hotel, get the tickets and telephone him later about dinner.

Now Gaye has called Flogdell and instructed him to pack his things for Finland. Flogdell agrees that the adventure promises to be quite exciting. "At this time of year you will find the climate still mild in Finland," he contributes. "The days will be getting shorter, but there will be autumn flowers. I think you will require your complete wardrobe for Helsingfors is a remarkably cosmopolitan center, and you will also find—"

Gaye has interrupted excitedly to call Linda. He would dictate some last minute letters. One to Benham, saying that by the time it is received Gaye will be on the "Ile de France" on his way to Southampton, with Finland to follow.

"Forget 'Old Love,' dash, and save yourself a lot of headaches," he dictates. "Nobody cares about that old fool, anyway. . . ." He has moved gayly around Linda, patting her shoulder as he passes. "What do you think of it, Linda? I'm quitting! I'm going to live! For the first time in my life I've stopped being a playwright—I'm a man, that's what I am, I don't mean maybe."

" 'Nobody cares about that old fool, anyway,' " Linda repeats, her eyes on her notebook.

GAYE—Yes. Period. Bill, Bill, Bill, dash, I've retired. Period. . . . I really have, Linda. What a wonderful feeling! (*He*

*picks up one of the copies of the play from coffee table and drops
it into the wastebasket. Indicates a row of books on a shelf.)*
There are my collected works, nineteen comedies. I'm a success,
and I've got money. Why do I have to write tragedies? You
stick your head in the clouds, what does it get you—a crown of
thorns. You put your feet on the ground, what does that get
you—bunions. . . . Make a note. Advertisement. House for
rent, eight rooms, view of East River. . . . I've retired! . . .
What's the last thing I said?

LINDA *(reads)*—Bill, Bill, Bill, I've retired. Period.

GAYE—I've never lived before. Period. I'm going to do all
the things I was always about to do. Period. I'll learn golf. Exclamation point. It keeps you out in the open air. Period. Then
there's all those books I was going to read some day. Period.
And all the people I was going to meet, dash, think of it, colon,
you could kill all the actors, writers and directors in the world,
comma, and there'd still be fishermen in Capri, comma, peasants
in France, comma, bandits in Sicily. Period. And I wouldn't be
surprised if I found romance in Finland. Two exclamation
points. . . . Why, Bill, this is something you ought to do, too.
Period. To us Nature has never been anything but a set against
which dramas have to be played. Period. . . . Just think of it,
Linda! *I don't give a damn about that first-act love scene.* I
don't give a damn about *any* scene. I never have to worry again
about lines, characters, transitions, curtains—will *this* get a laugh,
will *that* get a tear. I don't have to worry about audiences. To
hell with audiences! I've retired! . . . What have you got?

LINDA *(reads)*—To us Nature has never been anything but a
set against which dramas have to be played. Period.

GAYE—I'm afraid this letter'll be over Benham's head. . . .
Kill it. I'll send him a radiogram from the boat. *(Sits on sofa.
LINDA shuts her book. There is a long pause.)* And, Linda—
you're discharged—with my compliments, my gratitude, my affection. . . . Now, we'll have to give you a nice present. What
would you like most in the world?

LINDA—Nothing, thank you.

GAYE—Come, come, Linda. I'm serious. Would you like a
car, a trip to Europe, maybe a trousseau? Haven't you got a boy
friend?

LINDA—No.

GAYE—Don't be silly. You're a fine-looking girl. You'd make
any man a splendid wife. Tell you what—write yourself a check
for six months' salary. (LINDA, *after a moment's thought, goes*

to desk, takes the checkbook out and begins to write.)   Sure.
You retire, too!   Here's an idea: go down to Saks' and order
yourself a complete outfit.   Charge it to me.   Then take a trip
somewhere.   Take your mother along.

LINDA—I haven't got a mother.

GAYE—Oh, of course.   I forgot.   I'm sorry. . . . Take a girl-
friend along.   Two nice young girls, Honolulu, ukuleles—Yellow-
stone Park, cowboys and Indians—see America first. . . . Or
maybe Havana.   It's romantic—

Linda has been writing the check.   She brings it to him now.
It is for the forty-one dollars and sixty-five cents she feels is due
her.   That is all she wants, all she will take.   For the rest—he
will find his letters finished, his manuscripts in order, his notes
filed away—

For a moment Gaye hesitates about signing the check.   He is
plainly annoyed.   Suddenly he makes up his mind, the check is
signed and handed to Linda with curt ceremony.   Linda takes
the check and then calmly proceeds to reëstablish their relations.
They are through now, she assumes.   He is no longer her em-
ployer, and she is no longer his secretary.   They are just two
human beings, a man and a woman.   That being admitted, Linda
proceeds—

"Well—before I say good-by, I want you to know that I love
you."   She is folding her check and putting it in her purse.   "I
want you to know that the three years and two months I've spent
with you have been the most wonderful, painful, happiest years
I've ever had or hope to have.   You hardly knew I was on earth—
but you've given me more than you could have given your wife,
or any other woman, or your friends, or your audiences.   I had
you when you were alone.—You've spoiled every man I know for
me.   You did that in the first month.   I don't think I'll ever
forget a single look of your face, a single word you said.   You've
done a terrible thing: you've opened my eyes, my heart, my brain
—and you never touched me.   It hurt—every bit of it hurt—how
could it not hurt, it was so beautiful.—And if you think I can
walk out of this house quietly—that you can smile me away
with money and a few new dresses—if you think I can walk out
of here without wanting to kill you, without wanting to cut my
initials into every day you're going to live, you're crazy.   (*A
pause—she controls herself.*)   Good-by—and try to forget me!"

Now Gaye, stunned for a second, has rushed after Linda and
brought her back into the room.

"Hey! Let me look at you!" he shouts. "You strange creature! You lovely creature!" He has lifted her head and is staring into her eyes. Linda is embarrassed now and would start
again for the door.

"Don't go away! Let me look at you some more!" Steven
persists. "I'm not patronizing you. I'm *seeing* you. You're
grand. . . . If I only were thirty-five, or forty, instead of fifty-
one. . . . What do you want of me, Linda?"

LINDA—Nothing.

GAYE—That's not true.

LINDA (*breaking*)—I know it's not true.

GAYE—What do you want of me, Linda?

LINDA—I don't know. . . . Everything. . . . Anything.

GAYE—Sit down. (*He gently leads her to the sofa, then paces
the room thoughtfully.*) Of course. . . . Of course. . . . Most
natural thing in the world. Where do you live, Linda?

LINDA—West Tenth Street.

GAYE—Apartment?

LINDA—Yes.

GAYE—And your parents are dead. You went to college or
something, didn't you?

LINDA—Three years.

GAYE (*musingly*)—Why, certainly. A girl like that—I come
into her life—and it happens. Suddenly, like a banquet, she gets
Broadway, literature, personalities, and me. . . . Linda, I know
you won't believe it—but you'll get over this.

LINDA (*despairingly*)—Will I?

GAYE—Yes, you will. You're young, and you made yourself
ready. The world is full of fascinating people—much more fascinating people—much more fascinating than I am.

LINDA—You know that isn't so.

GAYE—I suppose there's something in what you say. Am I
physically attractive?

LINDA—Yes.

GAYE—Funny, when you get right down to it. I can't think
offhand of a man—you know—who could make you forget me.
I'm beginning to see what a spot you're in! I *am* a unique combination—witty, sensitive, imaginative, worldly, gay and yet with
a feeling for tragedy. . . . And I know myself too well. I've
been around too much, to deny that I'm charming.

LINDA—You're wonderful.

GAYE—Dammit—I know I am! . . . But, Linda, my sweet,

I don't love you—I don't love anybody.

LINDA (*suffering*)—I know that. You don't have to tell me—I know that.

GAYE—And if I did love you. Suppose for the sake of argument, I fell in love with you. It would be worse. Picture a man of fifty-one—why, it's like the situation in "Old Love." . . . (*He stops, completely smitten with an idea.*) Oh, my God. . . . (*He turns to her, staring at her but not seeing her. He leaps to his feet.*) Linda—get your notebook. (*She takes up notebook and pencil.*) Ready?

LINDA—Ready.

GAYE (*thrilled, boyish*)—God, Linda, this is marvelous! How can I ever repay you? Do you realize what you've done for me? Angel—you've saved my play!

It is all quite simple as he sees it now. He cannot understand why it has not occurred to him before. The girl makes love to the older hero! That whitewashes the old man completely!

"I'm in love with the play all over again—aren't you?" he shouts, gleefully.

"I always was," she answers.

Now he would go back to the scene she herself has given him. He wants that speech, just as she delivered it, beginning with "Good-by, but before I go I want you to know—"

The light goes out of Linda's eyes. She understands now what has happened. It is only the playwright who has been moved. But she tries honestly to remember what she said. There are tears in her eyes as she repeats it. In his excitement over the new twist for the play Gaye does not notice. He is going on with the dictation, picking up a word here and there as he remembers Linda's farewell.

"The years I've spent with you have been pure hell—every hour, every second, every day. Period. But I'd rather have that hell than ten heavens with any other man. Period. Lousy! Too melodramatic. You said it better. I'm too excited. Kill the last speech—"

He starts again. Now he remembers a phrase or two. " 'You opened my eyes, my heart, my brain—and you never touched me.' "

Linda remembers now, but cannot write. On he goes, recalling the words she spoke. He notices that she is not writing. She tries again to get control of herself. She repeats his last line—

"It hurt—every bit of it hurt—how could it not hurt, it was so beautiful—"

Suddenly he is conscious that she is breaking. Now he has gone to her with comforting words He is a brute, he admits, but that shouldn't be news to her. . . .

The telephone is ringing. Linda answers. It is Genevieve Lang. Gaye takes the phone. He is looking steadily at Linda as he places his free hand over the mouthpiece.

"Linda, dear—do you love this play as much as I do?" he asks.

"More," she answers.

"Do you think this new scene is going to make a difference?"

"Yes, I do."

"Will you type it?"

Linda has taken up her notes and gone into the other room. Gaye is still staring abstractedly at the phone when the clicking of the typewriter is heard. Suddenly he takes the plunge—

"Hello, Genevieve," he calls. His expression changes to one of dismay. "You did? . . . Yes. . . . Yes. . . . The what? . . . The bridal suite on the 'Ile de France!!' " He has taken a deep breath. "Well, I tell you, Genevieve—I don't know if you'll quite understand this. . . . No, no, no. Listen. You'll go through the ceiling when you hear this . . . but on the other hand it means a wonderful part for you— (*He stops as if cut by a whip. He stands stricken as he listens to a harangue.*) Yes. . . . Yes. . . . Yes, but— (*Finally, in a defiant summing-up:*) Yes, Genevieve—that's exactly what I'm trying to tell you! (*Talking very fast.*) And all I ask is that you let me read you that scene when it's written. It changes *everything*—now listen, Genevieve, I switch the scene from Galloway to you—it's *your* scene, and at the same time it makes that old fellow as romantic, as colorful, as exciting, as any— Genevieve! Hello! Hello! . . . (*With mixed emotion he puts the telephone back on the receiver. He pauses a moment and then pulls the bell. He goes to desk and replaces his passport.* FLOGDELL *appears in the doorway.*) Flogdell.

FLOGDELL—Yes, sir.

GAYE—I'm not going to Finland.

FLOGDELL (*after a split-second's hesitation*)—Very well, sir.

(FLOGDELL *goes.* GAYE *stands quietly. Throughout the last few minutes we hear, in little spasmodic tappings,* LINDA'S *occasional typing. . . . Now suddenly* GAYE *hastens to the waste-basket, rummages through its contents, unearths the little box of*

*pills, takes one of them and follows it by a drink of water from
the glass which* LINDA *had put on the table. As he does this*

THE CURTAIN FALLS

ACT II

It is seven months later. Steven Gaye's study has undergone
certain attractive changes, indicating a woman's presence. A
piano has been added to the furnishings; also a framed photo of
Linda Brown. There is a new hand-painted lamp shade.

It is eleven o'clock Monday morning. The room is empty until
Flogdell shows in Frank Galloway. Mr. Galloway looks a bit
bedraggled. He wears a dark top coat, but underneath he is still
in evening clothes. It has, Mr. Galloway admits, been rather a
night. By his count he had danced three young women under
the table. Now he realizes that he should be at home, but one
is usually wise, under such circumstances, to telephone first. It
would seem a particularly wise thing for Mr. Galloway to do, seeing that he is still under the impression that this is Sunday. He
has lost a day somewhere.

When Galloway does try to telephone he is informed that Mrs.
Galloway is not interested. She has not been trying to get him,
nor will she come to the phone. The speech, with explanations,
which he has rehearsed so perfectly, is of no use to him. His situation, he feels, is more or less desperate.

"I stand before you a dying man," Galloway admits to Flogdell, moving away from the phone; "cast out of my home, dis-
owned by my wife— And for what? Is it my fault that I have
created a new romantic type? Can I help it if women fancy
me?"

"These things are chemistry, sir," suggests Flogdell, comfort-
ingly.

Galloway would like to talk with Steven Gaye, but that is not
possible, either. Mr. Gaye is not at home. Mr. Gaye has gone
to call upon Miss Brown at her apartment. Flogdell would not
take the liberty of calling him there.

"Why? Who is Linda Brown?" demands Galloway, warmly.
"An insignificant little accident of the theatre—type casting!—
Did you read the reviews? Did she get a single good notice?"

"She didn't get any bad ones, sir."

"—And I—I taught her to act. I sweated and slaved over her.
And what do I get for it? I'm kicked out of Steven Gaye's

house."

It is Flogdell's suggestion that a Turkish bath might help, but Galloway does not appear to be impressed as he leaves. . . .

Linda Brown, in a street costume, "looking extremely chic and expensive from head to toe," comes into the study, slamming the door behind her. She is plainly excited and she is looking for Gaye.

Mr. Gaye, Flogdell still has reason to believe, is at Miss Linda's apartment. He had gone there about a half hour before, after having tried to telephone Miss Linda all night. It was Mr. Gaye's intention, reports Flogdell, to break down the door of Miss Linda's apartment this morning. Yesterday? Mr. Gaye had dined at home yesterday. He was alone and victim of an air of melancholy, a strange brooding loneliness—

Linda does not blame Flogdell for his loyalty to his master. He has reason to be loyal. She hasn't. The expected has happened and she has come for her things. There are seven photos of her in that house and she wants them. The piano can stay— it may be Mr. Gaye will continue with his lessons. But the photos and her knitting and the lampshade—

Linda is making the collection when Steven Gaye comes excitedly into the room. He stops short at sight of her. He is not surprised to find her gathering her possessions. He had expected that. He finds her attitude fairly astounding, however.

"Well—haven't you anything to say for yourself?" demands Linda.

"Haven't *I* anything to say for *myself?* What for instance?" answers Gaye, curtly.

"Well—for instance: Good-by—I don't love you—and I hope I never see you again. We agreed—didn't we?—to be brutal, to be honest, the moment the moment came."

"Are you crazy?"

LINDA (*putting her things on the piano*)—Of course I'm crazy. Don't pretend you just discovered it. And *you're* crazy. That's why, when a time like this comes, we shouldn't lower ourselves to the level of sanity. I demand that we keep our hate on the same high mountain where you put our love.—Do you know what day yesterday was? It was the ninth of May. Seven months ago yesterday I was nothing to you—and you were everything to me.—You discharged me. I was willing to go. I told you I loved you, but it was an exit speech. I didn't ask for mercy. You dragged me back. *You* begged *me* to rehearse in your play.

I never wanted to be an actress.—Well, I became an actress. Then, on the opening night, you said you fell in love with me. I didn't believe it. I knew you too well. And then—then I did believe it.—We promised each other it would be breathless and magical, or nothing at all. We swore, as we sat in the dawn, that the moment the glory stopped, whichever one of us the glory stopped for would cut like a knife. You said, "The wonder that's in us is our love—and when that wonder goes, let's not live kindly, sweetly, disgustingly, with just each other." Did you or did you not say it?

GAYE—It's rather naïvely phrased, but I said it.

LINDA—Did you or did you not mean it?

GAYE—Of course I meant it.

LINDA—Then how could you—how *could* you—yesterday, on the seventh monthly anniversary of the day you discharged me—when I had bought a beautiful evening gown for two hundred and seventy-five dollars just for our dinner together—*how* could you break our date!

GAYE—Did you read my note?

LINDA—Of course I read it.

GAYE—I think it was very clear.

LINDA—What was clear about it? You walked into my apartment at six-thirty—

GAYE—And I found your young leading man in your bed.

LINDA—And you left.

GAYE—What did you expect me to do?

LINDA—If you had the least bit of poetry in you, you would have waited for me to come out of the shower.

GAYE—Would you have liked it if you had found me standing there?

LINDA—I would have loved it.

GAYE—You—you would have enjoyed explaining?

LINDA—Explaining? I should have refused to explain!

GAYE—That makes everything clear!—I find Dickie Reynolds asleep in your bed, I tactfully pretend nothing has happened, the three of us go out to dinner, and then, after the theatre, we all have a little night-cap, go to a hotel, ask for a triple bed, say our prayers, and turn in together!

Linda is not impressed. She still demands to know why Gaye has not answered her telephone calls; why he left the note on Dickie's chest. What if Dickie had read it! Linda is not angry, she is just unhappy because of Steven's loss of faith in her.

That Gaye denies. His faith is as strong as ever, but he is too worldly-wise not to know what has happened. Youth has again called to youth. Linda has turned quite naturally to her handsome young leading man. Gaye, if Linda must have the truth, is dying of jealousy.

But, Linda demands, couldn't he see that Dickie was drunk? Couldn't he see—

She has come to him now and he has impulsively thrown his arms about her. She is crying a little as he kisses her.

"Steven—do you love me?" she asks.

"What do you think?"

LINDA—I think yes—and I love you. (*They kiss.*) I'm tired of asking you to marry me. But we must let the world know we belong to each other. Otherwise, why shouldn't a young man come to see me?—If you're afraid of the word mistress, let's say we're engaged. I'll never sue you for breach of promise.

GAYE—But I *want* young men to come to see you—every one of them. The field is free: that's the way I want it. I didn't buy you in a market place.—And you don't have to tell me what Dickie was doing in your bedroom. I know nothing happened. I'm positive of it. All night long I was telling myself that. The reason I called you on the telephone so many times, and the reason I went to your apartment was only to tell you that it's all right, and please to forget it.

LINDA—Oh, Steven—darling— (*They embrace again.*) Let's never do things like this to each other again, shall we?

GAYE—Never! (*They are quiet in each other's arms.*)— Darling—

LINDA—Yes, dear?

GAYE—What was it Shakespeare said about men dying, but not for love?—Well, it might be true about men over twenty-five, and men under fifty . . . But I could die for love of you.

LINDA—. . . I'm so glad.

GAYE—I'm not. I see no peace ahead.

LINDA—Since when do you want peace?

GAYE—Since I've found adventure.

LINDA—Do you—really?

GAYE—No, I don't, *really.*

LINDA—I'm glad, because you're never going to have peace. You're an artist—you're never going to be middle-aged. You're going to stay young until suddenly one day you'll die, and on

your death-bed you'll say to the doctor, "What am I dying of?"
And the doctor will say, "Old age, you fool."

GAYE—Darling—

LINDA—Yes, dear?

GAYE—What did he do—just walk in?

LINDA—Who?

GAYE—Dickie.

LINDA—Oh, you angel, haven't I told you about that yet?

GAYE—Not that I can remember.

LINDA—He walked in unannounced, and very tight. I was
surprised—(*She takes his handkerchief and wipes rouge from his
lips.*) you know Dickie never drinks or smokes. And I couldn't
figure out what he came for, because I don't think I've exchanged
more than fifty words with the boy during the six months we've
been in the show.—He talked about the traffic, and I talked
about the weather—making a grand total of maybe sixty words—
and then suddenly, like a gentleman of the old school, he fell
asleep in his chair. Well, it got time for me to dress for dinner,
so I went in to dress. When I came out from my shower, there
on my bed was your note, and under it was Dickie.

Gaye has taken a jewel case from his pocket. In it is a bracelet he had intended as yesterday's anniversary present. These
monthly anniversaries, thinks the pleased Linda, are becoming
far too expensive, what with Gaye's presents and her new dinner
gowns—

Dickie Reynolds is calling. Linda gathers her things together
and disappears. Dickie has come to warn Gaye that he is quitting the play. Dickie is fed up with actors and acting. He has
bought himself a ranch in Wyoming with some money his father
left him. Hereafter he intends going in strong for the outdoor,
he-man sort of life. Everybody in the theatre is crazy. Especially the women. What actress is normal? How many of them
are willing to marry, settle down, have children and take some
interest in the next generation. How man—

Flogdell has announced Linda Brown. Dickie thinks he had
better be going, but Gaye urges him to stay. Dickie should
know Linda better. She's the best secretary Gaye ever had. He
thinks perhaps he made a mistake making an actress of her. . . .

Linda is most gracious. Surprised to hear that Dickie is leaving the show, but thinks perhaps they can get Oscar Feroni for
the part. Come to think of it, Dickie must tell Gaye all about
the fun he had yesterday in her apartment. Dickie is dumb-

founded.

"Yesterday afternoon?" he repeats, staring at Linda. "Oh . . . So that's where I was!—Gee, Linda, that's terrible. I—I don't quite know what to say. You see, I never drink—and yesterday I bought the ranch and—and the real estate man and I had a couple of drinks—"

"A couple?"

"Exactly two—that I can remember. Did you have any trouble getting rid of me?"

"I don't know. I left you there. You might call on my maid and get the rest of the story." . . .

Benham is on the phone. Gaye has gone to the extension to talk to the manager. Probably something about Dickie leaving the show. He hopes Linda will stay and entertain Dickie until he comes back.

Dickie is not difficult to entertain. He is quite excited once Gaye is out of the room. Linda is his trouble.

"I'm quitting the show on account of you," he says, tensely. "Don't look at me like that. That's the way you've been looking at me for six months, as if I was the wallpaper on the wall. It drove me crazy.—*I remember yesterday.* I didn't buy a ranch.— I had to see you. I couldn't stand it any longer. I took a couple of drinks—I don't know how many—so I could break through that look of yours."

"Dickie—you poor boy—you poor, foolish boy." Linda has moved slightly toward him. "What have I done to you?"

"Nothing. I love you so damn much I can't see straight— that's all."

Linda has recoiled from Dickie as though he had struck her. He stands for a second looking at her, both defiant and afraid. Then he dashes out of the room. . . .

Gaye is back, surprised to find Dickie gone. Linda had let him go, she says, because he wanted to go. Now she wants to talk seriously to Steven. She wants him to marry her. Right away. And when he admits that he is weakening—that he always has wanted to marry her, but felt that first he must be sure she really loved him—Linda is very happy. They are prepared to go to Greenwich the next morning.

It is time for Steven to practice his piano lesson. He has become quite proficient with one of the less complicated Schubert études and—

"Have you ever heard a great artist play the scales?" he calls, from the piano.

"The scales—that's by Beethoven, isn't it?" asks Linda. She has fetched her knitting from the drawer, arranged the cigarettes within reach and is lying comfortably on the sofa.

GAYE—I can play and address remarks to my concert audience at the same time.

LINDA—A dual personality. Steven—you're really doing it nicely. I'm proud of you.

GAYE—What do you make of Dickie, anyway?

LINDA—He's a fool.

GAYE—Funny that he came to see you. (*Pausing in his playing.*) Couldn't he remember why?

LINDA (*on guard*)—Apparently not.

GAYE—Funny . . .

LINDA—I figure he stepped out of the Waldorf Bar, walked a block, looked up and saw where I live— What do you think?

GAYE—Well—it's hard to say. If it were in a play, I'd have a theory; but in real life—well, life never makes sense. (*He turns back to the piano and continues his scales.*) Happy?

LINDA—Blissfully.

GAYE—You know—if I were writing a play, I'd have Dickie in love with you.

LINDA (*startled*)—Why?

GAYE (*still playing*)—It's a better reason for leaving a show than a cow ranch.—Then I'd hint to the audience either that he's not really going away, or that you like him more than you're telling. . . . (*He continues to play.*) But, thank the Lord, I'm a pianist, not a playwright.

He continues cheerfully with his scales as the curtain slowly falls.

At six o'clock that afternoon Flogdell is arranging flowers and generally straightening up the room. Answering the telephone he assures Miss Linda that Mr. Gaye is dressing. Flogdell quite understands the seating plans for the dinner. Miss Linda is to be at Mr. Gaye's right, Mrs. Benham at his left, Mr. and Mrs. Galloway next, and, then—

Gaye has appeared. He is in evening clothes, over which he is wearing a lounging robe. He takes up the telephone as Flogdell retires.

"Yes, darling. . . . Yes, my sweet. . . . No, darling. . . . Yes, my love. . . . Yes, my dearest. Can't you come over now? . . . Of course I want you to look beautiful, but hurry. . . .

It's six now. . . . Six-thirty? Swell. That'll give us an hour and a half before the other guests arrive. . . ."

Gaye is very happy as he leaves the phone—so happy that he is insistent on learning whether or not the returning Flogdell is really his friend. That having been settled to his satisfaction he declares his intention of making a momentous announcement at the dinner which will be the "ultimate test of a gentleman's gentleman."

Flogdell is neither surprised nor distressed. As a matter of fact, he also has been planning to be married—to the housemaid across the street. This, in turn, is happy news to Gaye. In his exuberance he proposes that he and Flogdell do a bit of a dance, and they are waltzing about the room humming "The Merry Widow," when the door opens and Dickie Reynolds appears, dressed precisely as he was when he left and appearing unmistakably distraught.

Dickie had been passing, he explains, and thought he would drop in. He knows about Gaye's dinner to the company. Dickie had not been invited, Gaye explains, because he is no longer a member of the company and had talked as though he didn't longer care for theatre people.

As it happens Dickie is quite anxious to come to the party. Linda is to be there and he must see Linda. He has been trying to see her all day, but she has not been home to him. He might as well confess to Gaye. He is desperately in love with Linda, and has told her so—

"So that's why you quit the show?" says Gaye, thoughtfully.

"Sure, that's why I quit. I couldn't stand it—her acting as if I wasn't on earth—me holding her in my arms every night, and her acting as if I wasn't on earth. . . . Every time I came near her—to tell her—I couldn't."

GAYE (slowly)—But this morning, you could. . . . What did you tell her?

DICKIE—What I'm telling you.

GAYE—You're sure she understood what you were saying?

DICKIE—She heard me all right.

GAYE— . . . What did she say?

DICKIE—I didn't wait to find out. I lost my nerve. I—I bolted.

GAYE—Why didn't you stay? (Savagely.) You damn fool, she'd have jumped into your arms.

DICKIE—Oh, gee—do you really think so! No, you're wrong.

—What's the matter with me, Mr. Gaye? You know me. You're a man of the world—you've lived—you're old enough to be my father. Tell me what's the matter with me.

GAYE (*bitterly*)—Nothing's the matter with you. You've got everything. Youth—and everything. . . . If you want her, go after her.

DICKIE—If it were any other girl. I never had trouble like this before—but she's different. You know her, Mr. Gaye. You've known her a long time. She thinks all the world of you— anyone can see that? She looks up to you.—You've been in love yourself, haven't you?

GAYE—Well—go on. What do you want?

DICKIE—Understanding. I don't know who to turn to.—Let me come tonight. I'll shoot the works the first chance I get. I've got to have my break with her. I never really had it. Every man has a right to have one break, anyway, if he's in love with a woman.—You're a man and I'm a man—and she doesn't mean anything to you— (*Suddenly staring at* GAYE.) Or does she?

GAYE (*slowly*)—Not a damn thing.

DICKIE—Then will you help me?

GAYE—Help you? Hell, I'll give her to you. You want your break—well, I'll hand it to you on a silver platter. She's due here at six-thirty—you know, ex-secretary helping with the place cards. —Well, I'll be gone, and she'll find you— (*Going to the bedroom door.*) The guests don't arrive until eight. That gives you an hour and a half. . . . You should be able to—get your message over in an hour and a half, don't you think?

DICKIE—I—I'll try.

GAYE (*at the door*)—Well—the stage is yours.

A moment later Gaye has reappeared, carrying his hat and coat. If Linda should inquire for him, he says, Dickie is to tell her that he has got a great idea for a play and has gone down to the river to think it over.

Dickie would hold the playwright back. Dickie is worried about what he is to say to Linda. He would have Gaye tell him what to say. He wishes very much he had Gaye's brains. He has the feelings and thoughts, but he can't find the words. He never has been able to find words when he is with Linda.

Now the playwright in Gaye is beginning again to take charge. The idea, he admits, is getting him. He *could* write a love scene for Dickie that couldn't miss, if in her heart Linda really cares a damn about him.

"Gee, Mr. Gaye—would you?" Dickie is flushed with the idea. "Nothing like it has ever been done before," muses Gaye, a little awed at himself. "Of course, there was Cyrano—but this is different. . . . Let's see.—(*Completely the artist now*.) . . . You're sitting here. The door opens. She comes in. At first, she doesn't see you.—What's the matter with me, am I going insane? The hell with you!"

DICKIE—Mr. Gaye—if you've really got an idea, you *must* help me. I know writing is your profession—and if it's money, my father left me fifteen hundred shares of American Tel. and Tel.—

GAYE—Don't interrupt me. . . . I'd be the sap of the world to do it—and yet I can't walk out on it. . . . If Molnar were in a spot like this, he'd go through with it. . . . So would Sheridan. . . . (*He stops short and turns to* DICKIE.) Well, Dickie—you win. Let's shoot the works.—We'll all of us shoot the works. . . . Now look—

DICKIE—I'm sitting here.

GAYE—Doesn't matter where you sit.—She comes in. You tell her, as simply as you can, that you're leaving for Europe tonight on—fake it—say the "Ile de France." Tell her you're all packed. (*Slowly.*) You're going because of her. Whether she likes it or not, she has changed your whole life. She has made life more beautiful, more exciting, more painful. Be sure to get that in.

DICKIE—More beautiful, more exciting, more painful.

GAYE—Right.—There's nothing as dull as just "I love you."—Now, this is a good-by scene. That's what makes it strong. You're going away forever. You're never going to see her again—you're never going to see this country again—all because of her. *She's* never going to see *you* again. . . .

DICKIE—Say, that's swell—she may even think I'm going to kill myself!

GAYE—No, no! No suicide. No hint of suicide. That's unfair—to all parties concerned.

DICKIE—Okay.

GAYE—Now. Carry that good-by scene right to the door.—She'll come to you. Start out of the door. Then turn. Ask her to kiss you good-by.—Think you can do that?

DICKIE—I know I can.

GAYE—All right. . . . The rest is up to you.

DICKIE— . . . Suppose she won't kiss me?

GAYE—She will. Any woman would. It's a good-by scene.

And after that it's up to the actors, not the playwright. The emotion is there, the moment has been created—and your bodies are there. . . . You'll find out all you need to know—we'll all find out.

DICKIE—Mr. Gaye. . . . Gee—you're brilliant.

GAYE—Maybe I am—(*Slowly*)—and maybe I'm not.

Gaye has gone. Dickie has paced the floor restlessly. Then Linda bursts in, calling happily to Steven. She finds Dickie instead and is not pleased. If Dickie is to be invited to the party she will not come. She doesn't want to see Dickie. She doesn't want to stay in the same room with him any longer than she has to. She—

Dickie has grabbed her roughly by the shoulders. She will have to listen, he says, but he cannot remember what it was he was going to say. For want of words he draws her closer to him and kisses her lips. She fights him off.

"What's the matter with you—are you crazy?" demands the struggling Linda frantically.

"I love you!" answers Dickie.

"I hate you. Oh, how I hate you!"

"I love you, I love you, I love you."

Again Linda tries to resist. He kisses her again and holds her close. Her resistance weakens. Now she is kissing as well as being kissed. The door opens. Gaye is standing there, wearing his top hat and carrying his light overcoat. The sight of the embracing couple holds him through the kiss. When Linda looks up and sees Gaye she is paralyzed at the sight of him, and speechless.

"Excuse me," says Gaye, walking to the table. "I came for my walking stick." He has taken the stick and gone back to the door. There he turns. They are still staring at him.

"You may not know it," he says, "but that was a curtain line."

THE CURTAIN FALLS

ACT III

Five months later Steven Gaye's study has reverted to its suggestion of bachelor disorder. The piano is gone. There are no photographs of Linda Brown in sight.

It is ten o'clock in the evening. Gaye and Galloway are devoting deep study to a checkerboard while Flogdell is busy mixing

whiskey and soda. This job completed and the drinks served it
transpires that Flogdell is the Galloway opponent, Gaye being
merely an onlooker. Flogdell is not alone playing the game, but
making something of an exposure of Galloway.

The game having been settled in Flogdell's favor, the talk turns
to the Galloway promise to be at home early and from that drifts
to his present work, which is that of writing his memoirs. He
has just passed his childhood period and has been frequently reminded of how thoroughly unpleasant a period it was.

Not so with Master Flogdell. His childhood memories are
among his sweetest ones. Flogdell was very handy with his fists
and proud of his muscles, when he was a lad. They may, if they
like, feel his muscles now. He is also prepared to show them
that, despite his considerable girth, he can still touch the floor
with his fists. At least he could earlier in the day, in his pyjamas.

They have got as far as Indian wrestling, in which Flogdell
also displays his prowess by toppling Galloway quite handily,
and are pouring their nightcaps when Galloway is reminded that
he misses "Old Love" very much. Steven, on the other hand,
is glad it is over.

"That play affected my life. . . . It did something to all of
us," insists Galloway. "Linda marrying Dickie; Miss Darling
getting a Hollywood contract. . . . I thought either it would be
a smash hit, like a Eugene O'Neill play, or a dreadful failure,
like—like a Eugene O'Neill play. But who would have predicted
that it would turn out just a show."

The thought is depressing to Gaye. Nor has he any notion of
writing a comedy as a sequel to "Old Love." He's getting old
and feels it. It is Galloway's idea that Gaye is taking life much
too seriously. He should be getting around more, seeing more
people, traveling more, enjoying life more.

"I've been thinking about it, Frank," admits Gaye, "but every
time I sit down with a map and a travel folder, I realize there's
no trip as beautiful as Act One of a new play."

A moment later Genevieve Lang is announced and Galloway
has gone hurriedly to keep his homecoming promise with Mrs.
Galloway.

Genevieve has just popped in. She was at the opera when she
noticed the date in the program. It was October ninth. The
luckiest day of Genevieve's life, because it was on October nine
that she went to Finland. In Finland Genevieve found a Finn
and brought him home with her. Now she is buying a trousseau
and next Monday Gaye is invited to a wedding. Being in love

has completely changed Genevieve. She thinks Gaye should try
it sometime.

Gaye has tried it, and found love unpleasant. He lost. Genevieve decides she must know more of that story.

"Knut can wait," she says, settling herself for a stay. "It'll do
him good. Tell me about it. When did you meet her?"

"October the ninth."

GENEVIEVE—Oh!—how interesting! . . . Do I know her?"

GAYE (*wearily*)—What's the difference? (*Pause.*)

GENEVIEVE—How's the work?

GAYE—There isn't any. . . .

GENEVIEVE—Now, Steven, love is the greatest thing on earth
and all that—but don't be a baby.

GAYE—I'm not. I'm an old man.

GENEVIEVE—Somehow I can't imagine you losing a girl if you
really wanted to hold her.

GAYE (*savagely*)—I *gave* her away! Why, he wouldn't have
had a chance. But I saw something between them—*he* didn't
know it was there—and I, *I* wrote his love scene, *I* staged it, *I*
gave him the setting—I put the words in his mouth. . . . Well,
I did a good job. And now they're happily married.

GENEVIEVE—Do you think that was very bright?

GAYE—There's no fool like an old playwright. . . . Genevieve,
Genevieve, I always thought when you got older, you got wiser.
Well, it doesn't help. You know what it's all about, but don't
let anybody tell you that lessens the pain.

GENEVIEVE—Steven, why don't you travel? Look what it's
done for me! . . . See new places, new faces—get out in the open
air—play golf.

GAYE (*patiently*)—Listen, Genevieve—I don't like golf.

GENEVIEVE—I'll tell you what—join us at the opera, and then
we'll all go somewhere.

GAYE—I don't like opera.

GENEVIEVE—Well—there's only one thing left for you to do.

GAYE—I don't like suicide!

Suddenly the door has swept open and Linda Brown stands revealed. She is wearing a sports coat over a dinner gown and
she carries a huge bouquet of flowers. For a moment the sight
of Genevieve and Gaye gives her pause, but soon she has swept
into the room with a gay hello and found a place for her flowers
by unceremoniously lifting those that Genevieve has brought from

the vase and putting them in the wastebasket.

"Do you know what day this is?" Linda calls, cheerily, to Gaye.

"Tuesday," he answers maliciously.

"It's October the ninth," she says. . . . "I brought you some flowers. . . . I think yellow goes better in this room."

"Well—!" It is all Genevieve can say. In considerable agitation she recovers her flowers, and the wastebasket, and leaves the room abruptly.

For a moment neither Linda nor Gaye can think of anything to say. Then Linda asks to be taken back. She has been living a life of torture for five months, she reports, and Gaye is the only man who can save her. True, she thought she loved Dickie when she married him. But it all happened so quickly and Steven was so mean about everything—Linda hated Steven that night.

"I could have loved him; I wanted to; I tried," she says, recalling Dickie. "And then came the honeymoon. . . . I never want to go through anything like it again. Oh, Steven, why didn't you tell me what a dreadful thing youth was—why didn't anybody tell me! . . . We went to Santa Barbara. Here's a typical honeymoon day: out of bed at seven—A.M. not P.M.— three hasty kisses, a shower, then we play tennis—what do I know about tennis? Then sweating and limping, another shower, two hasty kisses, and swimming, while I sit on the beach and burn. Did you ever see the rich men's sons in their bathing suits waiting for the depression to pass? They're broad-shouldered, handsome, tan—every one of them was once an All-American something—and ten feet away you can't tell one from the other. . . . And you couldn't tell Dickie from any of them. Then he gets a rub-down and it's time for lunch. Oh, Steven, after sitting with a clean-cut outdoors man and watching him eat vitamins, starches and spinach, you and your pills are a Midsummer Night's Dream.—Going to bed with him was just like going to bed with the front page of a physical culture magazine—in the first place, I was too exhausted by that time to care for him even if I hadn't begun to hate him; and there you lie, unable to sleep because the lights are on—and *why* are the lights on? Because Lionel Strongfort has to do his setting-up exercises: it seems that somewhere during the day he missed out on a couple of muscles.— Then a home in Connecticut, fox-hunting, golf, polo. . . . Five months of it, Steven—five months without night life, without the theatre, without glasses of beer pounding the table because somebody has got something crazy and beautiful and passionate to say to somebody else, without cigarettes and poetry and laughter and bad ventilation, and dialogue—without you, Steven. . . .”

Steven wants to know where Dickie is. Learning he is at the Waldorf and that Linda had left him a note telling him good-by and saying she wanted a divorce, Steven goes to the telephone and calls Dickie. He would have Linda's husband come and get her.

Linda's husband, as it happens, is even then in Steven's building, accompanied by two of his college friends. They are looking for Linda and for evidence and they are accompanied by a detective. Flogdell thinks perhaps they could all be dissuaded from entering, if Mr. Gaye will give the word, but Gaye wants them to enter. He sends Linda into the bedroom and finds himself a book.

Dickie and his friends, two tanned and broad-shouldered young men cut from a similar college pattern, are not to be fooled by appearances. They know Linda is there. Having heard nothing for five months except Steven Gaye it was natural for Dickie to suspect the playwright first when he had found Linda gone and her note requesting a divorce. He knows that Linda, with a bouquet of flowers, had walked around Steven's building five times and then had entered. And if he thinks she is going to fool him; if she thinks she is going to get any alimony—

The door of the bedroom has opened and Linda walks calmly into the room. “She has taken off her dress and her shoes. Over her slip she wears an old bathrobe of Gaye's and on her feet she wears a pair of Gaye's bedroom slippers.”

Linda greets Dickie cheerily and recognizes both his pals, “Butch” and “Chuck,” though she never can be sure which is which. Now she has asked Steven for a cigarette and, getting it, found a place on the sofa, ready for a nice long chat. Dickie and the college boys can do nothing but stare.

Flogdell is back, though no one has rung for him, and Linda, with an air, orders champagne. It is an order that Gaye is pleased to confirm and it is the last bit of evidence that Dickie wanted. He and the fellows have their evidence now.

“We'll see who's going to get the divorce,” sneers Dickie, preparing to go. “And you—thought you were smart, didn't you?” he adds, turning to Gaye. “Deliberately giving me a love lesson—teaching me how to win her—passing your ex-mistress off on me! Well, your lesson wasn't so hot. She was so glad to get a husband, she just fell into my arms and I didn't have to say a word except I love you.”

The three young men have stormed out and Flogdell has followed them. Left alone, both Linda and Gaye are speechless. “The crudeness of Dickie's attack has stripped them of all gay-

ety." Linda is weeping softly and Gaye is still staring after the
departed visitors. Slowly Linda gets up, walks across the room
and stubs out her cigarette in an ash try. She turns then and
faces Gaye.

"Steven," she begins.

"Yes?"

LINDA—When I came in, I thought I wanted you—and I
thought you would *have* to want me if I wanted you. So I
thought to myself, as I was walking around and around and
around the block, "In another five years he'll be almost sixty and
interested in bigger things than love, and I'll be thirty which
nowadays is very young, and then we'll really be through with
each other, and by that time somebody else will probably fall in
love with me whom I'll be able to endure, because although I'm
not a Garbo, people do seem to be falling in love with me recently—there were two up in Connecticut—" You see, Steven,
I've become quite mature and realistic, don't you think, and not
the romantic girl who once thought life was a flame just because
you lived and breathed, and to tell the truth I even thought so
when I was walking around the block—but you must agree that
I am being sensible now.

GAYE—You are, Linda. Very sensible.

LINDA—And I *have* changed, haven't I?

GAYE—Yes—you have.

LINDA—And knowing you as well as I do. . . . Well, after
all, you've had your affairs, you've been married even, and I'm
sure in each case you thought this is the one great love, this is
the mountain tip, this is the glory that will never end, just as
you did with me. . . . Didn't you? (GAYE *doesn't answer; he
hasn't heard her; he is very busy with his own thoughts. She
waits a pitiful moment and then bravely goes over to him and
continues.*) So the way I sum it up is that you can't warm over
cold mutton, not unless you're a weakling, and you yourself once
said there's nothing uglier than ex-lovers being friends. . . . So
I'm going to say good-by, Steven. (*She holds out her hand.*)

GAYE—Good-by, Linda. Listen—is that all he said—just "I
love you"?

LINDA—Yes, Steven.

GAYE (*sadly*)—Well, no matter what I do—it seems I can't
escape from tragedy. (*Gradually an idea dawns.*) I think I've
got the most exquisitely lyrical damned idea anybody ever had
since time began. (LINDA *looks at him with growing surprise.*

Suddenly, she goes to the desk, gets a pad and pencil. She hurries to the upper end of the sofa and sits, waiting.)

GAYE—Ready?

LINDA (*a look of happiness dawning on her face*)—Ready.

GAYE (*dictating*)—Act One. . . . Scene One. . . . A penthouse apartment in New York City—change that—The Bedroom of a Castle in Spain.

As he talks, and as Linda writes,

THE CURTAIN FALLS

MERRILY WE ROLL ALONG
A Drama in Three Acts

BY GEORGE KAUFMAN AND MOSS HART

THIS play might be classed with other experiments that are noble in purpose in the sense that they break new ground. In form it violates most of the rules of dramaturgy, deliberately making mock of the accepted convention, less important now than it was before the movies introduced the flashback, that a play to be well made must have a beginning, a middle and an end and must be based on a story that in interest follows an ascending scale. There have been dream plays in which the sleeper's consciousness was projected through past experiences, or through fantastic imaginings. But even the recovered story employing the flashback screen method, as did Elmer Rice's "On Trial," or plays employing the mechanics of "Lorelei, or the Artist's Dream," had their beginning in the present and came back in the end to their starting point, as by the rules of musical composition a song or a symphony must end on the key in which it is begun.

"Merrily We Roll Along" introduces its protagonist as a failure at forty. His life is not over, but his career is finished. From that point his life is revealed, not through dream scenes, but through scenes of actuality which carry him back twenty-odd years to the day he spoke as the valedictorian of his college class, eloquently inspired by the ideals of youth.

The result was an inspiring tragedy to some, a puzzling but interesting novelty to others. Produced September 29 at the Music Box in New York, "Merrily We Roll Along" continued successfully until February 9. Taken on tour, the reaction of Philadelphia audiences was unfavorable and rather than risk the possibility of a similar reaction in other cities the play was withdrawn.

As the drama opens on a certain evening in September, 1934, Richard Niles, playwright, is entertaining in his country house at Sands Point, L. I. We, as observing guests, are ushered into an oval room, fringed with French windows looking out upon Long Island Sound.

"It is the kind of room you have often seen as a full-page illustration in *Town and Country,* over a caption reading: 'This un-usual décor is a glimpse of the drawing room in the Long Island home of . . .' "

The party is variously disposed. There is a game of back-gammon going on. Also a game of bridge. There is more or less desultory conversation. "A dark-haired young man is at the piano, playing, with a good deal of skill, one of the popular tunes of the day. . . ." "A lady with a highball in her hand sits a little apart, surveying the scene with a certain detachment. There is a relaxed air about all of these people—it is merely an informal Sunday evening on Long Island."

As some sort of order evolves from the party confusion, we are conscious of the detached lady with the highball. "Julia Glenn is a woman close to forty. She is not unpretty, but on her face are the marks of years and years of quiet and steady drinking—eight, ten hours a day. In contrast to the modish eve-ning clothes of the other women, Julia wears something from about three years ago, and which wasn't quite right then. Withal, there is about her definitely an air. Here is a person."

David Haskell, "an ardent young man of about twenty-six with a rather sensitive face," has mixed himself a drink at the liquor table. Noticing Julia he turns and raises his glass in salute. She responds brightly. "Know what *I'm* having?" she queries. "What?" he asks. "Not much fun!" answers Julia. And you believe her.

A flaxen-haired young man has been standing at the piano, humming. Now he breaks into full voice, finishes the song and joins another group. He is, it transpires, Val Burnett and he croons for the radio. It is possible for him to be present tonight, he is telling a Mrs. Ogden, because he has just changed his broad-cast from the Miracle Mayonnaise hour to the Black Star Axle Grease hour—Tuesdays and Fridays—

"Mayonnaise to axle grease. Just a step," mutters Julia Glenn, gazing into her drink.

Burnett is never quite sure whether Julia is kidding him or not, but he hopes she likes his singing as well as he likes her stories. Often he reads them over and over, especially the one about the boy and the girl. Perhaps, Julia suggests, he doesn't get them the first time.

Now, briefly, interest turns to Sam Frankl, the pianist. Sam is a serious musician and seriously interested in the work of Sam Frankl. He gives a good deal of time to composing, is about to have a concerto played and is at work on a symphony, in addition to his light opera scores—

"You see, the trouble with me is I've got three different careers," explains Sam to inquiring admirers; "my light music, my serious music, and my sculpture."

The bridge game has arrived at a point at which Richard Niles finds himself dummy. Laying down his cards he rises to assume for the moment the obligations of host. Niles, at forty, "is the layman's idea of what a fashionable playwright should look like. His portrait by Pirie MacDonald has long been familiar to readers of *Vanity Fair*. He is faultlessly attired, has that distinguished touch of gray at the temples."

Richard moves over to the backgammon table to find his producer, Everett Nash, playing in great luck. There is some talk of the Nileses joining the Nashes on the Riviera at Christmas time, and then going on to the Antibes together. Richard has taken the Elliott place at Antibes. It is a big place but Richard likes big places, and lots of people—

"I think if we come back to Long Island next summer we'll take the Atherton place instead of this," he says.

"Really? This is a charming place. Seems quite large," suggests Cyrus Winthrop.

"Ye-es, but there's no place to dock the boat—you've got to land at Manhasset and have the car meet you," explains Richard.

A distressed "O-oh!" escapes Julia, still gazing into her drink.

"Well, next summer's a long way off," quickly adds Richard. "First I'm going down to Carolina—I've got to get away. Those four weeks of rehearsal and the two weeks out of town—pretty wearing. But if I get some good shooting, and a month in London before St. Moritz, I'll be ready to start work again when we get to Antibes."

"I've got *my* year pretty well laid out, too," confesses Julia, without being urged. "I'm going to spend November in Tony's, if they'll give me credit, and December trying to keep from getting thrown out of my apartment. I think in January I'll put a piece of paper in the typewriter, and if anything comes of that I'll be very much surprised. February and March are going to be tough sledding, but in April it's warm again and I can go right back to the gutter, only next year I'm going to give up the *little* gutter and take a great, big *hell* of a gutter. Hi, Richard!"

"Will you stop drinking?" demands Richard. His tone is low but earnest.

"Will I stop drinking? No, I won't stop drinking!" replies Julia, in a tone as high as his was low.

"Julia—"

But David Haskell has come dashing through the windows with the announcement that, it being twelve-thirty, the morning papers should be out. Several of the others are interested. The trouble with Saturday night play openings, it appears, is that you have to wait until Monday morning to get the reviews. David thinks he will jump in the car and dash to town for them.

Richard is less concerned with what the reviews may say about his play than are his guests. He has become reconciled. Ivy Carroll, "an extremely beautiful girl," has come in from the garden and sidled up to him to reassure him of her gratitude. Whatever the papers say, Richard had given Ivy her great chance and she will be forever grateful.

"Ivy, believe me, no matter what they say about the play, they're certain to say that you were magnificent," Richard assures her.

"I'm sure they will. No matter what they say about the play," adds a voice from the stairway. The speaker is Althea Niles, Richard's wife, who has entered so unobtrusively no one has noticed her. Now all heads are turned in her direction.

Althea is just over forty and still a beautiful woman. "She moves with a certain conscious grace—the result of many years of hearing people say 'There goes Althea Royce!' when she entered a restaurant or passed down a theatre aisle."

Althea has turned to her guests. A moment later the party is beginning to break up. The Winthrops must be going, though why, it is difficult for the others to understand. A man who has made a million in cellopaper should not have to worry much about being at his office early the next day. Silly thing to make a fortune with anyway—cellopaper—the stuff they put around cigarettes to make it harder to get at them.

Yet, Winthrop protests, ten years ago he had begged people to invest in cellopaper and everybody thought him crazy. Now he has money, yes, but the art galleries get most of it. Still, Winthrop gets fun out of speculating in genius—

"When you look at a canvas that's got that spark in it, and you feel it is going to mean something three hundred years from now, and *you* can *own* it—that's got horse racing beat a mile," says he. "Because you're betting on a man's talent—whether you're right about it—and that's more important than you, or your money, or anything else. Right now, I'm betting on a man named Jonathan Crale. You know Jonathan Crale? Well, it's a name your grandchildren are going to know. Every hundred years or so there's a Jonathan Crale, and when he comes along it's history. Know what I mean?"

Winthrop has turned to the others for corroboration, but no one answers. The silence would indicate that he has said something that he shouldn't. Julia Glenn confirms the suspicion.

"Why, Cyrus Winthrop! Don't you know you shouldn't mention Jonathan Crale in this house? You'll never be invited again," she says.

"Julia, for God's sake," interposes Albert Ogden.

"Where have you been all these years—wrapped in cellopaper?" continues Julia, plowing straight ahead. "Don't you know Jonathan Crale painted a horrid picture of our host?"

"Julia, please!" Richard adds his objection.

"And our hostess! Althea was in it, too! With a hundred arms, like an octopus!" Julia is not to be stopped.

"Julia, I told you that if you came into my house—" Althea is white with rage. . . .

David Haskell is back with the papers and highly excited over the notices. His arrival breaks the tension.

"I got 'em!" he shouts. "They're wonderful—every single notice! It's a hit, Richard! It's a hit!"

There is a scrambling for the papers and quotations from the critics are enthusiastically read—

"'Richard Niles, whose flair for smart comedy is exceeded by none. . . .'" "'Our most fashionable playwright has written what will unquestionably be the most fashionable play of the season. It is Park Avenue's own. . . .'" "And Ivy, my dear, you're a star," calls Laura Nash, reading: "'Ivy Carroll, loveliest of our younger actresses, comes into her own in "Silver Spoon."'" . . . "'Starry-eyed and beautiful, her translucent performance . . .'"

"Here's that next play, Richard," calls Nash, reading: "'Ivy Carroll is the perfect instrument for the deft and sparkling comedy of Richard Niles. Playwright and actress form an ideal combination.'"

Ivy takes their congratulations gracefully, holding a kerchief to her lips the while funny little choking sounds catch her throat. Richard, too, beams modestly. It is, he agrees, about as nice a birthday gift as a man could expect. The rest had not known or had forgotten it was Richard's birthday and there is more excitement in consequence. Albert Ogden, who has been with Richard on many birthdays since they left college, thinks this the best of all.

"A new hit, his friends around him, right in the prime of life—"

There is a chorus of loud and merry protest. This isn't a banquet. But, if speeches are in order, says Julia Glenn, rising unsteadily to her feet, she would like to make one.

"To Richard Niles! Our most fashionable playwright! The man who has everything! And I'd rather be what *I* am—a drunken whore!"

There is a horrified pause, followed by a short gasp from one of the women. The tension is punctuated with repeated declarations of the guests that they really must be going. Julia still has a few side remarks to make, as Richard decides finally to take her glass away from her.

"Disgraced myself again, have I, Richard?" she asks. She turns to Val Burnett and asks him to take her home. She is weaving her way unsteadily toward the door, muttering: "Well, I guess I'll never see the inside of this house again. And that's O.K. with—"

She has lurched uncertainly forward, fallen against the table with the drinks on it and borne it crashing to the floor, glasses, bottles, ice bowl and all. The men rush forward and help Julia to her feet. As she stands alone she discovers an ice cube in her hand. "Ooh! Look what I got!" she cries in childish glee, pressing it against one breast and then the other. "The very latest! Can be worn here. . . . Here . . . Or as a brooch!" The brooch, Julia indicates as a parting gesture, should be worn very low in the back.

The guests are sympathetic, Althea is white-lipped with rage. Now the departing crowd has trooped down from the upper rooms with their wraps and spoken their good-bys. Only the Nashes, Ivy Carroll and David Haskell are left. Ivy, someone notices, has cut her hand. She had been picking up the broken glass. David is quite concerned. He must rush upstairs for the iodine. Ivy doesn't wait. The cut is nothing. She has rushed out on the lawn before they can do more. . . .

The Nashes have gone to bed. David is back with the iodine and gone to find Ivy. Facing Richard, Althea is of a mind to discuss the sensation of the evening. Certainly, she says, he must be quite satisfied with the entertainment furnished by his friend Miss Glenn. Richard would avoid a row. Althea is not to be so easily quieted. She has something to say and she is going to say it.

"If you think I don't know what's going on between you

and Ivy Carroll, you're crazy!" shrieks Althea.
"That's not true!" answers Richard sharply.

ALTHEA—You're a liar! I know how you work!

RICHARD (*anything for peace*)—All right. It's true—if that's the way you want it.

ALTHEA—Oh, now you're the martyred husband, eh? It won't do. I knew it was true the minute Everett told me I wasn't right for the part. And I knew it last year, too, with Judith Marshall. I suppose *that* wasn't true, either. The idea is I'm finished, eh? Well, I know damn well who's helping to finish me.

RICHARD—Lower your voice, will you?

ALTHEA—Shut up! Althea Royce—not right for the part! I was all right for you to use as a stepladder, though, wasn't I? Where do you think you'd have been if I hadn't played Penelope for you in "The Ostrich"? I made P. J. produce it. . . . And I needed this play. I needed it to come back in, and you killed it! What do you think they're saying, not seeing me in that part?

RICHARD (*forcing himself to be calm*)—Althea, believe me, if I'd thought you were right for that part—

ALTHEA—You! You don't care about anybody but yourself! You'd sell your soul to get a hit. Fashionable playwright! Fashionable prostitute—that's what you are!

RICHARD (*stung*)—What did you want me to do? Let you play a nineteen-year-old girl? You can see yourself, can't you, playing that balcony scene in a negligee! Why, they'd have laughed you off the stage!

ALTHEA (*in a low voice*)—You . . . dirty . . . bastard! (*She takes a breath.*) Well, maybe I am through, but you're not far behind me. Your trick won't last. You may write a couple more of these powder puffs, but they're on to you even now. And when you go you're going to go quick. *Then* see how you like it. Wait till you write those three straight flops and see who's out here on Sunday nights! Because you haven't got any *real* friends. No snob ever has.

RICHARD (*with a dangerous calm*)—I see. Well, you asked for this and you're going to get it. It's true about Ivy, and it was true about Judith, and it's going to be true about all of them. How do you like *that?*

ALTHEA—I like it fine. Because you're never going to get rid of me. Never, never, never!

RICHARD (*slowly*)—I know that. And a pretty prospect it is, too.

ALTHEA—God, but it's funny! That *you* should be telling *me*—why, I picked you up out of the Provincetown Theatre—a sniveling little failure—and gave you your chance. You were so frightened—you were going to be so grateful. Well, I can see now that you just used every one of us—me, and Julia, and Helen, and P. J.—all of us! You never made a move without knowing exactly where you were going. The only one you never fooled was Crale. How right he was! You don't see *him* hanging around. He recognized you for what you were—a money-loving, social-climbing, second-rate hack. And he put it all on canvas.

RICHARD (*bitterly*)—Well, God knows he was right about you, too. If I'd listened to him I might still be writing those failures for the Provincetown Theatre, but I wouldn't be bored and fed up with myself and sick of my life. You think these plays mean anything to me? I do them because I can't do anything else—I don't dare stop and take a look at myself. But all they bring with them is more of *this*—and I don't give a goddam what happens to me, or anything else. I'd just as soon have that tombstone over my head right now.

ALTHEA—Oh, don't ask me to feel sorry for you—you knew what you wanted and you've got it. But if you think I'm going to stand around—

Ivy comes bursting through the windows, "vibrant with youth." David is with her. There never has been such a night as this, Ivy is sure. The stars hang so low it would be easy to reach up and touch them—

A silence falls on the group. Richard breaks it with a suggestion that perhaps David can drive Miss Carroll into town—

"I have just discovered, Miss Carroll, why you were so right for the part," interrupts Althea. " 'Most beautiful of our younger actresses.' 'Starry-eyed and translucent!' . . . Well, perhaps you won't be so starry-eyed now—"

With that Althea has grabbed up the bottle of iodine that David has set on the table and dashed the contents into Ivy's face, the dark stains splotching her white evening gown. Ivy screams. The men rush to her side.

"There goes your hit, Richard," shrieks Althea, laughing and crying hysterically. "Didn't think I'd do that, did you? . . . I'll do it all the time! . . . To your hits and your women!"

"Richard! My eyes!" cries Ivy. "My eyes! It's my eyes!"

David has rushed to the telephone and is calling Dr. Pritchard
in Manhasset. The Nashes have come downstairs in their bath-
robes, yelling to know what's happened.

"I did it! I threw it at her, Laura! All over that beautiful
face! . . . Starry-eyed!" Althea laughs hysterically. "You
wouldn't give the part to me, Everett! And now you've got no
one!"

The butler and a maid have rushed in. Richard is trying to
comfort Ivy. David's voice can be heard summoning Dr. Pritchard.

"He was sleeping with her, Laura! That's why I did it!"
screeches Althea. "He was sleeping with her! And he told me
I was finished. Well, this'll finish everything—Ivy and me and
everything!"

The curtain is down.

1927—

The scene changes to that of a corner in the Restaurant Le
Coq D'Or, "the afternoon rendezvous of the social and theatrical
élite." It is seven years prior to the preceding act. The orchestra is playing song hits of the day, "Old Man River," "Blue
Skies," etc.

At one of the three or four tables visible a young couple has
reached the demi-tasse and liqueur stage of their luncheon. She
is trying to recall to him the things that happened after they had
left the El-Fay club the night before. Now they are going on to
see Nora Bayes at the Palace.

An angry headwaiter calls the busboy who is over by the orchestra, as usual, and we discover the busboy is none other than
the Val Burnett who, seven years later, is to become the favorite
crooner of 1934 and Richard Niles' party. "If someone had killed
Val Burnett at this particular moment, there would be no crooners
today," suggest the authors.

Two young girls come backing in from the main dining room.
They are giggling with excitement. They have just seen their
favorite actress in the flesh. Now she is coming this way. She
is Althea Royce at her height. "Her very gesture denotes the
actress who has New York at her feet."

Althea is there to meet Richard Niles, she tells the headwaiter,
but she has seen another person she is trying to avoid. She is
not displeased by the attentions of the giggling girls, one of whom
has summoned the courage to speak to her. They had seen a
picture of her wedding in the Sunday paper and wanted to con-

gratulate her. Also they would like to know if her husband is
going to write all her plays from now on.

"I hope so," says Althea, with a light laugh. "He is my favorite playwright."

The person Althea had hoped to avoid has followed her. "He
is somewhere in the early sixties, gray-haired, on the shabby side.
But instinctively you feel that he had been someone in his day.
His name is P. J. Morton."

P. J. is hoping to borrow. Five hundred if she has it. He
can get hold of a fine play with that— But Althea cannot go
on letting him have five hundred dollar loans, so he takes what
she can spare and is gone.

Althea has gone back to the main dining room when Julia
Glenn and Jonathan Crale come in. "The Julia of 1927 is just
beginning to show the faint traces of the woman we have seen in
1934." . . . "Jonathan Crale is Richard's age, which means that
just now he is thirty-three. He is, however, the very opposite of
Richard in looks, dress, and manner. He is none too particular
about the daily shave, and it is a long time since his suit was
pressed. One forgets all this, however, under the spell of his personality." . . . "The headwaiter regards them with a certain
hauteur. They so definitely do not belong in the Restaurant
Le Coq D'Or."

Jonathan Crale is rather evasive as to the reason he has brought
Julia to this haunt of the rich, in which she orders a Scotch highball to pair with the breakfast of wheat cakes and sausage that
he orders.

Jonathan is worried about Julie. And she about him. He
doesn't like the idea of a Scotch highball breakfast, and she
doesn't like to hear that he has spent the last three days in bed
just because he saw no good reason for getting up. Her asser-
tion that she is never going to write another line is disturbing.

"You've got to get hold of yourself, Julie—quick," he says.
"You can't go ahead this way—drinking Scotch highballs in the
morning, sitting in speakeasies all night. That just gets worse
and worse, you know. You've got no right to let that happen
to you."

JULIA—I've got a right to do anything that'll make it easier
for me. Because if I live to be a hundred I'm still going to be
in love with you. Only I hope to God I don't live to be a hundred. (*The* HEADWAITER *comes importantly into view, gives a
rather suspicious glance at* CRALE *and* JULIA, *and goes on out*

again. JULIA *looks venomously after him.*) What did you think we were doing? Stealing the napkins? (*She turns on* CRALE.) In God's name, will you tell me why you brought me here? I hate it.

CRALE—Certainly I'll tell you. I wanted to see Richard. (JULIA'S *highball glass comes down on the plate with a little bang.*) It's nothing to do with you, Julie. I want to see him myself. He won't talk to me on the telephone and he won't answer my letters. I know this is where he generally lunches, so I came here.

JULIA (*after a moment*)—It was wrong of you, Jonny. You never should have shown that picture.

CRALE—Oh, I suppose not. You never should do anything where your friends are concerned. But I didn't know it was going to stir up all this fuss.

JULIA—You knew people would see it.

CRALE—No, I didn't. Nobody ever saw any of my pictures before. It was just tough luck this one happened to get into the newspapers. Only I didn't know Richard was going to get so mad. God, he won't answer my letters; he won't talk to me; he told Albert he never wants to see me again. I can't believe it. What's he so mad about?

JULIA—You didn't think he'd be pleased, did you? A picture of himself embracing a cash register with one arm and Althea with the other. Why did you ever paint it in the first place?

CRALE—Because I felt it. The way I feel about things has got to come out. And I'm a *painter.*

JULIA—I'm sorry you did it, Jonny.

CRALE—So am I—now. I wouldn't have anything come between Richard and me for anything in the world. God, he's my best friend. I love him. The big baby. But I know if I run into him that we'll wind up with our arms around each other and everything'll be all right.

JULIA—And how do I fit into this touching scene of reconciliation?

CRALE—Because I wanted you here. The three of us have always been together, and—I wanted you here.

Something good has come from the Niles picture, Jonathan reports. For the first time he finds his work in demand. Letters from *Cosmopolitan* magazine—which is "something Fannie Hurst writes every month," Julia tells him—and letters from other magazines. But when Jonathan looks for the letters he can only find a top in his pocket. A gay little top that hums when it spins. In a second he is on his knees showing Julie the top. The head-waiter passes through again, steps haughtily over the top and disappears.

"Jonny, you're 33," protests Julia. "People are going to quit making allowances pretty soon."

Crale is not impressed. He is gayly recalling the jokes he and Richard and Julie used to play on the town— For instance, the time they telephoned hundreds of people in the Bronx that the water was to be shut off. Now Richard has come.

"Hello, Richard," Jonathan calls cheerily. Richard does not answer. Instead he steps quickly forward and strikes Crale with his fist. Crale hits back. They are pounding each other viciously while Julia, white and stricken, keeps yelling:

"Richard! Jonny! Don't! It mustn't end this way! It mustn't!"

A crowd of excited persons is gathering as the curtain falls.

1926—

It is the fall of the year before. We are in Richard Niles' rooms in an apartment hotel just off Park Avenue. "An interior decorator has clearly been given a free hand, and the result is a modernistic room done to the hilt." There is a breakfast table set for two.

Ito, Richard's Japanese servant, has told Althea Royce over the phone that he will give Mr. Niles her message and ushered in Richard's brother George before Richard is through with his shaving. When he comes out he still is in bathrobe and pajamas, and both are "Finchley's best."

Brother George is just in to say good-by. He's going back home and it has occurred to him that it would be a fine thing for his kid brother, Dick, if he would take a trip home for a change—

"Get away from all this," suggests George.—"New York; running around; restaurants. Get some good fresh air in your lungs, and some home cooking under your belt, and I bet you'd write better. I couldn't write a letter in this place."

The family, George excitedly reports, would get a terrific kick out of seeing Dick again. Mom and Pop especially.

Richard's telephone is busy this morning. Now there is a message from a Mr. Wertheimer which prompts Richard to agree to let Helen Niles have their child for another six months. "I'm foregoing my privilege," says Richard, adding: "She might send me a snapshot of the youngster."

Marriage sure is a lottery, George agrees. It seems like yesterday that Richard and Helen were in Evansville on their honeymoon, and now their son is five years old!

Everett Nash bursts in to report that Metro has called from
Hollywood and raised its bid for the picture rights to Richard's
play to seventy-five thousand dollars, which, to the astonished
George, is simply incredible. He's seen the play. Nice enough,
but—

"Seventy-five thousand dollars," repeats George. "Well, I
guess it was worth it—Ed and I putting you through college.
Ed working all those years in the knitting mill, and me nights
in the drug-store, just so you could go to college and earn all
this money. Yes, *sir*. Ed and I never regretted doing it, either—
not for one minute. No, *sir*."

There is a look in George's eyes that Richard has no difficulty
interpreting. A moment later he has written a check for George's
oldest boy and George has departed.

Jonathan Crale has arrived. It is for him the breakfast table
has been set. It has been weeks since these two have seen each
other and their meeting is enthusiastic, bubbling with an enduring
friendship.

At table Jonathan has several interesting adventures to report.
He has been in jail for one thing. Picked up as a picket in the
garment workers' strike. He has seen Richard's new play, too,
and resented it frightfully.

"My God, Richard, what do you want me to say?" Crale demands spiritedly. "You know how I feel about those plays. I
liked it; I laughed. And by the time I got to Broadway and
Forty-fifth Street I'd forgotten all about it. It's a carbon copy
of the other two you wrote. This year's model."

"Well, a lot of people don't agree with you."

"Oh, I know it's a hit. But what are you going to do? Keep
on writing those things? You're better than that, Richard. My
God, you wrote a fine play once."

"All right, and what happened to it? Two weeks at the Provincetown Playhouse."

"Yes, and you were better off then with a failure than you are
now with a hit, whichever way you look at it."

Richard recognizes the modern argument. If the play's a hit
it can't be a good play. A man ought to starve and write for the
art theatres, and so on. Being successful is a crime—

Crale doesn't mean that. Crale means that the whole scheme

of Richard's life is wrong, all the things that are interesting him now are wrong, they're doing things to him.

"You're getting away from the guts of things into a whole mess of nice, polite *nothing*," fumes Jonathan. "And that's what your plays are about. Why, I used to come into the studio and find you bubbling over with ideas—good, juicy ones. And in the past year all I've heard you talk about is how much the play grossed, and what you got for the movie rights, and you met Noel Coward."

RICHARD—All right—now let me tell *you* something. I *like* my life the way it is now. I like meeting Noel Coward, and I like being successful. I'm enjoying myself for the first time. I had plenty of the other thing—all those years with Helen. Working in a shoe store all day and writing that fine play at night. And what for? So that you and Julia could tell me how great I was? I don't see myself writing plays for two people, and being miserable the rest of the time. Why has that got to be a part of it? Why do you have to be poor to write a fine play?

CRALE—Because when you're rich you never write it. That's why.

RICHARD—I don't want to be *rich*, Jonny. But give me a chance. Give me a chance to get a little money in the bank and I'll write you a fine play. I'll write you the finest play that ever closed in a week.

CRALE—No, you won't. The longer you wait the tougher it gets. It's like a man saying he's going to take up reading when he's forty. You start reading at ten or you don't read at all. Besides, the trouble with these plays you're doing is you don't dare stop. You've got to write one a year or they'll forget you ever wrote a line. But you write one good play and they'll *always* know who you are. If I paint one good picture they'll remember *me*.

RICHARD—But I'm not like you, Jonny. That's the answer to the whole thing. I'm not like you!

CRALE—But you *are*, Richard. I know you too well for you to tell me that. You *are*, but you *won't* be if you go on living this way, getting in deeper and deeper with these people. I know all this isn't hard to take—(*a gesture that takes in the room*)—it must be very pleasant. It's fine for Ogden and Nash, and people like that, but you and I have got no right to it. I get my fun in front of an easel, and it's the only fun I'm entitled to. And that's where you ought to get yours—in front of a typewriter. I don't know whether you ever get any reward for it, but I do know this: you've only got so many good years, and when they're gone—and that may come sooner than you think, Richard—if you haven't made use of them, it's very tough. Because then you've got nothing.

RICHARD (*says nothing for a long moment. Then: pacing, thinking*)—It's hard, Jonny. I'd rather have your respect than anything. But it's hard to know which way to turn. When you've had nothing all your life, and suddenly get all this, maybe you have to be stronger than I am to push it aside. That's what I meant by a couple of years more—

CRALE—No, Richard. You've got to make a clean cut. (*He pauses a moment.*) Right from the very core.

The first thing Richard should do, Crale insists, is to cut Althea Royce completely out of his life. His attachment for her represents nothing but sex and is deadening to his higher ambitions. Richard wouldn't marry Althea, even if she was not already married. Therefore—

Richard is suddenly thoughtful. He thinks perhaps he and Jonny should take the afternoon off and have a good old-time talk about everything. Jonny is enthusiastic. They will go around and pick up Julie and make the reunion an event. Richard is agreeable. He has been feeling a little guilty about Julie. He understands that she has been drinking a good deal—

There is a reason for that, Crale insists. Julie is desperately in love with Richard and has been for a long time; so in love with him that she can't bear what is going on.

"Why—I never thought of Julia in that way," insists Richard, finding it difficult to credit Crale's words. "She's the swellest person in the world to be with, but Julia's like—well, she's like *you*. She's someone you talk to, like a man. I never thought of her as—"

"Well, there you have it. Come on—get your things on."

Richard starts for the bedroom and then remembers that there is something that must be attended to first. Let Jonny go on. He will pick him up at Julie's in about an hour.

"Listen, you dirty capitalist—you still love me, after all the things I said?" asks Jonny, as he prepares to go.

"Don't be an idiot," laughs Richard. "Nothing can ever change that, no matter what you say or do. Now, get the hell out of here, before we both bust out crying."

Crale has been gone but a few minutes before Althea Royce

arrives. She is carrying a small over-night bag, and obviously is in a state of great emotional stress. Now she has flung herself into Richard's arms and is excitedly telling him the story of a sleepless night during which her husband had followed her from room to room, hammering on the doors. She had told her husband that she was leaving him and that she wanted a divorce. She has come to Richard. He is all she cares about—

The phone is ringing. Althea's maid is calling. For a moment Althea listens tensely to the message. Her face goes white. She is staring straight in front of her as she hangs up the phone.

"It's Harry!" she says. "He's killed himself."

With a muttered "My God!" Richard stands staring dully as Althea throws herself into his arms. Her arms are around his neck and she is sobbing.

"Richard! . . . Richard! . . . Richard!"

THE CURTAIN FALLS

ACT II

Time has turned backward to 1925. It is approximately 10 o'clock of a bright spring morning. We are in Jonathan Crale's studio, "a skylight room on the top floor of an old house, somewhere in the East Twenties."

"It is cluttered up, of course, with all the traditional paraphernalia of the artist—easel, model stand, brushes, canvases. In addition, however, there are several objects around that are much more difficult to explain. A huge brass telescope, on a tripod, stands near the window. There is an old-fashioned Russian samovar, enormous, pushed into a corner. A pair of ice skates have been tossed onto a chair, and a pogo stick leans against the wall."

Crale, still in his pajamas, over which he has thrown a coat—a woman's coat with an imitation fox fur—is trying seriously to play an accordion. His first interruption is that of a girl's voice calling from the bedroom. She is dressing and can't find her step-ins. Crale is of little help. Soon she appears, "something very attractive in the early twenties," carrying a small suitcase and her hat.

The girl is hurt. She sees no good reason why she should be put out just because Crale's friend, Niles, is getting back. Niles knows what it is all about and there are two beds. Besides, Crale hasn't painted her picture yet—

A buzz of the doorbell hurries her departure. A moment later, while Crale is at the telescope looking for the sun, Julia Glenn arrives. "The Julia of 1925 is fresh, buoyant, youthful, happy. There is a definite glow about her."

Julia is dressed up and excited. In sheer joy she throws her arms about Crale's neck. Who wouldn't be happy the day Richard is coming back? And they've got to hurry if they are to meet the boat.

"Oh, Jonny! I never realized how much I wanted to see that man!" exults Julia. "Eight months! For God's sake get out of those pajamas! I was up at five o'clock. . . . Make it fast. I want to see that boat come up the bay, I want to wave to him from the end of the pier. I want to see him walk down the gangplank! Have you got money for a taxi?"

Crale is in the bedroom dressing. And wondering about money for a taxi. Wondering a moment later where the "Rosamond" is going to dock. Where do they dock private yachts anyway? It might be in the paper, but Jonathan does not take a paper. Does Mr. Hearst buy his paintings? Now Jonathan has an idea. He will call his old friend, Captain Peterson, at Sailors' Home. Captain Peterson knows all about every boat that comes into the harbor. Spends his days keeping track of them.

"Listen, Captain," Jonny calls into the phone, "there's a private yacht coming in today and I want to know where it docks. . . . Huh? . . . It's called the 'Rosamond' . . . 'Rosamond.' Owner, Albert J. Ogden. And it's got a lot of rich bastards on board, if that'll help you any. . . ."

After some research Captain Peterson reports the "Rosamond" as docking at Twenty-sixth Street, Brooklyn, which is going to take hours, and Jonny still not dressed—

Julia is tidying up the room and calling to Crale through the bedroom door.

"Jonny, won't it be wonderful to have him back! Fresh, and starting all over again! That whole terrible business behind him. I'm so excited I could sing! I *will* sing! (*And she does. A phrase of 'Look for the Silver Lining.'*)"

"You're terrible!" calls Crale.

"I don't care! I don't care about anything! (*She stands for a moment, smiling at nothing in particular.*) You know, Jonny, I was thinking this morning—it's funny how things work out. For the best, I mean. Everything seemed so hopeless eight months ago, but when you look at it now it seems as if it was all planned. He *had* to go through all that. That one taste of success was bad for him anyway, Jonny—he liked it. That shake-up was just what he needed. We were able to get him away."

Julia hopes Richard has finished his play. He had one act done in Cairo. She has news for Richard, too. She has started her novel. Got thirty-five pages done and she thinks it good. Julia, at the moment, is terribly glad that she was born—

There is the buzz of the doorbell. Jonathan calls down to see who it is. It's Richard! He's on his way up—

They have dashed pell-mell through the door to meet him. They are clattering down the stairs. "Richard!" "We are coming to meet you!" "Look at him, Julie—he's ten pounds heavier!" "We'd have been there hours ago, but he wouldn't put his pants on!" "Say! I know you two! I'm surprised you remembered the day, even!"

They have brought him triumphantly into the room, Richard in the middle, the other two clinging to him. Behind them, with beaming face, appears Albert Ogden. "Except for a coat of tan, Richard Niles has the beginnings of the man we have already seen—well-tailored, an air of assurance. His appearance and bearing, however, are in the nature of a surprise to Crale and Julia. Even the mustache is a product of the trip."

In the room their exuberant greeting is continued. Questions fly thick and fast, without the answers registering with any certainty. Was the trip wonderful? Where'd he get the English outfit? Is it paid for? Where'd he get the mustache? What about the new play? When can they hear it?

Richard is a little flustered at reference to the play, but Ogden speaks up for him. The play is finished, he reports—

"Just wait! You'll die laughing!" reports Ogden. "He read it to us and we almost fell overboard! Novel as hell—the whole thing takes place on a yacht! Everybody's wife gets into the wrong cabin! 'All on Deck'—isn't that the name of it, Richard?"

"Ah—yes," admits Richard, with a nervous laugh. "It's not as funny as all that, Albert."

"But, Richard—that isn't the play you wrote us about."

"No—it isn't, Julia."

"But—what happened to that? It—sounded—so swell."

"You mean the coal mine play? Well, I did an act of it—*you* know, I wrote you—but I was afraid of it. I don't think they want plays like that right now."

"I should say not," agrees Ogden. "There's enough trouble in real life without going to the theatre for it. People want to laugh."

He had read the coal mine play to the crowd, Richard explains, and they didn't seem to think—

There are two or three peremptory buzzings of the bell. It is Rosamond Ogden downstairs. She is getting impatient. She and some of the crowd are waiting, explains Ogden. They just stopped with Richard to say hello. No, they won't come up. Richard is coming with them.

RICHARD—We're spending the week-end at the Flemings'. We kind of made arrangements on the boat for a farewell get-together. The whole crowd are going out, and—I couldn't—I'll be back Monday morning. (*The buzzer sounds again—a long, imperative summons.*)

OGDEN (*yelling down the stairs*)—Oh, all right! . . . We'd better go down. Good-by, people! Coming, Richard?

RICHARD—Ah—just a second.

OGDEN—Okay! (*The bell again. Still more demanding.*) Coming down! Lay off the bell, will you? (*He is gone.*)

CRALE (*making the best of it—giving* RICHARD *a pat on the back*)—All right, kid—have a good time. When are you coming in—Monday? Leave me your trunk keys and I'll have you all unpacked.

RICHARD—Well, look, Jonny—would you care a lot if—if I didn't come back here to live? You see, I found on the boat— I could work better being alone, and—anyway it puts you to a lot of trouble having me here. I thought I'd just take a room at the Lombardy or somewhere until I can get a place of my own. You don't mind, do you?

CRALE (*masking his disappointment*)—Why—no. If you think you can work better that way, Richard—that's all right.

RICHARD—It isn't as if we can't see each other just as much. I—I want to talk to you both about the coal mine play. Maybe I could go back to it, if—you liked it. Ah—how about dinner Monday night? Are you both free?

CRALE—We're both free. If you are.

RICHARD—Fine. I'll keep it open. (*There is an awkward pause.*) Well—I guess I'd better go down before they start ringing again. Good-by, Jonny, you old fool. See you Monday. . . . Good-by, Julia. (*He blows her a kiss.*) Can't tell you how good it's been to see you two again.

CRALE—Good-by, Richard.

RICHARD—Good-by.

JULIA (*as he goes through the door*)—Good-by, Richard. (*She*

looks down the stairs after him.) Good-by. (*Slowly she pulls
the door shut and leans with her back against it. Her voice takes
on a new meaning.*) Good-by, Richard. . . . (*She gives a shrill,
unpleasant laugh.*) Hail and farewell! . . . Jonny, we saw the
last of Richard Niles eight months ago—the day he got on that
boat. He's met The Crowd, Jonny! He's met The Crowd, and
there he goes! And do you remember something, Jonny? *We
did it!* You and I. That day in the court-house. We made him
get on that boat. Everything works out for the best, eh? Did
I say that? Well, if I did I was a God-damned fool!

Crale, who has slumped into the easy chair, gives a single blast
of discord on the accordion as the curtain falls.

1924—

Two attendants guard the door of a courtroom, through which
the droning voice of the Judge can be heard announcing an ad-
journment, and threatening to have the newspaper photographers
up for contempt if one of them dares attempt to take another
picture.

The voices of the bailiffs repeat the announcement of adjourn-
ment, "and from the doors there emerges The Public—or, at
least, those lovely representatives thereof as are inevitably drawn
to any legal procedure that promises cheaply sensational develop-
ments. The women are sleazy, cheaply dressed, sensation-hungry.
There is, however, a sprinkling of Bronx housewives and two or
three over-dressed West End Avenue ladies. The men are of the
variety generally referred to as loafers, but among them too there
are a few who are better dressed."

From the remarks of the dispersing crowd it is made known that
tomorrow's testimony promises to be juicy; that Niles is looking
paler and paler; that there is a lot of sympathy for Mrs. Niles
and the baby; that the testimony about the leopard skin has
been pretty warm; that tomorrow Mrs. Niles will tell how she
found Althea Royce and Niles on the leopard skin.

Mrs. Niles appears leaning rather heavily on the arm of her
mother. She is "a frail, rather distraught young woman." They
are followed by several men, including Richardson, Mrs. Niles'
lawyer. He is anxious that Mrs. Niles should have a good night's
sleep so she will be rested if he has to put her on the stand again.
It has been a good day for them.

Albert Ogden and a man named Wertheimer are talking over
the seriousness of the situation so far as Richard is concerned.

He is sensitive and the ordeal is telling on him. He can't stand much more of the staring crowd and the sort of publicity the tabloids are giving him.

"Well, you've got to expect that in a case of this kind," says Wertheimer. "Women like Althea Royce—all those sexy plays she's been in. It was made to order for the tabloids."

Wertheimer is convinced that not only should the case never have been permitted to come to trial, but that it is going to get worse and worse.

"Tomorrow they are going to have some of those people testify that were at the party," he says. "The last ones to go. You see, Mr. Ogden, it all ties in too well. His wife leaves the party in tears—comes back with her brother at ten minutes to four—and there they were. On that damned leopard skin. Trust the tabloids to pick up that leopard skin. It was all they needed."

Richard Niles comes out of the courtroom with Jonathan Crale and Julia Glenn. Richard's "white, drawn face is the face of a man shaken to the very roots." He wants to get away. The photographers have swarmed in and are pestering him for another pose. Julia and Crale shield him from the cameras.

It is Wertheimer's advice that they drop the case. Richard is too tired to care. He will do whatever they say. There is relief at the decision. There will be no more trial, no more scenes. Richard brightens perceptibly at the thought. He is tremendously grateful to everybody—to Ogden and Wertheimer, to Julia—

"Julia, you've been so wonderful. I don't think I ever could have faced it if it hadn't been for the way you and Jonny—"

JULIA—But, Richard—we love you. We're always going to be with you—whenever you need us. Always.

CRALE—Just you forget about us, Dickie. Right now you've got to think about yourself.

JULIA—Richard, what you've got to do is to get away—get away as quickly as possible. Just think—in ten days you can be on Albert's boat, and this'll all seem like a bad dream.

RICHARD—No, no. I don't want to go away.

CRALE—It's what you need, Richard. You've got to.

JULIA—You won't be alone. You'll have Albert with you, and all his friends.

OGDEN—You'll love it, Richard. She's a beautiful boat, if I do say so myself. And it's a swell crowd that's going.

JULIA—Richard, think of it! The Mediterranean, Egypt, India!

RICHARD—No. Just let me stay with you and Jonny. I'll be all right if you and Jonny are with me.

JULIA—Listen, Richard. You're worn out. You're on the ragged edge. If you're ever going to work again you've got to get fresh strength—you've got to see new people, new places— this is a heaven-sent chance. If you stay here, even with Jonny and me at your side, you'll be constantly reminded of it—the whole city'll remind you of it. Richard, you must go. Won't you do it for *me*, Richard—for Jonny and me?

RICHARD—Julia, I'm afraid to go away now—the way I feel. I'm afraid to—

A photographer has rushed up behind Richard with a leopard skin, which he holds up as a background. Another levels a camera and a third springs a flashlight. Crale rushes in to stop them, Julia has turned sympathetically to Richard—

"All right, Julia, I'll go," he says. "Only get me away quick. I can't stand it. I can't stand it!"

He is sobbing. The others try to quiet him.

The curtain falls.

1923—

Althea Royce's apartment includes an assortment of what the hotel has furnished and favorite pieces taken from this and that production in which Althea has appeared, including a leopard skin thrown casually over a couch. Preparations are going forward for an after-theatre party. Waiters and maids are busy bringing in glassware and distributing them under the direction of a captain.

Two early arrivals are Harry Nixon, Miss Royce's husband, and Sid Kramer, a vaudeville agent. "Nixon is in his middle forties, a trifle gray. It is not long ago that he was considered a handsome juvenile. He still looks a trifle dashing in his evening clothes, but there is an indefinable air of sadness about him."

It is the night of Miss Royce's first appearance in Richard Niles' first play, and all indications point to a hit. Hundreds of telegrams of congratulation from all the big people of the profession—Elsie Ferguson, Glenn Hunter, Lenore Ulric, Condé Nast, Irene Fenwick, Al Woods, Oliver Morosco, David Belasco —are stuffed in Nixon's pocket.

It is a big night, but there are features about it that Kramer doesn't like. If he were Harry Nixon he'd be so sore he couldn't sleep. To think that if it hadn't been for Nixon there would be

no success for Althea tonight! Hadn't Nixon taken her out of
the chorus and put her into his vaudeville act? Hadn't he taught
her everything she knows? And she without a shred of gratitude! She's forgotten now that her husband ever had anything
to do with her beginnings, and it makes Sid Kramer boil.

Harry Nixon doesn't feel that way. Althea has become an
important actress. It is right she should have attention. It is
natural that he should have faded from the picture. But it does
get pretty lonesome sometimes. Harry can't even go to the
Lamb's Club with any enthusiasm any more. The boys were
always riding him about having it pretty easy, now that his wife
is a hit.

There is another thing Sid feels he should speak about. It's
Althea's going around with other men. The town's talking a good
deal about that, too. Harry ought to do something about it.
But again Harry is content. He is still very much in love with
Althea.

"I'm so in love with her that if she'll just let me stay around,
I don't care what she does," says Harry. "That's the only thing
that scares me, Sid—if she ever left me. Because if that ever
happens, then there's no reason for me at all."

Suddenly there appears in the doorway "a lady of formidable
proportions. It is Althea's mother, Maggie Riley. She has one
of those emphatic Irish faces, which just at the moment is labor-
ing under such loads of make-up that it is difficult to tell her
age, and she is wearing what would be considered evening clothes
on anybody else. Something happens, during the course of the
evening, to anything that *Maggie Riley* puts on. Her long white
gloves are dirty at the fingertips; her evening cape, obviously
handed down from Althea, is a trifle askew on her shoulders; the
edge of her petticoat shows beneath her dress. People *like* Maggie
Riley *enormously—because she is not* their *mother*."

Mrs. Riley will not let the servants have her wraps. She is
not a guest. She has just dropped in for a bottle of beer, and she
may be thrown out any time. But she's determined to get something out of the wake. Mrs. Riley doesn't think much of Althea's
play. Most of the plays of today give her a pain, and most of
the acting, too. She swings easily into an imitation of what she
considers the modern actress—

" 'There's no one here, Alfred. They've all gone into the garden. Shall we dawnce?' . . . 'I can face anything, dearest, as
long as I know that I have you. Shall we dawnce?' . . . 'Edgar!
Father just has shot himself! Shall we dawnce?' Dawnce my

behind! Believe me, that show could *use* a couple of ostriches. And they call it acting, too—that's what beats me. 'Won't you have a cup of tea?' 'Yes, it *is* warm.' Acting, for Christ's sake! Leslie Carter swinging on that bell in 'The Heart of Maryland'— that was acting. That blood dripping down in 'The Girl of the Golden West'—that was acting!"

Now Althea has appeared in the entrance hall. "She is resplendent. Great bursts of orchids peep out through the fur of her evening wrap, while behind her stand two maids, laden with flower boxes."

For a moment Althea does not see her mother. When she does she greets her with a studied sweetness that indicates a positive loathing for Mrs. Riley. The old lady is not at all impressed. Not with Althea's upstage attitude, nor with Nixon's explanation that Althea is always tired out after a performance.

"Tired?" echoes mother, with great scorn. "What the hell from? I sat in the first row of the balcony and couldn't hear a goddam word you said."

"Oh, really?" answers Althea, as from a great height. "The rest of the audience heard every word."

MRS. RILEY—They must have good ears. What were you doing with your back to the audience all the time? I thought you were going right *up* that fireplace.

ALTHEA (*icily*)—Well, mother, I'm sure you're right and everyone else is wrong. That's why P. J. Morton pays me two thousand dollars a week and puts my name up in lights.

MRS. RILEY—Say, get it while you can, Annie—before they get onto you.

ALTHEA (*unable to stay calm any longer*)—Mother, will you please stop calling me Annie?

MRS. RILEY—Well, for Christ's sake, that's your name, ain't it? That's what you were born. Annie Riley to Althea Royce— *that's* a sleeper jump for you. And I see by the program—(*She unfolds it.*)—where your grandfather was the founder of the Irish Theatre. Old Patrick Royce. The only place *he* was ever found was under the seat drunk. (*She consults the program.*) "Comes from a long line of distinguished Irish actors.' You should know some of them. Your great-grandfather was a horse-thief; old Patrick Royce was sent up for wife-beating, when he wasn't busy founding the Irish Theatre, and—

ALTHEA (*with repressed fury*)—Mother, are you going home or aren't you?

MRS. RILEY (*squaring off*)—Oh, I see. I'm not good enough for your fine friends. Listen—just because they wear ermine wraps and a lot of jewelry don't fool *me*. I'm on to them all. Irene Bordoni! Where do you think she came from—Tiffany's?

ALTHEA—Now, that's one thing I will not stand for! I will not have you saying things like that about my friends!

MRS. RILEY—Oh, save that for someone who doesn't know you. You're just shanty Irish, that's all you are! You're not lace-curtain Irish—you're *shanty!* And don't you forget it!

ALTHEA (*losing all control*)—Get out of here! Get out of here before I throw something at you!

Mrs. Riley and Harry Nixon have gone. The party begins to take shape. Sam Frankl, a piano player from Harms, arrives and proceeds to his job. The guests appear in groups; six, eight, ten at a time. There is the usual buzz of greetings and explanations. Now the early comers have seen Althea and the air is palpitant with compliments.

"Oh, my darlings, was I terrible?" Althea asks anxiously. "I want you to tell me the truth, my dears, because I know when I'm bad."

"Althea, my darling, you were wonderful," they assure her. "My dear, we loved you. We've never seen you better." . . . "My dear, didn't you hear that audience? They practically cheered—they *never* do that! . . . You were brilliant, Althea darling. That's all I can say—brilliant!"

Althea is also quite certain that the success is not hers, really. It is Mr. Niles' beautiful play.

The party grows and the gushing grows with it. Now P. J. Morton, the leading producer of his day, is there, very proud to be Althea's manager. Tonight P. J. is certain, though he has handled all the biggest stars, that Althea is the biggest of them all.

"That means more to me, P. J., than all the critics in the world," says Althea, huskily. "As long as I am able to walk onto a stage, I want you to be my producer."

And now the much heralded Richard Niles arrives. "We see him framed in the doorway—Richard at 29—youthful, eager, scared. Clinging to his arm, as though she were afraid ever to let go, is his wife, Helen. She is very pretty, with the kind of good looks that go at thirty—one of those women whose chief allure is an excessive femininity, of the helpless, appealing kind. At the moment her bewilderment, almost her fright at her surroundings, is plain on her face."

Althea has pushed her way through the crowd to greet Richard and to give his wife a perfunctory welcome. She stops the music and the buzzing while she introduces her attractive young playwright and the crowd gathers around to congratulate him. Helen Niles hangs onto her husband's arm and tries her best to rise to the greetings of the guests.

Now Althea has taken charge of Richard and, whisking him through the crowd to meet someone else, leaves Helen stranded. For a time she attempts to exchange comments with those who speak to her, but it is a strange world they are discussing and she knows little about it. Soon the crowd and the waiters have hemmed her off.

There is a good deal of excitement as some of the guests raise Althea to a bench and are lifting the bench into the air. From that height Althea must make a speech, an honor she insists Richard shall share. Gayly the friends raise the playwright to a place beside Althea. When he speaks he gives all the credit to her.

"It isn't only the wonderful performance she gives, but—no one can ever know what a great help she's been right through it all. I can only say—thank you, Althea."

"Why, Richard! Aren't you a darling!" Althea has impulsively thrown her arms about Richard and kissed him full upon the mouth. Helen Niles, at the edge of the crowd, is trying to take what is happening like a good fellow, but not succeeding very well. A moment later she has seen Althea playfully rub her cheek against Richard's cheek, and draw away from that intimate touch to rumple his hair.

It is a little more than Helen can stand. She starts working her way through the crowd to the door. The party is going full blast as

THE CURTAIN FALLS

ACT III

In 1922 the Murneys are living in an apartment in West 111th Street, just below Morningside Heights. "The living room itself, which also serves as a dining room, is a replica of countless other living rooms all over New York. The wall paper is characterless, the furniture equally so. . . . All in all, it is not the pleasantest room to be in on a hot summer's night, and this is one of the hottest. The family is just finishing the evening meal; Mrs. Murney and Helen are carrying out the plates. Mr. Murney . . . has shed his coat, collar and tie—even loosened his belt. . . . Richard is not present, but the other male member of the household, Buddy Murney, is seated in front of that new wonder of 1922, the radio. He has the ear phones over his head, and is intently working with the copper wire, trying to find a sensitive spot in the crystal."

The clearing of the table goes on to the accompaniment of remarks about the heat and Buddy's repeated assurances that he is about to get something. Buddy is right. He gets a ukulele, but it makes little impression on Mr. Murney.

Richard's absence finally becomes a subject of comment. Richard, reports Helen, is mad. She had found a pocketbook with eleven dollars in it at the butcher shop. Richard insisted she should try to find out who owned it. Helen as firmly declared that finders should be keepers. She could use that eleven dollars as well as anyone else. So she kept it. When Richard appears in the door he speaks like a man who is still mad. He has come to tell Helen that the baby is crying. Richard is not popular with the Murneys. He is always writing in Buddy's room, or anywhere he can find a light. Mr. Murney thinks he should be taken off his high horse.

Mr. Weintraub has called. "If the Murneys but knew it they are at this moment in the presence of a future millionaire, a man who is destined to change the entire surface of industrial America. For Simon Weintraub is none other than that future art connoisseur and cellopaper king, Cyrus Winthrop."

Mr. Weintraub has brought with him in a little black satchel samples of his cellopaper wrapping which, he assures the Murneys, is certain one day to revolutionize the whole paper and twine business. He has a loaf of bread, neatly wrapped in cellopaper. Also a pack of cigarettes and a toothbrush.

"No, no, this isn't tissue paper," Mr. Weintraub corrects Mrs. Murney. "This is called cellopaper. That's my invention. That's the whole idea. It not only protects the article—it makes it look better. And for the first time people will be able to see what they're buying. Now, you take this toothbrush, Mr. Murney. Ordinarily you go into a drugstore and you ask for a toothbrush and the clerk digs it up out of some old drawer. But if it was wrapped in cellopaper it could be lying right on the counter and—"

"Hold on a minute, Weintraub," protests Mr. Murney. "Not so fast. Wait a minute. Let me see that stuff once. (*He has taken the loaf in his hand.*) Why is it any better than regular paper?"

"Well, the way it makes things look, in the first place. It makes the merchandise attractive. And not only that, Mr. Murney—"

"Now, wait a minute, Weintraub. Wait a minute. (*He turns to* MRS. MURNEY.) Let me ask you something, Rose. If you were to go into the grocery store to buy a loaf of bread, would you want it wrapped up in this—er—stuff of Weintraub's?"

"No, I don't see any sense in it," answers Mrs. Murney, after a judicial inspection of the loaf.

"But, Mrs. Murney, outside of the way it looks, don't you see how much cleaner it is, how much more sanitary?"

"Mr. Weintraub, the grocery store I deal with, you could eat off the floor. Besides, it'd have to be wrapped up in regular paper before I could take it home. I wouldn't want people on the street to see what I was carrying. So what good is it?"

"You see, Weintraub, I'm afraid it's no good. My wife is no different from millions of other women."

The Murneys are not impressed by any of the Weintraub arguments. You can't sell the public something it doesn't want.

"It's like that radio thing over there—I bet you the fellow that invented that thought he had something, too," ventures Mr. Murney. "Take a tip from me, Weintraub—stop wasting your time with this thing."

Mr. Weintraub at least stops wasting his time with the Murneys. He is gone, now, and they are congratulating themselves that Mr. Murney was not simple enough to buy a half interest in the future of cellopaper for two thousand dollars. To Mrs. Murney the nerve of some people is beyond belief.

Helen is back and in a mood. Richard, she complains, keeps walking up and down the hall. The baby keeps waking up. No wonder. He's a new kind of writer, this Richard. You've got to take a college course to understand one of his plays. For three years now Helen has been putting up with Richard, and the only thing he has produced is a crazy kind of a play in a crazy kind of theatre for which he didn't get a nickel. And if that's what she's bringing up her baby for she's through.

Mrs. Murney is sorry Helen and Richard can't get along better, but Mr. Murney understands. It all comes from marrying a man like that. Someone has always got to support them—

Richard appears, carrying his hat. He is going across the street to the park. He is going to meet Jonny Crale. He does not even try to reply to Helen's taunting suggestion that if she were good enough for Jonny Crale he might come to the house. That's what intellectuals are. They don't care about their wives or their baby or anything. All they care about—

Jonny Crale is at the door. He has brought Julia Glenn to see Richard. They are on their way to hear Eugene Debs speak. Jonny thought Richard would like to go along. Richard would, but he thinks perhaps he should stay with Helen. She has had a hard day, with the baby and all. Which is okay with Jonny. And Julia. What she really wanted to meet Mr. Niles for was to tell him how much she had liked his play at the Provincetown Theatre. She thought it was almost a great play—

"Oh, did you see the play?" brightens Richard. "I'm so glad you liked it."

"Liked it? I thought it said more than any other play I'd ever seen in my life. I thought it was beautiful. I saw it twice, Mr. Niles."

"Did you really? I can't tell you how happy that makes me. Not many people seemed to like it."

"Not many people liked Ibsen in the beginning either. Oh, Mr. Niles, you mustn't let anything stand in your way. You're going to do great things in the theatre."

"You needn't worry about him, Julie. He's the Rock of Gibraltar. Why, he just turned down an offer from P. J. Morton to write a play for Althea Royce."

"I should think he would," says Julia, significantly.

Jonny and Julia have gone now and the Murneys have turned on Richard. How dared he turn down an offer from P. J. Morton? How dared he refuse probably five hundred dollars, while he's letting the Murneys support him?

"You've got no right to turn down anything," chimes in Mr. Murney, with feeling. "You ought to be damned glad of a chance to pay back some of what you owe."

HELEN—He doesn't care! He doesn't care about anything but himself! (*She wheels on* RICHARD.) What did you marry me for? Just to shut me up in a room? Just to tie me down with a baby, so I couldn't ever go any place or have a good time again!

MR. MURNEY (*shouting*)—You ought to be ashamed of yourself!

MRS. MURNEY—Alfred, the neighbors!

MR. MURNEY—I don't care! Let 'em hear! They know it anyway.

HELEN—How do you think I feel when I haven't got a dress

to go out in? How do you think I feel when I meet all my friends? What are we going to do—go on like this? Pinching and scraping! Well, I won't do it! I won't!

RICHARD (*taking a deep breath*)—Now, listen. I want to try to explain to you—all of you—how I feel about this. I've tried very hard, Helen, to give you the things you want—and that you ought to have. I was a floorwalker, and—I tried selling that coffee, and—for pretty near two years I worked in a shoe store. Didn't I? I've got a duty toward you, Helen. I know that. But I see a little further than you do. I know what I'm trying to do. If I could only make you understand that. I know the kind of plays I've got to write, and what I want to say, and that's everything to me. It's all I've got. I know it's hard on you, but—if you'll only come along with me, Helen—if you'll only help me fight it out. (*He is met with dogged silence.*) You see, Helen, I know what it would mean—writing a play for Althea Royce. It's just the opposite of—everything I'm trying to do. (*She remains silent.*) I'm doing all this for you, Helen—for both of us. And I need your help. I need your help if we're ever going to get there. Don't you see that? Because if you don't see that, then—there's nothing more I can say.

MR. MURNEY—I'll tell you what *I* see. I see what I've been telling my wife and daughter ever since I first laid eyes on you. You're a lazy good-for-nothing who doesn't want to work, that's what's the matter with you. And I'll tell you something else. I'm through supporting you. You can go out and get a job or you can get out of here! Because I'm through supporting you! (*He storms out of the room. There is a fractional pause; then, from over the areaway, come once more the strains of "Pretty Baby."*)

HELEN (*in a low tone*)—I wish I was dead. I wish the baby was dead. I wish I'd never seen you.

MRS. MURNEY—Helen, you mustn't say such things. That's a terrible thing to say.

HELEN (*shaking off her mother's hand*)—Oh, let me alone! (*She stalks out of the room.*)

MRS. MURNEY (*following her*)—Helen, please! He's your husband. Helen! (RICHARD *stands stock still for a second, then his steps carry him slowly over to the window. He stands there, staring vacantly out. There is a long pause.* MR. MURNEY *appears in the doorway.*)

MR. MURNEY—As long as you're not paying for it, perhaps you won't mind if I put the lights out. (*He switches off the*

*lights, and goes. The room is in darkness except for the light
from the apartment across the areaway, where the piano continues
to grind out "Pretty Baby.")*

Richard stands motionless in the little circle of light as the
curtain falls.

1918—

The scene is Madison Square. The Metropolitan Life Insurance tower looms in the background, a bit of the park, with trees
and scattered benches in the foreground. As secluded a corner
as the park affords.

A policeman strolls in, and a man with a dog. The man and
the policeman usually exchange a few words in the evening. Tonight their talk is of the armistice celebration that is about over.
The man had been let off his job at ten o'clock in the morning
and he and his wife had stood at the corner of Forty-second Street
and Fifth Avenue all day long.

"I figured we'd never see anything like that again," he says.

"You bet your life you won't," the policeman agrees.

Two boys roller-skate their way down the walk, singing "You'd
Be Surprised." Two girls wander through. One has her hair
bobbed. A scary thing to do, but a great relief once it's done.

Now Helen and Richard appear. Their arms are interlocked
and they are walking slowly. Richard is in uniform. Helen is
saying that all day the day the armistice was signed she could
think of nothing but that Richard was safe. Richard, too, could
think of nothing but Helen when the news came.

"It didn't mean that the greatest war in the history of the
world was ended," he says; "somehow it just meant you. Curious
how, even at a great moment like that, one thinks selfishly."

It will be six weeks, maybe longer, before Richard is out of the
army. Then they will get married. The very first day. Whether
Richard has a job or not. They will live, says Richard, on air, if
necessary; "pure, rarefied, ecstatic air." He expects, however, to
find a job and write at night.

"I've thought a good deal lately about our marriage, Helen,"
says Richard. "I want our love to be something that nothing can
disturb, nothing uproot—something that will always be there
for us to fall back on, no matter what happens."

"I love to hear you talk that way, Richard. It makes me feel
all trembly inside."

"We mustn't ever be like other people, Helen. You see so
many people who are disillusioned, bitter. We mustn't ever let

our marriage become tattered and shopworn."

"Richard, I love you so."

He has pushed the hair back from her forehead and kissed her again, lightly. Now he would continue the speculation as to what their life will be together. Sometimes, when he is lying awake thinking of all it may mean, "it is like hearing great music for the first time—you want to rush out into the street and stop the first person you see, and tell him about it."

"The world isn't what it was yesterday," says Richard. "It's all new. The war has changed everything. Things are going to be fresher, and cleaner—more honest, somehow. And we're part of it, Helen—you and I. In our own small way we're part of it. You can feel it in the air. People are breathing again. They're lifting up their heads to a new America. All over the country, like millions of invisible wires, people are reaching out to be part of it, to shape their lives to this new world."

"Yes, Richard! And I want to do it all with you!" Helen, caught up in the sweep of his idealism, clings closer to him.

"How lucky we are, Helen! How lucky we are to be young just at the start of it!"

Transported, Richard turns to poetry. "Oh, world, be nobler for her sake!" he begins. . . . Now he has swept her into his arms, as she gives him her lips, passionately.

For a minute they are locked in a close embrace. Then the Metropolitan chimes strike the hour.

"Richard, we'd better go," says Helen. "If we take the bus it'll be almost ten before I get home."

He kisses her again. The chimes are still tolling the hour as the curtain falls.

1916—

We are in a college chapel. The year is at the spring. "Gothic pillars frame a towering stained-glass window, through which floods a stream of sunlight. In half shadow, on the platform, sit a solid mass of students and faculty." Jonny Crale is there. And Albert Ogden. Richard stands in the center of the platform, the sun streaming over his gown. He is speaking and is near the close of his address.

RICHARD— . . . All of these things, and more, college has given us. (*He pauses.*) And now, fellow students—and this, in the way of all things, is the last time I shall be able to address you as fellow students—I stand before you as your valedictorian to speak for you and for myself. I have touched upon the educational aspects of these four years, I have dwelt with gratitude upon the stimulating influence of our teachers. But I have purposely left until the last the two things that lie closest to my heart, the two things which this college has helped to foster, and which will remain ever green so long as memory lasts. I have waited until the last to talk about *you*—you as I know you, not in the classroom or on the field, but in those small, chosen hours, those all-revealing hours when we sat and talked about ourselves and each other—talked with a richness and a warmth that never can be recaptured. Those were the hours when we discovered and embraced that greatest of all glories—friendship. Of all the things I take away with me, the one that I most treasure, for which I am the most humbly grateful, is a friendship that I have formed here. (*He makes a slight gesture toward* JONATHAN CRALE.) I hope he will always be beside me, all through my life. Many are the things that vanish in this changing world, but a real friendship will always endure. If I could make one wish for you—for all of you—I would ask that you be given a great friendship. (*He pauses momentously.*) Lastly, this I have learned. I have learned to value ideals above all else. Let them ever be our heritage, our guiding force. As we go out in the world, as we take up our chosen professions, we are clad, as it were, in shining armor. Let nothing sully that. With you goes a new hope, a new idealism. Carry your banners high; compromise them never. I give you the words of Polonius;

> "This above all; to thine own self be true,
> And it must follow, as the night the day,
> Thou canst not then be false to any man.
> Farewell: my blessing season this in thee!"

The organ peals thunderously forth.

THE CURTAIN FALLS

AWAKE AND SING

A Drama in Three Acts

By Clifford Odets

WHATEVER the future may hold for him as a dramatist, Clifford Odets, author of "Awake and Sing," will always be able to look back upon the theatre season of 1934-35 with great personal satisfaction. That season at least he dominated his particular division of playwriting, which is that of the propagandists. Three of his plays, coming to production within comparatively a few weeks of each other, all registered definitely with the publics for which they were written, and with the reviewers who reported their introductory performances.

Two of these, "Waiting for Lefty" and "Till the Day I Die," are one-act plays. The first, a vivid and dramatic study of a recent taxi strike in New York from the viewpoint of the strikers engaged, had been given frequently on special Sunday night programs and at various labor meetings. The second is Mr. Odets' contribution to the drama's attacks upon the early Hitler régime in Nazi Germany.

"Awake and Sing," however, follows the conventional three-act form. It reveals an intimate study of Jewish-American family life in the Bronx section of New York. Although it may be classified as an embittered protest against the injustices put upon the poor by the workings of the capitalist system, it escapes most of those extravagances of statement and situation that frequently nullify propagandist drama. The Odets support of and sympathy for his protagonists are vital factors in his writing and of unquestioned importance in the results he obtains. But, while he is not one who would permit a too close adherence to cold logic to rob him of an effective scene, he is, in this instance, also restrained by quite as strong a conviction that truth in itself is the successful dramatist's chief aid to success.

It is a Fall evening in New York at the opening of this drama, the title of which derives from Isaiah 26: 19: "Awake and sing, ye that dwell in dust." The view is of a divided scene showing part of both dining room and living room in a Bronx apartment. The Berger family is just finishing the evening meal. The table

236

conversation is desultory, but at the moment high-pitched and a little strident because of the protests of Ralph Berger, a lad in his early twenties. "Ralph is a boy with a clean spirit. He wants to know, wants to learn. He is ardent, he is romantic, he is sensitive."

Ralph is also pretty disgusted with life in general and with his particular part of it. Doesn't like his job; doesn't believe he has a chance for advancement. A stock clerk in a silk house! Five dollars a week for expenses and the rest he gives to the house! What chance?

Ralph gets little sympathy from Bessie Berger, his mother; some understanding from Myron, his father; most understanding from Jacob, his grandfather; a gentle razzing from Hennie, his sister. But none can answer his reiterated query as to what life is all about.

To Myron life's a cakewalk. To Hennie all it gets you is a four-car funeral. To Jacob life has its objectives—

"If this life leads to a revolution it's a good life. Otherwise it's for nothing," says Jacob.

"It's crazy," protests Ralph, shrilly. "All my life I want a pair of black and white shoes and can't get them. It's crazy."

Such talk is too much for Bessie, who is "not only the mother but the father in this home." She can't eat another bite, so upset is she over the wrangling. And Bessie, doing her living best, on her feet twenty-four hours—

"What do I do? Go to nightclubs with Greta Garbo?" shrills Ralph, accepting the challenge. "Then when I come home can't even have my own room? Sleep on a day-bed in the front room!" His voice is choked as he rushes out.

"When Hennie here marries you'll have her room," Bessie calls after him, adding prayerfully: "I should only live to see the day!"

"Me, too," echoes Hennie.

The talk turns to family affairs and neighbor gossip. Has the dog been fed? . . . There are ants in the sink. . . . A butcher on Beck Street has won eighty thousand dollars in an Irish Sweepstakes. . . . Yesterday they threw out a family on Dawson Street with all the furniture on the street.

There's something that Myron forgot. Sam Feinschreiber sent Hennie a present and he had forgotten to give it to her. Sam's crazy about Hennie. But Hennie will have none of Sam or his chocolate peanuts. Only Bessie is interested.

"It's time you already had in your head a serious thought," her mother warns Hennie. "A girl twenty-six don't grow younger.

When I was your age it was already a big family with responsibilities."

"Maybe that's what ails you, Mom," laughs Hennie. . . .

The dinner is over, table clearing begun. Hennie waxes generous. She'll take her mother and father to the vaudeville at the Franklin. Nor let a reported date she had with Moe Axelrod keep her home.

"Don't break appointments, Beauty, and hurt people's feelings," advises her father.

"His hands got free wheeling," explains Hennie, defensively.

Ralph has come back and silently finished his supper. Bessie and Myron have gone to dress for the vaudeville. Only Jacob is there to hear Ralph's further protests against his lot.

"There's an expression: 'Strong as iron you must be,' " quotes Jacob.

"It's a cockeyed world," protests Ralph.

"Boys like you could fix it some day," promises the grandfather. "Look on the world, not on yourself so much. Every country with starving millions, no? In Germany and Poland a Jew couldn't walk in the street. Everybody hates, nobody loves."

"I don't get all that."

"For years, I watched you grow up. Wait! You'll graduate from my university."

Ralph is not cheered. After the others have left for the theatre he is still bitter.

"I never in my life even had a birthday party," he protests. "Every time I went and cried in the toilet when my birthday came."

Tonight Ralph is going out, and going out right—with a clean shirt. Ralph's got a girl. A girl who lives in Yorkville with an aunt and an uncle; a bunch of relatives but no parents—

RALPH—But she's got me! Boy, I'm telling you I could sing! Jake, she's like stars. She's so beautiful you look at her and cry! She's like French words! We went to the park the other night. Heard the last band concert.

JACOB—Music. . . .

RALPH—It got cold and I gave her my coat to wear. We just walked along like that, see, without a word, see? I never was so happy in all my life. It got late . . . we just sat there. She looked at me—you know what I mean, how a girl looks at you—right in the eyes? "I love you," she says. I took her home. . . . I wanted to cry. That's how I felt!

JACOB—It's a beautiful feeling.

RALPH—You said a mouthful!

JACOB—Her name is—

RALPH—Blanche.

JACOB—A fine name. Bring her sometimes here.

RALPH—She's scared to meet Mom.

JACOB—Why?

RALPH—You know Mom's not letting my sixteen bucks out of the house if she can help it. She'd take one look at Blanche and insult her in a minute—a kid who's got nothing.

JACOB—Boychick!

RALPH—What's the diff?

JACOB—It's no difference—a plain bourgeois prejudice—but when they find out a poor girl—it ain't so kosher.

RALPH—They don't have to know I've got a girl.

JACOB—What's in the end?

RALPH—Out I go! I don't mean maybe!

JACOB—And then what?

RALPH—Life begins.

JACOB—What life?

RALPH—Life with my girl. Boy, I could sing when I think about it! Her and me together—that's a new life!

JACOB—Don't make a mistake! A new death!

RALPH—What's the idea?

JACOB—Me, I'm the idea! Once I had in my heart a dream, a vision, but came marriage and then you forget. Children come and you forget because—

RALPH—Don't worry, Jake.

JACOB—Remember, a woman insults a man's soul like no other thing in the whole world!

RALPH—Why get so excited? No one—

JACOB—Boychick, wake up! Be something! Make your life something good. For the love of an old man who sees in your young days his new life, for such love take the world in your two hands and make it like new. Go out and fight so life shouldn't be printed on dollar bills. A woman waits.

RALPH—Say, I'm no fool!

Moe Axelrod is at the door. "Moe lost a leg in the war. He seldom forgets that fact. He has killed two men in extra-martial activity. He is mordant, bitter. Life has taught him a disbelief in everything, but he will fight his way through."

Moe has come thinking he had a date with Hennie. Finding

her gone he covers his disappointment in chatter with Jacob. It is Jacob's opinion that Moe is a no-good and that he will never change, but he likes him. And so he should, thinks Moe—

"Didn't I go fight in France for democracy? Didn't I get my goddam leg shot off in that war the day before the armistice? Uncle Sam give me the Order of the Purple Heart, didn't he? What'd you mean, a no-good!"

Jacob has opened the door to his room and put a Caruso record on his phonograph. He and Moe are about to settle down to a quiet game of pinochle for ten cents a deck when the Bergers come excitedly back.

Hennie isn't feeling well. For two weeks she hasn't been feeling well, but tonight she got sick on Prospect Avenue and Bessie had to bring her home. Now Bessie would have Hennie lie down and wait for a doctor. Hennie will not have a doctor, nor will she lie down. There is nothing the matter with her, except the tuna fish she had for lunch.

"Last week you also ate tuna fish?" Bessie queries, suspiciously.

"Yeah, I'm funny for tuna fish," snaps Hennie. "Go to the show—have a good time."

"I don't understand what I did to God He blessed me with such children—" Bessie would wail a further protest, but Moe shuts her up and carries the conversation over to the alleged excuse for his visit. Dabbling in making book on the races Moe has come to bring Myron $6.50 a fifty-cent bet had won for him on a twelve-and-a-half-to-one shot. Bessie is disgusted Myron didn't bet more, so long as Moe said it was a sure thing.

Moe had gone to get change to pay Myron and Bessie goes back to getting Hennie to bed. Hennie is still obdurate. Again she isn't sick. She doesn't want a doctor. Slowly, as her excitement rises and her protests grow shrill, Bessie understands. She would send Jacob to the roof with the dog while she confirms her suspicions, but Hennie doesn't care whether her grandfather goes or stays. Suddenly she is defiant. There is confession in her eyes. Bessie, her face blanched with pain, towers above her.

"Who's the man?" demands Bessie.

"The Prince of Wales!" sneers Hennie.

BESSIE—My gall is busting in me. In two seconds—

HENNIE (*in a violent outburst*)—Shut up! Shut up! I'll jump out the window in a minute! Shut up! (*Finally she gains control of herself, says in a low hard voice:*) You don't know him.

JACOB—Bessie. . . .

BESSIE—He's a Bronx boy?

HENNIE—From out of town.

BESSIE—What do you mean?

HENNIE—From out of town!!

BESSIE—A long time you know him? You were sleeping by a girl from the office Saturday nights? You slept good, my lovely lady. You'll go to him . . . he'll marry you.

HENNIE—That's what you say.

BESSIE—That's what I say! He'll do it, take *my* word he'll do it!

HENNIE—Where? (*To* JACOB.) Give her the letter. (JACOB *does so.*)

BESSIE—What? (*Reads.*) "Dear Sir: In reply to your request of the 14th inst., we can state that no Mr. Ben Grossman has ever been connected with our organization. . . ." You don't know where he is?

HENNIE—No.

BESSIE (*walking back and forth*)—Stop crying like a baby, Myron.

MYRON—It's like a play on the stage. . . .

BESSIE—To a mother you couldn't say something before. I'm old-fashioned—like your friends I'm not smart—I don't eat chopsuey and run around Coney Island with tramps. (*She walks reflectively to a buffet, picks up a box of candy, puts it down, says to* MYRON.) Tomorrow night bring Sam Feinschreiber for supper.

HENNIE—I won't do it.

BESSIE—You'll do it, my fine beauty, you'll do it!

HENNIE—I'm not marrying a poor foreigner like him. Can't even speak an English word. Not me! I'll go to my grave without a husband.

BESSIE—You don't say! We'll find for you somewhere a millionaire with a pleasure boat. He's going to night school, Sam. For a boy only three years in the country he speaks very nice. In three years he put enough in the bank, a good living.

JACOB—This is serious?

BESSIE—What then? I'm talking for my health? He'll come tomorrow night for supper. By Saturday they're engaged.

Jacob is disgusted to think Bessie would deliberately plan such a thing, but there is no shame in Bessie. She has worked hard to raise a family and she is determined it shall be respected. Nor does she intend taking advice from a man as much a failure as her father has been. A good barber who can't hold a job a week! Let him keep his mouth shut and go to his room.

"But Ralph you don't make like you," Jacob threatens, excitedly, as he shuffles toward his room. "Before you do it I'll die first. He'll find a girl. He'll go in a fresh world with her. This is a house? Marx said it—abolish such families." And as he reaches his door he turns to repeat: "Ralph you don't make like you."

Moe is back with the six-fifty for Myron, but he pays it to Bessie. She tells him of Hennie's engagement and her approaching marriage. The news is bitter to Moe. Not because he has any use for marriage, or for women, but on Hennie's account.

"Who's it—some dope pullin' down twenty bucks a week?" Moe demands, facing Hennie. "Cut your throat, sweetheart. Save time. I say what I think, that's me!"

"That's you," snaps Hennie; "a lousy fourflusher who'd steal the glasses off a blind man! My God, do I need it—to listen to this mutt shoot his mouth off!"

Moe is stopped, but not crushed by Hennie's spirit. After she has gone he is willing to confess to Bessie that he thinks a lot of Hennie. He'd even think of marrying her himself. This is a new idea to Bessie. Moe and Hennie. That should work out fine for all of them.

"You said she was engaged," reminds Moe.

"But maybe she don't know her own mind—" Bessie qualifies. "Say, it's—"

"I need a wife like a hole in the head," Moe presses on. "What's to know about women, I know. Even if I asked her. She won't do it! A guy with one leg—it gives her the heebie-jeebies. I know what she's looking for. An arrow collar guy, a hero, but with a wad of jack. Only the two don't go together. But I got what it takes . . . plenty, and more where it comes from. . . ."

Moe isn't paying much attention when Bessie would urge tea and cake upon him. He is still staring at the door through which Hennie has passed.

"No wet smack . . . a fine girl. . . . She'll burn that guy out in a month," he mutters.

The victrola in Jacob's room is playing a lament from "The Pearl Fishers." Moe is spinning a quarter on the dining room table.

"She wantsa see me crawl—my head on a plate she wants!"

sneers Moe. "A snowball in hell's got a better chance."
He is matching Myron for the quarter as

THE CURTAIN FALLS.

ACT II

It is a year later. In the front room of the Berger apartment
Jacob has reverted for the moment to his old trade of barbering.
He is cutting the hair of his son, Mordecai, seated high in a chair
in the center of the room, with papers spread on the floor. "Mordecai is a successful American business man with five good senses;
. . . a rich relative to the Berger family; . . . he can blink in
the sun for hours; a fat tomcat; . . . he lives in a penthouse
with a real Japanese butler to serve him; . . . he sleeps with
dress models, but not from his own showrooms; . . . he sees
every Mickey Mouse cartoon which appears; . . . he is a 32nd
degree Mason; . . . he is really deeply intolerant finally."

Uncle Morty is reading jokes during the haircutting process.
Moe Axelrod and Ralph are reading the Sunday papers spas-
modically. Bessie is in and out, interested in the preparation of
a duck for dinner. Uncle Morty prefers goose, but today he is
going to get duck. Goose next time, perhaps. Uncle Morty is
also going to have a little seltzer if Bessie can induce Ralph to
fetch it. Ralph is waiting for a telephone call and is not inclined
to stir, but he goes finally for the seltzer. Misses his call, too.
He has just left when Bessie answers the phone and assures a
Miss Hirsch that she has a wrong number. . . .

The gossip is general. Moe finds the newspapers reporting
more and more suicides by roof jumping. Morty was witness to
one. Fearful sight when the victim struck the sidewalk. He
had to be swept up. Times are terrible and getting worse. Ralph
has had another wage cut. Myron is working only three days a
week. Hennie is married with a baby—and no money coming in.
"I never saw conditions should be so bad," wails Bessie.

Business is terrible with Uncle Morty too. So terrible that he
could lay all day in a Turkish bath and lose nothing. Yet he
sends his five dollars every week for Jacob's care with Bessie.

Hennie has been looking after the baby. Now she would call
Sam, her husband, to take the baby's washing. . . .

Moe has a couple of grievances. He doesn't want his morning
paper disturbed before he reads it. And he doesn't want any of
the Bergers using his razors. Moe, as a star boarder, is par-

ticular. . . .

The haircut is finished and paid for with a dollar bill, though Jacob's charge is only a nickel. Jacob takes advantage of the moment to ask Morty to take care of a large envelope for him. It contains his life insurance policy. Some day Ralph will have three thousand dollars from that policy. Jacob doesn't think it necessary to tell Bessie, but he is anxious that Morty shall be careful of the policy.

Ralph is back with the seltzer and anxious to hear about his expected telephone call. He is furious with his mother when he is certain she is lying about the wrong number call. Bessie, on the defensive before Uncle Morty, would explain that Ralph has been very disappointing, running around with a girl for a year now, a girl with no parents, an orphan—

"I could die from shame," protests Bessie. "A year already he runs around with her. He brought her once for supper. Believe me, she didn't come again, no!"

"Don't think I didn't ask her," shouts Ralph.

BESSIE (*to* MORTY)—You hear? You raise them and what's in the end for all your trouble?

JACOB—When you lay in a grave, no more trouble. (*Exits.*)

MORTY—Quack, quack.

BESSIE—A girl like that he wants to marry. A skinny consumptive-looking . . . six months already she's not working— taking charity from an aunt. You should see her. In a year she's dead on his hands.

RALPH—You'd cut her throat if you could.

BESSIE—That's right! Before she'd ruin a nice boy's life I would first go to prison. Miss Nobody should step in the picture and I'll stand by with my mouth shut.

RALPH—Miss Nobody! Who am I? Al Jolson?

BESSIE—Fix your tie!

RALPH—I'll take care of my own life.

BESSIE—You'll take care? Excuse my expression, you can't even wipe your nose yet! He'll take care!

MORTY (*to* BESSIE)—I'm surprised. Don't worry so much, Bessie. When it's time to settle down he won't marry a poor girl, will you? In the long run common sense is thicker than love. I'm a great boy for live and let live.

BESSIE—Sure, it's easy to say. In the meantime he eats out my heart. You know I'm not strong.

MORTY—I know . . . a pussy cat . . . ha, ha, ha.

BESSIE—You got money and money talks. But without the dollar who sleeps at night?

RALPH—I been working for years, bringing in money here—putting it in your hand like a kid. All right, I can't get my teeth fixed. All right, that a new suit's like trying to buy the Chrysler Building. You never in your life bought me a pair of skates even—things I died for when I was a kid. I don't care about that stuff, see. Only just remember I pay some of the bills around here, just a few . . . and if my girl calls me on the phone I'll talk any time I please. (*He exits.* HENNIE *applauds.*)

BESSIE—Don't be so smart! Miss America! (*To* MORTY.) He didn't have skates! But when he got sick, a twelve-year-old boy, who called a big specialist for the last $25 in the house? Skates!

Bessie has gone to hurry the dinner. Uncle Morty has had a few comforting words with Hennie, the doleful. She can, if she will, come down to Uncle Morty's place and pick out a couple of the "eleven-eighty line," if she'll promise not to sing her uncle the blues. . . .

Myron has taken Morty in to have a taste of schnapps. He knows where Bessie keeps it. Moe is standing in the door watching Sam Feinschreiber as he starts for the kitchen to fix the baby's bottle. Moe thinks perhaps Hennie's hired a nurse, not married a husband. There's a story in the paper about a woman who strangled her husband with picture wire because she didn't like him. Hennie might brain Sam with an ax—

"Christ, you coulda had a guy with some guts instead of a cluck stands around boilin' baby nipples," sneers Moe.

"Meaning you?"

"Meaning me, sweetheart."

HENNIE—Think you're pretty good.

MOE—You'd know if I slept with you again.

HENNIE—I'll smack your face in a minute.

MOE—You do and I'll break your arm. (*Holds up paper.*) Take a look. (*Reads.*) "Ten-day luxury cruise to Havana." That's the stuff you coulda had. Put up at ritzy hotels, frenchie soap, champagne. Now you're tied down to "Snake-Eye" here. What for? What's it get you? . . . a 2 by 4 flat on 108th Street . . . a pain in the bustle it gets you.

HENNIE—What's it to you?

MOE—I know you from the old days. How you like to spend

it! What I mean! Lizard skin shoes, perfumed behind the ears. . . . You're in a mess, Paradise! Paradise—that's a hot one—yah, crazy to eat a knish at your own wedding.

HENNIE—I get it—you're jealous. You can't get me.

MOE—Don't make me laugh.

HENNIE—Kid Jailbird's been trying to make me for years. You'd give your other leg. I'm hooked? Maybe, but you're in the same boat. Only it's worse for you. I don't give a damn no more, but you gotta yen makes you—

MOE—Don't make me laugh.

HENNIE—Compared to you I'm sittin' on the top of the world.

MOE—You're losing your looks. A dame don't stay young forever.

HENNIE—You're a liar. I'm only twenty-four.

MOE—When you comin' home to stay?

HENNIE—Wouldn't you like to know?

MOE—I'll get you again.

HENNIE—Think so?

MOE—Sure, whatever goes up comes down. You're easy—you remember—two for a nickel—a pushover! (*Suddenly she slaps him. They both seem stunned.*) What's the idea?

HENNIE—Go on . . . break my arm.

MOE (*as if saying "I love you"*)—Listen, lousy.

HENNIE—Go on . . . do something!

MOE—Listen—

HENNIE—You're so damned tough!

MOE—You like me. (*He takes her.*)

HENNIE—Take your hand off! (*Pushes him away.*) Come around when it's a flood again and they put you in the ark with the animals. Not even then—if you was the last man!

MOE—Baby, if you had a dog I'd love the dog.

HENNIE—Gorilla!

Hennie has bolted out of the room. Now it is Ralph who is troubled. He must know from Moe more about the telephone call. He is worried about his girl. If Bessie has insulted her again it may be she has gone away. She has been having trouble at home, too. Her family "shove her around like a freight train." Twice they had thrown Ralph down the stairs. No, Ralph can't take Moe's suggestion and hire "a clubroom for two members." She isn't that kind of a girl.

That's something Moe can laugh at. But he can be serious, too. He doesn't want to ride Ralph. Wants him to grow up.

Wants him to get independent. "Get what it takes and be yourself. Do what you like!" is Moe's advice. "Pick out a racket. Shake down the cocoanuts. See what that does."

"It's all a racket—from horse racing down," Moe says to Uncle Morty, Morty being strong for the law. "Marriage, politics, big business—everybody plays cops and robbers. You, you're a racketeer yourself."

MORTY—Who? Me? Personally I manufacture dresses.

MOE—Horse feathers!

MORTY (*seriously*)—Don't make such remarks to me without proof. I'm a great one for proof. That's why I made a success in business. Proof—put up or shut up, like a game of cards. I heard this remark before—a rich man's a crook who steals from the poor. Personally, I don't like it. It's a big lie!

MOE—If you don't like it, buy yourself a fife and drum—and go fight your own war.

MORTY—Sweatshop talk. Every Jew and Wop in the shop eats my bread and behind my back says, "a sonofabitch." I started from a poor boy who worked on an ice wagon for two dollars a week. Pop's right here—he'll tell you. I made it honest. In the whole industry nobody's got a better name.

JACOB—It's an exception, such success.

MORTY—Ralph can't do the same thing?

JACOB—No, Morty, I don't think. In a house like this he don't realize even the possibilities of life. Economics comes down like a ton of coal on the head.

MOE—Red rover, red rover, let Jacob come over!

JACOB—In my day the propaganda was for God. Now it's for success. A boy don't turn around without having shoved in him he should make success.

MORTY—Pop, you're a comedian, a regular Charlie Chaplin.

JACOB—He dreams all night of fortunes. Why not? Don't it say in the movies he should have a personal steamshop, pyjamas for fifty dollars a pair and a toilet like a monument? But in the morning he wakes up and for ten dollars he can't fix the teeth. And millions more worse off in the mills of the South— starvation wages. The blood from the worker's heart. (MORTY *laughs loud and long.*) Laugh, laugh . . . tomorrow not.

MORTY—A real, a real Boob McNutt you're getting to be.

JACOB—Laugh, my son. . . .

MORTY—Here is the North, Pop.

JACOB—North, south, it's one country.

MORTY—The country's all right. A duck quacks in every pot!

JACOB—You never heard how they shoot down men and women which ask a better wage? Kentucky 1932?

MORTY—That's a pile of chopped liver, Pop. (BESSIE *enters*.)

JACOB—Pittsburgh, Passaic, Illinois—slavery—it begins where success begins in a competitive system. (MORTY *howls with delight*.)

MORTY—Oh, Pop, what are you bothering? Why? Tell me why? Ha, ha, ha. I bought you a phonograph . . . stick to Caruso.

BESSIE—He's starting up again.

MORTY—Don't bother with Kentucky. It's full of moonshiners.

JACOB—Sure, sure. . . .

MORTY—You don't know practical affairs. Stay home and cut hair to fit the face.

JACOB—It says in the Bible how the Red Sea opened and the Egyptians went in and the sea rolled over them. (*Quotes two lines of Hebrew*.) In this boy's life a Red Sea will happen again. I see it!

Morty is pretty mad by this time. Bessie is mad, too. Ralph is the only one with any sympathy for Jacob, and they shut Ralph up quickly. Jacob would go on, arguing an old man's rights. In Russia they know how to treat an old man. In Russia they got Marx—

"Who's Marx?" scoffs Morty.

"An outfielder for the Yanks," shouts Moe, and Morty is convulsed. Russia is funny, too. Myron and Bessie are agreed to that. Let anybody read the papers. Here, insists Sam Feinschreiber, is opportunity.

"People can't believe in God in Russia. The papers tell the truth, they do," insists Myron.

"So you believe in God . . . you got something for it?" demands Jacob, keen for argument. "You! You worked for all the capitalists. You harvested the fruit from your labor? You got God! But the past comforts you? The present smiles on you, yes? It promises you the future something? Did you found a piece of earth where you could like a human being and die with the sun on your face? Tell me, yes, tell me. I would like to know myself. But on these questions, on this theme—the struggle for existence—you can't make an answer. The answer I see in your face . . . the answer is your mouth can't talk. In

this dark corner you sit and you die. But abolish private property!"

Bessie would settle the issue now. Let Jacob go fight City
Hall if he wants to. It is Morty's opinion that Jacob is drunk,
anyway. Drunk and a nut. In the park the squirrels could get
him.

They've finally gone into dinner. All except Jacob and Ralph.
The phone rings again and Ralph is quick to answer this time.
Jacob stands guard at the door. Then he turns on the radio and
gives Ralph a chance to talk.

Ralph gets the news now. Things are happening at the
Hirsches'. They're sending Blanche away. Sending her to Cleveland. Sending her out West in a week or two! But they can't
get away with that. It's a put-up job! Ralph hangs up the
phone. He's going down there.

"We'll find something," consoles Jacob.

"Sure, the angels of Heaven'll come down on her uncle's cab
and whisper in his ear," answers Ralph, bitterly, tears in his
voice.

JACOB—Come eat. . . . We'll find something.

RALPH—I'm meeting her tonight, but I know— (BESSIE
throws open the curtain between the two rooms and enters.)

BESSIE—Maybe we'll serve for you a special blue plate supper
in the garden?

JACOB—All right, all right. (BESSIE *goes over to the window,
levels the shade and on her way out, clicks off the radio.*)

MORTY (*within*)—Leave the music, Bessie. (*She clicks it on
again, looks at them, exits.*)

RALPH—I know . . .

JACOB—Don't cry, Boychick. Why should you make like this?
Tell me why you should cry, just tell me. . . . (JACOB *takes*
RALPH *in his arms and both, trying to keep back the tears, trying
fearfully not to be heard by the others in the dining room, begin
crying.*) You mustn't cry. . . .

"The tango twists on. Inside the clatter of dishes and the clash
of cutlery sound. Morty begins to howl with laughter" as the
curtain falls.

It is later the same night. The living room is dark. A light
shines through the door of Jacob's room. Inside the room Jacob
can be heard reading from a sheet, "declaiming aloud as to an

audience—"

"They are there to remind us of the horrors—under those crosses lie hundreds of thousands of workers and farmers who murdered each other in uniform for the greater glory of capitalism. (*Comes out of his room.*) The new imperialist war will send millions to their death, will bring prosperity to the pockets of the capitalists—aie, Morty—and will bring only greater hunger and misery to the masses of workers and farmers. The memories of the last world slaughter are still vivid in our minds."

Ralph disturbs the soliloquy. Ralph has found it cold outside. He is not inclined to talk about anything else at first. He is pretty low. Nor does Jacob's forced optimism cheer him. Finally he tells something of his evening. He had waited in Mount Morris Park until Blanche came. She explained. They wanted her to marry a millionaire, too. Ralph met that with his own offer of marriage—on sixteen bucks a week and knowing that his mother would get Uncle Morty to fire him in a second!

"I'd fight the whole goddam world with her, but not her," wails Ralph. "No guts! The hell with her! If she wantsa go—all right—I'll get along."

"For sure, there's more important things than girls. . . ."

"You said a mouthful . . . and maybe I don't see it. She'll see what I can do. No one stops me when I get going. . . ."

Ralph is near to tears now. Jacob would cheer him with an old man's philosophy. All an old man can do is talk. But Ralph can do. Ralph should act.

"DO! Do what is in your heart and you carry in yourself a revolution," prompts Jacob. "But you should act. Not like me. A man who had golden opportunities but drank instead a glass of tea. No . . ."

Sam Feinschreiber has burst into the room. He is wild-eyed and disheveled. He is looking for Mom. He can't sit down. He can't keep quiet. The signs indicate that Sam has had another fight with Hennie, suggests Ralph. Incoherently Sam is ready to admit it, and to add that one day Hennie will fight once too often. Sam's a person with a bad heart. In the old country the Cossacks had caught his father and cut off his beard. The old man had gone to bed, and covered his face. In two days he was dead—dead of shame. Dead from a broken heart. Sam, too, could die of shame.

"Hennie told you something?" suggests Jacob.

"Straight out she said it," wails Sam; "like a lightning from the sky. The baby ain't mine. She said it."

"Don't be a dope!" scoffs Ralph.

"For sure, a joke!" echoes Jacob.

"She's kidding you!"

"She should kid a policeman, not Sam Feinschreiber," protests the unhappy Sam. "Please . . . you don't know her like me. I wake up in the nighttime and she sits watching me like I don't know what. I make a nice living from the store. But it's no use—she looks for a star in the sky. I'm afraid like anything. You could go crazy from less even. What I shall do I'll ask Mom."

" 'Go home and sleep,' she'll say," promises Jacob. " 'It's a bad dream.' "

But Sam isn't convinced. He's too nervous—so nervous that twice he weighed himself on the subway station. . . .

Bessie and Myron have come home and Sam is ready to burst through again with the story of Hennie. Ralph and Jacob manage to retire discreetly. Now Sam can talk freely. Hennie had said he was a second fiddle in his own house, he repeats. Like a knife in the heart it stabbed him. Like a dead he fell in the chair. For ten miles everybody could hear, Hennie had yelled so.

"Hennie don't feel well, Sam," explains Myron. "You see, she—"

BESSIE—What then?—a sick girl. Believe me, a mother knows. Nerves. Our Hennie's got a bad temper. You'll let her she says anything. She takes after me—nervous. (*To* MYRON.) You ever heard such a remark in all your life? She should make such a statement! Bughouse.

MYRON—The little one's been sick all these months. Hennie needs a rest. No doubt.

BESSIE—Sam don't think she means it—

MYRON—Oh, I know he don't, of course—

BESSIE—I'll say the truth, Sam. We didn't half the time understand her ourselves. A girl with her own mind. When she makes it up, wild horses wouldn't change her.

SAM—She don't love me.

BESSIE—This is sensible, Sam?

SAM—Not for a nickel.

BESSIE—What do you think? She married you for your money? For your looks? You ain't no John Barrymore, Sam. No, she liked you.

SAM—Please, not for a nickel. (JACOB *stands in the doorway.*)

BESSIE—We stood right here the first time she said it. "Sam

Feinschreiber's a nice boy," she said it, "a boy he's got good common sense, with a business head." Right here she said it, in this room. You sent her two boxes of candy together, you remember?

MYRON—Loft's candy.

BESSIE—This is when she said it. What do you think?

MYRON—You were just the only boy she cared for.

BESSIE—So she married you. Such a world . . . plenty of boy friends she had, believe me!

JACOB—A popular girl . . .

MYRON—Y-e-s.

BESSIE—I'll say it plain out—Moe Axelrod offered her plenty —a servant, a house . . . she don't have to pick up a hand.

MYRON—Oh, Moe? Just wild about her . . .

SAM—Moe Axelrod? He wanted to—

BESSIE—But she didn't care. A girl like Hennie you don't buy. I should never live to see another day if I'm telling a lie.

SAM—She was kidding me.

BESSIE—What then? You shouldn't be foolish.

Sam is reassured at last. The baby *has* got Feinschreiber eyes. And they do say he looks like Sam. It would be easy, as Bessie points out, for Hennie to pick a name out of the phone book, if it's only the father's name that worries him—

Sam has gone. Jacob is getting ready to take Tootsie, the dog, on the roof. Ralph has come in, hoping to have a word with his mother. Bessie is not inclined to listen. Less inclined when she hears it's about his girl that Ralph wants to talk. Bessie has no intention of doing anything to help along Ralph's affair. She wouldn't think of having Blanche in the house, even for a few weeks, as Ralph pleads. Neither as Ralph's wife "or as a girl he might sleep with without marriage—"

"Make up your mind for your own good, Ralphie," Bessie concludes; "if she dropped in the ocean I don't lift a finger."

"That's all, I suppose," says Ralph.

"With me it's one thing—a boy should have respect for his future. Go to sleep, you look tired. In the morning you'll forget."

" 'Awake and sing, ye that dwell in dust, and the earth shall cast out the dead,' " quotes Jacob.

Something that Myron says about Hennie and Sam stirs Ralph to a new resentment. So that's how things are! They talk about respect and then they trap a guy like Sam! And Jacob knew, and let them do it! What a laugh!

"Let me say something, son," pleads Myron, laying a paternal hand on Ralph's arm.

"Take your hand away!" shouts Ralph. "Sit in a corner and wag your tail. Keep on boasting you went to law school for two years."

MYRON—I want to tell you—

RALPH—You never in your life had a thing to tell me.

BESSIE (*bitterly*)—Don't say a word. Let him, let him run and tell Sam. Publish in the papers, give a broadcast on the radio. To him it don't matter nothing his family sits with tears pouring from the eyes. (*To* JACOB.) What are you waiting for? I didn't tell you twice already about the dog? You'll stand around with Caruso and make a bughouse. It ain't enough all day long. Fifty times I told you I'll break every record in the house. (*She brushes past him, breaks the records, comes out.*) The next time I say something you'll maybe believe it. Now maybe you learned a lesson. (*Pause.*)

JACOB (*quietly*)—Bessie, new lessons . . . not for an old dog.

MYRON—You didn't have to do it, Momma. (MOE *enters.*)

BESSIE—Talk better to your son, Mr. Berger! Me, I don't lay down and die for him and Poppa no more. I'll work like a nigger? For what? Wait, the day comes when you'll be punished. When it's too late you'll remember how you sucked away a mother's life. Talk to him, tell him how I don't sleep at night. (*Bursts into tears and exits.*)

MOE (*sings*)—"Good-by to all your sorrows. You never hear them talk about the war, in the land of Yama Yama . . ."

MYRON—Yes, Momma's a sick woman, Ralphie.

RALPH—Yeah?

MOE—We'll be out of the trenches by Christmas. Putt, putt, putt, . . . here, stinker . . . (*Picks up Tootsie, a small, white poodle that just then enters from the hall.*) If there's reincarnation in the next life I wanna be a dog and lay in a fat lady's lap.

Jacob has taken Tootsie and started for the roof. It is cold out, but Jacob has been cold before. It is snowing, too. But there are no snows like the old snows that Myron remembers. The Great Blizzard, for instance.

Moe is singing of the land of Yama Yama and dealing himself a card hand. Myron is still trying to make friends with his son. Suddenly there is a violent ringing of the downstairs door-bell.

It is late and everybody's accounted for. Why the ringing?
Now there is someone at the upstairs door. It is Schlosser, the
janitor. Myron has let him in. The family crowds about him.
What's the trouble?

It's Jacob! He slipped, maybe, off the roof. Bessie can't
understand. In a daze she listens.

"Your fadder fall off the roof, ja!" repeats Schlosser.

"Myron . . . Call Morty!" Bessie shouts, staring dazedly
ahead of her. "Call Morty on the phone!" Then, as Myron
starts, she calls: "No! I'll do it myself! I'll . . . do it!"

Schlosser has gone. Moe goes on with his card game. Bessie
fumbles with the phone dials, muttering to herself. "He slipped!"
she says.

"I can't see the numbers," says Bessie, brushing the mist out
of her eyes. "Make it, Moe. Make it—"

"Make it yourself," answers Moe, going back to his card game.

"Riverside 7—" Slowly the dials whizz around.

"Don't . . . make me laugh . . ." sneers Moe, turning over his
cards.

THE CURTAIN FALLS

ACT III

A week later Uncle Morty, Bessie and Myron are having a bite
in the dining room, while Moe Axelrod, in the living room adjoining, is pretending to mark a dope sheet. His ears are cocked,
however, and he is hearing much of what is being said.

The discussion in the dining room is concerned with the im-
pending call of the insurance man. Morty, who has "shtupped"
him $10, is sure he will come. It is Morty's idea that Bessie
should make a quick settlement, considering the expense she has
been under.

"Ralphie don't know papa left the insurance in his name,"
says Myron.

"It's not his business," answers Morty, shortly. "And I'll tell
him."

Ralph has come into the front room and is talking with Moe.
Ralph has had a letter from Blanche. She is giving Ralph up
because, she says, if he cared he would have been to see her before. She sends him a locket on a chain and will phone before
she goes. . . .

"They're trying to rook you—a freeze-out," Moe reports, holding Ralph back when he starts to go

"Who?"

"That bunch stuffin' their gut with hot pastrami. Morty in particular. Jake left the insurance—three thousand dollars—for you."

"For me?"

"Now you got wings, kid. Pop figured you could use it. That's why . . ."

"That's why what?"

"It ain't the only reason he done it."

"He done it?"

"You think a breeze blew him off?"

"I'm not sure what I think."

Hennie has come in. Moe has shoved Ralph into Jacob's room to get a little sleep before the insurance man comes. Now Sam has followed Hennie. Sam is ready to go home, if Hennie is. The baby has been all day with Mrs. Strasberg. But Hennie is not ready to go. If she were Moe would hold her back. He has something he wants to tell her. Moe's leaving. Leaving tonight. He—

The family interrupts. Morty is getting ready to go. It is raining. The thought that Jacob is lying in the rain disturbs Sam. But not Morty.

"Personally, Pop was a fine man," agrees Morty. "But I'm a great boy for an honest opinion. He had enough crazy ideas for a regiment."

Ralph has joined the circle. His serious expression attracts their attention. Morty is the first to notice it.

"What's the matter, Ralphie?" he asks. "What are you looking funny?"

"I hear I'm left insurance and the man's coming tonight," answers Ralph.

MORTY—Poppa didn't leave no insurance for you.

RALPH—What?

MORTY—In your name he left it—but not for you.

RALPH—It's my name on the paper.

MORTY—Who said so?

RALPH (to his mother)—The insurance man's coming to‹ night?

MORTY—What's the matter?

RALPH—I'm not talking to you. (To his mother.) Why?

BESSIE—I don't know why.

RALPH—He don't come in this house tonight.

MORTY—That's what *you* say.

RALPH—I'm not talking to you, Uncle Morty, but I'll tell you, too, he don't come here tonight when there's still mud on a grave. (*To his mother.*)   Couldn't you give the house a chance to cool off?

MORTY—Is this a way to talk to your mother?

RALPH—Was that a way to talk to your father?

MORTY—Don't be so smart with me, Mr. Ralph Berger!

RALPH—Don't be so smart with *me*.

MORTY—What'll you do?   I say he's coming tonight.   Who says no?

MOE (*suddenly, from the background*)—Me.

MORTY—Take a back seat, Axelrod.   When you re in the family—

MOE—I got a little document here.   (*Produces paper.*)   I found it under his pillow that night.   A guy who slips off a roof don't leave a note before he does it.

MORTY (*starting for* MOE *after a horrified silence*)—Let me see this note.

BESSIE—Morty, don't touch it!

MOE—Not if you crawled.

MORTY—It's a fake.   Poppa wouldn't—

MOE—Get the insurance guy here and we'll see how—   (*The bell rings.*)   Speak of the devil . . .   Answer it, see what happens.   (MORTY *starts for the ticker.*)

BESSIE—Morty, don't!

MORTY (*stopping*)—Be practical, Bessie.

MOE—Sometimes you don't collect on suicides if they know about it.

MORTY—You should let . . .   You should let him . . .   (*A pause in which* all *seem dazed.   Bell rings insistently.*)

MOE—Well, we're waiting.

MORTY—Give me the note.

MOE—I'll give you the head off your shoulders.

MORTY—Bessie, you'll stand for this?   (*Points to* RALPH.) Pull down his pants and give him with a strap.

RALPH (*as bell rings again*)—How about it?

BESSIE—Don't be crazy.   It's not my fault.   Morty said he should come tonight.   It's not nice so soon.   I didn't—

MORTY—I said it?   Me?

BESSIE—Who then?

MORTY—You didn't sing a song in my ear a whole week to settle quick?

BESSIE—I'm surprised. Morty, you're a big liar.

MYRON—Momma's telling the truth, she is!

MORTY—Lissen. In two shakes of a lamb's tail, we'll start a real fight and then nobody won't like nobody. Where's my fur gloves? I'm going downtown.

Sam decides to go with Morty, even without Hennie. Hennie is nervous, she explains, with more than her accustomed gentleness. She will sleep there and come home in the morning. She kisses him with feeling. She loves him, she says. Sam is happy.

They have come back to the question of insurance now. Bessie believes it belongs to the whole family. Ralph will get his teeth fixed; Hennie needs a vacation; a family needs for a rainy day, and times are getting worse—

BESSIE—Ralphie, I worked too hard all my years to be treated like dirt. It's no law we should be stuck together like Siamese twins. Summer shoes you didn't have, skates you never had, but I bought a new dress every week. A lover I kept—Mr. Gigolo! Did I ever play a game of cards like Mrs. Marcus? Or was Bessie Berger's children always the cleanest on the block? Here I'm not only the mother, but also the father. The first two years I worked in a stocking factory for six dollars while Myron Berger went to law school. If I didn't worry about the family who would? On the calendar it's a different place, but here without a dollar you don't look the world in the eye. Talk from now to next year—this is life in America.

RALPH—Then it's wrong. It don't make sense. If life made you this way, then it's wrong!

BESSIE—Maybe you wanted me to give up twenty years ago. Where would you be now? You'll excuse my expression—a bum in the park!

RALPH—I'm not blaming you, Mom. Sink or swim—I see it. But it can't stay like this.

BESSIE—My foolish boy . . .

RALPH—No, I see every house lousy with lies and hate. He said it, Grandpa—Brooklyn hates the Bronx. Smacked on the nose twice a day. But girls and boys can get ahead like that, Mom. We don't want life printed on dollar bills, Mom!

BESSIE—So go out and change the world if you don't like it.

RALPH—I will! And why? 'Cause life's different in my head. Gimme the earth in two hands. I'm strong. There . . . hear him? The air mail off to Boston. Day or night, he flies away, a job to do. That's us and it's no time to die. (*The airplane sound fades off as* MYRON *gives alarm clock to* BESSIE *which she begins to wind.*)

BESSIE—"Mom, what does she know? She's old-fashioned!" But I tell you a big secret: My whole life I wanted to go away too, but with children a woman stays home. A fire burned in *my* heart too, but now it's too late. I'm no spring chicken. The clock goes and Bessie goes. Only my machinery can't be fixed.

Bessie and Myron have gone to bed. At the phone Ralph hears again from Blanche. Before he can say anything she hangs up. He can't understand, but no girl can mean anything to him until he can take care of her. Ralph knows that. He has a new idea of life these last few weeks. Still newer ideas since he has found Jacob's books. He has brought an armful of them out of Jacob's room now.

"I got them, too," he says; "the pages ain't cut in half of them. Does it prove something? Damn tootin'! A ten-cent nail-file cuts them. Uptown, downtown, I'll read them on the way. Get a big lamp over the bed. (*Picks one up.*) My eyes are good. (*Puts book in pocket.*) Sure, inventory tomorrow. Coletti to Driscoll to Berger—that's how we work. It's a team down the warehouse. Driscoll's a show-off, a wise guy, and Joe talks pigeons day and night. But they're like me, looking for a chance to get to first base too. Joe razzed me about my girl. But he don't know why. I'll tell him. Hell, he might tell me something I don't know. Get teams together all over. Spit on your hands and get to work. And with enough teams together maybe we'll get steam in the warehouse so our fingers don't freeze off. Maybe we'll fix it so life won't be printed on dollar bills."

Ralph is going back to the room when he remembers the note that his grandfather left. He would have a look at that. Moe gives him the paper. It is blank. . . .

Hennie, who has never cried in her life, is crying now. Moe notices it. He has noticed, too, that she told Sam she loved him. "If I'm sore on life why take it out on him?" explains Hennie.

MOE—You won't forget me to your dyin' day—I was the first guy. Part of your insides. You won't forget. I wrote my name on you—indelible ink!

HENNIE—One thing I won't forget—how you left me crying on the bed like I was two for a cent!

MOE—Listen, do you think—

Hennie—Sure. Waits till the family goes to the open air movie. He brings me perfume. . . . He grabs my arms—

Moe—You won't forget me!

Hennie—How you left the next week?

Moe—So I made a mistake. For chris' sake, don't act like the Queen of Roumania!

Hennie—Don't make me laugh!

Moe—What the hell do you want, my head on a plate? Was my life so happy? Chris', my old man was a bum. I supported the whole damn family—five kids and Mom. When they grew up they beat it the hell away like rabbits. Mom died. I went to the war; got clapped down like a bedbug; woke up in a room without a leg. What the hell do you think, anyone's got it better than you? I never had a home either. I'm lookin' too!

Hennie—So what?

Moe—So you're it—you're home for me, a place to live! That's the whole parade, sickness, eating out your heart! Sometimes you meet a girl—she stops it—that's love. . . . So take a chance! Be with me, Paradise. What's to lose?

Hennie—My pride!

Moe (*grabbing her*)—What do you want? Say the word—I'll tango on a dime. Don't gimme ice when your heart's on fire!

Hennie—Let me go! (*He stops her.*)

Moe—Where?!!

Hennie—What do you want, Moe, what do you want?

Moe—You!

Hennie—You'll be sorry you ever started—

Moe—You!

Hennie—Moe, lemme go— (*Trying to leave.*) I'm getting up early—lemme go.

Moe—No! . . . I got enough fever to blow the whole damn town to hell. (*He suddenly releases her and half stumbles backwards. Forces himself to quiet down.*) You wanna go back to him? Say the word. I'll know what to do. . . .

Hennie (*helplessly*)—Moe, I don't know what to say.

Moe—Listen to me.

Hennie—What?

Moe—Come away. A certain place where it's moonlight and roses. We'll lay down, count stars. Hear the big ocean making noise. You lay under the trees. Champagne flows like—

The phone is ringing. It is Sam. Hennie starts to answer, then changes her mind. "I'm sleeping," she says. It is Sam. He had only wanted to tell her that he got home O.K.

Now Hennie has made up her mind. She has never loved Sam. All her life she has waited for this minute. Her baby? She can't give him up—

"Make a break or spend the rest of your life in a coffin," counsels Moe.

"Oh, God, I don't know where I stand," pleads Hennie.

"Don't look up there," says Moe. "Paradise, you're on a big boat headed south! No more pins and needles in your heart, no snake juice squirted in your arm! The whole world's green grass and when you cry it's because you're happy."

"I didn't hear a word, but do it, Hennie, do it!" Ralph calls from the door.

MOE—Mom can mind the kid. She'll go on forever, Mom. We'll send money back, and Easter eggs.

RALPH—I'll be here.

MOE—Get your coat . . . get it.

HENNIE—Moe!

MOE—I know . . . but get your coat and hat and kiss the house good-by.

HENNIE—The man I love . . . (MYRON *entering.*) I left my coat in Mom's room. (*Exits.*)

MYRON—Don't wake her up, Beauty. Momma fell asleep as soon as her head hit the pillow. I can't sleep. It was a long day. Hmmm. (*Examines his tongue in buffet mirror.*) I was reading the other day a person with a thick tongue is feeble-minded. I can do anything with my tongue. Make it thick, flat. No fruit in the house lately. Just a lone apple. (*He gets apple and paring knife and starts paring.*) Must be something wrong with me—I say I won't eat but I eat. (HENNIE *enters dressed to go out.*) Where are you going, little Red Riding Hood?

HENNIE—Nobody knows, Peter Rabbit.

MYRON—You're looking very pretty tonight. You were a beautiful baby too. 1910, that was the year you was born. The same year Teddy Roosevelt come home from Africa.

HENNIE—Gee, Pop; you're such a funny guy.

MYRON—He was a boisterous man, Teddy. Good night. (*He exits paring apple.*)

RALPH—When I look at him, I'm sad. Let me die like a dog, if I can't get more from life.

HENNIE—Where?

RALPH—Right here in the house! My days won't be for

nothing. Let Mom have the dough. I'm twenty-two and kickin'! I'll get along. Did Jake die for us to fight about nickels? No! "Awake and sing," he said. Right here he stood and said it. The night he died, I saw it like a thunderbolt! I saw he was dead and I was born! I swear to God, I'm one week old! I want the whole city to hear it—fresh blood, arms. We got 'em. We're glad we're living.

Moe—I wouldn't trade you for two pitchers and an outfielder. Hold the fort!

Ralph—So long.

Moe—So long. (*They go and* Ralph *stands full and strong in the doorway seeing them off.*)

THE CURTAIN SLOWLY FALLS

THE FARMER TAKES A WIFE

A Comedy in Three Acts

BY FRANK B. ELSER

NO one had thought to write a play about the old Erie canal until the late Frank B. Elser read Walter D. Edmond's novel called "Rome Haul." Then it occurred to Mr. Elser as something that should be done, both because of the subject's value as a contribution to human comedy and the Erie's historically significant background.

Mr. Elser's first dramatization of Mr. Edmond's book was called "Low Bridge" and was variously produced by those organizations that decorate the fringe of the theatre, including two midwestern universities and one semi-amateur company in New York.

When options on the play lapsed Mr. Elser decided that, inasmuch as he had rewritten it a half dozen times and still was not satisfied, a fresh mind should be called in. He consulted with and aroused the interest of Marc Connelly, who is pretty hard to interest since the success of "The Green Pastures" has made him financially independent. Together they worked the manuscript over and "The Farmer Takes a Wife" is the result.

The play was cast and directed by Connelly and produced at the Forty-sixth Street Theatre in New York, October 30, 1934. Its early reception was enthusiastic, but having satisfied that part of the New York playgoing public interested in early American folk plays, business fell off and the run was concluded in late January with a record of one hundred and four performances.

The Elser-Connelly recital is the homely and human annals of those pioneer boaters who helped make history on the greatest of the inland waterways in 1853. They filled the bars of the canalers' hotels and walked the towpaths of the Big Ditch in perfect confidence that they were kinfolk of the lords of the earth, and they took their defeat by the encroaching railroads with complete befuddlement and little grace. No one of them missed being a character full rounded and amusingly individual. These "canawlers" provide the decoration for the basic romance of a cook-lady who loved the canal and a young farmer from up Black River way who was determined that she should forget it.

At the opening of "The Farmer Takes a Wife" we are in the main room of Hennessy's Hotel in Rome, N. Y. The time is April, 1853. In the center of the room is a large stove of the old-time barrel pattern. At one side is a counter desk, and back of that a mail rack. A barroom, to which frequent reference is made, adjoins the main room.

"Gay wallpaper picks up the halation of the afternoon sun. Posted about the walls are bills of Levi J. North's Circus, Joe Pentland's Circus, Dan Rice's Equestrian Troupe. On the bulletin board to the left of the door up stage is a printed notice addressed 'Captains of the Swiftsure Line'; an announcement of the Ohio Lottery; four or five newspaper clippings; an almanac hanging from a string; a $50 reward sign for a stolen horse and wagon; an announcement from the Canal Commissioner's office signed 'N. J. Beach, Secretary Canal Commissioners.' "

The room at the moment is variously peopled. At one table sits Mrs. Lucy Gurget, plump and middle aged, an operator of a canal boat, and opposite her is Solomon Tinker, her boater. Mrs. Gurget has just finished a drink; Solomon is still occupied with a game of solitaire.

In a kind of alcove at back glimpses may be had of a man at work at some task, the nature of which is kept from the audience by a semi-circle of interested onlookers. Later it is made plain that the worker is Fortune Friendly and that his task is the extraction of a tooth from the upper jaw of one Ivy Elliott, a fancy lady from up Uticy way.

Snatches of conversation from the adjoining barroom can be heard but not easily understood. Occasionally the sound of conch and metal boat horns are heard as coming from the immediate distance.

At the counter two or three boatmen are talking business. Most of it concerns the loading and capacities of boats, the length of the expected haul and the general activities attendant upon the official opening of the canal, scheduled for the next day.

At a side table one Fisher, a scalper, or freight agent, is principally concerned with the assignment of cargoes. Fisher is optimistic regarding the outlook for the season. The ice is reported out of all the feeders, the Black River boats have already started and it is Fisher's prediction that the old canawl will be open all the way a week earlier than she was the year before. Strollers from the barroom pick up the gossip of the canawl.

"Hi, Joseph!" Mrs. Gurget calls to a newcomer.

"Hello, Lucy!" he answers heartily. "Hi, Sol! You startin' tomorrow?"

"If we can git away. You startin' from Rome?"

"No. My boat's at Whitesboro, haulin' butter to Albany. You eastbound?"

"Naw. Surracuse."

"Well, see you on the Big Ditch!"

Harry Emory finds himself in a discussion with the agent Fisher about a cargo of hogs. Harry is tired of hauling hogs, but Fisher insists that once a boat has hauled 'em it ain't fit for much else. Harry has been working on his boat to get the hog smell out, and he wants a new kind of cargo. Nobody ought to haul hogs but pea-soupers anyway. "Them Frenchmen eat garlic and they don't mind it," explains Harry. "But I weren't born to be a hog man, Mr. Fisher. Now I got my boat to smellin' decent again I want to git my wife back."

The boys in the bar have started a song of the canawl. The boys at the counter are ready to take up the tune. Fortune Friendly emerges from the circle surrounding Ivy Elliott with a protest. He is a man of about sixty, wears rimmed spectacles, carries an old-fashioned dentist's turnkey, or "pulican," and is greatly worried.

"Hey, for God's sake, stop that singing!" protests Fortune. "Don't you realize I'm trying to do a delicate operation? You got me so upset I come near pullin' the wrong tooth again. A woman's jaw is at stake!"

"I can't git over him pullin' teeth," says Lucy Gurget, as Fortune returns to his patient. "I didn't think there was anybody between Albany and Buffalo but would know he's no dentist."

"These here announcements is pretty convincin'," ventures Sol.

"Convincin' to who?"

"Anybody that reads 'em. 'Teeth drawn or filled with pure crystal gold without pain.' That's a fair honest statement."

"Well, I don't wish him no harm," concludes Lucy, "but I'm never goin' to itch to have him work on me."

There has been a good deal of horn blowing from time to time. One long, one short blast. It is, we are told, Molly Larkins calling her boater, Jotham Klore; not only calling him to supper, but warning him to come at once. More horn blasts indicate increasing impatience on the part of Miss Larkins.

Now Klore has come from the bar. He is young and good looking, but typically the physical bully. He is also a little drunk and, so far as Molly's horn blasts are concerned, it is his announced intention to "let 'er blow."

"And I'll tell you why I'm taking my time," he explains, sensing the opposition of Mrs. Gurget and the others. "She's gittin' too independent. She gits notional and wants to be the Cook and the Captain too. She bossed her pa around like he was a driver boy. This year she's signed up with a canawler that's goin' to learn her *different*."

"Mebbe you're goin' to learn somethin' too."

"What would *that* be?"

"No good cook likes to keep supper waitin'," declares Mrs. Gurget. "Especially when she's the best cook on the Erie. Why do you suppose all them fellers used to visit Captain Larkin's so much for? Just to see how *he* was feelin'?"

"That don't cause me anguish. You notice they ain't bothered her none since her pa died? By God, I licked the two of them comin' home from the funeral."

There is no denying that Klore has stood up for Molly, Sol admits, nor that "all gals is fools for boaters that fight for 'em," but Mrs. Gurget is of the opinion that if some of the other fellows "had a little gristle on their bellies" Molly Larkins might get a better article. . . .

Fortune Friendly has completed his operation and Ivy Elliott, a little wobbly from the effects of the rum they have fed her, is content with the loss of her teeth. She is not, however, a very good sales argument for Fortune. A Mr. Otway, who is paying Miss Elliott's bill, is doubtful as to whether he should pay Fortune for the tooth extracted by mistake, but Fortune makes a convincing point of the fact that the tooth pulled was the tooth Ivy pointed to, for which he has eye-witness. And his unvarying rate is a dollar a tooth.

"It's ironical," Fortune insists, after Ivy and her friend have left. "I give up preaching to be a dentist, and my first patient is a Magdalene from a parlor house."

Fortune takes a stimulating drink and feels refreshed, but he has no intention of gambling his two dollars away. He plans to frame these particular bills, the first dollars earned in a new career, and hang them in his office, when he has an office, either in Philadelphia or New York. He has practically given up gambling for all time—

"Except occasionally for pleasure," he explains. "The only good luck I've really had in the last year was winning this set of tools from that dentist in Albany. I might go back next month. He's got a mighty nice drill that works with a foot pedal."

"Why don't you go back to preachin'? You're a good preacher."

"The trouble is, people won't hire you to give one sermon. They want you to stay in the town and give five or six. I've got one or two that're wizards. But when I got to do five or six, I just run out of gospel."

With the arrival of Sam Weaver, an old boater, and a younger man named Stark, the talk has turned to the possibility of a new-fangled kind of engine and train supplanting the canawl. Stark is apprehensive. Trains can run in winter, when the canawl's froze, and cut their rates in the summer. Weaver refuses to be impressed. Trains or no trains, the canawl will keep a-movin'.

"The trains!" sneers Sam. "Don't you know the canawl's the greatest thing this country ever done? It's the greatest thing it ever will do! Look at Oneida County! Look at this here town. Why, Rome's due to be one of the biggest cities in the world. (STARK *and* HOWARD *laugh.*) Bigger'n Albany or New York even. She's all unfroze and ready for another season. The horns is startin' today. Tomorrow, by grab, it'll be a swarming *hive*. Why, the old Erie is the bowels of the *nation!* It's the whole shebang of *life!*"

There is excuse for Sam Weaver's unsettled state of mind. He's got a load of mill machinery for a Mr. Butterfield in Uticy; his driver's quit and his cook, Annie, has run off with a tug boat feller, younger'n Sam. Being younger he could eat more, and that is what appealed to Annie.

Sam is still there when Molly Larkins barges angrily through the door. She is an attractive young woman of about twenty, and wears a shawl over the clothes she has been cooking in. She goes straight over to the door letting into the bar and searchingly surveys the crowd inside. She is looking for Jotham Klore. She is tired of blowin' for him.

"I've had supper ready for half an hour," reports Molly, in reply to Sam Weaver's friendly query. "We're supposed to be loadin' in Herkimer tomorrow mornin', and he wanted to git away early. Watch me next time. Settin' in that cabin like a *married woman!*"

"It's a cook's job, Molly!"

MOLLY—I told myself that. But that didn't stop me gittin' mad.

SAM—Sit down, Molly. You're too excited.

MOLLY—I know I am. Do you suppose Klore's right about

me? He says I'm gittin' too notional.

SAM—Well, you *are* notional! You've been notional ever since you was born. Jotham just don't understand why.

MOLLY—Well, what is it?

SAM—He don't feel things quite the same way we do. It's awful important to you, ain't it, when the Grand Canawl opens?

MOLLY—It's the most excitin' time of the whole year. When I was little I like to died.

SAM—Well, that's it. Two weeks ago they began lettin' the water in. That started you off. That made you restless. It always *does,* if you're born on the canawl. And on the day before the Big Ditch opens, your boater decides to *stop* your notions by *not* comin' to supper. That's all it is.

MOLLY—That might be it. (*She thinks it over.*) I'm still mad, though. It was a special *nice* supper.

SAM (*casually*)—You're goin' to marry him, ain't you?

MOLLY—That was my plan. I hired out to him last month. I went on board on the tenth, when the freeze ended. He was jest as nice as pie. (*Crosses to table and shows a bracelet.*) He bought me that in Albany.

SAM—Ain't jealous, is he?

MOLLY (*simply*)—Why should he be? He knows I ain't never cooked for anyone except Pa. Wouldn't you think *he'd* be excited about tomorrow?

SAM—Maybe he is. He's just goin' *about it* in a different way. He takes it out like most young fellers would *like* to.

MOLLY—He's the best *fighter* on the whole *canawl.* Even in Albany they admit he's the *bully* now. This year no one will race *us* to a lock. Maybe he'll be all right.

The report is that Klore is not so very drunk. He has gone in search of a keg of liquor for the boat. Molly thinks perhaps she should go after him, but Weaver agrees to fetch him back. Let Molly stay where she is. If a driver boy comes looking for Weaver, she can hold him.

Molly is sitting at a table reading a newspaper when Dan Harrow comes through the door. "Dan is about twenty-three, tall, and a bit self-conscious. He carries a carpet bag." He stands for a moment taking in the room. The bar, Molly tells him, looking over the top of her newspaper, is in the next room. Dan isn't looking for the bar. He is looking for Samson Weaver. He is expecting to drive for Weaver. Dan is new to the canawl. Molly could see that right away. He'd been in the bar by now

if he wasn't new. He's so new he didn't know the difference between canawl hotels. Didn't know, as Molly explains to him,
that the bad hotels all have their chimneys whitewashed. Hennessy's is just plain brick and respectable.

They have stared at each other pretty hard, and that has
flustered Dan more than it has Molly. Now they feel that the
mention of names would help some with the informality of their
meeting. Molly also feels impelled to state her position. She
is a cook. Her price is twelve dollars, if anyone's interested. She
cooks for Jotham Klore, and anyone who stays around the canawl
will soon know who Klore is.

Dan, for his part, doesn't know whether he's going to stay
long on the canawl or not. He likes a farm better. He aims to
drive for a while, to give himself a lift. He gets along fine with
horses, but he likes cows better.

"I couldn't stand a farm," says Molly. "Too lonesome."

"Depends. There's good farms and bad," insists Dan.

MOLLY—Not with me. I got to be on the move. What you
quit for?

DAN—It weren't mine. I was jest hired on to milk and such.
I like milkin' when the pasture's good and the stock's got some
heft to them. But on this farm they jest had little cross-breed
dinkeys. Couldn't hardly fetch a-hold of their tits. But if I had
red cattle or Holsteins. . . .

MOLLY—You could fetch a-hold of them, huh?

DAN—Yes, ma'am.

MOLLY—I've seen Holsteins. Black and white.

DAN—Dairy stock.

MOLLY—Like John Butterfield's got.

DAN—You know Mr. Butterfield?

MOLLY—Sure. Why?

DAN—I got a letter to him. (*Goes to his pocket and takes
it out.*) That's why I want a lift if it's goin' East. He lives in
Uticy.

MOLLY—Mr. Butterfield's all over the place from hell to
breakfast. My Pa used to work for him. So does most everybody. He's got propositions all up and down the canawl. Right
now he's puttin' up a new barn outside Uticy, as big as a church.

DAN—Jeepers! He started as a poor young man, didn't he?

MOLLY—He's the richest man up state ever since my time.

DAN—I passed one of his farms up near the Five Combines.
Must be fine to have land all your own.

Molly—The canawl's all *our* own.

Dan (*smiling*)—You ain't got a deed.

Molly—*My* part's mine. I'd like to see anybody try to take *it*.

Dan—What about the railroads?

Molly (*belligerently*)—*What* about them?

Dan—I don't know. Some say the canawl's done. Anyway, it ain't the whole of life.

Molly—Ain't it? *Well,* to me it *is* the whole of life. I love it. Things *happen* on the Canawl. There's boats comin' and there's boats goin' passin' you all the while. All day long you hear their horns blowin'; and, like as not, there's a fight at every lock. There's all kinds of people and they're goin' all the time. (*Pause.*) Naturally you wouldn't like it, though, if you've took such a frenzy for a farm.

Dan (*gallantly*)—There's some things I like about it.

Molly (*flattered*)—Well, you'll like Samson Weaver. He's a little sickly, but he's a nice old fellow. (*Looks at* Dan.) Hope you get the job.

Dan—I do too.

Molly—Maybe the canawl will grow on you.

Sam Weaver is back from the bar to report that he has found Jotham Klore and given him hell. Jotham is sorry and wants Molly to wait. Now Sam meets Dan Harrow and is properly surprised to discover that he is Henry Harrow's boy—old Hank, who used to have the "Golden City" that made the wonderful run: "From Schenectady to Buffalo in three days, eleven hours and thirty-seven minutes," explodes Sam, with enthusiasm. "Three hunderd and forty-six miles. Dang sight better than four miles an hour!"

The elder Harrow, Dan explains, got himself a farm north of Booneville after leaving the canawl. He's been dead five years now, and Dan has been working for another man. Dan's ma is dead, too, a year before his pa.

Sam Weaver is sympathetic. Of course he will hire Hank Harrow's son, and he doesn't want any recommendations, either. Dan's wages will be regular, too—twelve dollars a month.

Jotham Klore is still absent. Mrs. Gurget invites Sam and Dan to go with her and Sol to dinner, seein' they haven't got any cook. She would take Molly along, too, but Molly thinks she will wait for Klore.

"Good-by, Miss Larkins. Hope I ain't seen the last of you,"

ventures diffident Dan, as they are about to herd him out of Hennessey's.

"No. I'll see you on the Big Ditch," answers Molly, lightly. "Our boat's called 'The Emma.'"

"I don't know the name of ours."

"'Sarsey Sal. Rome, New York,' painted right across the back of her," Molly tells him. "Red belly with green stripes. I hope you like her, Dan."

"I'm beginnin' to think I will."

It is possible they will be meeting in Little Falls, Weaver thinks, seeing both boats are going there. Molly thinks perhaps they may.

Fisher has returned to the business of assigning cargoes. The boys in the bar are swinging into the canal song "Ee-ri-ee," being encouraged by a virtuoso of the harmonicy named Riley. The words of the song come floating in—

> "Drop a tear for Big-foot Sal,
> The best damned cook on the Erie Canal;
> Aimed for Heaven but went to Hell—
> Fifteen years on the Erie Canal.
> (The) Missioner said she died in sin;
> Hennery said it was too much gin;
> There weren't no bar where she hadn't been,
> From Albany to Buffalo.

> Chorus

> "Low bridge! Everybody down!
> Low bridge! We're comin' to a town!
> You'll always know your neighbor,
> You'll always know your pal,
> If you've ever navigated on the Erie Canal."

Jotham Klore has come in, considerably sobered. His manner toward Molly is surprisingly kindly.

"We'll go have supper in a little bit now," he says. "I got to see Mr. Fisher."

"All right, Jotham," Molly answers, meekly.

KLORE (to FISHER)—My name is Jotham Klore. Ever hear of me?

FISHER—We certainly have.

KLORE—I was to start East with dairy stuff tomorrow, but it's so puny 't won't make a cargo to Albany. What *you* got?

FISHER—I can give you grain to Rochester right up to the hatches. (MOLLY *crosses to right of* KLORE.)

KLORE—That's all right.

FISHER—What's your boat?

KLORE—One-eight-four-six. "The Emma."

FISHER—Oh, yes. You work two teams, don't you?

KLORE—That's right.

MOLLY—Jotham! (KLORE *turns.*) Ain't we goin' to Little Falls?

KLORE—No, Rochester. It won't pay to go East this trip. Unless your mind's set on it. Is it?

MOLLY—No, of course not. I'll do whatever you *want* to do, Jotham.

KLORE—That's a good cook! (*He pats her face, then turns to sign slip.* MOLLY *turns and slowly walks to table.*)

FISHER (*as* KLORE *signs*)—Looks like we're goin' to have a very nice season this year.

KLORE—Yes, it looks good.

MOLLY—It's much the best for us to go the other way. (KLORE *has signed the slip. He calls a "Good night" into the bar, takes* MOLLY'S *hand and starts to exit.*)

FISHER—All right, Howard. I'm ready for you. (HOWARD *enters from bar.*)

THE CURTAIN FALLS

ACT II

It is a foggy morning at the Utica weighlock. The early dawn discloses the towpath of the canal at back, with two boats tied, bow to stern. Bentley's hotel is still open, though the feeble light shining through the door indicates little activity inside. The hoarse voices of two men raised uncertainly in song suggest the last two customers of the night.

The outline of Fry's stable and blacksmith shop can barely be made out with the help of the light of a forge shining through the door. The sound of hammer on anvil in the smithy locates one early worker. A man appears with a lantern and continues on his way down the towpath. A Mrs. Howard comes in search of the two who are singing. She thinks they should be ready to come to breakfast by this time. After they eat they can go to bed. Don't look as though the fog was going to lift for quite a spell.

Dan Harrow wanders in. It is his team the smithy is shoeing, and Dan has his own ideas as to how the job should be done. You can't shoe horses that have to pull against weight as you do trotters, whether Fry knows it or not.

Now Molly Larkins has appeared suddenly with a market basket on her arm. She is a great surprise to Dan. He thought she was in Buffalo, but it seems Jotham Klore is short-haulin' for the Six-Day Line. That job has brought him to Uticy.

"We're right up here in front of you," reports Molly. "Come in last night. I thought we'd like to scrape your deck house off when we threw the ropes over. You must've been asleep."

"Yes, I go to bed early."

"On account of you're bein' a farmer, I suppose, eh?"

"I suppose so."

"Well, if you're goin' to live like a farmer, why do you keep workin' on the canawl? Thought you told me last month you was only goin' to Uticy."

"I've been delayed about the farm. I found out Mr. Butterfield was goin' to be in New York City for two or three weeks. Mr. Weaver's been ailin' and I'm sort of helpin' him out."

Joe Teethem comes through the fog leading a horse down the towpath. Stopping to pass the time Joe is full of news about the Ohio lottery. The drawing was held Monday and the winning numbers should be in Uticy today. Klore has six tickets in that lottery, Molly reports proudly. She doesn't suspect Dan would think of buyin' even one. Dan admits that he wouldn't be prone to.

It appears that Dan and Sam Weaver are still without a cook. Sam is waiting for the old cook to come back. Meantime they are taking turns cooking. They have been livin' on fried steak mostly.

It doesn't look as though the fog was going to lift for hours, and that is distressing to Dan. He has an appointment with Mr. Butterfield at 9, and it doesn't look now as though he was going to make it.

"You've still got yours plans, huh?" ventures Molly, when it appears that Dan is not going to volunteer further information.

"Yes, ma'am."

MOLLY (*coming down a step*)—H'm. Don't you *like* the canawl?

DAN (*after an effort*)—Yes. It jest don't seem staple. I like the people on it! 'Course, it's nice now with Spring comin' on.

The last three days have been *fine* for plantin'.

MOLLY—Oh, it was pretty *yesterday mornin'* comin' down to Oneida. I sat out in that chair there in the sun and watched the *birds* comin' North. Do you like flowers?

DAN—Yes, ma'am.

MOLLY—There certainly is a mess of violets and patty-cutters this side of Rome. I had the urge to git off and *git* some.

DAN—You ought to pick some of them elderberry blossoms and make some wine.

MOLLY—I never made any wine. Boaters don't like anythin' so weak as that. That is, *real* boaters. Mr. Weaver used to drink wine for his stomach. But he gave it up way back when he was workin' for my Pa. Said it only aggravated him.

DAN—He can certainly drink *hard liquor*.

MOLLY (*intimately*)—He can drink more than any two men on the canawl, except one. You've never met *my* boater.

DAN—No, ma'am.

MOLLY—He can drink more than any two men on the canawl, *plus* Sam Weaver. He's been down there at the Ætna House ever since we tied up last night. I went down to git some eggs jest now and he wasn't ready to come home *yit*.

DAN—Was he still drinkin'?

MOLLY—Old Mr. Purcell, the bartender, jest told me he's busted all records. Pretty soon I'm going to git ready and call him for breakfast.

DAN—Maybe he won't want any.

MOLLY—You don't *know* him!

Now Klore appears, walking slowly, with great dignity and just the suggestion of a lurch. He is making for the door of Bentley's hotel, but it does not seem at all certain he will make it. Molly would greet her boater civilly and introduce him to Mr. Harrow. The fact that Klore is still able to walk is a point of pride with Molly, though his manners are not what she could wish. Still Klore insists that he is not drunk. Just disgusted with the fog and the Ohio lottery. His six tickets have not won him a cent. He has heard that Sam Weaver has won something; a hundred dollars, probably.

Neither is Mr. Klore interested in breakfast. He isn't drunk enough yet, even though, on the testimony of eye-witnesses, he has beaten all drinkin' records. He will go git his last drink when he wants to, he announces; he'll get on his boat when he wants to; and he's pretty sore about Molly standin' there talking to whoever-it-is she's talking to. It's against his principles.

"Why did you keep her from cookin' my breakfast?" demands Klore, turning suddenly on Dan.

"I ain't stopped her," answers Dan.

"Now, you don't know Mr. Harrow," interrupts Molly, injecting herself between the men and turning on Klore. "You got to be *polite*."

KLORE (*turning on* MOLLY)—Git on that boat!

MOLLY (*her good nature dissipated*)—*You* git on it! Either that or go git a drink. (*To* DAN.) Don't pay no notice to him.

KLORE—You're my cook, ain't you?

MOLLY—Yes, when you're nice. Here I've been braggin' 'bout your reputation with your liquor and you are actin' like a baby.

KLORE (*wobbling and menacing*)—Mebbe the time has come to give you a good *lacin'!*

MOLLY—That time ain't never goin' to come, Klore! You go on and git on to that boat. I'm sick and tired of humorin' you. You want any breakfast or not? (*Her tirade has sobered* KLORE *slightly, and he has watched her intently during the last speech.*)

KLORE (*starts raggedly up the ramp*)—Mebbe I do and mebbe I don't. Come on and cook it. Does he want to watch you too?

MOLLY—No. He's had his.

KLORE—Is there any liquor left in that kag?

MOLLY—I s'pose so.

KLORE—Well, I'm goin' to work some more on my reputation.

MOLLY (*to* DAN)—Danged if I like him like that.

DAN—He was talkin' mean to you.

MOLLY (*looking at the boat*)—He knew *well* I told Mr. Purcell to send him home so it would be worth while gittin' breakfast ready. I even heard Mr. Purcell tell him jest that. I didn't say it *was all* ready. That makes me mad.

DAN—You mean him up and callin' you a liar?

MOLLY—No, he knows I ain't a liar, so I don't mind that. It was the goin' out of his way to be so mean. I ain't never blamed him when he's got mad, 'cause I git mad too, when I'm notional.

DAN (*smiling*)—Are you mad now?

MOLLY—By God, I'm gittin' to be.

DAN—If you find out you really are, why don't you transfer to Mr. Weaver. He'd admire to *have you.*

MOLLY—Oh, I could git a job easy enough.

DAN—It's jest that he needs a cook, and his boat's so handy.

MOLLY—I ain't worked up enough yit. Maybe he was jest

showin' off in front of you. Boaters are very peculiar, you know.
(*She starts up.*) Well, I'm still signed up, so I guess I'll cook his
breakfast. See you when the fog lifts.

DAN—I hope so, but maybe you won't.

MOLLY (*from the deck of the boat*)—Oh. You're quittin' the
canawl today?

DAN—If I hire out to Mr. Butterfield.

Molly is still wondering a little how a big strong fellow like
Dan can go on hankerin' after a farm as she goes to her boat to
get Klore his breakfast. . . .

Lucy Gurget and Sol Tinker have arrived with news of Sam
Weaver. Sam has, as Joe Teethem reported, won a prize in the
Ohio lottery and he and Fortune Friendly have stayed in town
celebratin'. Nobody knows how much Sam won, but—

There is some commotion on Klore's boat. Molly Larkins has
suddenly appeared on deck and is pacing back and forth. They
call to her to know what the trouble is and Molly is quick to tell
them, with emphasis. It's Klore! She's stood about as much of
Klore as she can. She ain't intendin' to take a lacin' and she
ain't wiping no egg off his face—

"What's the egg doin' there?" Sol wants to know.

"I put it there!" admits Molly, coming down the canal ramp
to join them. "Said he wanted to sleep and didn't want no breakfast, and I said: 'All right, go sleep!' I told him the fog was
goin' to lift and I'd wake him in an hour. He said he wasn't
takin' no orders from me and he was goin' to give me a lacin'.
What a dang fool I was to be proud he could drink so much. I
ought to have thrown the hull dozen at him."

Molly is ready to leave Klore after this experience. Lucy
Gurget can't see why she doesn't go to work for Sam Weaver,
knowing as she does that Sam would like to have her. Molly
is inclined to think perhaps she will, only Sam, being frail, is
not much of an eater, and Dan isn't likely to be there long, seeing
he is set on farmin'.

"How long since you had a good meal?" asks Molly, turning
to Dan.

"Not since that night we et on *her* boat," Dan confesses, pointing at Lucy.

MOLLY—Do you like chicken pie?

DAN—Yes, I *do*.

MOLLY—They tell me I make *them* pretty *good*. Mornin's like this do you like griddle cakes?

DAN—Yes, ma'am, I like them *fine*.

MOLLY—Why don't you stay with Mr. Weaver a *little* longer? (SOL and LUCY *enter and remain on the porch.*)

DAN—That ain't the point. I wouldn't like nothin' *better* than to eat some of your cookin'. It's that I'd never git anywhere on a canawl, and I know a hell of a lot about a *farm*.

MOLLY—If you had some *good* canawl *food* you might feel different.

DAN—I'll never feel any different about the farm.

MOLLY—Well, there's no use me goin' on Mr. Weaver's boat then.

DAN—He'll git another *driver*.

MOLLY—Well, I don't know whether I'd like *him* or not. (*She pauses as she realizes what she has said, and then turns to the ramp.*)

DAN—How about me askin' Mr. Butterfield about a cook's job on the farm?

MOLLY—I thought I told you I wasn't so crazy about farms. I thought I'd be kinda doin' you a favor by goin' on that boat. (*She goes up the ramp.*)

DAN—Yes, ma'am, and I sure appreciate it.

LUCY (*coming down*)—Well, git your things and come back to Rome with us, Molly. Then we'll see what there is at the agency.

MOLLY—All right.

The crowd is back from town now, with what Fortune describes as "news by the bellyfull." Sam Weaver has won third prize in the Ohio lottery! Five thousand dollars! They have just seen the official numbers posted in Uticy and Sam is going to Buffalo on Tuesday to collect.

Sam knows exactly what he is going to do with the money, too. He's going to buy him the finest vessel on the Grand Canawl. A ninety-six foot boat, a hundred and fifty tons. What's more, he is going to make Dan Harrow a present of a half interest in the "Sarcey Sal."

"I bought this ticket the day I hired you," beams Sam, as the surprised Dan tries to take in the news. "I had a feelin' you was good luck for me. You're her captain, beginnin' today. From now on we divide what she makes, even-steven."

Dan is properly grateful and a little flustered by Sam's generosity. He can, Sam points out, try being a boat owner for a year and then, if he still wants a farm, he can sell the boat and buy a farm. Dan thinks he'd like a little while to consider.

When the others are gone Dan calls to Molly Larkins. She is packing her things and busy, but she can give him a minute.

"Mr. Weaver's jest won a lot of money in a lottery," explains Dan nervously. "He's given me a half interest in the boat."

"Ain't that wonderful!"

"Yes, ma'am. Are you quittin' Klore?"

"Yes."

"Well, then—will you marry me?"

It takes Molly a second or two to get that. When she does she is still hesitant. She likes Dan. Liked him the first day she saw him. But she isn't sure he is going to stay on the canawl.

Dan agrees he would be willing to stay awhile if at the end he could buy a farm that Molly would like. That is what she is afraid of, too. Wouldn't it be awful if she should learn to like a farm!

"Well—I'll come and cook for you," she says finally.

"All right. You don't want to get married now?"

"Not yet, Dan. We don't know."

"All right. It ain't part of my plan to make you unhappy," he says.

The fog is clearing. Molly has transferred her things from Klore's boat to the "Sarcey Sal" and Dan is trying to find a driver. Fortune Friendly thinks he might take the job temporarily. He isn't doing anything at the moment and it doesn't look as though there was to be much dentist business. Ivy Elliott's been spreading reports about Fortune. It seems the second tooth he pulled for her wasn't the right one either.

Molly has blown a couple of defiant blasts on the horn as a good-by to Klore, but that boater does not even wake up. Fortune has gone for the horses. He won't have to get his things, seeing he hasn't any, excepting some pants in Oneida.

Molly has had Dan retrieve her rocking chair from the Klore boat and put it on the bow end of the "Sarcey Sal."

"I want to keep my eyes open for elderberry blossoms," she explains, as they get ready to cast off. Fortune is fooling with the towline as the curtain falls.

September of that year finds the "Sarcey Sal" tied up at Whitesboro. Looking into her cabin we see the sleeping "cuddies" at the back, and in front of them Molly's stove and kitchen table. There are cupboards in the walls and a stairway leads to the deck.

It is a snug and habitable cabin.

Gammy Hennessey is visiting Molly and there is a deal of gossip about canawl folk. Some of it about Jotham Klore, who has been in jail in Buffalo all summer. Jotham had thrown a couple of men through a window in Lockport.

Molly hasn't seen Klore since she left him, and Dan, who certainly is a grand man, hasn't even mentioned him. Tonight Molly and Dan are goin' to the fair. There is a new dress for the occasion, which came from Albany, and there is to be a lace parasol to go with it when they get to the fair. Dan is going to buy it. Molly's got quite an exhibit at the fair. Tomater and plum butter and about eighteen kinds of preserves. She isn't counting on winning any of the prizes, but it would be nice if she did. Dan would like that. Her sending the things in was Dan's idea. . . .

Fortune Friendly stops in a minute. He is carrying a fairly cumbersome camera—a camera obscura, he explains, with which he expects to take daguerreotypes. He had come by the camera when he went to have his picture taken and the photographer suggested a card game Everything went fine for Fortune until the photographer got a straight flush. Then he had to give back a few parts, including a piece of glass that goes with the camera. He expects to get the glass back when he meets the photographer at the fair.

Dan has been doing a lot of short-hauling all summer, Molly tells Fortune, and she is hoping that they will get a long trip west for a change. There has been a good deal of talk about the progress the railroads are making, and that is disturbing to Molly. They've got the road finished all the way from Philadelphia to Pittsburgh, Fortune reports, and are expecting to have the Oswego and Syracuse ready by Fall.

"Fortune, the canawl ain't goin' to be whipped, is it?" asks Molly anxiously.

"I don't know, Molly," answers the philosophical Fortune. "Everyone is so happy, you'd think nothing *could* lick it. But it seems that's what *does* happen to everything *pleasant* in life. Tempus fugit."

"What does that mean?"

"Time is flying! Not only time, but everything else. We don't stay satisfied with what's wonderful. We've always got to make *perfection* better. The railroads will give us more speed, all right, but they'll make people forget how fine the world could go at *four miles an hour.*"

Molly recalls Dan's prophecies about the canawl when they first met. Since then he hasn't said anything, they having agreed that if Molly didn't talk against farms and farmin' Dan wouldn't say anything about the canawl. Not until the end of the season, when they would see how they felt. Molly is hoping that if she does win a cooking prize at the Fair it will at least prove to Dan that you can get better things to eat on a boat than you can on land.

Molly has an idea that Dan is getting a little used to the canawl. He certainly is a new kind of boater. Doesn't get drunk; doesn't get mad; hasn't had a fight all summer. He isn't afraid of things in general, like cholery reports. And other things just don't excite him. Dan's a funny fellow.

Now Dan has appeared lugging a huge package. This turns out to be a mirror for Molly to see her new dress in, and when she pirouettes in front of it Dan is convinced she is about as pretty as anything he ever saw.

"She's as pretty as the face that launched a thousand ships," asserts Fortune.

"Who was that?" asks Dan.

"Helen of Troy."

"Gosh, Molly's prettier than any girl in the whole state!" insists Dan.

Dan has news. He has signed for two long hauls to Buffalo before the season ends, and that pleases Molly. She's been wanting to see Niagara Falls again. Pleases Fortune, too. He has pleasant memories of that part of the country, associated with the early days of the canawl. Fortune even remembers that wonderful day in 1825 when the canawl was opened.

"There were cannons strung within earshot of each other all the way from Buffalo to New York," he tells Dan. "I helped fire one. She bucked, but we shot her twice. The minute the canawl was opened and the water came in it, first muddy and slow, like a little crick, the guns went off one after another, all the way to New York. They had the news there eighty minutes later. Then they began firing them toward the West and in about an hour we knew *New York* knew all about it. The minute she was filled, *everybody cheered*. Do you know the first *boat* to move on her?—Governor Clinton's. She was painted *red* and *yellow* and was drawn by four matched grays. But what everybody was looking at was a beautiful kag right in the middle of her. Had the American Eagle painted on it and the Star-spangled Banner draped *over* it. It was a barrel of water from *Lake*

Erie on its way to New York *bay*. It was quite a sight to see."

Now Fortune has left them. He wants to go back to the photographers to see if he can't get a little more equipment for the camera. He has discovered the piece of glass he's missing is pretty important.

Molly and Dan are happy together. He has playfully held her up in her new dress and announced soberly that he never wants any other girl but her. Molly is quick to notice the serious note in his voice.

"Don't be too solemn, Dan," she chides him playfully. "Not tonight anyway. You look as if we'd been talkin' about what we said we *wouldn't* talk about. Mister, the season ain't over yit and tonight I've got a new dress, you've got a hair-cut and we're goin' to the County Fair."

"You're jest so dang sweet-lookin'," explodes Dan. "What kind of a parasol are you goin' to git?"

"A French one with lace on it. I'd ruther have that than anythin'. Is it all right, Dan, to spend so much money on me?"

" 'Course it is. All *summer* I ain't bought you anythin'. I added up my books this mornin'. We've made a lot more than I figured we would."

"Enough to buy the other half of the boat—" Molly knows as soon as she has spoken that this is something she should not have said.

"I got a letter from Mr. Weaver this mornin'," answers Dan uncomfortably. "His stomach's ailin' him ag'in."

"We'll see him when we git to Durhamville, won't we? The new boat ought to be finished by now. . . . That came out quick, Dan, before I thought."

"That's all right."

"I'm sorry. I didn't mean to break my word. . . ."

Lucy Gurget has appeared with Sol Tinker at the head of the companionway. She is so mad she can be heard sputtering explosively before she puts in an appearance. Lucy has just come from the Fair and the judges have refused to accept Molly's pickles and preserves in competition. Molly isn't a resident of Oneida County, and that bars her.

" 'What county does the lady live in?' " Lucy reports the Judge having asked her. " 'She don't live in no county,' " Lucy answered. " 'She lives on a boat—and she's the first canawl cook that ever sent anythin' to your Fair.' By God, I'm goin' back and slap his face!"

It is a great disappointment to Molly, but she accepts it gracefully. After all, everybody on the canawl knows she can cook. Soon there is other news to take her mind off the incident. Lucy and Sol have seen Jotham Klore at the Fair. He's been out of jail since Thursday and he's tied up about four boats back. Dan had seen him, too. Klore was getting drunk. He had enquired of Lucy about Molly, but had been given but little information.

It is about Klore that Molly want to talk to Dan, after Lucy and Sol have left the boat. Molly is worried. She doesn't think Dan is afraid of Klore, but she isn't certain. He hadn't said anything about seeing Klore at the Fair, and he was unusually excited about the haul to Buffalo. He's never been excited about leaving a place before. And as long as he thought Klore was working in the West he'd never talked of going there.

"Molly, what's got into you?" demands Dan. "I've told you I ain't afraid of him. Why, you ought to know I ain't."

"You ought to know I don't want to believe you are," answers Molly. "Why, till tonight I never had doubt but what you'd stand up to him. Dan, I ain't jest notional. You *know* you *did* act funny when you came home tonight. You was excited about somethin' *besides* a *full haul to Buffalo.* Ain't that so?"

DAN—It's nothin' you want to *talk* about.

MOLLY—I *do* want to talk about it.

DAN—It's somethin' we said we wouldn't talk about till the end of the season.

MOLLY—You mean, it's somethin' about a farm?

DAN—What about our promise?

MOLLY—Dan, I mustn't think you're a *coward.*

DAN—Now, you're jest goin' to spoil things for both of us. We've been mighty happy. Let's stay happy till they let the *water* out.

MOLLY—I *ain't* happy *now.* I busted the promise tonight. I'm sorry I did it, but I did. So what was it about a farm? (*Thinking.*) You were checkin' up your *money* this mornin'. My God, did you go an' *buy* a farm?

DAN—Yes, I did. I bought an option on it and paid somethin' down. We've got two months to decide if we want it. If it's what I think it is, it's the best farmland north of Rome. *Now* you know why I was *excited.*

MOLLY—Then you've made your mind up *already?*

DAN—I said from the beginnin' I didn't think I could stay on the Erie. When the season ended I planned to take you up there so's you could see how fine it was. Molly, I think it *is* fine. It's *that* one Mr. Butterfield owns at the Five Combines. I've been thinkin' about it all *summer*. Last week I talked it over with him when we was in Uticy. This afternoon I fixed it up with his agent here. You 'n' me promised not to pester each other with arguments. I wasn't goin' to mention it; especially today when you were *feelin'* so good. Then on top of your gittin' them things back, there was all the *more* reason not to talk about it. By God, this is the most I ever talked in my life!

MOLLY—And you've had the idea all summer. You *kept your promise* about our arguin' all right, but you never gave the Grand Canawl a chance to argue with *you*. You never *bothered* to notice how *beautiful* it is. You've never bothered to notice that you've been happier than you ever was in your life.

DAN—That's because I've been in love with *you*.

MOLLY—Oh! You've been thinkin' all along that you could jest snap your fingers and I'd change my mind. And all them things you've been buyin' for the boat; things that are too *big* fer it. That lookin' glass—that kitchen oven up there—them two rockin' chairs—that we don't need—and all them other things. You've been buyin' them for a *farm!*

DAN—Well, they'd be *handy* on a farm.

MOLLY—So that's playin' fair!

DAN—Molly, there ain't a thing in the world I wouldn't do for you except this one; and that's jest because I *can't* do it. Will you come and let me show you the farm? (MOLLY *laughs hysterically at the idea.*)

MOLLY—Hah! Gittin' well-known as a dependable boater! Workin' up a fine business! Captain Henry Harrow's son! And all the time makin' money and buyin' furniture 'n' things and every bit of it for a farm. You—ain't bought a damn thing for this boat that ain't fer the farm. Except this dress—I'll bet you got that fer me to go to church in.

DAN—I thought maybe you might git married in it.

MOLLY—You're certain sure of about nearly everythin', ain't you? Well, I'm gittin' sure about somethin' too. I'm gittin' sure I ain't never goin' to marry *you*.

DAN—Yes, you are, Molly.

MOLLY—Oh, am I? Well, it happens that I'm changin' my mind. I thought Klore was mean, but he's nothin' to what you are! I ought to call him over and apologize for *ever sayin'* he was mean.

DAN—Don't talk like that, Molly! I'm a lot better man than Klore is.

Molly—Are you afraid to face him?
Dan—Do you think so? Call him over.

Molly has taken Dan at his word and is at the head of the
stairway blowing the familiar Klore call on her horn. From
down the canal Klore answers with enthusiasm, if a little thickly.
Dan has gone into his cuddy and a moment later he is out with
his bag. He isn't, however, running away. He is waiting for
Klore. After that he will make up his mind as to what he
will do.

Now Klore has appeared at the top of the companionway and
is backing down the steps. He is very drunk and he is looking
for what sounds like "the dirty cuss f'm Boo'ville" who stole his
cook. Molly can come back, Klore allows, but not until he has
fixed the dirty cuss. He draws back his right arm to annihilate
Dan, but before he can swing Dan has turned him around, pushed
him into a chair and advised him to go to sleep.

"Want me to take him home?" Dan asks Molly.

"Leave him there," she answers. "What are you going to do?"

"Maybe you *are* tired of me," answers Dan, with some spirit.
"I'm goin' to give you a chance to find out. You said I've
thought of nothin' but the farm. I'm provin' that ain't so. I
ain't so mean. From now on, my half of the boat is yours, Molly.
I'll write Mr. Weaver tomorrow. Everythin' I bought fer the
boat's yours, too. Lisle and Denning are the agents for the cargo
to Buffalo. On account of Mr. Weaver, I'd like you to keep
haulin' until the season ends. *There's* money enough to keep you
goin'. You and Fortune kin git the help you need. (Klore
snores.) Him, if you want him when he sobers up. I guess that's
all. (*He picks up the bag and starts up the steps.*)

"And where you goin'?"

"I'm leavin' the Erie Canawl (*starts to steps*), like my Pa
done. Because in his heart he was a farmer, jest like *his* Pa was
and like I am now. If you ever find out you want me ag'in—
I'll be waitin' fer you at the Five Combines, on the Black River
Canawl."

"That's a fine thing to do," calls Molly, as Dan disappears up
the stairs. "I don't want your damned boat. I hate your boat.
I despise it. I—" She has gone to the foot of the steps to see if
Dan has really gone. "No, I don't either, Dan! I love the boat,
Dan, but I can't take it. Dan!!"

Her last despairing call has awakened the sleeping Klore. He
gets unsteadily to his feet and lurches toward Molly. He's glad

Harrow has gone, he mumbles. Now he won't have to tear him to pieces. Molly pays little attention to him. She is still talking to herself—

"Runnin' a boat all alone. . . . I don't want to take a boat all the way to Buffalo. . . . Give me half the boat. . . . Who wants half the boat? . . . I . . . hope it's a terrible farm. . . . I hope you starve to death on it. . . . I don't know where Lisle and Denning's is. . . . I've never been to Lisle and Denning's."

"He's gone, huh? We got rid of 'm," runs Klore's accompanying obbligato. "You blew the horn 'n' I came back, didn't I? I fergive you, Molly. 'N' here y'are. Back on the 'Emma' ag'in. Le's shake hands."

He has lurched toward Molly and she avoids him. There is a large frosted cake on the table. It, too, was to have gone to the Fair. Now she picks it up and hurls it in Klore's face. It musses the boater up considerably. He is still trying to be rid of the frosting when Fortune Friendly comes into the cabin. Fortune had passed Dan. Dan said he was going to the railroad station, but he probably was joking.

Dan wasn't joking, Molly confesses. Dan was going to a farm he bought.

"Oh, Fortune!" she wails. "He gave me the boat! And he's gone away on a damned old railroad train!" Her head is on his shoulder.

THE CURTAIN FALLS

ACT III

It is cold enough in November to keep a good fire in the stove at Hennessy's Hotel. Otherwise the room is but little changed from its April appearance. The wall posters, however, are now advertising loudly for workers on the Black River and Utica Railroad, and the J. L. Fisher who was assigning cargoes to canal boats in the spring has taken over the job of rounding up railroad workers for these new jobs.

It is early forenoon. Sol Tinker is again trying to beat solitaire. Gammy Hennessey is filling three lamps with kerosene. Two boaters are interested in the bulletin board notices. It is a dull morning at Hennessey's. . . .

There is a rumor that Molly Larkins is in town, and the appearance of Fortune Friendly, her driver, confirms the rumor. Molly had emptied her last haul in Buffalo and written Sam Weaver to meet her at Hennessey's. So far as Fortune knows she has no

intention of making things up with Dan Harrow. The last time
he had tried to bring up the subject of Dan, says Fortune, Molly
acted a good deal like a wildcat up a tree. After that the subject
was never again open for discussion.

Fortune's newest investment is in almanacs. He had met a
fellow with a stock of them and had talked him out of the lot at
four cents apiece. He can, Fortune insists, sell the almanacs,
which are filled with funny sayings, to a large feedstore at six
cents apiece, and he has five hundred of them at his hotel.

Talk turns again to the onsweep of the railroads. Luke has
heard they aim to keep workin' on the Watertown and Rome
right through the winter, and Fisher has been hiring canawlers
for the Black River and Uticy right and left. Sam Weaver is
pretty mad about it. The idea of half the boaters on the canawl
spendin' practically all summer haulin' for people that were tryin'
to cut their throats! The only relief that Sam can get is to drink
rum and cuss the cars. He has a mind to go over to the new
depot of the Surracuse and Uticy and cuss the next train in right
to its face. When he hears the train whistle he is ready to carry
out his threat.

Now Molly Larkins has arrived, hale and hearty, ready to correct all rumors and announce her winter plans. She was goin' to
winter in Buffalo, but she changed her mind. And as for marryin'
Dan Harrow, she wouldn't do that for anything in the world.
Neither does she intend winterin' on her boat. She wants a room
in Gammy Hennessey's hotel, and will be movin' right in.

Jotham Klore is in the bar. Molly isn't surprised to hear that.
But Jotham is also sober, which doesn't sound reasonable. She
will have to investigate that report. She calls Klore in.

It's true. Klore admits it, though he doesn't intend to be
mocked for it. Not for being sober or the fact that Dan Harrow
licked him when he was sick, and then run away. Klore is a
little hazy about the fight with Harrow, bein' sick as he was, but
Dan had hurt the side of his head and had jumped on his chest.
Fortune Friendly had seen the end of it, and been a little surprised that Klore hadn't put up a better fight. Which wasn't
very fair to a sick man.

"Well, perhaps you would like to know just what happened,"
interrupts Molly finally. "The only thing that struck you was
the cake. Fortune says you fell down while he was luggin' you
home. *That's* where you must have hurt your chest and your
head. You didn't fight Dan Harrow at all. And as for the cake
—you received that from me!"

"Well, why did that Fortune let me think Harrow *licked* me?"

"I guess he just imagined it."

"Well, for God's sake!" Klore is excitedly resentful. "I thought he'd seen it, and I went and followed his advice."

"What advice?"

"He was so damned sympathetic and he said I couldn't git vengeance unless I stopped drinking entirely, and on his advice, I went and joined the Cold Water Society. For God's sake! I've took the pledge."

It is all mystifying to Klore. Why did Molly throw a cake at him? Because he was gettin' to be a bother? That's nothin' to say to a man who has always been ready to marry her, and is considerin' the same again. Molly isn't interested.

A moment later Klore has torn off his white ribbon pledge and invited Fortune Friendly to have a drink. He feels that he has wasted six weeks. Fortune is ready for a small drink. He has just learned that the almanacs in which he had invested were already the property of the feedstore. The store had hired the man who sold them to Fortune to distribute them around the town. Now Fortune will have to do the distributing in order to retrieve two of the twenty dollars he had invested.

Sam Weaver is back from his defiance of the railroads still disgusted. Molly wants to settle with him for the long hauls she made with his boat. She doesn't feel she is a partner and she won't take half the boat from Dan, nor run it the next year for Sam.

"I don't want to run a boat," Molly explains, with some feeling. "Don't want the *burden* of it. I'm just a cook. It's the job I like, and it's the one I'm goin' to stick to. I ain't goin' to take favors from nobody."

"What's behind this, Molly? You're just as upset as you was that day last spring when you had your first fight with Klore."

"That was nothin'. I was just mad then. Now I ain't got anythin' to git mad about. I'm all tired out in here." (*Touches breast.*)

"I'm awful sorry, Molly. You're all through with *Dan*, I s'pose?"

"I'm as through as a person kin be. I'll fergit about him in time. I *know* I kin. Maybe it's just the responsibilities of bein' a captain that's busted me down. Anyway, there it is. The teams are on the boat at the basin, and thanks very much for your kindness."

Molly is going to her room. She is wintering in Rome. No,

she doesn't expect to meet Dan Harrow, seeing he has a farm and a village near by where he can do his buying. If she should see Dan, and speak to him, it would only be to tell him that she's settled on the canawl. . . .

Dan Harrow has come through the center doors. He, too, is looking for Sam Weaver. Wants to buy his big team, if Sam will sell. Dan can use the team in his plowin'. Sam thinks the sale can be arranged, but thinks they had better talk to Molly about it. Dan wasn't countin' on meetin' Molly, but he does want the horses. Of course he isn't mad at Molly. How could he be?

Sam has called to Molly and she has come down the stairs before she sees Dan. She would turn around and go back, but Sam calls sharply to her that it is only business they want to talk about. He has got to have some sort of release from her before he can sell Dan the team. She'll have to covenant and bear witness to something. He is ready to fix up a paper, but just at that moment he hears another of those train whistles and rushes out to keep his cussin' engagement.

Molly would be going now, but Dan asks her to stay a minute. He'd like to know how she's been and where she is going to stay through the winter. He would like to ask her, if she happens to be boatin' up Black River way in the spring, to stop and see his farm.

"Thanks. I might if I'm passin' that way," agrees Molly. "Is it big?"

"When she's all cleared, there'll be four hundred acres."

Molly—A lot of it's woods, huh?

Dan—Yes. Maple and beech, birch and cherry, and a nice little stand of pine—must be a thousand cord.

Molly—Was it paying Mr. Butterfield?

Dan—He worked two hundred acres. On the meadowland he cleared this year he had red bush-clover under a cover crop of oats and the barley and rye was fine.

Molly—A lot of cattle, I s'pose.

Dan (*starts to creep up on her*)—Yeah. Fine sheep. There's some grand Southdowns and merinos. He's leavin' twenty head of 'em for me. Gittin' 'em served this month.

Molly—Chickens, I s'pose, too.

Dan (*turns*)—Yep, Spanish blacks, sea-brights, shanghais—all healthy as can be.

Molly—It's goin' to git awful cold for them soon.

Dan—Yeah, I know it is. It's a good hen house though. And the main dwellin' house is good too. One of the French settlers put it up in 1800. Knew his business. It's got a grand side-hill barn. Runnin' water right by the horse stalls.

Molly—I trust you got a good cellar?

Dan—Yes, ma'am. And pump right in the house, so I let the water in the cellar yesterday to keep the potaters from freezin'. Next week I'm goin' to bank it with manure. That will keep the roots and the hams and other things from freezin'.

Molly—Got anybody working in the house?

Dan—Yeah. I got a big fat Dutch woman that's all right. Last week I bought her a machine to do the washin' with. She's scared of it.

Molly—Oh, they're so ignorant. Got a lot of maple sugar this winter, I guess, eh?

Dan—I will in the Spring.

Molly—That'll be very nice for you.

Dan—I'm orderin' some apple trees from the nurseries in Rochester.

Molly—In a few years you kin have apples.

Dan—There's some there now. There's darn near everything there, Molly, that a person would want. I think even you would like the kitchen. It's big and bright, with a pump right in it.

Molly—Of course, I like little ones.

Dan—Well, this ain't little. You'd like the dairy stock though. I've got some Holsteins. (*Crosses to her.*) It's fine dairy land.

Gammy Hennessey has barged in before Molly can ask further information and soon Fisher is back with a crowd of canawlers he is herding toward the railroad station. Again Molly tries to say good-by to Dan, and again he tries to hold her with further attractive facts about the farm. Finally she has to be downright positive with him, saying flatly and once and for all that she isn't interested in anything he does. At which moment the agent Fisher is heard calling lustily for Klore. That gives Molly something of a start.

"Mr. Butterfield says the spring house I'm buildin' is the best he ever heard of," persists Dan. "There's goin' to be runnin' water in it too!"

"Do you know who's comin' out here?" demands Molly, a little excitedly.

"I don't give a damn who's comin' out!" snaps Dan. "Molly, it won't be any colder up there than it is in this place."

"Jotham Klore is comin' out here and he ain't so drunk this time!" she warns.

Klore has appeared in the door. Gammy yells to Molly to get Dan out. Molly turns first to Klore to distract his attention. She will walk to the station with him if he'd like her to—

Dan isn't to be put aside like that. Not even when Molly pointedly addresses him as Mr. Jones. His name isn't Jones. His name is Dan Harrow. At which statement Klore pushes Molly aside and comes back.

"I've been lookin' for you for some time," says Klore, advancing belligerently.

"I've been around," answers Dan calmly.

"Maybe from now on you won't be around so *much*," sneers Klore, beginning to take off his coat.

"Dan, git out! He's sober!" screams Molly.

Dan isn't paying much attention to Klore. He still wants to tell Molly about the farm. Nor will he pay any heed to her plea that he get out before he is killed. He is taking off his coat, too, now and Klore, in his shirtsleeves, is waiting.

Gammy is excited. They can't fight in there, with kerosene lamps around. If they're going to fight, let them do it outside. The crowd agrees. Several of the men grab Klore and force him toward the door. Another group holds Harrow. The movement in general is toward the door and up the towpath.

"We'll go to the stores this afternoon and buy the things you think you'll need out there," calls Dan from the door.

"Oh, Gammy! I don't want him to git killed!" wails Molly.

Outside the door the two fighters have broken loose and are at each other. They are masked by the boaters crowding around them, but bits of the fight can be seen as the crowd moves to one side or the other. There is a good deal of shouting.

"That's right, kill him, Dan!" . . . "Kick him in the privates!" . . . "He's got him!" . . . "My Gad, look what Harrow's doin' to him!" . . . "Looks like a new bully!"

The fight has moved past the windows. The boaters who couldn't get through before, rush out to join the crowd.

"That's right! That's right! Throw him in!" yells someone.

There is a roar of laughter. The crowd moves back toward the door, cheering and laughing.

"Gammy! He throwed him in the canawl!" calls Riley gleefully.

"He's swimming to the other side!" adds Emory. "My God! He's salivated him!"

It is a highly pleased crowd that comes crowding back into the hotel. Everybody is wanting to buy Dan a drink to celebrate. The hero himself is not at all fussed. He is getting back into his coat and calling—

"Well, Molly, let's git started!"

"But, Dan, don't you see what's happened? You're the bully of the canawl now!" Molly's eyes are shining with tears.

"That's got nothin' to do with it!" answers Dan.

"But you've licked Klore! Now you're the boss of the Erie!"

"No, I ain't. I'm jest a farmer. Tryin' to fit you to go on a farm. I didn't fight him jest to be the bully. Come here, talk to me jest a minute."

Dan has led Molly away to a corner of the room and Gammy is trying to keep the excited boaters away. So's they can talk private. Suddenly in the doorway appears Sam Weaver. He is supported by a conductor of the railway train and he is pretty well mussed up.

"Damn fool! He was right in front of us and we knocked him down with the cowcatcher," explains the conductor explosively. "It's a wonder he ain't dead."

Sam, coming to, is strong enough to order a little Jamaicy rum and to push the conductor aside. He's all right, he says. No bones broken and, as a matter of fact, his stomach is feelin' a lot better. . . .

Fisher had finally rounded up his men and they have started for the railroad. Gammy Hennessey has lured Molly and Dan out of the corner.

"But it'll only be for four months," Dan is saying earnestly. "I tell you it ain't the canawl you hate to leave. You're jest hatin' to grow up and take responsibilities. I'm only askin' you now to try it fer four months. You kin come back when she opens. Ain't that a fair proposition? I'll let you come back if you don't like it up there."

"All right," Molly agrees. "But he'll find some way to make me stay," she adds, turning to Gammy.

"Would you like to come along with us?" Molly calls to Lucy Gurget.

"Where you goin'?"

"We're goin' to git a license to git married."

"Can I be of any service, Dan?" speaks up Fortune Friendly, just back from peddling almanacs and collecting his two dollars. "I used to be a preacher."

"No one else could do it, Fortune," answers Molly.

"Are you goin' to take a honeymoon trip on a train?" asks
Sol Tinker.

"No. We're goin' to OUR farm in a horse and buggy!" laughs
Molly.

She has taken Fortune's arm and is leading him out the door.
Dan gives his arm to Gammy and they follow after, with Sol,
Lucy and Sam after them.

"Git ready a bottle o' champagne wine," calls Sam from the
door. "We'll be right back!"

The last of Fisher's boaters have come from the bar. They are
singing and gathering up their bags. There is a great shouting of
good-bys.

THE CURTAIN FALLS

LOST HORIZONS

A Dramatic Fantasy in Three Acts

By John Hayden

"LOST HORIZONS" is another play with a history as exciting as the story of the drama itself. It was originally conceived and written by Harry Segall, whose "The Behavior of Mrs. Crane" earned him written words of modest praise but practically no royalties a year or so ago.

Mr. Segall submitted the script to the Rowland Stebbins who produced "The Green Pastures" and has a fondness for dramas of spiritual import and Mr. Stebbins suggested certain revisions. Mr. Segall agreed and suggested that Philip Dunning be called in. Mr. Dunning made suggestions but he and Mr. Segall were never able to work out a new version. Mr. Segall then submitted the play to A. H. Woods, who took an option on it, also with the agreement that the play be partly rewritten. It was not rewritten and the option lapsed. Segall went to Hollywood to write scenarios and while there did a second version of "Lost Horizons" which Mr. Stebbins bought.

Still it was thought something should be done to strengthen certain scenes in the play and a David Hertz was called in as a collaborator. Mr. Hertz wrote an entirely new version, which apparently no one liked except Mr. Hertz. Then John Hayden entered the picture. He was the Stebbins stage director and he thought he would like to write a third version of the play. While Hayden was at work Segall sold all his rights in the script to the Metro-Goldwyn-Mayer motion picture corporation, which later agreed to permit Mr. Stebbins to make a production of the Hayden version.

This script was then submitted to Mr. Segall and he did not care for it. At least he did not feel that he should share either such praise as it might earn or be held responsible for mistakes laid against it.

The play finally was hopefully produced in October, with Jane Wyatt as the heroine, and met a divided reception. A third of the reviews were favorable, a third unfavorable, a third noncommittal. Audiences were similarly divided. One week's poor business would be followed by another of encouraging gains. The play was twice scheduled to close and twice continued.

The first scene of the play is that of a bungalow in Los Angeles. An attractive, tastefully but not elaborately furnished room, similar to hundreds in that part of the country, including all the familiar features, from a tiled kitchenette to a Murphy wall bed.

It is an early evening in September. The room is empty until Janet Evans comes from the kitchen with a bowl of flowers. She is an attractive girl of twenty-five, alert and happy at the moment. She wears a freshly laundered bungalow apron with a certain air of pride.

Janet has no more than placed the roses on the gate-leg table than there is a knock at the door anouncing Rita Rogers, friend and former stage associate. A jolly, wise-cracking type of actress, Rita had started for Kansas City and a stock company job but had missed her train. Now she is hoping a final talk with Janet will induce her to go along. Janet has real talent, insists Rita, and there should be a great chance for her in the East. Especially in a company run by a gifted gentleman named Thayer.

Janet is not interested. Janet, in fact, has made her final decision. She is leaving the stage; she is marrying Ralph Bondley and she had rather be a young lawyer's wife in love with her husband than even a successful actress.

When Ralph Bondley arrives he is discovered to be a "well-built, assertive chap of thirty-five." Ralph is a little preoccupied, but cheerful and friendly. He has come with news for Janet which Rita would let them share without her embarrassing presence, but they hold her long enough to hear it. Ralph has been appointed an Assistant District Attorney in New York.

Rita is properly impressed. Janet glows with pride and they drink a cocktail with Ralph in celebration. Then Rita goes back to wait for another train and Ralph reveals the second half of the message he has for Janet.

It has occurred to Ralph that Janet is still ambitious for a stage success. That is where she should be, on the stage, playing good parts.

"There is only one part I want to play," smiles Janet, loyally, throwing her arms about Ralph. "When do we leave?"

Ralph must be ready the fifteenth. Janet is thrilled. Doesn't give them much time, but—

"Janet—I—I'm going alone," announces Ralph.

Janet stops as one stunned and stands mutely facing him as he continues with an explanation:

"The truth is, Janet, I've thought it all out very carefully, and I feel that we're not ready for marriage yet. Not nearly ready. (*She does not move.*) I've wanted to tell you this before, but you were planning on it so much, I just couldn't. But last night I decided it wasn't fair to you to let you go on planning. I decided it was best to tell you at once just how matters stand. (*Hesitates.*) I told you I didn't want to get married until I'd gotten the appointment and made good, but that's not *all* the truth! (*He hesitates.*) The fact is, Janet, to be honest about it, I—I've changed entirely about the whole thing! About getting married—about us—about everything! . . . I can't explain it! You certainly haven't done anything to change me; you've been as sweet, as nice, as helpful as always, but just the same— something's gone! . . . I'm tremendously fond of you, Janet, and I'd do anything in the world for you, but—that's all."

Janet winces at the finality of his tone, but she does not speak. He continues, repeating the same argument, feeling more uncomfortable with every word. Some day, he says, she will see that he is right; some day, when she has got to the very top of her profession; some day— If she hears him she gives no sign. She is staring straight ahead. He has taken his hat and started for the door. Won't she even say good-by? She does not move—

"Oh, come, Janet—smile a little, can't you?" (*She turns away from him.*) "Say something! Don't look as though I'd stuck a knife in you! . . . Please, Janet, don't let's part this way. Don't let there be any bitterness. Why not smile and be thankful we discovered our mistake in time? It's the way I'd take it if it were the other way around."

Still she does not answer. Now he loses patience.

"Oh, stop acting, Janet! Save it for where it'll do you some good . . . All right, then! Have it your own way! Be tragic! Good-by!"

He has slammed the door behind him. Janet stands for a moment looking after him, like a stricken animal, dazed, bewildered. She moves slowly, sadly, from one thing to another, without decision. She has picked up Ralph's cocktail glass. Mechanically she starts for the dinette and puts it on the table. She continues wearily on into the kitchen. A moment later the report of a revolver shot is heard, followed by the thud of a falling body. The curtain falls.

The scene changes to a Hall of Records that greatly resembles the reading room of a public library. At one side of the room a woman, evidently an attendant, is sorting and filing cards. At one of the long reading tables are two men, one young, one old; the young man an intellectual type, carelessly dressed; the older man the executive, high-class business type. At another table a middle-aged, worn-looking woman is reading and weeping softly. Here is a banker, and there a clerk. A Guide is talking to one who looks as though she might have been a scrub woman.

A second Guide ushers Janet into the room. She is still wearing the bungalow apron and is plainly puzzled. The Guide is explaining to her that she will find the record of her life in this room where are filed the accounts of all mortal life.

"Mortal life! . . . Then am I . . . Is this death?" demands Janet.

"If you think so," answers the Guide, leaving her with the Attendant. She gives her name and her address. The Attendant starts slightly at the designation of Los Angeles as Janet's home. "It is nothing," she is quick to explain, "only we get such *young* people from there."

"Could you tell me—is everyone sent here to read the record of their life?" asks Janet.

"No. Only those, like yourself, who did not complete their earthly existence. Here they learn what the unfinished part held in store for them," he answers.

JANET—But why must they know? That is what they wished to escape. *I* don't want to know.

GUIDE—You must. You tried to escape from your own imagination—your own conclusions. Now you must learn what was actually in store for you.

JANET—But all I ask is for forgetfulness—for peace. Is there no place where a soul may rest?

GUIDE—You had no right to avoid your destiny; to draw a line and say, "Thus far will I go and no farther."

JANET—I couldn't go on. I am sorry if I have done wrong, but in my senses I couldn't go on.

GUIDE—Others have been as unhappy as you, but have kept on and found the journey good.

JANET—But it can't matter now. And it couldn't have mattered then—without him. . . . May I talk to you about him?

GUIDE—If it will help.

JANET—I think it will.

GUIDE—That is why I was sent to meet you—to help.

JANET—I worshiped him . . . I worshiped him . . . I had never known affection of any sort before he came! I had never mattered to anyone! Perhaps that's why his love meant so much to me! I just stood there listening to him while something seemed to be crushing all the life out of me. I can't even remember his saying good-by, I just turned and suddenly he was gone. All I can remember is that I felt I had to do something at once to stifle the pain—anything! (*Shudders.*) He left me nothing to hope for! Nothing to cling to! Nothing to live for!

The Messenger has brought several books to Janet's table. One is thick, the others comparatively thin. The smaller books are marked with other names—David Prescott, Diane Reynolds, Elsie Marshall, Adam Thayer—

So many books indicate that Janet had been desperately needed on earth, the Guide explains. These are the records of lives that were linked with hers.

"But I don't know them," protests Janet, picking up one and reading its title. " 'Adam Thayer'—except for him, I never even heard their names before. They are all utter strangers to me."

GUIDE—And some of them would always have remained strangers. Some you might have met, but the others would never have known of your existence or you of theirs.

JANET—Then why must I read their lives?

GUIDE—Because at some point in your existence they would have depended on you. Had you gone on, you would have been instrumental in some way in shaping their lives; in creating circumstances that would have affected them. . . .

JANET—Even though I never knew them?

GUIDE—Even though you never saw them. You might have passed them in the street or in a crowded lobby—and never have known it. Your life would have affected many others, but these are the ones who need you.

JANET—I couldn't help them. I couldn't help anyone. I couldn't even help myself.

GUIDE—You could have helped them all.

JANET—How?

GUIDE—Merely by living! (*He selects a book at random.*)

See, you are given to read only the parts of their lives that you would have influenced—whenever that might be. (*He opens the book to a page at the end.*)   Here is the situation of the man whose name you know, Adam Thayer.   Broken in spirit; discouraged beyond hope; contemplating an act like yours—you would have prevented that.

JANET—It isn't true!   It can't be true!

GUIDE (*opens another book*)—And this young man, David Prescott, accused of murder, unable to save himself.   Had you lived, his innocence would have been established.

JANET—No—no.

GUIDE—. . . and this lovely young girl—Diane Reynolds— throwing away her chances of happiness through her infatuation for Gary Farwell, a worthless scamp, who ruined, tricked and deserted—this other girl— (*Taking another book.*)   Elsie Marshall, little more than a child.   Deserted her—left her desperate in her miserable room.   Read them!   Learn their need of you! Begin with Elsie Marshall!   (JANET *stares down at* ELSIE's *open book as the curtain falls.*

The third scene reveals a small furnished room in Montreal. It is barely furnished, and yet is a grade above being squalid or uninviting.   It is a bright August morning.   The door opens to admit the occupant, Elsie Marshall, a frail girl of about twenty, rather pretty, but obviously helpless and a little pathetic.   She has brought with her two paper parcels, one a bottle of milk in a bag.   She has no more than set them in a washstand cupboard than there is a knock at the door followed by the appearance of the landlady, Mrs. Kondos, towels over her arm; a thin woman, past middle age, with a deeply lined face, who speaks in a Scottish-Canadian accent.

Mrs. Kondos is in a normal state of mind, at least a normal state of mind for a landlady.   She has been watching Elsie, her goings and her comings; she suspects there has been cooking in the room, which is against the rules of the house; she has little faith that Elsie will ever hear from her husband again, seeing it is three weeks now since he went away and there is a matter of two weeks' rent due.

Elsie finds it hard to explain, both her trust in her husband and her confidence in the future; she will give Mrs. Kondos the few dollars she has; she has pawned what jewelry she had; she is confident Mr. Farwell will either come back or send for her to join him, and she doesn't like Mrs. Kondos' familiarity.

"Listen to me," bristles the landlady. "You're not the first girl I've seen in your predicament, so don't get on your high horse with me. The best thing you can do is get in touch with your folks."

Elsie cannot do that. She has only a brother and a mother; they are not wealthy; brother is a doctor; Mrs. Kondos has no right to go on insisting Mr. Farwell will not be back.

Mrs. Kondos may not have a right, but she says it just the same; that Gary Farwell was just amusing himself; that his story of his divorce not being final in the States is what they all say; that he has gone for good and the quicker Elsie admits it and decides what she is going to do the better. She has no money and she can't live there on charity.

"There's only three things a girl in your predicament can do," announces Mrs. Kondos with finality: "Go back to her folks; get a job; or find a man to pay her bills."

"Well, I can do that, too," announces Elsie, with spirit, reaching for her hat and her pocketbook. "I may be too proud to go home, but I'm not too proud to work."

"And half of Montreal unemployed!" sneers Mrs. Kondos.

"I'm not going to sit here idly until you throw me out," continues Elsie, defiantly; . . . and I'm not going to appeal to anyone for help. . . . You needn't be afraid of having me on your hands, Mrs. Kondos. . . . I'll have a job before night . . . You'll see . . . you'll see. . . ."

She is out of the door and gone. Mrs. Kondos picks up the money Elsie has left on the dresser and counts it "with a sour and knowing smile," as the curtain falls.

The scene changes to a bright and cheerful drawing room in the home of people of means and social standing. It is the New York home of Oliver Reynolds, who has just come in and is trying to learn from Dobbs, his servant, the situation at home.

There have been several telephone messages, Dobbs reports. Miss Diane is home and dressing, expecting Mr. Farwell to come in for a cocktail. Mr. Reynolds is fixing himself a highball when his daughter comes downstairs.

Diane is an attractive well-poised girl of twenty and a great pal of her father. Just now he is particularly interested in the Gary Farwell with whom she has been going about a good deal. He is hoping to know more about Farwell than he has so far learned before he is asked finally to trust Diane to his keeping.

An unexpected caller is Robert Potter, a personable youth a few years older than Diane. It is Potter's first call in some time; he has been sticking pretty close to his laboratory, but his experiments have been worth it. Potter is about to isolate a germ that will benefit all humanity. With that accomplished he has something he would like to say to Diane. She advises him not to say it. Diane has other plans. She is fond of Bob, too fond of him to want to hurt his feelings—but there is someone else—

Gary Farwell is announced. He, too, is an attractive young man, though a less substantial and frank type than Potter. They accept each other politely but with reservations. Potter is soon gone.

Now Diane is in Gary's arms, and very happy to be there. It has been a long time since last night.

"Being in love with you is such fun," sighs Diane. "It can't last."

"Nonsense," answers Gary, quickly. "Being in love ought to be fun. People who don't make fun out of it aren't in love. We're just going to laugh our way through life. . . . What will we do tonight?"

Diane thinks perhaps a dinner, a theatre and then the Cotton Club. But Gary frowns on the Cotton Club suggestion. He would prefer a quieter place, where he can have Diane more to himself. And when will Diane marry him? Very soon, Diane promises. Just as soon as her Dad agrees.

"But why should he make any objection?" demands Gary, a little testily. "I've told him all about myself."

"He doesn't object to you, dear," explains Diane. "It's just that it's hard for him to think anyone is quite good enough for his only child."

Diane has called her father and explained to him that she and Gary are going out. Then Albert Grayson is announced. Grayson is a friend of Mr. Reynolds, a fine, distinguished-looking man. He greets the Reynolds family cheerily and is glad to know Mr. Farwell. It seems to Grayson, the more intimately he studies Farwell, that they have met before, though Gary doubts it. It must be, Reynolds suggests, that the famous Grayson memory is slipping.

Grayson is not one to give up easily. He is sure he remembers Farwell. Remembers him as a fellow boat passenger. When he hears that Gary is proposing to marry Diane, his interest increases.

"I am an old friend of this family," explains Grayson, as Farwell and Diane are preparing to leave; "and after what Mr. Reynolds has just said, you must realize that there is nothing I can do but put him in possession of such facts as I have."

"I can't imagine what you have in mind, Mr. Grayson," protests Gary, amiably, "but you evidently mistake me for someone else."

GRAYSON—I'm not mistaken.

REYNOLDS—Is there any reason why Mr. Farwell should prefer not to recall your meeting?

GRAYSON—I think so. . . . On the occasion in question there was a very unpleasant incident connected with a card game. I don't think I need be more explicit.

GARY—I can only repeat—you are mistaking me for someone else. I never sailed on that boat.

REYNOLDS—Thanks for speaking out, Al. Such a thing is easily verified.

GARY—Exactly. You won't even find my name on the passenger list.

GRAYSON—The name was Fiske at that time—George Fiske.

REYNOLDS—I know Mr. Grayson would not make such a statement without every justification.

DIANE (to GRAYSON)—That isn't fair . . . You could be mistaken . . . and I'm sure you are. . . . So sure that . . . Gary, you asked me to set a date for our wedding . . . I am ready to do so.

REYNOLDS—Diane!

GARY (to REYNOLDS)—Just a moment, please . . . (To DIANE.) I appreciate your faith in me, Diane, and you are going to find it justified. . . . But I want this matter thrashed out as much as your father does.

REYNOLDS—Thanks, Farwell, that is very white of you.

GRAYSON (to REYNOLDS)—Bluff! (GARY looks at GRAYSON.)

DIANE (to GRAYSON)—You have no right to judge Gary until you can prove your case. He says he never sailed on the "Empress of Britain."

REYNOLDS—My dear, I have been associated with Mr. Grayson for a great many years. I know him. . . .

DIANE—And I know Gary. . . . Gary, you asked me when I

would marry you. The answer is—whenever you wish.

The curtain falls.

The fifth scene is in the library of Albert Grayson in uptown New York. It is a darkly paneled, heavily furnished room, definitely masculine in suggestion. The walls are lined with book shelves filled with handsomely bound volumes.

The room is dimly lighted. Lying face up on a rug in front of a desk is the body of Grayson in evening dress. Seated at the desk and using the telephone is Detective Keegan, an officer of the more intelligent type. At least he does not wear his hat in the house.

Keegan is making a report to headquarters and asking that someone be sent to bring in a man who seems to have been the last man to have seen Grayson alive. As Keegan talks Daniels, an assistant, appears with a series of fingerprint photographs. They include those of the dead man, which are not the same as those found on the handle of a heavy letter opener on the table.

This fact established, Keegan dismisses Daniels and sends for Harry Wormser, Grayson's butler. Wormser is able to add little to what he has already told: That he had worked for Mr. Grayson for three weeks; that his master had left the dinner table and had come to the library leaving instructions that he was not to be disturbed; that a Mr. Prescott had called about 10 o'clock and insisted on seeing Mr. Grayson; that he (Wormser) had tried to keep Prescott out but was finally forced to tell Mr. Grayson; that Grayson agreed to see Prescott, with whom he had had several quarrels the last week; that there were no other callers during the evening and that when he had come to bring Mr. Grayson his coffee, which he always did, he had found the body. He had immediately notified the police.

Wormser had always found Mr. Grayson a good sort, but extremely irritable; a fine man to work for; a man of reasonably good habits; some women friends, naturally, but none that would have any cause to want to put him, a generous patron, out of the way. . . .

Detective Daniels has found David Prescott, "a fine-looking, sturdy, wholesome chap of twenty-five." Wormser identifies him as the caller who had forced his way into the library. Prescott demands to see Mr. Grayson and is horrified to find him slain. He frankly admits that he had had words with the dead man. Their quarrel was over property that had been left Prescott and which he suspected Grayson of trying to cheat him out of. He had accused Grayson, Grayson had explained his side and Prescott had accepted the explanation.

"You don't look as though you would let a man slip a fast one over on you; talk his way out of it and not even try to get even," ventures Keegan.

"I came here intending to get even with him. I told him I would," admits Prescott.

KEEGAN (*picking up letter opener*)—And so you grabbed this letter opener—

PRESCOTT—I didn't. I didn't. I never touched it.

KEEGAN (*throwing it down in disgust*)—Why, your fingerprints are all over it.

PRESCOTT—Well, I may have handled it while I as talking with him. . . . I was sitting right there by the desk . . . I . . . I was nervous—probably I was fooling with it . . . what does that prove?

KEEGAN—This is what he was killed with. . . . You had a motive for doing it . . . you had quarreled with him . . . threatened him . . . (*Rises.*) and you were the only person who came here tonight.

PRESCOTT (*rises*)—I tell you I didn't do it! I—I couldn't. . . . Someone might have been here after I left. . . .

KEEGAN—The butler says not.

PRESCOTT—They could have gotten in without his knowing it—

KEEGAN—But they couldn't have handled this and not left a fingerprint!

PRESCOTT—They must have! They must have!

KEEGAN (*turns*)—Not this time. Prescott . . . you are under arrest for the murder of Albert Grayson. . . . Come on.

Keegan reaches for his hat as the curtain falls.

The sixth scene is the office of Adam Thayer, stage director of a Kansas City stock company. It is a cheaply furnished room and had been used as a dressing room before the shelves were ripped out. There is a wash basin and running water, a roll-top desk and an old swivel chair. The walls are covered with flashlight photographs and a few posters, the most conspicuous of the posters announcing the current week's production of "Bird Cage Walk," the first time on any stage.

Thayer comes through the door from the stage. He is thirty-eight, a good-looking actor type without the gloss of a matinee idol. He evidently is in a state of great depression and wearily throws himself into a chair at the desk. Soon Eddie, a lean and gangling stage manager, is in for instructions. Thayer hands him the parts for next week's show, tells him to call rehearsal as usual at 10.30.

Maude Trevor, the company's leading woman, would have a word with Thayer. She is a fading actress of thirty-five, still wearing her stage make-up and part of her costume. She has come to thank Mr. Thayer for writing her so wonderful a part, the most wonderful part she ever played; and wasn't the house wonderful? Miss Trevor is ever and ever so grateful! And they say Dohlman, of New York, was in front! It thrills Miss Trevor to think of Dohlman coming all the way from New York to see her in this new play. She wishes he had waited until a little later in the week. . . .

Miss Trevor has gone to her dressing room. Thayer and Eddie are free to express their thought—

"God, she was lousy!" says Thayer.

"Stinkin'!" agrees Eddie.

"Even if she couldn't *play* the part—"

"She might at least *learn* it."

Rita Rogers sticks her head in the door to say good night. Thayer would stop her long enough to thank her for saving the show. Eddie, too. If it hadn't been for Rita, when Trevor went up in her lines Eddie would have had to ring down the curtain—

"And 'Bird Cage Walk' would have been right in the middle of the Missouri river."

"If you hadn't jumped in, Rita, she'd have been standing there yet," says Thayer. "Don't think I don't appreciate it. . . . You gave the only decent performance in the troupe. I never saw a bunch go to pieces so."

Next time, allows Thayer, he will follow his hunch and send for someone to play as important a part as this heroine. Still, the play must be wrong, too. Otherwise the audience would have found something to applaud. Nor can anything that Eddie and Rita say lift Thayer out of this mood. Dohlman, he admits, is his only chance.

"You don't suppose he is going to pass up a piece of property just because an actress forgets a few lines," ventures Rita.

"A few lines!" explodes Thayer, his anger getting the better of him for the first time. "She forgot more lines than I wrote in the God d— Ouch!" He has banged his fist on the table and cut his hand on a paper knife.

Eddie and Rita are excited. It's a cut like that, if you get a

little dirt in it, that causes trouble. Rita goes for some iodine. . . .

Dohlman has appeared. He liked the production; agrees with
Thayer that Rita is an actress worth watching. He doesn't want
Thayer to be too discouraged. Someone else may like "Bird
Cage Walk." . . .

Dohlman has gone. Eddie finds Thayer very depressed. He
had banked a lot on this play. It's a year's work wasted and a
blow to his pride. He is pretty sure now he was never meant to
be an author.

Eddie leaves. The bottle of iodine tablets Rita has sent in
lies on the table. It fascinates Thayer. He stares at it as he
pours himself a drink. He picks up the iodine and reads the
poison label on the bottle. He is dropping a tablet in his drink
as the curtain falls.

We are back in the Hall of Records. Janet has finished reading the books, but still cannot understand.

"I don't even know these people," she protests to the Guide.
"A friend of mine is mentioned. . . . Oh, I feel for them . . . I
pity them. . . . They are in trouble—yes—but so was I—and
their difficulties are not of my making."

"But their salvation was in your hands," insists the Guide.

"I can't believe that. I was so ineffectual in my own life—
I can't believe I could have mattered to them."

"You might have saved them all," the Guide insists, calmly,
handing her the larger book. "This is your book. . . . It is the
chronicle of your life—as it might have been."

"What does it matter what would have happened in my life—
I don't want to know."

"You must. The pattern of life's tapestry is so intricate, that
the cutting of one thread is unforgiveable. You are to read, not
only what would have happened in your own life from this point
on—but the events in the lives of these others which you would
have seriously affected—had you lived—had you the courage to
live. . . . This is your book. Read it."

THE CURTAIN FALLS

PART TWO

A month or more has passed since we first met Janet Evans in
her California bungalow. It is now ten days before Adam Thayer

is producing "Bird Cage Walk" in his Kansas City theatre. The scene is the Green Room of the theatre, a long room beneath the stage with benches around its sides, the walls of painted plaster covered generously with posters and framed photos of bygone stars.

A rehearsal of the week's bill is in progress. Thayer, as director, is seated at a kitchen table at the front of the room; Eddie, his stage manager, is near by with a clip board on his lap making notes. Maude Trevor, leading woman, looking a good forty without her make-up, and Rita Rogers, second lead, are finishing a scene. At the fringes of the room are groups of actors and extra people.

"So and so and so and so and so and so," intones Miss Trevor, finishing a speech she does not know; "long speech ending with: 'No one can do that to me!'"

Eddie has held up his watch. The rehearsal is over for the day. The call is for next morning at 10, "and everybody perfect." Several of the players are anxious to explain why they were not perfect today. Maude Trevor, however, has more serious business to discuss with Thayer. She wants to know about this new play of his. From what she has heard it is to go into rehearsal on Monday. She also has heard that there is a plan to lay her off that week and send to Chicago for some new girl to play the lead.

"To be honest with you, Maude, we have talked of it, but it isn't definitely settled yet," explains Thayer.

"Well, it's going to be settled right now," answers Maude, snappily. "Is there any valid reason why I shouldn't play it?"

"Yes, it isn't suited to you."

"Ha! Not suited to me! Don't make me laugh! It fits me down to the ground. . . . I read the play . . . it couldn't suit me better if it was written for me."

"Well, I have to be the judge of that."

"And I have to be the judge of whether or not I'll allow you to humiliate me. Now, get this, Thayer, either I play that part in 'Bird Cage Walk' or I quit."

Without wanting to quarrel, Thayer would like to point out that Miss Trevor was engaged to play "as cast"; that he cannot consistently cast her as a nineteen-year-old girl, whatever she may think; if he does get someone else for the part Maude will have a week off with pay—

"But what about my following—what about my prestige?" cries Maude.

"Please, Maude, I wish you wouldn't make an issue of it. If it didn't mean so much to me, I'd let you do it. But here's the layout—Dohlman is coming on from New York to look at it. If it goes over right, he may let me stage it for him on Broadway. It's my big chance, Maude, and it might be the means of getting me out of stock and on to the main street."

"Well, it's my big chance, too. If Dohlman sees me in that part, it'll put me *back* on Broadway. All I need to put me right back in the swim is one good part."

Maude is obdurate. Does she get the part or doesn't she? She doesn't? Very well, here is her notice, and to hell with Thayer and to hell with his play! She has stormed out of the room.

Eddie is pleased. Now Thayer will have to get someone else. But Thayer is worried. He has tried the agencies, and nothing has happened. He is of a mind to give the whole thing up. Eddie gets him to promise that he will wait a couple of days. If he can't get anyone then he can let Maude think she has whipped him and let her do her best. Or worst.

"If this didn't mean so much to me, I'd let it ride with Maude in the part," explains Thayer. "But I've banked a lot on this play—a whole year's work . . . and I just have a hunch that she'd kill it . . . and your first hunch is always right. . . ."

Thayer looks up to see Janet Evans standing in an arch at the end of the room. She is looking for Rita Rogers. But she would like to speak to Mr. Thayer, too. She is an actress. There might be extra work—

Perfunctorily Thayer would take Janet's name and address, and some record of her experience. Where has she played before? With Duffy? In Oakland? Thayer remembers. He had seen Janet in "Mary Dugan." Very good, too. An idea—

"I wonder if you could play that part," Thayer is mumbling to himself.

"I'd like to try—whatever it is," says Janet, eagerly. She has had a rather distressing personal experience, and she wants to work, she explains. "I've done some good things—but I won't mind playing a bit—anything—if I can only be occupied," she adds.

"What's your idea of money?"

"That really won't matter, Mr. Thayer. . . . I'll leave it to you to give me whatever it's worth. . . . If you can use me—I will be very grateful."

Eddie barges in with a telegram to a Chicago agency. He

would get Thayer's O.K. on it. Thayer takes the telegram and tears it up without taking his eyes off Janet.

"The position is filled," he says, as the curtain falls.

We are back in Adam Thayer's office. It is about the same hour of a similar day. Thayer comes from the stage, a little wearily, but with a faint smile of satisfaction shining through the weariness. Eddie, the stage manager, follows shortly. It is the same old routine—rehearsal at 10.30 in the morning, and won't the new leading woman beef when she gets a load of the skinny part she is to have in the next show!

The new leading woman, this time, is Janet Evans. She has given what Eddie thinks was a pretty good performance in "Bird Cage Walk." Thayer goes farther. To him Janet was swell. . . .

Janet is in to thank Thayer for the fine chance he gave her, and happy to have his complimentary thanks in return. It is all quite amusing to Janet. She has to laugh a little, which excites the Thayer curiosity.

"Well, it is amusing," says Janet, in answer to his query as to why she laughs. "I just came in here—a stranger—looking for extra work—a bit of any kind—and you take a chance by allowing me to play 'Flora.' I do appreciate it, Mr. Thayer. She is a lovely part, you know."

Janet has gone happily homeward before Dohlman arrives. He is as business-like as before, but this time his voice has a cheerier note. He cannot wait to see another performance, but he has seen enough to convince himself that "Bird Cage Walk" is a good buy. He was only anxious about one thing—would the spiritual values he found in the script come through in the playing? They did.

Dohlman would also like to have Thayer come to New York and direct the rehearsals. He will plan to hire an English leading man, of course, and he likes Rita Rogers a lot. He will take her if she will come. How about Miss Evans? Well, Dohlman liked Janet's performance very much, but they should have a name in that part.

"I think she is just right for it," declares Thayer. "She has the quality—"

"But not the reputation," counters Dohlman. "No, Thayer, we need a name in that part . . . Audrey Wood, if we can get her. . . . And I think we can. . . . Well, I can just make a train. . . . Anything else you want to take up?"

"Not a thing . . . and thanks a lot."

"Hope we both make a lot of money."

"I hope so."

Eddie is tickled, but not surprised. Rita is thrilled. Thayer is ready to take a drink in celebration. Still, there's Janet. What about Janet? Rita wants to know. Thayer explains Dohlman's decision in favor of a name. Which, as Eddie explains, is just the breaks—

"And it's all due to her," muses Rita.

"What's all due to her?" demands Eddie.

"Everything," continues Rita, quietly. "Your going to New York . . . Ad's selling the play . . . my getting the job. . . . Suppose she hadn't been here. She put the play over."

The curtain falls.

Still in Kansas City. This is a reasonably pleasant furnished apartment occupied by Janet and Rita. It is evening and three or four weeks have elapsed since the production of "Bird Cage Walk."

At the moment Rita, attractively but scantily clad in her undies, is doing her native best to pick out a popular song on the ukulele. The fact that it happens to be "The Last Round-Up" doesn't make it any easier.

The outer door opens suddenly and Janet bursts in with the announcement that "he" is following her. She is being followed and she is afraid of being pestered to death, but Rita assures her that "he" is reputed to be worth a million. Nothing over fifty thousand is a pester.

It transpires that the person following Janet is a playboy named Paul Duttine; that he has been haunting the theatre for days; sending Janet orchids at every performance and candy at every opportunity. Janet will have none of him. She is "concentrating on stage lovers this season." She has not thought of Ralph Bondley in weeks and she is gradually getting herself back into whistling condition. She wants to stay there. So— If that ringing of the bell is Mr. Duttine, Janet is not at home, or doesn't live there—

Janet has run for the bedroom and Rita has answered the house phone. It is Mr. Duttine and Rita promptly asks him to come up. The poor boy appeals to her material nature.

Duttine is a well-dressed, good-looking chap, but obviously the playboy. He is ever so eager to have five minutes with Miss Evans. Rita thinks it might be arranged. Rita could be bribed.

A fur coat? That would be swell. Let Mr. Duttine call back in fifteen minutes.

The next caller is Adam Thayer, come to take the girls to dinner. It is, concludes Rita, a fine chance to repeat her conviction that when she and Thayer go on to New York Saturday for the Broadway production of Thayer's play it is going to be pretty sad for Janet, who is secretly eating her heart out at not having a chance to play the part. Janet would deny the charge. This is Thayer's big chance and she is awfully happy for him. But, as Thayer notices, her voice doesn't sound as cheerful as she may think.

"She sounds just the way she feels . . . lousy!" says Rita. "She's dying to play 'Flora MacDonald' on Broadway!"

"Don't pay any attention to her, Ad," pleads Janet.

RITA—She's too damn retiring. . . . Afraid to speak up for what's coming to her.

THAYER—Well, just what do you mean by "coming to her"?

RITA—I mean that Janet's performance was what sold that play.

JANET—Rita is speaking for herself, Ad, not for me. I don't feel that way at all.

THAYER—I agree with you, Rita.

RITA—And I hate to think of what your play would have looked like with someone else . . . Maude Trevor, for instance. . . . God, I can just hear her chanting away in her best voice. . . . When she meets a long speech, it sounds like High Mass.

JANET—Don't pay a bit of attention to her. If Audrey Wood likes the part and will play it . . . I think it's a great break for you.

RITA—Scallions!

THAYER—Thanks, Janet. (*The phone bell rings.*)

JANET—And now, let's get going.

RITA (*at phone*)—Hello . . . Oh, it's you, Paul.

JANET—Hang up. (RITA *obeys without a word.*)

THAYER—Some chap, Janet?

RITA—Wants to give me a fur coat.

JANET—He'll probably follow me to California.

THAYER—You're not going to California.

RITA—With no coat, *I'd* better go to California.

THAYER—I don't think he'll bother you after next Saturday.

JANET—What makes you say that?

THAYER—Read this. (*He hands* JANET *a telegram.*)

JANET (*reading*)—"Audrey Wood not available stop arrange Evans report rehearsal stop regards. . . . Dohlman."

RITA—There is a Santa Claus!

JANET—It can't be true.

THAYER—Why not?

JANET—It's too wonderful—I—I'm dreaming. (*Without otherwise moving* RITA *lifts one foot and gives* JANET *a gentle kick which produces an "Ouch."*)

RITA—You're awake.

THAYER—You get ready to leave after the performance next Saturday night. . . . Can you make it?

JANET—Can I? (*Throws her arms around* THAYER'S *neck.*) You old darling.

RITA (*rising*)—Hey! What about money? Any more?

THAYER—A little.

JANET—Oh, let's not be little. (*The phone bell rings.*)

RITA—Come on . . . the hell with it.

The curtain falls.

The scene changes to that of a pent-house apartment in New York. In the center of the handsome drawing-room Paul Duttine, late of Kansas City, is busily collecting his belongings and putting them in a large Gladstone bag. He gets along quite well until he is interrupted by Edna Winters, a tall attractive girl, elaborately dressed and at the moment of an inquiring mind.

Edna would know what it is Paul is doing. Paul is packing for a trip, but it is not the trip Edna thinks it is. Paul is not going to Bermuda, as promised. Paul is going away from there and without Edna.

Edna is not perturbed. Edna has her own plans and she knows every move that Paul has made for days; knows all about Janet Evans being in New York; knows all about her opening in a new play in Atlantic City; even knows about the fur coat Paul has bought, the bill for which has just come.

"So," concludes Edna, "you're going with me."

"I'm laughing right heartily, my sweet," answers Paul, looking as though he might.

"You'll weep right copiously if you don't, my pet," replies Edna, looking as though she meant it.

Paul is not to be moved by threats. He is, he repeats, through. There is only one way to hold him, and that is without hitching. He will not be bossed and he will not be bullied. He's through! Besides, he could not go to Bermuda even if he were not through.

His sister Helen is coming home from Paris.

That announcement is good news to Edna. That makes every-ing fine. Edna is anxious to meet Helen, too. But first she must know definitely: Is Paul walking out on her?

Paul is. For the first time in his life Paul has met a girl he would like to make Mrs. Paul Duttine. Edna is not good enough for that job, though she rates a good second choice.

"Just your hard luck, that's all," Paul explains.

"Yeah! Well, listen, it's going to be just *your* hard luck! Nobody dumps me and gets away with it! Nobody!"

"Listen, you! When I'm through, I'm through!" shouts Paul, angrily. "Start any kind of fireworks you like! I don't scare one little bit, understand?"

"No? We'll see!"

Paul has gathered up his Gladstone and is at the door. He has one regret. He should have smacked Edna one. On second thought he does.

"I'm glad you did that!" cries Edna, rubbing her cheek. "Now, nothing you can say or do will stop me."

"What the hell I ever saw in you, I don't know!" says Paul.

"Blow!" yells Edna, grabbing a bowl of flowers and hurling it after him. As the bowl crashes against the door Edna rushes to the phone. "Hello. . . . Operator . . ." she calls. "This is room 508. I want to send a cable . . . to Miss Helen Duttine . . . Hotel Crillon, Paris. . . . 'To tip you off. . . . Am telling Paul everything . . .' signed Edna."

The curtain falls.

On the Boardwalk at Atlantic City, facing the interior of a shop. It is Monday afternoon. There has been some sort of accident. Several people are crowding into the shop. This is exciting but also confusing to the proprietor, who is bobbing about anxiously. Presently Adam Thayer, Eddie Lewis, Janet Evans and Rita Rogers come through the crowd. They are helping Eddie, who has one leg drawn up and his face contorted with pain.

The proprietor solicitously finds a chair into which Eddie is gradually eased. They get a second chair, and lift his feet onto that. While they are making Eddie as comfortable as possible a stranger pushes his way through the crowd, a pleasant-spoken stranger with the poised air of a professional man. The stranger, it transpires, is a doctor who had seen Eddie slip on the steps and fall as the Thayer party was coming back to the Boardwalk from the beach. He would like to be of such assistance as he can.

After a hurried examination, painful and irritating to Eddie, the Doctor decides there has been no break but a bad sprain. He has sent Janet to the drug store for surgical tape and proceeds to bandage the ankle, before moving Eddie back to his hotel. There it will be necessary for him to go to bed and stay in bed for some time.

But—Eddie can't go to bed! How can they open the show without him? How can they run it without him? Not in a million years! Eddie is positive about that.

The Doctor is interested to learn that these are theatre people. He thinks perhaps, in such an emergency, after he bandages Eddie's ankle, he can let the stage manager hobble through the night on crutches.

Eddie can call his own doctor to have a look at him after the performance. He might be running a temperature.

"Well—how about you doing that?" asks Thayer.

"I'd be glad to, if you have no one else. You see I don't practice here. I live in the Middle West. I'm on here for a convention."

"It's awfully kind of you to help us out—but in all this excitement, no one has thought to ask your name."

"Marshall. Alan Marshall," answers the Doctor, as the curtain falls.

Back in Elsie Marshall's furnished room in Montreal. At the end of another unsuccessful day job hunting Elsie meets Mrs. Kondos. It has been five weeks since the rent has been paid and it seems to Mrs. Kondos a foolish thing for Elsie to go on. Elsie won't let her folks know her situation, she won't even tell Mrs. Kondos where she is from. She has had one job and lost it. She is losing flesh so rapidly that soon she will not be able to work— nor be attractive to any man.

"You'd best get yourself a man," concludes Mrs. Kondos. "You've small cause for pride, remember. It's the shame of living with one man prevents you from going home."

"I couldn't! You don't understand! I couldn't!" sobs Elsie.

"There's naught else for you to do. . . . Here you are, getting thinner by the minute for lack of proper food. . . . Do you think I want you to be left on my hands—ailing? You're a pretty thing, and there's many a nice man would take kindly to you. It's better than starving, Elsie. . . . And it's not like you were in the business . . . and a heap sight better than walking the

streets. . . . There's a man here in the house that likes the look
of you. You know the one . . . Stevens . . . has the parlor on
the ground floor. . . . He'd like to meet you. . . . Several times
he's mentioned you to me. . . . I tell you what to do. . . .
Freshen yourself up a bit and come down to the kitchen and
have a bit of hot supper with me. . . . Later on, I'll send him
up to see you."

Mrs. Kondos has gone out quietly, leaving Elsie crying softly
on the bed as the curtain falls.

We are back in the Reynolds home. It is late afternoon, the
time co-incident with the two previous scenes. Diane Reynolds
is at the telephone trying to explain to someone (Gary Farwell
by the evidence) that she could not refuse to go away with her
father, but that she will expect to see him before she goes.

Mr. Reynolds is in in time to hear Diane tell Dobbs that she
is expecting Mr. Farwell. The trunks have gone, Dobbs reports,
and the hand luggage is downstairs, ready to go in the car with
them.

Reynolds is not surprised that Diane is expecting Farwell, nor
particularly pleased. He has suspected that Diane has been seeing Farwell; he hadn't said anything about it because he doesn't
enjoy having rows with his daughter. He is sorry this misunder-
standing had to come between them. So is Diane.

"Damn good of you to say you'd make this trip with me,"
admits Reynolds.

"What else could I do?"

"Well, you might have refused to go, you know . . . made it
pretty awkward."

"You think these months abroad are going to change me, don't
you?"

"I hope they will prove to you that Gary isn't as important
to your life as you think he is right now."

"And I hope . . . that when we come back next Fall you will
find that separation has made no difference to Gary and me . . .
that we still feel just the same about each other."

For a moment father and daughter hold each other close. Then
Diane wants to know what it is that Reynolds has against Gary.
Reynolds frankly admits that he still thinks Farwell is after
Diane's money. Diane is sure Gary has plenty of his own, be-
cause he has said he has. And as for what Mr. Grayson had said
about the card cheat, that never was proved. . . .

Mr. Reynolds has gone to attend to last minute business. If

he is not back he will meet Diane at the dock. Gary passes him
at the door and stops to wish him bon voyage, for which he is
coldly thanked.

Gary is emotionally eager. He would hold Diane in his arms
and make passionate love to her to prove how desperately he is
going to miss her. Diane is afraid. She doesn't want to be made
love to now. It is going to be hard enough to give Gary up without that.

For Gary it is worse. Diane will have her father . . . and
the interest of the trip. He will have nothing but his burning
memories.

"Oh, my darling—my life was so lonely until I found you. I
have been alone so long—and now—I must again face it—made
more unbearable by having known you," pleads Gary.

"But it's the only way."

"It's useless."

"Don't say that."

"You know it's true. Your father is taking you away from
me. . . . He'll never bring you back, and I don't blame him.
. . . He's right, but he is cruel. If he knew how I love you,
he'd consent today."

Gary has taken Diane in his arms again. Her protests are
weakening. The spell of sex is working. Gary's voice has sunk
to a tremulous murmur. He cannot bear going to the boat to
say good-by—

"I want you to lie forever in my arms, where you belong,"
Gary is saying. "It's my own fault. . . . That day when you
said you would marry me, I should have taken you at your
word."

"Why didn't you?" whispers Diane.

GARY—I was a fool. . . . Think of all the time we've lost.
. . . All those days together that we can never regain. . . .
There's only one thing that will convince your father.

DIANE—What?

GARY—Your happiness after we are married. And I will make
you happy, dear. I'll devote my life to it. When he sees that,
he will be glad for you.

DIANE—If I only believed that.

GARY—You must. It's true. . . . You know how you dread
this separation. . . . Why should we consent to it?

DIANE—What can we do?

GARY (ringing for DOBBS)—Marry me tonight.

DIANE—Tonight?

GARY—My car's out front. . . . Let's go now. Don't stop to think. . . . I do love you.

DIANE—Where would we go?

GARY—Almost anywhere. . . . You know I can't be married in New York of course . . . my divorce won't allow it. . . . Oh, Darling, say you will. I can't bear to let you go. I need you so.

DOBBS (*entering*)—You rang, Miss?

DIANE (*a slight pause*)—Yes, Dobbs. . . . Bring my hat and coat, and put my bags in Mr. Farwell's car.

Dobbs bows and exits. Diane and Gary are in each other's arms as the lights dim out.

The curtain falls.

This is the Green Room of a theatre in Atlantic City. A small rather dingy room with a sliding fire door leading to the stage, and stairways leading to the upper dressing rooms. Two stage hands are sitting on a bench against the wall, waiting. One is reading *Variety*. The other is absorbed in thought. There is a burst of applause from the auditorium. The stage hands move into action. It is the signal that the show is over.

The applause dies down and comes up again. Actors come running down the stairs ready to take their calls with the company. A couple of them are too late and greatly perturbed. "I wait for it ever since the first act, and then I miss it," wails one; "and my girl's out front!"

The actors are coming from the stage. They are pretty proud of each other. Adam Thayer is in from the front of the house. He is satisfied but not beaming.

"Nice show, folks," he flings at those in sight. "Thanks a lot. . . . I have a few notes for you. . . . One o'clock tomorrow."

Janet has come from the stage. And Rita. Thayer kisses them both as he thanks them. They were swell.

Eddie hobbles in on his crutches. They are all O.K. so far as Eddie is concerned.

Now Dohlman and Paul Duttine have arrived. Janet, Paul would like to shout, was superb. Janet was very good, admits Dohlman. He thinks they should all get together in his room. He might even buy a little drink. . . . Paul would take Janet to the hotel; but she thinks Mr. Thayer is waiting for her. She'll probably see Paul later. . . .

The street door has opened. Ralph Bondley comes through.
He, too, is looking for Miss Evans. Told she is in Room 1 he
raps on the door. A moment later Janet comes out in her dressing gown. She starts slightly at sight of Ralph, then greets him
in a perfectly friendly, straightforward manner.

"How nice to see you again," she murmurs, perfunctorily. "I
want you to meet our manager, Mr. Dohlman—and Mr. Duttine. . . . This is Ralph Bondley."

Both Dohlman and Paul know the name. Ralph has made
quite a name for himself with his first case. Janet hasn't followed the news very closely but she is sure Ralph made good—

"You two are old friends, I take it," says Dohlman.

"Indeed we are," admits Janet.

"Yes, I knew Janet when the chance to play in a New York
production was just a dream," smiles Ralph.

Dohlman includes Ralph in the invitation to meet in his rooms
at the hotel, and Ralph is quick to accept. Now Dohlman and
Duttine have gone and Ralph has his chance to talk with Janet.
He beams amiably as he congratulates the little girl who made
good. He knew she would. He thinks, too, that it is swell the
way she is taking his reappearance.

"Why?" queries Janet, sweetly. "Did you think I'd be resentful? . . . I'm not. I'm really grateful. . . . I wasn't at
first . . . but I have been since . . . how right you were!"

"That's great," beams Ralph. "Now that you've had success—
realized your own ambition—you can give it up whenever you
like—without regret. Otherwise, you would have had a feeling
all your life—that you had missed something—that by giving up
the stage, you had sacrificed something that is far sweeter than it
really is."

"You sound as if you were moving right in."

"I am . . . you're not going to lose me this time."

"But I wouldn't have missed it for anything."

"That's the spirit. . . ."

Ralph suggests lunch next day. Janet will be rehearsing.
Then how about dinner? He is moving much too fast, suggests
Janet.

Oh, well, if Janet wants to be courted again Ralph is agreeable.
He is about to move toward an embrace when Rita appears. She,
too, is a bit shocked to see Ralph again. But she can make use
of him. She has a cripple to take to the hotel and Ralph can
fetch her a wheel chair.

"My God, you haven't married an invalid!" explodes Ralph.

"All you men see is the mother in me. . . . Get that chair!" answers Rita.

"All right. I'll be back for you, Janet."

"No, thanks. There is someone waiting for me. I'll see you at the hotel."

Thayer has appeared on the stairs, back of Janet. He stops there and hears Ralph call back:

"All right. . . . But whoever he is, he is going to find me strong competition."

Janet hasn't taken her eyes off the door through which Ralph has passed. "Just think, Rita—once I didn't want to live because that man wouldn't marry me," she says.

Thayer, starting down, stops dead in his tracks. Rita is the only one who sees him. She is looking directly at Thayer.

THE CURTAIN FALLS

PART III

Back of the desk in the lobby of the Atlantic City hotel at which the "Bird Cage Walk" principals are stopping, the night clerk, a Mr. Flusser, is just coming on duty. It is about 11.30 at night. Mr. Dohlman and Mr. Duttine, arriving first from the theatre, have gone on up to Mr. Dohlman's rooms.

Otherwise it has been the usual dull evening, according to Miss Smith, whom Mr. Flusser is relieving at the desk. Nothing ever happens in Atlantic City just before the holidays. It's dead, if you ask her.

"That's the way with you young girls, Miss Smith," observes Mr. Flusser, brightly. "Always looking for what you call thrills."

"And looking is as far as we get," answers Miss Smith, sharply. " 'The excitement of a big hotel,' eh? . . . 'The drama of all those contrasting and varying personalities brought together under one roof.' Burp!"

"You take your moving pictures too literally, Miss Smith."

There is a call for sandwiches, set-ups, rye and Scotch from the Dohlman suite, which indicates to Mr. Flusser that the new play has a chance. If the notices are good, tomorrow will be the day to strike for a pass. . . .

Ralph Bondley has arrived, followed by Rita and Eddie. They get their keys and go to their rooms. Dr. Marshall is in, expecting to have a look at Eddie's ankle. He is making the usual room inquiries at the desk when Gary Farwell and Diane come happily through the door. They see only his back.

"You have reservations for us," Gary tells Mr. Flusser. "I phoned from Camden."

"Yes, sir. What was the name?"

"Gary Farwell."

Marshall has wheeled suddenly at the sound of the name. Flusser has turned back from the book after confirming the registration.

"Mr. Farwell and Miss Reynolds. Five thirteen and five fifteen," he says.

Marshall calmly walks over, takes Gary by the arm and turns him around to a facing position.

"I've been looking for you," he says. "Where's my sister?"

Gary and Diane are startled into quick exclamations. Gary doesn't know what the man is talking about. Diane can't understand.

"Where is Elsie?" demands Dr. Marshall, his voice rising and his grip on Farwell's arms tightening. "Tell me what you've done with her?"

Mr. Flusser and Miss Smith would take a hand if they could think quickly of anything to say or do. Gary continues to protest that he knows nothing about anyone's sister.

"You'll tell me or, by God, I'll choke it out of you!" continues Marshall, grabbing Farwell by the throat.

Mr. Flusser would call the police. That would suit Dr. Marshall, who has reached into his pocket and brought out a revolver. He doesn't intend that Farwell shall try to run.

"No! Don't call the cops in," says Farwell, quickly turning to Diane. "Would you mind leaving us alone for a few minutes, Diane?"

Diane would mind very much. She wants to know what this is all about. She is going to stay. What is it Dr. Marshall wants Gary to tell him about his sister? Why does he imagine Gary can tell?

"Are you married to this man?" Dr. Marshall demands.

"Not yet. We are to be married tomorrow."

DR. MARSHALL—Five months ago my sister eloped with him, too . . . and they were going to be married—tomorrow. But they never were. I had a note from her telling me that much. That was sent from Chicago. But I can't find her there. She said I wouldn't because she was going on with you. You didn't marry her—and she wouldn't come home after what had happened.

DIANE—Oh, no!

DR. MARSHALL—I hope you heard that story in time. (*To* GARY.) Now. Where is she?

GARY—How should I know?

DR. MARSHALL—Farwell—I've been carrying this gun for five months—and there hasn't been a moment in all that time that I haven't longed for the opportunity to use it on you. . . . You can't undo what you have done to my sister—but, by God, you're going to tell me where she is.

GARY—I left her in Montreal.

DR. MARSHALL—Whereabouts in Montreal?

GARY—In a rooming house on King Street—Mrs. Kondos.

DR. MARSHALL—Get it on the phone.

SMITH—Yes, sir. (*To her switchboard and puts in the call.*)

GARY (*attempting to recover his poise*)—And now I don't suppose there is anything else you want of me?

DR. MARSHALL (*very quietly*)—There is just one thing I want of you . . . to keep you here until this phone call is completed . . . and then—when I am sure that I have found my sister—get out of my sight and don't ever let me lay eyes on you again, because if I do, I think I'll kill you, and you're not worth swinging for.

Gary would laugh off the situation if he could. He is sorry he and Diane had not stopped in Asbury, as they first planned. Diane's eyes are flashing. She doesn't want Gary to speak to her. She would like to send a telegram.

Dr. Marshall has herded Gary into the next room to wait for the long distance call from Montreal. He still keeps the revolver leveled.

Janet and Thayer have arrived. Flusser has recovered his clerk's urbanity. He wants to congratulate Miss Evans most heartily. Whatever may be wrong with the play, it certainly is not her fault. It's the author's.

"Of course, I am terribly flattered," smiles Janet, indicating Thayer, "but have you met the author?"

"Oh, is it your play?" Mr. Flusser is quite flustered. "Well, the lay mind is easily mistaken. Perhaps all your intentions were not clearly brought out by the direction."

"No doubt you are right," smiles Thayer.

Diane is back with her wire. She would also know the time

of the next train for New York. One fifteen? She has rushed off to collect her luggage.

"Phone this in, Miss Smith," instructs Mr. Flusser.

" 'Oliver Reynolds. "Berengaria." You were right. Following on next boat.' "

Miss Smith is repeating the words of the wire as the curtain falls.

The entrance hall to Mrs. Kondos' lodging house in Montreal is seen in semi-darkness. It is after midnight. There is a bluish moonlight filtering through a transom and a faint gas flame flickers an all-night vigil. On the wall a nickel-in-the-slot telephone is dimly outlined. Attention is called to it by a persistent ringing, with slight intervals.

After a pause Mrs. Kondos shuffles in. She has thrown a faded wrapper over her nightgown. She answers the phone in a hushed voice, hoping, evidently, not to disturb her roomers.

The call is from Atlantic City. Mrs. Kondos doesn't know anyone in Atlantic City. Yet it is the number and this is Mrs. Kondos. This— A startled look flashes across Mrs. Kondos' face—

"Who is this?" she demands quickly. "Gary? . . . What? . . . Oh, I see. . . . Yes, she's still here. . . . But she's in bed by now. . . . No, she's all right. . . . But it's after 11 o'clock. . . . I can't be rousing folks at this hour. . . . All right, hold the line. . . . I'll call her. . . ."

The telephone receiver dangles at the end of the cord as Mrs. Kondos goes to the foot of the stairs and calls Elsie in a stage whisper. A moment later Elsie appears, dressed as she was in the previous scene.

"Who is it?" Elsie asks.

"Find out for yourself," answers Mrs. Kondos roughly.

"Hello. . . . Yes. . . . Yes. . . . Yes, I know—it's Alan," calls Elsie excitedly into the phone. "Where are you? . . . I'm all right. . . . How did you find out where I was? . . . Oh! . . . he's with you . . . you must know why I didn't come home. . . . I couldn't write you after what happened. . . . It made a difference to me. . . . I'm sorry, Al. . . . Yes, of course I knew you'd worry . . . but I couldn't write. I just couldn't. . . . No, I haven't a cent. . . . I had a job for a while, but . . . What? . . . You'll wire me. . . . I owe her for five weeks now . . . twenty dollars. . . . All right, Al. . . . Yes, dear. . . . No, I won't fail you. . . . You don't have to come here. I'll start as soon as I get your wire. . . . As soon as I can cash it at the telegraph office. . . . Yes. . . . Yes, dear . . . and thank you. . . . I—I'll see you tomorrow night. . . . It *was* fortunate you met him. . . . Good night, my dear. (*She hangs up as she murmurs:*) It was fortunate!"

Elsie's hand have gone to her face as she leans heavily against the wall. She is pretty close to a state of collapse. Slowly she rouses herself and walks over to the entrance through which Mrs. Kondos has disappeared.

"Mrs. Kondos," she calls huskily. "Mrs. Kondos. . . . Get that man Stevens out of my room!" The lights fade.

The Dohlman suite is the best the hotel can boast. The parlor, set for the after-theatre party, is a good-sized room liberally supplied with comfortable chairs, a table for the drinks, several sofas, occasional tables for cigarettes, etc.

Dohlman and Paul Duttine are the first in and the first to sample the drinks. Rita and Eddie follow and Ralph Bondley. The conversation is general and choppy, concerned principally with the new play and the spreading of congratulations. Duttine does manage to get in a few serious words. He would like to buy the play if Dohlman, by any chance, has lost faith in it. Dohlman hasn't lost faith, but he is willing to sell up to twenty-five per cent. Duttine wants the whole thing. . . .

Thayer and Janet arrive and are served with a good deal of ostentation by Duttine, clowning to boost the evening's fun. Everybody is set with a drink and Mr. Dohlman makes a speech of thanks to the company and of hope for the show when it gets to the big town.

Duttine would interrupt to suggest that Janet be starred. When Dohlman evades the question Duttine renews his offer to buy. But Dohlman will not sell. Nor will Janet work for any other manager. Dohlman was willing to take a chance on an unknown actress, she says firmly, and his shall be the reward, if any.

A moment later there is a knock at the door and Dohlman opens it to admit Edna Winters. Edna is a surprise and hopes she is not breaking up a party. The party appears able to adjust itself, but Paul Duttine is stunned.

Edna, who used to work with Dohlman, is pleased to meet the guests. Especially the brilliant young district attorney, Mr. Bondley, who has just scored so perfect a conviction in the Grayson murder case. That was a fine triumph for Bondley, Edna admits, but not so good for young David Prescott, who was convicted.

"Mr. Bondley, no doubt it will surprise you to learn that he was innocent," says Edna.

"Why do you think that?" demands Bondley, calmly.

"I *know* it, but you'll have to let me tell this my own way."

"That isn't what you came here for," interjects Paul.

"Oh, yes, it is. . . . I told you last night that after what you did NOTHING COULD STOP ME . . . just keep that in mind, because nothing can."

Paul is ready to apologize now. He is sorry for what happened. But he is sorry too late. Edna thinks he had better get a grip on something firm while he hears the rest of what she has to say.

"Mr. Bondley, in spite of all the circumstantial evidence you produced at that trial, young Prescott is innocent. Albert Grayson was killed by a woman."

Bondley is unconvinced. Why has this not been told before? Because of the people it would involve. What was the motive? The woman had caught Grayson cheating—she was his mistress. How did she get in the house? She had a key. Why were there no fingerprints? She wore gloves. Who was she? Paul Duttine's sister!

"How do you know?" demands Ralph.

"I was there. I was with her," triumphantly answers Edna.

Bondley has snapped into action now. Duttine's sister is still at the Hotel Crillon in Paris, Edna tells him. She (Edna) is perfectly willing to be held as a material witness. But what about Prescott in Sing Sing under sentence of death? Ralph will fix that. A phone message to the Governor and he will grant a stay of execution.

"Prescott ought to send you a vote of thanks, Miss Evans," calls Edna, as Ralph starts through the door with her.

"But—what had I to do with it?" innocently demands Janet. The lights fade.

A few minutes later the sound of a key in the lock of a door is heard. As the scene lightens it is seen to be Janet's hotel room, conventionally furnished.

It is Thayer at the door. He snaps on the lights and lets Janet in, transfers the key to the inside of the door and is ready to go. She asks him in. She has something that she wants him to hear.

It is, as it transpires, only her great thanks for his goodness and understanding; thanks for his giving her the chance in the play; thanks and more for a volume of Tagore inscribed: "To Janet—who so perfectly embodies Flora MacDonald—with the love and admiration of Adam Thayer."

Janet is moved by the gift. It is she who is deeply in his debt, yet he insists that had it not been for her there would have been no success for the play.

"You are never out of my thoughts," Thayer is saying.

"Really, Ad? . . . That makes me very happy. . . . You don't know how happy."

THAYER (*hopefully*)—Does it mean that much to you? . . . I've wanted to speak before but—

JANET—Why didn't you?

THAYER—Your gratitude. . . . You've mentioned it so often that I knew—no matter what you might say, or think, that what you really feel for me is an intense gratitude. . . . I don't want that.

JANET (*seeing through*)—What did you think I had to tell you when I asked you to stop just now?

THAYER—What you have every right to tell me. . . . Oh, I'm no fool, Janet. . . . I realize how much these other fellows have to offer you. Duttine can give you wealth—great wealth. Bondley can give you position. And he is an old suitor—

JANET (*very simply*)—I love you, Ad.

THAYER—My dear. (*He has her in his arms.*)

JANET—I knew it out there in Kansas City. . . . When I thought you were coming East without me. . . . Don't ever leave me.

THAYER—I never shall.

JANET—Just you and I together—for always.

THAYER—Now I am the one without words.

JANET—We don't need them. . . . I know you understand all my thoughts—and I do yours. I'm no sentimental schoolgirl, to simper while you protest your love. . . . I'm a woman, Dear . . . my love for you is a grown-up thing. . . . It's fine—and calm—and beautiful.

Impetuously, now, Thayer would have her set the day for their wedding, but Janet will let nothing disturb the serene beauty of her present happiness. It is enough tonight to know such happiness; all else can be discussed tomorrow, and all through the to-morrows to follow.

"You're right, my love," Thayer agrees.

"I feel—enchanted—as though I were some third person—some disembodied spirit—looking down on this little part of life—and I—find it—beautiful. (JANET *turns her face to him.*) Kiss me, my dear. (*He does so. It is a very reverent kiss.*) Now go. . . . Leave me alone to hold and cherish my happiness. . . . There is one poem I want to read."

"Which one?"

" 'There is an anguish in my heart, the burden of its riches not given to you. Put out your hand through the night— Let me hold it and fill it and keep it. Let me feel its touch along the lengthening stretch of my loneliness.' "

"Good night, sweetheart . . . until tomorrow."

Janet is sitting at the table, the open book before her, looking straight ahead with eyes that glow. The lights fade slowly.

The curtain falls.

We are back in the Hall of Records. It is some time after the final scene of the first act. Janet is still reading. The three others who were there have finished their records and departed. Janet, half way through the record of her own life, is sobbing. She has put down the book and is wiping her tears away when she hears the Guide enter with a man and leave him with the Attendant.

"I was told to ask for the record of my life," the man is saying. At the sound of the voice Janet starts.

"Name?" asks the attendant.

"Adam Thayer," answers the man.

Janet is sobbing. She turns and stretches out her hand toward Adam.

"My dear."

Only her lips form the words. There is no sound of her voice. The Man has turned and is looking at Janet.

"Where were you born?" the Attendant is asking.

The Man stares blankly at Janet and turns slowly back to the Attendant. Janet's head falls on her arms.

"Her shoulders move with her sobs as she realizes what we do, that he does not even know her."

THE CURTAIN FALLS

THE DISTAFF SIDE

A Comedy in Three Acts

By John Van Druten

FEWER plays than usual came from foreign sources to supplement the Broadway list the season of 1934-35. There was the extensively debated "Within the Gates" of the Irish dramatist, Sean O'Casey; the Theatre Guild's offering of James Bridie's "A Sleeping Clergyman" and Margaret Kennedy's "Escape Me Never," with Elizabeth Bergner. Gilbert Miller brought over J. B. Priestley's "Laburnum Grove," with Edmund Gwenn; Katharine Cornell produced John Van Druten's "Flowers of the Forest" and Dwight Deere Wiman joined Auriol Lee in the transference of Van Druten's "The Distaff Side" from the London stage to ours. There were a few others, including Friedrich Wolf's "Sailors of Cattaro," offered by one of the groups interested in the propaganda drama, but none of outstanding importance.

We have chosen the Van Druten "Distaff Side" to represent the foreign list in these pages. It was, excepting "Escape Me Never," which was a personal success for Elizabeth Bergner, the best supported of the foreign plays and as well written as any. It also appeals directly to those most consistent of drama supporters, the women playgoers, being concerned frankly with an observing male's study of five feminine types—a widowed mother who in a way absorbs and seeks to compose the sex and marital problems of both a lightly unconventional daughter and a socially rebellious sister; a querulous and exacting granddam and a small-town wife wearied of the dull monotony of a dull marriage.

It is a frankly spoken play that approaches the subject of present-day sex freedom openly and with results that are steadily absorbing if never dramatically exciting.

The sitting room on the ground floor of Millward's house in St. John's Wood, London, is spacious and comfortable. At ten o'clock the evening "The Distaff Side" opens, it is also briefly quiet and restful. Mrs. Millward, "a graceful, pretty and charming woman of fifty," is sitting in an armchair before the fire, reading. Her mother, Mrs. Venables, "a bunchy old lady of seventy-five, dressed in black," sits just above the fire, a novel in her hand, her bag, spectacle case and a box of chocolates on a table at her side.

The curtain has been up a moment or two before Mrs. Venables decides that she must protest against the type of modern fiction her book represents. It is, she declares, sheer twaddle. To prove which she reads:

"Monica stood at the cottage door and watched her lover go, tall and straight into the sunset. She knew now she would never see him again. As he turned the bend of the road, a bird began to sing. The end!"

Nor is Mrs. Venables particularly impressed with the book her daughter, Eve Millward, is reading, which happens to be a work on education by Bertrand Russell. Why Mrs. Millward should want to be reading a book on education when her children are already grown is more than Mrs. Venables can understand. Especially a book that seems to be mostly about Russia.

The discussion is interrupted by the arrival of Mrs. Millward's daughter Alex, an attractive young woman of twenty-one. Alex, however, is in for just a moment. She has come home to change before going on to a party with Charles Hubbard. She had had dinner with young Hubbard, too. He has been quite attentive the last two weeks. He is Seton Hubbard's son and Seton Hubbard is the playwright in whose last comedy Alex had played a small part. There is a chance, she thinks, that she may get even a better part in his next play.

Another of Alex's young men, Toby Chegwidden, has called earlier in the evening to say that he would be around later with some rather important news for Alex, Mrs. Millward reports. It is news that Mr. Chegwidden wants to have the excitement of telling Alex himself. He told Mrs. Millward what it was, but made her promise she would not tell Alex.

Alex has been rather neglecting Toby recently, or so it seems to her mother. Neglecting Toby and paying a good deal of attention to Charles Hubbard.

"I should have thought you'd have been glad if I had found someone more . . . eligible," ventures Alex. "Charles is a wealthy young man and influential, too."

"Is he at all . . . serious?"

"Is any rich young man ever serious?" counters Alex, and makes no further answer. . . .

The Millwards are anticipating the arrival of a second sister, Liz, who is Mrs. Frobisher, and Alex is excited at the thought of seeing her aunt again.

"You know, she used to be my idea of everything that was smart and fascinating," confesses Alex. "Roland and I used to think she was . . . fast."

"Well, in a sort of way I suppose she is," admits Mrs. Millward, with a faintly embarrassed smile.

"Oh, for an aunt," agrees Alex. "But I'm not thrilled any more at the idea of people living together."

It appears that Mrs. Frobisher had married the wrong man, out of spite, when her parents stopped her seeing the married man she really was in love with. After a lapse of years she had met the married man again. After her husband divorced her she had taken up living with her first love, though he was still married.

Now Mrs. Frobisher has arrived, attended by the usual confusion at the front door. "Liz is about forty-five; very smart; rather Continental looking. She is not nearly so pretty as her sister, but far more fascinating and chic. She has a gay, rather silly, extravagant manner of speech, underlining her words, and bubbles with high spirits. She wears extremely smart traveling clothes."

Mrs. Frobisher's greetings are hearty. She is glad to see Evie again. She is pleased that Alex looks such a smart West End actress, but is disappointed she is not acting at present. She is glad to hear that Mother Venables is well—and in bed. She hopes that may delay the maternal greetings for the night, but it won't. Mrs. Venables is even now waiting impatiently to see Liz. . . .

Roland Millward, Evie's twenty-two-year-old son, has come in from the car with his aunt's bags. Roland is a medical student, "a little off-hand and casual," but pleasant.

"I was thrilled to have someone so young and attractive as Roland to come and meet me," says Liz. "You know, he looks much too nice for a medical student. You'd never think that he knows all the disgusting things he must about women's insides. . . . One day I want you to draw me an exact diagram of everything I've got, and tell me just how it works."

"We'll have a nice new parlor game like 'Snakes and Ladders.' Call it 'Through the Large Intestine.' "

"Roland, don't be revolting," protests Mrs. Millward. . . .

"You've nice children, Evie," admits Liz, when Roland has gone to put up the car. "Are Roland and Alex friends?"

MRS. MILLWARD—Brother and sister. Now, tell me about yourself. Where did you leave Gillie?

LIZ—Down South.

MRS. MILLWARD—Is he all right?

LIZ—As far as I know.

MRS. MILLWARD—I didn't know whether he was coming with you or not. (*Pause.*) Is anything the matter?

LIZ—I've left him.

MRS. MILLWARD—What?

LIZ—I've left him.

MRS. MILLWARD—When?

LIZ—Two weeks ago.

MRS. MILLWARD—Liz! Why?

LIZ (*a little theatrically*)—I'd had just too much. You know what Gillie is . . . what he's always been.

MRS. MILLWARD (*tentatively*)—Women?

LIZ (*assenting*)—They flatter him, and he falls for it. His behavior's all of a piece. He's in with the most frightful crowd, and expects me to run with them. Lets them sponge on him, goes on some awful bat with his winnings . . . *when* he wins . . . and then if I complain tells me I nag him to death.

MRS. MILLWARD—Oh, Liz!

LIZ—Well, I do complain. We had a climax two weeks ago . . . perfectly calm and reasoned . . . at least, *I* was. But it seems to me so obvious that if he cared for me he wouldn't do it, knowing how I hate it. He does do it. Therefore he doesn't care for me. Well . . . that's all right with *me*.

MRS. MILLWARD—Don't *you* care for *him* any more?

LIZ (*violently*)—I hate and loathe and despise him. It's true, Evie.

MRS. MILLWARD—Did you tell him you were leaving him? (LIZ *nods*.) What did he say?

LIZ—Swore at me, and said good riddance.

MRS. MILLWARD—Well, I rather think it is . . . for you.

LIZ—I know it is. I only wish to God I'd done it before, when his wife first said she'd never divorce him. I might have known she meant it! I ought to have left him years ago, when you and Andrew begged me to. I'm getting old, Evie.

MRS. MILLWARD (*smiling*)—What rubbish!

Liz—It isn't rubbish. (*She takes out her pocket mirror.*)
Look at me. What a sight I am.

After her quarrel with Gillie Mrs. Frobisher had gone to Brussels. In Brussels she had renewed an acquaintance with a Belgian, a widower. His name is De Bruyn and she had met him at Cannes the year before. Now she is thinking of marrying him. She is not in love with him, but he is a kind man, has been a saint to Liz and is enormously rich.

Mrs. Millward is disturbed by this report. It would be nice to think of Liz being married, even if she did have to live in Brussels, but if she does not love her Belgian, wouldn't she be taking a big risk? Also there is the physical side to consider—

"As if that made any difference," laughs Liz. "Isn't that all that Gillie and I ever had in common, really, and what good has it done us? I don't expect Marcel would be . . . (*With a tiny giggle.*) exorbitant in his demands. He isn't young. And, after all, one has to take the rough with the smooth in life."

"Well, if that's how you look at it . . ."

"It's all very well for you, Evie. You had your husband whom you loved. It lasted for you."

"Lasted!"

"Well, you had him for over twenty years. You've still got your home and your children. What's my life been since I left home? Egypt and the army with Fred. Then, all the bust-up of the divorce. And now these last ten years with Gillie. I want to grow roots like you."

Spicer, Mrs. Venables' companion, has come to report Liz's mother as impatiently waiting to greet her.

"Are the birthday celebrations going to be very grim this year?" asks Liz.

"The usual . . . with perhaps a shade more trimming because she's seventy-five," reports Mrs. Millward.

It is planned that this year's theatre party shall be at the Palace, where there is a musical play. There will be ten in all, including the dear cousins, Theresa and Christopher, and a third sister, Nellie, married to a Professor Fletcher and living in Newcastle with her four children and her husband, whom she seems to like, however dull the family may find him. . . .

Toby Chegwidden is back, and inquiring for Alex. "He is a young man of twenty-seven; slight in build, untidy and careless in his dress. He is eager, excitable and rather self-centered."

Toby is a motion picture director, or hopes to be. He has already had some success at home. One of his pictures, a sort of impression of Hyde Park on a Sunday morning, with only Alex and himself playing story characters against a background of park scenes, had attracted the attention of a Hollywood director and he has offered Toby a job as his assistant. Toby will be sailing, he thinks, in a couple of weeks, and will be gone probably for three years.

"I thought people who made your kind of films despised Hollywood and all its works," suggests Liz.

"One says one despises a lot of things," says Toby, smiling. "There's plenty they can teach me that I want to know."

"And after that, you'll teach them?"

"It would be nice to think so."

Alex is wearing a very pretty evening dress when she comes down the stairs to greet Toby. Her tone is bantering as she accuses him of having secrets with her mother, and her impatience to learn what the secret is grows keen as the others leave them alone while they go to appease the impatience of Mrs. Venables, already at the martyred stage.

Now Toby can tell Alex his news. He hands her a letter to read making him the offer of the assistant directorship in Hollywood. Alex reads, and is delighted. It means a great chance for him and she is glad. But—she doesn't like the thought of his being away three years. That brings him to the matter he had come to suggest. Why shouldn't Alex come with him?

"We've always said we'd get married one day," Toby reminds her.

"One day . . . yes," she answers, hesitantly.

Toby—Well, today is the day, or rather . . . some time next week. I think I can support you now on this. Don't you?

Alex—Yes, I . . . I suppose so.

Toby—Well, then . . . Alex, won't you come? You know I love you, don't you? (*He puts his head against hers.*) You ought to. You and my work are the only two things I do care about. Alex . . . us two together . . . Hollywood . . . I know it's a rotten place and they make lousy pictures, but it's something.

Alex—It's marvelous!

Toby—Well, all right, then. It's pretty good, even if it is denying everything I said. I'll admit it, I'm excited. But I want you there, too. You've seen me start from almost nothing.

Wouldn't it be rather good to do it all together right up to the top?

ALEX—Oh, Toby, you must give me *time*.

TOBY—Time?

ALEX—To get used to the idea. When do you go?

TOBY—Hegerman sails in a couple of weeks. I should think I'd go with him. I'm going to Paris in the morning to talk to him. We'll fix everything up then. I'll be back in a couple of days . . . just in time to get a few things together and then sail . . . both of us, I hope.

ALEX (*with an uncomfortable laugh*)—You've got it all planned out.

TOBY—Well . . .

ALEX—You didn't tell Mother you were going to ask me to come with you?

TOBY—Good Lord, no. But you will, though, won't you?

ALEX—I can't tell you like this. Give me a day to think about it. After all, Toby, I've got *my* life and *my* career.

TOBY—Oh, all right. We'll make a film star of you.

ALEX—Likely. You know I'd have no chance in the films except as an extra. If I'd made a success on the stage already . . .

TOBY—Well, just how important *is* the career . . . to you?

ALEX—It *is* important. I'm nowhere near where you are, nor ever likely to be. I know that. But I *am* getting my foot in. Charles thinks there might be something in his father's new play for me. Not the lead, of course, but a real part.

TOBY—So that's why you're running around with him!

ALEX—Well, partly. Do you think that's mercenary? You've got to do it in the theatre.

TOBY—Have you? It's something I couldn't do . . . toady to someone for a job . . . go to parties for one. I've got this on my own, and on my work. That's how one *should* get there.

ALEX—It's all very well for you.

TOBY (*suddenly appealing*)—Alex, don't you *want* to marry me? Don't you love me—don't you?

ALEX—Yes, Toby, I do—I do. (*Kissing him.*) I do! (CHARLES's *voice is heard off stage, speaking to* ROSE.) There is Charles.

TOBY (*surlily*)—You won't put him off and come out with me?

ALEX (*appealingly*)—I can't . . . really I can't. Oh, Toby, don't be angry with me. Look. Go to Paris in the morning

. . . see Hegerman . . . and when you come back we'll talk again. I'll have had time to think then. Please.

Charles Hubbard is calling for Alex. "He is a well-dressed, suave young man of thirty." He has been delayed somewhat by the fog and he thinks he may possibly have grazed the Baby Austin car in front of the house, which he assumes belongs to Toby. He is sure, however, that his Rolls had done no real damage.

Mr. Hubbard is glad to meet Mr. Chegwidden and Mrs. Millward, too. He fears he and Alex will have to hurry, considering the traffic. His governor is giving the party at Ciro's and there will probably be quite a few theatrical celebrities there.

"It must be such fun to meet them all," says Toby, with a bitter suavity. "Will Gloria Swanson be there? She's *so* lovely! I think her pictures are *so* . . . don't you? You might get her autograph for me, Alex."

"Shut up, Toby!" commands Alex.

"What's the matter with *him?*" asks Charles, with a smile.

"He's going to Hollywood."

"Poor blighter!"

Alex and Charles have gone now. Toby follows shortly after. Roland is back from the garage. The talk turns to Liz and her apparent good spirits.

"By the way, did you notice anyone special at Victoria, anyone *with* her, I mean?" asks Mrs. Millward.

ROLAND—Oh, there was a sort of baby beaver, who seemed to be hovering a bit. Called her Elise, and said 'à tantôt.' Why?

MRS. MILLWARD—I just wondered. She told me she'd come over with a friend. What was he like?

ROLAND—Bloody awful, I thought. Well, I'll say good night, Mother. When does Aunt Nellie arrive, by the way?

MRS. MILLWARD—Tomorrow or the next day. She's bringing Christine.

ROLAND—Oh, the polypus. Charming child, so communicative. All she wants is crowning.

MRS. MILLWARD—I'm putting them in the guest room, and Liz in Alex's.

ROLAND—Standees only, for the next few days. How lovely! (*He kisses her.*)

MRS. MILLWARD (*smiling*)—You haven't a lot of family feeling, have you, Roland? (LIZ *enters. Overhears the remark.*)

ROLAND—I shall have a good deal less before the week's out.

LIZ—That's a nice thing to say!

ROLAND—My regard for you, Liz, isn't family feeling. It's passion within the prohibited degrees. Good night. (*He goes out.*)

LIZ—Mother's been very difficult about Gillie not coming with me. I ought to ring up the Savoy, and say good night to Marcel. But not just yet. It's lovely being here, Evie.

MRS. MILLWARD—It's lovely having you. (*She sits on the arm of* LIZ's *chair and puts her arm around* LIZ's *shoulder.*)

LIZ—It's a nice house. There's something complete about it . . . something fulfilled. I don't know what . . . the life you've led in it, I suppose. Just as you're a sort of . . . complete person. (*With a smile.*) What is it about you?

MRS. MILLWARD—I haven't an idea. (*She smiles, too, and they remain sitting together.*)

THE CURTAIN FALLS

ACT II

Six o'clock one afternoon three days later Alex Millward opens the door to Evie Millward's sitting room and peeps in. She is surveying the coast before she asks Charles Hubbard to follow. It is the night of Grandma Venables' birthday dinner, scheduled for seven o'clock, and what Alex and Charles have come upon is the lull before the storm.

Alex rings for Rose, who brings cocktails, and there is a moment for an intimate sort of talk before the others finish dressing. Charles is acquiring an interest in the Millwards. He is interested in hearing that Alex's mother has been a widow for five years; that she adored Alex's father, who was a good man—a terribly good man. (Why is one always frightened of good people? Alex wonders.) She thinks her mother should marry again, but she doesn't believe she ever will. There is a barrister cousin who has a crush on Mother, but Evie is pretty much a one-man woman.

Charles has been conscious all afternoon that there is something troubling Alex, but she is of no mind to discuss it with him, even if his conclusions are true. It is nice of him to be interested, and she is pleased at his confession that he is fond of her and that he really is trying to put in a good word for her with his play-writing dad. But for the time being she is in no mood for further confidences.

Happily the two aunts, Mrs. Frobisher and Mrs. Fletcher, put in an appearance. The newcomer, Mrs. Fletcher (Nellie) "is a woman of forty; plump, with the after effects of prettiness and a strenuous life as a wife and mother." Liz Frobisher is pleased to see the cocktails and is in no mood to wait for other glasses to be brought. She will take hers in Alex's glass, because she needs it. Nellie is less excited. She can do without a cocktail, but she might manage a cherry.

It has been a hard afternoon for the aunts. Grandma Venables has been entertaining old friends and Cousin Theresa has arrived. Cousin Theresa has also spent her time going on at Mrs. Venables about social reform and telling Nellie, the mother of four, how to bring up children. . . .

Alex is back from taking Charles to the door. Nellie has gone to dress for dinner and Liz would talk with Alex about her young men. She finds Hubbard a personable young man. She is interested to know, too, that Toby Chegwidden is expected back that afternoon. But how does Alex feel about it? Alex admits that she is worried about Toby—

"He wants me to marry him and go with him to Hollywood," Alex reports.

"Does he? Are you going?"

ALEX—I don't know. Liz . . . do you think things like success and money and position are very important?

LIZ—What do you mean?

ALEX—Well, this Hollywood job is a marvelous chance, but . . . it's only a beginning. I know it would be an adventure . . . but ought one to risk things?

LIZ—Are you in love with him?

ALEX—We've lived together. . . .

LIZ (sharply)—What's that?

ALEX—I said we'd lived together.

LIZ—Alex! (She rises.)

ALEX—Are you shocked?

LIZ—Of course I'm shocked. Do you know what you're saying?

ALEX—Yes.

LIZ—What do you suppose your mother would say if she knew? She'd never get over it.

ALEX—Well, there's no reason why she *should* know, unless you tell her.

THE DISTAFF SIDE

335

LIZ—God forbid! And don't *you*, either. He wants to marry
you, you say? But now *you're* not sure. Is that it?

ALEX—Yes.

LIZ—What made you do it? (*Goes to her.*) You weren't unhappy at home? It isn't as if you were alone in the world.
What possessed you? It's fantastic that a girl brought up as you
have been . . .

ALEX—Oh. (*Pause.*) I'm sorry . . . I'm sorry I told you.
I thought I *could* tell *you*.

LIZ—Why me? Oh! Because of Gillie? (*With a laugh that
is not too friendly.*) Ha! As one fast woman to another!

ALEX (*protesting*)—No! But . . .

LIZ (*contemptuously*)—Really! Don't you see that was entirely different? I wasn't a child like you, protected and unmar-
ried. I'd been married. I got married because I wouldn't do the
very thing you've done. Afterwards . . . well, I was unhappy.
My marriage was a failure. But *you?* What excuse had you?

ALEX—I didn't think I needed any. Does one, nowadays?
Everyone has affairs.

LIZ—Not girls like you.

ALEX—I think so. Aren't you taking it all a little seriously?
Do you think I ought to marry Toby . . . *because* of that?

LIZ—Your mother would think so.

ALEX (*with a slightly twisted smile*)—I've even been old-
fashioned enough to wonder myself.

LIZ—Then you're taking it seriously, too.

ALEX—I think it's silly of me to do so. I hoped you'd tell me
it was.

LIZ—Oh, did you? Well, I'm not going to.

Alex is persistent. If she could marry Charles Hubbard,
would her aunt think she should do that, as things stand? Liz
thinks that Alex has been a fool and worse, but if she isn't sure
about Toby and can marry Charles and obliterate everything she
would be wise to do so.

"And I wanted you to tell me to marry Toby . . . love and
the world well lost. I can tell myself the other thing," sighs Alex.

"Now you're contradicting yourself. You said just now . . ."

"I'm contradicting myself all day. That's why I came to you.
Oh, damn!" . . .

Toby Chegwidden has arrived. He is more untidy than ever.
Aunt Liz stares rather frankly at him and leaves "with a rigid
back." Toby doesn't feel well. Alex is sure he has a fever. He

admits he has been going pretty fast. He is packing and expects to sail in two days. Hegerman, the picture director, has unexpected orders to get back to Hollywood and start a picture in a fortnight. He wants Toby to go with him and Toby wants Alex to go, too.

"I want you to come *with* me," pleads Toby. "Alex, darling, *darling,* isn't it just as easy to do it tomorrow as in six weeks' time, and so much more exciting? You promised me my answer today."

ALEX—I know, but I was going to ask for a little more time . . . and now you come and spring this on me.

TOBY—Then you're still not sure? (*Pause.*) You said the other evening that you loved me. Why? Why did you say it? Just to . . . keep me going?

ALEX—No, it was true. Oh, Toby, this has all been so queer. Till the other evening I had hardly seen you for two weeks. . . .

TOBY—That wasn't *my* fault. I'd been wanting you.

ALEX—Had you?

TOBY—Terribly. More, these last days.

ALEX—Oh, Toby! (*Goes to him.*)

TOBY—But I don't want to use that as a lever . . . now.

ALEX—What do you mean?

TOBY—Just that. . . . What is it? Charles Hubbard after all?

ALEX—Not Charles himself. . . .

TOBY—I see—but what he stands for. Comfortable success, without any of the fun of having worked for it . . . a sort of twilight sleep. And then what? Your future assured forever . . . and sheer sterility. I thought you liked the battle of getting there.

ALEX—I'm afraid of it.

TOBY—Then you're not the girl I took you for.

ALEX (*helplessly*)—I'm sorry. I don't think I can.

TOBY—I've seen that side of you before. I didn't think that was the real you. I thought *I* had the real you. But if that was just a flash in the pan and the other's what you really want . . . (*He puts his hand to his head.*) I say. I feel rather peculiar. I must sit down for a minute.

ALEX—Toby, you're ill. (*She goes to him.*)

TOBY (*sitting, with his hand to his forehead*)—Well, I'm a bit odd. I've been doing too much. Could I have a drink?

ALEX (*rather frightened*)—Of course. I'll ring for some

brandy.

Toby (*relaxing*)—I really do feel very strange.

There is a good deal of excitement about Toby's illness and Mrs. Millward rather takes charge of things. Roland is brought, half dressed, from his room, to take the sick man's temperature, which he finds a bit alarming. It is shortly apparent that Toby must be put to bed, despite his protests that he cannot afford to give up now. As there is no one at his own rooms to look after him he will have to be put in Roland's room for the time being and Roland can sleep on a cot in the study.

Mrs. Venables is a little disgusted with the interruption to her birthday plans. She suspects that Roland is just practicing on the young man, and she is sure Mr. Chegwidden will be quite all right when they get him to bed.

"I've never seen such a commotion in all my life," protests Mrs. Venables, excitedly. "What's a bit of a temperature? And who's Mr. Chinkumpoop, anyway, to make such a fuss over?"

"Mother, the poor boy's ill."

"Who is he?"

"A friend of Alex's."

"Is she going to marry him?"

"I really don't know, Mother."

"Apparently you hope she is, the way you're fussing over him." . . .

Christopher Venables, the barrister cousin, has joined the party. "He is a man of fifty, tall, good-looking, distinguished." He has brought a large box of chocolates for Mrs. Venables and a corsage spray for Evie. This has been his custom for a matter of years.

The gathering is settling nicely into its accustomed anniversary ways when there is a ringing at the telephone. The call is from Lichfield and is for Mrs. Frobisher, who recalls with a start that "Gillie's" father is one of the canons at Lichfield cathedral.

At the phone Liz is learning the news. The family listens rather impatiently for her report, and this is too much for her. She can't talk to Gillie now. Let him ring up again in the morning.—

"Well? What's it all about?" demands Mrs. Venables, as Liz hangs up.

"His father's dead. He came over for the funeral," reports Liz.

Mrs. Venables—It must have been very sudden. He was barely eighty.

LIZ (*crosses to* MRS. VENABLES)—Gillie sent you his love, Mother. Wished you many happy returns.

MRS. VENABLES—When is he coming to London?

LIZ—Tomorrow.

MRS. VENABLES (*as gong goes*)—Dinner! (*Rising.*) Come along, come along! It's my party, and I'm not going to be kept waiting. Stop fidgeting with your bag, Spicer. You never can find anything in it. Come along, Nellie. Come along, Theresa. Oh, dear, I wish we had a few more men in the family! (*She goes out followed by the family.*)

CHRISTOPHER—You're looking tired, Eve.

MRS. MILLWARD—I've had a lot to do.

CHRISTOPHER—You look worried, too. Are you?

MRS. MILLWARD—A little.

CHRISTOPHER—What about?

MRS. MILLWARD—Oh . . . Alex . . . and Liz . . . and . . . oh, it's nothing, really. (*With a light laugh.*) We've got a young man upstairs in bed with 'flu.

CHRISTOPHER—You're pretty wonderful, Eve.

MRS. MILLWARD (*with a smile*)—Why?

CHRISTOPHER—The way you deal with things. You're so unselfish.

MRS. MILLWARD—Theresa wouldn't say so.

CHRISTOPHER—Has Tess been daring to criticize you?

MRS. MILLWARD—Oh, no. She's only been saying one shouldn't be bounded by personal relationships.

CHRISTOPHER—What rubbish.

MRS. MILLWARD—Well, her kind are the ones who *do* things. My trouble is that I've never wanted to. I've been happy to be bounded.

CHRISTOPHER—Don't you ever want to run away?

MRS. MILLWARD (*moving toward the door*)—Where to?

CHRISTOPHER—Somewhere where you'd be the important one for a change.

MRS. MILLWARD (*stopping*)—No. Do you know, I don't really? (*The gong goes again, loudly. She smiles.*) Mother!

They go out together as the curtain falls.

About 12 o'clock the night of the birthday party the Millward family and all the relatives have arrived home. In the hall outside Mrs. Millward's bedroom they can be heard saying their collective good nights, wishing Mrs. Venables well, hoping that now she will be good for another year and dispersing to their respective rooms.

Mrs. Millward, Roland and Alex come into her room. Roland has had a look at Toby. His report is that the boy is all right, but not likely to be able to sail Saturday unless his temperature comes down. . . .

With the others gone, Nellie Fletcher pops in for a good-night chat. She is envious of her sister Eve. Envious of her smoothly ordered life and her well-conducted home. On the table, quite close to a picture of Andrew Millward, she notices an open book of verse. Nellie picks it up, and finding one bit marked, reads it aloud:

> "When you have tidied all things for the night,
> And while your thoughts are fading to their sleep,
> You'll pause a moment in the late firelight,
> Too sorrowful to weep.
> The large and gentle furniture has stood
> In sympathetic silence all the day
> With that old kindness of domestic wood:
> Nevertheless the haunted room will say
> Someone must be away."

Nellie cannot understand why Eve can be lonesome with all she has. Nor why Liz can be unhappy looking as young and smart as she does. Neither does she credit Eve with being entirely sane when she says she would gladly change places with her.

"With me?" echoes Nellie. "What have I got?"

"You've got your husband," quietly answers Eve.

"I sometimes wonder if I wouldn't have been better off without one," admits Nellie. "Look at Theresa. She's free, and the things she does interest *her*, though they wouldn't me. But she can do what she likes and go where she likes. I'm tied hand and foot."

Nellie supposes that she loves her husband, but even so she doesn't think love is everything.

"Look at the marriages where it doesn't exist," says Eve; "Father and Mother, for example. . . ."

"What do you mean? Theirs wasn't an unhappy marriage," protests Nellie.

"It wasn't a marriage at all," insists Eve. "When Father died, all that Mother missed was her position as the spoiled head of the household. But then, poor old Mother's never really been able to care for anyone except herself."

Liz, looking for some place to smoke a peaceful cigarette, is of much the same mind regarding Mrs. Venables.

"I don't know how we've all put up with Mother all these years," she says with spirit. "Why don't we pop her into a boarding house? She'd be much happier there. She'd have so much more to grumble at."

Liz has been having a time with her mother trying to explain her men friends. She is of two minds herself in respect to Gillie, who has 'phoned asking to see her, and Marcel, with whom she is to lunch next day. Liz has no intention of going back to Gillie, even if that should be suggested, but she does feel that she ought to see him. Nor can she see any reason for letting her Belgian friend know.

"You're not still in love with Gillie, are you?" asks Eve.

"Really, Evie, you do ask the most uncomfortable questions," answers Liz. "That's got absolutely nothing to do with it. I'm not weakening, if that's what you mean. But after all, we did end rather violently and I'd like to have one last dispassionate look at him, just to *know* how right I am."

"You're quite sure you're not just enjoying playing with fire?"

"I'm only sure of two things. I want to see Gillie just once more, and I'm going to marry Marcel. Let me ask Gillie here to tea tomorrow afternoon and then you can chaperon us, if you're doubtful about the proprieties."

Alex is back in pyjamas and dressing gown and Liz is off to bed. Mrs. Millward is eager to have a talk with Alex. Eager to know what answer she is expecting to give Toby. Alex doesn't know. Alex is very unhappy and would like to get away and start all over. She loathes herself so. Mrs. Millward starts as the full purport of that phrase reaches her—

"Alex! Is there something you haven't told me?" she demands. Alex nods her head. "Will you tell me?"

"I can't."

"Why not?"

ALEX (*whispering*)—I don't want to hurt you.

MRS. MILLWARD—Darling, you know there's nothing you can't tell me. Won't you tell me?

ALEX (*with an effort*)—Well . . . Toby and I . . . No, can't.

MRS. MILLWARD—You've been lovers? (ALEX *nods*.) I see.

ALEX (*sobbing*)—Oh, Mother, I'm so sorry.

Mrs. Millward—Why are you sorry?

Alex (*amazed*)—Don't you *mind?*

Mrs. Millward—I want to understand. Why did you? (Alex *makes a gesture of "I don't know."*) You loved him?

Alex—I think so. I don't know. He was sweet, and there was . . . opportunity. We were together all the time. There seemed no need to look ahead. It didn't seem wrong, then.

Mrs. Millward—Does it now?

Alex—Telling you it does.

Mrs. Millward—Even if you love him . . . or you *did?*

Alex—Yes, but now that I've got to decide, suddenly and for ever . . . I don't know. That's why I wish we . . . *hadn't* now. It seems so big a thing.

Mrs. Millward—Well, isn't it?

Alex—It didn't seem so, then. (Mrs. Millward *moves away from her.*) You're angry with me?

Mrs. Millward—If you mean that.

Alex (*faintly mocking to protect herself*)—You'd have forgiven . . . a grand passion?

Mrs. Millward (*a shade sharply*)—You needn't put it like that.

Alex (*contrite*)—I'm sorry. But I didn't want to dramatize myself, and say (*Over-dramatically.*) "Do I love him enough to *give* myself to him?" It seemed making too much of it. I suppose that's what you can't forgive.

Mrs. Millward—Perhaps it is. I can't see why you'd balk at saying that and not at saying "Do I love him enough to marry him?"

Alex—You think I *ought* to marry him?

Mrs. Millward—Not if you don't want to . . . really want to. My point is only that you seem to be questioning now for the first time how much you care for him. I think you might have thought of that before.

Alex is convinced now that it might mean a great deal to her to stay in London and marry Charles. She has been thinking of that, even though she knows Toby despises her for it. She doesn't see why she should make her life Toby's life—

"I might as well say he doesn't love me enough to make his life mine. Why not?" Alex demands a little bitterly.

"Because that's not the way things are," Mrs. Millward answers. "Because you're a woman."

"What's that got to do with it?"

"Everything! Unless you're of the kind that lives impersonally like Theresa. And then I think you're unfulfilled. I think that's what being a woman means."

"To submerge yourself and everything you stand for, in a man? To give up everything to him?"

"It isn't giving up—it's an exchange for something so much more enriching than anything you could have alone. It's not a sacrifice—it's a fulfillment."

When a woman's husband dies, then, to all intends and purposes, her life is over, Mrs. Millward insists. Alex's father was her mother's life. Now her children are grown and do not need her. There is no one in whom she can exist. And yet there is no thought of "suttee" in Mrs. Millward's mind. Everyone must live his life out, in her philosophy.

"I think there's another kind of life that comes from inside you . . . after your own life's done," she says.

"After your married life, you mean?" asks Alex.

"After your own personal life. It comes from what you've made of it, almost like a reflection of it. Without it you wouldn't be complete. Can you understand that?"

"Yes . . . if you've the capacity. Oh, Mother!"

Alex has begun to cry, and as her mother crosses the room to comfort her the door opens slowly and Toby is standing within its frame. "He is in pyjamas, tousled, feverish and delirious."

Mrs. Millward has helped Toby to a chair and is gently urging him to go back to bed. A little wildly he insists his bed is too hot, and that he has to get the boat. He mustn't miss the "Bremen." She's sailing today. He must get his hair cut, too, because Alex says it is too long. Too long and too hot and there's too much of it. He wishes Mrs. Millward would cut it off for him—

Alex has gone for Roland's dressing gown, and Mrs. Millward, with a pair of nail scissors from the dressing table, pretends to cut the offending hair. It is falling all about him on the floor, she tells him, and he is relieved. Alex was quite right. It did need cutting.

Toby protests against being put into the dressing gown when Alex brings it, but Mrs. Millward gently convinces him that it is cool, and that if he will go back to bed for a little the boat will wait for him.

"No. They don't wait! They never wait!" wails Toby.

"This one will," soothingly promises Mrs. Millward. "They just rang up to say so."

TOBY—Did they? Oh, well, that's all right then. Alex mustn't miss it, either. She's coming too, you know. I think she wants to bring a party. I believe I told her she wasn't to, only (*Turning to* ALEX.) *you* tell her she can. She can bring anyone, as long as she comes. We can get rid of them later. There'll be lots of stops. Only she's got to come. Tell her for me, will you?

ALEX (*in a whisper*)—I'll tell her.

TOBY (*to* MRS. MILLWARD, *rising*)—You'll keep that other chap out, won't you? I don't want *him*. You know, Alex is awfully sweet, really. She's silly sometimes, but that's when she's young. It's the *Tatler* that does it. And I don't know why she wants to bother with all that lace. It's a damn fool thing to have around a studio, anyway. She's got to get rid of it.

MRS. MILLWARD—It's all gone . . . it's thrown away.

TOBY—Is it? Oh, I'm so glad. Did you make her? You know you're being awfully sweet to me. I do like you. (*He collapses suddenly, his knees giving way completely.* MRS. MILLWARD *stops him from falling, holding him against her for a moment.* ALEX *gives a little cry.* MRS. MILLWARD *helps* TOBY *straighten up.*)

MRS. MILLWARD—Come back to bed now. (*At the door she turns and says over her shoulder to* ALEX, *in a low decisive tone:*) Ring up Dr. Mackenzie at once. Tell him to come round. We'd better have a nurse. Tell him what's happened. (*She goes out with* TOBY.)

The 'phone rings. The call is from Charles Hubbard. He wants to tell Alex that his father would like to have her read a part in the new play next morning. There is not great enthusiasm in Alex's voice. Charles evidently notices that. But, as she explains, things are rather difficult at home at the moment. However, she will be there at half-past ten in the morning.

Alex is still sitting by the telephone a little dazed when Mrs. Millward comes back. She hasn't rung up Dr. Mackenzie because Charles was on the 'phone. But it is of Toby that she is thinking.

"Oh, Mother," she cries, "it was so awful. I've never seen anyone like that before. Toby didn't know who I was!"

"Alex, pull yourself together," commands Mrs. Millward, sharply; "he's all right. He'll be all right."

"Oh, Mother, he's not going to die, is he? **He's not going to die.**"

"Of course he's not going to die. Don't be so silly. . . . I think you might stop being an hysterical child and try and make an effort to control yourself, and behave properly," declares Mrs. Millward. "I have had about as much as I can stand today."

"I'm sorry. I'll try. I'll be good," promises Alex.

Mrs. Millward has started for the door when she turns for a reassuring look at Alex.

"All right now?" she calls. Alex nods. "I'll go down and boil a kettle," Mrs. Millward adds.

Alex is sitting staring after her mother, trying to control her tears.

THE CURTAIN FALLS

ACT III

It is late afternoon of the following day. Roland, short of sleep, has been dozing in a chair in the living room, but manages to arouse himself sufficiently to report to inquirers including Cousin Theresa, that his patient, Toby, has conquered his fever and is planning to sail for America next morning. Dr. Mackenzie had agreed with Roland that it would do Toby more harm to stay behind and fret than it would to make the effort and go. Mrs. Millward is around packing for him now.

It is Cousin Theresa's idea that Mrs. Millward does altogether too much for others and thinks too little of herself. Every woman should have some definite activity in her life as a kind of insurance against a lonely old age.

Liz Frobisher, following Theresa in this discussion, is of a similar opinion. She, too, wishes that Mrs. Millward could get more out of life. But Roland can think of nothing that he can do about "stirring his mother up."

Liz is also in a slightly worried state of mind. She is wearing a new and handsome wrist watch and she is expecting a caller. Roland might be worried about the watch, knowing his aunt as he does, but he is perfectly willing to get out and let her have the living room for the entertainment of her expected guest.

The guest, as it now turns out, is "Gillie." Gilbert Baize, if properly introduced. "A man of forty-eight, and attractive in a slightly 'flash' way."

Gillie is quite chipper. Casual with Roland, and confidently possessive with Liz when Roland is gone. At least he would be confidently possessive did she not hold him off with a show of firmness. Gillie does not seem to realize that Liz has left him, and is frank to admit that he has no intention of realizing it. He refuses to take seriously her threatened attachment for what he describes as her "Brave Petit Belge." Gillie is of a mind to talk things over fully, but he would get friendly first.

"*I'm* perfectly friendly," announces Liz, coldly.

"Well, then, give me a kiss," suggests Gillie.

"No," says Liz, moving away from him. "I'm damned if I do. If you've anything to say, say it. . . . I was sorry to hear your father was dead. Did you . . . see him?"

GILBERT—Yes. We had quite a chat.

LIZ—Did he forgive you?

GILBERT—He was inclined to forgive. I told him we were washed up, you and I, I mean.

LIZ—And that pleased him, of course.

GILBERT—Well, you know how he felt about those things. As a matter of fact, I rather gave him to understand . . . without actually saying so . . . that it was *I* who had left *you*. (LIZ *gasps*.) I thought you wouldn't mind. It comes to the same thing in the end, and if it eased his last hours . . . well, you *don't* mind, do you?

LIZ—I mind a very great deal.

GILBERT—Oh, I'm sorry. I don't know what I can do about it now.

LIZ—What did he say?

GILBERT—He said he was very glad I'd seen the light, or words to that effect, and wouldn't I consider going back to May if she'd forgive me. May was there, by the way.

LIZ—And you said?

GILBERT—I said, of course I'd consider it. May said she'd consider forgiving me. You've no idea the amount of consideration we worked up. The old boy went out wreathed in smiles.

LIZ (*very amused*)—Gillie, you are more of a disgrace . . . (*Then pulling herself together.*) And that's how you left it?

GILBERT—Yes.

LIZ (*not quite liking it*)—Well, it's all very satisfactory, isn't it? When do you and May set up house together?

GILBERT (*with an eye on her*)—I should think about the same time as you and Marcel. (*A pause. He walks away from her, turning his back. Then he speaks with a deliberate airy unconcern.*) As a matter of fact, May's consenting to divorce me.

Liz (*startled out of all her flippancy*)—What's that? After ten years? Why?

Gilbert—Well . . . I can make it worth her while now.

Liz—Oh! Have you come into money?

Gilbert—Quite a bit. We'd a long chat over the funeral baked meats. Am I a bit yellow about the eyes, by the way?

Liz—Yes. You drank too much sherry. It always got on your liver.

Gilbert—Well, anyway, we arranged terms for a settlement. She's filing her petition right away.

Liz (*a shade alarmed*)—Am I to be co-respondent?

Gilbert—No. I even got her to consent to spare you that.

Liz—That was very nice of you.

Gilbert—I told her it would make *her* look an awful bitch. So I should say that in something under a year, if you feel like it, you can be an honest woman again.

This is, in effect, Gilbert admits, a proposal of marriage. And he never was more serious in his life. He has always wanted Liz to marry him, when he wasn't wishing she would go drown herself, and he feels certain she will never be able to marry "that lump of Camembert" from Belgium any more than he could go back to May.

Soon Gillie's voice has taken on a pleading tone and his manner has lost something of its early assurance. Liz must know that he is fond of her; that he has missed her terribly; that he is perfectly willing to let her have her way about settling down wherever she wants to. In Paris, if she likes.

Now Liz has suddenly begun to cry, and now she is in Gillie's arms.

"Oh, Gillie, why—why do you do the things you do . . . behave as you used to and then come and be nice to me? You will be just as bad again in a week. I know you will. You don't think marriage is going to change you, do you?"

"It may have a sobering effect . . . if you really want me changed, that is. I don't want *you* changed, for all your tiresomeness. You know, I've always thought how awful it would be to meet people in heaven that you were fond of on earth and find them all cleaned up, with none of the things that you liked left about them . . . all your old drinking companions gone teetotal. . . ."

"Oh, Gillie, you are a fool."

"It's true. If you were sweet and gentle and uninteresting

like Evie, do you think I'd still want you, even though she's got
a far better character than you have?"

"Why *do* you want me?"

"Because you make me laugh, and you smell nice."

Mrs. Millward is home and surprised to find Gillie there. She
invites him to stay to tea, but Gillie had rather take Liz out to
dinner, if she doesn't mind. He doesn't feel quite up to meeting
Mrs. Venables just yet.

Roland comes back, helping Toby. Toby has made the stairs
all right but he does feel a bit like blotting paper. Everything
has been settled for him.

Dr. Mackenzie is to get a nurse to take him to Southampton
and see him on board. Mrs. Millward has packed all his things
and settled with his landlady. Toby is ever so grateful and a
little conscious. The experiences of the last several hours have
deeply impressed him. Impressed him with the differences between him and Alex. It has worried him a good deal.

"Did I say anything stupid last night?" Toby asks, suddenly,
after Roland has left him with Mrs. Millward.

"I don't think so."

TOBY—I seem to remember I said something about Alex coming with me.

MRS. MILLWARD—You said you wanted her to.

TOBY—Oh!

MRS. MILLWARD—I gathered from her you'd asked her to
marry you.

TOBY—And she told you she wouldn't?

MRS. MILLWARD—Not quite that.

TOBY—It comes to that.

MRS. MILLWARD—Would you mind *terribly* if she didn't?

TOBY—Yes, I'd mind, of course. But I've been sort of getting
used to the idea today. You see . . . can I talk to you about it?

MRS. MILLWARD—If it won't tire you.

TOBY—It won't. I'd like to. I've never talked to you before
and I feel now . . . now that you've been so frightfully good to
me . . . that I've been going a bit behind your back.

MRS. MILLWARD—I think more than you realize, Toby. (TOBY
looks up at her searchingly.) Alex told me last night.

TOBY (*looking away*)—I'm sorry.

MRS. MILLWARD—That I know?

TOBY—Not quite that. But I've suddenly realized that Alex
is an awful lot younger than I thought. I don't mean in age, but

. . . you see, I'd only known her, really, away from all this, and she puts on a sort of sophistication that rather took me in. I knew, of course, that it wasn't all real, but what I do see is that perhaps I've tried to make her go my way. I'm a bit headlong, and I think she got swept up. I'd always felt I'd like to marry her, but until now I couldn't possibly keep her, and the idea was just ruled out, except as a . . . possibility one day.

MRS. MILLWARD—I see.

TOBY—I do want to marry her, but I feel I mustn't try and force her. It wouldn't be any good unless it came, really spontaneously, from her, because even with what I'm getting in Hollywood, it's not going to be too easy. And besides, that may not last. I can wait if there's a chance. I did try to force her just on the sort of excitement of it all. But now I mustn't. I know that. (*With a smile.*) That's what being here for twenty-four hours and running a temperature has done for me.

MRS. MILLWARD (*smiling*)—I don't think it's only that. But thank you for talking to me.

TOBY—I'm awfully glad I have. She's lucky to have you.

MRS. MILLWARD—Try and rest a little now.

Alex has come in. She is still wearing her outdoor things and is a bit excited. Surprised and glad to see Toby up. Pleased that he is going to be able to sail next day. How did she get on reading the part? Oh, pretty well. She can have it if she wants it, she thinks. She's been shopping since she finished with the reading.

"Charles Hubbard rang up for you at lunch time," says Mrs. Millward. "He said would you ring him when you got in. He's asked you and me to go with them to the first night at the Playhouse next Wednesday. I thought it was very nice of him. Can you go?"

"I don't know. I don't think I can," Alex answers.

Mrs. Millward has gone to get ready for tea now. It is to be served in the drawing room so Toby can be quiet where he is.

Now Alex has found her pocketbook and fished out a large envelope. It is a present for Toby, she says. Let him open it and see what it is. And Toby does.

"My ticket and my passport," says Alex, coming over to sit on his knee. "I'm coming with you. That's what I've been doing all day. That, and buying a trunk and some things. That's why I was longing for Mother to go out of the room. I wanted to tell you alone."

"And the reading? Was that all made up?"

"No. I read the part. I wanted to prove I could before I chucked it."

"They really offered it to you?"

"God knows how I did it," Alex confesses. "My mind was miles away with all I had to do, and the terror of not being able to get it done. And the thought of walking in here like this. . . ."

Mrs. Venables has come in in time to see the kissing. She's rather caustic about that. Nor does she like the idea of having tea in the drawing room. Let them go in there for their love making, if they want to, and let her have her tea in the sitting room as usual.

Alex is in no mood to give way to her grandmother's whim. The drawing room is too cold for Toby and they will stay where they are, she decides. And they do, though with a proper explanation to Mrs. Millward when she comes back.

"I come in here and find her carrying on with a half-dressed young man in my armchair!" snaps Mrs. Venables, defensively.

"You may be interested to hear that I'm going to marry the half-dressed young man, Grandma," answers Alex.

MRS. VENABLES—And so you ought by the way you were behaving.

MRS. MILLWARD (*with half-delighted surprise*)—Alex!

ALEX—I'm sorry, Mother. I didn't mean to tell you like this, but it's true. I'm going *with* Toby to California.

MRS. VENABLES—What's that?

ALEX—Toby's going to America, Grandma. And I'm going with him in the morning.

MRS. VENABLES—In the morning? And when do you propose to get married?

ALEX—I really don't know, Grandma. On the boat, if we can . . . or when we get there. That doesn't seem to me very important.

MRS. VENABLES—Oh, really. Evie! Are you going to stand there and listen to such wicked nonsense?

MRS. MILLWARD—I don't know that I think it *is* nonsense, Mother.

MRS. VENABLES (*rising*)—Well, *I* do. I never heard such a thing in all my born days. Have you gone stark staring mad? Your own daughter tells you that she's going off to America with (*Spluttering.*) God knows what kind of a young man . . . and it doesn't matter whether she gets married or not.

MRS. MILLWARD—She didn't mean that.

MRS. VENABLES—I'm not so sure.

TOBY (*feebly*)—Please, please don't go on like this.

MRS. MILLWARD—Mother, Alex is old enough to get married if she wants to, and I'm very glad she does. You can't interfere. You mustn't interfere.

MRS. VENABLES—I mustn't interfere? Oh, very well. Now we know where we are. Now my own daughter turns against me!

ALEX—Grandma, will you please stop making a scene?

MRS. VENABLES—A scene! A scene! (*To* MRS. MILLWARD.) And you let her speak to me like that! (*During the last few speeches* TOBY, *unnoticed by the others, has struggled to his feet after a couple of unheard protests. He is swaying, and clutches at the mantelpiece for support. In doing so he knocks over an ornament, which calls attention to him.*)

ALEX—Toby! (*She goes to him quickly. Turning to the others.*) Look what you're doing to him. Mother, take Grandma away! (*She supports him.*) Mother, for God's sake take her away . . . take her away!

The curtain falls.

At seven o'clock next morning Mrs. Millward's bedroom is again the center of activity. The house is gradually coming to life, preparing for the leavetaking of Alex and Toby Chegwidden. Nobody has slept much. Mrs. Millward is not going to the station. Alex had asked her not to, and she thinks, too, it would be best.

There is a momentary exchange of confidences between mother and daughter. Alex admits to feeling a little funny inside, "but awfully important, too, as if I'd been put in charge of something . . . the War Office, perhaps."

"Mother . . . you don't . . . mind, do you? You've been so grand and splendid. But inside . . . do you mind?"

"I don't pretend that I like you're going away from me," admits Mrs. Millward. "But otherwise I'm very glad."

"You're responsible for it, you know, making me take the plunge. I told you that last night. . . . It wasn't what you said, but when I saw you . . . *with* him . . . and treating him as if he were one of us, like Roland and me, I mean . . . it . . . it did something to me."

"You told me."

"I know. I told it to myself all yesterday when I was running around. I kept reliving that scene in here. Do you know, in a funny way I felt jealous of you? It was like seeing someone else look after one's child, and knowing that they'd a perfect right to, because one was so inadequate oneself. That's when I knew . . . that nothing else counted. (*With a change of tone.*) Now let's have our tea. (*She starts to pour out.*) I've written to Charles. I know I've treated him rottenly, but I can't be sorry, really. I did my best to *write* sorry. (*Passing cup.*) Oh! Let me know who gets my part, won't you? It's the heroine's best friend—the one who gets told everything."

Alex has gone to see how her fiancé is getting along. Liz Frobisher pops in in a dressing gown. She would sympathize with her sister, but has a feeling the arrangement is entirely to Evie's liking. Liz has news of her own, too. She has decided to go back to Gillie. His father's death has made it possible for him to effect a settlement with his wife. She is to divorce him, and as soon as she has her evidence Gillie and Liz are to take a trip around the world to escape all the fuss about the divorce—

"Then we shall be married and respectable," says Liz, "and the vicar will call . . . or perhaps he won't. 'A brave man wedded her, after all, but the world said, frowning, we shall not call.' That'll be one comfort, anyway." . . .

Alex has decided to dispense with a nurse for Toby. She will take care of him herself. Which is not a surprising decision to her aunt. . . .

Mrs. Venables, in her dressing gown, and accompanied by Spicer, her companion, has come for a good-by. She is not surprised at Alex's decision to go with her young man. Alex is in a conciliatory mood.

"Have you forgiven me, Grandma?" she asks, pleasantly.

"I suppose I've got to, as it's probably the last time I'll ever set eyes on you," snaps Mrs. Venables.

"Oh, no, Grandma."

"Three years, you said? You don't expect me to be here when you come back, do you? I suppose you'll be taking your mother away from me to come and visit you? Though what Evie'll do in Hollywood I can't imagine."

"You'll have to go and keep an eye on her," suggests Spicer.

"We'll get you off with Ronald Colman," promises Alex.

"I think Wallace Beery's more in my line," says Grandma.

Nellie Fletcher arrives, and now Toby comes with Roland. He's feeling quite as well as could be expected, Toby thinks. He

agrees with Mrs. Venables that he does need a haircut—
"Give you something to do on the boat," says Mrs. Venables with a grin, "when you're not being 'quiet'!"
Now the good-bys have been said. Alex has kissed them all, reminding her tearful Aunt Nellie that she is being married and not buried.
"Oh, Alex," calls Mrs. Venables, after them. "I know it doesn't seem important . . . but don't forget to get married."
Christopher Venables has called and bidden the departing bride and bridegroom good-by downstairs. Now he would pay his respects to Mrs. Venables. From the window the departure can be seen and reported. Mrs. Millward is quite wonderful, the way she takes everything. . . .
Christopher would add his bit of comfort to Mrs. Millward when she comes back.
"Has this hit you very badly, Eve?" he asks.
"I don't think so," she answers, reflectively.

CHRISTOPHER—You're good at being lonely.
MRS. MILLWARD—I'm not really lonely.
CHRISTOPHER—I always think of you as that.
MRS. MILLWARD—That's where you make a mistake. Loneliness means that there's something you want, some companionship you're looking for.
CHRISTOPHER—And you're not.
MRS. MILLWARD—No.
CHRISTOPHER—Perhaps if instead of loneliness I called it "solitude" . . . ? (*He points to book.*)
MRS. MILLWARD—That's different.
CHRISTOPHER—Eve, couldn't I do something about that?
MRS. MILLWARD—No, Christopher. It's sweet of you. But that's something that just happens to one. And there's a kind of peace in it, really. That's what makes it different from loneliness. Loneliness aches. I believe you think of me as being unhappy. I'm not, you know.
CHRISTOPHER—I think of you as being very lovely, Eve.
MRS. MILLWARD—That's dear of you.
CHRISTOPHER—I've tried to let you know that. Eve, wouldn't you marry me and let me . . . help your solitude?
MRS. MILLWARD (*takes his hand*)—Christopher, I couldn't. I'm terribly, terribly sorry, but I couldn't. I like you. You know that. I'm deeply, deeply fond of you. But marriage and all it means is something different. That couldn't happen twice . . .

for me.

CHRISTOPHER—I wouldn't expect it to be the same.

MRS. MILLWARD—Even so . . . it just wouldn't be possible. I'm sorry. You're not angry with me?

CHRISTOPHER—I've always known it, really.

MRS. MILLWARD—You'll come and see me just the same?

CHRISTOPHER—Of course.

MRS. MILLWARD—I love being with you.

CHRISTOPHER—And I with you. Would you like me to get along now?

MRS. MILLWARD—If you wouldn't mind.

CHRISTOPHER—May I come in this afternoon?

MRS. MILLWARD—Please do.

CHRISTOPHER—Good-by, my dear. (*He bends down and kisses her gently on the cheek and then goes out.*) (MRS. MILLWARD *sits alone a moment. She cries a very little.* MISS SPICER *comes in.*)

SPICER (*at the door*)—Oh! Mrs. Millward, dear, Mrs. Venables says will you come in and talk to her?

MRS. MILLWARD—All right. I'll come in a moment, Miss Spicer. (MISS SPICER *goes out.* MRS. MILLWARD *goes over to the dressing table and takes up a photograph of her husband. She looks at it a long time. Whispering.*) Our girl's all right, dearest. She's all right.

She puts the photograph down and then quickly goes out of the room as the curtain falls.

THE PLAYS AND THEIR AUTHORS

"The Children's Hour." A drama in three acts by Lillian Hellman. Copyright, 1934, by the author. Copyright and published, 1934, by Alfred Knopf, New York.

This is Lillian Hellman's first appearance as a Best Play author, so far as the record of these volumes is concerned. For that
matter it is also Miss Hellman's first appearance as a Broadway
playwright. She is gracefully approaching thirty, she was born
in New York and she went to New York schools. Out of school
she laid the foundation for a career as a writer by doing a lot of
reading. She was a play reader for Herman Shumlin, who is the
producer of "The Children's Hour"; she was a reviewer of books
for the New York *Herald Tribune;* she was a reader of scenarios
for the Metro-Goldwyn-Mayer motion picture company. She has
been a contributor to many of the better magazines and did her
bit as a press agent, working one season for the good of a Rochester stock company. She had been co-author of one play before
"The Children's Hour." It was a farce, written with Louis
Kronenberger and called "Dear Queen." Nothing, so far as the
records indicate, ever came of that. In the writing of "The Children's Hour" Miss Hellman acknowledges as her inspiration "The
Great Drumsheugh Case," the record of a famous criminal trial
fought through the Scottish courts and reported in detail by William Roughead in an essay entitled "Closed Doors; or, The Great
Drumsheugh Case," published by Duffield and Green in 1931.

"Valley Forge." A drama in three acts by Maxwell Anderson.
Copyright, 1934, by the author. Copyright and published,
1935, by Anderson House, Washington, D. C. Distributed
by Dodd, Mead & Co., New York.

Maxwell Anderson has been a frequent contributor to the Best
Play series, having made his bow originally with Laurence Stallings as co-author of "What Price Glory." His recent appearances
have been as the author of the two historical plays, "Mary of
Scotland" and "Elizabeth the Queen," and also as the winner of
the Pulitzer prize award in 1932-33 with "Both Your Houses."

He was born in Atlantic, Pa., is the son of a minister, did a good deal of editorial writing for various newspapers before turning to playwrighting and is now one of the higher-priced literary advisers to the producers of motion pictures in Hollywood.

"The Petrified Forest." A drama in two acts by Robert Sherwood. Copyright, 1934, 1935, by the author. Copyright and published, 1935, by Charles Scribner's Sons, New York.

This, having been a year of general economies, was probably as good a time as any for Robert Emmet Sherwood to drop the Emmet from his name and become plain Robert Sherwood. His last previous appearance as a Best Play author was in the volume recording the success of his "Reunion in Vienna" the season of 1931-32. He acknowledges New Rochelle, N. Y., as the town of his birth, Harvard as the seat of learning from which he went to war in 1918. Back from war he became a magazine editor (*Life, Vanity Fair, Scribner's*), wrote motion picture reviews and finally decided on playwriting as the career he most cared to follow. His other plays have included "The Road to Rome," and "The Queen's Husband."

"The Old Maid." A drama in three acts by Zoe Akins, from a novel by Edith Wharton. Copyright, 1934, 1935, by Edith Wharton and Zoe Akins. Copyright and published, 1935, by the D. Appleton-Century Co., New York.

Zoe Akins had been a poet of promise in St. Louis for some time before she gained recognition as a playwright. Her first year of prominence was 1919, when three of her plays, two short and one long, came to notice. These were "Papa," "The Magical City" and "Declassee." The first two were produced by the Washington Square Players who afterward became the Theatre Guild in New York. The third served Ethel Barrymore well as a starring vehicle and was included in the first volume of "Best Plays" to be compiled, that covering the season of 1919-20. Since then Miss Akins has written many plays, including "Daddy's Gone A-Hunting," "The Varying Shore," "The Texas Nightingale," "The Furies," "The Love Duel" and her outstanding comedy success of five years ago, "The Greeks Had a Word for It." She was born in Missouri, in the Ozark Mountains, the town being Humansville. Of recent years she has spent much time in

Hollywood creating and adapting motion picture scenarios.

"The Old Maid," Edith Wharton's story from which Miss Akins has dramatized the play, was written in 1924 and was one of a series of stories of Old New York. Other novels by the same author that have been dramatized include "Ethan Frome" and "The Age of Innocence." Mrs. Wharton was born in New York in 1862. Her first novel, "The Greater Inclination," was published in 1899.

"Accent on Youth." A comedy in three acts by Samson Raphaelson. Copyright, 1934, by the author. Copyright and published, 1935, by Samuel French, New York.

Samson Raphaelson was born in New York but did not stay here long. He went to Chicago. Out of the Chicago high schools he worked his way through the University of Illinois, and is a little proud of his record as one of the best table waiters the university ever boasted. Out of college Raphaelson went in for newspaper work, first with the City Press in Chicago. Then he came to New York and worked on the *Times*. After that he had a whirl at writing advertising copy, which led naturally to other fiction and he became a contributor of short stories to the magazines. He wrote his first play, "The Jazz Singer," in 1925. As the story of a cantor's son who heeds the call of race it proved decidedly popular with large numbers of Jewish-American playgoers and was played, with George Jessel as a star, for two years. This was followed by "Young Love" and "Harlem." Mr. Raphaelson has been devoting a good deal of time recently to the motion pictures.

"Merrily We Roll Along." A drama in three acts by George S. Kaufman and Moss Hart. Copyright, 1934, by the authors. Copyright and published, 1934, by Random House, New York.

This is the second collaboration of George Kaufman and Moss Hart, the first having been the immensely successful "Once in a Lifetime." Mr. Kaufman has contributed many plays to this series of Best Play volumes. He will be found in the issue of 1921-22, when he collaborated with Marc Connelly on "Dulcy," and thereafter he appears frequently with Mr. Connelly and also with Edna Ferber, with whom he wrote "Dinner at Eight" and

"The Royal Family"; with the late Ring Lardner, with whom he
wrote "June Moon," and notably with Morrie Ryskind and the
Gershwin brothers, who were all concerned in the writing of "Of
Thee I Sing." Mr. Connelly is a Pennsylvanian, born in Pittsburgh, and was a hard-working and successful newspaper man before his playwrighting brought him a touch of fame and a sizable
fortune.

Moss Hart was born and went to school in New York. He
was always a great one to write sketches and short plays (folk
sketches for Jewish societies a good many of them), even while
he was a student at the Morris High School. Out of school he
took such jobs as offered, but kept up his writing. Finally he
became an office assistant for Gus Pitou, who was a booking
agent for the Erlanger interests. Knowing that Mr. Pitou was
looking for a play, Mr. Hart wrote him one. He used a pen name
that might as well have been Anonymous. The play was called
"The Hold-up Man," Mr. Pitou bought it and it lasted five weeks
in Chicago. Hart did the original draft of "Once in a Lifetime,"
which Mr. Kaufman revised, and since then he has written "Face
the Music" and "As Thousands Cheer," with Irving Berlin. He
was born in the Bronx in 1906.

"Awake and Sing." A drama in three acts by Clifford Odets.
    Copyright, 1935, by the author. Copyright and published,
    1935, by Covici-Friede, New York.

Clifford Odets was one of the Theatre Guild juniors (juniors
in point of membership rather than in years) who drew away
from the parent organization in the winter of 1931 and formed
the now prospering Group Theatre. There was no break with
the Guild. In fact the juniors were at first financed and coun-
seled by the Guild. A desire for greater activity and greater
opportunities in the way of play production caused the separation.
Odets had had three years with the Guild, and these years had
followed a considerable experience in the theatre devoted mostly
to acting a variety of small parts in stock. His playwrighting
activities began during a Group Theatre engagement in Boston a
year ago. He first wrote the one-act drama, "Waiting for Lefty,"
for a benefit performance to be given for the *New Theatre Magazine,* published by a group of young radicals. This was followed
by his first full-length play, "Awake and Sing," and a long one-
act anti-Nazi opus called "Till the Day I Die." These three
plays have gained Mr. Odets, who is still in his early thirties, the

reputation of being the most promising of America's newer dramatists. He was born in Philadelphia but has lived the greater part of his life in the Bronx section of New York. His sympathies are frankly radical and he likely will be concerned for some time with plays of a propagandist nature.

"The Farmer Takes a Wife." A comedy in three acts by Frank
    B. Elser and Marc Connelly, adapted from the novel, "Rome
    Haul," by Walter D. Edmonds. Copyright, 1934, by the
    authors.

The late Frank Ball Elser died in the British West Indies a week after "The Farmer Takes a Wife" closed on Broadway, following a run of three months. It was his second play to be produced in New York, the first being an adaptation of the Liam O'Flaherty novel, "Mr. Gilhooley." The first draft of "The Farmer Takes a Wife" was made by Mr. Elser and called "Low Bridge." It had been given semi-professional production before Mr. Connelly was called in as collaborator. Elser was born in Fort Worth, Texas, in 1885, and after a year and a half at Cornell had filled a variety of jobs that led him finally to newspaper work and to war assignments, first as a correspondent on the Western front and later with the Pershing chase of Villa in Mexico. He was night city editor of the New York *Times* for a year and a half before he withdrew from newspaper work to devote his time to writing.

Marc Connelly is a familiar contributor to this published record of the American theatre. He made his bow as co-author with George Kaufman of "Dulcy," and later "Beggar on Horseback" and "Merton of the Movies." His own play, "The Wisdom Tooth," was included in the issue of 1925-26 and his adaptation of "The Green Pastures," which won the Pulitzer award in 1929-30, also led the list of Best Plays selected for that year. Mr. Connelly is a Pennsylvanian, a native of McKeesport, and did a good deal of newspaper reporting before he turned dramatist.

"Lost Horizons." A dramatic fantasy in three acts, by John
    Hayden, based on an original play by Harry Segall. Copy-
    right, 1934, by the author.

John Hayden was a stage director for Rowland Stebbins (Laurence Rivers, Inc.) when the manuscript of this play by Harry

Segall was submitted for production, as is more fully related in the introduction of the digest herein published. He was born in Hartford, Conn., in 1889, and became actively interested in the theatre in 1911. He has been an actor in and a director of many stock companies, principally in the South. Since 1924 he has directed plays in New York and is the author of several one-act plays of his own. His work on "Lost Horizons" included a general clarifying and rearrangement of material and the rewriting of the last act.

"The Distaff Side." A drama in three acts by John Van Druten. Copyright, 1933, 1934, by the author. Copyright and published, 1934, by Alfred Knopf, New York.

John Van Druten did so well in his study of the law that after his graduation from the University College School in London, and his annexation of a degree as a Bachelor of Law at the London University, he lectured on English Law and English Legal History for three years at the University College of Wales, located in the pretty little town of Aberystwyth. It was during this time that he was attacked by the urge to write, and satisfied it to some extent by sending poems, short stories and such to London magazines. His first play to attract attention was his study of student life and adolescence entitled "Young Woodley," which, being banned by the London Censor as an attack upon the English school system, was produced in New York in 1925. After that the Censor removed the ban and the play had an eleven-month run in London. Mr. Van Druten has lectured in America extensively and his "There's Always Juliet" was a season's success in 1932. He was born in London in 1902. His father was Dutch, his mother English.

PLAYS PRODUCED IN NEW YORK

June 16, 1934—June 16, 1935

(Plays marked with asterisk were still playing June 16, 1935)

HER MAJESTY THE WIDOW

(32 performances)

A comedy in three acts by John Charles Brownell. Produced by Her Majesty Company at the Ritz Theatre, New York, June 18, 1934.

Cast of characters—

```
Sarah.........................................Grayce Hampton
Jane Seymour..................................Pauline Frederick
Judge Coolidge...............................Alexander Campbell
Robert Seymour...................................Thomas Beck
"Bunny" Williams..............................Frederick Bell
Veronica Day....................................Isobel Withers
Elsie Reynolds..............................Laurette Bullivant
Peter Stuyvesant.........................Charles Mitchell Harris
```
Acts I, II and III.—Living Room of Jane Seymour's Home in a Fashionable Suburb of Boston.

Staged by Pauline Frederick; settings by Karl Amend.

Jane Seymour, a widow of experience, seeks to save her son Robert from an entanglement with a lively young worldling named Veronica Day. The boy, having tossed over a nice girl, Elsie Reynolds, for the artificial Veronica, Jane invited them both to the house and lets nature, assisted by an old beau of her own, take its course. Nature and the nice girl win. And Mother marries her first love.

GYPSY BLONDE

(24 performances)

A musical comedy in three acts rewritten by Kenneth Johns; lyrics by Frank Gabrielson; from "Bohemian Girl" by Balfe. Produced by Dmitri Ostrov at the Lyric Theatre, New York, June 25, 1934.

Cast of characters—

```
Arline...........................................Isabel Henderson
Philip Arnheim...................................John Hendricks
Florrie...............................................Arthur Page
Devilshoof.........................................John Dunsmure
```

Trusty..Georges Trabert
Baba..Helene Arden
A Dancer...Belle Didjah
Dancers: Helen Ecklund, Betty Blake, Myra Scott, Madeline Mac-
    Donald, Zabelle Thall, Diane Demler, Suzanne Cort, Grace Gil-
    lern, Mildred Hamilton.
Singers: Nell Gebest, Vera Beaumont, Marie Falica, Maudeline
    Smith, Beulah Blake, Marla Forbes, Virginia Vallance, Helen
    Barricklow, Betty Gravier, Elizabeth Kerr, Evelyn Wycoff, Lotti
    Tilsen.
Men: Dan Meduri, Leon Sabater, Carl Robertson, Earl Mason, El-
    vin Howland, Zachary Carr, Frank Grinnell, Bernard Warren.
    Act I.—Westchester Estate of Philip Arnheim. Acts II and III.—
Gypsy Camp near State Fair.
    Staged by Dmitri Ostrov; settings by Karl Amend; dances by
Vaughn Godfrey; musical director, Fred Hoff.

In this modernized version of the Balfe opera the locale is
switched to Westchester county, which lies immediately to the
north of New York and is one of the big city's snootiest suburban
districts. The Devilshoof gypsies of the opera are camped in
the neighborhood and induce Arline, the daughter of the Philip
Arnheims', to go with them and become a singing gypsy to escape
the young man to whom she is engaged and who simply cannot
carry his liquor gracefully. As a gypsy Arline falls in love with
a tenor, called Trusty, because he has just escaped from Sing
Sing, and from the meeting a new romance and several familiar
duets are born.

DODSWORTH

(First engagement 147 performances. Return 168. Total 315.)

A drama in three acts by Sidney Howard dramatized from the
novel by Sinclair Lewis. Produced by Max Gordon at the Shubert Theatre, New York, February 24, 1934; withdrawn June 30,
1934; resumed August 20, 1934.

Cast of characters—

Samuel Dodsworth................................Walter Huston
A Sales Manager..................................Arthur Uttry
A Publicity Man..................................Nolan Leary
A Secretary......................................Betty Van Auken
Henry E. Hazzard.................................Charles Halton
Fran Dodsworth...................................Fay Bainter
Thomas J. Pearson, called "Tubby".................Harlan Briggs
Mrs. Pearson, called "Matey"......................Ethel Jackson
Emily McKee......................................Ethel Hampton
Harry McKee......................................Mervin Williams
Two Traveling Gentlemen................... { Nick Adams
                                           { William E. Morris
Clyde Lockert....................................John Williams
An American Lady.................................Beatrice Maude
Another American Lady ....Marie Falls
A Passenger......................................Bert Gardner
His Wife...Lucille Fenton
Edith Cortright..................................Nan Sunderland
A Steward..Charles Christensen
Another Steward..................................John Roberts

```
A Barman..........................................Jay Wilson
A. B. Hurd......................................Hal K. Dawson
Renee de Penable.............................Leonore Harris
Arnold Israel..................................Frederic Worlock
Kurt von Obersdorf..............................Kent Smith
A Cashier.......................................J. H. Kingsberry
An American Mother.............................Marie Falls
Her Daughter..................................Georgette Spelvin
A Tourist.......................................Frank W. Taylor
His Wife........................................Myrtle Tannehill
"Junior," His Son...............................Charles Powers
Information Clerk................................Ralph Simone
A Second Tourist..................................Marie Mallon
Baroness von Obersdorf........................Dorothy Raymond
Teresa..........................................Flora Fransioli
      Staged by Robert B. Sinclair; settings by Jo Mielziner.
```

The withdrawal of "Dodsworth" was occasioned by the desire of Walter Huston to play "Othello" in the Central City, Colorado, revival of that Shakespearean drama in July. The engagement was resumed in August with the original cast and continued until January 12, 1935. See "Best Plays of 1933-34."

KEEP MOVING

(20 performances)

A revue in two acts by Newman Levy and Jack School; music by Max Rich. Produced by the White Horse Productions, Inc., at the Forrest Theatre, New York, August 23, 1934.

Principals—

Tom Howard	Harriet Hutchins
Woods Miller	Joan Abbott
John Adair	Kay Picture
Billy Taylor	Nayan Pierce
Frank Delmar	Sally Gooding
John Delmar	Meta Carlyle
Clyde Hagar	Sonia Kasten
Dan Carthay	Singers' Midgets

Staged by George Rosener and Harry Losee; settings by Clark Robinson.

LIFE BEGINS AT 8.40

(237 performances)

A revue in two acts by David Freedman; music by Harold Arlen; lyrics by Ira Gershwin and E. Y. Harburg. Produced by the Messrs. Shubert at the Winter Garden, New York, August 27, 1934.

Principals—

Bert Lahr	Luella Gear
Ray Bolger	Frances Williams
Brian Donlevy	Adrienne Matzenauer

<pre>
Earl Oxford   Josephine Huston
James McColl   Winifred Harris
Charles Fowler   Dixie Dunbar
Ofelia and Pimento   Esther Junger
Weidman Dancers   Sally Gibbs
</pre>
Staged by John Murray Anderson; sketches staged by Philip Loeb; dances by Robert Alton and Charles Weidman; settings by Albert Johnson.

SALUTA

(39 performances)

A musical comedy satire in two acts by Will Morrissey, revised by Eugene Conrad and Maurice Marks; music by Frank D'Armond. Produced by R. A. Reppil at the Imperial Theatre, New York, August 28, 1934.

Cast of characters—

<pre>
Pete Fondana.....................................William Edmunds
Tony Carello.......................................Milton Watson
Moe Ginsberg.................................Edward J. Lambert
Nicholo Lorenzo................................Chaz. Chase
Guard..Cliff Whitcombe
"Windy" Walker...................................Milton Berle
George Palalis.....................................Ralph Sanford
Henry Bradley.................................Dudley Clements
Elinore Bradley..Ann Barrie
Betty Baxter.......................................Thelma White
Policeman..Cliff Whitcombe
Policeman..Otto Simanek
Captain Sardi.....................................L. C. Phillips
Sailors...The Maxcellas
Felicia Sorel
        and.......................................Themselves
Demetrios Vilan
Steward...Cliff Whitcombe
Officer..William Hargrave
Stephano Milano..............................Daniel Makarenko
Nina..Betty Gravier
Secretary.......................................Dorothy Bradshaw
Sergeant of Police............................William Hargrave
Priest...William Hargrave
Monk...George Ortell
The Dictator..Frank Marino
</pre>
Act I.—Scene 1—Jail. 2—Black Horse Tavern. 3—S.S. "Rex." 4—Ship's Concert. 5—Impresario's Office. 6—Opera Rehearsal. Act II.—Scene 1—Italian Street. 2—Dictator's Office. 3—Opera. 4—S.S. "Rex."
Staged by William Morrissey and Edwin Saulpaugh; dances by Boots McKenna; settings by Hugh Willoughby.

"Windy" Walker, master of ceremonies in a cheap New York café, is drafted by Nicholo Lorenzo and his spaghetti mob to go to Italy and stage an opera that shall compete with the state productions organized by Il Duce. Henry Bradley, millionaire, agrees to back the opera if his daughter, Elinore, has the prima donna rôle. Nicholo, who is also a tenor, falls in love with Elinore. Il Duce takes steps to repress the invasion, but not many.

D'OYLY CARTE OPERA COMPANY

(15 weeks engagement)

Presenting a repertory of Gilbert and Sullivan operettas at the Martin Beck Theatre, New York, beginning September 3, 1934.

THE GONDOLIERS

(19 performances)

Cast of characters—

```
The Duke of Plaza-Toro...........................Martyn Green
Luiz.............................................John Dean
Don Alhambra del Bolero.......................Sydney Granville
Marco Palmieri...................................Derek Oldham
Giuseppe Palmieri..................................Leslie Rands
Antonio.........................................Richard Walker
Francesco........................................Robert Wilson
Giorgio..........................................Radley Flynn
Annibale.........................................Frank Steward
The Duchess of Plaza-Toro.........................Dorothy Gill
Casilda..........................................Eileen Moody
Gianetta........................................Muriel Dickson
Tessa............................................Marjorie Eyre
Fiametta.........................................Doreen Denny
Vittoria..................................Elizabeth Nickell-Lean
Giulia.........................................Margaret O'Brien
Inez..........................................Josephine Curtis
```
Act I.—Venice. Act II.—Pavilion in the Palace of Barataria.

COX AND BOX

(September 6)

(13 performances)

By Maddison Morton, F. C. Burnand and Arthur Sullivan

Cast of characters—

```
Cox.............................................Martyn Green
Box...............................................John Dean
Bouncer......................................Darrell Fancourt
```
Scene—A Room in Bouncer's House.

THE PIRATES OF PENZANCE

(September 6)

(17 performances)

Cast of characters—

```
Major-General Stanley............................Martyn Green
The Pirate King.............................Darrell Fancourt
```

Samuel...Richard Walker
Frederic...Derek Oldham
Sergeant of Police..............................Sydney Granville
Mabel...Kathleen Frances
Edith...Marjorie Eyre
Kate...Maisie Baxter
Isabel......................................Elizabeth Nickell-Lean
Ruth..Dorothy Gill

Act I.—Rocky Seashore on the Coast of Cornwall. Act II.—Ruined Chapel, by Moonlight.

IOLANTHE

(September 10)

(15 performances)

Cast of characters—

The Lord Chancelor...............................Martyn Green
Earl Mountararat ....Darrell Fancourt
Earl Tolloller....................................Derek Oldham
Private Willis..................................Sydney Granville
Strephon..Leslie Rands
Queen of the Fairies............................Dorothy Gill
Iolanthe..................................Elizabeth Nickell-Lean
Celia..Kathleen Frances
Leila..Maisie Baxter
Fleta..Margaret O'Brien
Phyllis...Muriel Dickson

Act I.—An Arcadian Landscape. Act II.—Palace Yard, Westminster.

TRIAL BY JURY

(September 13)

(12 performances)

Cast of characters—

The Learned Judge..........................Sydney Granville
Counsel for the Plaintiff........................Leslie Rands
The Defendant..................................Robert Wilson
Foreman of the Jury............................Frank Steward
Usher...Richard Walker
Associate....................................C. William Morgan
The Plaintiff...................................Doreen Denny
First Bridesmaid.............................Kathleen Frances

H.M.S. "PINAFORE"

(September 13)

(11 performances)

Cast of characters—

Rt. Hon. Sir Joseph Porter, K.C.B...................Martyn Green
Captain Corcoran...................................Leslie Rands
Ralph Rackstraw...................................Derek Oldham
Dick Deadeye...................................Darrell Fancourt

Bill Bobstay......................................Richard Walker
Bob Becket...Radley Flynn
Josephine...Muriel Dickson
Hebe..Marjorie Eyre
Little Buttercup....................................Dorothy Gill
    Scene—Quarter Deck of the H.M.S. "Pinafore," off Portsmouth.

THE MIKADO

(September 17)

(19 performances)

Cast of characters—

The Mikado of Japan............................Darrell Fancourt
Nanki-Poo..Derek Oldham
Ko-Ko...Martyn Green
Pooh-Bah.......................................Sydney Granville
Pish-Tush..Leslie Rands
Go-To...Radley Flynn
Yum-Yum..Eileen Moody
Pitti-Sing...Marjorie Eyre
Peep-Bo....................................Elizabeth Nickell-Lean
Katisha..Dorothy Gill
    Act I.—Courtyard of Ko-Ko's Official Residence. Act II.—Ko-Ko's Garden.

THE YEOMEN OF THE GUARD

(September 20)

(11 performances)

Cast of characters—

Sir Richard Chalmondeley..........................Leslie Rands
Colonel Fairfax...................................Derek Oldham
Sergeant Meryll...............................Darrell Fancourt
Leonard Meryll......................................John Dean
Jack Point..Martyn Green
Wilfred Shadbolt...............................Sydney Granville
First Yeoman......................................Robert Wilson
Second Yeoman....................................Samuel Mooney
First Citizen................................C. William Morgan
Second Citizen...................................Frank Steward
Elsie Maynard....................................Muriel Dickson
Phoebe Meryll.....................................Marjorie Eyre
Dame Carruthers...................................Dorothy Gill
Kate (Her Niece)..............................Kathleen Frances
    Acts I and II.—Tower Green.

RUDDIGORE

(September 24)

(6 performances)

Cast of characters—

Sir Ruthven Murgatroyd............................Martyn Green
Richard Dauntless....................................John Dean
Sir Despard Murgatroyd.........................Sydney Granville

Old Adam Goodheart..............................Radley Flynn
Sir Roderic Murgatroyd.........................Darrell Fancourt
Rose Maybud....................................Eileen Moody
Mad Margaret...................................Marjorie Eyre
Dame Hannah....................................Dorothy Gill
Zorah..Kathleen Frances
Ruth...Elizabeth Nickell-Lean
    Act I.—Fishing Village of Rederring, in Cornwall. Act II.—Picture Gallery in Ruddigore Castle. Time—Early in the Last Century.

PRINCESS IDA

(September 27)

(11 performances)

Cast of characters—

King Hildebrand ....Sydney Granville
Hilarion.......................................Derek Oldham
Cyril..John Dean
Florian..Leslie Rands
King Gama......................................Martyn Green
Arac...Darrell Fancourt
Guron..Richard Walker
Scynthius......................................Radley Flynn
Princess Ida...................................Muriel Dickson
Lady Blanche...................................Dorothy Gill
Lady Psyche....................................Doreen Denny
Melissa..Marjorie Eyre
Sacharissa.....................................Kathleen Frances
Chloe..Maisie Baxter
Ada..Elizabeth Nickell-Lean
    Act I.—Pavilion in King Hildebrand's Palace. Act II.—Gardens of Castle Adamant. Act III.—Courtyard of Castle Adamant.

PATIENCE

(September 27)

(10 performances)

Cast of characters—

Colonel Calverley..............................Darrell Fancourt
Major Murgatroyd...............................Frank Steward
Lieut., The Duke of Dunstable..................John Dean
Reginald Bunthorne.............................Martyn Green
Archibald Grosvenor...........................Leslie Rands
Mr. Bunthorne's Solicitor......................W. F. Hodgkins
The Lady Angela................................Marjorie Eyre
The Lady Saphir................................Maisie Baxter
The Lady Ella..................................Kathleen Frances
The Lady Jane..................................Dorothy Gill
Patience.......................................Muriel Dickson
    Act I.—Exterior of Bunthorne Castle. Act II.—A Glade.

NO MORE LADIES

(16 performances)

A comedy in three acts by A. E. Thomas. Revived by Lee Shubert at the Morosco Theatre, New York, September 3, 1934.

Cast of characters—

```
Dickens..........................................John  Bramall
Oliver Allen......................................Bradley Cass
Mrs. Fanny Townsend............................Mary Sargent
Jacquette.......................................Isabel Delehanty
Mrs. Anderson Townsend............................Ann Dere
Mr. Anderson Townsend............................Roy Gordon
Sheridan Warren..............................Walter Pidgeon
Marcia Townsend.......................Daphne Warren Wilson
Stafford...........................................Boyd  Davis
James Salston....................................Robert Lowes
Diana............................................Betty Linley
The Earl of Moulton.............................Nicholas Joy
Teresa German.................................Marcella Swanson
```
     Act I.—New York Apartment of the Townsends. Acts II and III.
—Living Room of the Warrens, Southampton, L. I.
     Staged by Harry Wagstaff Gribble; settings by Watson Barratt.

This was a resumption of the original run which began January
23, 1934, at the Booth Theatre. (See "Best Plays of 1933-34.")
The play was moved February 12 to the Morosco, and closed
there temporarily June 9. The above company was organized to
tour with the comedy, starting out a fortnight later.

LADY JANE

(40 performances)

A comedy in three acts by H. M. Harwood. Produced by
Arch Selwyn and Harold B. Franklin, in association with Arthur
Hopkins, at the Plymouth Theatre, New York, September 10,
1934.

Cast of characters—

```
Lady Jane Kingdom.............................Frances Starr
Professor Charles Kingdom......................Reginald Mason
Lord Aldingham.................................Frank Elliott
Liza Kingdom.......................................Lila Lee
David Remington..............................Lowell Gilmore
Sybil Kingdom...............................Frieda Inescort
Hume..........................................Henry Vincent
Douglas Allenby...............................Paul McGrath
Maid..........................................Florence Selwyn
Steven Rains....................................Alan Marshal
```
     Acts I and III.—Breakfast Room. Act II.—Scene 1—A Bedroom.
2—Balcony. The Kingdoms' Country House, High Barrows.
     Staged by Mr. Harwood; settings by Woodman Thompson.

Lady Jane Kingdom is asked by her daughter-in-law, Sybil, to
help the latter get a divorce and keep her children. Sybil is in
love with a novelist, Douglas Allenby. Lady Jane, convinced
that "many a marriage has been saved by an unsuccessful infidelity," arranges adjoining rooms for Sybil and Douglas. Next
morning at breakfast the Sybil-Douglas affair is threatened with
collapse. To hasten that outcome Lady Jane confesses to Sybil
that she, too, as a young woman, had taken a lover to save her

home and had never told, nor ever regretted, her action. Sybil
goes back to her husband and her children.

TOO MANY BOATS

(7 performances)

A drama in three acts by Owen Davis, from a novel by Charles
L. Clifford. Produced by William A. Brady, Jr., at the Playhouse,
New York, September 11, 1934.

Cast of characters—

Colonel Hart	Mitchell Harris
Lt. Col. Mathewson	Charles Kennedy
Lt. Col. Decker	Brandon Peters
Major Von Kurtz	Horace Braham
Major Hunt	Henry Whittemore
Captain "Cork" Coates	Earle Larimore
Captain Withers	Donald McClelland
Captain Brannan	Harry Worth
Captain Chaplain Randolph	Alston Burleigh
Lieutenant Shard	Frank Shannon
Lieutenant Willard	Eric Mansfield
Mrs. Hart	Ruth Gates
Thelma Von Kurtz	Helen Flint
Betty Withers	Ruth Abbott
Julie Shaw	Anne Teeman
Nancy Carter	Shirley Gibbs
Barbara Lake	Nancy Dover
Juan	Richard Bond
1st Sergeant Warren	John Marriott
Sergeant Robert Washington	Jesse Gines
Corporal Murphy	Rudolph Toombs
Corporal Rivins	Percy Verwayne
Private Grumby	Hays Prior
Private Dinkin	Al Stokes
Private Brant	A. B. Comathiere
Private Franklin	Earl Goff
Sentry No. 5	Charles Stewart
Private Jeff Wendel	Joseph Tiggs
Private George Acorne	Ernest Evans
Private Louie Wadlin	Herman Lynn
Private Isiah Crowle	Mack McCoy
Private Tousant Greer	Eleazer Brice
Private Franklin Southern	Arnie Howard
Private Jeff Woodbury	Joseph Martin
Private Elisha Cunningham	Frank Williams
Private Joe Tompkins	Louis Teague
Private Marc Samson	Elmore Sanders
Private Peter Lee	James Gill
Private Thomas Jackson	William Smith
Private John Smith	John Ferguson
Private Joe Grey	John Davis
Private Peter Lazarus	Henderson Muziel
Private Paul Simon	James Dunmore
Private Anthony Cæsar	John Remy

Acts I, II and III.—Camp Blaisbell, Philippine Islands, 1918.
Staged by W. A. Brady, Jr.; setting by Robert Barnhart.

The army of the allegedly unfit shunted to the Philippines when
the U. S. entered the World War. Captain "Cork" Coates, a
hard drinker, hates Major Von Kurtz, suspected of German sym-

pathies. Mrs. Von Kurtz loves Coates, who tries to repulse her. Von Kurtz and Coates are fighting when Von Kurtz is shot. Coates is freed by a court-martial and is transferred to the states with a prospect of going over seas. Too late it is discovered that Mrs. Von Kurtz sailed on the same boat.

TIGHT BRITCHES

(23 performances)

A drama in three acts by John Tainter Foote and Hubert Hayes. Produced at the Avon Theatre, New York, September 11, 1934.

Cast of characters—

Vistie Edney	Ethel Wilson
Brad Palmer	Frank Camp
Ulys Palmer	Shepperd Strudwick
Doctor Clem Hooper	Robert Harrison
Sallie Tabor	Joanna Roos
Lou Cabe	Virginia Milne
Kom Kirrah	Boris Marshalov
Jesse Cabe	Doan Borup
Fairdy Tabor	Kathleen Comegys
Jarvie Tabor	Arthur Hughes

Acts I, II and III.—The Palmer Cabin in the Heart of the Great Smoky Mountains.

Staged by Miriam Doyle; setting by G. Bradford Ashworth.

JUDGMENT DAY

(93 performances)

A drama in three acts by Elmer Rice. Produced by the author at the Belasco Theatre, New York, September 12, 1934.

Cast of characters—

Dr. Michael Vlora	Lee Baker
Dr. Panayot Tsankov	Raymond Bramley
Colonel Jon Sturdza	William H. Barwald
Professor Paul Murusi	Philip Leigh
Count Leonid Slatarski	St. Clair Bayfield
Lydia Kuman	Josephine Victor
George Khitov	Walter N. Greaza
Kurt Schneider	Eric Wollencott
Dr. Wolfgang Bathory	Carroll Ashburn
Malinov	Charles Durand
Dr. Stambulov	James Moore
Dr. Mensch	Horace Casselberry
Conrad Noli	Vincent Sherman
Srazhimir	Joseph Julian
Gherea	W. J. Hackett
Gluca	Edward Mann
Pekmesi	Lionel Dante
Vidin	Aage Steenshorne
Jorga	Frank A. Lovejoy
Zogu	William Toubin
The Court Reporter	Ferdi Hoffman

```
Jonescu...............................................Louis La Bey
Lubin................................................St. John Terrell
Dr. Constantine Parvan..............................Hans Robert
Vasili Bassaraba.....................................Mark Schweid
Marthe Teodorova..................................Ethel Intropidi
Sonia Kuman.........................................Olga Druce
General Michael Rakovski.......................Romaine Callender
Giulia Crevelli....................................Fania Marinoff
Nekludov...........................................Edward Downes
Grigori Vesnic....................................House Jameson
Marek.........................................Brice Disque, Jr.
An Orthodox Priest...............................Ryder Keane
Attorneys' Clerks, Police Officers and Witnesses: Peggy Burt, Ted
   Erwin, Edward Hill, Thomas B. O'Connor, Robert Rice and
   Leslie Urbach. ..
   Acts I, II and II.—Room in Palace of Justice in a capital of
Southeastern Europe.
   Staged by Mr. Rice; setting by Aline Bernstein.
```

Lydia Kuman, George Khitov and Kurt Schneider are on trial as conspirators seeking the overthrow of the national government. Lydia and George are leaders of the People's party. Schneider is a drug addict who has been used by the Nationalists and their Leader in framing the case against them. The trial occupies three days covered by three acts. In the end the People's party revolution is successful and the persecutors of the people, including the Leader, are defeated.

THE BRIDE OF TOROZKO

(12 performances)

A comedy in three acts by Otto Indig, adapted by Ruth Langner. Produced by Gilbert Miller and Herman Shumlin at the Henry Miller Theatre, New York, September 13, 1934.

Cast of characters—

```
Comsa..............................................Francis Pierlot
Jonel.................................................Don Costello
Stephan...........................................Lionel Stander
Mate................................................Victor Kilian
Herschkowitz........................................Sam Jaffe
Andreas.............................................Van Heflin
Klari................................................Jean Arthur
Boeske.............................................Rose Keane
Franz Ambruz.....................................Frank Verigun
Josef Galfi.......................................Harry M. Cooke
Mrs. Blum.....................................Genevieve Belasco
   Act I.—Office of the Recorder.  Acts II and III.—Herschkowitz'
Inn.  Torozko.
   Staged by Herman Shumlin; settings by Stewart Chaney.
```

Klari would marry Andreas. When she applies for her birth certificate it is discovered she was a foundling, born of Jewish parents. Andreas is discouraged, the townsfolk contemptuous. Only Herschkowitz, the tavern keeper, is sympathetic. He takes

Klari and seeks to make her a good Jew. After two weeks of the Talmud the Recorder discovers a second error. Klari is not a Jew, but a Hungarian born of Protestant parents. Reluctantly Klari goes back to being a Hungarian Catholic and Andreas is forgiven his snobbishness.

STRANGERS AT HOME

(11 performances)

A comedy in three acts by Charles Divine. Produced by M. S. and G. S. Schlesinger at the Longacre Theatre, New York, September 14, 1934.

Cast of characters—

Mrs. Crosby	Eleanor Hicks
Russ Crosby	Philippe de Lacy
Mr. Crosby	Clyde Franklin
Aunt Phœbe	Marie Bruce
Jean Crosby	Joan Wheeler
Kay Crosby	Katherine Emery
Mrs. Humiston	Maud Durand
Stuart Mason	Robert Henderson
Tom Gibbs	William Post, Jr.
Mr. Humiston	Frederick Malcolm
Mrs. Fowler	Helen Ray
Mr. Fowler	Franklyn Munnell
Mr. Whittaker	Harold Grau
Helen Scott	Maxine King
Ethel Yates	Nancy Haswin
Mrs. Newton	Aline McDermott
Joe Stafford	John Deering

Acts I, II and III.—The Crosbys' Living Room, Kingston, N. Y. Staged by Walter Hart; setting by P. Dodd Ackerman.

The Crosbys are doing reasonably well when Mrs. Crosby is fired with an ambition to accommodate tourists with lodgings and make a little extra money. As a result of a growing avariciousness she drives her daughter Jean to New York, where she has a sad experience, and brings her husband to the verge of nervous prostration. The older daughter, Kay, loses a snobbish fiancé, but that is for the best. She acquires Tom Gibbs, the most attractive of the bachelor tourists.

FIRST EPISODE
(First called College Sinners)

(40 performances)

A comedy in three acts by Terence Rattigan and Philip Heimann. Produced by the Messrs. Shubert at the Ritz Theatre, New York, September 17, 1934.

Cast of characters—

Albert Arnold.....................................Max Adrian
Philip Kahn....................................Staats Cotsworth
Joan Taylor....................................Gerrie Worthing
Tony Wodehouse..................................John Halloran
David Lister................................Patrick Waddington
Margot Gresham..................................Leona Maricle
James..Stanley Harrison
A Butler..T. C. Dunham
    Acts I, II and III.—Living room in an undergraduates' lodging
house and at the King's Head hotel.
    Staged by Haddon Mason; setting by Rollo Wayne.

Tony Wodehouse plays Antony opposite the Cleopatra of the
beautiful London actress, Margot Gresham, invited down from
the city to take part in Oxford theatricals. Tony falls in love
with Margot and she with him, though she is ten years his senior.
David Lister, Tony's roommate, tries to break up the affair.
Tony tires of Margot after a few week-ends and retires of his
own accord. Margot, catching David off the reservation with a
town girl, reports him to the proctors and he is expelled. She
has hoped thus to win Tony back. No win.

ERRANT LADY

(40 performances)

A comedy in three acts by Nat N. Dorfman. Produced by
Harry Albert at the Fulton Theatre, New York, September 17,
1934.

Cast of characters—

Stella Kirchwey..........................Mary Horne Morrison
John...................................Reynolds Denniston
Clara Jessup..............................Leona Powers
Ralph Jessup................................Averell Harris
Ned Kirchwey..............................Dodson Mitchell
Sylvia Howard..............................Helen Walpole
Frank Howard..............................King Calder
Victor Rachmananov........................Donald Randolph
Walter Slocum..............................Stuart Fox
    Acts I, II and III.—The Jessup Living Room, Westchester.
    Staged by Priestly Morrison; setting by Victor Graziano.

Clara Jessup is a dominant and flighty lady. She dominates
her husband and most of her neighbors. When her daughter reports that she is about to divorce her husband and marry a Russian named Rachmananov Clara saves the situation by taking
over the Russian. This involves her in a threatened suit for
divorce on her husband's part. Clara is cured of her dominancy
and her husband goes duck shooting.

KILL THAT STORY

(117 performances)

A comedy in three acts by Harry Madden and Philip Dunning.
Produced by Abbott-Dunning, Inc., at the Booth Theatre, New
York, August 29, 1934; withdrawn September 8, 1934; resumed
September 17, 1934.

Cast of characters—

First Bell Boy	James Lane
Frank Martin	Buford Armitage
Second Bell Boy	Pedro Galvan
Sam Gersten	William Foran
Bayard Colton	William Lynn
Spike Taylor	Matt Briggs
Joe Blake	Oliver Barbour
John T. Horrigan	Alfred Webster
Paul Simpson	Royal Dana Tracy
Agatha	Claire Carleton
Duke Devlin	James Bell
Waiter	Fred Kaufman
Margaret McGuire	Emily Lowry
Millicent	Eleanor Audley
Emily	Joyce Arling
Joe McGuire	Wyrley Birch
J. Goodington Cartwright	Thomas F. Tracey
Mitzi Gray	Gloria Grafton
Detective	George Carleton

Acts I, II and III.—Parlor of a Hotel Suite in a Large American
City.

Staged by George Abbott; setting by Stewart Chaney.

Duke Devlin had befriended a stenographer working on the
same paper with him when she got into trouble. The girl kills
herself, leaving a note of thanks for Duke. Mrs. Devlin, accepting the note as evidence of an affair, divorces Duke. Duke, refusing to accept his dismissal without a fight, gets evidence that
his crooked publisher, Spike Taylor, was responsible for the
stenographer's condition. He follows Spike to an advertising convention where he meets the former Mrs. Devlin (Margaret Mc-
Guire) and finally forces Taylor to confess his guilt to her on pain
of exposing certain of his crooked newspaper deals, in one of
which Taylor planned to harm Margaret's father.

ALLEY CAT

(8 performances)

A comedy in three acts by Alan Dinehart and Samuel Shipman, from an original script by Lawrence Pohle. Produced by
Margaret Hewes at the 48th Street Theatre, New York, September 17, 1934.

Cast of characters—

Elsie Foster...Evelyn Varden
Carl Vinal...Alan Dinehart
Henry Foster..Harry Gribbon
Jean Wales...Audrey Christie
The Drunk..Frank Jaquet
Tony...Royal Beal
Linda Vinal..Kay Strozzi
May...Mozelle Brittonne
Doctor..Edward Broadley
          Acts I, II and III.—Top Floor of an Old House in Greenwich Village.
          Staged by Mr. Dinehart; setting by Tom Adrian Cracraft.

Carl Vinal, a financier out of funds and disgusted with life, hires a Greenwich Village room in which to turn on the gas. Jean Wales, a dress designer without a job, running away from a fat drunk, bursts into Vinal's room in time to turn off the gas and give the would-be suicide other things to think about. Jean and Vinal are getting along swell when Carl's wife notifies him that he is the father of a son. Carl thinks perhaps he should go back to his wife and his son, but wife was just fooling. It wasn't Carl's son after all. He goes on with Jean.

A SHIP COMES IN

(38 performances)

A drama in three acts by Joseph Anthony. Produced by Richard Herndon in association with John C. Mayer at the Morosco Theatre, New York, September 19, 1934.

Cast of characters—

Mr. and Mrs. Jenkins......................... { Edwin Cooper
                                             { Elizabeth Farrar
Johann...Frank Manning
Dr. Marvin.......................................William Packer
Dr. Sawyer.......................................Bjorn Koefoed
Mrs. Charlotte Strawbridge.........................Nana Bryant
Oblanitcheff.......................................Boris Korlin
Dr. Victor Bard...................................Jacob Ben-Ami
Dr. Carl Brenner.................................Manart Kippen
Stella Rickert.......................................Ann Lubowe
H. Gordon Mortimer..............................Calvin Thomas
Blanche Mortimer...............................Virginia Stevens
Ship's Steward......................................Arthur Row
Ship's Officer.....................................Rudolf Brooks
          Act I.—Scene 1—Room in Donau Coffee House, Vienna. 2—Dr. Bard's Office, Vienna. Act II.—Scene 1—Promenade Deck, S.S. "Manhattan." 2—Promenade Deck. 3—Dr. Bard's Cabin. 4—Promenade Deck. Act III.—Scene 1—Dr. Brenner's Cabin. 2—Salon of Mortimers' Suite. 3—Dr. Bard's Cabin. 4—Promenade Deck.
          Staged by Augustin Duncan; settings by Herbert Ward and Walter Harvey.

Dr. Victor Bard is the most famous of Vienna's psychologists H. Gordon Mortimer is richer than rich. Mortimer proposes to

endow a chain of psychological clinics in America and gives Dr.
Bard the job. On the way over in the steamer Blanche Mortimer,
H. Gordon's restless niece, forces her way into the Bard stateroom hoping to awaken the doctor's love. He gives her an emetic
in her whisky and that's that. But Millionaire Mortimer thinks
the worst and is about to withdraw his million. Then it is proved
that the great psychologist himself suffers from a neurosis. He is
afraid to be alone with a woman. Convinced that he had wronged
the psychologist Mortimer agrees to go through with his original
offer.

THE RED CAT

(13 performances)

A drama in three acts by Rudolph Lothar and Hans Adler,
adapted by Jessie Ernst. Produced by A. H. Woods, in association with the 20th Century Pictures Corporation, at the Broadhurst Theatre, New York, September 19, 1934.

Cast of characters—

Josephine	Florence Edney
Gabrielle	Marianne Davis
Tillie	Lorraine Hayes
Pauline	Edith Trivers
Baron Fernand Cassini	Francis Lister
Mimi	Tamara Geva
Perishot	Wylie Adams
Eugene Charlier	Francis Lister
Morrisot	Barnett Parker
Marquis Rene De Lac	Rex O'Malley
Henri Beneffe	Herbert Yost
John Charteris	Porter Hall
Genevieve (Baroness Cassini)	Ruth Weston
François	Gerald Oliver Smith
Second Servant	Lewis Dayton
Monsieur Paulet	Frederick Graham
Victor	Louis Tanno

Act I.—Scene 1—Dressing Rooms of "The Red Cat" Cabaret. 2—
Stage Box. Act II.—Reception Room at the Palais Cassini.
Staged by Bertram Harrison; settings by P. Dodd Ackerman.

Eugene Charlier is giving so amazingly perfect an impersona-
tion of the Baron Fernand Cassini, the great Parisian banker, in
the floor show at the Red Cat cabaret that the Baroness Cassini,
seeing the show, is quite stirred and insists on meeting Charlier.
A few days later, while the Baron is in London trying to raise a
loan to save the bank, a meeting is called in Paris which he positively must attend. His friends engage Charlier to take the
banker's place for twenty-four hours. This includes sleeping arrangements at the Cassini home, which interests the Baroness.
The Baron returns suddenly. The actor disappears suddenly.
But does the Baroness know? Even next morning she can't be
quite sure.

THE GREAT WALTZ

(298 performances)

A musical romance in two parts based on libretti by Dr. A. M. Willner, Heinz Reichert, Ernst Marischka, Caswell Garth; adapted by Moss Hart, lyrics by Desmond Carter; music by Johann Strauss, father and son. Produced by Max Gordon at the Center Theatre, New York, September 22, 1934.

Cast of characters—

Greta	Jessie Busley
Ebeseder	Ernest Cossart
Leopold (Poldi)	Dennis Noble
Therese (Resi)	Marion Claire
Johann Strauss, Jr. (Schani)	Guy Robertson
Augustina	Ruby Asquith
Lottie	Josephine McKendrick
Paul Heinrich	Lew Christensen
Hans Heinrich	Harold Christensen
Countess Olga Baranskaja	Marie Burke
Wilhelm	Richard Lambart
Lili	Frances Hayes
Franzi	Tanya Sanina
Tini	Diana Walker
Mali	Sandra Walters
Sini	Rosalynd Hutner
Mitzi	Nina Dean
Nini	Ruth Clayton
Betti	Dorothy Forsyth
Karl Hirsch	Ambrose Manning
Johann Strauss, Sr.	H. Reeves-Smith
Kathi Lanner	Alexandra Danilova
Dommayer	Solly Ward
Captain Boris Androff	Ralph Magelssen
Dreschler	Robert C. Fischer
Hartkopf	Richie Ling
Franz Ludwig	Charles Romano
Gretchen Ludwig	Aphie James
Lieutenant Carl Boch	Ralph Glover
Captain Hal Fredrich	Charles Brokaw
Lieutenant Ferdinand Holmann	Edgar Allan

Parts I and II.—Ebeseder's pastry shop and gardens, Dommayer's Gardens, Vienna.

Staged and supervised by Hassard Short; dances by Albertina Rasch; settings by Albert Johnson.

Johann Strauss the elder is waltz king in Vienna. Johann Strauss the younger is a hopeful young man who has written a waltz or two of his own, but can get no chance to play them. Father's lack of faith, inspired by father's jealousy, blocks the way. Comes the Countess Olga, an influential Russian lady. She evolves a plan. Has Father Strauss practically kidnaped the night of the opening of Dommayer's Gardens. Young Johann is there and gets a chance to play a little thing of his called "The Beautiful Blue Danube." A new waltz king is crowned shortly thereafter. He marries Therese and they are happy. Father goes on thinking what he thinks of the new-fangled music.

THE DISTAFF SIDE

(First engagement 153 performances. Return 24. Total 177.)

A comedy in three acts by John Van Druten. Produced by Dwight Deere Wiman and Auriol Lee at the Booth Theatre, New York, September 25, 1934.

Cast of characters—

Mrs. Venables	Mildred Natwick
Mrs. Millward	Sybil Thorndike
Mrs. Frobisher	Estelle Winwood
Mrs. Fletcher	Viola Roache
Roland	Bretaigne Windust
Alex	Viola Keats
Christopher Venables	Charles Bryant
Therese Venables	Lillian Brennard Tonge
Miss Spicer	Hilda Plowright
Rose	Doris Hall
Toby Chegwidden	Clifford Evans
Charles Hubbard	Charles Campbell
Gilbert Baize	Austin Fairman

Acts I, II and III.—Sitting Room and Bedroom in Mrs. Millward's House in St. John's Wood, London.

Staged by Auriol Lee; settings by Raymond Sovey.

See page 325.

SMALL MIRACLE

(117 performances)

A melodrama in three acts by Norman Krasna. Produced by Courtney Burr at the Golden Theatre, New York, September 26, 1934.

Cast of characters—

Carl Barrett, Jr.	Edward Crandall
Tony Mako	Joseph Spurin-Calleia
Joseph Taft	Joseph King
Ma	Eva Condon
Herman	William Wadsworth
William S. Johnson	G. Albert Smith
Eddie	Myron McCormick
Mae Danish	Elspeth Eric
Mac Mason	Wyrley Birch
Helen	Fraye Gilbert
Repair Man	James Lane
Sylvia Temple	Ilka Chase
Anna	Lucille Strudwick
Kitty	Jean Bellows
Twelve-Year-Old Girl	Edna Hagen
Stanley Madison	George Lambert
Mrs. Madison	Violet Barney
Donald Madison	Hitous Gray
Frank	Juan Varro
George Nelson	Allan Hale
Captain Seaver	Robert Middlemas
Healy	Herbert Duffy
Anderson	Owen Martin
First Girl	Helen Gardner

Second Girl..Nancy Vane
    Acts I, II and III.—Lounge of the 43rd Street Theatre, New York.
    Staged by George Abbott; setting by Boris Aronson.

Sections of an audience are gathering in the lounge of the 43rd Street Theatre, New York, for the performance of a play upstairs. Tony Mako, prisoner, is handcuffed to Joseph Taft, detective. They are on their way to Colorado, where Tony is to be hung for murder. Carl Barrett, Jr., has a rendezvous with Sylvia Temple, wife of a broker. Mae Danish, head usher, is stealing time while the performance is on to remind Eddie, the coatroom boy, that she is expecting him to raise $200 to help her through her trouble, or marry her. Helen, Eddie's honest fiancée, is determined to help him escape from Mae, even if she has to sacrifice herself to her employer to raise the $200. Before the performance is over Tony Mako escapes, shoots another crook who had sold him out, and is caught and killed. Tony's victim is Mae's husband, which frees Eddie. Helen has sacrificed herself needlessly. The Barrett-Temple affair is exposed and broken up, and the audience goes home.

DREAM CHILD

(24 performances)

A comedy in three acts by J. C. Nugent. Produced by Albert Ingalls, Jr., and the Westport Country Playhouse at the Vanderbilt Theatre, New York, September 27, 1934.

Cast of characters—

Elizabeth..Sara Floyd
Robert Jones, Jr.......................................Alan Bunce
"King Tut" Jones.......................................J. C. Nugent
Attie Brant..Helen Carew
Elsie Harper...Gale Huntington
Elmer Harper...John C. Brownell
Laurette Harper..Maida Reade
Mrs. Pitt..Alice Belmore Cliffe
Ted..David Morris
Molly..Jean Briggs
Gray...John G. Bertin
Kay Carmel...Ruth Nugent
    Acts I and III.—Jones' Living Room at Eastville, New Jersey.
Act II.—Parlor of Mrs. Pitt's Boarding House in Downtown New York.
    Staged by Julius Evans; settings by Stewart Chaney.

"King Tut" Jones, an honest real estater of Eastville, N. J., has hoped that his son Robert might get a chance at the romance that eluded his father. When he sees Robert about to marry the girl across the street and settle down to the usual hum-drum small town existence he is desperate. He induces Robert to go to New York on a bust; introduces him to the old theatrical boarding house where he (father) had met a dream girl. Robert's adventure is similarly interesting. He meets Kay Carmel, an artist, who, being independent, has been looking long for the right man to be the father of her child. She selects Robert— and then disappears. Years later Kay visits Eastville. Robert is married and settled. But not very happy. Kay goes away again.

MERRILY WE ROLL ALONG

(155 performances)

A play in three acts by George S. Kaufman and Moss Hart. Produced by Sam H. Harris at the Music Box Theatre, New York, September 29, 1934.

Cast of characters—

David Haskell	Gilbert Squarey
Julia Glenn	Mary Philips
Rosamond Ogden	Mary Howes
Val Burnett	Jack Edwards
Albert Ogden	Grant Mills
Sam Frankl	Herbert Steiner
Lady Patricia Dorson	Mary Heberden
Laura Nash	Jacqueline Logan
Ivy Carroll	Murial Williams
Richard Niles	Kenneth MacKenna
Everett Nash	Wilfrid Seagram
Cyrus Winthrop	Charles Halton
Althea Royce	Jessie Royce Landis
Butler	Edward Loud
Maid	Peggy Bancroft
A Man Lunching	John Cosby
A Woman Lunching	Otis Schaefer
Waiter	Burton Mallory
Headwaiter	George Jackson
Two Very Young Girls	{ Patricia Palmer { Betty Reynolds
P. J. Morton	George Alison
Jonathan Crale	Walter Abel
Ito	Biacouren Yoshiwara
George Niles	Harold Moffet
Molly	Beatrice Blinn
Chief Court Attendant	Leo Kennedy

Women Leaving the Trial: Elsa Ryan, Jenny Mac, Elizabeth Kennedy, Connie Madison, Doris Eaton, Patricia Allen, Geraldine Wall

Reporters	{ William MacFadden { John Kennedy
Mrs. Murney	Leslie Bingham
Helen	Adrienne Marden
Richardson	Charles Engel
Mr. Murney	Granville Bates
The Head Photographer	Louis Cruger
Wertheimer	George Parsons
Buddy Murney	Robert Griffith
A Captain of Waiters	James Seeley
Bell-Boy	Robert Stone
Della	Martha Brown
Harry Nixon	Malcolm Duncan

Sid Kramer..George McKay
Mrs. Riley..Cecilia Loftus
Janet Newcomb....................................Chouteau Dyer
Among the Guests: Otis Schaefer, Geraldine Wall, Henry Ephron, Irving Schneider
Courtroom Crowd, Party Guests, Students, etc.: Ariane Allen, Joan Adrian, Roaine Baker, Elsa Beamish, Elaine Blauvelt, Isis Brinn, Joan Brewster, Eleanor Whitney, Annette DuBois, Jean Ellyn, Gloria Gill, Dorothy Groman, Claire Greenwood, Sonya Jaffe, Helen Kim, Joan Marston, Annette Robinson, Hattie Ross, Toni Sorel, Emily Winston, Robert Adams, Paul Benson, Robert Bowen, Dan Carey, Cliff Furst, Henry Gallagher, Herbert Greenberg, John Hampshire, Lawrence Hutt, William Kruger, Howard Lane, Charles La Rue, Carl Rose, Robert Russell, Michael Stirling, Richard Stringfellow, Hudson Shotwell, Morris Tepper, Frank Waldecker.

Act I.—Scene 1—Home of Richard Niles, Long Island. 1934. 2—Restaurant Le Coq D'Or. 1927. 3—Niles' Apartment. 1926. Act II.—Scene 1—Jonathan Crale's Studio. 1925. 2—Court House Corridor. 1924. 3—Althea Royce's Apartment. 1923. Act III.—Scene 1—Living Room of the Murneys. 1922. 2—Madison Square Park. 1918. 3—College Chapel. 1916.

Staged by George S. Kaufman; settings by Jo Mielziner; costuming by John Hambleton.

See page 203.

SPRING SONG

(40 performances)

A play in three acts by Bella and Samuel Spewack. Produced by Max Gordon at the Morosco Theatre, New York, October 1, 1934.

Cast of characters—

Bessie..Angela Jacobs
Tillie Solomon....................................Frieda Altman
Girl...Sylvia Manners
Young Man.......................................Garson Kanin
Freiberg.......................................Joseph Greenwald
Dr. Schneider.....................................Sam Mann
Mrs. Blatt.......................................Bertha Walden
Birdie Blau.......................................Anne Loeb
Sidney Kurtz.....................................Norman Stuart
Florrie Solomon.............................Francine Larrimore
Mrs. Solomon....................................Helen Zelinskaya
Mrs. Faber....................................Yetta Schoengold
Delivery Man...............................Morris Strassberg
Milton..Sam Levene
Mrs. Ruben....................................Malka Kornstein
Mrs. Birnbaum....................................Alma Ross

Act I.—Mrs. Solomon's Stand on the East Side. Acts II and III. —Dining Room of the Solomons' Apartment.
Staged by Eddie Sobol; settings by Jo Mielziner.

Florrie Solomon, denied the comforting association of her own young man, an absent salesman, turns for company one moonlight night to the fiancé of her sister Tillie. Tillie's beau is a studious youth named Sidney Kurtz. He, too, is restless and of a mind in moonlight to follow recklessly where Florrie leads. This leads to a seduction and later a good deal of misery as Florrie

discovers her approaching motherhood and her growing dislike of
Sidney. Mrs. Solomon, deeply religious, insists on Florrie marrying Sidney to cleanse her soul and give her child a name. Florrie
later dies in childbirth.

THE FIRST LEGION

(112 performances)

A drama in three acts by Emmet Lavery. Produced by Bert
Lytell and Phil Green at the 46th Street Theatre, New York,
October 1, 1934.

Cast of characters—

Rev. Paul Duquesne, S.J.	William Ingersoll
Rev. Charles I. Keene, S.J.	Philip Wood
Dr. Peter Morell	Harland Tucker
Rev. Robert Stuart, S.J.	Thomas Findlay
Rev. Edward Quarterman, S.J.	Charles Coburn
Rev. Mark Ahern, S.J.	Bert Lytell
Rev. Thomas Rawleigh, S.J.	John Litel
Rev. John Fulton, S.J.	Harold Moulton
Rt. Rev. Monsignor Michael Carey	Whitford Kane
Rev. José Maria Sierra, S.J.	Pedro de Cordoba
Jimmie Magee	Frankie Thomas

Novices and Choir Played by: Charles Danforth, John J. Williams,
Thomas Ewell, Joseph Fitzmaurice, Joseph Mitchell, Jules
Schmidt, Lester Atwell, Bruce Parish, Robert Payson, Harry
Lane, John Foster, Tom Monahan, Raymond Wolber, Jerome
Thor, Robert Barrett, Arthur Zwerling, Rob Wood, Wayne Nel-
son, Frank Ray and Donald Wilson.

Act I.—Scenes 1 and 3—Community Room of St. Gregory's Noviti-
ate. 2—Father Fulton's Room. Act II.—Scenes 1, 2 and 4—Community Room. 3—Father Rawleigh's Room. 5—Chapel. Act III.—
Scenes 1, 2 and 3—Community Room.
Staged by Anthony Brown; settings by Edward Eddy.

The Revs. Thomas Rawleigh and John Fulton, after twenty
years of loyal service in the order of Jesuits, find themselves questioning the wisdom of having given up the world to serve God.
Their associate, Father Mark Ahern, has begun to have doubts
as to the stability of his faith, particularly his faith in miracles.
For a time the apparently miraculous healing of Father José
Sierra, who had been paralyzed but arose from his bed, composes
their doubts. In the confessional the physician of St. Gregory's,
Dr. Peter Morell, declares that the healing of Father Sierra can
easily be accounted for by men of medicine. Father Ahern is
about to leave the order and return to the world when Jimmie
Magee, 12-year-old victim of infantile paralysis, comes to St.
Gregory's as to a shrine and is healed. A great renewal of faith
on the part of all the doubters follows.

STEVEDORE

(64 performances)

A play in three acts by Paul Peters and George Sklar. Revived by The Theatre Union, Inc., at the Civic Repertory Theatre, New York, October 1, 1934.

Cast of characters—

Florrie	Millicent Green
Bill Larkin	David Lesan
Freddy Reynolds	Robert Caille
Sergeant	Jack Daley
Bobo Valentine	Carrington Lewis
Rag Williams	Tom Mosley
Angrum	Ray Yeates
Lonnie Thompson	Jack Carter
Joe Crump	G. Harry Bolden
Steve	Robert Simpson
Binnie	Abbie Mitchell
Ruby Oxley	Edna Thomas
Sam Oxley	Al Watts
Uncle Cato	William C. Elkins
Jim Veal	Leigh Whipper
Blacksnake	Canada Lee
Walcott	Thomas Coffin Cooke
Mike	Robert Caille
Detective	Donald Black
Lem Morris	Martin Wolfson
Marty Fox	Donald Black
Al Regan	Robert Simpson
Charley Freeman	Irving Gordon
Mitch	David Lesan
Pons	Robert Caille
Cop	Donald Black
Bertha Williams	Juanita Hall
Mose Venable	William C. Elkins
Victor	Arthur Bruce

Neighbors, Wharf Hands, Policemen and Mitch's Gang: Roy Gillespie, Dewey Armstrong, Wm. Myers, I. Peters, Cal Bellaver, Henry May, Emily Patterson, Esther Hall, Annis Davis.

Act I.—Scene 1—Backyard. 2—Police Station. 3—Binnie's Lunchroom. 4—Office of Oceanic Stevedore Co. Act II.—Scene 1—Union Headquarters. 2—Stuyvesant Dock. 3—Binnie's Lunch-room. Act III.—Scene 1—Bertha Williams' Attic. 2—Courtyard.

Staged by Michael Blankfort and Irving Gordon; settings by S. Syrjala.

"Stevedore" was produced originally at the Civic Repertory Theatre in April, 1934, and ran through July.

DIVIDED BY THREE

(31 performances)

A play in three acts by Margaret Leech and Beatrice Kaufman. Produced by Guthrie McClintic at the Ethel Barrymore Theatre, New York, October 2, 1934.

Cast of characters—

Miss Brooks...Vera G. Hurst
Teddy Parrish......................................James Stewart
Irene Potsford.....................................Hedda Hopper
Robert Parrish....................................Hunter Gardner
Hermine...Gertrude Davis
Lila..Judith Anderson
Hudson...Arthur Chatterton
Hugh Faraday......................................James Rennie
Cordelia Wetherell................................Hancey Castle
Jed Hyman...Tenen Holtz
    Acts I and III.—Mrs. Parrish's Sitting Room in the Parrishes'
Duplex Apartment in the East Sixties, New York City. Act II.—
Drawing Room.
    Staged by Guthrie McClintic; settings by Donald Oenslager.

Lila Parrish, wife of Robert and mother of Teddy Parrish, has accepted Hugh Faraday as her lover. After successfully hiding their love for some years they are threatened with exposure the time young Teddy is ready to announce his engagement to Cordelia Wetherell and likewise his association with others in the establishment of a publishing business. Cordelia, jealous of Teddy's devotion to his mother, reveals the scandal to him. The young man is utterly crushed by the revelation, contemplates numerous avenues of escape, but is finally induced to compromise by leaving his parents' home and going on his own, with forgiveness for Cordelia and pity for his mother.

ROLL, SWEET CHARIOT

(7 performances)

A symphonic play in four scenes by Paul Green; incidental music by Dolphe Martin. Produced by Margaret Hewes at the Cort Theatre, New York, October 2, 1934.

Cast of characters—

Quiviene Lockley.................................Eleanor Wallace
Willie Lockley....................................Lucius Carter, Jr.
Zeb Vance Lockley.................................Billy Andrews
Milly Wilson......................................Dorothea Archie
Bantam Wilson.....................................Luoneal Mason
Tom Sterling.......................................Ralf Coleman
Ed. Uzzell.......................................Lionel Monogas
Levin Farrow.......................................Frank Wilson
Seeny Gray..Pearl Gaines
Bad Eye Smith......................................Philip Carter
"John Henry"......................................Warren Coleman
Jim Parr..Fred Miller
Belle Utley.......................................Lillian Norris
Sport Womack.....................................Willard DeCosta
Dode Wilson..Lucian Ayers
Doodle Wilson......................................Lloyd Horton
Sudie Wilson......................................Rose McClendon
Flossie Tucker................................Marguerite Cartwright
First Guard.......................................John Morrissey
Second Guard......................................Bigelow Sayre

Chain Gang: Ralph Northern, Teddy Vaughn, Herbert Ellis, Joe
   Northern, Edward Pugh, William Hardaway, Billy Jones, Jay
   Thomas, Sam Tolson, Leonard Brown, Johnny Johnston.
Orchestral Choir, Conducted by Dolphe Martin: Rosalie King, Annie
   Wilson, Leona Avery, Maud Simmons, Sadie McGill, Dora Ba-
   cotte, Dora Thompson, Zelda Shelton, Ethel Hardie Smith, Olga
   Maillard, Rufus Brent, Mulford Lee, Thomas Anderson, Bobby
   Robinson, Lester Robinson, Albert McCoy, Paul Smelley, Arthur
   McLean, Edward Batten.
Baritone Soloist....................................Joseph James
Clarinet...Samuel Harris
Tuba..Virginia Criscuoli
Tympani..Everett L. Westcott
   Scenes 1, 2, 3 and 4—Potter's Field, A Negro Village Somewhere
in the South.
   Staged by Margaret Hewes, Emjo Basshe and Stanley Pratt; set-
tings by Tom Adrian Cracraft.

A "symphonic play of the Negro people," depicting the general moral and physical disintegration of Potter's Field, a shanty
town populated by Negroes in the South. A series of dramatic
episodes acted against a background of choral and orchestral
music.

CONTINENTAL VARIETIES

(77 performances)

A vaudeville revue in two parts. Presented by Arch Selwyn
and Harold B. Franklin at the Little Theatre, New York, October
3, 1934.

Principals engaged—

Lucienne Boyer	Vicente Escudero
Lydia Chaliapine	Raphael
Emma Runitch	De Roze
Carmita	Nikita Balieff
Iza Volpin Orchestra	Sacre Monte Gypsies

Mlle. Boyer, famed French diseuse, sang ten character songs,
including "Les Gueuses," "Attends!" "Viens Danser Quand
Meme," "Moi, J'Crache Dans l'Eau," "Parlez-moi d'Amour,"
"D'Amour en Amour," "Parle-moi d'Autre Chose," "Je ne Savais
Pas," "Si Petite," "Prenez Mes Roses." Escudero, Carmita and
a band of Sacre Monte Gypsies gave a series of dances. Raphael
played the concertina, Mesdames Chaliapine and Brunitch sang,
De Roze mysteriously poured a variety of drinks from a single
pitcher of pure water and Balieff served as master of ceremonies.

SPRING FRESHET

(12 performances)

A play in three acts by Owen Davis. Produced by Lee Shubert at the Plymouth Theatre, New York, October 4, 1934.

Cast of characters—

Isabel Levenseller......................................Esther Dale
Sylvia Merrill....................................Francesca Bruning
Clementina Lynch............................Elizabeth Patterson
Wesley Levenseller.............................Owen Davis, Jr.
Wade Hamlin....................................Alexander Clark
Lydia Mundy.....................................Eleanor Powers
Myrtle Hodge.......................................Lynn Beranger
Betty Eldridge......................................Viola Frayne
Ned Levenseller....................................Richard Whorf
Miss Abbie......................................Julia MacMahon
Miss Minnie.....................................Sydney Shields
Miss Ella...Leona Hogarth
Judge Ira Levenseller............................Thurston Hall
Rev. Doctor Brewster.............................Lionel Adams
Sue Colby.......................................Margaret Callahan

Acts I, II and III.—The Levensellers' "Sitting Room" in Bucksport, Maine.

Staged by Owen Davis; setting by Rollo Wayne.

Isabel Levenseller, matriarch of the Levenseller family of Bucksport, Maine, for two generations, determines that her grandson Ned shall marry Betty Eldredge and carry on the family name. Ned loves his distant cousin, Sylvia Merrill, and she him, but this love is crushed. Grandma Levenseller also remains ruler of the family after Ned's wife tries to take command. Ned and Betty quarrel and there is no hope of Levenseller issue. Not until Sue Colby, a town girl, dies in childbirth and names Ned as the father of her infant son. Ned confesses and Grandma Levenseller decides to rear the illegitimate Levenseller legitimately, that the family may go on.

YESTERDAY'S ORCHIDS

(3 performances)

A play in three acts by Henry Rosendahl. Produced by Vanhill Productions at the Fulton Theatre, New York, October 5, 1934.

Cast of characters—

Jean Standing....................................Helene Calahan
Sidney Farrow.......................................Ann Whitney
David Kinney....................................Carleton Young
Fred Morgan...Royal Stout
Caroline...Laura Bowman
Peony Rockwell.......................................Kay Linaker
Esmond Rockwell...............................William Balfour
Charlie Quince......................................Grant Erwin
Dee Dee Lawlor..................................Charles Dingle
Electrician.......................................Richard Reeves

Prologue—Telephone Room in Basement of New York *Times* Building. Act I.—Studio Apartment, New York. Act II.—Living Room. Act III.—Porch in Westchester.

Staged by Robert Ober; settings by P. Dodd Ackerman.

Sidney Farrow, cheat, after having accepted everything from numerous patrons, finally falls deeply in love with David Kinney and is blessed with a wedding ring when the claims of all rivals are adjusted in conference.

THE CHINESE NIGHTINGALE

(8 performances)

A fantasy in seven scenes by Hans Schmiedel and Lasar Galpern based on a Hans Christian Andersen story; adapted by James L. A. Burrell; music by Alan Shulman. Produced by The American Children's Theatre at the Theatre of Young America, New York, October 5, 1934.

Cast of characters—

```
Emperor.........................................Fuller Mellish
Captain of the Guards............................Sidney Packer
Umbrella Bearer..................................Baruch Lumet
Master of Ceremonies.............................Blake Scott
Prime Minister...................................Cooksey Curtiss
Zoölogist........................................Percival Vivian
Astronomer.......................................Lester Lonergan, Jr.
Physician........................................Oscar Stirling
Poet.............................................Rolla Nuckles
Kitchen Maid.....................................Flora Le Breton
Cook.............................................Herbert Fisher
First Court Lady.................................Vivian Gieson
Second Court Lady................................Frederica Going
Third Court Lady.................................Ruth Vivian
Fourth Court Lady................................Eugenia Tucker
Fifth Court Lady.................................Jacqueline Hoyt
Japanese Herald..................................Frederick Leland
First Japanese Doctor............................Richard Allen
Second Japanese Doctor...........................Howard Bird
Third Japanese Doctor............................Jerry Sylvon
Fourth Japanese Doctor...........................Jane Oakley
First Soldier....................................Richard Allen
Second Soldier...................................Howard Bird
```
   Staged by Lasar Galpern and Percival Vivian; settings by Serge Soudeikine; masks and marionettes by Remo Bufano.

An ancient Emperor of China is informed by his friends the Japanese that the nightingale is a bird of good omen and sweet song. None of his stupid court ever saw or heard a nightingale. Only the little kitchen maid knows where one may be found. She takes the Emperor there and he is so delighted he makes her a Nightingale Ambassadress and introduces her to the court, even if she does smell a little of onions. Japan sends the Emperor a golden nightingale that can be wound up. This drives the real nightingale back to the forest and the Emperor is like to die of disappointment until the kitchen maid brings the bird back.

DANCE WITH YOUR GODS

(9 performances)

A drama in three acts by Kenneth Perkins. Produced by Laurence Schwab at the Mansfield Theatre, New York, October 6, 1934.

Cast of characters—

William Simpson....................................Oliver Barbour
Bartender..O. J. Vanasse
A Tourist..Muriel Robert
Another Tourist....................................John Gordon
Jacques Boyean.....................................Ben Smith
Maitre Livers......................................Rex Ingram
Mother Bouche......................................Georgette Harvey
Baptiste...Barclay Trigg
Amos Juvenal.......................................Chas. D. Waldron
Ninon Juvenal......................................Pauline Moore
Jeffries...Dewey Brown
Maitre Bowles......................................Joseph Scott
Maitre Buffon......................................Al Stokes
Madame Chou..Olive Burgoyne
Madame De La Jones.................................Musa Williams
A Quadronne Girl...................................Lena Horne
Drummers: Jacques Vanderhouse, Louis Broges, Cuto Beauchamp, Iodilo Coker, Moses Mainns, Daifmore Martin, John Antiga.
Miscellaneous Negro Characters enacted by Edna Barr, Teddy Brown, Beatrice Elegore, Marjorie Fowlkes, Amelia Benskina, Ethel Purbello, Anita Bogart, Olive Gordon, Ella Smith, Eleanor Hines, Althea Weston, Lulu King, Peter Clark, Charles Hollis, Archer Savage, William Bodkin, George Hayes, Waddell Saunders, Grayson Walker, Clifton Lamb, Webster Elkins, Cecil Cunningham, Joseph Maxwell.
Act I.—Scene 1—Saloon and Street Corner Near the Parish Prison. 2—Front Yard of a Negro Cabin. 3—Main Hall of the Juvenal Manse, on the Outskirts of New Orleans. Act II.—Scene 1—Interior of a Cotton Warehouse. 2—Juvenal Manse. Act III.—Scene 1—Ninon's Bedroom. 2—Warehouse.
Staged by Robert B. Sinclair; settings by Donald Oenslager.

Jacques Boyean is showing a newspaper friend from the North around New Orleans. They come to a saloon in the Negro quarter and hear talk of old Mother Bouche, who has the power to put a voodoo curse on practically anybody. Jacques, urged on by the doubting Yankee, would test the Bouche power and demands that she curse the owner of a name he has taken casually from an old billboard, convinced no such character ever lived. Mother Bouche works her spell, swearing she will transfer the black soul of a recently executed murderer to the body of a living man who shall be the instrument of the forces of evil. Suddenly Jacques learns that the name he has chosen is that of the Juvenals, a fine old Southern gentleman living with a sweetly innocent daughter just home from a convent. He goes to warn them, is himself overcome by the voodoo curse. Now he takes on the habits of a tough Negro, threatens the honor of the girl and, when thwarted, runs off with her. Back at Mother Bouche's he is having his way until the Yankee bursts in and sets matters straight.

A SLEEPING CLERGYMAN

(40 performances)

A play in two acts by James Bridie. Produced by The Theatre Guild, Inc., at the Guild Theatre, New York, October 8, 1934.

Cast of characters—

A Sleeping Clergyman	Frank Kingdon
Dr. Cooper	J. Colvil Dunn
Dr. Coutts	Harry Mestayer
Wilkinson	Harry Joyner
Charles Cameron, the first	Glenn Anders
Mrs. Elspeth Hannah	Helen Westley
Dr. William Marshall	Ernest Thesiger
Harriet Marshall	Ruth Gordon
Aunt Walker	Alice John
Cousin Minnie	Gertrude Flynn
Wilhelmina Cameron	Ruth Gordon
John Hannah	Theodore Newton
A Sergeant	Walter Lawrence
A Constable	Donald Campbell
Charles Cameron, the second	Glenn Anders
Donovan	J. Malcolm Dunn
Sir Douglas Todd Walker	A. P. Kaye
Lady Todd Walker	Charlotte Walker
Hope Cameron	Ruth Gordon
A Prostitute	Sheila Trent
Lady Katherine Helliwell	Florence Britton
Dr. Purley	Malcolm Soltan
A Medical Student	Robert Haig

Doctors, Nurses, etc.: John Taylor, Frank Henderson, Elizabeth Valentine Phœbe Gilbert.

Prologue to Act I.—A Club in Glasgow. 193—. Act II.—Scene 1 —A Lodging Near the High Street, Glasgow. 1867. 2—A Victorian Bedroom. 1872. 3—A Seaside Cliff Near a Lighthouse. 1885. 4— Dr. Marshall's Consulting Room. 1886. Prologue to Act II.—A Club in Glasgow. 193—. Act II.—Scene 1—A Police Station in a Country Town. 1907. 2—Dr. Marshall's Drawing Room. 1916. 3—A Flat in London. 1916. 4—The Hotel Paradise. Northumberland Avenue, Converted into the Walker Institute. 193—.

Staged by Philip Moeller; settings by Lee Simonson.

While a clergyman friend sleeps quietly in a chair near them, the scene being a physicians' club in Glasgow, Dr. Coutts tells Dr. Cooper the story of the Camerons, in order to strengthen an argument that hereditary influences often are unpredictable. As Dr. Coutts begins with the story of Charles Cameron, the first, the scene fades into a Glasgow lodging back in 1867. Here young Cameron, a wild medical student of tubercular tendencies, dies of a hemorrhage the day Harriet Marshall, whom he has seduced, comes to tell him she expects him to marry her. Harriet's baby is born and later adopted by her uncle, Dr. Marshall, who had attended Cameron. The baby grown to womanhood as Wilhelmina

Cameron is also a wild one. She seduces Dr. Marshall's assistant, but when he would marry her and defeat her chances of a richer match she puts prussic acid in his wine. Later she gives birth to twins, who are also adopted by Dr. Marshall. The twins turn out rather brilliantly. Charles Cameron 2d becomes famous as a medical officer in the war and in 193— stamps out a world plague, and his sister, Hope Cameron, internationalist, is elected secretary of the League of Nations.

ORDER PLEASE

(23 performances)

A comedy in three acts by Edward Childs Carpenter from a play by Walter Hackett. Produced by George Bushar and John Tuerk at The Playhouse, New York, October 9, 1934.

Cast of characters—

Phœbe Weston	Vivienne Osborne
Willie Taylor	Robert Toms
Mrs. Potter	Suzanne Jackson
Blake	Henry Norell
Selby	Joseph R. Garry
Waiter	Pierre D'Ennery
Alice Stanhope	Delphine Doray
Gertrude Hatfield	Peggy Marlowe
Arthur Carlisle	Jack Soanes
Mrs. Stokes	Olive Briscoe
Mr. Stokes	Albert Andress
Robert Kent	Robert Shayne
Collis	Percy Moore
Ermine	Alney Alba
Charlie Matthews	Gregory Deane
Dr. Weisner	A. Fothringham Lysons
Doris Ripley	Gladis Griswold
Victor Neilson	William Hopper
Louise Broussiloff	Tala Birell
Dudley Hampton	Hermann Lieb
Foxhall Ridgway	James Bell
Tom	Paul Jacchia
Evelyn Grayson	Bernice Kenyon
George Sheridan	Matthew Smith
Betty	Lulu Mae Hubbard
Trench	Clifford Dempsey
Head Porter	Addison Pinckert

Act I.—Where You Telephone. Hotel Diplomat, New York City. Act II.—Room 307. Act III.—Scene 1—Room 307. 2—Where You Telephone.

Staged by Edward Childs Carpenter; setting by Louis Kennel.

Foxhall Ridgway, a Wyoming rancher, comes to New York in search of adventure and a brunette. He meets Phœbe Weston, telephone operator in the Hotel Diplomat, who is interesting but blonde. Ridgway is assigned a room and discovers a murdered man next door. Pursuit of the murderer is complicated by the suspicions of the police, the disappearance of the corpse, its discovery in Ridgway's trunk, and the increasing interest the Westerner is forced to take in Phœbe, blonde or not. At 11 P.M. the murderers are caught and Ridgway decides to take Phœbe back to Wyoming with him.

GREEN STICK

(16 performances)

A drama in three acts by Jay Doten. Produced by Vincent Mallory at the Provincetown Playhouse, New York, October 9, 1934.

Cast of characters—

Helen Morning	Betty Worth
Zoe Morning	May Gerald
Jason Morning	Richard Boegner
Annabel	Mary Strachan
Eric Hormon	Frank Howson
Janet Morning	Marguerite Walker
Paul Dorne	Thomas Anthony

Acts I, II and III.—Room in the Morning Home Near New Bedford, Mass.

Staged by Arthur Donaldson; setting by Vincent Mallory and Jay Doten.

Zoe Morning, another of those matriarchal New Englanders who would rule her family by Bible precept, comes finally to grips with a newer generation that intends to have its fun and enjoy it, too. After Zoe, widow of a roistering sea captain, has enforced her will upon the household for a spell of years, her niece Janet arrives home from school, bringing with her a taste for liquor and a friend who can take it. The old lady's will is finally beat down. She seems doomed to loneliness and defeat as the youngsters run out on her.

BRIDAL QUILT

(5 performances)

A play in three acts by Tom Powers. Produced by Vera Murray at the Biltmore Theatre, New York, October 10, 1934.

Cast of characters—

Granny Lawhead	Fredrica Slemons
Minnie Ella Givens	Eleanor Lynn
Washburn Alexander	Blaine Cordner
Les Givens	Larry John
Bert Beasley	Fred Herrick
Cathleen Hotchkiss Barton	Claudia Morgan
Holly	Horace Sinclair
Sarah Cheseldene	Eleanor Phelps
Ralph Cheseldene	James Todd
James Barton	Lester Vail

The Hon. Dally R. Carlton............................Fred Leslie
  Act I.—The Givens' Place Half Way Up the Mountain. Kentucky.
Act II.—The Drawing Room at the Bartons'. New Jersey. Act III.
  —Inside the Givens' House.
  Staged by Tom Powers; settings by John Biddle Whitelaw.

Washburn Alexander, living quietly in the mountains of Kentucky, comes upon a New York motor car stalled in a creek. Wash wades in and carries Cathleen Hotchkiss Barton of Englewood, N. J., to dry ground. The contact is exciting to both. Cathleen casually suggests that she would like to see her rescuer in New Jersey some time. Wash shortly thereafter packs his bag and goes visitin'. Cathleen's friends make sly sport of the hillbilly friend, but Cathleen is nice and so is her husband. Wash had not known there was a husband. When he meets him he goes back to his mount'ins and rediscovers Minnie Ella Givens, suddenly become 17 and purty.

LOST HORIZONS

(56 performances)

A fantasy in 21 scenes by Harry Segall, revised by John Hayden. Produced by Rowland Stebbins at the St. James Theatre, New York, October 15, 1934.

Cast of characters—

Janet Evans....................................Jane Wyatt
Rita Rogers....................................Kathryn Givney
Ralph Bondley..................................Arthur Pierson
A Youth..Vernon Crane
A Banker.......................................Robert Conness
A Guide..William Norton
A Scrubwoman...................................Mabel Paige
A Young Man....................................Robert Smith
Guide-in-Charge................................Thomas Louden
An Attendant...................................Francesca Lenni
Elsie Marshall.................................Betty Lancaster
Mrs. Condos....................................Kathleen Comegys
Oliver Reynolds................................Oswald Yorke
Dobbs..Alf Helton
Diane Reynolds.................................Cynthia Rogers
Robert Potter..................................Lex Lindsay
Gary Farwell...................................Gage Clarke
Albert Grayson.................................J. Arthur Young
Keegan...Grandon Rhodes
Daniels..Joseph Doncourt
Wormser..Wallace Widdecombe
David Prescott.................................Jonathan Hole
Adam Thayer....................................Walter Gilbert
Eddie Lewis....................................Forrest Orr
Maude Trevor...................................Irene Shirley
Charles Dahlman................................Lyster Chambers
Dudley...Clarence Rock
Sybil..Sally Washington
Character Woman................................Mabel Paige
Judge Riley....................................Harry Hanlon
Clerk of the Court.............................Edwin Hodge

Attorney for the Defense......................Robert Conness
Paul Duttine.....................................John Gallaudet
Edna Winters..Ruth Lee
An Astrologer....................................Fred Sutton
A Doctor.......................................Charles Laite
First Stagehand...................................Fred Sutton
Second Stagehand.............................Clarence Rock
First Actor..................................Burton McEvilly
Second Actor..................................Robert Conness
Third Actor...................................Joseph Doncourt
Fourth Actor...................................William Norton
First Actress....................................Mabel Paige
Second Actress..............................Sally Washington
Fifth Actor....................................Harry Hanlon
Maid...Ruth Carl
Mr. Flusser.....................................Edwin Hodge
Miss Smith....................................Brenda Dahlen

Act I.—Scene 1—Bungalow. Los Angeles, Cal. 2—Hall of Rec-
ords. 3—Lodging House. Montreal, Canada. 4—Oliver Reynolds's
Home. New York. 5—Albert Grayson's Library. New York. 6—
Adam Thayer's Office. Kansas City, Mo. 7—Hall of Records. Act
II.—Scene 1—Rehearsal Hall. Kansas City. 2—Adam Thayer's Of-
fice. Kansas City. 3—Courtroom. New York City, October 18. 4—
Janet and Rita's Apartment. Kansas City. 5—Pent House. New
York. 6—On the Boardwalk. Atlantic City. 7—Lodging House.
Montreal, Canada. 8—Reynolds's Home. 9—Green Room of a Thea-
tre. Atlantic City. Act III.—Scene 1—Lobby of the Claridge Hotel.
Atlantic City. 2—Lodging House. Montreal. 3—Richard Dahlman's
Suite. 4—Hotel Room. 5—Hall of Records.

Staged by John Hayden; settings by G. Bradford Ashworth.

See page 292.

*PERSONAL APPEARANCE

(286 performances)

A comedy in three acts by Lawrence Riley. Produced by
Brock Pemberton at the Henry Miller Theatre, New York, October 17, 1934.

Cast of characters—

In the Benjamin Z. Fineberg Production
"DRIFTING LADY"
Superfine Pictures, Inc.

Cacily Carewe....................................Carole Arden
                                                (Gladys George)
Gilbert Gordon...........................Franklin Crawford
                                                (Leonard Penn)

On the Stage
Carole Arden...In Person

In the Play
Clyde Pelton..................................Richard Kendrick
Gladys Kelcey.................................Florence Robinson
Aunt Kate Barnaby.................................Eula Guy
Joyce Struthers....................................Merna Pace
Chester Norton (Bud)..............................Philip Ober
Mrs. Struthers (Addie)..........................Minna Phillips
Gene Tuttle......................................Otto Hulette
Johnson..Phil Sheridan
Carole Arden...................................Gladys George
Jessie...Dorrit Kelton
Henry Bush..John Jones

Act I.—Scene 1—Grand Theatre in Scranton, Pa. During the
Showing of the Film, "Drifting Lady," and the Personal Appear-
ance of Its Star, Carole Arden. 2—Living Room of the Struthers'
House. Act II.—Living Room. Act III.—Scene 1—Living Room.
2—Colonial Theatre in Wilkes-Barre.
Staged by Antoinette Perry and Brock Pemberton.

Carole Arden, motion picture celebrity, is in the East making a
series of personal appearances in connection with the showing of
her latest screen success, "Drifting Lady." Between Wilkes-Barre
and Scranton her Isotta-Fraschini breaks down. Held in the tour-
ists-accommodated home of Addie Struthers, Carole takes note of
Bud Norton, handsome filling station attendant who is engaged
to Mrs. Struthers' daughter, Joyce. Bud has a gadget he is hoping to patent and sell to the producers of sound pictures. Carole
would take him with her back to Hollywood and introduce him
to her husband, Benjamin Z. Fineberg. With the sympathetic
interference of Gene Tuttle, Carole's public relations counsel,
Bud is saved to Joyce and the filling station.

HIPPER'S HOLIDAY

(4 performances)

A comedy in three acts by John Crump. Produced by Marian
T. Carter at the Maxine Elliott Theatre, October 18, 1934.

Cast of characters—

Charlie Mason	Shelton Earp
A Janitor	Hume Cronyn
Jim Hipper	Burgess Meredith
A Waiter	Jan Ullrich
Helen Tyson	Katherine Squire
A Man from Woonsocket	Charles Scott
Orange Juice Manager	Edward Forbes
A Lady from Los Angeles	Irene Cattell
Joel Lambert	John Boyd
Marie Aguilar	Lisa Berenda
José Aguilar	Carlos La Torre
A Salesman	Bigelow Sayre
Jerry Duggan	Clyde Franklin
A Detective	Dick Ellington

Orange-juice Addicts, Dog-walkers, Policemen, Detectives, and
Other Pedestrians
Act I.—Scene 1—Orange Juice Stand. 2—Jerry Duggan's Apart-
ment. Acts II and III.—Jerry Duggan's Apartment.
Staged by Alan Williams; settings by Louis Bromberg.

Jim Hipper, a young man down on his luck, proposes to Charlie
Mason, who runs an orange juice stand, that they hold somebody
up in order to get needed money. They take Joel Lambert in tow
and deposit him in a borrowed flat. Finding he has only a few
dollars they decide to hold him for ransom. Lambert manages to
get word to Marie Aguilar which brings her and her father to his
aid, but also adds to the complication. Aguilar has entrusted

$50,000 to Lambert to buy guns for a South American revolution. Lambert has the money in a bag tied round his neck and was preparing to elope to Canada with Marie. The owner of the borrowed apartment returns, and he, too, is wanted by the police. Hipper is finally rewarded for saving the Aguilar money.

WITHIN THE GATES

(First engagement 101 performances. Return 40. Total 141.)

A symbolic drama in four scenes by Sean O'Casey; incidental music by Milton Lusk and A. Lehman Engel. Produced by George Bushar and John Tuerk at the National Theatre, New York, October 22, 1934.

Cast of characters—

The Dreamer	Bramwell Fletcher
The Bishop	Moffat Johnston
The Bishop's Sister	Kathryn Collier
1st Chair Attendant	Barry Macollum
2nd Chair Attendant	John Daly Murphy
A Boy	Alexander Lewis
The Atheist	Morris Ankrum
The Policewoman	Jessamine Newcombe
The Young Man in Plus-Fours	Ralph Sumpter
The Scarlet Woman	Miriam Goldina
1st Nursemaid	Vera Fuller Mellish
2nd Nursemaid	Esther Mitchell
A Guardsman	James Jolley
The Gardener	Barry Kelley
1st Evangelist	Edward Broadley
2nd Evangelist	Arthur Villars
The Young Whore	Lillian Gish
A Young Salvation Army Officer	Byron McGrath
The Foreman	Ralph Cullinan
The Old Woman	Mary Morris
The Man in the Bowler Hat	Stanley G. Wood
The Man with the Stick	Phil Bishop
The Man in the Trilby Hat	Charles Angelo
1st Platform Speaker	Gordon Gould
2nd Platform Speaker	Dodson Mitchell
A Young Man	Arthur Gould Porter
The Man in the Burberry	Charles Keane

A Chorus of Down and Outs, Young Men and Girls, Salvationists, Strollers in the Park, etc.: Mildred Albert, Suzanne Black, Mary Brandt, Kathryn Curl, Martha Eaton, Betty Gladstone, Anne Goddard, Dorothy Higgins, Marjorie Hyder, Ellen Love, Elizabeth Morgan, Evangeline Raleigh, Ursula Seiler, Edith Shayne, Virginia Spottswood, Pauline Stokes, Peggy Strickland, Teddy Williams, George Augustin, Tony Barone, Mordecae Bauman, Victor Bryant, Tomes Chapman, Frank Gabrielson, Kenneth Bostock, Serge Gradoff, Serge Inga, Robert Kerr, Stanley Klein, Karl Kohrs, Ram Meyer, Gifford Nash, William Trieste, Clyde Walters, William Williams, Rodifer Wilson.

Symbol of the Seasons	Margaret Mower
The Woman Who Feeds the Birds	Ellen Larned

Scenes 1, 2, 3 and 4—Within a Park.

Staged by Melvyn Douglas; setting by James Reynolds; dance direction by Elsa Findlay.

The gates of an imaginary Hyde Park open to admit a varied assortment of muddled humans. Singly and in groups they have their day expressing themselves by symbol or by speech. The Young Prostitute, illegitimate daughter of the Bishop and the Old Woman, seeks release for her soul by appealing to the religion of her father, but is drawn into the fullness of physical life again by the call of the Dreamer. There are many debates as to the existence or non-existence of God and the value or purpose of religion. In the end the Young Prostitute comes again to the church and dies in the Bishop's arms. . . . Following a short road tour "Within the Gates" was brought back to New York for an additional four-week engagement.

CONVERSATION PIECE

(55 performances)

A romantic comedy in three acts by Noel Coward. Produced by Charles B. Cochran in association with Arch Selwyn and Harold B. Franklin at the 44th Street Theatre, New York, October 23, 1934.

Cast of characters—

Sophie Otford	Sylvia Leslie
Martha James	Moya Nugent
Mrs. Dragon	Betty Shale
Paul, Duc de Chaucigny-Varennes	Pierre Fresnay
Mélanie	Yvonne Printemps
Rose	Maidie Andrews
The Marquis of Sheere	Carl Harbord
The Earl of Harringford	George Sanders
Lord Braceworth	Pat Worsley
Lord Doyning	Anthony Brian
Mr. Hailsham	Sidney Grammer
The Duchess of Beneden	Winifred Davis
The Duke of Beneden	Athole Stewart
Lady Julia Charteris	Irene Browne
Hannah	Jill Anthony
A Tiger	Leonard Goodman
Miss Goslett	Phyllis Harding
Miss Mention	Dorothy Drover
Lord Kenyon	Penryn Bannerman
Lord St. Marys	George Sanders
Fishermen: Reginald Thurgood, William McGuigan, Evan Jones, Roy Hall	
Countess Harringford	Shela Pattrick
Lady Braceworth	Eileen Clifton
Mrs. Hailsham	Winifred Campbell
Hon. Julian Kane	St. John Lauri
Lord Mosscrock	Felix Hill
Mr. Amos	Alex Robertson
Butler	Claude Farrow
Mr. Jones	Leonard Michel
Courtesan	Brenda Clether

Acts I, II and III.—Brighton, Eng., 1811.
Staged by Noel Coward; setting by G. E. Calthrop.

The Duc de Chaucigny-Varennes, happening upon Mélanie, a beautiful young French girl, singing in a Paris café, takes her to Brighton, England, and introduces her as his ward. His hope is to marry Mélanie to a rich man, or a rich man's son, thus insuring his own and his ward's future. Mélanie, however, determining to follow the dictates of her secret heart, announces her love for her guardian and will have none of those other lovers who offer themselves. Resulting in the capitulation of the Duc.

GOOD-BYE PLEASE

(2 performances)

A comedy in three acts by Burt Clifton. Produced by Edward Mendelssohn at the Ritz Theatre, New York, October 24, 1934.

Cast of characters—

Marian	Selena Royle
Jack	Robert Keith
Bob	Eric Dressler
Sweeney	Molly Pearson
Anne	Ruth Hammond
Mrs. McCorkle	Marjorie Wood
Caleb	Percy Kilbride
Geraldine	Lois Huntington

Acts I and II.—An Apartment Overlooking the East River, New York City. Act III.—A Farm in Connecticut.

Staged by Edward Mendelssohn; settings by Theodore Kahn and William Mensching.

Marian and Jack had been living together for two years. Jack suddenly discovered that he did not love Marian anymore and asked to be released from their agreement. Marian let him go. In three months Jack was back but Marian would not let him stay. Jack married another woman and Marian adopted a child. Within the year Marian was back and found Jack giving a Christmas party at his Connecticut farm. Jack's wife was snowbound. Jack and Marian spent the evening discussing divorce and playing with an electric train Jack had bought for his caretaker's little boy.

BETWEEN TWO WORLDS

(32 performances)

A drama in nine scenes by Elmer Rice. Produced by the author at the Belasco Theatre, New York, October 25, 1934.

Cast of characters—

Eleanor Massey	Nelly Malcolm
Christine Massey	Tucker Maguire
Frederick Dodd	Conway Washburne
James Roberts	Thomas H. Manning
The Deck-steward	Alfred A. Hesse
Rita Dodd	Constance McKay
A News-Photographer	Ned Glass

Vivienne Sinclair...............................Josephine Dunn
Rose Henneford..................................Osceola Archer
Richard Neilson..................................Lee Ellsworth
Matilda Mason......................................Anne Tonetti
The Photographer's Assistant......................Samuel Bonnell
Hilda Bowen......................................Diantha Pattison
Elena Mikhailovna Golitzin.....................Margaret Waller
Margaret Bowen...............................Rachel Hartzell
Louberta Allenby.................................Gladys Feldman
The Smoke-room Steward........................Francis Compton
Lloyd Arthur.......................................Maurice Wells
Henry Ferguson...............................James Spottswood
N. N. Kovolev..................................Joseph Schildkraut
Assistant Purser Charles Holaday.................Cledge Roberts
Giuseppe Moretti.................................Frank Marino
Edward Maynard................................Eric Wollencott
Junior Eddington...........................Lester Lonergan, 3rd
Helen Eddington.................................Ruth Tomlinson
Edgar Howell..................................Wells Richardson
Clara Roberts......................................Sara Peyton
Dr. David MacKnight............................Elmer Brown
A Page-boy......................................Joie Brown, Jr.
Daisy Cooper.......................................Sue Moore
Chester Cooper...................................Ralph Sanford
An Assistant Deck-steward.......................John Cambridge
Harold Powers.......................................Jack Leslie
Captain John Whalley............................Clyde Fillmore
Eunice Stafford..................................Rose Burdick
Henri Deschamps.................................Leonard Penn
Billy Eddington..................................Buddy Farley
Two Nuns....................Edilou Bailhe, Polly de Loos
A Newspaper Vendor............................Buddy Proctor
An Englishwoman....................................Janet Fox
An Englishman.................................R. Birrell Rawls
    Scenes 1, 2, 3, 4, 5, 6, 7, 8 and 9—Aboard an Ocean Liner.
    Staged by Elmer Rice; settings by Aline Bernstein.

Margaret Bowen, crossing to Cherbourg with her mother and
her friend, the Princess Elena Mikhailovna Golitzin, meets N. N.
Kovolev, a motion picture director returning to Russia from an
unsatisfactory experience in Hollywood. Margaret, representa-
tive of the capitalistic class, and Kovonev, a ruthless bolshevik,
both repel and fascinate each other. Margaret, piqued by Kovolev's sneering charge that she is a parasite and too cowardly to
live independently of the conventions of her class, permits herself
to be led away to his cabin. The experience both disgusts and
awakens her and is somewhat sobering to Kovolev's self-confi-
dence. Margaret decides to break her engagement to a man of
her own social group, preparatory to making something of herself. Kovolev, leaving her at the gangplank, goes on to Russia
to continue his work for the party.

GERANIUMS IN MY WINDOW

(27 performances)

A comedy in three acts by Samuel Ornitz and Vera Caspary.
Produced by Phil Baker and Laura D. Wilck at the Longacre
Theatre, New York, October 26, 1934.

Cast of characters—

Louie..Harold Waldridge
Ryan...Ben Laughlin
Zabriskie...Clem Wilenchick
Denver..Thomas Ewell
Slater Jones (Toby Starr).....................Bruce MacFarlane
Rosabelle..Viola Richard
Nellie Quinn.....................................Audrey Christie
Weinstein...Robert Leonard
Policeman..Milano Tilden
Joe...Frank Shannon
Kathie Starr.......................................Ruth Matteson
Randolph Starr...................................Cyril Chadwick
Miss Windsor......................................Eda Heinemann
Michael Henry Cronin...............................Alan Goode
    Act I.—Scene 1—New Deal Employment Agency. 2—Toby Starr's
Library. Acts II and III.—Nellie Quinn's Room.
    Staged by Sidney Salkow; settings by Philip Gelb.

Toby Starr, eccentric son of an eccentric and wealthy father, meets Nellie Quinn, waitress, in a Sixth Avenue employment agency where both are looking for jobs. Toby, known as Slater Jones, protects Nellie from the too free attentions of a roughneck. Out of gratitude she gets him a job as a dishwasher in the restaurant where she goes to work. Later they are married and go to live in Nellie's one-room apartment. When Nellie discovers who her husband really is, her pride is flattened. The elder Starr has to convince her that Toby will lose his mind if she quits him before she will go on living with Toby.

ALLURE

(8 performances)

A drama in three acts by Leigh Burton Wells. Produced by Arthur Dreyfuss and Willard G. Gernhardt at the Empire Theatre, New York, October 29, 1934.

Cast of characters—

Mr. Corwin...John Miltern
Sep Corwin..Jess Barker
Barton...Alexander Frank
Dr. Edwards.....................................Ernest Woodward
Marion..Edith Barrett
Paul Seonie..Guido Nazdo
Fidela..Clara Mahr
Joan Corwin.....................................Florence Williams
Basilio...Saul Z. Martell
Jensen...Sydney G. Smith
Dr. Koppel..Robert T. Haines
    Act I.—Garden Terrace of the Corwins' Country Home. Acts II
and III.—Sun Room.
    Staged by Clifford Brooke; settings by Yellenti.

Marion Corwin had been sadistically minded from the day she, aged 8, pushed her little sister, Joan, 3, downstairs and so in-

jured her that Joan had to use crutches for years. In Europe
Marion married Paul Seonie, sculptor. When she brought him
home he met Joan in the garden after midnight without knowing
who she was and a great love was born. This made Marion
furious and meaner than ever. When Paul made a statue of Joan,
Marion destroyed it. The shock would have destroyed Joan, too,
if it had not been for Dr. Koppel, famed psychiatrist from Vienna.
Dr. Koppel exposed Marion's cruelties, which released Joan from
her fear of her sister, curing her paralysis and leaving her free to
marry Paul after Marion shot herself.

THE FARMER TAKES A WIFE

(104 performances)

A comedy in three acts by Frank B. Elser and Marc Connelly,
based on a novel, "Rome Haul," by Walter D. Edmonds. Produced by Max Gordon at the 46th Street Theatre, New York,
October 30, 1934.

Cast of characters—

Mr. Fisher	Joseph Sweeney
Luke	Lewis Martin
Lucas	Larry Oliver
Fortune Friendly	Herb Williams
Lucy Gurget	Margaret Hamilton
Calder	Frank Knight
Yazey	Jay Young
Sol Tinker	Francis Pierlot
Riley	Joe M. Fields
Joe Teetham	Jas. Francis-Robertson
Harry Emory	Morton L. Stevens
Jotham Klore	Gibbs Penrose
Howard	Bert J. Norton
Ivy	Mabel Kroman
Otway	Charles F. O'Connor
Sam Weaver	Ralph Riggs
Stark	Robert Ross
Molly Larkins	June Walker
Dan Harrow	Henry Fonda
Mrs. Howard	Ruth Gillmore
Fry	Walter Ayres
Gammy Hennessy	Kate Mayhew
Della	Mary McQuade
Conductor	Wylie Adams

Acts I and III.—Hennessy's Hotel at Rome, New York, 1853. Act
II.—Scene 1—Near Utica. 2—Cabin of "Sarsey Sal," Whitesboro.
Staged by Marc Connelly; settings by Donald Oenslager.

See page 262.

LADIES' MONEY

(36 performances)

A drama in three acts by George Abbott, previously written by
Lawrence Hazard and Richard Flournoy. Produced by Courtney

Burr at the Ethel Barrymore Theatre, New York, November 1, 1934.

Cast of characters—

Eddie	Eric Linden
Ruth Potter	Joyce Arling
Nelson Blummer	Jerome Cowan
Platt Touhey	Len Doyle
Clare Touhey	Eleanor Z. Audley
Jim Harriss	Robert R. Sloane
Mrs. Potter	Lora Rogers
Fruity	Hal K. Dawson
Betty Harriss	Margaret Mullen
Margie	Helen Lynd
Drunken Woman	Gertrude Mudge
June	Margaret Callahan
Red	Garson Kanin
Dr. Curtis	James P. Houston
Detective	Gordon Hamilton
Musician	Jack Rigo
2nd Detective	J. Ascher Smith
Fat Man	Frank Jaquet
Policeman	Nick Wiger
Mrs. Brown	Beatrice Behr
Mr. Brown	Boyd Crawford

Acts I, II and III.—First and Second Floor of Old Brown-stone House in 46th Street.

Staged by George Abbott.

Eddie, Fruity and Jim Harriss are all out of work and pretending to do the housework in Mrs. Potter's rooming house while their wives support them. Eddie and Fruity are vaudeville performers. Jim is a clerk. Across the hall from them Nelson Blummer, a gunman, has seduced the landlady's daughter, Ruth, and is about to make a getaway when the police close in on him. Blummer hides in the Harrisses' room. Jim Harriss sees him coming out and thinks Mrs. Harriss is cheating. Jim stabs Blummer. A pal of the gunman, cornered in the house, leaves his gun and a wad of money behind when he dives out the window of Eddie's and June's room. June takes the money and pays Eddie's debts with it.

L'AIGLON

(58 performances)

A tragedy in three acts adapted by Clemence Dane from the French of Edmond Rostand. Produced by Arch Selwyn and Harold B. Franklin at the Broadhurst Theatre, New York, November 3, 1934.

Cast of characters—

Marie-Louise, Duchess of Parma	Ethel Barrymore
First Lady	Stella Reynolds
Second Lady	Helena Glenn
Third Lady	Ruth Wilton

```
Count Bombelles...............................Stiano Braggiotti
Therese de Lorget..............................Helen Walpole
Tiburce de Lorget.............................Richard Waring
Metternich, Chancellor of Austria.............Charles Waldorn
Count Dietrichstein............................Lionel Hogarth
Gentz..........................................John H. Brewer
A French Attaché...............................Donald Cameron
The Archduchess................................Leona Roberts
A Lady-in-Waiting.............................Margaret Cloninger
"L'Aiglon," Franz, Duke of Reichstadt..........Eva Le Gallienne
Countess Camerata.............................Marion Evensen
A Tailor.......................................Horace Braham
A Maid.........................................Ysobel Martin
Baron D'Obenaus.................................Paul Leyssac
Fanny Elssler....................................Ethel Colt
Count Sedlinsky..................................Walter Beck
First Servant.................................Douglas Rowland
Second Servant..................................William Walsh
Third Servant.................................Charles Sedgwick
An Usher.......................................Edward McHugh
Flambeau.......................................Hugh Buckler
Foresti.........................................Joseph Kramm
Prokesch......................................William Whitehead
First Swiss Guard................................John Salzman
Second Swiss Guard...........................Larry Schwimmer
A Man..........................................Bennett Challis
An Old Woman..........................Georgie Drew Mendum
A Woman..........................................Mary Ward
An Old Peasant...................................Ted Tenley
A Young Countryman..............................Samuel Colt
A Farmer.........................................David Turk
Franz, Emperor of Austria........................Sayre Crawley
A Harlequin......................................Sam Pearce
First Lilac Domino.............................Stella Reynolds
Second Lilac Domino..............................Mary Ward
Third Lilac Domino............................Margaret Cloninger
Fourth Lilac Domino..............................Martha Crego
Fifth Lilac Domino...............................Ruth Wilton
Sixth Lilac Domino..............................Ysobel Martin
A Shepherdess...................................Helena Glenn
A Lackey.......................................Martin Pollock
A Folly.........................................Nelson Welch
A Princess...........................Georgie Drew Mendum
A Jester......................................Charles Sedgwick
A Fop............................................Ted Tenley
Marmont........................................Bennett Challis
First Conspirator...............................Joseph Kramm
Second Conspirator.............................Lionel Hogarth
Third Conspirator.............................Martin Pollock
Fourth Conspirator.............................Lawrence Hutt
Fifth Conspirator...............................Samuel Colt
Sixth Conspirator...............................Nelson Welch
A Doctor.........................................Sam Pearce
General Hartmann..........................Benedict MacQuarrie
A Prelate.....................................Lionel Hogarth
Acolytes................................. { Eugene Francis
                                          { Charles Sedgwick
```

Guests, Peasants, etc.: Gabrielle Morgan, Jane Kim, Barbara Coch-
rane, Betty Fouche, Richard Heath.
Singers: Ruth Wilton, Alice Swanson, Dorothy Johnson.
    Act I.—Scene 1—Marie-Louise's Salon at Baden, Near Vienna.
2—Duke's Study at Schoenbrunn. Act II.—Scene 1—Duke's Study.
2—Park at Schoenbrunn. Act III.—Scene 1—Plain of Wagram. 2—
Duke's Bedroom at Schoenbrunn.
    Staged by Eva Le Gallienne; settings by Aline Bernstein.

Mme. Sarah Bernhardt and company presented the original
Rostand version of "L'Aiglon" at the Globe Theatre, New York,
in December, 1910, and again in June, 1911. On a return visit
in 1916 she gave the sixth act, the death scene of the Duc de

Reichstadt, as one of a series of short plays. The Maude Adams production was staged in New York in October, 1900.

During the above engagement Miss Le Gallienne revived Ibsen's "Hedda Gabler" ("Best Plays of 1927-28"), and the Sierra "Cradle Song" (1926-27), from her Civic Theatre Repertory, giving four performances of each.

JAYHAWKER

(24 performances)

A comedy in three acts by Sinclair Lewis and Lloyd Lewis. Produced by Henry Hammond, Inc., at the Cort Theatre, New York, November 5, 1934.

Cast of characters—

Reverend Peavie	Ralph Theadore
Will Starling	Paul Guilfoyle
Wes	Douglas McMullen
Ike Swan	Tom Fadden
Ed Ridley	Clif Heckinger
Mrs. Carson	Margaret O'Donnell
Mrs. Swan	Katherine Rolin
Mrs. Ridley	Ludmilla Toretzka
Mrs. Elkins	Nancy Levering
Matt Carson	Edward Acuff
Vic Rousseau	Walter Baldwin
Sam Blevins	David Andrada
Mrs. Blevins	Gretchen Winkler
Luke Kildare	Edward McNamara
Asa ("Ace") Burdette	Fred Stone
Nettie Burdette	Carol Stone
Mr. Russell	Harry Worth
Artist	Donald Smith
Mose	Hayes Pryor
O'Reilly	Lawrence C. O'Brien
Gen. Philemon Smallwood	Walter C. Kelly
Hawkins	George Oliver Taylor
Eph Brown	Martin Howe
Fresh Fish	O. Z. Whitehead
Confederate Soldier	Milburn Stone

Act I.—Scene 1—Outdoor Camp-meeting Ground in Kansas. 2—Senator Burdette's Washington Home. Act II.—Scene 1—Burdette's Home. 2—Glory Hole on the Chickahominy River. Act III.—Burdette's Home.

Staged by Joe Losey; settings by Walter Walden.

Asa ("Ace") Burdette, leader of a band of Jayhawkers in the Kansas of the early '60's, is elected Senator on a strong abolitionist ticket. In Washington Asa is torn with regret by the prolongation of the war he helped encourage and would conspire with General Smallwood, a Southern General held prisoner in Washington, to propagandize both armies with a proposal that the armies of General Lee and General Grant adopt a truce and unite under Lee to march into Mexico and repel the French invaders. The failure of the conspiracy leaves Asa politically in a hole.

(31 performances)

A comedy in three acts by Irving Kaye Davis. Produced by
Joseph Pollak at the Ritz Theatre, New York, November 6, 1934.

Cast of characters—

```
A Young Man.......................................Allan Dailey
A Young Woman..................................Shirley Gibbs
An Old Man......................................Russell Thayer
A Girl...........................................Ruth Sheppard
A Spinster.......................................Rowena Aubert
A Motion Picture Executive.......................Carr Caddon
Josie Frampton..................................Violet Heming
Jack Huffaker...................................Thurston Hall
Minnie..........................................Ollie Burgoyne
Percival Lockwood............................Louis Jean Heydt
Robert Bradley...................................King Calder
Philip Frampton.............................William Harrigan
Miss Tobison....................................Shirley Gale
Mae...............................................Helene Dumas
Expressman........................................C. E. Smith
```
      Acts I, II and III.—Living Room at the Framptons'.
      Staged by Melville Burke; setting by Tom Adrian Cracraft.

Philip Frampton is a literary man of parts who is too preoccupied with his work as an essayist of national reputation to
pay any attention to his wife. Mrs. Frampton, bored by her husband's neglect and intent upon making a little money for household expenses, writes a sexy novel called "A Naked Lady" under
a masculine nom de plume. The novel enjoys a phenomenal sale,
Philip discovers his wife's authorship, suspects her of having living models for her love chapters, primes his courage with liquor,
gives two men black eyes, acquires one himself, and finally learns
that Mrs. Frampton has merely rewritten episodes already used
by Boccaccio, Voltaire and De Maupassant.

DARK VICTORY

(51 performances)

A drama in three acts by George Brewer and Bertram Bloch.
Produced by Alexander McKaig at the Plymouth Theatre, New
York, November 7, 1934.

Cast of characters—

```
Dr. Frederick Steele............................Earle Larimore
Miss Wainwright.................................Mildred Wall
Dr. Parsons...................................Frederick Leister
Judith Traherne..............................Tallulah Bankhead
Alden Blaine....................................Ann Andrews
Josie............................................Myra Hampton
Michael.........................................Edgar Norfolk
```

Leslie Clarke......................................Dwight Fiske
Miss Jenny......................................Helen Strickland
Postman..Lewis Dayton
　　Act I.—Dr. Steele's Office in New York. Act II.—Judith's House
on Long Island. Act III.—Living Room of Dr. Steele's House.
　　Staged by Robert Milton; settings by Robert Edmond Jones.

Judith Traherne, suffering a threatened breakdown, defiantly
refuses medical aid until she is led to the office of Dr. Frederick
Steele, who diagnoses her trouble as brain tumor. An operation
by Steele apparently restores Judith to health, but her physician
knows she cannot live more than six months. When she confesses
her love for him she suspects his secret and returns to the fast
society life she has been living in an effort to extract all she can
from life. Disgusted with this course, she seeks Steele out a
second time, induces him to marry her and lives happily with him
until the dread summons two months later.

SAY WHEN

(76 performances)

A musical comedy in two acts by Jack McGowan; music by
Ray Henderson; lyrics by Ted Koehler. Produced by Jack Mc-
Gowan and Ray Henderson at the Imperial Theatre, New York,
November 8, 1934.

Cast of characters—

Alice...Helen Buck
Freddie......................................J. Elliott Leonard
Betty...Betty Dell
Jane..Linda Watkins
Ellen...Lillian Emerson
Jimmy Blake.......................................Bob Hope
Bob Breese....................................Harry Richman
Deck Steward....................................John Albert
Reginald Pratt.................................Nick Long, Jr.
An Inspector.................................Martin Sheppard
Carter Holmes................................Charles Collins
Murphy......................................Frederick Manatt
Aimee Bates...................................Dennie Moore
Charles Palmer................................Taylor Holmes
Tompkins.......................................J. P. Wilson
Myra Palmer................................Cora Witherspoon
Prince Michael.............................Michael Romanoff
Pete, the Punk.................................Clyde Veaux
Junior..Donald Brown
Bank Guard...................................Jack Richards
Bank Guard......................................Joe Carroll
Bishop...Fred Lyon
　　Act I.—Scene 1—Deck of a Transatlantic Liner. 2—Pier 57,
New York City. 3—Living Room, Palmer Home, Southampton. 4—
Upstairs Corridor, Palmer Home. 5—The Veranda. Act II.—Scene
1—Outside of Waldorf-Astoria. 2—Garden of Palmer Home. 3—
Living Room of Aimee Bates' Apartment. 4—Vaults of the Palmer
Trust Company. 5—Living Room, Palmer Home.
　　Staged by Bertram Harrison and Russell Markert; settings by
Clark Robinson.

Bob Breese and Jimmy Blake, crossing on a transatlantic liner with their jazz orchestra, meet Jane and Betty Palmer, daughters of Banker Palmer. The boys follow the girls to the Palmer estate on Long Island and are eventually able to overcome the objections of Papa Palmer by discovering his affair with Aimee Bates. When he gives them an assignment to broadcast a thrift program from the vaults of the Palmer Trust Company everything is practically as good as settled.

THE ABBEY THEATRE PLAYERS

(5 weeks engagement)

A repertory of Irish plays presented by Elbert A. Wickes at the Golden Theatre, New York, beginning November 12, 1934.

THE PLOUGH AND THE STARS

By Sean O'Casey

(13 performances)

Cast of characters—

Commandant Jack Clitheroe	F. J. McCormick
Nora Clitheroe	Eileen Crowe
Peter Flynne	W. O'Gorman
The Young Covey	Michael J. Dolan
Fluther Good	Barry Fitzgerald
Bessie Burgess	Maureen Delany
Mrs. Gogan	May Craig
Mollser	Aideen O'Connor
Captain Brennan	Denis O'Dea
Lieut. Langan	U. Wright
Rosie Redmond	Frolie Mulhern
A Bargain	P. J. Carolan
A Voice	P. J. Carolan
Corporal Stoddard	P. J. Carolan
Sergeant Tinley	Arthur Shields

Act I.—Living Room of Clitheroes' Flat in Tenement in Dublin. Act II.—Public-house in Street Where Meeting Is Being Held. Act III.—Outside of Tenement House. Act IV.—Bessie Burgess's Room in Tenement House.

See "Best Plays of 1927-28."

THE NEW GOSSOON

By George Shiels

November 13, 1934

(2 performances)

Cast of characters—

Ellen Carey	Maureen Delany
Luke	Denis O'Dea
Peter Carey	Michael J. Dolan

```
Ned Shay............................................P. J. Carolan
May Kehoe .........................................May Craig
Rabit Hamil........................................F. J. McCormick
Sally Hamil.........................................Eileen Crowe
John Henly.........................................Arthur Shields
Biddy Henly........................................Aideen O'Connor
```
    The action takes place in Carey's kitchen.

See "Best Plays of 1932-33."

THE FAR-OFF HILLS

By LENNOX ROBINSON

November 14, 1934

(1 performance)

Cast of characters—

```
Patrick Clancy.....................................P. J. Carolan
Marion.............................................Eileen Crowe
Dorothea ("Ducky")................................Aideen O'Connor
Anna ("Pet")......................................Frolie Mulhern
Oliver O'Shaughnessy..............................Barry Fitzgerald
Dick Delany.......................................Michael J. Dolan
Harold Mahony.....................................F. J. McCormick
Susie Tynan........................................Maureen Delany
Pierce Hegarty....................................Arthur Shields
Ellen Nolan........................................May Craig
```
    Acts I and III.—Clancy's Dining Room.   Act II.—Ducky's and
Pet's Bedroom.

See "Best Plays of 1932-33."

DRAMA AT INISH

By LENNOX ROBINSON

November 14, 1934

(3 performances)

Cast of characters—

```
John Twohig.......................................W. O'Gorman
Annie Twohig......................................Maureen Delany
Lizzie Twohig.....................................Eileen Crowe
Eddie Twohig......................................Denis O'Dea
Peter Hurley, T.D.................................Michael J. Dolan
Helena.............................................Aideen O'Connor
Michael............................................Arthur Shields
Christine Lambert.................................Frolie Mulhern
Hector De La Mare.................................F. J. McCormick
Constance Constantia..............................May Craig
John Hegarty......................................Barry Fitzgerald
Tom Mooney.........................................P. J. Carolan
William Slattery...................................U. Wright
```
    Acts I, II and III.—Private Sitting Room in Sea-view Hotel.

See "Is Life Worth Living," "Best Plays of 1933-34."

LOOK AT THE HEFFERNANS

By Brinsley MacNamara

November 16, 1934

(1 performance)

Cast of characters—

Festus Darby....................................F. J. McCormick
James Heffernan...............................Michael J. Dolan
Paul Heffernan...............................Barry Fitzgerald
Marcella Molloy....................................Eileen Crowe
Marks Heffernan.................................P. J. Carolan
Alice Heffernan......................................May Craig
Sidney Heffernan..................................Denis O'Dea
Ignatious Crinnion.............................Arthur Shields
Mabel Scally....................................Frolie Mulhern
Roseanne Rooney...............................Maureen Delany
Tessie Malone..................................Aideen O'Connor
    Acts I and III.—House of James Heffernan in Garradice in the County Meath. Act II.—Shop of Molloy and Co. in Sheepstown.

James and Paul Heffernan take pride in the custom of their neighbors who point to the Heffernan achievements until Festus Darby, the town tailor, and Marcella Molloy, the town modiste, convince them that the frequent admonition to "look at the Heffernans" is inspired by contempt for their failure to establish themselves as solid, married citizens. James and Paul thereupon begin looking about at the girls, engage themselves to a couple, order their wedding clothes from the tailor and the modiste and then suffer a break in their plans.

THE SHADOW OF THE GLEN

By J. M. Synge

November 17, 1934

(1 performance)

Cast of characters—

Dan Burke.....................................F. J. McCormick
Nora Burke......................................Eileen Crowe
Michael Dara...................................Arthur Shields
A Tramp.......................................Barry Fitzgerald
    Scene—The last cottage at the head of a long glen in County Wicklow.

Dan Burke, suspicious of his wife's loyalty, plays dead and listens as she and Michael, a neighbor farmer, plan a marriage of property advantage to both. Comnig to life Dan would beat Michael, who pleads weakly for Nora's protection. Nora, disgusted with the two of them, accepts the invitation of a tramp to whom she has given shelter to go walking the roads with him.

THE PLAYBOY OF THE WESTERN WORLD

By J. M. Synge

November 17, 1934

(7 performances)

Cast of characters—

Margaret Flaherty	Eileen Crowe
Shawn Keogh	Michael J. Dolan
Michael James Flaherty	Barry Fitzgerald
Philly Cullen	F. J. McCormick
Jimmy Farrell	U. Wright
Christopher Mahon	Arthur Shields
The Widow Quinn	Maureen Delany
Sara Tansey	May Craig
Susan Brady	Frolie Mulhern
Honor Blake	Aideen O'Connor
Nellie	Joan Sullivan
Old Mahon	P. J. Carolan

Acts I, II and III.—Flaherty's Public-house on the Coast of Mayo.

See "Best Plays of 1929-30."

CHURCH STREET

By Lennox Robinson

November 19, 1934

(1 performance)

Cast of characters—

Joseph Riordan	Barry Fitzgerald
Kate Riordan	Maureen Delany
Hugh	Arthur Shields
Jack	Danny Malone
Mollie	Alma Schirmer
Aunt Moll	Eileen Crowe
Mrs. DeLacy	Joan Sullivan
Miss Pettigrew	May Craig
Jim Daly	F. J. McCormick
Honor Bewley	Aideen O'Connor
The Evoked Hugh	Denis O'Dea
Doctor Smith	Michael J. Dolan
A Clergyman	P. J. Carolan

Scene—Mrs. Riordan's Drawing Room, Knock.

Hugh Riordan, playwright, back from failure in London and looking for inspiration, finds it in the statement of his Aunt Moll that there are plenty of plots around him if he will see them. Four at least in his mother's supper party. Hugh sets his imagination working and in a fantasy brings in the supper guests to act out their individual tragedies. In the end he is put to it to tell how much is truth and how much he has imagined.

THE RESURRECTION

By W. B. Yeats

November 19, 1934

(1 performance)

Cast of characters—

The Hebrew.....................................Michael J. Dolan
The Greek..F. J. McCormick
The Syrian..Denis O'Dea
Attendants....................................... { P. J. Carolan
                                                 { W. O'Gorman
Scene—An ante-chamber in a house near Jerusalem.

A discussion of the tragedy of Calvary between a Hebrew and a Greek in which the Greek's contention that Jesus was a spirit is dramatically disproved by the appearance of the Savior on his way to the meeting with the disciples, after the departure from the tomb.

THE COINER

By Bernard Duffy

November 21, 1934

(3 performances)

Cast of characters—

James Canatt.....................................P. J. Carolan
Catherine Canatt..............................Maureen Delany
John Canatt.......................................W. O'Gorman
Tom McClippen...................................F. J. McCormick
A Police Sergeant.................................Denis O'Dea
The scene is laid in Canatt's kitchen.

Tom McClippen sells James Canatt the secret of how to make brand new half crowns by rubbing dirty old crowns on a brick. The cheater is himself cheated when he discovers that he has been paid for the secret in counterfeit coin.

THE WELL OF THE SAINTS

By J. M. Synge

November 21, 1934

(1 performance)

Cast of characters—

Martin Doul.....................................Barry Fitzgerald
Mary Doul...May Craig

```
Timmy the Smith..................................P. J. Carolan
Molly Byrne....................................Aideen O'Connor
Mat Simon.......................................Denis O'Dea
Patch Ruadh.......................................U. Wright
Bride.........................................Frolie Mulhern
The Saint.....................................F. J. McCormick
      Acts I and III.—Outside a Church in Lonely Mountainous District
in the East of Ireland.  Act II.—Outside the Smith's Forge.
```

See "Best Plays of 1931-32."

JUNO AND THE PAYCOCK

By Sean O'Casey

November 23, 1934

(9 performances)

Cast of characters—

```
"Captain" Jack Boyle...........................Barry Fitzgerald
"Juno" Boyle...................................Eileen Crowe
Johnny Boyle..................................Arthur Shields
Mary Boyle...................................Aideen O'Connor
"Joxer" Daly.................................F. J. McCormick
Maisie Madigan...............................Maureen Delany
"Needle" Nugents...............................U. Wright
Mrs. Tancred...................................May Craig
Jerry Devine..................................P. J. Carolan
Charlie Bentham..............................Michael J. Dolan
An Irregular...................................Denis O'Dea
      Acts I, II and III.—Living Apartment of the Boyle Family in
Dublin.
```

See "Best Plays of 1925-26."
The Abbey Theatre Players also included in their repertory
one performance of "Kathleen Ni Houlihan" by William Butler
Yeats; two performances of "Riders to the Sea" by J. M. Synge
and "Spring" by T. C. Murray.

BRITTLE HEAVEN

(23 performances)

A drama in three acts adapted by Vincent York and Frederick
Pohl from Josephine Pollitt's book, "Emily Dickinson"; incidental
music by Rudolf Forst. Produced by Dave Schooler at the
Vanderbilt Theatre, New York, November 13, 1934.

Cast of characters—

```
Austin Dickinson................................Earl McDonald
Sue Dickinson..................................Helen Huberth
Mrs. Dickinson...................................Helen Ray
Lavinia Dickinson.............................Katherine Hirsch
Emily Dickinson................................Dorothy Gish
Mr. Dickinson................................Robert Le Sueur
```

```
Helen Hunt.......................................Edith Atwater
Samuel Bowles....................................Herbert Warren
Captain Edward Bissell Hunt...................Albert Van Dekker
Horatio Turnbull................................Grant Gordon
Gilbert Dickinson..............................Edward Ryan, Jr.
Maggie..........................................Elizabeth Heaslip
```
    Acts I, II and III.—Parlor of the Dickinson Home in Amherst,
Mass.
    Staged by Clarence Derwent; setting by P. Dodd Ackerman.

Emily Dickinson, poet, meeting Major Edward Bissell Hunt,
husband of her dearest friend, for the first time discovers that the
Major has long been deeply in love with her, a passion stirred by
her letters to his wife. Swept away by the Major's declaration,
and piqued by the jealousy of her friend, Emily declares her will-
ingness to follow her love, but he is killed while carrying out a
civil war assignment.

*THE CHILDREN'S HOUR

(247 performances)

A tragedy in three acts by Lillian Hellman. Produced by Herman Shumlin at the Maxine Elliott Theatre, New York, November 20, 1934.

Cast of characters—
```
Peggy Rogers....................................Eugenia Rawls
Mrs. Lily Mortar...............................Aline McDermott
Evelyn Munn....................................Elizabeth Seckel
Helen Burton.....................................Lynne Fisher
Lois Fisher..................................Jacqueline Rusling
Catherine........................................Barbara Leeds
Rosalie Wells....................................Barbara Beals
Mary Tilford....................................Florence McGee
Karen Wright...................................Katherine Emery
Martha Dobie......................................Anne Revere
Doctor Joseph Cardin.............................Robert Keith
Agatha.........................................Edmonia Nolley
Mrs. Amelia Tilford...........................Katherine Emmet
A Grocery Boy......................................Jack Tyler
```
    Acts I and III.—Living Room of the Wright-Dobie School. Act
II.—Living Room at Mrs. Tilford's.
    Staged by Herman Shumlin; settings by Aline Bernstein and Sointu
Syrjala.

See page 33.

*ANYTHING GOES

(244 performances)

A musical comedy in two acts by Guy Bolton, P. G. Wode-
house, Howard Lindsey and Russel Crouse; music and lyrics by
Cole Porter. Produced by Vinton Freedley, Inc., at the Alvin
Theatre, New York, November 21, 1934.

Cast of characters—

Bartender......................................George E. Mack
Elisha J. Whitney................................Paul Everton
Billy Crocker.................................William Gaxton
Bell Boy...Irvin Pincus
Reno Sweeney....................................Ethel Merman
Reporter....................................Edward Delbridge
First Cameraman....................................Chet Bree
Second Cameraman...................................Neal Evans
Sir Evelyn Oakleigh.............................Leslie Barrie
Hope Harcourt....................................Bettina Hall
Mrs. Wadsworth T. Harcourt.....................Helen Raymond
Bishop Dodson....................................Pacie Ripple
Ching...Richard Wang
Ling..Charlie Fang
Snooks..Drucilla Strain
Steward...William Stamm
Assistant Purser..................................Val Vestoff
First Federal Man...............................Harry Wilson
Second Federal Man............................Arthur Imperato
Mrs. Wentworth....................................May Abbey
Mrs. Frick.....................................Florence Earle
Reverend Dr. Moon...............................Victor Moore
Bonnie Letour......................................Vera Dunn
Chief Officer.................................Houston Richards
Ship's Drunk....................................William Barry
Mr. Swift......................................Maurice Elliott
Little Boy.......................................Billy Curtis
Captain..John C. King
Babe...Vivian Vance
The Foursome.................................⎰ Marshall Smith
                                             ⎱ Ray Johnson
                                             ⎰ Dwight Snyder
                                             ⎱ Dee Porter
The Ritz Quartette...........................⎰ Chet Bree
                                             ⎱ Bill Stamm
                                             ⎰ Neal Evans
                                             ⎱ Ed. Delbridge
The Alvin Quartette..........................⎰ Arthur Imperato
                                             ⎱ David Glidden
                                             ⎰ Richard Nealy
                                             ⎱ Stuart Fraser
Ship's Orchestra...............................The Stylists
Reno's Angels: Ruth Bond, Norma Butler, Enes Early, Marjorie
  Fisher, Ruth Gomley, Irene Hamlin, Renee Johnson, Irene
  Kelly, Leoda Knapp, Doris Maye, Lillian Ostrom, Jackie Paige,
  Mary Philips, Cornelia Rogers, Frances Stewart, Ruth Shaw,
  Eleanore Sheridan.
Passengers: Kay Adams, Lola Dexter, Maurine Holmes, Helen Fol-
  som, Marquita Nicholai, Ethel Sommerville, Finette Walker,
  Evelyn Kelly.
  Act I.—Scene 1—Weylin Caprice Bar. 2 and 4—Afterdeck. 3—
Mr. Whitney's and Dr. Moon's Cabins. 5—Sir Evelyn's Cabin. 6—
Deck. Act II.—Scene 1—Lounge. 2—Brig. 3—Conservatory of Sir
Evelyn's Home in England.
  Staged by Howard Lindsay; dances by Robert Alton; settings by
Donald Oenslager.

Public Enemy No. 13, who happens to be Victor Moore, is
escaping trouble in the States by shipping aboard an Atlantic
liner as the Rev. Mr. Moon, carrying his putt-putt gun in a
clarinet case. Billy Crocker, who is really William Gaxton, is a
superior sort of stowaway on the same boat, having sailed without
a ticket to be near the love of his heart, who is Bettina Hall.
Complicating matters slightly is Reno Sweeney, or Ethel Merman,

pretending to be a night club hostess, taking her floor-show girls
to London and trying to annex Mr. Gaxton.

BUT NOT FOR LOVE

(8 performances)

A drama in three acts by Geraldine Emerson. Produced by
Shepard Traube at the Empire Theatre, New York, November
26, 1934.

Cast of characters—

Patricia Dodd	Helen Brooks
Mrs. Dodd	Effie Shannon
Jeff Dodd	Walter N. Greaza
Will Dodd	Ray Harper
Lois Dodd	Hortense Alden
Sam Parker	Ben Lackland

Acts I, II and III.—Living Room of the Jeff Dodd Home in
Marshall, Michigan.
Staged by Shepard Traube; setting by Arthur Segal.

Jeff Dodd, bank clerk, is selfish. Lois Dodd, his wife, is generous and forgiving. Lois, with an artistic bent, sells a poster
for $50. Jeff borrows the fifty to spend on a trip to a bankers'
convention hoping that it will help him out of his position as
teller. Lois hears that at the convention Jeff spent at least a part
of the fifty on his boss's stenographer. She is ready to walk out
when Patricia Dodd, her sister-in-law, dies in childbirth, leaving
a motherless infant Lois feels she should look out for. Ambushed
by circumstances she goes back to the job.

AFRICANA

(3 performances)

An operetta by Donald Heywood. Produced by Perry-Wood
Co., at the Venice Theatre, New York, November 26, 1934.

Principals engaged—

Jack Carr	Walter Richardson
Howard Gould	Nita Gale
Joseph Byrd	Dan C. Michaels
Earl Carter	Barrington Guy
Olivette Miller	Gretchen Branch

Staged by Peter Morell; settings by Anthony Continer.

THE NIGHT REMEMBERS

(23 performances)

A mystery melodrama in three acts by Martha Madison. Produced by B. Peters and Leslie J. Spiller at The Playhouse, New York, November 27, 1934.

Cast of characters—

Bell Hop	Robert Elwyn
Fred	Frank Collins
Hank	Harry Clarke
Mr. Ivins	Wilfred Jessop
Paul Ivins	Van Heflin
Van	Howard Ferguson
Flynn	Tom Morrison
Dr. Max Offner	André Salama
Bill	F. G. Cleveland
Jim	Philip Bourneuf
Speakeasy Proprietor	Ernst Robert
Waiter	Vincent Gerbino
Lola	Mary Holsman
"Shrimp" Yates	William Nunn
Night Clerk	Allen B. Nourse
Taxi Driver	Philip Van Zandt
Scrub Woman	Lizzie Cubitt
Flashy Woman	Marie Hunt
Fitzsimmons	Robert J. Mulligan
Mullen	Frank Coletti
Mooney	Hal Dearborn
Tough Boy	Bill Darwin
Inspector Kelly	Frank Dae
Momo Sebalios	Brandon Tynan
Tall Man	Sheldon Leonard
Maria Sebalios	Vera Hurst
A Nurse	Ann Martin
A Model	Margaret Seaman

Act I.—Scenes 1 and 3—Lounge in New York Athletic Club. 2—Speakeasy in Brooklyn. Act II.—Scenes 1 and 3—Detective's Room in Ninth Precinct, Brooklyn. 2—Lola's House. Act III.—Scene 1—Doctor Offner's Office. 2—Lola's House.
Staged by Leo Bulgakov.

Paul Ivins, meeting the beautiful Lola in a speakeasy, follows her home. The girl's father hypnotizes Paul, forces him to stay. Paul's weird experiences convince him that he and Lola are both victims of mysterious evil forces, which sends him searching for the police next day. The police can find no trace of either the house or the people described by Paul. A psychoanalyst explains it all as an illusion and perhaps it was.

PAGE MISS GLORY

(63 performances)

A comedy in two acts by Joseph Schrank and Philip Dunning. Produced by Laurence Schwab and Philip Dunning at the Mansfield Theatre, New York, November 27, 1934.

Cast of characters—

Dan (Click) Wiley	Charles D. Brown
Ed Olsen	James Stewart
Betty	Jane Seymour
Loretta	Dorothy Hall
Mr. Bates	Royal Beal
Gladys Russell	Peggy Shannon
"Bingo" Nelson	Bruce MacFarlane
Professor Noonan	Royal Dana Tracy
A Gentleman of the Press	Harold Grau
Slattery, of the *Mirror*	J. Anthony Hughes
Metz, of the *Times*	Frederic Voight

Telegram ⎫
Tribune ⎪
Journal ⎪
Sun ⎬ ....Reporters.......... ⎨ Betty Field / Jerry Sloane / Muriel Robert / Pedro A. Galvan
Daily Worker ⎪ ⎩ Edward Colebrook
News ⎪ Peggy Hart
American ⎭ Douglas Gregory

Mr. Grace	Chester Clute
Mr. Williams	Roy Gordon
First Bellboy	Carter Blake
Second Bellboy	Ralph Sternard
The Mother	Maud B. Sinclair
Blackie	Joseph Downing
Petey	Harry Bellaver
Nick	Joe Vitale

Associated Press ⎫
United Press ⎪ ⎧ H. S. Hopkins
Brooklyn Eagle ⎬ ....Reporters.......... ⎨ Harry Dee / John Fleming
Post ⎭ ⎩ Charles Strong

Detectives.........................O. J. Vanasse, Frank Sardo

Acts I and II.—In New York City.
Staged by George Abbott; settings by Arne Lundborg.

Dan Wiley and Ed Olsen, who live by their wits, are stranded in a New York hotel. Dan reads the offer of a health salts company agreeing to pay $2,500 for a picture of the most beautiful girl in America. Olsen, who has been a photographer, produces a synthetic photo of a girl with Garbo's eyes, Dietrich's legs, and all the visible assets of other Hollywood beauties. The picture is entered as that of Dawn Glory. The picture wins the prize and the boys are urged to produce the girl that she may cash in on various advertising contracts and a movie appearance. Loretta, a good-looking chambermaid, is caught trying on some of the sample clothes sent to Miss Glory and is thereafter forced into the part. Complications are many, adjustments satisfactory.

THE LORD BLESSES THE BISHOP

(7 performances)

A comedy in three acts by Hatcher Hughes. Produced by Glen McNaughton at the Adelphi Theatre, New York, November 27, 1934.

Cast of characters—

```
Barbara Kemble..................................Claudia Morgan
Hugh Kemble......................................Wilton Graff
Ben..............................................Robert Finch
Bishop Tupper....................................Jack Soanes
Harriet Gresham..................................Patricia Calvert
The Reverend Alan Gresham........................Hugh Rennie
Mlle. Suzanne Barres.............................Ann Dunnigan
Father Hanahan...................................Gerald Cornell
```
    Acts I, II and III.—Hugh Kemble's Studio. New York City.
    Staged by Hatcher Hughes; setting by Cleon Throckmorton.

Hugh Kemble, artist, wishes to become a father. Barbara
Kemble, his wife, prefers reform work in the theatre to motherhood. Following a disagreement Barbara goes home to her father,
a Bishop of the church, and Hugh engages a practical Suzanne
Barres to become the mother of his child. After the child is born
Barbara returns to Hugh's house and offers to buy his baby, but
the mother will not sell. There are hints of a reconciliation.

GOLD EAGLE GUY

(65 performances)

A drama in five scenes by Melvin Levy. Produced by The
Group Theatre, Inc., in association with D. A. Doran, Jr., at the
Morosco Theatre, New York, November 28, 1934.

Cast of characters—

```
                                    ⎧ Phœbe Brand
                                    ⎪ Helen Carrm
                                    ⎪ Paula Miller
                                    ⎪ Ruth Nelson
Girls of the "Mantic".............. ⎨ Eunice Stoddard
                                    ⎪ Florence Cooper
                                    ⎪ Evelyn Geller
                                    ⎪ Joan Madison
                                    ⎩ Dorothy Patten
Mrs. Kummer......................................Frances Williams
Macondray........................................Roman Bohnen
Tony Sorrenson...................................Gerrit Kraber
Adam Keane.......................................Walter Coy
Guy Button.......................................J. Edward Bromberg
Bartender........................................Herbert Ratner
Gus..............................................Bob Lewis
Burns............................................Clifford Odets
Will Parrott.....................................Morris Carnovsky
Ortega...........................................Sanford Meisner
Emperor Norton...................................Luther Adler
Pearly...........................................William Challee
Merg.............................................Art Smith
Polyzoides.......................................Elia Kazan
Sailor...........................................Jules Garfield
Adah Menken......................................Stella Adler
MacNaurty........................................Alan Baxter
A Miner..........................................Lewis Leverett
Another Miner....................................David Kortchmar
A Deserter.......................................Russell Collins
Captain Roberts..................................Lewis Leverett
```

```
Ed  Walker.....................................Russell  Collins
Jessie  Sargent.................................Margaret  Barker
Tang  Sin...........................................Luther  Adler
Jolais............................................Clifford  Odets
Joe.............................................Gerrit  Kraber
Mackay..........................................Jules  Garfield
Elizabeth  Jolais.................................Phœbe  Brand
Mrs.  DaSilva..................................Florence  Cooper
Mrs.  Muller......................................Joan  Madison
Miss  Simmonds................................Dorothy  Patten
Mrs.  Sheldon.....................................Paula  Miller
André..........................................Lewis  Leverett
Ah  Kee........................................William  Challee
Mrs.  Lemon...................................Eunice  Stoddard
Mrs.  Guadalla...............................Frances  Williams
Jacobs.........................................Herbert  Ratner
Wallin.............................................Art  Smith
Kohler...........................................Alan  Baxter
Lon  Firth...................................Alexander  Kirkland
Mrs.  Halstead...................................Helen  Carrm
Mrs.  McElvay....................................Ruth  Nelson
Guy,  Jr.  (Act  2)...................................John  Jordan
Rev.  Brown..................................David  Kortchmar
Postman.........................................Alan  Baxter
Guy,  Jr.  (Act  3).............................Sanford  Meisner
Okajima.........................................Bob  Lewis
A.  D.  T.  Boy..................................Herbert  Ratner
Mrs.  Nass.......................................Paula  Miller
Miss  Richards...................................Ruth  Nelson
```

Scene 1—"Mantic" Barroom, San Francisco, 1862. 2—Offices of the Keane Shipping Company, San Francisco, 1864. 3—Guy Button's California Street Home, San Francisco, 1879. 4—Offices of the Gold Eagle Lines, March, 1898. 5—Guy Button's Private Offices in the Home Office of Gold Eagle Lines, San Francisco, 1906.

Staged by Lee Strasberg; settings by Donald Oenslager; dances by Tamiris.

Guy Button, a tough sailor before the mast, jumps ship in San Francisco in 1862 and begins a ruthless climb toward the top of the shipping business of the gold coast. His mania for the possession of gold eagle pieces explains his soubriquet. In 1864 Guy has taken over the Keane Shipping Company and gone into the Chinese coolie trade to supply the California labor market. By 1879 he is head of a great line of steamships, married to a gentle Californian and able to take over a bank that is in trouble. By 1898 he is himself in danger of crashing. To avert disaster for his bank he scuttles the Wells-Fargo strong box on one of his ships and sinks the ship with all on board to cover the crime. In 1906 the pillars of his office fall in upon him at the first shake of the quake.

REVENGE WITH MUSIC

(158 performances)

A musical comedy in two acts and seventeen scenes by Howard Dietz and Arthur Schwartz. Produced by Arch Selwyn and Harold B. Franklin at the New Amsterdam Theatre, New York, November 28, 1934.

Cast of characters—

```
Manuelo.............................................Jay Wilson
Miguel Rodriguez, the Mayor......................Detmar Poppen
Pablo...........................................Rex O'Malley
Alonzo.......................................Joseph Macaulay
Doña Isabella....................................Ilka Chase
Don Emilio, Gobernador of the Province.........Charles Winninger
Maria...........................................Libby Holman
Margarita.......................................Margaret Lee
Eduardo........................................George Kirk
Carlos.........................................Georges Metaxa
Consuella.........................................Ivy Scott
Constantina...................................Natali Danesi
Salvador........................................Walter Armin
Josefa..........................................Helen Arden
Mule Driver..................................George Thornton
Rosalia..........................................Berta Donn
Juanita........................................Beatrice Berens
Guitarists................................Hernandez Brothers
Dancing Soloists: Rosita Ortega, Nuñez de Polanco, Omero Valencia,
  Frances Farnsworth, Tamara Doriva.
  Staged by Komisarjevsky; dances by Michael Mordkin; music di-
rection by Victor Baravalle; settings by Albert Johnson.
```

Don Emilio, governor of a Spanish province, lusts after many women and would steal Maria on her wedding night. He is serenading Maria when he falls into a handy pool. While he is drying off, Maria's bridegroom, young and handsome Carlos, believing that he has been deceived, seeks a personal revenge by making love to the governor's wife, Doña Isabella, who is not at all averse to his advances.

A ROMAN SERVANT

(9 performances)

A drama in three acts by Larry O'Connor. Produced by Arnaud and Connors Associates at the Longacre Theatre, New York, December 1, 1934.

Cast of characters—

```
Symes...............................Charles H. Croker-King
Prof. Wayne..................................Lester Alden
Lady Gylda...........................Lilian Kemble Cooper
Sybil Weyman................................Helene Millard
Dr. Samuel Weyman.......................Ernest Glendinning
Lord Cyril..................................Leslie Denison
  Acts I, II and III.—Study of Dr. Weyman's London Home.
  Staged by William B. Friedlander; settings by Watson Barratt.
```

Dr. Weyman, recognizing a former lover of his wife in a patient suffering an attack of amnesia, restores the man's memory despite his belief that he will again become his rival. The result is as the doctor had anticipated. Realizing that he stands in the way of his wife's happiness, the Doctor instructs his faithful servant, Symes, to prepare the lethal drops, which Symes does.

POST ROAD

(212 performances)

A comedy in two acts by Wilbur Daniel Steele and Norma Mitchell. Produced by Potter and Haight at the Masque Theatre, New York, December 4, 1934.

Cast of characters—

George Preble	Percy Kilbride
May Madison Preble	Mary Sargent
Wesley Cartwright	Romaine Callender
Bill	Dillon Deasy
Celia	Geraldine Brown
Emily Madison	Lucile Watson
Jeeby Cashler	Ada May Reed
Dr. Spender	Edward Fielding
Nurse Martin	Edna M. Holland
The Girl	Wendy Atkin
Matt	Henry Norell
Virgil Bemis	Edmon Ryan
Jay	Leonard Barker
Mrs. Canby	Caroline Newcombe
Mrs. Cashler	Virginia Tracy

Acts I and II.—Living Room of Emily Madison's Home in Connecticut.

Staged by H. C. Potter; setting by Raymond Sovey.

Emily Madison accommodates tourists as roomers in her home on the Boston Post Road. The night Dr. Spender asks that she take in his patient, a young woman taken ill while touring, Emily makes room for the sick girl, the doctor, a nurse and a chauffeur. A few hours later the girl is announced the mother of a baby. Dr. Spender thereupon engages the entire Madison cottage. A week later Emily becomes suddenly conscious of the fact that while there is an infant in her house there has been no birth. Piecing suspicious circumstances together she is convinced she is housing a kidnaped child. She maneuvers to get hold of the baby and contact the police before the crooks can do anything about it.

TOMORROW'S HARVEST

(4 performances)

A drama in three acts by Hans Rastede. Produced by Douglas G. Hertz at the 49th Street Theatre, New York, December 5, 1934.

Cast of characters—

Augusta Goerlich	Valerie Bergere
Emil Goerlich	Robert Henderson
Gretchen Goerlich	Sheila Trent
Anton Hieber	Howard St. John

```
Frieda.............................................Helen Salinger
Dr. Jerry Warder...................................Lester Vail
John Goerlich..............................Wm. F. Schoeller
Alma Goerlich..................................Greta Granstedt
Paula Goerlich.......................................Kay Strozzi
Fred Westlake...............................Chester Stratton
```
Acts I, II and III.—Living Room of the Goerlich Home in We-
tonka, Wisconsin.
Staged by Frank Merlin.

Paula Goerlich, having been married against her will to Anton
Hieber, at the command of her martinet of a father, runs away
and establishes herself as a buyer in New York. Later she returns home to ask her husband to divorce her. She finds her
father as domineering as ever, and suffering from a weak heart.
The family tells her she can solve all their family problems if she
will return to her husband. Paula is ready to make the sacrifice,
when her sister's threatened suicide, because of the father's opposition to her marriage, alters her decision. She denounces the father
bitterly. He curls up in his wrath and dies. The family turns
against Paula. She goes back to her job with a prospect of marrying a doctor friend.

SO MANY PATHS

(28 performances)

A drama in three acts by Irving Kaye Davis. Produced by
Cohn and Scanlon at the Ritz Theatre, New York, December 6,
1934.

Cast of characters—
```
Mrs. Kenny.........................................Sara Perry
Ruth Kenny.....................................Nancy Sheridan
Clara Kenny......................................Norma Terris
Walter Henderson............................George Blackwood
Howard Brown.....................................Matt Briggs
Margaret Kenny Brown..........................Natalie Schafer
Henry J. Stewart...............................Hermann Lieb
Miss Pearson..................................Blanche Fleming
Beulah...........................................Mary Barker
Madame Fuselli......................................Lea Penman
```
Acts I, II and III —Home of Mrs. Kenny in New York City.
Staged by Priestly Morrison; setting by Watson Barratt.

Clara Kenny has a voice and hopes for a career. She is engaged to ardent Walter Henderson, who wants her to marry him
and live and love in Texas. She tries to borrow money from her
brother-in-law for three years of voice training abroad. Brother-
in-law dodges the gamble. Clara turns to Henry J. Stewart,
millionaire, who has offered to back her at a price. Three years
in Europe with Henry and the voice teachers and Clara comes
home to startle Gatti-Casazza at the Metropolitan. But she has

lost her lover. Walter has married her sister and is the father of a son. Clara goes back to the Metropolitan, and probably to Henry, if he is still active.

VALLEY FORGE

(58 performances)

A drama in three acts by Maxwell Anderson. Produced by the Theatre Guild, Inc., at the Guild Theatre, New York, December 10, 1934.

Cast of characters—

Andrew	Thaddeus Clancy
Spad	Alan Bunce
Alcock	Victor Kilian
Teague	Grover Burgess
Mason	Charles Ellis
Jock	Jock McGraw
Oscar	Hans Hansen
Nick	Robert Thomsen
Minto	Harry Hermsen
Marty	Alexander Mirsky
Tavis	Frances Sage
Auntie	Florence Gerald
Neil	Hendrik Booraem
Lieutenant Cutting	George Coulouris
Rover	Bingo
Lieut. Col. Lucifer Tench	Stanley Ridges
An Aide	Philip Robinson
General George Washington	Philip Merivale
Marquis de Lafayette	Edward Trevor
Major André	John Hoysradt
A Brigadier	Charles Drummond
Sir William Howe	Reginald Mason
Mary Philipse	Margalo Gillmore
A Captain	Philip Foster
Fielding	Stephen Appleby
"The Washington" (Masquerade)	Charles Francis
First Soldier	Alan Bandler
Second Soldier	Philip Robinson
Third Soldier	Wallace Acton
A Civilian	George Spaulding
General Varnum	Harold Gould
General Stirling	Harold Elliott
Rafe	John Sennott
Mr. Harvie	Harold Tucker
Mr. Folsom	Erskine Sanford
General Conway	Charles Francis

Ladies: Cora Burlar, Eleanor Eckstein, Jean Sennott, Cynthia Sherwood, Katherine Standing.
Musicians: Max Weiser, Nicolai Pesce, Maurice Sackett.
Act I.—Scene 1—Bunk-house at Valley Forge, January, 1778. 2—Private Ballroom in General Howe's Headquarters, Philadelphia. 3—General Washington's Headquarters. Act II.—Scene 1—Bunk-house. 2—Washington's Headquarters. Act III.—Barn on Hay Island in the Delaware River.
Staged by Herbert Biberman and John Houseman; settings by Kate Drain Lawson; minuet staged by Martha Graham.

See page 66.

SAILORS OF CATTARO

(96 performances)

A drama in two acts by Friedrich Wolf, translated from the German by Keene Wallis and adapted by Michael Blankfort. Produced by the Theatre Union, Inc., at the Civic Repertory Theatre, New York, December 10, 1934.

Cast of characters—

Mate Bernicevic	Robert Reed
Jerko Sisgoric	Ernest Gann
Sepp Kriz	Howard da Silva
Kuddel Huck	Charles Thompson
Alois	George Tobias
Anton Grabar	Martin Wolfson
Franz Rasch	Tom Powers
Gustav Stonawski	John Boruff
Ensign Julio Sesan	Harold Johnsrud
Lieutenant	James McDonald
Captain	Frederick Roland
Hans Trulec	Abner Biberman
Officer of Archduke Karl	Paul Stein

Sailors and Soldiers: Wendell Phillips, Edwin Clare, William Schap-Kevisch, Edward Mann, Samson Gordon, David Kerman, Theodore Cohen, Bernard Zanville, William Nichols, Sidney Packer.

Act I.—Scene 1—Crew's Quarters on Battleship "Saint George," Flagship of the Austrian Fleet, in the Bay of Cattaro, an Inlet of the Adriatic Sea. 1918. 2—Fore-deck. 3—Chart Room. Act II.—Scenes 1 and 2—Chart Room. 3—Fore-deck.

Staged by Irving Gordon; settings by Mordecai Gorelik.

Led by Franz Rasch the sailors on the Austrian battleship "Saint George" join with six thousand other sailors in the harbor of Cattaro in a mutiny the last year of the World War. The first steps of the mutineers are successful, but they talk themselves out of a victory with too much bickering in their sailors' council and are defeated in the end. The mutiny is crushed and the ringleaders led away to be executed.

THE SKY'S THE LIMIT

(24 performances)

A farce in three acts by Pierce Johns and Hendrik Booraem. Produced by Raymond Golden at the Fulton Theatre, New York, December 17, 1934.

Cast of characters—

Connie	Norma Downey
Russell Brent	Russell Gleason
Vickers	Richard Clark
Fraser	Martin Gabel
Prof. Mungoe	Maurice Cass
Perry Nichols	John Kane

```
Olga...............................................Ruth Altman
Peggy.............................................Mary Mason
Enright...........................................Don Beddoe
Lew Briskin.........................................Joe Smith
Abe J. Pinkel.......................................Chas. Dale
Murgatroyd.......................................Lew Daniels
```
Act I.—Executive Office Hackett, Hitchcock & Hotchkiss, N. Y. C.
Acts II and III.—Scenes 1 and 3—Office. 2—On the Air.
Staged by Sidney Salkow; settings by Arthur Segal.

Lew Briskin, late of burlesque, becomes an advertising agent for radio. To snare the Yeast Sweetie account of Abe Finkel, Briskin organizes a program presenting Perry, tenor, and Peggy, soprano. Olga, Perry's sweetheart, jealously threatens to break up the deal. Briskin invites Yeast Sweeties patrons to vote on box-tops of the product as to whether Peggy or Olga shall be Perry's bride. Peggy is winning, Olga becomes increasingly nasty and the Yeast Sweeties outfit is forced to buy up its own output to switch the vote.

CALLING ALL STARS

(36 performances)

A revue in two acts by Lew Brown; music by Harry Akst. Produced by Lew Brown at the Hollywood Theatre, New York, December 13, 1934.

Principals engaged—

Lou Holtz	Mitzi Mayfair
Phil Baker	Gertrude Niesen
Everett Marshall	Patricia Bowman
Jack Whiting	Peggy Taylor
Al Bernie	Estelle Jayne
Harry McNaughton	Martha Ray
Arthur Auerbach	Strauss Dancers

Staged by Lew Brown and Thomas Mitchell; dance direction by Sara Mildred Strauss; music by Al Goodman; settings by Nat Karson.

ROMEO AND JULIET

(77 performances)

A tragedy by William Shakespeare, arranged in two parts and twenty-three scenes by Katharine Cornell; music by Paul Nordoff. Produced by Miss Cornell at the Martin Beck Theatre, New York, December 20, 1934.

Cast of characters—

```
Escalus, Prince of Verona.......................Reynolds Evans
Paris...........................................George Macready
Montague.........................................John Miltern
Capulet..........................................Moroni Olsen
```

```
An Old Man....................................Arthur Chatterton
Romeo.........................................Basil Rathbone
Mercutio......................................Brian Aherne
Benvolio......................................John Emery
Tybalt........................................Orson Welles
Friar Laurence................................Charles Waldron
Friar John....................................Paul Julian
Balthasar.....................................Franklyn Gray
Sampson.......................................Joseph Holland
Peter.........................................David Vivian
Gregory.......................................Robert Champlain
Abraham.......................................Irving Morrow
An Apothecary.................................Arthur Chatterton
Officer.......................................Irving Morrow
Lady Montague.................................Brenda Forbes
Lady Capulet..................................Irby Marshal
Juliet........................................Katharine Cornell
Nurse to Juliet...............................Edith Evans
A Street Singer...............................Edith Allaire
Guards..................................Angus Duncan, Ralph Nelson
```

Citizens of Verona, Kinsfolk of Both Houses, Maskers, Guards, Watchmen and Attendants: Margaret Craven, Jacqueline De Wit, Lois Jameson, Agnete Johannson, Ruth March, Pamela Simpson, Gilmore Bush, John Gordon Gage, William Hopper, Albert Mc-Cleery, Charles Thorne.

```
Chorus........................................Orson Welles
```

Part I.—Scenes 1 and 11—Public Place in Verona, Mantua. 2 and 4—Capulet's House. 3 and 8—Street in Verona. 5—By Wall of Capulet's Cell. 6 and 9—Capulet's Orchard. 7 and 10—Friar Laurence's Cell. Part II.—Scenes 12, 15, 18 and 20—Juliet's Bedroom. 13 and 16—Friar Laurence's Cell. 14, 17 and 19—Capulet's House. 21—Street in Mantua. 22—Outside Friar Laurence's Cell. 23—Tomb of the Capulets.

Staged by Guthrie McClintic; settings by Jo Mielziner; dance direction by Martha Graham.

The version of "Romeo and Juliet" used by Miss Cornell divides the play into two acts, intermission following Romeo's flight to Mantua. The last previous revival of the tragedy in New York was that of Eva Le Gallienne, staged as a feature of her Civic Theatre repertory in 1930.

ODE TO LIBERTY

(67 performances)

A comedy in three acts adapted from the French of Michel Duran's "Liberté Provisoire" by Sidney Howard. Produced by Gilbert Miller at the Lyceum Theatre, New York, December 21, 1934.

Cast of characters—

```
Madeleine.....................................Ina Claire
Barnaud.......................................Nicholas Joy
Dorlay........................................Paul McGrath
Policeman.....................................Walter Slezak
Inspector Roulet..............................Stanley Jessup
Sergeant Duval................................Allen Fagan
Benoite.......................................Katherine Stewart
Ducroux.......................................Hal K. Dawson
A Chauffeur...................................Colin Hunter
```

Acts I, II and III.—Studio Living Room of Madeleine's Apartment in Paris.
Staged by Sidney Howard; setting by Elsie de Wolfe, Inc.

Madeleine, married to Barnaud, a banker, has left her husband's
home, established herself in an apartment and found a job. She
is entertaining her friend Dorlay and her husband the night a
young policeman invades the apartment. He is a Communist in
disguise, escaping the police after having shot at Hitler and
missed. For four days Madeleine is obliged to keep the Communist hidden, or turn him over to the authorities. Her interest
in him ripens into love. She bargains with her husband, agreeing to go back to his home if he will use his influence to help
the Communist escape. Husband agrees, Communist starts on
a long walking tour and Madeleine orders a good stout pair of
walking shoes for herself.

MOTHER LODE

(9 performances)

A drama in three acts by Dan Totheroh and George O'Neil.
Produced by George Bushar and John Tuerk at the Cort Theatre,
New York, December 22, 1934.

Cast of characters—

Cassius	William Franklin
Brutus	John Troughton
Whiskey Truman (Later, Senator Truman)	Clifford Dempsey
Frank O'Malley	Thomas Chalmers
Irish Johnnie	Orrin Burke
Swede	Einar Svalbe
Little Breeches	Lester Lonergan
Pious Pete	Robert Thorne
Mother O'Brien	Lida Kane
Slim	Robert Kellard
Yank	Ivan Arbuckle
Red Dog	Tex Ritter
Curley	George Lamar
Julia Musette	Gertrude Flynn
Horace Fields	Robert Shayne
Carey Ried	Melvyn Douglas
Mrs. Kate Hawkins	Beulah Bondi
Speed Jake	C. Russell Sage
Hannah Hawkins	Helen Gahagan
Thomas Carter	Frank Camp
Sing	Arvid Paulson
Booth Ried	Lester Lonergan, 3rd
Clarissa Ried	Lenore Lonergan
Mrs. Thomas Carter	Edythe Elliott
Madame Lorska	Helen Freeman
Lord Berkeley Beresfield	Roland Bottomley
Evelyn	Kate Warriner
A Young Woman	Lillian Walker
Mrs. Schiller	Louise Beaudet
A Young Man	Robert Kellard
A Lieutenant	Einar Svalbe

```
A Man.........................................Lester Lonergan
Dick Condon....................................George Lamar
A Sailor........................................William Franklin
Mike...........................................C. Russell Sage
Another Man.......................................Tex Ritter
A Woman........................................Barbara O'Neil
Another Woman....................................Lillian Walker
Miners, Citizens, Guests at the Ball, etc.: Mary Reilly, Rosalie Van
    der Stucken, Cynthia Dane, Carolyn Hun, Barbara Brown, Jean
    Marwood, Valerie Tempest, Dorothea Cadwallader, Alice Dowd,
    Dorothy Bayley, Paul Porter, Willis Duncan, Franklin Reber,
    Frank Baer, Frank Burke, Frank Lambert, Al Guin, Sam Worth,
    Robert Wellman, J. James.
    Act I.—Continental Boarding House and First Class "Two-bit" Sa-
loon of Virginia City, Nevada.  Act II.—Ried Suite, Lick House on
Montgomery Street, San Francisco.  Act III.—Scenes 1 and 3—Ried
Mansion on Nob Hill, San Francisco.  Scene 2—Exterior of the Bank
of San Francisco.
    Staged by Melvyn Douglas; settings by Leigh Morrison.
```

Carey Ried dreams of building the San Francisco of the 60's into the world's most beautiful city. He meets and loves Hannah Hawkins when she is singing in a two-bit saloon in Virginia City. Hannah stakes Carey to a nugget with which he buys an interest in the Comstock lode. The investment makes Carey a rich man. In San Francisco he builds extravagantly in the people's interest and to his own profit. At the verge of a panic his partners desert him as a visionary. He is crushed and beaten until Hannah, overlooking his temporary passion for an actress, lifts him again to his feet with her courage and faith.

RAIN FROM HEAVEN

(99 performances)

A comedy in three acts by S. N. Behrman. Produced by The Theatre Guild, Inc., at the Golden Theatre, New York, December 24, 1934.

Cast of characters—

```
Joan...........................................Hancey Castle
Mrs. Dingle...................................Alice Belmore-Cliffe
Rand Eldridge......................................Ben Smith
Hobart Eldridge...................................Thurston Hall
Lady Violet Wyngate................................Jane Cowl
Hugo Willens....................................John Halliday
Sascha Barashaev................................Marshall Grant
Phœbe Eldridge.....................................Lily Cahill
Clendon Wyatt....................................Robert Woods
Nikolai Jurin......................................José Ruben
    Acts I, II and III.—Living Room of Lady Wyngate's Home Near
London.
    Staged by Philip Moeller; settings by Lee Simonson.
```

Lady Violet Wyngate, a lady of liberal tendencies and an open heart, is hostess to three interesting émigrés, Hugo Willens, a music critic barred from Berlin because of a strain of Jewish blood; Nikolai Jurin, a Russian scholar, and Sascha Barashaev, a Russian pianist, victims of the revolution. Her guests also include Hobart Eldridge, an American millionaire, and his younger brother, Rand. Rand is in love with Lady Violet, but her ladyship is afraid to risk marriage. Hugo Willens also loves her, but puts aside his love to go back into the fight for liberalism and culture on the German front. The American would unite the youth of England and America in a Fascist movement to save the rich, but is defeated.

HAMLET

(8 performances)

A tragedy in three acts by William Shakespeare. Revived by Walter Hampden at the 44th Street Theatre, New York, December 25, 1934.

Cast of characters—

Francisco	Howard Galt
Bernardo	Franklin Salisbury
Marcellus	Arthur Stenning
Horatio	Herbert Ranson
King Claudius	Ernest Rowan
Queen Gertrude	Mabel Moore
Ghost of Hamlet's Father	Edwin Cushman
Laertes	John D. Seymour
Polonius	P. J. Kelly
Hamlet	Walter Hampden
Ophelia	Eleanor Goodrich
Reynaldo	Edwin Ross
Rosencrantz	R. C. Schnitzer
Guildenstern	S. Thomas Gomez
Player King	Hannam Clark
Player Queen	Albon Lewis
Prologue } ....Players......... {	Katherine Lane
Lucianus	Richard Edward Bowler
First Grave-digger	Hannam Clark
Second Grave-digger	P. J. Kelly
A Priest	Elliott Leland
Osric	Le Roi Operti

Lords, Ladies, Guards, Attendants: Bradford Hatch, Richard Carewe, Murray D'Arcy, Robert Thompson, Mary Carter, Daphne Ruller, Rose Le Gant and others.

Act I.—Scenes 1 and 3—Platform of Castle. 2 and 5—Hall in Castle. 4—Curtained Lobby. Act II.—Scenes 1 and 3—Hall in Castle. 2—The Queen's Closet. Act III.—Scene 1—Churchyard. 2—Curtained Lobby. 3—Hall in Castle.

Staged by Walter Hampden; settings by Claude Bragdon.

Mr. Hampden's four weeks repertory also included six performances of "Macbeth," ten of "Richelieu" and eight of "Richard the Third."

FOOLS RUSH IN

(14 performances)

A revue by Norman Zeno, Will Irwin, Viola Brothers Shore, Richard Whorf, June Sillman and Richard Lewine. Produced by William A. Brady at the Playhouse, New York, December 25, 1934.

Principals engaged—

Leonard Sillman	Imogene Coca
Richard Whorf	Betzi Beaton
Billy Milton	Miriam Battista
O. Z. Whitehead	Cyrena Smith
Rinaldo Quigley	Ellen Howard
Teddy Lynch	Vandy Cape
Charles Walter	Mildred Todd
Lee Brody	Peggy Hovenden
Albert Whitley	Dorothy Fox
Robert Burton	Olga Vernon
Cliff Allen	Billie Haywood
Edward Potter	Virginia Campbell

The Strawbridge Dancers

Staged by Leonard Sillman; settings by Russell Patterson and Eugene Dunkel; dances by Edwin Strawbridge and Arthur Bradley.

PIPER PAID

(15 performances)

A drama in three acts by Sarah B. Smith and Viola Brothers Shore. Produced by Harold K. Berg in association with D. W. Lederman at the Ritz Theatre, New York, December 25, 1934.

Cast of characters—

Amy Minton	Spring Byington
A German Waiter	Walter Crane
A German Assistant Hotel Manager	Fred De Cordova
Elinor Crane	Katherine Warren
Dr. Martin Sperling	John Marston
Zelda Kay	Edith Barrett
David Crane	Donald Douglas
Larry Allen	Raymond Hackett
Basil Gainsborough	Harry Green

Acts I and II.—Adjoining Balconies of Two Suites—Royal Hotel, Karlsbad. Act III.—Living Room of Apartment on Boulevard. Raspain, Paris.

Staged by Clifford Brooke; settings, John Root.

Zelda Kay is engaged to Dr. Sperling, is in love with David Crane and has confessed a night of dalliance with Larry Allen. When all three meet in Karlsbad later Larry, hard hit by his love for Zelda, has tried to kill himself. Zelda thereupon dismisses her fiancé, tells her lover she can not marry him and devotes her time to nursing Larry back to health. But she goes back to David in the end.

* ACCENT ON YOUTH

(204 performances)

A comedy in three acts by Samson Raphaelson. Produced by Crosby Gaige, Inc., at the Plymouth Theatre, New York, December 25, 1934.

Cast of characters—

```
Miss Darling.....................................Eleanor Hicks
Frank Galloway..................................Ernest Lawford
Dickie Reynolds...............................Theodore Newton
Linda Brown..............................Constance Cummings
Steven Gaye....................................Nicholas Hannen
Flogdell..........................................Ernest Cossart
Genevieve Lang....................................Irene Purcell
Chuck.......................................William Carpenter
Butch..............................................Al. Moore
    Acts I, II and III.—Study of Steven Gaye's Penthouse Apartment
in New York City.
    Staged by Benn W. Levy; settings by Jo Mielziner.
```

See page 173.

RUTH DRAPER

(24 performances)

A repertory of dramatic sketches. Presented by Actor-Managers, Inc., at the Ethel Barrymore Theatre, New York, December 26, 1935.

Sketches—

```
Three Women and Mr. Clifford
Three Generations at a Court of Domestic Relations
In a Church in Italy
Opening a Bazar
The Italian Lesson
In a Railway Station on the Western Plains
In County Kerry
The Scottish Immigrant
A Dalmatian Peasant in the Hall of a New York Hospital
Doctors
At a Children's Party in Philadelphia
A Class in Greek Poise
A Class in Soul Culture
At an Art Exhibition
```

BIRTHDAY

(13 performances)

A drama in three acts by Aimee and Philip Stuart. Produced by Sidney Harmon and James R. Ullman at the 49th Street Theatre, New York, December 26, 1934.

THE BEST PLAYS OF 1934-35   431

Cast of characters—

Mrs. McNeil	Hilda Spong
Irene Lawrence	Antoinette Cellier
Baba Lawrence	Jeanne Dante
Mrs. Queen	Florence Edney
Jennifer Lawrence	Peggy Wood
Sir John Corbett, K.C.	Louis Calhern
Dr. Sloane	Lionel Pape

Acts I and II.—Sitting Room in Mrs. Lawrence's Flat in London.
Act III.—Scene 1—Irene and Baba's Bedroom. 2—Mrs. Lawrence's
Sitting Room.
Staged by William W. Schorr; settings by P. Dodd Ackerman.

Jennifer Lawrence, some years after the death of her husband, meets and loves Sir John Corbett and would marry him. Irene, her 16-year-old daughter, who idealizes her father's memory, thanks to the mother's glowing descriptions of his innate nobility of character, is thrown into an emotional state of mind by the thought of a strange man taking father's place. She tries to throw herself into the Thames, but lacks the courage. Only after her mother has returned to the truth and admitted that the dead Mr. Lawrence was really a good deal of a cheater is Irene brought out of her depression. Then she accepts Sir John as a stepfather.

THE O'FLYNN

(11 performances)

An operetta in four parts based on Justin Huntly McCarthy's novel and play, by Brian Hooker and Russell Janney; music by Franklin Hauser. Produced by Russell Janney at the Broadway Theatre, New York, December 27, 1934.

Cast of characters—

Hendrigg	William Balfour
The Captain of the Soleil d'Or	Hugo Baldi
The Lady Benedetta Mount-Michael	Lucy Monroe
The Cook	Jules Epeilly
Jacques	Will H. Philbrick
Captain Flynn O'Flynn, Known as "The O'Flynn"	George Houston
The Landlord	Walter Munroe
Conacier O'Rourke	Colin Campbell
Goslings	Thomas Williams
Coin	James Ross
Burden	H. H. McCollum
Beggles	Raymond O'Brien
Conamur	Lee Randall
Fancy Free	Anna Trockowna
Mrs. Oldmixon	Jean Newcombe
The Drummer Boy	Wilson Angel
The Dancer	Paula Lind
The Ham	Charles Homer
The Fat Player	Eugene W. King
Comedian	Don Valentine
Tall Player	John Zak
The Landlord	George Shields

```
The Landlord's Daughter..........................Merle Stevens
Lord Sedgemouth..................................Frank Fenton
His Majesty King James II........................H. Cooper-Cliffe
Sir George Mayhew...............................Henry Vincent
Lord Fawley......................................Edward Martyn
General Van Dronk...............................Chas. E. Galagher
The Duchess of Tyrconnel..........................Doris Rich
Lieutenant Trusham..............................John Mealey
The Bishop.......................................Walter Munroe
A Tailor.........................................John Cardini
```

Fancy Free Girls: Misses Beverly, Gotlieb, Collins, Svesson, Laney, Ideal, MacDonald, Brown, Knott, Constant, Garner, Hosier.

Sailors: Messrs. Race, Soback, Rollis, Cardozo, Mason, Franklyn, Monteer, Bell, Hamilton, Prock, O'Toole, Fulco, Cody, Howland, Cardini, Scandur.

Part I.—Scene 1—The Boat. 2—The Dock. 3—Castle Famine. Part II.—The Tavern. Part III.—Scene 1—The Camp. 2—Knockmore Tower. Part IV.—Scene 1—Great Hall of Tapestries. 2—Castle Famine.

Staged by Max Figman and Olga Treskoff; settings by James Reynolds.

Captain Flynn O'Flynn has a hand in the fighting and the conspiracies that circled the attempt to put James II back on the throne from which he had been thrust by William of Orange. During which he meets, woos, wins and sings to the Lady Benedetta Mount-Michael. Sings and sings. And she to him.

THUMBS UP

(156 performances)

A revue in two acts by H. I. Phillips, Harold Atteridge, Alan Baxter, Ballard MacDonald and Earle Crooker; music by James Hanley and Henry Sullivan. Produced by Eddie Dowling at the St. James Theatre, New York, December 27, 1934.

Principals engaged—

Eddie Dowling	Ray Dooley
Bobby Clark	Rose King
Eddie Garr	Sheila Barrett
J. Harold Murray	Eunice Healy
Al Sexton	Ruben Garcia
Hal Le Roy	Margaret Adams
Hugh Cameron	Alice Dudley
Paul McCullough	Irene McBride
Jack Cole	Sandra Gould
The Delmars Pickens Sisters	Falla Sisters

Staged by John Murray Anderson; dances by Robert Alton; settings by Ted Weidhaas, James Reynolds and Raoul René Dubois.

BABY POMPADOUR

(4 performances)

A comedy in three acts by Benjamin Graham. Produced by Arthur Dreifuss and Willard G. Garnhardt at the Vanderbilt Theatre, New York, December 27, 1934.

Cast of characters—

George Armstrong	Scott Kolk
Margie	Virginia Deane
Ferdinand Dike	Robert Lowe
General Sancho Guiterrez	Joseph Monneret de Villard
Elmer Tweed	Maurice F. Manson
Rear Admiral Wilfred Butler	Charles Wellesley
Señor Miguel Arboleda	Daniel Ocko
Daniel P. Atkinson	John Murray
Dr. Calloway	A. M. Putnam
E. Silas Buchanan	Herbert Rawlinson
Dorothy Hamilton	Gladys Shelley
Cora Hunt Buchanan	Nana Bryant
Angela Dike	Gladys Feldman
Herbert Woolsey	Ralph Locke
Genevieve	Lillian Brown
Jeffries	Maurice F. Manson

Staged by Clarence Derwent; settings by Nicholas Yellenti.

E. Silas Buchanan is an editorial columnist with two women in his life. One his wife, the other a blonde, Dorothy, from the chorus. It is Dorothy who has the greater influence with him and who keeps him up to snuff as a writer. Politicians and business tycoons seek her out in order to win her endorsement of their plans that she may pass the word on to E. Silas. Buchanan is indirectly responsible for sending the Marines to Nicaragua. Dorothy runs away with her boss's private secretary and ditches him for a sailor. Buchanan's work goes off and Mrs. Buchanan is forced to scheme to restore Dorothy to her husband's arms to get him in form again.

PORTRAIT OF GILBERT

(3 performances)

A drama in five scenes by Carlton Miles. Produced by Sam H. Grisman at the Longacre Theatre, New York, December 28, 1934.

Cast of characters—

Gladys Whitman	Alice John
Lacy Whitman	Ethel Wilson
Donald Whitman	Roy Le May
Amy	Ann Dere
Jerry Morse	William Harrigan
Henry Whitman	Frederick Forrester
Murphy	Charles Lawrence
Anne Choate Whitman	Selena Royle
John McVitty	Frank Rowan
Lucy Farren	Patricia Quinn

Scenes 1, 2, 3, 4 and 5—Living Room of Anne Whitman's Home.
Staged by Herbert V. Gellendre; setting by Raymond Sovey.

Anne Whitman, following the kidnaping and murder of her husband, Gilbert, is harassed by the brooding spirit of Gilbert and the activities of his hard-bitten sister, Lacy. Anne is also worried because Jerry Morse, engaged as bodyguard for her young son, is trying to influence her against identifying the kidnaping suspect on trial, whom she has recognized. It is Morse's idea that by letting the kidnaper off Anne can do more good to humankind than by sending him to his death in revenge for the loss of her husband. Anne sticks to her vow to prosecute Gilbert's murderer and leaves both Morse and her husband's home.

MUSIC HATH CHARMS

(29 performances)

A musical comedy by Rowland Leigh, George Rosener and John Shubert; music by Rudolf Friml. Produced by the Messrs. Shubert at the Majestic Theatre, New York, December 29, 1934.

Cast of characters—

PERIOD 1934

Spokesman	Robert Long
Theophilus Roberts	Andrew Tombes
Charles Parker	Robert Halliday
Maria, Marchese Del Monte Nee Di Orsano	Natalie Hall
Giovanni, Duke of Orsano	Harry Mestayer
Two Venetian Hooligans	{ Paul Haakon / Nina Whitney
Lovey	Billy Rey
Dovey	Gracie Worth
Rudolfo, Marchese Di Orsano	John Clarke
Isabella	Elizabeth Crandall
Giaconda	Constance Carpenter
Duke of Umbria	Cyril Chadwick
A Footman	Truman Gaige

Dancers in Interlude Between 1934 and 1770
Paul Haakon, Nina Whitney

A—Danse Moderne.   B—Polka 1880.
C—Gavotte 1810.   D—Tarantella 1770.

PERIOD 1770

A Villager	Robert Long
Angela	Betti Davis
Maria Sovrani	Natalie Hall
Vittorio Sovrani	John Clarke
Petronella	Elizabeth Crandall
Pappio	Andrew Tombes
Marella	Constance Carpenter
Senator Bellanqua	William Kent
Senator Nocio	Stanley Harrison
Senator Burranto	Paul Burns
Emilio	George Schiller
Pidgy	Billy Rey
Widgy	Gracie Worth
Signora Barbara Bellanqua	Sheila Harling
Spokesman	Robert Long
Fillipo	Truman Gaige
Duke of Orsano	Robert Halliday
Luigi	William Lilling
Old Duke	Harry Mestayer
Cornelia	Vona Norin
Signora Nocio	Jane Mackenzie
Nella	Ruth Reiter
Laspera	Salley Warren
Leonora	Isabel Lane
Senator Burranto	Marie Wilson

Bishop..Robert Long
Bridesmaids.............................. { Constance Carpenter
                                          { Frances Wallace
    Act I.—Scene 1—Grand Canal. 2—Street. 3—Palazzo Orsano
House. 4—Dance of Years. 5—Fishing Village—1770. 6—Square
in Venice—1770.   Act II.—Scene 1—Palazzo Orsano—1770. 2—
Corridor—1770. 3—Love Nest—Private Room of the Duke—1770. 4
—Corridor—1770. 5—Ballroom—1770. 6—Grand Canal—1770. 7—
Outside of St. Mark's Cathedral—1934.
    Staged by George Rosener; dances by Alex Yakovleñ; settings by
Watson Barratt.

Maria, Marchese Del Monte, is pursued by Charles Parker, a
brash but melodious baritone tourist from America.   Maria resents Charles, but listens to the story of her great-grandmother
as it is related to her by her grandfather, the Duke of Orsano,
and that helps her make up her mind.   During the telling of the
story Maria appears as her great-grandmother, a peasant, and
Parker is the Duke of Orsano, her suitor.

SLIGHTLY DELIRIOUS

(8 performances)

A comedy in three acts by Bernard J. McOwen and Robert F.
Adkins. Produced by Willo Productions at the Little Theatre,
New York, December 31, 1934.

Cast of characters—

Gracie...Ruth Amos
Prof. Judson Hargraves............................Hall Shelton
Millicent Hargraves................................Lee Patrick
Ruth Waters....................................Audrey Douglas
Dr. Arthur Wyatt..................................Edwin Evans
    Acts I, II and III.—Penthouse Apartment of Prof. Judson Har-
graves in the East 60's. Manhattan.
    Staged by G. T. Clarke; setting by Karl Amend.

Judson Hargraves, a college professor, marries Millicent with
the idea that theirs is to be a marriage of minds rather than
bodies.   But Judson, going wandering, contacts a nudist colony,
achieves amnesia and returns to Millicent a changed man.   Without recognizing his wife, or her friend Ruth or the maid, Judson
seeks intimate acquaintance with each of them.   After which it
is indicated that Judson was faking his amnesia.

* THE PETRIFIED FOREST

(181 performances)

A drama in two acts by Robert Emmett Sherwood. Produced
by Gilbert Miller and Leslie Howard in association with Arthur
Hopkins at the Broadhurst Theatre, New York, January 7, 1935.

Cast of characters—

A Telegrapher.....................................Milo Boulton
Another Telegrapher..............................James Doody
Boze Hertzlinger..................................Frank Milan
Jason Maple......................................Walter Vonnegut
Paula...................................... Esther Leeming
Gramp Maple..............................Charles Dow Clark
Gabby Maple....................................Peggy Conklin
Alan Squier.....................................Leslie Howard
Herb...Robert Porterfield
Mrs. Chisholm..................................Blanche Sweet
Mr. Chisholm...................................Robert Hudson
Joseph...John Alexander
Jackie..Ross Hertz
Ruby...Tom Fadden
Duke Mantee................................Humphrey Bogart
Pyles..Slim Thompson
Commander Klepp..........................Aloysius Cunningham
Hendy..Guy Conradi
Sheriff..Frank Tweddell
A Deputy......................................Eugene Keith
Another Deputy.................................Harry Sherwin
      Acts I and II.—Black Mesa Bar-B-Q, a Gas Station and Lunch
Room at a Lonely Crossroads in the Eastern Arizona Desert.
      Staged by Arthur Hopkins; setting by Raymond Sovey.

See page 115.

* THE OLD MAID

(190 performances)

A drama in three acts by Zoe Akins, founded on a novel by
Edith Wharton. Produced by Harry Moses at the Empire Theatre, New York, January 7, 1935.

Cast of characters—

Delia Lovell (later Mrs. James Ralston)............Judith Anderson
Charlotte Lovell..................................Helen Menken
Mrs. Jennie Meade................................Mary Ricard
Bridget...Hope Landin
Clementina......................................Yvonne Mann
Dr. Lanskell....................................⌣...George Nash
Mrs. Mingott...................................Margaret Dale
Joseph Ralston.................................Robert Wallsten
James Ralston..................................Frederick Voight
Servant..Gail Reade
Dee...Florence Williams
John Halsey......................................Warren Trent
Lanning Halsey..................................John Cromwell
Tina...Margaret Anderson
      Act I.—Scene 1—Delia Lovell's Room, Lovell Place, New York.
2—A Nursery in Mercer Street. Acts II and III.—Ralston Draw-
ing Room, Gramercy Park, New York.
      Staged by Guthrie McClintic; settings by Stewart Chaney.

See page 144.

A LADY DETAINED

(13 performances)

A comedy in two acts by Samuel Shipman and John B. Hymer.
Produced by S. L. Latham at the Ambassador Theatre, New York,
January 9, 1935.

Cast of characters—

Frank Cavola	Sydney Mason
Buzz Willett	Jack Hartley
Duke Bradford	Oscar Shaw
Happy Jackson	Tom Tempest
Joe Darcy	Calvin Thomas
Joan Palmer	Claudia Morgan
Helen Palmer	Jane Grey
Craig Palmer	Clifford Brooke
Clara	Gae Fortune
George Merrill	William David
Inspector Wheeler	John M. Kline
Chi-Chi	Helene Petri
Louise	Shirley Gibbs
Jimmie	Ralph Holmes

Act I.—Scenes 1, 4 and 5—Duke Bradford's Camp in the Adirondacks, New York. 2 and 3—Living Room in Palmer House, Larchmont, New York. Act II.—Scene 1—Palmer Living Room. 2, 3 and 4—Camp.

Staged by Clifford Brooke; settings by P. Dodd Ackerman.

Joan Palmer is a society aviatrix and rich. Flying the Adirondacks she is forced down and finds herself in the camp of Duke Bradford, ex-bootlegger. Joe Darcy, erstwhile partner of Bradford, proposes holding Joan for ransom, forcing Bradford to agree. Bradford is made the go-between and in the end is able to save both Joan and himself, after they had been ticketed for a ride by the bootleggers.

LIVING DANGEROUSLY

(9 performances)

A drama in three acts by Reginald Simpson and Frank Gregory. Produced by the Messrs. Shubert at the Morosco Theatre, New York, January 12, 1935.

Cast of characters—

David Norton	Conway Tearle
Lady Annerley	Gertrude Maitland
Vera Kennedy	Renée Gadd
Helen	Phœbe Foster
Detective Inspector Webster	Boyd Davis
Henry Pryor	Percy Waram
Mr. Lloyd, K.C.	Kenneth Hunter
Sir George Parker, K.C.	A. P. Kaye
Dr. Lingard	Frank Kingdon
Garrett Gale	John Harrington
Logan	John Bramall
Members of the General Medical Council:	
Sir Barnaby Rutland	Reginald Carrington
Sir Guy Wells	Fuller Mellish
George Winthrop	Herbert Standing
H. Ashley Montague	Charles Esdale
H. A. C. Tomlinson	Charles Martin
Major Courtney Williams	Neville Percy
Ashton Barnes	Jack Daniels
Edward Tottenham	Alf Helton
Sir James Bolton	Arthur W. Rowe

Act I.—Surgery in Wimpole Street. London. Act II.—Medical
Council Chamber. Act III.—David Norton's Apartment.
Staged by Harry Wagstaff Gribble; settings by Watson Barratt.

David Norton and Henry Pryor, physicians, have combined
their practices in London. Dr. Norton is in love with Mrs.
Pryor and she with him, but they are scrupulously loyal to Pryor.
Scotland Yard, tracing a narcotic leak, fasten it upon Pryor.
Norton breaks off their business arrangement. To be even Pryor
brings charges against Norton before the Medical Council, accusing him of having seduced Mrs. Pryor. The trial goes against
Norton. He and Mrs. Pryor sail for America, Norton changes
his name to Stanley and builds a new practice. Pryor ferrets
them out and would create a scandal. Norton shoots him and is
absolved by a district attorney friend.

LABURNUM GROVE

(131 performances)

A comedy by J. B. Priestley. Produced by Gilbert Miller and
Lee Shubert at the Booth Theatre, New York, January 14, 1935.

Cast of characters—

Elsie Radfern...............................Margery Pickard
Mrs. Lucy Baxley.............................Elisabeth Risdon
Bernard Baxley...............................Melville Cooper
George Radfern...............................Edmund Gwenn
Harold Russ..................................Lloyd Gough
Joe Fletten..................................A. G. Andrews
Mrs. Dorothy Radfern.........................Molly Pearson
Inspector Stack..............................Reynolds Denniston
Sergeant Morris..............................George Anderson
    Acts I, II and III.—Living Room of the Radferns' House, Fern-
dale, Laburnum Grove, Shooters Green, a Suburb of London.
    Staged by Lewis Allen; settings by Watson Barratt.

For many years George Radfern has been a respected resident
of Laburnum Grove, a London suburb. Suddenly out of a clear
sky he confesses to his visiting relatives, the Baxleys, and Harold
Russ, who wants to marry Elsie Radfern, that he is a lawbreaker,
a counterfeiter, and has been living on tainted money for years.
The Baxleys and young Russ, both of whom had been trying to
borrow money from Radfern, draw suspiciously away. Later
they are led to believe Radfern was only spoofing, but still later,
when a Scotland Yard man appears looking for him, they are not
so sure. Neither is the audience.

* FLY AWAY HOME

(179 performances)

A comedy in three acts by Dorothy Bennett and Irving White. Produced by Theron Bamberger at the 48th Street Theatre, New York, January 15, 1935.

Cast of characters—

Harmer Masters	Montgomery Clift
Buff Masters	Georgette McKee
Linda Masters	Joan Tompkins
Corey Masters	Edwin Philips
Penny	Clare Woodbury
Tinka Collingsby	Lili Zehner
Johnny Heming	Philip Faversham
James Masters	Thomas Mitchell
Armand Sloan	Albert Van Dekker
Maria	Geraldine Kay
Gabriel	Sheldon Leonard
Taxi Driver	Elmer Brown
Nan Masters	Ann Mason

Acts I, II and III.—Living Room of the Masters' Summer Home in Provincetown, Mass.

Staged by Thomas Mitchell; setting by Raymond Sovey.

James Masters has not seen his four children since their mother, Nan, divorced him and undertook their rearing, a matter of twelve years. Invited to Nan's second marriage to Prof. Armand Sloan of Ann Arbor, James discovers that the children have been left to their own devices, that they have gone violently radical and that, with Prof. Sloan, they believe in leading the lives of free, healthy animals. They freely acquaint their father with all the facts of life. James protests but is outvoted until Prof. Sloan discovers something of the cost of rearing a grown family. Sloan withdraws and the children and Nan are glad to have James back.

CREEPING FIRE

(23 performances)

A melodrama in three acts by Marie Baumer. Produced by Glen N. W. McNaughton and John Cameron at the Vanderbilt Theatre, New York, January 16, 1935.

Cast of characters—

John Connors	Maurice Wells
Frankie Connors	Marjorie Peterson
Paul Connors	Theodore Fetter
Dot	Hope Richards
Joe	Ralph Morris
Scotty	Eric Dressler
Mr. Greenberg	Frank Manning

```
First Vendor....................................Walter Vaughn
Second Vendor.....................................Ralph Herzt
A Fortune Teller..............................Fernanda Eliscu
First Reporter..................................William Shea
Second Reporter..................................Butler Hixon
Third Reporter...................................Mark Preston
State Trooper..................................Gordon Gould
Mr. Goodman...................................Bernard Gorcey
A Singer..........................................Leslie King
Mamma.........................................Adelina Roatinno
Papa..........................................Frank S. Marino
Boy..............................................Tommy Emma
Girl..........................................Josephine De Vito
Jim...............................................Jack Harwood
A Young Wife..................................Joan Meredith
Captain Johnson...............................Alfred Webster
Ed................................................Morris Armor
Dr. Bentley.......................................Alvin Dexter
A Nurse...........................................Jean Colbert
              Spectators, Boaters, Tourists, etc.
```

Act I.—John Connors's Boating Pavilion in a Resort on the Delaware River. Act II.—On a Hillside Above the Cave. Act III.—Scene 1—Corridor in a Hospital. 2—Room in the Hospital.
Staged by John Cameron; settings by Cleon Throckmorton.

John Connors has married a second time, taking Frankie Connors to wife. Frankie is loyal to John, but secretly in love with Scotty, a guide to a nearby cave visited by tourists. Paul Connors, also in love with his stepmother, thinking to save her from Scotty, blows up the cave when he thinks the guide is there, seriously injuring his father, John, who was taking Scotty's place. Circumstantial evidence is convicting Scotty, when John Connors recovers sufficiently to place the blame on his son.

POINT VALAINE

(55 performances)

A play in three acts by Noel Coward. Produced by John C. Wilson at the Ethel Barrymore Theatre, New York, January 16, 1935.

Cast of characters—

```
Stefan..............................................Alfred Lunt
Lola.................................................Ruth Boyd
May...............................................Alberta Perkins
Mrs. Tillett.....................................Grayce Hampton
Major Tillett.......................................Fred Leslie
Mrs. Birling......................................Lillian Tonge
Elise Birling...................................Phyllis Connard
Mortimer Quinn..................................Osgood Perkins
George Fox........................................Brod Crawford
Ted Burchell......................................Philip Tonge
Linda Valaine...................................Lynn Fontanne
Mrs. Hall-Fenton................................Gladys Henson
Phyllis.........................................Margaret Curtis
Gladys..........................................Phyllis Harding
Sylvia..........................................Valerie Cossart
Hilda James....................................Everley Gregg
```

Martin Welford...............................Louis Hayward
    Acts I, II and III.—Linda's Sitting Room and the Veranda of the
Point Valaine Hotel.
    Staged by Noel Coward; settings by G. E. Calthrop.

Linda Valaine is proprietress of the Hotel Valaine at the point
of a tropical island. Her headwaiter, Stefan, is a primitive Russian who has served Linda and the hotel for seven years. Secretly
Stefan also has had access to Linda's boudoir. Among the hotel's
guests is a young English aviator, Martin Welford. Welford
falls in love with Linda. She gives way to him a night when
Stefan is away. Stefan gets back, discovers the assignation, exposes Linda, disgusts Martin. Being repulsed by Linda when
he pleads for forgiveness, Stefan slashes his wrist and throws himself into the sea.

LITTLE SHOT

(4 performances)

A comedy in three acts by Percival Wilde. Produced by Malcolm L. Pearson and Donald E. Baruch at the Playhouse, New
York, January 17, 1935.

Cast of characters—

Clyde Middleton.............................Donald Macdonald
Sturge Peabody...................................Frank Wilcox
Henry James Atherton...........................Eric Wollencott
Scarlatti.....................................Robert Middlemass
Pat Vining...Lillian Bond
Mildred East...................................Cynthia Rogers
    Act I.—Scenes 1 and 3—At Middleton's. 2—At Scarlatti's. Acts
II and III.—At Middleton's.
    Staged by Bretaigne Windust; settings by P. Dodd Ackerman.

Clyde Middleton, fiancé and guardian of the inheritance of
Patricia Vining, discovers that the girl's money has been lost in
the market and his own indebtedness is considerable on the eve
of their wedding. Carrying a million-dollar insurance policy
with a suicide clause attached Middleton decides that the only
way he can leave Pat his insurance money safely is to have himself bumped off by gangsters. He makes all arrangements with
Big Shot Scarlatti and then learns he has been left eleven million
dollars by a Cincinnati uncle. He spends the rest of the evening trying to call off the gunmen. Saved finally, he gives Pat
her money and marries Mildred East, his secretary.

BATTLESHIP GERTIE

(2 performances)

A farce in two acts by Frederick Hazlett Brennan. Produced by Courtney Burr at the Lyceum Theatre, New York, January 18, 1935.

Cast of characters—

Secretary Hollingshead	Frank Jaquet
Senator Gale	George Lessey
Senator Heffermeister	Harry Davenport
Senator Blowney	Walter Baldwin
Admiral Spenks	Herbert A. Yost
Aide	Claude McNair
Wo Pu Cheng	Frederick Banker
Lieutenant Commander Brophy	Philip Wood
Ensign Harriss	Oliver Barbour
Mildred	Gladys Griswold
Gertie	Helen Lynd
Mrs. Schumpf	Lora Rogers
Ensign McGurk	Boyd Crawford
Seaman Jones	Burgess Meredith
Marine Sergeant Grogan	Horace MacMahon
Marines	William Culloo / Richard Toms
Captain Buford	Richard Gordon
Price	Philip Truex
Commander McClintic	Ernest Woodward
Commander Black	George R. Taylor
Toma	Richard Taber
Koda	Moana Chu
Radio Messenger	Joseph P. Harris

Act I.—Scene 1—Headquarters of U. S. Naval District, Pearl Harbor, Honolulu. 2—Gertie's Room, Honolulu. 3 and 5—Ensign Harriss's Stateroom Aboard U.S.S. "Rhode Island." 4, 6 and 8—Captain Buford's Cabin. 7—Mrs. Schumpf's Kitchen. Act II.—Scenes 1 and 3—Buford's Cabin. 2—Hotel Suite, Honolulu.
Staged by Arthur Sircom; settings by Boris Aronson.

Gertrude Stumph is movie crazy and marooned in Honolulu. To get to Hollywood she stows away on the Battleship "Rhode Island." Hides herself in Ensign Harriss's room. Throws herself upon the mercy of Seaman Jones who, falling for Gertie, tries to save her. Scandal threatens the commander of the "Rhode Island." International complications are threatened when Gertie is accused of being a Japanese spy. An exchange of extravagantly satirical navy orders and department notes of inquiry follow. The "Rhode Island" finally is ordered back to Honolulu. Gertie and Seaman Jones are released in each other's custody.

ESCAPE ME NEVER

(96 performances)

A drama in three acts by Margaret Kennedy. Produced by The Theatre Guild, Inc., in association with Charles B. Cochran, at the Shubert Theatre, New York, January 21, 1935.

Cast of characters—

Sir Ivor McClean..............................Leon Quartermaine
Lady McClean.......................................Katie Johnson
Fenella McClean......................................Eve Turner
Woman Tourist.......................................Betty Lynne
1st Tourist..Cyril Horrocks
2nd Tourist..John Boxer
Caryl Sanger.......................................Griffith Jones
Butler...Bruno Barnabe
Herr Heinrich.................................William F. Schoeller
Gemma Jones...................................Elisabeth Bergner
Sebastian Sanger...................................Hugh Sinclair
Waiter...Peter Bull
1st Spinster.....................................Ann Stephenson
2nd Spinster.....................................Muriel Johnston
Mrs. Brown.......................................Ann Stephenson
Wilson...John Boxer
Petrova...Nina Bucknall
Dresser..Muriel Johnston
Pianist...Cyril Horrocks
Messenger...William Mills
Miss Regan...Susan Brown
1st Man..Peter Bull
2nd Man..John Boxer
3rd Man..A. J. Felix
Stallkeeper.......................................Cyril Horrocks
Man..Bruno Barnabe
Woman...Muriel Johnston
Girl...Jane Vaughan
    Act I.—Salon of the Palazzo Neroni, Venice. Act II.—Scene 1—
Terrace of Hotel in the Dolomites. 2—Caryl's Rooms in London.
Act III.—Scenes 1 and 4—Studio in a Mews. 2—Practice Room at
a Theatre. 3—Street Corner.
    Staged by Komisarjevsky; settings by Komisarjevsky.

Gemma Jones, origin misty, intentions hazy, history clouded, steals a uniform from a girls' school and enters the palazzo leased by the Sir Ivor McCleans in Venice. Caught, Gemma tells of her adventures as a waif, her experience as a child-mother and the friendship of a young man named Sanger with whom she and her child are living. The McCleans are upset. Their lovely daughter Fenella is about to marry a Sanger. He turns out to be Caryl Sanger. Gemma's friend is his brother Sebastian. The McCleans take Fenella to the Dolomites. The Sanger boys and Gemma follow. Both Sangers make love to Fenella. Gemma's baby dies. She tries to quit Sebastian. They discover that, come what may, they are bound to each other.

CRIME AND PUNISHMENT

(15 performances)

A drama in three acts by Fyodor Dostioevsky, adapted from the dramatization by Victor Trivas and Georg Schdanoff by Victor Wolfson and Victor Trivas, translated by Sonia Gordon Brown. Produced by Wolfson and Sherry at the Biltmore Theatre, New York, January 22, 1935.

Cast of characters—

Raskolnikoff . . . . Morgan Farley
Nastasia . . . . Barna Ostertag
First Painter . . . . Edward Mann
Second Painter . . . . Frederic Giuliano
Aliona . . . . Marfa Pasternak
Pestrakoff . . . . Philip Remer
Koch . . . . Lee J. Cobb
Janitor . . . . Robert Finch
Madame Margot . . . . Babette Feist
First Girl . . . . Anne Gerlette
Second Girl . . . . Katherine Locke
Third Girl . . . . Mary Whitbrook
Marmeladoff . . . . Harry D. Southard
Sonia . . . . Juliana Taberna
Razoumkin . . . . Sam Wren
Loushin . . . . Edward Forbes
Saloonkeeper . . . . Lee J. Cobb
Police Officer . . . . William Toubin
Porphyry . . . . Thomas Coffin Cooke
Clerk . . . . Robert Finch
Madame Raskolnikoff . . . . Irene Oshier
Dounia Raskolnikoff . . . . Katharine Phelan

Act I.—Scenes 1, 3 and 5—Raskolnikoff's Room in St. Petersburg. 2—Staircase. 4—Parlor of a Pleasure House. 6—Bar of the Tavern. 7—Police Station. Act II.—Scene 1—Private Room in Tavern. 2—Raskolnikoff's Room. 3—Staircase. 4—Niche in the Park Wall. Act III.—Scene 1—Porphyry's Study. 2—Mme. Raskolnikoff's Furnished Room. 3—Sonia's Room. 4—Staircase.

Staged by Victor Wolfson; settings by Irene Sharaff.

Rodion Raskolnikoff commits what he believes to be a humane murder by killing an aging pawnbroker who has preyed on the poor. Little by little the law, aided by his torturing conscience, brings him to a confession and justice. A new version of the Dostoievsky novel that furnished the basis for Richard Mansfield's "Rodion the Student" and E. H. Sothern's "A Fool There Was."

NOWHERE BOUND

(15 performances)

A melodrama in three acts by Leo Birinski. Produced by Birinski, Inc., at the Imperial Theatre, New York, January 22, 1935.

Cast of characters—

Tomski . . . . Pierre de Ramey
McTavish . . . . Allen Lee
Schwartz . . . . Fred Kaufman
Grasso . . . . Joseph Monneret de Villard
Pat . . . . Don Beddoe
Maureen . . . . Patricia Deering
Maxa . . . . Marshall Hale
Weber . . . . Herbert Treitel
Basil Oxley . . . . C. H. Croker-King
A Dope Peddler . . . . G. Frederick
Guzik . . . . Alexander Danaroff
Lajos . . . . Nicholas Bela
Ilona . . . . Clara Mahr

Mrs. Blum..Helene Rapport
Mr. Blum...Naum Zemach
Chester...Sherling Oliver
Federal Official..........................W. W. Shuttleworth
Al Pomo......................................Edward Raquello
Von Prellwitz...........................Frederick Giermann
Dobbs..John Alexander
Jack Thurston.....................................Matt Briggs
A Young Turk...............................Henry DeKoven
Another Turk..............................Franklin Heller
Ipolita Romanescu..............................Miriam Goldina
Police Sergeant................................G. Swayne Gordon
State Senator Dalton..............................Oswald Yorke
A Policeman....................................Robert Williams
     Act I.—Pullman Car of Deportation Train on Sidetrack of Chicago
Station.   Act II.—En Route.   Act III.—Arriving at Toledo Station.
     Staged by A. H. Van Buren; settings by Karl Amend.

A trainload of deportees is en route from Chicago to New York.
Prominent in the list is Al Pomo, public enemy No. 1. Al is the
only one who wants to be deported. He is rich and plans to
retire in Italy. Other public enemies in the group want to keep
him in America. The only way they can do it is to concoct a
murder and force the government to hold them all as material
witnesses. A murder is committed, but it turns out to be phony.
Drama becomes farce. The deportees are variously disposed of.

PRISONERS OF WAR

(8 performances)

A drama in three acts by J. R. Ackerly.   Produced by Frank
Merlin at the Ritz Theatre, New York, January 28, 1935.

Cast of characters—

Second Lieutenant Grayle...........................Ben Starkie
Lieutenant Tetford................................Lowell Gilmore
Captain Rickman............................Charles McClelland
Marie...Dorothee Nolan
Lieutenant Adelby...............................Francis Compton
Captain Conrad...................................Barton Hepburn
Jellerton..John Parrish
Mrs. Prendergast..................................Daisy Belmore
Madame Louis.......................................Zola Talma
Dr. Croz..Alfred Hesse
     Acts I, II and III.—Captain Conrad's Sitting Room in Hotel in
Murren, Switzerland.
     Staged by Frank Merlin; setting by Cleon Throckmorton.

During their internment in Switzerland through the last years
of the war the sensitive Captain Conrad is conscious of a growing fondness for Second Lieutenant Grayle. Unfortunate con-
structions are placed on the friendship by their associate officers,
a group of caged neurotics. Conrad and Grayle eventually come
to blows. As a result of worry over his disturbing impulses and
the trouble with Grayle, Conrad temporarily loses his mind and
transfers his affection to a potted plant.

*THREE MEN ON A HORSE

(164 performances)

A farce by John Cecil Holm and George Abbott. Produced by Alex Yokel at The Playhouse, New York, January 30, 1935.

Cast of characters—

Audrey Trowbridge	Joyce Arling
The Tailor	J. Asher Smith
Erwin Trowbridge	William Lynn
Clarence Dobbins	Fleming Ward
Delivery Boy	Nick Wiger
Harry	James Lane
Charlie	Millard Mitchell
Frankie	Teddy Hart
Patsy	Sam Levene
Mabel	Shirley Booth
Moses	Richard Huey
Gloria	Edith Van Cleve
Al	Garson Kanin
Mr. Carver	Frank Camp
Hotel Maid	Susan Smithers

Act I.—Scene 1—Living Room of Trowbridge House, Ozone Heights, New Jersey. 2—Bar Room in Basement of Lavillere Hotel. Acts II and III.—Ozone Heights and a Room in Lavillere Hotel.
Staged by George Abbott; settings by Boris Aronson.

Erwin Trowbridge is a timid greeting card poet. Between inspirations for appropriate Mother's Day sentiments he occupies his mind doping out the probable winners at the racetracks. Having quarreled with Mrs. Trowbridge over a forty dollar dress bill Edwin gets off the bus one morning and buys himself a drink. In a barroom he hears a trio of small-time racketeers discussing horse racing. Gives them tips from his red book. They try a few and win. Then they shanghai Erwin and set him picking winners for them. In the end much money is made, but Erwin is very unhappy. As soon as they make him bet on a race the charm is gone. He can no longer pick winners. He goes back to his greeting card job.

LOOSE MOMENTS

(8 performances)

A comedy in three acts by Courtenay Savage and Bertram Hobbs. Produced by Walter Hartwig at the Vanderbilt Theatre, New York, February 4, 1935.

Cast of characters—

Mrs. Gandle	Pearl Hight
Lilla	Artie Belle McGinty
Woman Looking for Lodgings	Carol Day

Mary Bartlett....................................Elizabeth Love
Constance Trowbridge.............................Lenore Sorsby
Henry Clay Penny.................................Russell Rhodes
Sophie Tuttle....................................Doro Merande
Lena Tarbutton...................................Edward Garvie
H. Augustus Tarbutton............................Irene Cattell
Ralph Merkes.....................................Joseph Cotten
Bruce Hamilton...................................Grant Gordon
Miss Markham.....................................Catherine Collins
    Acts I, II and III.—Bartlett Home in Rockville, North Carolina.
Staged by Walter Hartwig; setting by Cirker and Robbins.

Mary Bartlett is running her mother's "Tourists Accommodated" homestead on the road to Florida. Ralph Merkes is the
village grocery boy who is in love with Mary. Mary thinks she
prefers a city feller and Ralph is persistently pursued by half
a dozen other females who want to set him up in business: object
matrimony. Ralph escapes the pursuing ladies and Mary learns
about the ways of city slickers in the nick of time.

ON TO FORTUNE

(8 performances)

A play in three acts by Lawrence Langner and Armina Marshall. Produced by Crosby Gaige and Charles Heidt at the Fulton Theatre, New York, February 4, 1935.

Cast of characters—

Eleanor Sloan....................................Ilka Chase
Donald Sloan.....................................Myron McCormick
Anne...Mary Rogers
Miss Hedda Sloan.................................Josephine Hull
Peters...Edward Broadley
Ella...Martha Hodge
Chester Digges...................................Glenn Anders
Talbot Sloan.....................................Roy Atwell
Walter Sloan.....................................Hugh Rennie
Tracy..Worthington Miner
State Senator Parmelee...........................Robert T. Haines
Captain Halligan.................................Edward McNamara
Grimm..Percy Helton
    Acts I, II and III.—Living Room of Residence of Talbot Sloan in
Melrose, Ohio.
Staged by Worthington Miner; setting by Stewart Chaney.

Talbot Sloan, the fifth in line of the banker Sloans, is horrified
and indignant when a clerk, Grimm, confesses having speculatively
misapplied $25,000 of the Sloan bank's funds. He would send
Grimm to jail and collect his bond. Donald Sloan, the banker's
second son, turned lightly socialistic, protests that Grimm has
done nothing more than bankers frequently do. To prove his
point he takes a million in bonds from the bank and hides them
in the Sloan piano. The bank examiners are coming and Banker
Sloan borrows from his niece's estate to cover the loss. Threat-

ened with exposure he sees the light and agrees to let Grimm
retain his job and repay the bank with the help of a salary in-
crease.

IT'S YOU I WANT

(15 performances)

A farce in three acts by Maurice Braddell, adapted by George
Bradshaw. Produced by J. H. Del Bondio and Forrest C. Haring
at the Cort Theatre, New York, February 5, 1935.

Cast of characters—

Braille	Donald Randolph
Sheridan Delaney	Earle Larimore
Constance Gilbert	Cora Witherspoon
Otto Gilbert	Taylor Holmes
Melisande Montgomery	Leona Maricle
Jimmy Watts	Karl Swenson
Anne Vernon	Helen Chandler
Paul Entwhistle	J. Malcolm Dunn

Acts I, II and III.—Sheridan Delaney's London Living Room.
Staged by Forrest C. Haring and Joshua Logan; setting by Jo
Mielziner.

Sheridan Delaney is tired of the women who tire him and about
to leave for Scotland for the fishing and a rest. Sheridan rents
his London apartment to Otto Gilbert whose wife, Constance, is
one of the reasons Sheridan is leaving town. Mr. Gilbert installs
Melisande Montgomery, his mistress, in the apartment. Then
Sheridan, intrigued by the pursuit of Anne Vernon, does not go
to Scotland and everybody tries to hide from everybody else in
his apartment. He accepts Anne in the end.

FIELD OF ERMINE

(11 performances)

A play in three acts by Jacinto Benavente, adapted by John
Garrett Underhill. Produced by Crosby Gaige, Inc., at the Mansfield Theatre, New York, February 8, 1935.

Cast of characters—

Luisa	Alice Alworth
Natalia	Nedda Harrigan
Dorotea	Janet Leland
Gerardo	Charles Bellin
Demetria	Harriet Sterling
Cesar Estevez	Clarence Derwent
Santiago Solana	Courtney White
Irene	Frances Starr
The Duke of Santa Olalla	St. Clair Bayfield
Paco Utrillo	David Leonard
Butler	Francis French

```
Porter.......................................Harmanus Van Wie
Baltasar.........................................Gerald Cornell
Martin..............................................Frank Ray
Count of San Ricardo............................Harold West
José Maria.......................................Leonard Penn
Felisa............................................Alma Kruger
Carolina.....................................Lenore Chippendale
Maria Antonia....................................Mary Mason
Beatriz.......................................Frances Tannehill
    Act I.—Natalia's Boudoir.  Madrid.  Acts II and III.—Drawing
Room of the Marchioness of Montalbar.
    Staged by Ben Ali Haggin.
```

Irene, Marchioness of Montalban, would take Gerardo, the illegitimate son of her beloved and deceased brother, into her own home, despite the protests of her proud and greedy family. Gerardo is happy in the change and Irene grows very fond of him. The relatives continue to protest and offer proof of the boy's paternity being doubtful. Gerardo's cousins induce him to drink too much wine. Irene, disappointed, sends the boy back to his mother. Instead of going Gerardo walks the streets for two days. When he returns to Irene, to ask her pardon, she is so relieved she takes him again to her heart and burns all the proofs derogatory to his birth.

BITTER OLEANDER

(24 performances)

A drama in three acts by Federico Garcia Lorca, translated by José A. Weissman. Produced by The Neighborhood Playhouse at the Lyceum Theatre, New York, February 11, 1935.

Cast of characters—

```
Mother................................................Nance O'Neil
Novio (The Bridegroom)..........................Edgar Barrier
Neighbor........................................Alice Ann Baker
Leonardo's Wife..................................Louise Glover
Her Mother...................................Genevieve Belasco
Leonardo........................................William Lawson
Girl..............................................Rose Lieder
Servant..........................................Effie Shannon
Novio's Father.............................Thomas Coffin Cooke
Novia (The Bride)...........................Eugenie Leontovich
First Girl.......................................Dazma Minty
Second Girl.....................................Jane Haverhill
Third Girl......................................Dora Southern
Fourth Girl...................................Gertrude Stone
Fifth Girl........................................Sana Martin
First Man.........................................Jerome Thor
Second Man.........................................Paul Mann
Woodcutters.....................................{ Arthur Singer
                                                 Eric Kelton
                                                 Yisrol Libman
Spinning Girls..................................{ Beatrice St. Ives
                                                 Marian Barnes
                                                 Grace Carey
Woman........................................Ludmilla Toretska
              Wedding Guests and Musicians
    Act I.—Scene 1—Room in House of The Novio's Mother, District
```

of Guadix, Andalusia, Spain. 2—Room in Leonardo's House. 3—
Room in House of The Novia's Father. Act II.—Courtyard of House
of The Novia's Father. Act III.—Scene 1—A Forest. 2—Room in
House of The Novio's Mother.
    Staged by Irene Lewisohn; settings by Cleon Throckmorton from
sketches by Santiago Ontanon.

Novia, the bride, and Novio, the bridegroom, are preparing for
their wedding. Novia is secretly unhappy because she had been
in love with Leonardo and had quarreled with him. Leonardo
married another and Novia decided to do likewise. Now she
knows she can never love another. Novia and Novio are married,
but directly after the wedding Novia runs away to the forest
with Leonardo. After a night in the moonlight they are found
by the angry wedding party and Leonardo and Novio fight a duel
in which both are killed.

THE ELDEST

(24 performances)

A comedy in three acts by Eugenie Courtright. Produced by
Sam H. Grisman at the Ritz Theatre, New York, February 11,
1935.

Cast of characters—

Janet Janeway.....................................Helen Claire
Jimmy Wilson..................................Damian O'Flynn
Mrs. Wilson....................................Suzanne Jackson
Mrs. Trent......................................Minnie Dupree
Nancy Janeway.................................Nancy Sheridan
John Sales....................................William Post, Jr.
Aurelia Janeway...................................Lillian Foster
Alec Janeway....................................Richard Jack
1st Photographer...................................Paul Clare
2nd Photographer.............................Charles Lawrence
Samuelson....................................Joseph Greenwald
Mervin Strong..................................James Spottswood
    Acts I, II and III.—Living Room in Home of the Janeways in
Small Town in Middle West.
    Staged by Anthony Brown; setting by Raymond Sovey.

Aurelia Janeway, sentenced to life imprisonment for the murder of her husband, into whose soup she sprinkled a liberal portion of poison, is given a new trial and wrongfully acquitted after
serving six years. She returns home to take charge of the up-
bringing of her children and the care of her aging mother.
Aurelia is a flighty person who goes in strongly for publicity and
resumes her relations with a lover, Mervin Strong, for whom she
had committed the murder. In the end Aurelia runs away with
Mervin, the grandmother dies and the house reverts to the care
of Nancy Janeway, the eldest daughter.

RAIN

(47 performances)

A drama in three acts by John Colton and Clemence Randolph from a story by Somerset Maugham. Revived by Sam H. Harris at the Music Box Theatre, New York, February 12, 1935.

Cast of characters—

A Native Girl	Elizabeth Dewing
A Native Policeman	K. A. Fernando
Two Natives	{ John Waller { Frank De Silva
Ameena	Emma Wilcox
Private Griggs, U.S.M.C.	Kent Thurber
Corporal Hodgson, U.S.M.C.	Jack McKee
Sergeant O'Hara, U.S.M.C.	Walter Gilbert
Joe Horn	Granville Bates
Mrs. Alfred Davidson	Ethel Wilson
Doctor McPhail	Nicholas Joy
Mrs. McPhail	Ethel Intropodi
Quartermaster Bates (of the "Orduna")	Harold De Becker
Sadie Thompson	Tallulah Bankhead
Reverend Alfred Davidson	Herbert Ranson

Acts I, II and III.—Hotel Store of Trader Joe Horn, on the Island of Tutuila, Port of Pago Pago, South Seas.

Staged by Sam Forrest; setting by W. Oden Waller.

"Rain" was produced originally at Maxine Elliott's theatre, New York, November 7, 1922, following a fortnight's engagement in Philadelphia. The original New York run covered 648 performances. With the late Jeanne Eagels as its star the play continued on tour the following four years, playing one return engagement in New York in September, 1924. A digest of the drama was included in the 1922-23 edition of "The Best Plays."

NOAH

(45 performances)

A fantasy in three acts by André Obey, adapted by Arthur Wilmurt; music by Louis Horst. Produced by Jerome Mayer at the Longacre Theatre, New York, February 13, 1935.

Cast of characters—

Noah	Pierre Fresnay
Mamma	Margaret Arrow
Shem	David Friedkin
Ham	Harry Bellaver
Japhet	Norman Lloyd
Norma	Fraye Gilbert
Sella	Cora Burlar
Ada	Gertrude Flynn
A Man	Royal Beal
The Bear	Charles Holden

```
The  Lion...........................................Richard  Spater
The  Monkey........................................Milton  Feher
The  Elephant......................................Joseph  Willis
The  Cow...........................................Igene  Stuart
The  Tiger.........................................Richard  Fleming
The  Wolf..........................................Jane  Churchill
The  Lamb..........................................Georgia  Graham
```
    Act I.—A Clearing. Act II.—The Ark. Act III.—Scene 1—The
Ark. 2—The Top of Mt. Ararat.
    Staged by Jerome Mayer; settings by Cleon Throckmorton; animals
and masks by Remo Bufano and Ludwig Bemelmans; dances directed
by Anna Sokolow and Louis Horst.

Noah has finished the ark and is a little puzzled that God
has no intention of asking him to add a rudder. In response to
divine command Noah summons his sons, Ham, Shem and Japhet,
and three neighbor girls, Norma, Sella and Ada; calls in representatives of the animal world; bundles Mamma Noah and himself aboard and prepares to set sail when the rains descend. For
forty days the ark sails the wastes of water. Often Noah's faith
is tried by thoughts of God's desertion. The dark-skinned Ham
is ready to start a rebellion. Only the animals are understanding. When Ararat is reached the six children go forth in pairs,
the animals scatter into the forest and Mamma and Noah are left
wondering on the mountain top.

MOSCOW ART PLAYERS

(52 performances)

A repertory of modern Soviet plays and Russian classics. Produced by S. Hurok at the Majestic Theatre, New York, February
16, 1935.

REVISOR

A satiric comedy in four acts by Nikolai Gogol.

Cast of characters—

```
Anton Antonovich Skvoznik-Dluhanovsky.................P.  Pavlov
Anna Andreyevna.......................................V.  Gretch
Marya Antonovna...................................M.  Krijanowskaia
Luka Lukich Khlopov...................................V.  Zelitzky
His Wife..............................................N.  Tokarskaya
Ammos Fyodorovich Lyapkin-Tyapkin.................G.  Chmara
Piotr Ivanovich Bobchinsky........................S.  Strenkovsky
Piotr Ivanovich Dobchinsky.........................M.  Rasomov
Artemy Filipovich Zemlyanika.....................B.  Kremenetzky
Ivan Kuzmich Shpekin..................................A.  Zilinsky
Ivan Alexandrovich Chlestakov.......................M.  Chekhov
Ossip.................................................G.  Zagrebelsky
Gibner................................................B.  Alekin
Korobkin..............................................S.  Petrov
Chief of Police.......................................G.  Svoboda
Svistunov.............................................M.  Michon
Derjimorda............................................P.  Rostoff
Abdulin...............................................A.  Naletoff
```

```
Poshlepkina.........................................B. Martinova
Sergeant's Wife.....................................V. Solovieva
Mishka.............................................E. Korsak
Waiter at the Inn..................................A. Bogdanov
     Acts I, III and IV.—Mayor's Home.  Act II.—Room at Inn
     Staged by Michel Chekov; settings by Youri Annankov.
```

The Moscow Art Players also produced "Poverty Is No Crime," by Ostrovsky; "Strange Child," a Soviet comedy by Shkvarkin; "Marriage," by Gogol; "The White Guard," a Soviet drama by Bulgakov; "The Deluge," by Henning Berger; Chekov's "I Forgot"; and "Enemies" by B. Lavrenoff.

Following a tour the Moscow Art Players returned and gave an additional twenty-eight performances at the Public Theatre.

THE SIMPLETON OF THE UNEXPECTED ISLES

(40 performances)

A fantasy in a prologue and two acts by George Bernard Shaw. Produced by The Theatre Guild, Inc., at the Guild Theatre, February 18, 1935.

Cast of characters—

```
The Emigration Officer.............................Rex O'Malley
Wilks..............................................Lionel Pape
The Young Woman....................................Patricia Calvert
The Station Master.................................Reginald Malcolm
The Priest, Pra....................................McKay Morris
The Priestess, Prola...............................Nazimova
The Lady Tourist...................................Viola Roache
Sir Charles Farwaters..............................Lawrence Grossmith
The Clergyman......................................Romney Brent
Janga..............................................Leon Janney
Kanchin............................................Franklin Gray
Maya...............................................Alma Lloyd
Vashti.............................................Rita Vale
The Angel..........................................Louis Hector
     Prologue.—Scene 1—Emigration Office, Tropical Port in British
     Empire.  2—A Cliff Top.  3—Half-way Down the Cliff.  Acts I and
     II.—Garden of Government House, Tropical Port in British Empire.
     Staged by Harry Wagstaff Gribble; settings by Lee Simonson.
```

Four citizens of the British Empire join with Pra and Prola, priest and priestess of an ancient race living upon a tropical island in the British possessions, to form a community which shall experiment in joining the civilizations of the East and West. In twenty years four brilliant half-castes have been born to the community. Thinking to carry the experiment in eugenics further they induce a British clergyman to marry the half-caste daughters. The clergyman proves useless as a father and the arrival of Judgment Day, when all useless, selfish and mischievous persons who cannot justify their existence disappear into space, does for both half castes and Britishers. Pra and Prola are left to continue the rule of the island.

*AWAKE AND SING

(137 performances)

A drama in three acts by Clifford Odets. Produced by The Group Theatre, Inc., at the Belasco Theatre, New York, February 19, 1935.

Cast of characters—

```
Myron Berger...........................................Art Smith
Bessie Berger.........................................Stella Adler
Jacob.............................................Morris Carnovsky
Hennie Berger.......................................Phœbe Brand
Ralph Berger.........................................Jules Garfield
Schlosser...........................................Roman Bohnen
Moe Axelrod..........................................Luther Adler
Uncle Morty.........................................J. E. Bromberg
Sam Feinschreiber...............................Sanford Meisner
    Acts I, II and III.—In a Bronx Apartment.
    Staged by Harold Clurman; setting by Boris Aronson.
```

See page 236.

CROSS RUFF

(7 performances)

A comedy in three acts by Noel Taylor. Produced by Delos Chappell at the Masque Theatre, New York, February 19, 1935.

Cast of characters—

```
Alfred Rouff...........................................Jay Fassett
Leda...................................................Edith King
Doris..................................................Janet Fox
Wilbur Hanley...................................Raymond Bramley
Juniper.............................................Helen Brooks
Peter..................................................Noel Taylor
    Acts I, II and III.—Apartment of Alfred and Leda, New York City.
    Staged by Karl Nielson; setting by John Root.
```

Alfred and Leda are living happily in sin when Leda's daughter by a former husband returns from Paris. The daughter, Juniper, thinks nothing of her mother's living arrangements and later falls in love with Alfred's son, Peter. Alfred and Leda are pleased but a little shocked when Juniper and Peter insist upon being formally married.

THE BISHOP MISBEHAVES

(121 performances)

A comedy in three acts by Frederick Jackson. Produced by John Golden at the Cort Theatre, New York, February 20, 1935.

Cast of characters—

```
Red Eagan.............................................A. P. Kaye
Donald Meadows......................................Alan Marshal
Hester Grantham......................................Jane Wyatt
Guy Waller...................................Reynolds Denniston
Mrs. Waller........................................Phyllis Joyce
The Bishop of Broadminster.......................Walter Connolly
Lady Emily Lyons..............................Lucy Beaumont
Collins...............................................James Jolley
Frenchy...........................................Charles Laite
Mr. Brooke.......................................Horace Sinclair
```
Act I.—Taproom of The Queen's Head at Tadworth in Surrey.
Acts II and III.—Hall of the Bishop's Palace at Broadminster.
Staged by Ira Hards; settings by Woodman Thompson.

The Bishop of Broadminster and his sister, Lady Emily Lyons, take shelter in a London pub when caught in a sudden storm. The Bishop, whose minor passion is the reading of detective stories, discovers that they have accidentally followed close upon a holdup. Following the usual clews the Bishop discovers the jewels, which the robber had left for a confederate to pick up, and takes them home with him, leaving his professional card in their place. The robbers, bent on recovering their swag and adding to it the gold plate of the rectory, call on the Bishop. He maneuvers them into a vault and arranges not only for the recovery of the jewels, but their return to Hester Grantham, from whom they had been wrongfully taken by her guardian. Hester's young man, Donald Meadows, had staged the robbery in Hester's interest.

THE DISTANT SHORE

(13 performances)

A drama in three acts by Donald Blackwell and Theodore St. John. Produced by Dwight Deere Wiman at The Morosco Theatre, New York, February 21, 1935.

Cast of characters—

```
Elsie Hallett.........................................Ruth Vivian
Sophie Lancaster...................................Mabel Gore
Millie Caulfield...................................Violet Besson
Dorothea Gerhardt.................................Edith Angold
Dora Bond.......................................Jeanne Casselle
Edgar Bond.......................................Roland Young
Hotel Clerk...................................James MacDonald
Sylvia Sheldon......................................Sylvia Field
Buttons.............................................Roy Le May
George Lancaster..................................Harry Green
Inspector Ross...................................Hale Norcross
Sergeant Barnes....................................Edgar Kent
Doctor Nichols..............................Kenneth Treseder
Captain Graham.............................Francis Compton
Quartermaster Swan...............................Dennis Gurney
```
In the Street Scene: Barbara Allen, Andy Anderson, Sybil Campbell, William Fender, Jr., William M. Griffith, Roy Le May, Eric Mansfield, James McKay, Mary Michael, William Postance,

Roger Stearns, Morton Stevens, Jean Tate, Elizabeth Valentine, Dean West.

Act I.—Scenes 1 and 3—Sitting Room of Dr. Bond's House in London. 2—Bedroom in small London Hotel. Act II.—Dr. Bond's Sitting Room. Act III.—Scene 1—Exterior of Dr. Bond's House. 2—Aboard Steamship "Mont Royal." 3—Doctor Bond's Cabin. 4—London.

Staged by Robert Ross; settings by Raymond Sovey.

Dr. Edgar Bond, driven frantic by the rasping crudities of a cockney wife, deliberately or accidentally gives her an overdose of a sleeping potion. When she is found dead the doctor buries her body in the cellar. A police investigation frightens the doctor into running away with his secretary, with whom he is in love and who insists on sharing his exile. They are overtaken by the Marconi wireless, arrested on board a boat headed for Montreal and returned to London, where the doctor is sentenced to be hanged. The play is an adaptation of the Crippen murder exposed in London in 1910.

THE BARRETTS OF WIMPOLE STREET

(24 performances)

A drama in three acts by Rudolf Besier. Revived by Katharine Cornell at the Martin Beck Theatre, New York, February 25, 1935.

Cast of characters—

Doctor Chambers....................................Moroni Olsen
Elizabeth Barrett Moulton-Barrett.................Katharine Cornell
Wilson..Brenda Forbes
Henrietta Moulton-Barrett.........................Margalo Gillmore
Arabel Moulton-Barrett.............................Joyce Carey
Octavius Moulton-Barrett..........................Burgess Meredith
Septimus Moulton-Barrett..........................David Vivian
Alfred Moulton-Barrett............................Robert Champlain
Charles Moulton-Barrett...........................John Gordon-Gage
Henry Moulton-Barrett.............................Gilmore Bush
George Moulton-Barrett............................Irving Morrow
Edward Moulton-Barrett............................Charles Waldron
Bella Hedley......................................Margot Stevenson
Henry Bevan.......................................John Hoysradt
Robert Browning...................................Brian Aherne
Doctor Ford-Waterlow..............................Reynolds Evans
Captain Surtees Cook..............................John Emery
Flush...Flush

Acts I, II and III.—Elizabeth Barrett's Bed-Sitting Room at 50 Wimpole Street, London.

Staged by Guthrie McClintic; setting by Jo Mielziner.

"The Barretts of Wimpole Street" was produced originally at the Hanna Theatre, Cleveland, Ohio, January 29, 1931, and at the Empire Theatre, New York, February 9 the same year. The New York run was 370 performances. Miss Cornell later included the play in her repertory when she made a 17,000 mile tour of the United States the season of 1934-35.

TIMES HAVE CHANGED

(32 performances)

A drama in three acts by Edouard Bourdet, adapted by Louis Bromfield. Produced by Feodor Rolbein at the National Theatre, New York, February 25, 1935.

Cast of characters—

Hester Pentland.....................................Thais Lawton
Phyllis Pentland....................................Jane Buchanan
Mrs. Pentland.......................................Cecilia Loftus
Bates...Henry Vincent
Melanie Burnham.....................................Mary Sargent
Bob Burnham...Eric Wollencott
Forbes Pentland.....................................Robert Loraine
Morgan Pentland.....................................Lucien Self
Dr. William Pierce..................................Maurice Burke
Marianne Pentland...................................Elena Miramova
Peter Pentland......................................Owen Davis, Jr.
Harry Pentland......................................Moffat Johnston
Suzanne Pentland....................................Fania Marinoff
Rose..May Martyn
    Act I.—Scene 1—Pentland House on the North Shore, Mass. 2—Harry Pentland's Studio, Bridgeport.   Act II.—Pentland House. Act III.—Melanie Burnham's House, Park Avenue, New York.
    Staged by Auriol Lee; settings by Stewart Chaney.

Forbes Pentland, head of the aristocratic New England family of that name, is led to seek a reconciliation with his brother Harry, cut off from the family when he married a French actress. Harry still owns stock in the Pentland mills which will be helpful to Forbes in a threatened company crisis. When trouble continues to threaten Forbes proposes that Harry's daughter Marianne marry Bob Burnham, the mentally deficient son of a rich neighbor, and thus strengthen the Pentland credit. Marianne agrees to the arrangement but later comes to loathe her husband, recoiling from his beast-like passion. Following an emotional outbreak Bob Burnham shoots himself and Marianne returns to her father's house.

GREEN PASTURES

(73 performances)

A fable play by Marc Connelly, suggested by Roark Bradford's Southern Sketches, "Ol' Man Adam an' His Chillun." Revived by Laurence Rivers, Inc., at the 44th Street Theatre, New York, February 26, 1935.

Cast of characters—

Mr. Deshee....................................Charles H. Moore
Myrtle..Nonie Simmons

```
First Boy...........................................Willis Morton
Second Boy........................................Franklin Brown
Third Boy.........................................Billie Richards
Randolph..........................................Edward Yancey
A Cook...................................................Irene Watts
Custard Maker....................................Randall Homer
First Mammy Angel..............................Anna Mae Fritz
A Stout Angel....................................Laura Anderson
A Slender Angel..................................Dinks Thomas
Archangel.........................................Allen Charles
Gabriel...................................................Oscar Polk
The Lawd.....................................Richard B. Harrison
Choir Leader.......................................Roy McKinley
Adam...........................................Daniel L. Haynes
Eve.............................................Geraldine Gooding
Cain..............................................Thomas Russell
Cain's Girl....................................Benveneta Washington
Zeba..............................................Edna M. Harris
Cain the Sixth.....................................James Fuller
Boy Gambler...................................Richard Henderson
First Gambler......................................Richard Emory
Second Gambler.....................................Harold Hines
Voice in Shanty..................................Mary Frances
Noah.........................................Morris McKinney
Noah's Wife.........................................Susie Sutton
Shem.........................................Milton J. Williams
First Woman......................................Harriet Hoyt
Second Woman.....................................Janet Stevens
Third Woman.......................................Alice Geneva
Fourth Woman....................................Mildred Allison
First Man..........................................Henry Blake
Flatfoot........................................Freddy Archibald
Ham.................................................J. Homer Tutt
Japheth.........................................Harry Thompson
First Cleaner.....................................Florence Fields
Second Cleaner....................................Frances Smith
Abraham....................................Charles Winter Wood
Isaac.............................................John Charles
Jacob............................................John McAllister
Moses.............................................Frank Wilson
Zipporah.........................................Mercedes Gilbert
Aaron...........................................McKinney Reeves
A Candidate Magician........................Reginald Fenderson
Pharaoh...........................................George Randol
The General.......................................Charles Winter
The Admiral.......................................James Lindsay
First Wizard......................................George Milton
Second Wizard.......................................Carl Shorter
Head Magician.....................................Arthur Porter
Outer Guard........................................George Brown
Joshua.........................................William McFarland
First Scout.........................................Ivan Sharp
Master of Ceremonies.................................Jack Mann
King of Babylon..................................William Fenton
Prophet.............................................Ivan Sharp
High Priest...........................................J. Homer
```

The King's Favorites: Benveneta Washington, Leona Winkler, Gertrude Wilson, Nonie Simmons, Viola Mickens.

```
Officer............................................Martin Quinn
Hezdrel........................................Daniel L. Haynes
Another Officer..................................James Morrison
```

The Children: Gertrude De Verney, Viola Mickens, Gertrude Wilson, Nonie Simmons, Willis Martin, Franklin Brown.

Babylonian Band: Carl Shorter, Richard Henderson, Thomas Russell, Edgar Yancey.

Sopranos: Bertha Wright, Geraldine Gooding, Almalillie Hubbard, Nell Hunter, Mattie Harris, Gertrude DeVerney, Marie Warren, Mabel Ridley.

Altos: Olive Ball, Willie Mays, Viola Mickens, Benveneta Washington.

Tenors: Robert P. Ecton, Arthur Porter, James Taylor, Jr., McKinley

Reeves, William McFarland, Augustus Simons.
Baritones: T. Lloyd Hickman, Jerome Addison, Dow K. Williams,
Benjamin Ragsdale.
Bassos: Walter Meadows, Frank Horace, J. E. Lightfoot.
Part I.—Scene 1—Sunday School.   2—Fish Fry.   3—Garden.   4—
Outside the Garden.   5—Roadside.   6—Private Office.   7—Another
Roadside.   8—House.   9—Hillside.   10—Mountain Top.   Part II.—
Scene 1—Private Office.   2—Mouth of a Cave.   3—A Throne Room.
4—Foot of a Mountain.   5—Cabaret.   6—Private Office.   7—Outside
a Temple.   8—Another Fish Fry.
Staged by Marc Connelly; settings by Robert Edmund Jones; choir
directed by Evelyn Burwell and Oliver Foster.

"The Green Pastures" was produced originally at the Mansfield
Theatre, New York, February 2, 1930. It was played for five
years on tour, achieving a total of 1,642 performances, including
the 640 performances of the original New York run. Richard B.
Harrison, playing de Lawd and later made the star of the troupe,
had not missed a single performance at the time of this anniversary engagement. He died early in March and was succeeded
by his understudy, Charles Winter Wood.

AMERICAN BALLET

A repertoire of dance dramas. Presented by The American
Ballet Company at the Adelphi Theatre, New York, March 1,
1935.

Principals engaged—

Tamara Geva	Paul Haakon
Leyda Anchutina	William Dollar
Elena de Rivas	Charles Laskey
Annabelle Lyon	Boris Levinoff
Elise Reiman	Heidi Vosseler
Katherine Mallowney	Edward Caton
Ruthanna Boris	Eugene Loring
Giselle	Holly Howard

Staged by George Balanchine, maître de ballet.

The repertoire included "Alma Mater," a satire on college
athletics by Edward M. M. Warburg, music by Kay Swift, costumes by John Held, Jr.; "Serenade" with music by Peter Tchaikovsky, costumes by Paul Tchelichew; "Reminiscence" arranged
by Henry Brant from Godard's score, settings and costumes by
Sergei Soudeikine; "Dreams" with music by Antheil, settings and
costumes by Derain; "Transcendence," music by Liszt, costumes
by Franklin Watkins, setting by Gaston Longchamp. "Alma
Mater," completely American in theme and composed and de-
signed by Americans, and "Reminiscence" were presented for the
first time on any stage.

Other repertoires of dance drama during the season included:
Ballet Russe, presented by S. Hurok at the Majestic Theatre

for five performances beginning March 20, 1935.   Repertory—
"Firebird" music by Stravinsky, scenery and costumes by Gont-
charova; "Boutique Fantasque," music by Rossini, choreography
by Massine, scenery and costumes by Derain; "Bal," music by
Rieti, libretto by Boris Kochno, choreography by Massine, scenery and costumes by Chirico; "Aurora's Wedding," music by
Tchaikovsky, choreography after Petipa, scenery by Bakst, costumes by Benois; "Public Gardens," from a novel by André
Gide, music by Vladimir Dukelsky, choreography by Massine,
scenery and costumes by Jean Lurcot; "Three Cornered Hat,"
music by de Falla, choreography by Massine, scenery and costumes by Picasso; "Petrouchka," music by Stravinsky, choreography after Fokine, scenery and costumes by Benois; "Union
Pacific" libretto by MacLeish, music by Nabakoff, scenery by Albert Johnson, costumes by Irene Sharoff, choreography by Massine.

Tamaris and her group presented at the Civic Repertory Theatre January 13, 1935, a program including Brant's "Conflict,"
"Dance of War," "Work and Play"; Pitot's "Walt Whitman
Cycle"; Seigmeister's "Cycle of Unrest" and "Protest Cama-
raderie"; Hindemith's "The Individual and the Mass"; Mosso-
low's "Affirmation"; Powell's "Dirge"; Satie's "Hypocrisy" and
Gruenberg's "Twentieth Century Bacchante."

Ted Shawn and his men dancers at Carnegie Hall Oct. 27,
1934, presented a program including the "Hopi Indian Eagle
Dance," "Labor Symphony," "The Hound of Heaven," and
others.

* PETTICOAT FEVER

(121 performances)

A farce in three acts by Mark Reed. Produced by Richard
Aldrich and Alfred de Liagre, Jr., at the Ritz Theatre, New
York, March 4, 1935.

Cast of characters—

```
Dascom Dinsmore...................................Dennis King
Kimo..............................................Goo Chong
Sir James Fenton...............................Leo G. Carroll
Ethel Campion....................................Doris Dalton
Little Seal.........................................Naoe Kondo
Snow Bird.......................................Frances Hogan
Rev. Arthur Shapham.........................Joaquin Souther
Captain George Landry............................Leo Curley
Scotty.........................................Robert Bentzen
Clara Wilson......................................Ona Munson
```
    Acts I, II and III.—A Wireless Station on the Coast of Labrador.
    Staged by Alfred de Liagre, Jr.; setting by Robert Barnhart.

Dascom insmore, a wireless operator stationed in Labrador, has had little or no contact with the female sex over a period of months. Sir James Fenton and his fiancée, Ethel Campion, are flying to Montreal for their wedding when they are forced down at Dinsmore's station. While they are awaiting a rescue party Dinsmore does his best to entertain them, which includes making feverish love to Miss Campion. His campaign is temporarily interrupted by the arrival on a sealer of a discarded sweetheart of his own. In the end Dinsmore succeeds in substituting for Sir James with Miss Ethel and turning his own Clara Wilson over to Sir James.

DE LUXE

(15 performances)

A drama in two parts by Louis Bromfield and John Gearon. Produced by Chester Erskin at the Booth Theatre, New York, March 5, 1935.

Cast of characters—

Pat Dantry	Melvyn Douglas
Fanny Altemus	Cora Witherspoon
Janny Travis	Claudia Morgan
Sabine Brandon	Violet Heming
Ogden Travis	Clyde Fillmore
Marie	Beverly Sitgreaves
First Porter	Tabor Von Jany
Second Porter	David Hughes
Lady Daisy Dantry	Ann Andrews
Lottie Moore	Elsa Maxwell
Sophie Bashly	Blanche Ring
Hank McDonald	Alan Bunce
The Grand Duke Sacha (Zizi)	Pierre DeRamey
Tony Acolia	"Peppy" DeAlbrew
Princess D'Orobelli (Ena)	Ivy Troutman
Lady Dextries	Florence Edney
Bobby Triplett	Maurice Sommers
Mons. Du Pont	Robert LeSuer
Waiter	Tom Elwell

Part I.—Scene 1—Pat Dantry's Flat, Paris. 2 and 3—Salon of Sabine Brandon's House Near the Invalides. Part II.—Scene 1—The Ritz in Paris. 2—Sabine Brandon's Salon.
Staged by Chester Erskin; settings by Jo Mielziner.

Pat Dantry, one of a set of disillusioned and unhappy American expatriates in Paris, throws over Fanny Altemus, an amorous lady of middle years who has been keeping him. Sabine Brandon, at the end of her resources, is about to marry Ogden Travis, whom she does not love, in order to recoup her fortunes. Janny Travis, heiress daughter of Ogden Travis, is in love with Hank McDonald, a poor newspaper man, but afraid to marry him at the cost of being disinherited. In a succession of emotional readjustments one Armistice day Sabine gives up Ogden and agrees to marry Pat, taking a chance with poverty, and Janny runs away with her reporter.

PANIC

(2 performances)

A tragedy in verse by Archibald MacLeish. Produced by the Phœnix Theatre, Inc., at the Imperial Theatre, New York, March 14 and 15, 1935.

Cast of characters—

An Old Woman	Rose McClendon
A Man	Russell Collins
A Man	Harold McGee
A Girl	Joanna Roos
A Man	Gerrit Kraber
A Young Man	Bernard Zanville
A Young Girl	Eva Langbord
A Woman	Paula Trueman
A Young Man	Karl Swenson
McGafferty	Orson Welles
Immelman	George Glass
Bankers	Clifford Heckinger Gordon Nelson Walter Coy Joseph Eggenton
Guard	Edward Mann
Unemployed	Abner Biberman William Challee Albert Lewis Paul Genge Wesley Addy Robin Batcheller
Blind Man	Harold Johnsrud
Ione	Zita Johann
Griggs	Richard Whorf

Chorus—Men: Edward Mann, Paul Genge, Wesley Addy, Albert Lewis, Arthur Singer, Yisrol Libman, Eric Walz, Robin Batcheller, John O'Shaughnessy, Jerome Thor.

Women: Elizabeth Morison, Deirdre Hurst, La Verne Pine, Virginia Welles, Amelia Barleon, Elizabeth Timberman, Osceola Archer, Beatrice Pons, Lucille Strudwick, Mary Tarcai, Margaret Craven, Margot Loines, Elaine Basil.

The action takes place in a street before an electric news bulletin and in the office of a great American banker.

Staged by James Light; setting by Jo Mielziner; choral movement by Martha Graham.

The last stand of Banker McGafferty against the forces of fear that engulfed him the time the banks were closing and there was little hope in men. McGafferty, the leading industrialist and financier of his time, goes into conference with his fellow bankers to induce them to pool their credits and halt the threatened collapse. The bankers are interested only in saving themselves. Panic finally seizes McGafferty and he is crushed.

BLACK PIT

(85 performances)

A play in three acts by Albert Maltz. Produced by The Theatre Union, Inc., at the Civic Repertory Theatre, New York, March 20, 1935.

Cast of characters—

Justice of the Peace	Royal C. Stout
Joe Kovarsky	Alan Baxter
Iola	Millicent Green
Mary Lakavitch	Hester Sondergaard
Anna	Nonnie Edwards
Vincent	Elliott Fisher
Tony Lakavitch	Martin Wolfson
Tex	Harold Johnsrud
Bakovchen	George Tobias
Mansky	Tony Ross
Schnabelt	Royal C. Stout
Barolla	Vincent Sherman
Prescott	Clyde Franklin
Pop	Royal C. Stout
Terry Jarkowski	Tony Ross
Mrs. Anetsky	Alice Brooks
A Miner	Sidney Packer
Mrs. Floyd	Frances Bavier
Hansy McCulloh	Howard da Silva
Josaf Anetsky	Royal C. Stout
Pauline	Helen Waren
Lyster	George Tobias
Blind Jimmie	Harold Johnsrud
Old Freddie	Sidney Packer

Prologue.—A Room with Bars. Act I.—Scenes 1 and 3—Quarters of Tony Lakavitch in Company House No. 12, Henrietta Mine Patch No. 4, McCulloh's Run, Northern West Virginia. 2—Boarding House, Munson Mine in Pennsylvania. Act II.—Scene 1—Office of the Mine Superintendent. 2 and 3—In Front of Company House No. 12. 4—Quarters of Tony Lakavitch. Act III.—Scene 1—In Front of Company House No. 12. 2—Quarters of Tony Lakavitch. Staged by Irving Gordon; settings by Tom Adrian Cracraft.

Joe Kovarsky, arrested for picketing, is sent to jail for three years. The day of his sentence he marries Iola Lakavitch. Out of prison Joe tries to get a job and finds he is blacklisted. He changes his name and goes to another state. The company detectives still hound him. Growing panicky when Iola is to have a baby he agrees to accept a job with the old company and remain friendly with the bosses. He hopes to salve his conscience as a stoolpigeon by not reporting what he is expected to report. In the end his fellows find him out. In an effort to regain his self-esteem Joe goes on strike with the men.

A WOMAN OF THE SOIL

(24 performances)

A play in three acts by John Charles Brownell. Produced by John Cameron at the 49th Street Theatre, New York, March 25, 1935.

Cast of characters—

Margaret Young	Evelyn Varden
Ruth Young	Ellen Brewster
Steve Baldwin	Brandon Peters
Doctor Wade	Dodson Mitchell
The Rev. Donald Ferguson	Maurice Wells
Bert Mason	Frank Monroe
Weir Douglas	Alfred Kappeler
Robert Young	Arthur Pierson

Acts I, II and III.—Living Room of Margaret Young's Farmhouse in Vermont.

Staged by John Cameron; setting by Yellenti.

Ruth Young, the adopted daughter of Margaret Young, has grown up with the idea that she is to marry Robert Young, her foster brother, who is an actor with the cocaine habit. Two other men are in love with Ruth, Steve Baldwin, a farmer, and Donald Ferguson, the village preacher. The Rev. Ferguson decides heroic measures are necessary to save Ruth from Robert. He takes Robert out in a rowboat and dumps him into the lake. The Rev. Ferguson is drowned and Robert dies from exposure, leaving the field clear to Steve Baldwin.

* TILL THE DAY I DIE

(96 performances)

A play in seven scenes by Clifford Odets. Produced by The Group Theatre, Inc., at the Longacre Theatre, New York, March 26, 1935.

Cast of characters—

Karl Taussig	Walter Coy
Baum	Elia Kazan
Ernst Taussig	Alexander Kirkland
Tillie	Margaret Barker
Zelda	Eunice Stoddard
Detective Popper	Lee J. Cobb
Martin, an Orderly	Bob Lewis
Another Orderly	Harry Stone
Captain Schlegel	Lewis Leverett
Adolph	Herbert Ratner
Zeltner	David Kortchmar
Schlupp	Russell Collins
Edsel Peltz	William Challee
1st Orderly	Samuel Roland
2nd Orderly	Harry Stone

```
3rd Orderly...................................Gerritt Kraber
4th Orderly..................................Abner Biberman
Boy....................................Wendell Keith Phillips
Other Prisoners......................Elia Kazan, Paul Morrison
Major Duhring..............................Roman Bohnen
Frau Duhring.............................Dorothy Patten
1st Detective.................................Gerritt Kraber
2nd Detective...............................David Kortchmar
Secretary.......................................George Heller
Arno...........................................Samuel Roland
Stieglitz..........................................Lee Martin
Julius......................................Bernard Zanville
Women................................Ruth Nelson, Paula Miller
```
    Scenes 1 and 6—An Underground Room. 2 and 4—Office Room
in the Columbia Brown House. 3—Barracks Room, Brown House.
5 and 7—Tillie's Room.
    Staged by Cheryl Crawford.

Fighting proletarians in Germany are meeting in underground
halls against the day they can take arms against the feurer.
Ernst Taussig, a young leader, is taken in a raid and subjected
to torture in an effort to force him to tell who his associates are.
Gradually the inquisitors break Taussig down. Fearing he will
eventually weaken he commits suicide, but not until after his
suspicious associates have blacklisted him as false to the party.

* WAITING FOR LEFTY

(96 performances)

A play in six scenes by Clifford Odets. Produced by The
Group Theatre, Inc., at the Longacre Theatre, New York, March
26, 1935.

Cast of characters—

```
Fatt............................................Russell Collins
Joe.............................................Lewis Leverett
Edna..............................................Ruth Nelson
Miller..........................................Gerritt Kraber
Fayette.........................................Russell Collins
Irv...............................................Walter Coy
Florrie...........................................Paula Miller
Sid............................................Herbert Ratner
Clayton............................................Bob Lewis
Agate Keller......................................Elia Kazan
Henchman.....................................Abner Biberman
Secretary......................................Dorothy Patten
Actor..........................................William Challee
Reilly...........................................Russell Collins
Dr. Barnes.....................................Roman Bohnen
Dr. Benjamin..................................Clifford Odets
A Man..........................................George Heller
```
    Voices: Sam Roland, Lee Cobb, Wendell Keith Phillips, Harry Stone,
        Bernard Zanville.
    Action Takes Place in Taxi Union Committee Meeting Room with
Six Miniature Spotlight Scenes.
    Staged by Sanford Meisner and Clifford Odets; setting by Alex-
ander Chertoff.

At a meeting of the Taxi Drivers' union the membership is
harangued by union officers, labor racketeers and radical mem-

bers. The officers and racketeers try to prevent a strike, the radicals plead for definite and immediate action. As each man relates the incident that has brought his courage to the sticking point the scene is acted out. The meeting is awaiting the return of a delegate named Lefty. Word comes finally that Lefty has been shot.

LADY OF LETTERS

(20 performances)

A comedy in three acts by Turner Bullock. Produced by Dmitri Ostrov at the Mansfield Theatre, New York, March 28, 1935.

Cast of characters—

Julia Pace	Anne Sutherland
Mr. Creepmore	Edward Broadley
Professor Gilbert Willifer	William Williams
Susie Willifer	Betty Bourjaily
Stella McDonald	Irene Shirley
Adelaide Willifer	Muriel Kirkland
Henrietta	Georgette Harvey
Cornelia Lawrence	Roberta Beatty
Richard Mays	Shepperd Strudwick
Warren Ainsley	Peter Powers
Dr. Newberry	Leslie King
Winifred Shaw	Katherine Squire

Acts I, II and III.—Living Room of Professor Gilbert Willifer's Home in a Small College Town in Southern Texas.

Staged by Dmitri Ostrov; setting by Metropolitan Studio; costumes by Mildred Manning.

Adelaide Willifer, the young second wife of Prof. Gilbert Willifer of a Texas college, knows little or nothing about books save that they are very important to the people who write them, including her husband. When she has a chance to buy the unsold manuscript of Richard Mays she is happy to put her name on it and send it to a publisher. The publisher buys the book and it becomes a minor sensation. When Adelaide's deception is exposed the college faculty is kept busy explaining things.

THE DOMINANT SEX

(16 performances)

A comedy in three acts by Michael Egan. Produced by George Bushar and John Tuerk at the Cort Theatre, New York, April 1, 1935.

Cast of characters—

Alec Winstone	Eric Dressler
Dick Shale	Bramwell Fletcher

```
Angela Shale...................................Helen Chandler
Lucy Webster...................................Rosalind Moore
Mr. Webster....................................Ralph Cullinan
Mrs. Webster...................................Kathryn Collier
Gwen Clayton...................................Ruth Weston
Joe Clayton....................................A. E. Matthews
```
    Acts I and II.—The Shales' flat in Bayswater, London. Act III.
—All-electric House in Blissboro.
    Staged by Edward Clarke Lilley; settings by Raymond Sovey.

Dick Shale, married to and in love with Angela, has invented
a compact electric motor which he plans to market and make
enough money to buy himself a farm. Angela, with a wife's
ambition to run things, insists he shall sell his invention to a
trust and be satisfied with a small but secure profit. The disagreement extends over a period of weeks, at the end of which
time Dick is induced to sell his patent, but he takes the money
and buys the farm. Angela, victorious but hardly triumphant,
agrees to settle down to an ordered domesticity and raise a family.

MANSION ON THE HUDSON

(16 performances)

A mono-drama in six scenes by Cornelia Otis Skinner. Produced by Miss Skinner at the Booth Theatre, New York, April
2, 1935.

Characters played by Miss Skinner—
    Julia (Mrs. Stanley Howland), 1880
    Sally (Mrs. Stanley Howland, Jr.), 1898
    Carrie Howland, 1920
    Mrs. Joseph Kelly, 1927
    Tony's Wife, 1934
    A Young Society Woman, 1934
    Scenes 1, 2, 3, 4, 5 and 6—Living Room of "Tall Trees," a large
estate on the Hudson.
    Staged by Miss Skinner; music arranged by Mischa Raginsky; cos-
tumes by Helene Pons.

During this engagement Miss Skinner repeated her successes
of other seasons: "The Empress Eugenie," "The Loves of Charles
II," with music arranged by Amelia Umnitz, and "The Wives of
Henry VIII," with music by Lowell Patton. Character sketches
included "Nurse's Day Out," "Times Square," "Being Presented,"
"A Southern Girl in the Sistine Chapel," "In a Gondola," "A
Lady Explorer," "Motoring in the 90's," "Eve of Departure,"
"Hotel Porch," and "Home Work."

POTASH AND PERLMUTTER

(19 performances)

A comedy in three acts by Montague Glass and Charles Klein. Revived by United Players, Inc., at the Park Theatre, New York, April 5, 1935.

Cast of characters—

Miss Cohen	Nancy Evans
Boris Andrieff	Waldo Edwards
Expressman	Frank Jaquet
Abe Potash	Arthur S. Ross
Mawruss Perlmutter	Robert Leonard
Miss Nelson	Ethel Harris
Mozart Rabiner	Frank Allworth
Henry D. Feldman	Walter Fenner
Ruth Goldman	Betty Hanna
Marks Pasinsky	Joseph K. Watson
Miss O'Brien	Paula Denning
Miss Levin	Gaile Watson
Irma Potash	Sylvia Leigh
Ferguson	Milano Tilden
Farrell	Harry Eshbach
Mrs. Potash	Bertha Walden
A Gentleman	Louis Morrell
Steuerman	Sam Sidman
Senator Murphy	Willard Dashiell
Katie	Hazel Drury

Act I.—Potash and Perlmutter, Division St., New York. Act II.—Potash and Perlmutter, Seventh Avenue, New York. Act III.—Potash Home in Washington Heights, New York.

Staged by Robert Leonard; settings by Karl Amend.

"Potash and Perlmutter" was produced originally on August 16, 1913, at the Cohan Theatre, New York, by A. H. Woods. The cast was headed by Barney Bernard and Alexander Carr, and the play ran for a total of 441 performances. A second version, written by Montague Glass and Roi Cooper Megrue, called "Abe and Mawruss," was produced in October, 1915, with Bernard and Julius Tannen in the name parts. The title was later changed to "Potash and Perlmutter in Society." With Robert Leonard of the above cast playing Mawruss the comedy ran for 665 performances in London.

FLOWERS OF THE FOREST

(40 performances)

A drama in three acts by John van Druten. Produced by Katharine Cornell at the Martin Beck Theatre, New York, April 8, 1935.

Cast of characters—

Beryl Hodgson	Brenda Forbes
Naomi Jacklin	Katharine Cornell

Lewis Jacklin....................................Moffat Johnston
Matheson.......................................Arthur Chatterton
Mercia Huntbach...............................Margalo Gillmore
Leonard Dobie.................................Burgess Meredith
Mrs. Huntbach..................................Leslie Bingham
Thomas Lindsay.....................................John Emery
Richard Newton-Clare............................Hugh Williams
Rev. Percy Huntbach...........................Charles Waldron
Mrs. Ettles...................................Alice Belmore Cliffe

    Acts I and III.—The Jacklins' House in Bloomsbury, England,
1934. Act II.—The Vicarage in Sussex, England, 1914, 1916.
    Staged by Auriol Lee; settings by Jo Mielziner; supervised by
Guthrie McClintic.

Naomi Jacklin, contentedly married in 1934, is led to recollec-
tions of her war-time experiences by the taunting charge of her
embittered sister, Mercia Huntbach, that her (Naomi's) real love
was Richard Newton-Clare, a soldier-poet killed in the war.
Naomi's mind wanders back to 1914 and her impassioned love
affair with Richard. Then forward to the return of Richard from
his first years of service at the front, an embittered and cynical
pacifist, hating the thought of fathering Naomi's expected child.
Again in the present Naomi is conscious of the years of misery
she spent following the operation that had taken her child, and
her hunger for some sign of understanding from her dead lover.
During a visit to the Jacklins, Leonard Dobie, a strange youth
given to trance-like spells, is inspired to repeat a last message
that Richard had spoken on his deathbed in the hospital, reassuring Naomi of his love and crying out a prayer for the glory of
living. Which helps Naomi compose her doubts and accept her
destiny.

* CEILING ZERO

(80 performances)

A play in three acts by Frank Wead. Produced by Brock Pemberton at the Music Box, New York, April 10, 1935.

Cast of characters—

Buzz Gordon......................................John Boruff
Doc Wilson....................................Joseph Downing
Baldy Wright....................................Chester Clute
Les Bogan..John Bohn
Jake Lee......................................Osgood Perkins
Tommy Thomas.................................Margaret Perry
Lou Clark..Hope Lawder
Texas Clark...................................G. Albert Smith
Tay Lawson.......................................Allan Hale
Al Stone.....................................Walter N. Greaza
Eddie Payson.....................................Ben Starkie
Dodo Harvey..................................Gladys Griswold
Dizzy Davis.......................................John Litel
Joe Allen....................................John Huntington
Mike Owens..................................John F. Hamilton
Mary Lee.....................................Nedda Harrigan

```
Dick Peterson...................................John Drew Colt
Fred Adams......................................Grandon Rhodes
Jerry Stevens.....................................Philip Remar
Smiley Johnson...................................James Todd
Bob Wilkins.....................................Geoffrey Bryant
B. P. Jenkins....................................Walter Hill
```
    Acts I, II and III.—Operations Office of Federal Air Lines, Had-
ley Field, Newark, N. J.
    Staged by Antoinette Perry; setting by John Root.

Jake Lee, Texas Clark and Dizzy Davis were aviator pals before and throughout the war.   In 1934 Jake is in command of a
New Jersey airport from which the mail planes take off.   Texas
and Dizzy are pilots under him.   Dizzy is an irresponsible but
likeable playboy and reckless in the air.   There is a suspicion
that he has been more than a good friend to Jake's wife and he
is planning a new campaign to seduce Tommy Thomas, an air
hostess betrothed to another flyer.   To make a girl date possible
Dizzy gets Texas to fly his ship in bad weather.   The ship
crashes, Texas is killed.   Overcome by remorse and realizing the
mess he has made of his life, Dizzy flies into the fog against
orders and never comes back.

A JOURNEY BY NIGHT

(7 performances)

A drama in prologue, three acts and epilogue adapted by Arthur
Goodrich from the original German by Leo Perutz.   Produced by
the Messrs. Shubert at the Shubert Theatre, New York, April 16,
1935.

Cast of characters—

```
Janet Fleming...................................Jane Buchanan
Warren Fleming..................................Frank Wilcox
Max.............................................Eduardo Ciannelli
Otto............................................Waldemar Klavun
Hilda...........................................Mary Murray
Schimke.........................................Jack Hartley
Franz Urban.....................................Albert Van Dekker
Anna............................................Elizabeth Kendall
Fritz...........................................Fuller Mellish
Guardsman.......................................Hobart Amory
Adolph..........................................Francis Pierlot
Ferdie..........................................Richard Taber
Hedwig..........................................Mimi Bontemps
Lisa............................................Otis Schaeffer
Carl............................................James Stewart
Julie...........................................Beatrice Swanson
Director General Metzger........................Nicholas Joy
Claire..........................................Greta Maren
Trudie..........................................Isabel Delehanty
Vilma...........................................Annette Downes
Weinigl.........................................Kate Mayhew
Anton Zimmerman.................................Edmund George
Policeman.......................................George Barr
Police Officer..................................Joseph McInerney
```

Guests at the Night Bar: Ann Dere, John Ray, John Meehan, Sara
  Allen, Jerome Leng, Tom Coyle, Martin Corne, Harold Eidel-
  seim, P. Phillips.
Prologue and Epilogue.—The Fleming Suite at the Arcadia Hotel,
Vienna. Act I.—Portion of the Night Bar. Act II.—Scene 1—Room
at Frau Weinigl's. 2—The Night Bar. 3—Room in Hotel Excelsior.
Act III.—Scene 1—Frau Weinigl's. 2—Embankment of the Danube.
3—Night Bar.
  Staged by Robert Sinclair; settings by Rollo Wayne.

Claire, the divorced wife of Franz Urban, proprietor of the
Night Bar, stops over in Vienna on her way to Pressburg, where
she expects to enter a house of ill repute. By accident Claire
meets Carl Urban, brother of Franz. Carl, a bank clerk enamored
of the gay life, is fascinated by Claire, who lets him believe she
is a grand lady. He steals money from the bank that employs
him to elope with her. Learning from Franz the truth about
Claire's past, Carl drowns her in the Danube.

RECRUITS

(132 performances)

A comedy in three acts by L. Resnick; music by Ben Yomen.
Produced by the Jewish Workers' Art Theatre at the Artef Theatre, New York, April 18, 1935.

Cast of characters—

Nachman	S. Levin
Gavriel "Shed"	M. Friedman
Chaim Plut	L. Freilich
Reb-Motele Chernobiler	S. Nagoshiner
Tsalie	A. Cohen
Rochele	L. Eisenberg-B. Lelchuk
Shloime Psayoches	O. Schreiber
Broche	Ch. Shpiner
Hersh Lieb	J. Levenstein
Pinches der Roiter	S. Anisfeld
Frumele	G. Russler
Velvl Gulevate	H. Bender
Isroel Ukrainer	M. Eisenberg
Aaron Kluger	S. Eisikoff
Perele	F. Biro
Lifshe	L. Rymer
Econom	M. Schneiderman
Young Peasant	M. Goldstein
Old Peasant	D. Holtz
Vasil	A. Horwitz
Agofonovitch	M. Kirsch
First Invalid	S. Kulman
Second Invalid	N. Gwirtzman
Leizer Krivoshei	I. Velichansky
First Tailor Apprentice	H. Rosen
Second Tailor Apprentice	J. Shrogin
Butcher	A. Hirshbein
Cobbler	A. Shapiro
Bahelfer	Ch. Brisman
Chantze	Ch. Fraiman
Boy	Ch. Kramer
Woman	A. Eisen

Nachmen's Mother....................................T. Todrina
A Lackey...M. Kirsch
First Dayon...T. Wendi
Second Dayon....................................N. Gwirtzman
First Haidamack.................................M. Pitkiowitz
Second Haidamack..................................D. Farber
A Drummer..J. Gostinsky
    Act I.—Scene 1—Street in Nibivale-Russ-Poland in 1828.   2—The
Rabbi's House.   3—The Inn.   Act II.—Scene 1—Schloime's House.
2—Kluger's House.   3—The Market Place.   Act III.—Scene 1—The
Street.   2—Leizer's Tailor Shop.   3—Kluger's House.
    Staged by Benno Schneider; settings by M. Solotaroff; dances by
Lily Mailman.

The Russian village of Nibivala is thrown into a state of fear
in 1827 as a result of the Czar's ukase impressing Jews into military service.   The elders of the town decide the punishment of
conscription has been visited upon them because of the presence
of Rochele, a widow who is not without sin, in their community.
Nachman, the tailor, opposes the elders and saves Rochele.   Re-
senting his activities the elders trick Nachman into signing enlist-
ment papers and he is taken into the army for twenty-five years.

During their season the Artef Players also gave 56 perform-
ances of Maxim Gorky's "Dostigayev," 4 performances of Gorky's
"Yegor Bulitchev" and 11 performances of Sholem Aleichem's
"Aristocrats."

JACKSON WHITE

(17 performances)

A drama in three acts by David Arnold Balch.   Produced by
A. Lawton McElhone at the Provincetown Playhouse, New York,
April 20, 1935.

Cast of characters—

Mrs. Bark..Marjorie Main
Birdie...Ruth Conley
Elijah Bark....................................Frank McCormack
Rance..John Galedon
Bert Rink......................................William Phillips
Emanuel Sisko...................................William Balfour
Ella..Katherine Hirsch
Ruth Davison......................................Mary Talbot
Martin Carey......................................Kirke Lucas
Kelsey...Ross Forrester
    Acts I, II and III.—Bark's Cabin in the Ramapo Mountains.
    Staged by David Balch.

Ruth Davison, nurse, brings Ella Bark back to her home in
the Ramapo mountains after Ella, an unwed mother at fifteen,
has spent three years in a state institution for defectives.   Ruth
is determined to protect Ella from her defective kin.   Despite
her watchfulness the girl is seduced by Emanuel Sisko, a villainous
hex doctor, and Ruth, threatened for her interference, might have
fared badly but for the protection afforded by Martin Carey, a

young biologist hunting snakes in the neighborhood. A further misery is added to the lot of the Barks when the son, Rance, shoots and kills his father, Elijah, who is caught lusting after Rance's wife, Birdie.

* KIND LADY

(66 performances)

A drama in three acts adapted by Edward Chodorov from a story by Hugh Walpole. Produced by Potter and Haight at the Booth Theatre, New York, April 23, 1935.

Cast of characters—

Annie	Hope Winchester
Mr. Foster	Francis Compton
Mary Herries	Grace George
Lucy Weston	Irby Marshal
Rose	Marie Paxton
Phyllis Glenning	Florence Britton
Peter Santard	Alan Bunce
Henry Abbott	Henry Daniell
Ada Abbott	Justine Chase
Doctor	Alfred Rowe
Mr. Edwards	Thomas Chalmers
Mrs. Edwards	Elfrida Derwent
Aggie Edwards	Barbara Shields
Gustav Rosenberg	Jules Epailly

Acts I, II and III.—Living Room of Mary Herries' Home in Montague Square, London.

Staged by H. C. Potter; setting by Jo Mielziner.

Mary Herries, slightly eccentric spinster of middle years, invites Henry Abbott, whom she finds shabbily dressed at her door, into her home for tea, and discovers him to be an art connoisseur. Abbott lifts her jade cigarette case on the way out. Days later Henry is back with the case and the story that he has pawned it to help a sick wife and child, who are in the street waiting for him. Miss Herries has them in and sends Henry for a doctor. Within the week the Abbotts, aided by three supposed relatives, move in upon Miss Herries to stay. They dismiss the servants, hold Miss Herries prisoner, spread word that she has sailed suddenly for a trip around the world and board up the house. For weeks Miss Herries is held incommunicado while the crooks strip the house of art treasures and try to force her to sign various commitments. By a ruse the victim of the plot effects her release.

SYMPHONY

(3 performances)

A drama in two acts by Charles March. Produced by Michael Myerberg at the Cort Theatre, New York, April 25, 1935.

Cast of characters—

```
Priest............................................Seth Arnold
Girl..........................................Patricia Randolph
Prudence Chandler..............................Edith Barrett
Monte.......................................Suzanne Caubaye
Marylou.......................................Ruth Matteson
Diane............................................Ann Thomas
Flo............................................Lillian Green
Priscilla........................................Hene Damur
Estelle.......................................Margot Stevenson
Constance....................................Patricia Randolph
Dorothy....................................Adrienne Matzenauer
Mrs. Chandler..................................Beverly Bayne
Whitly........................................Tom Stevenson
Mr. Chandler..................................Herbert Warren
Bob Bennett..................................Shirling Oliver
Mrs. Fawcett....................................Alice Fisher
Arlova...............................................Batami
Walter Winchell (electrical trans.).................Ted de Corsia
Bartender.......................................Seth Arnold
Charles Crane..................................Oliver Barbour
Arthur........................................Fred de Cordova
Dick.........................................Richard S. Stark
Mrs. Ralston......................................Marie Hunt
Baranoff.....................................Adia Kuznetzoff
Tramp..........................................Seth Arnold
```

Act I.—Scene 1—St. Patrick's Cathedral, New York City. 2—Boudoir of Chandler Home. 3—Bennett's Apartment. Act II.—Scene 1—Bill's Gay Nineties Bar. 2—A Bookstore. 3 and 6—Bennett's Apartment. 4—A Wharf. 5—Study in Chandler Home. Staged by Felix Weissberger; settings by Tom Adrian Cracraft.

Prudence Chandler, engaged to marry Charles Crane, confesses to a priest at St. Patrick's that she loves only Bob Bennett, a poverty-stricken writer. She is advised that to deny love is to sin against God, since true love exalts the spirit even though it crucify the body. Prudence leaves her groom at the altar and rushes to Bob. For two years they live poorly but happily. Bob, unbalanced by his failure to support Prudence in a manner to which she has been accustomed, kills himself. His widow, gazing rapturously upon the features of their year-old child, recalls the words of the priest and is content.

* SOMETHING GAY

(56 performances)

A comedy in three acts by Adelaide Heilbron. Produced by the Messrs. Shubert at the Morosco Theatre, New York, April 29, 1935.

Cast of characters—

```
Hatters.........................................Percy Ames
Nick..........................................Kent Thurber
Herbert Grey..................................Walter Pidgeon
Julia Freyne...................................Nancy Ryan
John Cochran...................................Hugh Sinclair
Monica Grey..................................Tallulah Bankhead
```

Marie..Elizabeth Dewing
Richard Rogers..................................Roy Gordon
    Acts I, II and III.—Drawing Room of the Greys' New York Pent-
house.
    Staged by Thomas Mitchell; setting by Donald Oenslager.

Monica Grey, returning to her penthouse in New York, discovers that her husband, Herbert, has been carrying on rather
brazenly with Julia Freyne, a widow from two floors below.
Monica seeks the advice of Jay Cochran, British playwright, with
whom she once was in love, as to what she should do. Jay suggests the old trick of making the husband jealous. Let Monica
call up a man friend and make a date for dinner. Monica tries,
but all her men friends refuse to react with anything resembling
ardor. Then Jay suggests that, inasmuch as he is sailing next day,
they let Herbert catch them planning to elope. Herbert overhears the plan and plays bravely up to it, not knowing that during
their scene of pretending Monica and Jay had revived their old
love and actually are on the high seas while he is laughingly
awaiting Monica's return.

TO SEE OURSELVES

(23 performances)

A comedy in three acts by E. M. Delafield. Produced by
J. H. Del Bondia and Joshua Logan at the Ethel Barrymore Theatre, New York, April 30, 1935.

Cast of characters—
Caroline Allerton...............................Patricia Collinge
Freddie Allerton................................Reginald Mason
Jill Charteris..................................Helen Trenholme
Michael Dennison................................Earle Larimore
Emma..Chouteau Dyer
    Acts I and III.—Drawing Room in the Allertons' House in South
Devon, England. Act II.—Scene 1—Allerton Drawing Room. 2—
Caroline's Bedroom.
    Staged by Joshua Logan; settings by Kate Drain Lawson.

Caroline Allerton, married to Freddie and the mother of two
children, suffers pangs of regret that her unimaginative husband
has come to take her for granted. Life is barren and dull for
Caroline until Jill Charteris and Michael Dennison come down
for a week end. Michael is also in a state of mind because Jill
cannot make up her mind to marry him and risk growing as dull
and unhappy as the Allertons. One night when Jill and Freddie
Allerton are away Michael and Caroline talk their problems out
and end by falling into each others' arms. Caroline goes to bed
for four days after that. When she is up and about again she has

recovered a sense of balance. Jill, sensing something of what has happened, decides to take no further chances with Michael. Freddie, urged on by Jill, agrees to take a bit more notice of Caroline.

IF A BODY

(45 performances)

A mystery drama in three acts by Edward Knoblock and George Rosener. Produced by Pierre de Reeder at the Biltmore Theatre, New York, April 30, 1935.

Cast of characters—

```
Chang..........................................Honorable  Wu
Druce Greywater...............................Courtney  White
Noah............................................Harry  Mestayer
Gerry Vincent.....................................Hal  Conklin
Dapper Dan Carmody...........................Morgan  Conway
Dinty Hackett..................................Greta  Granstedt
Justin Flowers..................................Anthony  Blair
Dick Rainsford.................................Arthur  Pierson
Helen Rainsford...............................Katherine  Locke
Jimmy Gage......................................Joseph  Allen
Rocca Angelo.....................................Louis  Tanno
Porky Quinn..................................Frank  S.  Marino
Puss Hyman....................................Marie  Hartman
Blackie Bannister...............................Rollin  Grimes
Dorgan..........................................Robert  O'Neill
Sammy................................................Himself
```
    Act I.—Druce Greywater's Living Room in Paradise House, a Rebuilt Private Dwelling in the Fifties of Manhattan. Act II.—Scene 1—Dinty Hackett's Living Room on Floor Below. 2—The Cellar. Act III.—Scene 1—Greywater's Living Room. 2—The Lobby.
    Staged by George Rosener; settings by Rollo Wayne.

Druce Greywater, student of occultism, discovering that Gerry Vincent is about to place Dick Rainsford in jeopardy, hypnotizes Gerry and stands him in a closet. Racketeers in an adjoining apartment engage Rainsford in a crooked game, which is frustrated by a friendly janitor. The hypnotized Gerry spends the evening falling out of closets, into windows and through coal holes. Druce finally restores Gerry to consciousness and the police herd the gamblers into the patrol wagon.

REPRISE

(1 performance)

A drama in three acts by W. D. Bristol. Produced by Frederick E. Mailey at the Vanderbilt Theatre, New York, May 1, 1935.

Cast of characters—

```
Madame.....................................Zamah  Cunningham
Roy...........................................Donald  Randolph
```

Julie...Barbara O'Neil
Peter...George Blackwood
    Acts I, II and III.—The Terrace of Roy's Penthouse.
    Staged by George Somnes; setting by John Biddle Whitelaw.

Roy Carter, finding Peter about to jump off the fifteenth story of an apartment house, draws him back and promises to make him happy in a month. Peter lives with the Carters and falls in love with Julie, Roy's sister. When he needs money to run away with Julie, Peter sells Roy's business to a rival. Roy is terribly hurt and a little jealous and Grandma Carter is so mad she goads Peter into carrying out his original jumping plan.

SAILOR, BEWARE!

(16 performances)

A comedy in two acts by Kenyon Nicholson and Charles Robinson. Revived by the Harlem Players at the Lafayette Theatre, New York, May 3, 1935.

Cast of characters—

Mattie Matthews...............................Carrington Lewis
Flip Edwards...................................Paul N. Johnson
Spud Newton...................................Milton Williams
Barney Waters..................................James Dunmore
Pee Wee Moore...................................Henry Davis
Herb Marley.......................................Canada Lee
Chester "Dynamite" Jones.....................Juano Hernandez
Lieut. Loomis, U.S.N............................Tom Moseley
Texas Patton.................................Reginald Fenderson
Ruby Keefer.......................................Lulu King
Bernice Dooley.................................Dorothy Sinclair
Hazel de Fay....................................Florence Lee
Dode Bronson....................................Juanita Hall
Humpty Singer....................................Hayes Pryor
Louie..Frank Ross
Billie "Stonewall" Jackson.....................Christola Williams
Señor Gomez.......................................Ken Renard
    Act I.—Scenes 1 and 4—Compartment 108, Aboard U.S.S. "Dakota," Panama Bay, Canal Zone. 2 and 5—Patio of the Idle Hour Café, Panama City. 3—Billie's Room. Act II.—Scene 1—A Nearby Beach. 2—Compartment 108. 3—Billie's Room.
    Staged by Shepard Traube and Mack Hilliard.

See "Best Plays of 1933-34." The Harlem Players also revived "The Front Page," for eight performances.

THE HOOK-UP

(21 performances)

A comedy in three acts by Jack Lait and Stephen Gross. Produced by Leslie J. Spiller at the Cort Theatre, New York, May 7, 1935.

Cast of characters—

Florence.....................................Mary Jane Barrett
Lawrence.....................................Russell Morrison
Etta Lynch...................................Grace Valentine
"Maestro" Ciccolini..........................Aristides de Leon
Grant..Frederic Howard
Roper..Peter Powers
Victor Vance.................................Ernest Truex
Mary Bainbridge..............................Edith Taliaferro
Virginia Bryce...............................Helen Lynd
A Page Boy...................................Richard Abert
Another Page Boy.............................Robert Elwyn
A. J. Lamb...................................Harold Moffet
Miss Hemingway...............................Olive Miller
An Announcer.................................Edward Ferguson
Radio Engineer...............................Charles Engel
Tappin.......................................Percy Helton
A Blonde.....................................Gloria Castle
Mother Bryce.................................Eva Condon
Bloomberg....................................Philip Van Zandt
Hollis.......................................Douglas Gregory
Seth...C. Jay Straight, Jr.
Misha..Saul Z. Martell
Jerry..Wells Richardson
Ruby...Georgette Harvey
Kay Palmer...................................Ruth Fallows
Betty..Patricia Peardon
Harry..Philip **Truex**
Bishop Thorndyke.............................Frederick Graham
A Bridesmaid.................................Margaret O'Donnell
Another Bridesmaid...........................Elaine Blauvelt

Act I.—Scenes 1 and 3—Program Room of Amalgamated Broadcasting Company. 2—Studio "F" at ABC. Act II.—Scene 1—Studio "F." 2—Virginia's Apartment. Act III.—Scene 1—Program Board Room. 2—Studio "R."

Staged by Frank Merlin; settings by Nat Karson.

Victor Vance is a radio actor with a reputation for his characterization of a country lawyer, Uncle Abe. To save the account of a rejuvenating pill sponsor Victor agrees to a thirteen weeks radio romance that shall culminate in his marriage to Virginia Bryce, the Orphan Nell of his studio troupe. Victor, being engaged to Mary Bainbridge, doesn't want to marry Virginia Bryce but is forced to go through with his contract up to and including the broadcast ceremony itself. At which point he is able to trick himself out of the picture.

* PARADE

(32 performances)

A satirical revue in two acts by Paul Peters, George Sklar, Frank Gabrielson, David Lesan and Kyle Crichton; music by Jerome Moross. Produced by The Theatre Guild at the Guild Theatre, May 20, 1935.

Principals engaged—

Jimmy Savo	Earl Oxford	Leon Janney
Edgar Allan	Eve Arden	Vera Marche

Dorothy Fox	Esther Junger	Lois Leng
Avis Andrews	Charles Walters	Irwin Shurack
J. Elliott Leonard	Jean Travers	Evelyn Dall
David Lawrence	Modern Dance Group	George Ali
Parade Quartet	André Cherise	David Lesan
Roger Logan	Yisrol Libman	Bob Long
Evelyn Monte	Melton Moore	Susanne Remos
Polly Rose	Stella Sanders	Ezra Stone
Charles D. Brown	Ralph Riggs	

Staged by Philip Loeb; dances by Robert Alton; settings by Lee Simonson.

WEATHER PERMITTING

(4 performances)

A comedy in three acts by Edward Sargent Brown. Presented by the author at the Masque Theatre, New York, May 23, 1935.

Cast of characters—

Frederick	Matthew Smith
Beevers	Harold DeBecker
Virginia	Viola Frayne
Josephine	Ruth Holden
Tony	Len Doyle
Oscar	Marcel Rousseau
Miss Hillman	Marjorie Dalton

Acts I, II and III.—Frederick's Bachelor Suite in a Boston Hotel. Staged by Edward Sargent Brown; setting by Ed. Sundquist.

Virginia, hero-hunter, compiles scrapbooks of the press notices of three favorites—Frederick, a society poloist; Tony, a racketeer, and Hemingway, a great aviator. Virginia is hopeful of enjoying a grand romance with one of them. Calling first on Tony she finds him both noble and cautious, particularly after she tells him she is only 17. Flying from Tony to Frederick she encounters a similar reception, though Freddie does permit her to get out of her wet clothes (Virginia always comes out of a storm) and into a suit of dry pajamas (which she had thoughtfully thrown into an overnight bag). Tony follows Virginia to Frederick's and would contest the poloist's possession of her. Frederick is interested, but already engaged. Following complications Virginia decides to try Hemingway next.

* THE YOUNG GO FIRST

(23 performances)

A comedy in three acts by Peter Martin, George Scudder and Charles Friedman. Produced by The Theatre of Action at the Park Theatre, New York, May 28, 1935.

Cast of characters—

```
Captain Hood...................................Philip Robinson
Christy Stark...................................Stephen Karnot
Sergeant Thrush.................................Paul Enders
Lieutenant Mullins.............................Mitchell Grayson
Orderly.........................................Jack Arnold
Beebie Menucci..................................Will Lee
Jeff Patten....................................Edward Mann
Lempi Sawicki..................................Harry J. Lessin
Giuseppe Calderone.............................Perry Bruskin
Hymie Kucher...................................Ben Ross
Glenn Campbell.................................Nik Ray
Paul Crosby....................................Earl Robinson
Frank Clark....................................David Kerman
Edmund Burke O'Leary...........................Curtis Conwaye
Miss Ferris....................................Roslyn Harvey
Mrs. Ruth Kent Menzies.........................Catherine Engels
Clifford Stedman...............................Roger Anderson
Florence Stedman...............................Joan Madison
Robin Stedman..................................Jean Harper
Polly..........................................Greta Karnot
Mrs. Stedman...................................Rhoda Rammelkamp
Colonel Hager..................................Joseph Lerner
"Dizzy" Scanlon................................George Parke
```
    Act I.—Scenes 1, 3 and 4—Blue Hill Camp, Civilian Conservation
Corps. 2—Work Field. Act II.—Scene 1—Porch of Stedman Home.
2 and 3—Blue Hill Camp. 4—Another Work Field. Act III.—Blue
Hill Camp.
    Staged by Alfred Saxe and Elia Kazan; settings by Mordecai
Gorelik.

A fairly tough unit of eight boys from New York is accepted into the C. C. C. camp at Blue Hill Mountain. They find Captain Hood and Lieutenant Mullins tough hombres and start a series of incipient rebellions against the food, against military drill, against the special privileges allowed officers and denied the men and against a shortage of lorries that keeps them from their pleasures in town. They band together for mutual protection, are brought before the Colonel and separated, each one being assigned a different camp to break their solidarity. They go away happily resigned because each hopes to start a new rebellion against any wrongs he finds in the camp to which he is sent.

KNOCK ON WOOD

(11 performances)

A comedy in three acts by Allen Rivkin. Produced by Elias Weinstock at the Cort Theatre, New York, May 28, 1935.

Cast of characters—

```
Christian Hugo.................................Bruce MacFarlane
Jake...........................................Richard Taber
Pat Moran......................................Lee Patrick
Edith..........................................Beverly Parker
Harry..........................................Walter Wilson
Nick Hugo......................................James Rennie
Mort Chandler..................................Calvin Thomas
```

Lurleen Marlowe.................................Sallie Phipps
Joan Wexley...................................Beatrice Swanson
Stuart Schuyler...............................Albert Van Dekker
Francis Z. Barrington...........................Tom Morrison
The Major..Nicholas Joy
Pink Wilson..................................James Spottswood
Gary "Slug" Green..............................Donald Black
Potts Jackson................................Horace MacMahon
Elmer McGurk...............................Charles Comoroda
John Greylock..................................William David
Two Hoodlums....................................{ Robert Gray
                                               { Harry Seton
    Acts I, II and III.—Office of Nick Hugo, of Schuyler & Hugo,
Artists' Representatives, Hollywood.
    Staged by John Hayden; setting by Watson Barratt.

Nick Hugo and Stuart Schuyler are artists' representatives in
Hollywood, running their business on lines that suggest the more
familiar rackets. Lurleen Marlowe, from the mountains of Virginia, is looking for a job. Nick's brother Christian falls in love
with her. Nick can get Lurleen a job and a fat commission for
the firm if Lurleen will be nice to the Major on a yachting party.
Business is business with Nick, until he suffers a change of heart.

SEVEN KEYS TO BALDPATE

(8 performances)

A comedy in prologue, two acts and epilogue adapted by George
M. Cohan from a novel by Earl Derr Biggers. Revived by The
Players at the National Theatre, New York, May 27, 1935.

Cast of characters—

Elijah Quimby..................................Francis Conlan
Mrs. Quimby...................................Josephine Hull
William Hallowell McGee......................George M. Cohan
John Bland................................Ernest Glendinning
Mary Norton.....................................Zita Johann
Mrs. Rhodes.......................................Irene Rich
Peters..James T. Powers
Myra Thornhill...................................Ruth Weston
Lou Max..Ben Lackland
Jim Cargan...................................Edward MacNamara
Thomas Hayden................................George Christie
Jiggs Kennedy................................James Kirkwood
First Policeman................................Percy Moore
Second Policeman.................................Allen Delano
Hal Bentley..................................Walter Hampden
    Acts I and II.—Office of Baldpate Inn.
    Staged by Sam Forrest; setting by W. Oden Waller.

Trial performances of "Seven Keys to Baldpate" were given in
Hartford, Conn., the week of September 15, 1913. The New
York run started a week later. Cohan played his own hero in
Hartford, following an automobile accident that incapacitated
Wallace Eddinger, who was assigned the rôle of McGee, novelist,
who wagered Hal Bentley that he, McGee, could write a complete

novel in twenty-four hours if he had complete quiet. Bentley opened Baldpate Inn, a summer resort, for McGee in the dead of winter. There the story was written to involve all of the author's imagined adventures in winning the wager.

THEM'S THE REPORTERS

(6 performances)

A comedy in three acts by Phil Kanter. Produced by Fourth Estate Productions, Inc., at the Ethel Barrymore Theatre, New York, May 29, 1935.

Cast of characters—

Scoop	Frederick Sherman
Pincus	Nat Burns
Cassady	Dave Burns
Reiley	Howard Negley
Peter	Cledge Roberts
Speed	John Neill
Miriam Jordan	Helen Kingsley

Acts I, II and III.—District Police Reporters' "Shack."
Staged by Addison Pitt; setting by Karl Amend.

Peter, cub reporter, resents the attitude of his associates of the police run in sacrificing everything, including reputations, in building up scandal stories. Miriam Jordan, one-time fiancée of Peter's, is involved in a gunman's automobile accident. Peter fights to save her the notoriety to which she is subjected, thereby winning her renewed esteem and reviving love.

* EARL CARROLL SKETCH BOOK

(15 performances)

A revue in two acts by Eugene Conrad and Charles Sherman; music and lyrics by Charles Tobias, Murray Mencher, Charles Newman, Norman Zeno and Will Irwin. Produced by Earl Carroll at the Winter Garden, New York, June 4, 1935.

Principals engaged—

Ken Murray	Peter Higgins	Lillian Carmen
Sibyl Bowan	Bert Lynn	Milton Charleston
Elaine Arden	George Lessey	Matt Duffin
Arthur Griffin	Jessie Draper	Billy Rayes
Billy Revel	Jane Moore	Brenton Beattie
Charlotte Arren	Sunnie O'Dea	Betty Dell
Beryl Wallace	Johnny Broderick	Mlle. Nirska
Julia Mooney	Robert Williams	
Allen Lee	The Hudson Wonders	

Staged by Earl Carroll, dialogue staged by Edward Clarke Lilley; dances by Boots McKenna; settings by Clark Robinson. Music directed by Ray Kavanaugh.

OFF BROADWAY

The Red Flannel Players revived "Greed for Gold," "Wide Awake Lil" and other old time melodramas at the Greenwich Village Music Hall, November 20, 1934. The Forum Theatre revived "Singing Jailbirds" at the Heckscher Theatre, November 24, 1934. This was an Upton Sinclair play presented six years ago at the Provincetown Theatre. They also produced "Races," May 13, 1935.

The Morayell Productions revived "Ticket of Leave Man" by Tom Taylor (also called "Hawkshaw the Detective"), a revival of the vintage of 1863, at the New Palm Garden Music Hall June 24, 1934. Butler Davenport, March 31 and April 2, in commemoration of the twentieth anniversary of the Davenport Theatre, revived "Hamlet." The Morningside Players of Columbia revived John Gay's "The Beggar's Opera" at the Heckscher Theatre July 16, 1934, playing 16 performances. Asadata Dafora Horton brought "Kykundor" back and housed the dance drama in the Chanin Building Auditorium, the first of January, 1935.

The Nudist Theatre Guild revived "A Girl from Childs" by Al Jackson and Archie Colby at the Sutton Theatre April 16, 1935. The Sutton Theatre also housed "A Character Intrudes" by Charles S. Costello and produced by the Ensemble Theatre December 11, 1934.

At the Roerich Theatre the Group Players staged "Heavenly Rackets" by Alexander Kavanau and Maxwell Bressler, May 6, 1935, and "Summer on Parade," a musical show by Arthur C. Leach with music by Irving Bibo and Jerry Lang, June 22, 1934. The Group Theatre also produced "Spring Varieties" in conjunction with the New Dance League and the Theatre of Action at Mecca Auditorium, May 19, 1935. Clifford Odets contributed "I Can't Sleep," a one-act play in which Morris Carnovsky interpreted a Jewish shopworker, and Art Smith contributed "Tide Rises," a strike play in nine scenes.

The Ibsen Theatre, a coöperative group of stagehands, actors, playwrights, electricians, etc., started an Ibsen repertoire with "Ghosts" in East Houston Street. The Moscow Art Players ended their season June 15, 1935, with an evening of satirical one-act plays in Russian and Yiddish at the Public Theatre.

Catherine Bammen started the third season of the intimate revue, "Sunday Nights at Nine," at the Barbizon-Plaza November 11 with such talent as Nina Tarasova, Billy Milton, Shirley

Booth, Jacques Krakeur, Felicia Sorel, Demetrios Vilan, etc.

Mme. Mimi Aguglia returned to New York after a long absence in a farce comedy in Italian, "Gentlemen, the Baby Is Born," produced by Clemente Giglio at the Venice Theatre June 7, 1935. Clemente Giglio had been producing Italian plays at the Venice since February. Helen Howe, with a program of monologues and monodramas, was at the Belasco Jan. 31, 1935, and Sydney Thompson, another monologuist, gave sketches from the Decameron and scenes from Guy de Maupassant at the Little Theatre Feb. 17, 1935.

Puppets

Tony Sarg in association with the United Parents Association gave seven marionette performances during the Christmas season at Carnegie Hall. The Yale Puppeteers presented "Gulliver's Travels" Dec. 27 and 28 at Lenox Little Theatre and "Mister Punch at Home" during the Easter Holiday at the Barbizon-Plaza and the A. W. A. Clubhouse. Sue Hastings presented "Cinderella," Dec. 26; "Jack and the Beanstalk," Dec. 27; "The Wishing Fairy and the Discontented Donkey" Dec. 28 and "Winnie the Pooh" Dec. 29 at the Barbizon-Plaza. The Workers Laboratory opened a marionette show at the Irving Plaza with Lou Bunin, Yosel Cutler and Ben Yano in charge, August 22, 1934.

Children's Theatre

The American Children's Theatre, a group of adult actors, opened the Theatre of Young America (formerly Cosmopolitan Theatre) Oct. 5 with "The Chinese Nightingale." At Carnegie Hall the United Parents Associations of New York and Carnegie Hall gave a series of Saturday performances for children including "Toto, the Clown," Oct. 6, 1934; "Tom Sawyer," Oct. 13; "Ted Shawn and His Dancers" Oct. 20; Sigmund Spaeth, Oct. 27; Commander Macmillan, Nov. 3; "Indoor Circus" Nov. 10; "Western Folkways" Nov. 17; Dr. Raymond Ditmars, Nov. 24; "Hansel and Gretel" Dec. 1; and "Neighborhood Playhouse Revue" Dec. 8. Directed by Helen Arthur and Helen Snider.

The Children's Theatre of New York under the direction of Clare Tree Major started its 11th year with "Under the Lilacs" Nov. 17, 1934, at the Hotel Barbizon. Other presentations were "Aladdin and His Wonderful Lamp," "Pocahontas," "Nobody's Girl," "Dick Whittington and His Cat" and "The Prince's Secret" (with Mabel Taliaferro) closing the series April 27, 1935.

At the Guild Theatre December 26, 28 and 30, Robert Reinhart, sponsored by the Theatre Guild, presented a variety show called "Hocus Pocus" with George Chaffee, Hazel Kranz, Al Baker and a large cast to entertain the children with "Punch and Judy," magic, juggling, shadowgraphs, a dance fantasy, etc.

The Metropolitan Opera Association gave its regular Christmas matinee performance for children Christmas day. Editha Fleisher sang Hansel, Queena Mario the Gretel in Humperdinck's "Hansel and Gretel." Geraldine Farrar was radio interpreter. The National Music League gave the same opera at Carnegie Hall Dec. 22, 1934 and Charlotte Lund directed it at the Music Hall from December 12 to 21.

"The Enchanted Forest" was given at Radio City Dec. 20, 1934; "Romance in a Toy Shop," an operetta by children, at the Town Hall April 22, 1935; "Dream in Fairyland," a ballet by the Mikhail Mordkin dancers, at Roerich Hall and "Strike Me Red," an operetta played by sixty children directed by Will Lee, at the Fifth Ave. Theatre, New York, November 10, 1934.

STATISTICAL SUMMARY

(LAST SEASON PLAYS WHICH ENDED RUNS AFTER JUNE 16, 1934)

Plays	Number Performances	Plays	Number Performances
Are You Decent	188	Men in White	351
As Thousands Cheer	400	Milky Way, The	63
Caviar	20	New Faces	149
Dodsworth (revival)	147	Roberta	295
Drunkard, The (revival)	277	Sailor, Beware!	500
Every Thursday	60	She Loves Me Not	360
Invitation to a Murder	53	Stevedore	111
Kykundor	65	Tobacco Road	658

LONG RUNS ON BROADWAY

To June 16, 1935

Plays	Number Performances	Plays	Number Performances
Abie's Irish Rose	2,532	Street Scene	601
Lightnin'	1,291	Kiki	600
The Bat	867	Blossom Time	592
The Ladder	789	Show Boat	572
The First Year	760	The Show-Off	571
Seventh Heaven	704	Sally	570
Peg o' My Heart	692	Strictly Dishonorable	557
East Is West	680	Good News	551
Irene	670	The Music Master	540
Tobacco Road	658	The Boomerang	522
A Trip to Chinatown	657	Blackbirds	518
Rain	648	Sunny	517
The Green Pastures	640	The Vagabond King	511
Is Zat So	618	The New Moon	509
Student Prince	608	Shuffle Along	504
Broadway	603	Bird in Hand	500
Adonis	603	Sailor, Beware!	500

PULITZER PRIZE WINNERS

"For the original American play performed in New York which shall best represent the educational value and power of the stage in raising the standard of good morals, good taste and good manners."—The Will of Joseph Pulitzer, dated April 16, 1904.

In 1929 the advisory board, which, according to the terms of the will, "shall have the power in its discretion to suspend or to change any subject or subjects . . . if in the judgment of the board such suspension, changes or substitutions shall be conducive to the public good," decided to eliminate from the above paragraph relating to the prize-winning play the words "in raising the standard of good morals, good taste and good manners."

The committee awards to date have been:

1917-18—Why Marry? by Jesse Lynch Williams
1918-19—None
1919-20—Miss Lulu Bett, by Zona Gale
1920-21—Beyond the Horizon, by Eugene O'Neill
1921-22—Anna Christie, by Eugene O'Neill
1922-23—Icebound, by Owen Davis
1923-24—Hell-bent fer Heaven, by Hatcher Hughes
1924-25—They Knew What They Wanted, by Sidney Howard
1925-26—Craig's Wife, by George Kelly
1926-27—In Abraham's Bosom, by Paul Green
1927-28—Strange Interlude, by Eugene O'Neill
1928-29—Street Scene, by Elmer Rice
1929-30—The Green Pastures, by Marc Connelly
1930-31—Alison's House, by Susan Glaspell
1931-32—Of Thee I Sing, by George S. Kaufman, Morrie
        Ryskind, Ira and George Gershwin
1932-33—Both Your Houses, by Maxwell Anderson
1933-34—Men in White, by Sidney Kingsley.
1934-35—The Old Maid, by Zoe Akins

PREVIOUS VOLUMES OF BEST PLAYS

Plays chosen to represent the theatre seasons from 1909 to 1934 are as follows:

1909-1919

"The Easiest Way," by Eugene Walters. Published by G. W. Dillingham, New York; Houghton Mifflin Co., Boston.

"Mrs. Bumpstead-Leigh," by Harry James Smith. Published by Samuel French, New York.

"Disraeli," by Louis N. Parker. Published by Dodd, Mead and Co., New York.

"Romance," by Edward Sheldon. Published by the Macmillan Co., New York.

"Seven Keys to Baldpate," by George M. Cohan. Published by Bobbs-Merrill Co., Indianapolis, as a novel by Earl Derr Biggers; as a play by Samuel French, New York.

"On Trial," by Elmer Reizenstein. Published by Samuel French, New York.

"The Unchastened Woman," by Louis Kaufman Anspacher. Published by Harcourt, Brace and Howe, Inc., New York.

"Good Gracious Annabelle," by Clare Kummer. Published by Samuel French, New York.

"Why Marry?" by Jesse Lynch Williams. Published by Charles Scribner's Sons, New York.

"John Ferguson," by St. John Ervine. Published by the Macmillan Co., New York.

1919-1920

"Abraham Lincoln," by John Drinkwater. Published by Houghton Mifflin Co., Boston.

"Clarence," by Booth Tarkington. Published by Samuel French, New York.

"Beyond the Horizon," by Eugene G. O'Neill. Published by Boni & Liveright, Inc., New York.

"Déclassée," by Zoe Akins. Published by Liveright, Inc., New York.

"The Famous Mrs. Fair," by James Forbes. Published by Samuel French, New York.

"The Jest," by Sem Benelli. (American adaptation by Edward Sheldon.)

"Jane Clegg," by St. John Ervine. Published by Henry Holt & Co., New York.

"Mamma's Affair," by Rachel Barton Butler. Published by Samuel French, New York.

"Wedding Bells," by Salisbury Field. Published by Samuel French, New York.

"Adam and Eva," by George Middleton and Guy Bolton. Published by Samuel French, New York.

1920-1921

"Deburau," adapted from the French of Sacha Guitry by H. Granville Barker. Published by G. P. Putnam's Sons, New York.

"The First Year," by Frank Craven. Published by Samuel French, New York.

"Enter Madame," by Gilda Varesi and Dolly Byrne. Published by G. P. Putnam's Sons, New York.

"The Green Goddess," by William Archer. Published by Alfred A. Knopf, New York.

"Liliom," by Ferenc Molnar. Published by Boni & Liveright, New York.

"Mary Rose," by James M. Barrie. Published by Charles Scribner's Sons, New York.

"Nice People," by Rachel Crothers. Published by Charles Scribner's Sons, New York.

"The Bad Man," by Porter Emerson Browne. Published by G. P. Putnam's Sons, New York.

"The Emperor Jones," by Eugene G. O'Neill. Published by Boni & Liveright, New York.

"The Skin Game," by John Galsworthy. Published by Charles Scribner's Sons, New York.

1921-1922

"Anna Christie," by Eugene G. O'Neill. Published by Boni & Liveright, New York.

"A Bill of Divorcement," by Clemence Dane. Published by the Macmillan Company, New York.

"Dulcy," by George S. Kaufman and Marc Connelly. Published by G. P. Putnam's Sons, New York.

"He Who Gets Slapped," adapted from the Russian of Leonid Andreyev by Gregory Zilboorg. Published by Brentano's, New York.

"Six Cylinder Love," by William Anthony McGuire.

"The Hero," by Gilbert Emery.

"The Dover Road," by Alan Alexander Milne. Published by Samuel French, New York.

"Ambush," by Arthur Richman.

"The Circle," by William Somerset Maugham.

"The Nest," by Paul Geraldy and Grace George.

1922-1923

"Rain," by John Colton and Clemence Randolph. Published by Liveright, Inc., New York.

"Loyalties," by John Galsworthy. Published by Charles Scribner's Sons, New York.

"Icebound," by Owen Davis. Published by Little, Brown & Company, Boston.

"You and I," by Philip Barry. Published by Brentano's, New York.

"The Fool," by Channing Pollock. Published by Brentano's, New York.

"Merton of the Movies," by George Kaufman and Marc Connelly, based on the novel of the same name by Harry Leon Wilson.

"Why Not?" by Jesse Lynch Williams. Published by Walter H. Baker Co., Boston.

"The Old Soak," by Don Marquis. Published by Doubleday, Page & Company, New York.

"R.U.R.," by Karel Capek. Translated by Paul Selver. Published by Doubleday, Page & Company.

"Mary the 3d," by Rachel Crothers. Published by Brentano's, New York.

1923-1924

"The Swan," translated from the Hungarian of Ferenc Molnar by Melville Baker. Published by Boni & Liveright, New York.

"Outward Bound," by Sutton Vane. Published by Boni & Liveright, New York.

"The Show-off," by George Kelly. Published by Little, Brown & Company, Boston.

"The Changelings," by Lee Wilson Dodd. Published by E. P. Dutton & Company, New York.

"Chicken Feed," by Guy Bolton. Published by Samuel French

New York and London.

"Sun-Up," by Lula Vollmer. Published by Brentano's, New York.

"Beggar on Horseback," by George Kaufman and Marc Connelly. Published by Boni & Liveright, New York.

"Tarnish," by Gilbert Emery. Published by Brentano's, New York.

"The Goose Hangs High," by Lewis Beach. Published by Little, Brown & Company, Boston.

"Hell-bent fer Heaven," by Hatcher Hughes. Published by Harper Bros., New York.

1924-1925

"What Price Glory?" by Laurence Stallings and Maxwell Anderson. Published by Harcourt, Brace & Co., New York.

"They Knew What They Wanted," by Sidney Howard. Published by Doubleday, Page & Company, New York.

"Desire Under the Elms," by Eugene G. O'Neill. Published by Boni & Liveright, New York.

"The Firebrand," by Edwin Justus Mayer. Published by Boni & Liveright, New York.

"Dancing Mothers," by Edgar Selwyn and Edmund Goulding.

"Mrs. Partridge Presents," by Mary Kennedy and Ruth Warren. Published by Samuel French, New York.

"The Fall Guy," by James Gleason and George Abbott. Published by Samuel French, New York.

"The Youngest," by Philip Barry. Published by Samuel French, New York.

"Minick," by Edna Ferber and George S. Kaufman. Published by Doubleday, Page & Company, New York.

"Wild Birds," by Dan Totheroh. Published by Doubleday, Page & Company, New York.

1925-1926

"Craig's Wife," by George Kelly. Published by Little, Brown & Company, Boston.

"The Great God Brown," by Eugene G. O'Neill. Published by Boni & Liveright, New York.

"The Green Hat," by Michael Arlen.

"The Dybbuk," by S. Ansky, Henry G. Alsberg-Winifred Katzin translation. Published by Boni & Liveright, New York.

"The Enemy," by Channing Pollock. Published by Brentano's,

New York.

"The Last of Mrs. Cheyney," by Frederick Lonsdale. Published by Samuel French, New York.

"Bride of the Lamb," by William Hurlbut. Published by Boni & Liveright, New York.

"The Wisdom Tooth," by Marc Connelly. Published by George H. Doran & Company, New York.

"The Butter and Egg Man," by George Kaufman. Published by Boni & Liveright, New York.

"Young Woodley," by John Van Druten. Published by Simon and Schuster, New York.

1926-1927

"Broadway," by Philip Dunning and George Abbott. Published by George H. Doran Company, New York.

"Saturday's Children," by Maxwell Anderson. Published by Longmans, Green & Company, New York.

"Chicago," by Maurine Watkins. Published by Alfred A. Knopf, Inc., New York.

"The Constant Wife," by William Somerset Maugham. Published by George H. Doran Company, New York.

"The Play's the Thing," by Ferenc Molnar and P. G. Wodehouse. Published by Brentano's, New York.

"The Road to Rome," by Robert Emmet Sherwood. Published by Charles Scribner's Sons, New York.

"The Silver Cord," by Sidney Howard. Published by Charles Scribner's Sons, New York.

"The Cradle Song," translated from the Spanish of G. Martinez Sierra by John Garrett Underhill. Published by E. P. Dutton & Company, New York.

"Daisy Mayme," by George Kelly. Published by Little, Brown & Company, Boston.

"In Abraham's Bosom," by Paul Green. Published by Robert M. McBride & Company, New York.

1927-1928

"Strange Interlude," by Eugene G. O'Neill. Published by Boni & Liveright, New York.

"The Royal Family," by Edna Ferber and George Kaufman. Published by Doubleday, Doran & Company, New York.

"Burlesque," by George Manker Watters. Published by Doubleday, Doran & Company, New York.

"Coquette," by George Abbott and Ann Bridgers. Published by Longmans, Green & Company, New York, London, Toronto.

"Behold the Bridegroom," by George Kelly. Published by Little, Brown & Company, Boston.

"Porgy," by DuBose Heyward. Published by Doubleday, Doran & Company, New York.

"Paris Bound," by Philip Barry. Published by Samuel French, New York.

"Escape," by John Galsworthy. Published by Charles Scribner's Sons, New York.

"The Racket," by Bartlett Cormack. Published by Samuel French, New York.

"The Plough and the Stars," by Sean O'Casey. Published by the Macmillan Company, New York.

1928-1929

"Street Scene," by Elmer Rice. Published by Samuel French, New York.

"Journey's End," by R. C. Sheriff. Published by Brentano's, New York.

"Wings Over Europe," by Robert Nichols and Maurice Browne. Published by Covici-Friede, New York.

"Holiday," by Philip Barry. Published by Samuel French, New York.

"The Front Page," by Ben Hecht and Charles MacArthur. Published by Covici-Friede, New York.

"Let Us Be Gay," by Rachel Crothers. Published by Samuel French, New York.

"Machinal," by Sophie Treadwell.

"Little Accident," by Floyd Dell and Thomas Mitchell.

"Gypsy," by Maxwell Anderson.

"The Kingdom of God," by G. Martinez Sierra; English version by Helen and Harley Granville-Barker. Published by E. P. Dutton & Company, New York.

1929-1930

"The Green Pastures," by Marc Connelly (adapted from "Ol' Man Adam and His Chillun," by Roark Bradford). Published by Farrar & Rinehart, Inc., New York.

"The Criminal Code," by Martin Flavin. Published by Horace Liveright, New York.

"Berkeley Square," by John Balderstone. Published by the Macmillan Company, New York.

"Strictly Dishonorable," by Preston Sturges. Published by Horace Liveright, New York.

"The First Mrs. Fraser," by St. John Ervine. Published by the Macmillan Company, New York.

"The Last Mile," by John Wexley. Published by Samuel French, New York.

"June Moon," by Ring W. Lardner and George S. Kaufman. Published by Charles Scribner's Sons, New York.

"Michael and Mary," by A. A. Milne. Published by Chatto & Windus, London.

"Death Takes a Holiday," by Walter Ferris (adapted from the Italian of Alberto Casella). Published by Samuel French, New York.

"Rebound," by Donald Ogden Stewart. Published by Samuel French, New York.

1930-1931

"Elizabeth the Queen," by Maxwell Anderson. Published by Longmans, Green & Co., New York.

"Tomorrow and Tomorrow," by Philip Barry. Published by Samuel French, New York.

"Once in a Lifetime," by George S. Kaufman and Moss Hart. Published by Farrar and Rinehart, New York.

"Green Grow the Lilacs," by Lynn Riggs. Published by Samuel French, New York and London.

"As Husbands Go," by Rachel Crothers. Published by Samuel French, New York.

"Alison's House," by Susan Glasgow. Published by Samuel French, New York.

"Five-Star Final," by Louis Weitzenkorn. Published by Samuel French, New York.

"Overture," by William Bolitho. Published by Simon & Schuster, New York.

"The Barretts of Wimpole Street," by Rudolf Besier. Published by Little, Brown & Company, Boston.

"Grand Hotel," adapted from the German of Vicki Baum by W. A. Drake.

1931-1932

"Of Thee I Sing," by George S. Kaufman and Morrie Ryskind; music and lyrics by George and Ira Gershwin. Published by Alfred Knopf, New York.

"Mourning Becomes Electra," by Eugene G. O'Neill. Published by Horace Liveright, Inc., New York.

"Reunion in Vienna," by Robert Emmet Sherwood. Published

by Charles Scribner's Sons, New York.

"The House of Connelly," by Paul Green. Published by Samuel French, New York.

"The Animal Kingdom," by Philip Barry. Published by Samuel French, New York.

"The Left Bank," by Elmer Rice. Published by Samuel French, New York.

"Another Language," by Rose Franken. Published by Samuel French, New York.

"Brief Moment," by S. N. Behrman. Published by Farrar & Rinehart, New York.

"The Devil Passes," by Ben W. Levy. Published by Martin Secker, London.

"Cynara," by H. M. Harwood and R. F. Gore-Browne. Published by Samuel French, New York.

1932-1933

"Both Your Houses," by Maxwell Anderson. Published by Samuel French, New York.

"Dinner at Eight," by George S. Kaufman and Edna Ferber. Published by Doubleday, Doran & Co., Inc., Garden City, New York.

"When Ladies Meet," by Rachel Crothers. Published by Samuel French, New York.

"Design for Living," by Noel Coward. Published by Doubleday, Doran & Co., Inc., Garden City, New York.

"Biography," by S. N. Behrman. Published by Farrar & Rinehart, Inc., New York.

"Alien Corn," by Sidney Howard. Published by Charles Scribner's Sons, New York.

"The Late Christopher Bean," adapted from the French of René Fauchois by Sidney Howard. Published by Samuel French, New York.

"We, the People," by Elmer Rice. Published by Coward-McCann, Inc., New York.

"Pigeons and People," by George M. Cohan.

"One Sunday Afternoon," by James Hagan. Published by Samuel French, New York.

1933-1934

"Mary of Scotland," by Maxwell Anderson. Published by Doubleday, Doran & Co., Inc., Garden City, N. Y.

"Men in White," by Sidney Kingsley. Published by Covici, Friede, Inc., New York.

"Dodsworth," by Sinclair Lewis and Sidney Howard. Published by Harcourt, Brace & Co., New York.

"Ah, Wilderness," by Eugene O'Neill. Published by Random House, New York.

"They Shall Not Die," by John Wexley. Published by Alfred A. Knopf, New York.

"Her Master's Voice," by Clare Kummer. Published by Samuel French, New York.

"No More Ladies," by A. E. Thomas.

"Wednesday's Child," by Leopold Atlas. Published by Samuel French, New York.

"The Shining Hour," by Keith Winter. Published by Doubleday, Doran & Co., Inc., Garden City, New York.

"The Green Bay Tree," by Mordaunt Shairp. Published by Baker International Play Bureau, Boston, Mass.

WHERE AND WHEN THEY WERE BORN

Abbott, George	Hamburg, N. Y.	1895
Abel, Walter	St. Paul, Minn.	1898
Aborn, Milton	Marysville, Cal.	1864
Adams, Maude	Salt Lake City, Utah	1872
Adler, Stella	New York	1904
Aherne, Brian	King's Norton, England	1902
Akins, Zoe	Humansville, Mo.	1886
Alexander, Katherine	Arkansas	1901
Alexander, Ross	Brooklyn, N. Y.	1904
Allanby, Peggy	New York	1905
Allen, Adrianne	Manchester, England	1907
Allen, Viola	Huntsville, Ala.	1869
Ames, Robert	Hartford, Conn.	1893
Ames, Winthrop	North Easton, Mass.	1871
Anders, Glenn	Los Angeles, Cal.	1890
Anderson, Judith	Australia	1898
Anderson, Maxwell	Atlantic City, Pa.	1888
Andrews, Ann	Los Angeles, Cal.	1895
Anglin, Margaret	Ottawa, Canada	1876
Anson, A. E.	London, England	1879
Anspacher, Louis K.	Cincinnati, Ohio	1878
Arliss, George	London, England	1868
Arthur, Julia	Hamilton, Ont.	1869
Astaire, Fred	Omaha, Neb.	1899
Atwell, Roy	Syracuse, N. Y.	1880
Atwill, Lionel	London, England	1885
Bainter, Fay	Los Angeles, Cal.	1892
Baker, Lee	Michigan	1880
Bankhead, Tallulah	Huntsville, Ala.	1902
Banks, Leslie J.	West Derby, England	1890
Barbee, Richard	Lafayette, Ind.	1887
Barrett, Edith	Roxbury, Mass.	1904
Barrie, James Matthew	Kirriemuir, N. B.	1860
Barry, Philip	Rochester, N. Y.	1896
Barrymore, Ethel	Philadelphia, Pa.	1879
Barrymore, John	Philadelphia, Pa.	1882

Barrymore, Lionel ....London, England 1878
Bates, Blanche ....Portland, Ore. 1873
Baxter, Lora ....New York 1907
Beatty, Roberta ....Rochester, N. Y. 1900
Beecher, Janet ....Chicago, Ill. 1884
Behrman, S. N. ....Worcester, Mass. 1893
Ben-Ami, Jacob ....Minsk, Russia 1890
Bennett, Richard ....Cass County, Ind. 1873
Bennett, Wilda ....Asbury Park, N. J. 1894
Bergner, Elizabeth ....Vienna 1901
Berlin, Irving ....Russia 1888
Best, Edna ....Sussex, England 1900
Binney, Constance ....Philadelphia, Pa. 1900
Blackmer, Sidney ....Salisbury, N. C. 1896
Boland, Mary ....Detroit, Mich. 1880
Bondi, Beulah ....Chicago, Ill. 1892
Bordoni, Irene ....Paris, France 1895
Brady, Alice ....New York 1892
Brady, William A. ....San Francisco, Cal. 1863
Brady, William A., Jr. ....New York 1900
Braham, Horace ....London, England 1896
Brian, Donald ....St. Johns, N. F. 1877
Brice, Fannie ....Brooklyn, N. Y. 1891
Broadhurst, George H. ....England 1866
Broderick, Helen ....New York 1891
Bromberg, J. Edward ....Hungary 1903
Bryant, Charles ....England 1879
Buchanan, Jack ....England 1892
Buchanan, Thompson ....Louisville, Ky. 1877
Buckler, Hugh ....Southampton, England ...1886
Burke, Billie ....Washington, D. C. 1885
Burton, Frederick ....Indiana 1871
Byington, Spring ....Colorado Springs, Colo. ...1898
Byron, Arthur ....Brooklyn, N. Y. 1872

Cagney, James ....New York 1904
Cahill, Lily ....Texas 1885
Cahill, Marie ....Brooklyn, N. Y. 1871
Calhern, Louis ....New York 1895
Cantor, Eddie ....New York 1894
Campbell, Mrs. Patrick ....England 1865
Carle, Richard ....Somerville, Mass. 1871
Carlisle, Alexandra ....Yorkshire, England 1886
Carminati, Tullio ....Zara, Dalmatia 1894

Carpenter, Edward Childs .....Philadelphia, Pa. 1871
Carr, Alexander ....Russia 1878
Carroll, Earl ....Pittsburgh, Pa. 1892
Carter, Mrs. Leslie ....Lexington, Ky. 1862
Catlett, Walter ....San Francisco, Cal. 1889
Cawthorne, Joseph ....New York 1868
Chandler, Helen ....Charleston, N. C. 1906
Chaplin, Charles Spencer .....London 1889
Chase, Ilka ....New York 1900
Chatterton, Ruth ....New York 1893
Cherry, Charles ....England 1872
Christians, Mady ....Vienna, Austria 1907
Churchill, Burton ....Toronto, Can. 1876
Claire, Ina ....Washington, D. C. 1892
Clarke, Marguerite ....Cincinnati, Ohio 1887
Cliffe, H. Cooper ....England 1862
Clifford, Kathleen ....Charlottesville, Va. 1887
Clive, Colin ....St. Malo, France 1900
Coburn, Charles ....Macon, Ga. 1877
Coghlan, Gertrude ....England 1879
Coghlan, Rose ....Petersborough, England ...1850
Cohan, George M. ....Providence, R. I. 1878
Cohan, Georgette ....Los Angeles, Cal. 1900
Colbert, Claudette ....Paris 1905
Collier, Constance ....Windsor, England 1882
Collier, William ....New York 1866
Collinge, Patricia ....Dublin, Ireland 1894
Collins, José ....London, England 1896
Colt, Ethel Barrymore ....Mamaroneck, N. Y. 1911
Colt, John Drew ....New York 1914
Conklin, Peggy ....Dobbs Ferry, N. Y. 1912
Connolly, Walter ....Cincinnati, Ohio 1888
Conroy, Frank ....London, England 1885
Cook, Joe ....Evansville, Ind. 1890
Cooper, Gladys ....Lewisham, England 1888
Cooper, Violet Kemble ......London, England 1890
Cornell, Katharine ....Buffalo, N. Y. 1900
Corrigan, Emmett ....Amsterdam, Holland 1871
Corthell, Herbert ....Boston, Mass. 1875
Cossart, Ernest ....Cheltenham, England 1876
Courtenay, William ....Worcester, Mass. 1875
Courtleigh, William ....Guelph, Ont. 1869
Coward, Noel ....England 1899

Cowl, Jane ....Boston, Mass. 1887
Craven, Frank ....Boston, Mass. 1880
Crews, Laura Hope ....San Francisco, Cal. 1880
Crosman, Henrietta ....Wheeling, W. Va. 1865
Crothers, Rachel ....Bloomington, Ill. 1878
Cumberland, John ....St. John, N. B. 1880
Cummings, Constance ....Seattle, Wash. 1911

Dale, Margaret ....Philadelphia, Pa. 1880
Dalton, Charles ....England 1864
Daly, Blyth ....New York 1902
Danforth, William ....Syracuse 1869
Daniels, Frank ....Dayton, Ohio 1860
Davis, Owen ....Portland, Me. 1874
Davis, Owen, Jr. ....New York 1907
Dawn, Hazel ....Ogden, Utah 1891
Day, Edith ....Minneapolis, Minn. 1896
De Angelis, Jefferson ....San Francisco, Cal. 1859
Dean, Julia ....St. Paul, Minn. 1880
De Cordoba, Pedro ....New York 1881
Dillingham, Charles B. ....Hartford, Conn. 1868
Dinehart, Allan ....Missoula, Mont. 1889
Dixey, Henry E. ....Boston, Mass. 1859
Dixon, Jean ....Waterbury, Conn. 1905
Dodson, John E. ....London, England 1857
Doro, Marie ....Duncannon, Pa. 1882
D'Orsay, Lawrence ....England 1860
Dressler, Eric ....Brooklyn, N. Y. 1900
Dressler, Marie ....Cobourg, Canada 1869
Drew, Louise ....New York 1884
Duncan, Augustin ....San Francisco 1873
Dunn, Emma ....England 1875
Dunning, Philip ....Meriden, Conn. 1890
Dupree, Minnie ....San Francisco, Cal. 1875

Edeson, Robert ....Baltimore, Md. 1868
Eldridge, Florence ....Brooklyn, N. Y. 1901
Ellis, Mary ....New York 1900
Elliston, Grace ....Wheeling, W. Va. 1881
Ellinger, Desirée ....Manchester, Vt. 1895
Elliott, Gertrude ....Rockland, Me. 1874
Elliott, Maxine ....Rockland, Me. 1871
Eltinge, Julian ....Boston, Mass. 1883
Emery, Gilbert ....Naples, New York 1875

Greenstreet, Sydney ....England 1880
Grey, Katherine ....San Francisco, Cal. 1873
Groody, Louise ....Waco, Texas 1897
Gwenn, Edmund ....Glamorgan, Wales 1875

Haines, Robert T. ....Muncie, Ind. 1870
Hale, Louise Closser ....Chicago, Ill. 1872
Hall, Bettina ....North Easton, Mass. 1906
Hall, Laura Nelson ....Philadelphia, Pa. 1876
Hall, Natalie ....North Easton, Mass. 1904
Hall, Thurston ....Boston, Mass. 1882
Hamilton, Hale ....Topeka, Kansas 1880
Hampden, Walter ....Brooklyn, N. Y. 1879
Hannen, Nicholas ....London, Eng. 1881
Hanson, Gladys ....Atlanta, Ga. 1887
Harding, Lyn ....Newport, England 1867
Harrigan, William ....New York 1893
Harris, Sam H. ....New York 1872
Harrison, Richard B. ....London, Ontario 1864
Hayes, Helen ....Washington, D. C. 1900
Hazzard, John E. ....New York 1881
Hedman, Martha ....Sweden 1888
Heggie, O. P. ....Australia 1879
Heming, Violet ....Leeds, England 1893
Hepburn, Katharine ....Hartford, Conn. 1907
Herbert, Evelyn ....Brooklyn, N. Y. 1900
Herne, Chrystal ....Dorchester, Mass. 1883
Hobart, Rose ....New York 1906
Hodge, William ....Albion, N. Y. 1874
Hopkins, Arthur ....Cleveland, Ohio 1878
Hopkins, Miriam ....Bainbridge, Ga. 1904
Hopper, de Wolf ....New York 1858
Hopper, Edna Wallace ....San Francisco, Cal. 1874
Holmes, Taylor ....Newark, N. J. 1872
Howard, Leslie ....London, England 1890
Hull, Henry ....Louisville, Ky. 1893
Hunter, Glenn ....Highland Mills, N. Y. 1896
Huston, Walter ....Toronto 1884
Hutchinson, Josephine ....Seattle, Wash. 1898

Inescort, Frieda ....Hitchin, Scotland 1905
Irving, Isabel ....Bridgeport, Conn. 1871
Irwin, May ....Whitby, Ont. 1862

Janis, Elsie ....Delaware, Ohio 1889
Joel, Clara ....Jersey City, N. J. 1890

Johann, Zita ....Hungary 1904
Jolson, Al ....Washington, D. C. 1883
Johnston, Moffat ....Edinburgh, Scotland 1886

Kaufman, George S. ....Pittsburgh, Pa. 1889
Keane, Doris ....Michigan 1885
Keith, Robert ....Scotland 1899
Kelly, Walter C. ....Mineville, N. Y. 1875
Kennedy, Madge ....Chicago, Ill. 1890
Kerrigan, J. M. ....Dublin, Ireland 1885
Kerr, Geoffrey ....London, England 1895
Kershaw, Willette ....Clifton Heights, Mo. 1890
Kingsford, Walter ....England 1876
Kirkland, Alexander ....Mexico City 1904
Kosta, Tessa ....Chicago, Ill. 1893
Kruger, Alma ....Pittsburgh, Pa. 1880
Kruger, Otto ....Toledo, Ohio 1895

Lackaye, Wilton ....Virginia 1862
Larimore, Earl ....Portland, Oregon 1899
Larrimore, Francine ....Russia 1898
La Rue, Grace ....Kansas City, Mo. 1882
Lauder, Harry ....Portobello, England 1870
Lawrence, Gertrude ....London 1898
Lawton, Thais ....Louisville, Ky. 1881
Lean, Cecil ....Illinois 1878
Lederer, Francis ....Karlin, Prague 1906
Le Gallienne, Eva ....London, England 1900
Leiber, Fritz ....Chicago, Ill. 1884
Leontovich, Eugenie ....Moscow, Russia 1894
Levey, Ethel ....San Francisco, Cal. 1881
Lewis, Mabel Terry ....London, England 1872
Lillie, Beatrice ....Toronto, Canada 1898
Logan, Stanley ....Earlsfield, England 1885
Loraine, Robert ....New Brighton, England ...1876
Lord, Pauline ....Hanford, Cal. 1890
Lorraine, Lillian ....San Francisco, Cal. 1892
Lou-Tellegen ....Holland 1881
Love, Montagu ....Portsmouth, Hants 1877
Lowell, Helen ....New York 1866
Lunt, Alfred ....Milwaukee, Wis. 1893

Mack, Andrew ....Boston, Mass. 1863
Mack, Willard ....Ontario, Canado 1873

Mackay, Elsie ....London, England 1894
MacKellar, Helen ....Canada 1896
Marlowe, Julia ....Caldbeck, England 1870
Marshall, Herbert...........London, England 1890
Massey, Raymond ....Toronto, Canada 1896
Matthews, A. E. ....Bridlington, England 1869
Matthison, Edith Wynne .....England 1875
Maude, Cyril ....London, England 1862
McClintic, Guthrie ....Seattle, Wash. 1893
McIntyre, Frank ....Ann Arbor, Mich. 1879
Meek, Donald ....Glasgow, Scotland 1880
Meighan, Thomas ....Pittsburgh, Pa. 1879
Melba, Nellie ....Melbourne, Australia 1866
Menken, Helen ....New York 1901
Mercer, Beryl ....Seville, Spain 1882
Merivale, Philip ....Rehutia, India 1886
Miller, Gilbert ....New York 1884
Miller, Marilyn ....Findlay, Ohio 1898
Mitchell, Grant ....Columbus, Ohio 1874
Mitchell, Thomas ....Elizabeth, N. J. 1892
Mitzi (Hajos) ....Budapest 1891
Moore, Grace ....Del Rio, Tenn. 1901
Moore, Victor ....Hammonton, N. J. 1876
Moran, Lois ....Pittsburgh, Pa. 1909
Morgan, Claudia............New York 1912
Morgan, Helen ....Danville, Ill. 1900
Morgan, Ralph ....New York City 1889
Morris, Mary ....Boston 1894
Morris, McKay ....San Antonio, Texas 1890
Muni, Paul ....Lemberg, Austria 1895

Nagel, Conrad ....Keokuk, Iowa 1897
Nash, Florence ....Troy, N. Y. 1888
Nash, Mary ....Troy, N. Y. 1885
Nazimova, Alla ....Crimea, Russia 1879
Nielsen, Alice ....Nashville, Tenn. 1876
Nolan, Lloyd ....San Francisco, Cal. 1903
Nugent, J. C. ....Miles, Ohio 1875
Nugent, Elliott ....Dover, Ohio 1900

O'Connell, Hugh ....New York 1891
Olcott, Chauncey ....Buffalo, N. Y. 1862
O'Neill, Eugene Gladstone ....New York 1888

NECROLOGY

June 16, 1934—June 15, 1935

Anderson, Dallas, actor, 60. Popular juvenile for many years; member of Walter Hampden's company for past decade. Died Richmond, Va., November 16, 1935.

Askin, Harry, manager and producer, 67. Widely known as manager of the Sousa band and the Paul Whiteman and George Gershwin concert tours; directed tours for James O'Neill, Lillian Russell, Eleanor Robson, Otis Skinner, Ada Rehan, Viola Allen and William Hodge. Born Philadelphia, Pa.; died New York City, September 30, 1934.

Baker, George Pierce, author and professor of drama, 68. Creator of first important collegiate course in dramatic construction, "English 47" at Harvard; later head of similar "Drama 47" at Yale; wrote "The Development of Shakespeare as a Dramatist" and "Dramatic Technique." Born Providence, R. I.; died New York City, January 6, 1935.

Berkeley, Reginald, novelist, playwright and scenarist, 54. Wrote "French Leave" and "The Lady with a Lamp" for stage; "Cavalcade," "Carolina," "Marie Galante" (adapted) and "House of Connelly" (adapted) for screen; elected to Parliament, 1924. Born London, England; died Los Angeles, Calif., March 30, 1935.

Boyd, William, actor, 45. Leading man with Maude Adams, Mrs. Fiske and Ethel Barrymore; success as Sergeant Quirt in "What Price Glory?" Born New York City; died Hollywood, March 20, 1935.

Bradley, Leonora, actress, 80. Played in support of many notable actors including Otis Skinner and E. H. Sothern. Born London; died Boston, Mass., May 31, 1935.

Browne, Porter Emerson, dramatic author, 55. Wrote "A Fool There Was," "The Spendthrift," "Wild Oats," "A Girl of Today" and "The Bad Man. Born Beverly, Mass.; died Norwalk, Conn., September 20, 1934.

Burt, Harriet, actress, 47. Played The Girl in "The Time, the Place and the Girl," "The Jewel of Asia" and "The Jersey Lily"; one of the founders of Actors' Equity Association. Born Troy, New York; died Kansas City, May 22, 1935.

Crosby, Edward Harold, dramatic author and critic, 75. Critic of Boston *Post* for 44 years; author of "The Catspaw," "The Hour of Reckoning," "A Modern Parasite," "The Man Who Grew Young," "My Greenwich Village Girl" and "The Taming of Helen." Born Boston, Mass.; died Boston, December 2, 1934.

Daniels, Frank, actor, 74. Well-known comedian; toured in "Little Puck" seven seasons; remembered for "The Wizard of the Nile," "The Ameer," "The Tattooed Man," "The Office Boy" and "Miss Hook of Holland"; retired in 1913. Born Dayton, Ohio; died West Palm Beach, Fla., January 12, 1935.

De Forest, Marian. Playwright and dramatic critic, 70. Best known for dramatization of "Little Women"; wrote "Erstwhile Susan" for Mrs. Fiske. Born Buffalo, New York; died Buffalo, New York, February 17, 1935.

Dillingham, Charles Bancroft, producing manager, 66. Newsman; dramatic critic New York *Evening Sun;* publicity man for Charles Frohman; member of firm of Dillingham, Klaw and Erlanger; associated with Florenz Ziegfeld and Erlanger in A. L. Erlanger Amusement Enterprises, Inc., and founded the Dillingham Theatre Corporation; produced many Victor Herbert operas and Montgomery-Stone repertory. Born Hartford, Conn.; died New York City, August 30, 1934.

Dodge, Henry I., author and playwright, 73. Wrote "Skinner's Dress Suit," "The Higher Court," "Counsel for the Defense," "The Whirlpool," etc. Born Kasoag, Oswego County, New York; died New York City, July 28, 1934.

Douglas, Byron, actor, 70. With Charles Frohman in "Held by the Enemy," "Secret Service," "Under the Red Robe," etc.; played with Clara Morris in "Denise." Married Marie Booth, niece of Edwin Booth. Died New York City, April 21, 1935.

Dressler, Marie (Lelia Koerber), comedienne, 64. Toured in light opera; played in "The Princess Nicotine," "Tillie's Nightmare," "The Rivals" and at Weber's Music Hall in "Higgledy-Piggledy," "The College Widower" and "Twiddle Twaddle"; pictures include "Min and Bill," "Dinner at Eight," "Tugboat Annie" and "Christopher Bean." Born Cobourg, Canada; died Santa Barbara, California, July 28, 1934.

Elser, Frank B., novelist and playwright, 50. Left city editorship of the New York *Times* to write plays; adapted Liam

O'Flaherty's "Mr. Gilhooley"; adapted "The Farmer Takes a Wife" with Marc Connelly. Born Fort Worth, Texas; died St. George's, Grenada, British West Indies, January 31, 1935.

Eric, Fred, actor, 61. With Sothern-Marlowe company in Shakespearean repertory; Maude Adams in "Quality Street" and "Twelfth Night"; Margaret Anglin in "Electra and Medea." Born Peru, Indiana; died New York City, April 17, 1935.

Farren, George Francis, actor, 74. Well-known character actor with stock companies in Boston, Cincinnati, Chicago, Kansas City and Denver; played in support of Eleanor Robson, Mrs. Fiske, Blanche Bates, Henry Miller and many other stars. Born Boston, Mass.; died New York City, April 21, 1935.

Fowler, Gertrude, actress, 42. Appeared in "The Power Behind the Throne," "The Man of the Hour," "Seven Days" and "The Show-Off." Died New York City, June 5, 1935.

Grossmith, George, author and comedian, 61. Son of famous Gilbert and Sullivan comedian; first American tour in "The Shop Girl," 1895; last appeared in America 1930 in "Princess Charming" and "Meet My Sister"; extensive career in England, both as comedian and author of revues. Born London, England; died London, June 6, 1935.

Hale, Philip, author and dramatic critic, 80. Critic of music and drama, Boston *Herald;* author and compiler of Boston Symphony program notes and annotations. Born Norwich, Vermont; died Boston, Mass., November 30, 1934.

Hale, Ruth, critic and publicist, 48. Newspaper writer for New York, Philadelphia and Chicago papers; critic for Philadelphia *Public Ledger;* adapted "The Venetian Glass Nephew"; married Heywood Broun. Born Rogersville, Tenn.; died New York City, September 18, 1934.

Harrison, Richard Berry, actor, 70. Début at age of 66 as De Lawd in "Green Pastures"; played rôle for 1,659 consecutive performances; headed drama department of Agricultural and Technical College, North Carolina; Spingarn Medal (1932) for highest achievement of American Negro. Born London, Ontario, Canada; died New York City, March 14, 1935.

Lou-Tellegen (Isador Louis Bernard van Dameler), actor, 52. Played in support of Sarah Bernhardt in Paris; toured America with her in 1910-11, first appearing as Raymond in "Madame X"; part author and played in "Blind Youth" and "The Lust of Gold"; married Comtesse de Bronchen; Geraldine Farrar; Nina Romano and Eva Casanova. Born Holland; died Hollywood, October 29, 1934.

Mack, Willard (Charles W. McLaughlin), actor, playwright and director, 61. Wrote "Madame X," "Tiger Rose," "Cheating Cheaters," "The Dove," and "The Ziegfeld Follies of 1921" (with Channing Pollock). Born Morrisburg, Ontario, Canada; died Brentwood Heights, California, November 18, 1934.

Marion, Dave (David Marion Graves), manager, playwright, actor, 73. Fifty-eight years in theatre as actor, producer and song and dialogue writer; was with Weber and Fields and Gus Hill. Born Toledo, Ohio; died New York City, September 15, 1934.

Moissi, Alexander, actor, 55. Famous European star; protégé of Max Reinhardt; toured United States in 1928 in Tolstoy's "The Living Corpse," "Everyman," "Ghosts," Danton's "Tod," etc. Born Triest, Austria; died Vienna, March 22, 1935.

Moore, Florence, actress and singer, 48. First Broadway success in "Hanky Panky" in 1912; last appearance in revival of "Cradle Snatchers" in 1932. Born Philadelphia, Pa.; died Darby, Pa., March 9, 1935.

Mulle, Ida, actress, singer, 75. Successful light opera star; sang Little Buttercup in "H.M.S. Pinafore" at the age of nine; created many light opera rôles; with Blanche Yurka in "The Squall" 1926. Born Boston, Mass.; died New York, August 5, 1934.

Murphy, John Daly (John Daly Conlon), actor, 61. Forty years a character actor; with Sarah Bernhardt in "La Tosca"; Blanche Bates in "Hedda Gabler"; Mrs. Fiske in "Erstwhile Susan"; Polonius in Norman Bel-Geddes' "Hamlet"; died of heart attack on way to rehearsal with Mary Pickford for radio. Born County Kildare, Ireland; died New York City, November 20, 1934.

Nairn, Ralph, comedian, 61. Came from England for part in "Preserving Mr. Panmure" with Gertrude Elliott; in "The Play's the Thing" with Holbrook Blinn. Born Scotland; died London, December, 1934.

Nicholson, John, actor, 61. Produced melodramas in Chicago; toured in "The Call of the Heart," "The Price She Paid," "Daybreak," etc.; in "The Bad Man" with Holbrook Blinn; "The Padra" with Leo Carrillo. Born Charleston, Ill.; died New York City, June 24, 1934.

Pinero, Sir Arthur Wing, actor and dramatic author, 79. Left practice of law for theatre; acted briefly with Wyndham and Henry Irving; wrote 48 plays, including "The Second Mrs. Tanqueray," "The Gay Lord Quex," "Sweet Lavender," "The Amazons," "Iris," "Letty," "His House in Order," "Midchannel" and "Trelawney of the Wells." Born London; died London, November 23, 1934.

Playfair, Sir Nigel, actor, playwright and producer, 60. Produced John Drinkwater's "Abraham Lincoln" and "The Beggar's Opera"; fourteen-year period of continuous actor-management, Lyric Theatre, London. Born London; died London, August 19, 1934.

Powers, Arba Eugene, actor, 62. Known as Maine's "most distinguished actor," seven years in stock; prominently cast in "The Trial of Jeanne d'Arc," "Outward Bound" and "The Green Hat." Born Houlton, Maine; died Saranac Lake, New York, January 7, 1935.

Price, Eleazer D., manager and press agent, 86. Fifty years advance agent and theatrical manager; started with John McCullough; ended with Klaw, Erlanger and Ziegfeld. Born Tecumseh, Michigan; died New York City, May 24, 1935.

Rankin, Phyllis (Mrs. Harry Davenport), actress, 60. Daughter of Arthur McKee Rankin and Kitty Blanchard; wife of Harry Davenport; started as child of ten in her parents' company in "Stormbeaten"; sang in "The Belle of New York" and "Floradora." Born New York City; died Canton, Pa., November 17, 1934.

Ruhl, Arthur, dramatic critic, 58. World War correspondent, expert reporter and lecturer; authority on Central American and Caribbean affairs; author of "Second Nights." Born Rockford, Illinois; died Jackson Heights, New York, June 6, 1935.

Sawyer, Charles P., music and drama critic, 80. Assistant to J. Ranken Towse on New York *Post* for many years. Born Newbury, Mass.; died New York City, May 8, 1935.

Sears, Zelda, actress and playwright, 62. Prominent in Clyde Fitch comedies; author of "Heart of a Child" (adaptation), "Lollopop," and "A Lucky Break." Born Brockway, Michigan; died Hollywood, February 19, 1935.

Sembrich, Marcella, operatic soprano, 76. Star of Metropolitan Opera Company many years; played piano and violin at 4, professionally at 12; début as singer in 1877 in Athens; gained fame as teacher in Curtiss School, Philadelphia, and

Juilliard School, New York. Born Lemberg, Austria; died New York City, January 10, 1935.

Serrano, Vincent, actor, 65. Began with Augustin Daly in 1893; appeared as Lieutenant Denton in "Arizona" over a thousand times; supported many stars; last appearance in "Rio Rita" in 1927. Born New York; died New York, January 10, 1935.

Sherman, Lowell J., actor. New York début in "The Girl of the Golden West"; supported Leslie Carter, Nat Goodwin, Nance O'Neill; stock with Pauline Lord, Ruth Chatterton and Leonore Ulric; played many leading rôles; successful as picture director. Born San Francisco, California; died Hollywood, December 28, 1934.

Stevenson, Douglas, actor, 52. Musical comedy actor since 1903, playing with Weber and Fields, Montgomery and Stone and in many Dillingham plays. Born Versailles, Ky.; died Versailles, December 31, 1934.

Thomas, Augustus, playwright, 77. Wrote some fifty plays including "Arizona," "Alabama," "In Mizzoura," "The Witching Hour," "Mrs. Leffingwell's Boots," "The Earl of Pawtucket," "The Copperhead" and "On the Quiet;" last play "Still Waters" in 1926. Born St. Louis, Mo.; died Nyack, New York, August 12, 1934.

Tighe, Harry, actor, 50. Thirty years ago in vaudeville and musical comedy; took up radio and pictures. Born New Haven, Conn.; died Old Lyme, Conn., February 10, 1935.

Titheradge, Dion, actor, author and producer, 45. Member of famous English theatrical family; first appearance in New York in "Henry V," supporting Lewis Waller; last appearance here in 1925 in "Loose Ends." Born Melbourne, Australia; died London, November 16, 1934.

Vincent, Charles, actor, playwright, 76. On stage fifteen years; wrote 23 plays; among them "The Man from Mexico," "Gentleman Jack," "A Naval Cadet" (for J. J. Corbett) and "Dolly Varden." Born Bristol, England; died Glen Cove, L. I., March 21, 1935.

Warde, Frederick B., actor, 83. Contemporary of Edwin Booth, Lawrence Barrett, Tom Keene, John McCullough and Louis James; toured America eighties and nineties, co-starring with Louis James and Kathryn Kidder; lectured on Shakespeare and wrote "Shakespeare's Fools"; retired in 1923. Born Wardington, Oxfordshire, England; died Brooklyn, New York, February 7, 1935.

Wheatley, Jane (Jane Simpson), actress, 53. In "The Christian" with Viola Allen; many years in stock; several seasons with Theatre Guild; last appeared in "Dangerous Corner" in 1932. Born Roslyn, L. I., New York; died New York City, February 17, 1935.

Witherspoon, Herbert, singer and manager, 62. Sang in "Parsifal" with New York Philharmonic and Metropolitan Opera Company; operatic début with Henry W. Savage Company; director of Chicago Civic Opera Company and Cincinnati Conservatory of Music; made director Metropolitan shortly before death. Born Buffalo, New York; died New York City, May 10, 1935.

THE DECADES' TOLL

(Players of Outstanding Prominence Who Have Died in Recent Years)

	Born	Died
Aborn, Milton	1864	1933
Bacon, Frank	1864	1922
Baker, George Pierce	1866	1935
Belasco, David	1856	1931
Bernhardt, Sarah	1845	1923
Coghlan, Rose	1851	1932
Crabtree, Charlotte (Lotta)	1847	1924
Crane, William H.	1845	1928
De Koven, Reginald	1861	1920
De Reszke, Jean	1850	1925
Dillingham, Charles Bancroft	1868	1934
Ditrichstein, Leo	1865	1928
Dressler, Marie	1869	1934
Drew, John	1853	1927
Du Maurier, Sir Gerald	1873	1934
Duse, Eleanora	1859	1924
Fiske, Minnie Maddern	1865	1932
Galsworthy, John	1867	1933
Goodwin, Nathaniel	1857	1920
Hawtrey, Sir Charles	1858	1923
Herbert, Victor	1859	1924
Lackaye, Wilton	1862	1932
Mantell, Robert Bruce	1854	1928
Miller, Henry	1858	1926
Morris, Clara	1848	1925
O'Neill, James	1850	1920
Patti, Adelina	1843	1919
Pinero, Sir Arthur Wing	1855	1934
Rejane, Gabrielle	1857	1920
Russell, Lillian	1861	1922
Sembrich, Marcella	1859	1935
Shaw, Mary	1860	1929
Smith, Winchell	1862	1933

	Born	*Died*
Sothern, Edwin Hugh	1859	1933
Terry, Ellen	1848	1928
Thomas, Augustus	1857	1934
Warde, Frederick	1851	1935
Ziegfeld, Florenz	1869	1932

INDEX OF AUTHORS

INDEX OF PLAYS AND CASTS

524

INDEX OF PLAYS AND CASTS 527